THE SCOTTISH EMPIRE

The Scottish Empire

MICHAEL FRY

TUCKWELL PRESS and

First published in Great Britain in 2001. First published in paperback in 2002 by

Tuckwell Press   Birlinn Ltd
The Mill House   West Newington House
Phantassie   10 Newington Road
East Lothian   Edinburgh
EH40 3DG   EH9 1QS

ISBN 1 84158 259 X

The publishers gratefully acknowledge
subsidy from the Scottish Arts Council
towards the publication of this volume

British Library Cataloguing in Publication Data

A catalogue record for this book is available
on request from the British Library

Typeset by Hewer Text Ltd, Edinburgh
Printed and bound by RDC Group

Contents

PART ONE. A COMMERCIAL EMPIRE

PART TWO. A CHRISTIAN EMPIRE

Foreword

In my work on Scottish history over the last quarter of a century I have been concerned to fill in some of the black holes which blot the subject's visage. If Scotland had always had a healthy historiography, my task would have been redundant, for then the nation's past could have benefited from continual reassessment according to the advance of scholarship and the needs of each generation. This has unhappily not been the case so that, at least till the recent revival, much of the existing corpus of Scottish history remained inadequate, while many major aspects of it had never been written up at all. Even the revival does not quite solve the problem, since it has taken place largely in groves of academe pervaded by British agendas with their own priorities, regardless of what might be needed in Scotland to make the historiography more whole.

In the first instance I devoted myself to political history, and so set out against the tide of Whig or Anglo-British historiography, which claimed that Scotland had no political history worth the name, as of Marxist or vulgar Marxist historiography, which claimed that such history would anyway be worthless unless it vindicated the experience of the working class, as of Nationalist historiography, which claimed that such history could only be of value if it supported the case for Scottish independence. I shall write more political history but meanwhile, prompted by my earlier enthusiasm for Henry Dundas, I have turned aside to this imperial history.

It is meant as a contribution in equal measure to the history of Scotland and the history of the British Empire. It incorporates previous primary research of my own, filled out with reading as wide as I could manage in all other primary printed and secondary sources with some bearing on Scottish imperial experience. After several years of research round the globe, however, I became uncannily aware of standing on the shore of an ocean. There are untold masses of manuscripts in exotic archives which will serve on particular points to modify, sometimes no doubt to invalidate, what I have written here. But I thought it as well in opening up a new field of Scottish history, at least on anything like this scale, to be bold. In order to reduce to governable order the mass of material I had gathered myself, I resorted to a rigid structure, finally of four broadly chronological sections with ten chapters each (except for two cases of double chapters, as it were, on themes of special importance, namely, imperial economics and imperial politics in the nineteenth century). This obliged me to leave out some interesting episodes, such as Reginald Wingate's regime in the Sudan and George Scott's salvation of the Shan States. I regretted it, but nobody can do everything. The discipline of selection served to concentrate my mind on what was peculiarly Scottish about the nation's experience of Empire.

In my conclusions I assert that the Empire was never a monolith, in the way it tended to be depicted in the semi-official accounts conceived during the era of high imperialism. On the contrary, it existed in many forms which looked different according to the origin, status and activity of the individual or collective spectators. In this light I trust that my title, *The Scottish Empire*, will turn out not to seem so provocative as it might do at first sight. As for Scotland proper, I remark near the end of that last chapter how the nation's historical, political and economic circumstances have always made its sense of itself strangely intangible, compelling Scots to search elsewhere for promises of fulfilment. The compulsion was at once greater and lesser than the imperial one as such, though Empire provided the mould into which it had in the event to fit.

What I have written in this respect is a kind of external history of Scotland to match the internal history which by the work of many hands is now getting into better shape. I hope as a result to influence the future general course of our historiography, in showing that the external history is as crucial as the internal history to answer the questions which in these stirring times constantly confront us, of what Scotland is and what Scotland means. Hugh MacDiarmid's "Scotland small? Our multiform, our infinite Scotland *small*?" says something about that, though not as much on the metaphysics of the matter as the verses by Rainer Maria Rilke which in the end I have preferred for my epigraph: he is the finer poet, his Austrian nationality may offer affinity enough and he lived out his life, much more so than MacDiarmid, amid dissolution. He can scarcely be translated but he puts into incomparable poetic language the last sentence of my book, which may possess a special resonance for all those Scots who out in the world have been made to feel they belong to a non-existent nation. Above the sphere of being nowhere, writes Rilke, extends a sphere of being everywhere. See, if we throw – if we dare to throw – a ball up into it. Does the ball not fill our hands in a different way with its return? Purely by the weight of its homecoming, it is more.

I have the great pleasure of recording my debt to three benefactions which made my work possible. The first came from Brown University, Providence, Rhode Island, USA, where I held a fellowship in 1993–4 at the John Carter Brown Library. For the documentation of early colonialism, above all in the Americas, it is unrivalled. I offer my deep gratitude to the director, Norman Fiering, for his unfailing generosity, for his astounding tolerance of my foibles and for his continued interest in my project. A second benefaction came from the Huntington Library, Santa Monica, California, USA, where I held a fellowship in 1995–6. The director, Roy Ritchie, a migrant son of Scotland, was no less encouraging, and in idyllic surroundings assured me of the peace and quiet I needed to complete a crucial stage of my writing. At a different point I was fortunate enough to receive a third benefaction, a writer's bursary from the Scottish Arts Council, with the support of its former literature director, Walter Cairns. As a freelance with no regular income of any kind I have always first to make sure I eat, and the bursary relieved me of such cares for as long as was necessary to finish a further large part of the book. Numerous people have aided me with information or other support for my labours, which had to be performed in the interstices of an ever busier life. Without the help of those friends and the gratuitous kindness of so many passing acquaintances in so many distant places, the book could not have been finished. I thank them all.

Michael Fry

Illustrations

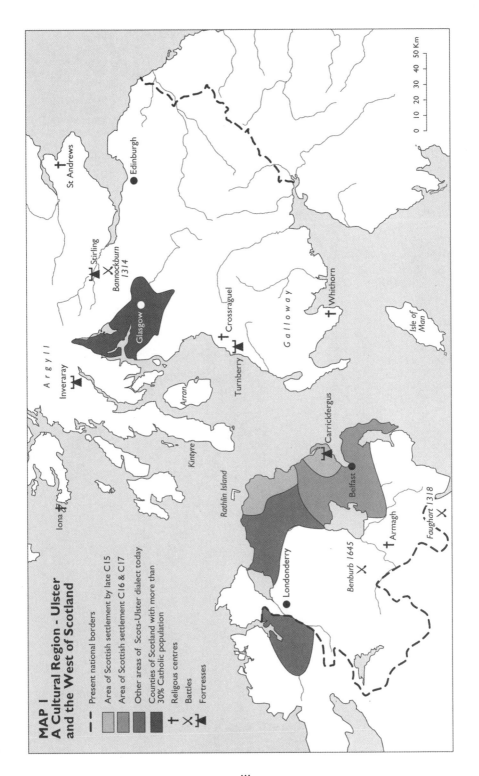

MAP 1
A Cultural Region - Ulster
and the West of Scotland

Present national borders

Area of Scottish settlement by late C15

Area of Scottish settlement C16 & C17

Other areas of Scots-Ulster dialect today

Counties of Scotland with more than
30% Catholic population

✝ Religous centres

✗ Battles

⚑ Fortresses

St Andrews ✝

● Edinburgh

Stirling ⚑
✗ Bannockburn
1314

A r g y l l

Inveraray ⚑

Glasgow ○

Crossraguel ✝
⚑

Turnberry ✝

G a l l o w a y

✝ Whithorn

Isle of
Man

Iona ✝

Arran

Kintyre

Rathlin Island

Carrickfergus ⚑✝

● Belfast

● Londonderry

Benburb 1645 ✗

✝ Armagh

Faughart 1318
✗

0 10 20 30 40 50 Km

xiii

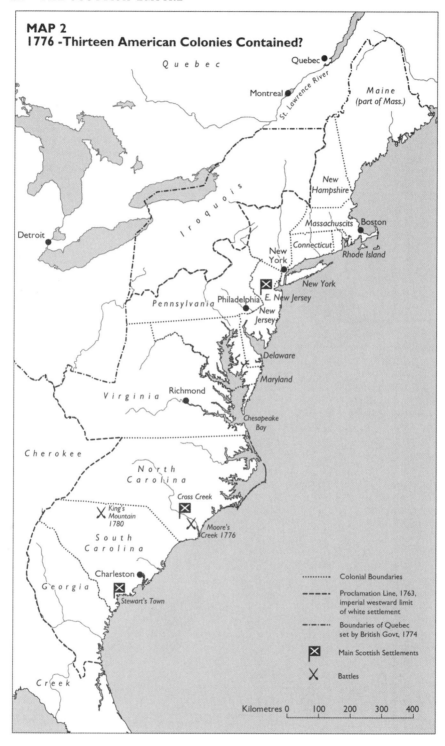

MAP 2
1776 -Thirteen American Colonies Contained?

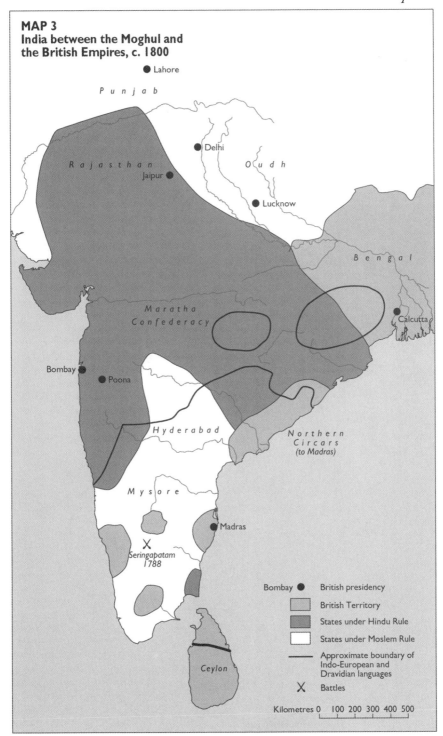

MAP 3
India between the Moghul and
the British Empires, c. 1800

● Lahore

P u n j a b

● Delhi

O u d h

R a j a s t h a n

Jaipur ●

● Lucknow

B e n g a l

M a r a t h a
C o n f e d e r a c y

● Calcutta

Bombay ●

● Poona

H y d e r a b a d

N o r t h e r n
C i r c a r s
(to Madras)

M y s o r e

● Madras

X
Seringapatam
1788

Bombay ●   British presidency

     British Territory

     States under Hindu Rule

     States under Moslem Rule

———   Approximate boundary of
     Indo-European and
     Dravidian languages

X   Battles

Ceylon

Kilometres 0   100 200 300 400 500

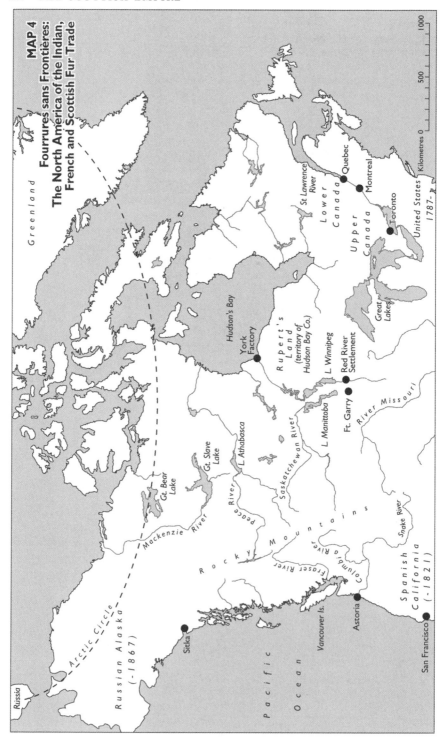

MAP 4
Fourrures sans Frontières:
The North America of the Indian,
French and Scottish Fur Trade

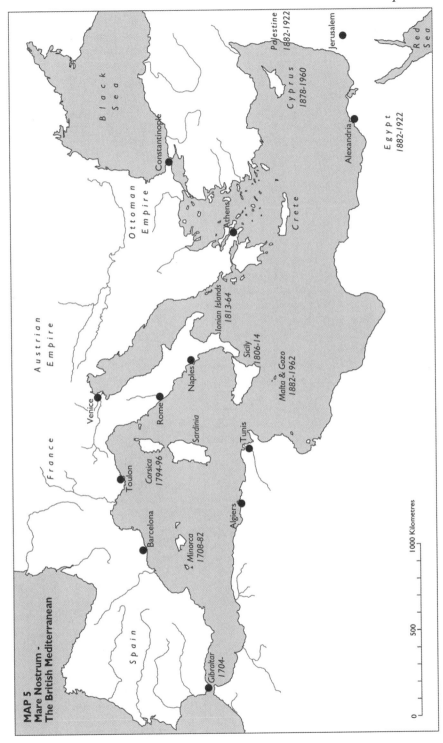

MAP 5
Mare Nostrum -
The British Mediterranean

Spain

France

Austrian Empire

Ottoman Empire

Black Sea

Constantinople

Venice

Athens

Toulon

Corsica
1794-96

Sardinia

Rome

Naples

Tunis

Algiers

Barcelona

Minorca
1708-82

Gibraltar
1704-

Ionian Islands
1813-64

Sicily
1806-14

Malta & Gozo
1882-1962

Crete

Cyprus
1878-1960

Palestine
1882-1922

Jerusalem

Alexandria

Egypt
1882-1922

Red Sea

0   500   1000 Kilometres

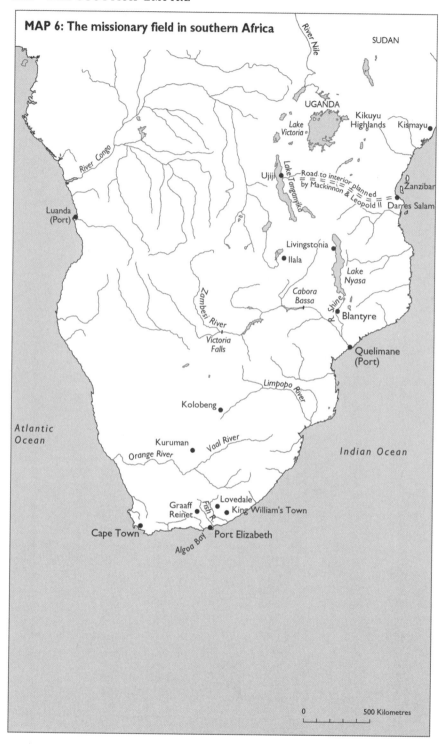

MAP 6: The missionary field in southern Africa

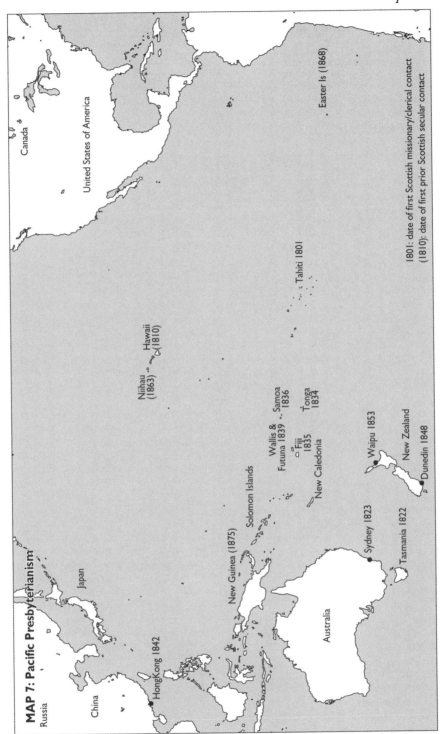

MAP 7: Pacific Presbyterianism

Russia

Canada

United States of America

Easter Is (1868)

1801: date of first Scottish missionary/clerical contact
(1810): date of first prior Scottish secular contact

Tahiti 1801

Hawaii
(1810)

Niihau
(1863)

Wallis &
Futuna 1839 ~ Samoa
1836
Fiji
1835
Tonga
1834

New Caledonia

Waipu 1853

New Zealand

Dunedin 1848

Solomon Islands

Sydney 1823

New Guinea (1875)

Tasmania 1822

Japan

Australia

China

Hong Kong 1842

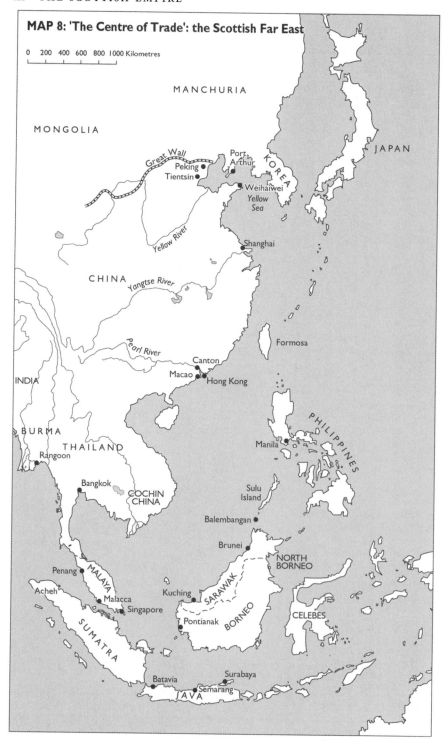

MAP 8: 'The Centre of Trade': the Scottish Far East

0   200 400 600 800 1000 Kilometres

MANCHURIA

MONGOLIA

JAPAN

Great Wall

Port Arthur

Peking

Tientsin

KOREA

Weihaiwei

Yellow Sea

Yellow River

Shanghai

CHINA

Yangtse River

Formosa

Pearl River

Canton

Macao   Hong Kong

INDIA

PHILIPPINES

BURMA

THAILAND

Manila

Rangoon

Bangkok

COCHIN CHINA

Sulu Island

Balembangan

Brunei

NORTH BORNEO

Penang   MALAYA

Acheh

Kuching

SARAWAK

Malacca

Singapore

Pontianak   BORNEO

CELEBES

SUMATRA

Batavia   Surabaya

Semarang

JAVA

Chronology

1603 Union of Crowns: James VI of Scotland becomes James I of England.
1610 Scottish plantation in *Ulster*.
1611 Voyage from Leith to *West Indies*.
1618 James VI grants patent for Scottish East India Company.
1621 *Nova Scotia* granted by James VI to Sir William Alexander.
1626 Antrim Meeting: Presbyterianism constituted in *Ireland*.
1629 Scottish colony in *Nova Scotia*.
1633 *Nova Scotia* abandoned by Scots.
1634 Scottish Guinea Company formed.
1638 National Covenant in Scotland.
1640 First cargo to Scotland of tobacco from *Virginia*.
1641 War of Three Kingdoms breaks out; rebellion in *Ireland*, atrocities against Protestant settlers.
1642 Scottish army invades *Ireland*.
1643 Scottish army invades England.
1644 Irish army, under Marquis of Montrose, invades Scotland.
1645 Scottish defeat at Benburb and withdrawal from *Ireland*.
1651 Oliver Cromwell conquers Scotland.
1660 Scottish independence restored under Charles II.
1668 Port Glasgow built for trade to *America*.
1672 *Regium donum* to Irish Presbyterians.
1681 Privy council at Holyroodhouse under Duke of Albany (later James VII) decides on mercantilist policy.
1684 Scottish colonies founded in *East New Jersey* and *South Carolina*.
1688 Glorious Revolution.
1690 Presbyterian settlement in Scotland.
1695 Foundation of Company of Scotland Trading to Africa and the Indies; foundation of Bank of Scotland.
1698 Scottish colony at *Darien*.
1700 *Darien* abandoned.
1706 Presbyterian synod formed in *America*.
1707 Union of Parliaments of Scotland and England.
1709 Foundation of Society in Scotland for the Propagation of Christian Knowledge.
1710 Reconquest of *Nova Scotia*, first colonial territory taken by Scots and English together.
1711 After capturing *Minorca*, Duke of Argyll becomes its Governor.
1714 Hanoverian succession.
1715 Jacobite rebellion of Old Pretender fails.
1727 Foundation of Royal Bank of Scotland.

1729 Francis Hutcheson, from *Ulster,* becomes professor of moral philosophy at Glasgow.

1745 Jacobite rebellion of Young Pretender fails; office of Secretary of State for Scotland abolished.

1759 British capture of *Quebec.*

1763 Treaty of Paris ends Seven Years' War and confirms British conquests in *India* and *Canada.*

1770 James Bruce of Kinnaird discovers source of Blue Nile in *Abyssinia.*

1773 First settlement of Highlanders in *Nova Scotia,* at Pictou Harbour.

1775 Henry Dundas Lord Advocate of Scotland.

1776 Declaration of Independence by 13 British colonies in *America.* Adam Smith publishes *The Wealth of Nations.*

1778 Verdict in case of Joseph Knight declares slavery illegal in Scotland.

1779 North West Company formed by Scots fur-traders in *Canada.*

1780 Free trade between Great Britain and *Ireland.*

1783 Treaty of Versailles recognises independence of *United States.*

1788 Alexander Mackenzie reaches *Arctic Sea* along Mackenzie River.

1791 Movement of United Irishmen formed. Division of *Lower Canada,* largely French, from *Upper Canada,* economically and politically dominated by Scots fur-traders.

1793 War with revolutionary France. Dundas Secretary of State for War and President of the Board of Control for *India.* Alexander Mackenzie traverses *Canada* overland.

1794 Gilbert Elliot of Minto negotiates Union of Great Britain and *Corsica.*

1795 Orange Order formed. George Keith Elphinstone captures *Cape of Good Hope.* Mungo Park's first expedition to *River Niger.* Secession synod constituted in *Nova Scotia.*

1796 Elliot leaves *Corsica.* Missionary societies formed in Edinburgh, which sends an inaugural mission to *Jamaica,* and in Glasgow, which sends one to *Sierra Leone,* received by Zachary Macaulay, the Governor.

1798 Rebellion in *Ireland.*

1799 Battle of Seringapatam: General David Baird defeats and kills Tipu Sultan of *Mysore.* General Ralph Abercromby occupies *Malta.*

1801 Union of Great Britain and *Ireland;* Dundas resigns on George III's refusal of Catholic emancipation.

1806 1st Earl of Minto Governor-General of *India.* Mungo Park killed after tracing true course of *River Niger.*

1807 Abolition of slave trade in British Empire.

1809 Lachlan Macquarie Governor of *New South Wales.*

1811 Lord Moira Governor-General of *India.*

1812 Earl of Selkirk's settlement on Red River in *Canada.*

1813 David Livingstone born at Blantyre, Lanarkshire.

1815 End of wars with Napoleonic France: under Treaty of Vienna, Britain retains almost all conquests and becomes the sole colonial power of any importance. Scots kirk opened in *Calcutta.*

1816 Battle of Seven Oaks: fur-traders massacre Highland settlers on Red River.

1817 Thomas Brisbane Governor of *New South Wales.* James Mill publishes *History of India* advocating westernisation. Secession presbyteries constituted in *Upper and Lower Canada.*

1818 9th Earl of Dalhousie Governor-General of *Canada.*

1821 North West Company unites with Hudson's Bay Company, under George Simpson as Governor of the entire *Canadian West*. Guthrie & Co founded in *Singapore*.

1823 Scots kirk opened in *Sydney*.

1824 In *South Africa*, synod of Dutch Reformed Church constituted, with mostly Scots clergy; Glasgow Missionary Society founds station at Lovedale.

1825 Standard Life Assurance Company formed in Edinburgh. J. & P. Coats starts manufacture of thread at Paisley.

1826 Government of Straits Settlements (*Penang, Malacca, Singapore*) organised by Robert Fullerton. Alexander Laing reaches *Timbuktu*.

1827 Presbyterianism constituted in *South Africa*, admitting non-whites.

1829 Presbyterians found College of South Africa, later University of Cape Town.

1830 George Maclean sets up Merchant Government on *Gold Coast*. Church of Scotland initiates missions in *Bombay* and *Calcutta*.

1831 John Ross discovers *Magnetic Pole*.

1832 Scottish Reform Act. Presbytery constituted in *New South Wales*; Scots open Australian College in *Sydney*. William Jardine and Alexander Matheson enter into partnership in *Canton*.

1833 Abolition of slavery in British Empire.

1834 Botanist David Douglas killed on *Hawaii*.

1836 Church of Scotland sets up Colonial Committee. Clyde Company formed in Glasgow to finance agriculture in *Australia*.

1836 William Lyon Mackenzie leads rebellion in *Canada*.

1839 Church of Scotland constitutes synod in *Canada*. Mission sent to the Jews in *Palestine*.

1840 First Opium War breaks out between Britain and *China*. Jardine Matheson moves to *Hong Kong*. Arthur Anderson founds Peninsular & Orient shipping line. Samuel Cunard, with Glaswegian partners, founds his shipping line.

1841 Britain annexes *Hong Kong*. Livingstone arrives in *South Africa*, received first by John Philip in Cape Town, then by Robert Moffat at Kuruman. John Crawford inaugural president of the Ethnological Society.

1842 Scots massacre Aborigines at Warrigal Creek, *Australia*.

1843 Disruption of the Church of Scotland: almost all missionaries enter Free Church. Stock exchanges set up in Edinburgh and Glasgow.

1844 Disruption in *Canada*.

1845 Banking (Scotland) Act ends Scottish monetary independence.

1846 Repeal of Corn Laws. 10th Earl of Dalhousie Governor-General of *India*. Disruption in *Australia*. Mission of Jamaican Presbyterians to Calabar, *West Africa*. John Rae begins explorations in *Arctic*.

1847 Earl of Elgin Governor-General of *Canada*. Livingstone sets up missionary station at Kolobeng.

1848 Dalhousie annexes *Punjab*. Elgin introduces responsible government to *Canada*. Free Church founds colony at Dunedin, *New Zealand*. Ranald MacDonald sent by Hudson's Bay Company to *Japan*.

1849 Repeal of Navigation Acts.

1850 Robert Knox publishes *The Races of Man*.

1852 Canadian Parliament burned down during riots against Elgin in *Montreal*. In *Australia*, gold rush and abolition of transportation herald end of squatting age. Dalhousie annexes *Lower Burma*.

1853 Livingstone begins traverse of *Africa*, completed in 1856. James Wilson inaugurates Chartered Bank in *India*.

1855 Dundonians begin manufacture of jute in *Calcutta*.

1857 Indian Mutiny. Second Opium War breaks out between Britain and *China*. Livingstone publishes *Missionary Travels*, and tours Britain.

1858 Livingstone, finding the Zambesi blocked at Cabora Bassa, ascends the Shire to *Lake Nyasa*. Presbytery constituted at Calabar.

1860 8th Earl of Elgin and General Hope Grant burn down Summer Palace in *Peking*.

1861 Elgin Viceroy of *India*.

1862 William Mackinnon and others found British India Steam Navigation Company. Disruption of the Dutch Reformed Church in *South Africa*. United Presbyterian mission to *China*.

1863 Britain cedes *Ionian Islands* to Greece.

1864 Thomas Sutherland inaugurates Hongkong and Shanghai Bank.

1865 Rebellion in *Jamaica* and execution of George William Gordon.

1866 Registration of joint-stock companies becomes possible in Scots law.

1867 Confederation of *Canada*.

1869 Hudson's Bay Company surrenders chartered rights to *Canada*; rebellion in Manitoba. Suez Canal opened in *Egypt*.

1871 H.M. Stanley finds Livingstone at Ujiji on *Lake Tanganyika*. Alfred Nobel helps to form British Dynamite Company in Glasgow. Presbyterians lose *regium donum* on disestablishment of Church of *Ireland*.

1873 Death of Livingstone. Robert Fleming launches first investment trust, Scottish American.

1875 Free Church of Scotland founds mission at Livingstonia, *Nyasaland*. Reunion of Presbyterians to form *Canada*'s largest Protestant Church.

1876 Mary Slessor arrives in *West Africa*. Jardine Matheson builds first railway in *China*.

1877 Church of Scotland founds mission at Blantyre, *Nyasaland*. Distillers Company formed.

1879 William Gladstone's Midlothian Campaign.

1881 William Robertson Smith deposed from his chair at Aberdeen. African Lakes Company formed.

1884 Inauguration of Imperial Federation League. Congress of Berlin, a defeat for British diplomacy, prompts scramble for *Africa*. John Mackenzie becomes commissioner to *Bechuanaland*, first High Commission Territory. Church of Scotland sets up mission at Tiberias, *Palestine*.

1885 Scottish Office established. In *Canada*, Donald Smith drives in last spike at Craigellachie to complete Canadian Pacific Railway. Inaugural Indian National Congess in *Bombay* under Allan Octavian Hume as general secretary.

1886 William Gladstone's first Home Rule Bill for *Ireland* causes Liberal schism and formation of Unionist party. Scottish Home Rule Association set up. Burmah Oil Company incorporated in Glasgow. Partition of *East Africa* between Britain and Germany, and resignation of John Kirk as consul in Zanzibar.

1888 Imperial British East Africa Company formed by Mackinnon and Kirk.

1889 *Nyasaland* and *Niger Coast* declared British protectorates. Arthur Gordon Governor of *New Zealand*.

1890 James Frazer publishes *The Golden Bough*.
1891 Presbyterian mission in *Kenya*.
1893 With sponsorship of Free Church, Presbyterian Church of Africa constituted for blacks at the *Cape*.
1894 Second Home Rule Bill for *Ireland* fails. Lord Rosebery Prime Minister. 9th Earl of Elgin Viceroy of *India*. British protectorate over *Uganda*. Robert Louis Stevenson dies on *Samoa*.
1895 Leander Starr Jameson leads raid on *Transvaal*. British protectorate over *Kenya*.
1898 4th Earl of Minto Governor-General of *Canada*. Britain leases Weihaiwei, *China*. British and Chinese Corporation set up.
1899 In *South Africa*, outbreak of Boer War; defeat of Highland Brigade at Magersfontein and death of General Wauchope.
1900 Khaki Election: Liberals lose majority in Scotland to Unionists.
1901 Federation of *Australia*. Martyrdom of James Chalmers in *New Guinea*.
1902 North British Locomotive Company formed.
1903 Arthur Balfour Prime Minister. Robert Williams begins building of Benguela Railway in *Angola*.
1905 Henry Campbell-Bannerman Prime Minister. Minto Viceroy of *India*.
1910 Union of *South Africa*. World Missionary Conference in Edinburgh: beginning of ecumenical movement.
1911 Revolution in *China*.
1912 Third Home Rule Bill for *Ireland*; Covenant in *Ulster* to resist it. First Native Association formed in *Nyasaland*.
1914 Scottish Home Rule Bill. Presbyterian Church formed in *China*. Lord Inchcape merges P & O and British India. Outbreak of First World War.
1915 General Douglas Haig appointed British commander on *Western Front*. John Chilembwe leads rising in *Nyasaland*.
1916 Easter rising in *Ireland*. Native College opened at Fort Hare, *South Africa*.
1917 Balfour Declaration in favour of a national home for the Jewish people in *Palestine*.
1918 Presbyterian synod constituted in *Gold Coast*. End of First World War.
1919 William Macmillan publishes *The South African Agrarian Problem*.
1920 Presbytery constituted in *Kenya*. Government of *Ireland* Act concedes Home Rule.
1921 Treaty, superseding Act, recognises Irish Free State and establishes *Northern Ireland* with Home Rule.
1922 Andrew Bonar Law Prime Minister. British mandate in *Palestine*.
1923 Bantu Presbyterian Church constituted in *South Africa*.
1924 Ramsay MacDonald Prime Minister of first Labour Government. Presbyterian Church of *Central Africa* constituted.
1925 Most Canadian Presbyterians join United Church of *Canada*.
1928 National Party of Scotland founded.
1929 Ramsay MacDonald again Prime Minister.
1930 Weihaiwei returned to *China*.
1931 Statute of Westminster defines legal basis of Commonwealth. Onset of Great Depression: Imperial Conference agrees system of preferences.
1935 John Buchan Governor-General of *Canada*.
1936 Marquis of Linlithgow Viceroy of *India*. Patrick Duncan Governor-General of *South Africa*.

1939 Outbreak of Second World War.

1944 Cullen Young and Hastings Banda publish *Our African Way of Life.*

1945 End of Second World War.

1947 Independence and partition of *India.*

1948 End of British mandate and partition of *Palestine.* Apartheid instituted in *South Africa.*

1949 *Irish Republic* leaves Commonwealth.

1953 Central African Federation formed.

1957 *Ghana* is first British territory in black Africa to win independence.

1959 Emergency in *Nyasaland* and arrest of Dr Banda.

1961 Independence of *Tanganyika.*

1964 Independence of *Kenya, Malawi* and *Zambia.*

1967 Colonel Colin Mitchell occupies the town of Crater, *Aden;* victory at Hamilton by-election heralds rise of Scottish Nationalism.

1979 Scottish devolution defeated in referendum.

1981 Takeover of Royal Bank of Scotland by either Hongkong and Shanghai Bank or Standard Chartered Bank averted.

1994 Overthrow of Dr Banda in *Malawi.*

1997 End of British rule in *Hong Kong;* referendum approves proposals for Scottish devolution.

1999 Scottish Parliament inaugurated.

Introduction

The first son of Scotland whose name has come down to us, Calgacus the Swordsman, is already given, by the Roman historian who immortalised him, a sense of living at the extremity, on the precarious edge of things. 'Sed nulla jam ultra gens, nihil nisi fluctus et saxa,' Tacitus has him say, 'There is nobody beyond us, nothing but the rocks and the surging sea.'[1] And so, he goes on in an oration to his assembled warriors, they can only stand and fight, throw back the army under Julius Agricola sent by Rome to conquer them, to make a desert of their homeland and call it peace. This scene took place, if at all, in or about 80 AD, perhaps on the slopes of Bennachie. That great, conical hill, still topped by a rough-hewn ancient fortress, today overlooks the howes of Aberdeenshire, verdant monuments to the triumph of toil over a bleak earth and clime. Then it stood sentinel on the track through the Caledonian forest up which Agricola was resolved to push and meet his fleet riding in the Moray Firth. Thus he would demonstrate to the barbarians, with their wild, red hair and their crudely tattooed bodies, that they were encircled, helpless and must submit. Instead they did make a stand, but proved no match for the discipline of the legions. Beaten and slaughtered in their thousands, enough of them yet escaped into the mountains and lived to fight another day. The Romans, thinking their task done, retreated to a kinder country. As we know, they had not subdued Scotland. The patterns of her history were set early.

Calgacus would have been head of a tribal confederacy, chosen no doubt for brutal and implacable prowess in war. Whether eloquence was in truth also required of a Celtic chieftain we cannot tell. But the speech put in his mouth by Tacitus may not have erred in evoking that sense of where he stood in relation to the known world. The peoples then living in the north of Britain were not so savage that they refused to enter into peaceful exchange, to trade, with others. One traffic led down through the comparatively sheltered waters of the Irish Sea, to Cornwall with its tin, along the Bay of Biscay with its access to the fruits of Gaul, to Spain with its iron and oil, to the Mediterranean with its plenitude of luxuries. Nor were the wider and more perilous tracts of the North Sea impassable. The Celts of Europe formed in many respects a common culture. A few, perhaps even Calgacus, would have been aware of its limits, and that beyond them stretched an apparently boundless ocean.

Of course the ocean was not boundless. A crossing may have been pioneered by Irish monks who set themselves adrift in penance, or by Nordic navigators driven far off course in storms. But what had once happened by chance could be repeated by skill and courage. Skill and courage were not wanting, for these peoples of Europe's north-western littoral had come by the end of the first Christian millennium into ample contact with one another through advances in seamanship. They did so in war, yet later in peace as well, trading and settling together. Maritime dominions fitfully formed, where Norseman and Gael at first fought each other, then fought alongside each other against rival bands, in time saw their children intermarry and bring forth a mixed race, long-limbed and fair-skinned. The world of the new generations was not girt by narrow glen and firth, but open to strangers and strangeness.

Only by such mingling of peoples, at any rate, could Herjulf the Viking have numbered among his crew a Christian from the Hebrides. They got lost in bad weather on a voyage sometime just before the year 1000 round Greenland. With the returning calm, they found themselves in unfamiliar waters amid icy, barren islands. Because they were fearful in the chill and silence, the Hebridean composed a prayer, a Song of the Tidal Wave, to solace them. They dared not land, but when with relief they reached their destination, they told Leif Eriksson of what they had seen, of regions further to the west than even the boldest Norseman had yet ventured. Leif, among the boldest of the bold, sought and explored them. Others followed. One, Thorfin Karlsefni, had on board two Scots, a man and a woman. The saga even gives their names, Hake and Hekja. These he set ashore, ordering them to scout southwards and see what sort of country it was, then meet him three days later down the coast. This was doubtless an unnerving errand, but they fulfilled it, bringing back the most useful of their discoveries, self-sown wheat and grapes. Thorfin thereupon called the region Vinland. From this evidence, later interpreters have argued, they must have been somewhere about Cape Cod or Long Island Sound. It is a charming little tale, but may not be true, since it comes as an interpolation in the text and this is not the only saga thus corrupted. Yet a single word gives it the ring of authenticity. For some reason, mention is made of Hake's and Hekja's clothing, a *kjafal*, a sleeveless tunic with a hood. The term, not otherwise attested in Old Norse, probably represents the Gaelic *cabhail*, the body of a shirt, or *gioball*, a garment. How could the detail have been recorded at all if it was not genuine? Should this confirm the story, Scotland can fairly count Hake and Hekja with the first Europeans to have set foot in the New World.[2]

That may not be taking too much liberty with history, for the Kingdom of the Scots had already been created, had indeed made itself by then perhaps the most successful of the monarchies in the British Isles. But only the supreme trial, 300 years later, of the Wars of Independence would render Scottish nationhood ineffaceable. The heroic struggle also produced, indisputably authentic this time, an expression of how the Scots saw themselves in the world, the Declaration of Arbroath (1320). Held traditionally to have been composed by Bernard de Linton, it was a dignified appeal to the Pope, thus far by no means on the Scots' side. It asked him to admonish the King of England 'ut nos Scotos in exili degentes Scotia, ultra quam habitatio non est, nihilque nisi nostrum cupientes, in pace dimittat.'[3] This is no picture of a restless, ambitious race, though three decades of fighting for survival had doubtless forced them to narrow their horizons. They wish to live quietly in their faraway country, seeking nothing but their own, above all to be left in peace by the English. Yet there is also here a verbal echo of Calgacus, that sense of being on the furthest edge of civilisation, with nobody beyond. And the sense has persisted: we shall find still more distant echoes of it even in the twentieth century.

Once the Scots had secured their place among the nations, they became again an outward-looking people. The experience of trial – often repeated, if in less dire form – perhaps also let them see in looking out how thin the crust of civilisation is, how easily it can be broken and dissolved in violence and chaos. They were anyway aware that nature's niggardly gifts to their homeland must drive many of them furth of it to earn a livelihood overseas. A small, poor country could never think of domination, but at best persuade larger and richer ones to treat it on equal terms. So they sought to make themselves useful, to thrive through adventure and enterprise, and to approach other societies not with a desire of conquering, ruling and changing, but of understanding them. These were, however, lessons of history. First, they had to be learned.

Part One

A Commercial Empire

CHAPTER ONE

'The special friendship': Ireland

The hill of Faughart stands at the point, three miles north of Dundalk, where the route from Ulster starts to descend to the coastal plain. Soon after midday on October 14, 1318, Edward Bruce, King of Ireland, stood and surveyed its slopes in satisfaction, covered as they were with the corpses of his foes. He had just won a victory, not so glorious as his brother Robert's at Bannockburn four years before, but pregnant with a promise that it could lead to the expulsion from this country of its English occupiers. A mauled army of them had taken flight down the road towards Dublin, leaving his 2000 Scots veterans and 1000 Irish allies in possession of the field. Emaciated from hard campaigning in a stormy year of bad harvests, and wracked now in their limbs, their hearts yet rose in confidence and pride at his valour. They had come marching over the brow of the hill that morning to find the enemy blocking their way. Hardly were they arrayed for battle than the feared English archers got to work and forced them from their positions, exposing them to attack from cavalry and infantry. Some of Edward's captains urged him to withdraw and await reinforcement, the Irish indeed refusing to fight on unless he did. A fierce, stubborn man, he would have none of it. Instead he rallied his soldiers and himself killed three knights who came at him. His inspired army poured down on the English and drove them to the foot of the hill, where they broke and fled.

Now, as the Celts sat in comradeship wolfing down the meagre rations saved till after the fray, a strange ragamuffin wandered across the battlefield. Though he carried an iron flail, a fearsome weapon of ball and chain, they hooted in derision. He sought out Edward and offered to entertain him with juggling tricks. The captains railed at his impudence, but the King, in high good humour, laughed too and told him to go on. It soon became clear that he was a fool who knew no tricks. Suddenly, as they grew bored and turned away, he rushed at Edward and smashed the flail on his head. A dozen swords transfixed the fellow. Too late: the King of Ireland fell dead. The success of this absurd ruse by, it later transpired, a disguised English burgess of Dundalk at once spread horror and dismay through the Celtic camp, rapidly communicated to enemy scouts still lurking round it. They carried the tidings to their general, John de Bermingham, who somehow gathered his own exhausted troops to renew the assault. The stunned Celts just fell back, their victory all at once turned into defeat. After driving them off, Bermingham ordered Edward's body to be found and gruesome insult to be visited on it. The cadaver was sliced open, the heart ripped out, a hand chopped off, the rest quartered. Heart, hand and one quarter were to be displayed in Dublin, other bits in the main Irish towns. The head was salted in a wooden pail, to be sent for the delectation of the homosexual King of England, Edward II. He made sure to show the sickening sight to the Scottish ambassador, before rewarding Bermingham with an earldom.[1]

It was necessary to dishonour Edward Bruce because he had posed such a danger. He had in the last three years established himself in mastery of Ulster, and his assumption of the Irish Crown showed ambitions not confined to that province. Using it for his base, he rampaged all over the island, as far away as Kilkenny, Tipperary and Limerick, striking at the sinews of the English occupation. With the military dash he and his brother shared, he proved victorious even when superior forces were marshalled against him. Gradually he bottled the English up in Dublin. If he could have captured their capital, as he was setting out to do on this march from the north, he would have destroyed them in Ireland, with who knew what consequences for their own country. He had gambled and lost, yet the reward would have been beyond price, to end England's aggression on the sister isle, perhaps end it for ever through an alliance of Scotland and Ireland.[2]

It was the last occasion when eventual English hegemony over the three kingdoms, which with hindsight destiny seems so clearly to have decreed, might have been averted, to allow some more equitable balance among them. Whether this was an actual object of Scotland's policy remains obscure. Geoffrey Barrow, biographer of King Robert I, believes rather that the policy was opportunistic, and that the relations of the two Celtic peoples should not be sentimentalised. Yet it is possible to read into the King's own words a more deeply laid, indeed greater, purpose: of opening a second front against England, even of combining with the Welsh in a pan-Celtic grand alliance that could meet the Saxon on more equal terms. Robert I, to keep up the momentum after Bannockburn, circulated the Irish chiefs in 1315 with a letter addressed to 'the inhabitants of all Ireland, his friends'. He reminded them that they had been 'free since ancient times'. Now he wanted to set about 'permanently strengthening and maintaining inviolate the special friendship between us and you, so that with God's will our nation may be able to recover her ancient liberty'. And by 'our nation', the authorities agree, he meant Scots and Irish together. To him, son of Carrick and native Gael, this would have been natural. His wife, Elizabeth de Burgh, was an Ulsterwoman. He held lands on both coasts of the North Channel, separated by only 13 miles of sea. His family had long involved itself in politics on the other side. During his darkest days, seeking refuge in 1306 from the English invaders of Scotland, he had found it on Rathlin Island. The Gaeltachd anyway did form a linguistic and cultural continuum from the South of Ireland to the North of Scotland, and Carrick lay at its crossroads. To the King, this never excluded loyalty from those of a different tradition. He spoke Norman-French with his paladins, had doubtless got passable Latin from his education by the monks at Crossraguel, though it is unsure whether he knew English; but even if through an interpreter he won devotion from those who had it for a mother-tongue, the Scots burgesses and the peasants of Lothian. It was his genius as a leader that he could go among all sorts and conditions of men, and make them feel he was one of their own.[3]

The Irish indeed rejoiced when Robert I crossed to join his brother on campaign in 1316. The Annals of Connacht exulted that he had come 'to expel the Gaill [the English] from Ireland' – surely the language of national liberation. Though the Bruces' efforts ended in failure, and in death for Edward, they were still the main cause of the decline in England's domination of Ireland during the later middle ages, of what historians now call the Gaelic resurgence, restoration of native lordships, recapture of lost lands, revival of hallowed institutions. To the extent that the King tried to unite two peoples he saw as essentially the same, his exertions are perhaps to be distinguished from properly imperial ones. Yet presumably he expected sovereignty among the Celts to be vested in some form in his house, and so at least the power of his own kingdom would reach overseas. Such ambitions were not less imperial than those, often dignified by the term, of his arch-enemy, Edward I of England.[4]

In the middle as opposed to the dark ages, the Scots usually intervened among the Irish rather than the reverse, if only because the Scots were better organised. The English did employ men and money from Ireland in their attacks on Scotland. But encroachment in the other direction had started well before the Wars of Independence, with the mercenaries who aided Gaelic chieftains against the same English aggression. They were known as *gall oglach*, or gallowglasses, which might be translated as fit young foreigners. They would continue crossing the water so long as fighting was to be done there, and some stayed: this was the origin of the MacSweeneys of Donegal and Munster, for example. A peaceable migration began after the marriage in 1399 between John Mor MacDonnell of Islay, Lord of the Isles, and the heiress of the Glynns of Antrim. The dynastic link opened the way for settlement by clansmen from his bare, windswept shores on that fertile one where, for their characteristic appearance, they were called Redshanks. The common Northern Irish surname of MacDonnell (in Scotland more often MacDonald) stems from this movement. It would accelerate as the clan collapsed, finally at the grasping hands of the Campbells. But the Lordship of the Isles would remain in about equal measure Irish and Scottish till the middle of the sixteenth century.

By then tension among the three kingdoms was sharpening again, not least because of the strategic position of the two smaller ones in European politics. From 1533 the authorities in Dublin repeatedly warned their masters in London about the danger of a new Celtic alliance. In a notably vain gesture, the Irish Parliament passed in 1558 an Act forbidding Scottish settlement. This was in the reign of Bloody Mary, whose Spanish marriage dragged England into war with France. Scotland's Auld Alliance with her enemy gave Anglo-Irish forces the pretext to try and dislodge by force the Redshanks, with raids on their cousins in Kintyre, Arran and the Cumbraes for good measure. Not that all was harmony on the Celtic side: Shane O'Neill, aiming to make himself master of Ulster, fought and beat the Scots in 1565 at

Ballycastle, for which they revenged themselves by murdering him two years later. The English at last acknowledged that the settlers, now several thousand strong, could not be expelled. Elizabeth I made a grant in 1586 to Sorley Boy MacDonnell of the lands which *de facto* he already held. He covered his Irish flank too by marrying a daughter of the Earl of Tyrone. At the end of the century his people were as secure as the country's circumstances allowed, one precondition of the great migration from Scotland which followed. Most MacDonnells were Catholics and Gaels, however. Their gradual assimilation was in train. In fact they would fight on the Irish side against protestant Scots and English alike during the wars of the 1640s.[5]

It is to the Union of the Crowns in 1603 that we must date the establishment of a Scottish colony in Ulster which, reformed in religion and English in speech, would define itself against indigenous culture and maintain this identity whatever befell, right to the present. James VI and I was conscious of being the first sovereign over the whole British Isles: he meant to make a reality of that. He declared all Scotsmen and Englishmen born after 1603 to be his natural subjects in both kingdoms, thus entitled to the same rights in either. He kept away from European entanglements which might have encouraged interest by foreign powers in the outlying parts of his dominions. Within them, he proceeded by peaceful means if he could, but by violence and retribution if he had to. The turbulent Scottish Borders were soon permanently subdued. Further away, he hit on the novel policy of intruding on the lawless Highlands and on the still more lawless Ireland – not to speak of primitive America – bodies of settlers from more civilised regions. He was eager to give the Scots their share of such enterprises at home and abroad. The Lowlanders, a plenteous people, proved most useful to him. Oddly, they showed more tenacity in Ireland than in Scotland herself. Plantations in Lewis, Lochaber and Kintyre either took no hold or were at length overrun by the natives. But in Ulster they struck root and flourished, to effect indeed a profound change in the whole course of Irish history.[6]

At once in 1603, James VI granted more land in Ulster to Scots, to Sir Ranald MacDonnell in Antrim and to Hugh Montgomery in Down. Then in 1610, after the Flight of the Earls and the forfeiture of their lands, anyway ravaged and depopulated by war, he distributed 81,000 acres to 59 Scots 'adventurers' over six of the province's nine counties. Within a dozen years, more than 7000 of their countrymen, many with a family, took up tenancies under them, and further waves followed from time to time. Trade burgeoned across the North Channel in textiles and grain, while the ports on each side boomed and plump Scots merchants sat on the new corporations of Belfast and Derry. Most of the immigrants originated from the south-western region closest to Ireland, though with large contingents from the Borders and the valley of the Clyde, some from as far off as Stirlingshire. Many were younger sons of the gentry in Scotland, or people who had found no economic opportunities there. For these, and especially for their children, Ulster was really the only home they knew. But they kept alive their sense of being Scots, maintaining such close links with the homeland that the plantation was rather an extension of it than a separate colony. The Government in Edinburgh, wanting in 1624 to regulate commerce between the two, raised the matter not with the authorities in Dublin but with the leaders of the Scottish community on the other side.

Religion furnished the firmest link, for the migrants took Presbyterianism with them. During James VI's reign, at least 65 Scottish ministers served in Ireland. The Church of Scotland was also by the King's decree again episcopal, and he appointed 12 Scots to Irish bishoprics, seven in Ulster. Under this hybrid system presbytery never languished, however. With the Antrim Meeting of 1626, it formally constituted itself in Ireland. As in Scotland, the ministers were held to be adherents of the established Church. The compromise, no doubt uneasy but far from unworkable, was overthrown by the rashness of Charles I, with his insistence on English notions of royal prerogative in a confessional state. He matched his attacks on Scottish Presbyterianism by an assault on its Irish offshoot, starting with deposition of the ministers in 1632. As the appalled Scots of Scotland turned against him, they did not forget their kinsmen in Ulster, and circulated the National Covenant among them. The King and his Irish lieutenant, Thomas Wentworth, countered by suppressing all nonconformity with the Church of Ireland in 1637. Two years later they required the Scots of Ulster to swear the so-called Black Oath, in 'abjuration of their abominable Covenant'. Most did swear, because refusal would have meant expulsion from Ireland. Foolish policies had made of these people, once bulwarks of the Crown's authority, a threat to it, and they were treated as such.[7]

It was thus an already troubled Ireland, fallen from one of her brief spells of peace and prosperity, that full-scale war overtook in 1641. English historians have traditionally regarded this and its results as a sideshow to their own Civil War, though it is scarcely comprehensible in such a context. In Scotland and Ireland, it has been more sensibly and properly seen as the onset of the War of the Three Kingdoms, during which several centres of political and military power struggled to sustain and aggrandise themselves, over a theatre of complex conflict which at one time or another embraced almost the whole British Isles. Since 1603 the thought had awakened that they formed one realm. Was it in fact to be one realm, how was it to be ruled and who was to rule it? These were the questions at stake.

Scotland had already laid out her defiant claims with the triumph of the Covenanters' revolution in 1638, which the English had prevented from spreading to Ulster. In August 1641 the King came to Edinburgh on a visit marking, among other things, his acceptance of this new order. It also allowed him to embark on reconstruction of a royalist party in Scotland, to help if needed in his contest with the English Parliament. Meanwhile, as a result of that contest, his rule in Ireland was crumbling. There during the autumn a rebellion of Catholics broke out, accompanied by terrifying atrocities. Ulster trembled, for restoration of the old faith could only mean destruction to the settlers. England was in no state to control the situation. Charles therefore turned to the Scots, who at length agreed to send over an army provided that the Parliament in London paid for it. Led by General Robert Monro, a veteran mercenary of Sweden's wars, it landed in 1642 and campaigned all through the next year. It managed to dominate Ulster, without fully protecting the province against Irish guerrillas.

Meanwhile in England, the Civil War had begun. In the early battles, fortune attended the King's arms. Scotland's interest lay in keeping check on the monarchy, and it was to prevent a quick royalist victory that in 1643 she sent into England a second army. War on two fronts was meant to bolster her security. But, always dangerous, in this case it provoked a reaction from her own royalists. Under the Marquis of Montrose, they brought in Irish forces, unleashing here too a Civil War which continued till 1646. It also left the Scots army in Ireland out on a limb. Some troops were withdrawn to defend the homeland. The rest retired after defeat by the Catholics at Benburb in 1645, able to do nothing more. All that remained to the Scots of Ulster was to submit with as much grace as they could muster to an English parliamentary army, called in by royal authorities in the last extremity to defend the Pale from the native Irish, and now, having routed these at Dangan Hill, over-running the whole island.[8]

The perils and reverses put Ulster's Presbyterian colony on its mettle. Though it had developed slowly, it was now spread across all social classes and stood united against its enemies. In the process its links with Scotland, and with her Kirk in particular, were confirmed, even strengthened, forestalling any assimilation to other elements in the Irish population. A legacy of bloodshed and bitterness endured to sour relations with the Catholics. Nor had the English settled in Ireland chosen to treat their fellow-protestants on equal terms, while those intervening from the mainland had shown themselves perfidious. Scotland herself was not powerful enough to lend security against every threat. A sense of embattled isolation built itself into the character of the Scots of Ulster. They were and would remain an awkward element in Irish politics, but their ordeal had proved that their colony could not be wiped out.[9]

It was not left quite at ease even by the victory of radical Protestantism in these wars, and the imposition of Oliver Cromwell's military dictatorship from London, with a parliamentary union of the three kingdoms for form's sake. That reflected as yet no real British unity. Scots, while resolved to maintain their Presbyterian religion, also stayed in large part faithful to their ancient royal line. The signal feature of their constitutional doctrine was dualism, strict separation of Church and state, which the English with their unitary polity could neither stomach nor usually understand. Thus, in Scottish theory at least, presbytery and monarchy might coexist. The upheavals of the 1640s drove Scots to the conclusion that what they needed to make practical reality of the theory was a covenanted King, sworn to respect the Kirk's own definition of its status. After the execution of Charles I – which horrified them – that was what they had, or thought they had, in his son, Charles II. When Scotland rose in the young King's favour in 1651, the Scots of Ulster came under suspicion too.

Cromwell contemplated deporting them all to Connaught, but found it unnecessary after the battles of Dunbar and Worcester. In fact Irish Presbyterianism flourished during the Commonwealth.[10]

But hopes raised amid rejoicing at the Restoration in 1660 of a covenanted King were soon dashed. In all three kingdoms, he revived episcopacy. The Irish Parliament's subsequent Act of Uniformity (1662) again forced Presbyterian ministers from their parishes. This further defined the character of the Scots of Ulster. It is a peculiar trait of presbytery that, when established, no religion could be more regular and loyal; but, disestablished or dissenting, it may turn radical to the point of sedition. The Church of Scotland had struck such deep root, now so fully commanded the people's allegiance, that its definition of its status was almost bound to be accepted by a Crown once forced to defer to the general will of the nation. This would happen with the settlement of 1690. But the Irish Presbyterians – even if their population, on modern estimates, approached 100,000 – could never have the strength to extract such a concession. They were doomed to a condition of dissent, and to the consequences. They already had the best they could hope for, simply that their presence in Ulster should be accepted by London.

The position could anyway hardly improve while royalist Governments in Edinburgh and Dublin alike harboured suspicions of a natural sympathy between the Ulstermen and the Covenanters. But the latter's insurrection in the South-West of Scotland, remembered by the grimly appropriate name of the Killing Time, had little effect on the other side of the water, though thousands of refugees fled across it. This keeping of the peace by Irish Presbyterians merited some recognition. They possessed a friend in one trusted servant of the Government, Sir Arthur Forbes, later Earl of Granard, a Scot who had fought with Montrose before settling in County Longford. On his intercession, the *regium donum*, an official grant for clerical stipends, was instituted in 1672. In the next reign, James VII made Granard one of his Irish Ministers. By the Declaration of Indulgence (1687), Presbyterianism in Ireland, along with all other religious dissent in the British Isles, was fully tolerated. This did not win the King its support, for the Scots of Ulster discerned his ulterior motive, the advancement of Romanism. In the Glorious Revolution of 1688 they sided with William of Orange. And the new King on his white horse, riding across the River Boyne to victory over James VII, remains the great icon of their communal solidarity to this day.[11]

The potency of that icon marks the Revolution as a further major stage in the formation of the community. It was now large, important and well-organised. When its Church could call a general synod in 1697, the first since 1661, it comprised seven presbyteries. It swelled with another wave of immigration from Scotland, totalling perhaps 50,000 families by the 1720s. They came attracted by, among other things, the offer of lands which Catholics were forced to vacate under draconian new penal laws. Earlier, this movement might have worried the authorities in London. Now it did not. Links between Scotland and Ireland were in fact to be of little further concern to them, for the evolution of one British realm, defined above all by its Protestantism, was proceeding, in sentiment if not yet in legal form. However outraged the Scots of Ulster felt about their treatment after 1688 – and they justly thought they were treated with black ingratitude – they had little choice but to stand by the settlement then reached, as they still do. Nor before long would Presbyterian nationalism in Scotland be any threat to British unity, certainly not after the Union of 1707; the danger then came from Jacobites rather than Covenanters. The political common cause which earlier had united the Presbyterians of the two kingdoms lost its force. By the same token, they were reconciled to British authority and power.

In politics, then, the bond was loosed of simmering disaffection from a confessional state of episcopalian predilections. While religious travails in Scotland also ceased with the final establishment of Presbyterianism, little respite came for Ulster. This was because presbyterianism remained unestablished there. Yet its increase alarmed the Anglo-Irish elite, gathered in the Church of Ireland. Scottish episcopacy had been overthrown: why should Irish episcopacy not follow? The presence of a dangerously growing rival prompted a persecution of it which in retrospect seems utter folly, and seemed so to many then. The grateful William of Orange actually wanted to remove Presbyterian disabilities, but had not enough control of the Irish Parliament to push that through. The accession of Queen Anne in 1702 magnified high Anglican influence. In 1704 a Test Act was passed in Dublin which had the effect of excluding Presbyterians from public service. The *regium donum* came under attack, was indeed briefly suspended in 1714. A further Schism Act of that year threatened to suppress Presbyterian schools. Almost immediately the Queen died, however, and the Hanoverian succession put an end to this sectarian fury.

The wonder was that the Scots of Ulster maintained a cool estimation of their interests. The Jacobite rising of 1715 revealed as much. Irish Catholics never stirred, well aware what retribution might await them. Though Presbyterians were nominally barred from the militia raised as a precaution, they simply ignored the law and joined up in thousands. Even this did not suffice to win them relief from the Test Act, despite efforts in London on their behalf. But the *regium donum* had already been restored, and soon was augmented. A Toleration Act (1719) formally permitted dissenting worship.[12]

The religious bond between Scotland and Ulster, if rendered apolitical, remained all the same strong. Presbyterians had brought with them to Ireland a sense of being a Church of the people. They also still saw themselves as an extension of the Scots Kirk, which enjoyed the privileges and liberties of establishment. They never lost the aspiration that at least a little of the same might one day be enjoyed in Ulster too. It was therefore important to keep up the standards of an establishment. Also imported from Scotland was the ideal of a learned, that is to say, graduate ministry. Barred from Trinity College, Dublin, many of the clergy were trained at the universities of Glasgow or Edinburgh. Of ordinands in the synod of Ulster between 1730 and 1760, more than one-third had a Scottish degree. Developments in the Kirk thus quickly crossed the water. Just as in Scotland, Presbyterianism was now pulled between its pristine evangelical fervour and a new impulse towards culture and politeness, so that ministers might hold their own amid advances in secular thought. During the century, this Moderatism, as it was dubbed, came to prevail on both sides of the North Channel. But along the way the Irish Church proved if anything more fissile than its parent. Even some Moderates were driven into schism, which never happened in Scotland. The so-called New Lights appeared in the synod of Ulster in 1719, latitudinarians influenced by the emergence of more liberal attitudes in the Scottish universities. They disgusted their orthodox brethren who, through efforts to exact from them rigorous adherence to the Westminster Confession, forced them out in 1726. But the tide was about to turn against the strict Calvinists. When the General Assembly of the Kirk deposed the Rev Ebenezer Erskine in 1733 for attacking the Scots law of ecclesiastical patronage, he left to form what became the Original Secession Church. Some Irish congregations felt in their turn that it was time to take a stand against compromise with secularism. They followed him, and there were enough of them to form a presbytery by 1750. Other sects descended from the Covenanters managed to maintain themselves in Ulster.

Altogether, the province's intellectual climate was remarkably similar to the mother country's. The link found embodiment in Francis Hutcheson, the Ulster-man who became professor of moral philosophy at the university of Glasgow in 1729–46, taught Adam Smith and helped father the Scottish Enlightenment. But every bright schoolboy in Antrim and Down would have been brought up in the Presbyterian love of controversy, resting on the conviction that all believers should possess personal knowledge of Scripture, and be educated so that they could. Ulster had no legal provision for a national system of education open to the whole people, as in Scotland. The province was, however, dedicated enough to the ideal of the democratic intellect to erect a passable imitation by voluntary effort. Even small towns usually boasted a school. After the Scottish example, instruction began to cover subjects unconnected with religion: mathematics, surveying, bookkeeping, navigation. Ulster too fitted itself to send trained, energetic, practical men out into the world. Yet this was never to the detriment of the intellect. Academies like those of Scotland opened in Strabane in 1785, then in Belfast. The Belfast Academical Institution, though it would turn into a secondary school, was founded on the model of the Scottish universities in 1814.[13]

By any standards the Presbyterian community of farmers and tradesmen, a certain number of lairds and a growing number of rich merchants, ought to have been regarded as good citizens. They formed besides, there being so few Catholics left among them, a population more homogeneous than in other Irish regions, which assured the reliability of this one. In retrospect it seems incredibly short-sighted that the loyal and God-fearing character of Ulster should have counted for nothing. But the Church of Ireland, increasingly a body concerned first with its own privileges, was determined to keep the Presbyterians on the margin of society. The great Irish landowners, too, doubtless saw the disabilities as a useful way to hold down a rising middle class. Of course, neither pillar of the Ascendancy succeeded in halting, only in delaying the rise: which was true also in respect of the vast Catholic underclass. In any event the Scots, though excluded from political power, never accepted their subordination. That brought two further developments important not only for them, but for the Empire.[14]

The first was a great emigration to America, not at all discouraged by the Irish authorities, of those embittered by the bigotry. This way out already counted as traditional. The earliest party had crossed, to escape the persecutions, as early as 1636. Others went in the 1680s, and more after 1715, once it became clear that the Presbyterians' exertions against Jacobitism would not earn them equal rights. A third wave followed in the 1770s, at a time of widespread emigration, usually on economic grounds, from several parts of the British Isles, including Scotland. In the course of the century, tens of thousands of Ulstermen took this path. In America, they often settled on the frontier, especially the slopes of the Alleghenies. They went there partly because the seaboard had already been peopled, so that newcomers found it easiest to fill up the back-country where land and living were cheap. But they liked it there anyway, for civil authority had been to them a mere mask for oppression. On virgin territory they could work and worship as they pleased. They were too remote to play much part in the unfolding of the struggle for American independence. Yet they had little love for the British Government, and most witnesses attest to their commitment to the colonists' cause. This conduct of the Scotch-Irish, as posterity has dubbed them (though they called themselves Scotch), stood in marked contrast to that of the Scots who had immigrated directly from Scotland. It can be traced to their dissenting Presbyterianism. On the other side of the Atlantic, it easily translated into solidarity with radical American ideas of freedom.[15]

Nor did those distant events leave unmoved the Scots staying behind in Ulster. A province so unfairly treated was susceptible to political liberalism. In the self-reliant, Presbyterian middle class, notably in the synod of Ulster, America won for her fight a sympathy again conspicuous by its absence in Scotland. With the blow struck in defeat to the moral authority of King and Parliament, the Irish seized the chance to assert their own rights. This was done first through the Volunteers, raised ostensibly to meet a threat of invasion as colonial rebellion turned into general European war. They even recruited Catholics, and soon voiced nationalist demands: to these, Scots such as Adam Smith and Henry Dundas urged concession. Some barriers to free trade between Ireland and Great Britain came down in 1780, when the hated Test Act was also repealed. Yet gestures were not enough. The Dungannon Convention (1782) demanded for the Irish Parliament the legislative independence lost three centuries before, and its resolutions were adopted by the Volunteers. There was no choice but for the Government in London to give in, unless it wanted Ireland to explode. Under the leadership of Henry Grattan, her Parliament snatched back its freedom from limp British hands. The coup could hardly have succeeded, however, without support well beyond the narrow circles of the Anglo-Irish. In particular it brought the Presbyterians of Ulster, who willingly or not had tended to stand apart from the rest, into a strong sense of common interest with their compatriots.[16]

That crisis was resolved to Ireland's satisfaction, but matters did not stop there. The appetite for liberty now whetted grew mightily amid the convulsions unleashed on Europe by the French Revolution. In Scotland they met a minimal popular response and were easily controlled. But Irish Presbyterians, perforce dissenters from the established order in Church and state, seemed to have passed the stage of staid loyalty. They took part in and provided some leadership for the movement of United Irishmen, set up in Belfast in 1791 to demand popular rights. Even so, this national consensus proved deceptive. War with France in 1793 split the Irish again by reminding Ulstermen of their overwhelming interest in the British connection. A patriotic reaction prompted the formation of the Orange Order in 1795. To the Catholics, however, the conflict offered a chance to throw off the English yoke, which they tried to seize with the rising of 1798, aided by a French expedition. It was soon suppressed, amid massacres of the rebels. But it also gave the Government in London the excuse needed to try a new and decisive solution to the Irish problem. Dundas, inculcated from his youth in enlightened Edinburgh with the ideal of religious toleration, had been urging a Union of Great Britain and Ireland accompanied by emancipation of the Catholics. He wanted Grattan in the Cabinet, to do for Irish interests what he had himself done for Scottish interests, assuring them a place and giving them a voice at the centre of affairs of a truly United Kingdom. His Prime Minister, William Pitt the younger, was well-disposed and needed little persuasion. The scheme foundered, however, on King George III's refusal to yield anything to popery. The Act of Union itself went through in 1801. But Pitt and Dundas, unable to carry Catholic relief subsequently, then resigned. Their vision of the Union thus remained imperfectly realised, the greatest single reason why it never worked.[17]

With the Irish Union, we must bring to an end the account of Ulster as a Scottish colony. Legally, Ireland and Scotland were now parts of a single country. For the Scots of Ulster, it allowed integration in a British political community, something they had never really managed in an Irish political community. This was why, no doubt, they had always looked in adversity first to their link with Scotland, as probably the sole one on which they could rely, even if it had seldom been able to do much for them. From now on, especially with an industrial revolution enriching the province, they came to a conviction that their loyalty lay to Britain as a whole, though their closest emotional and cultural ties remained Scottish. The influences of Scotland on Ireland had thus far been greater than the reverse. For the future, as we shall see, the influences were to flow strongly the other way.

The imperial relationship of Scotland and Ireland will appear in the present work as an eccentric case. Still, their interaction raised basic questions about the Empire. If the Scottish colony in Ulster could be seen at the start as an extension of the mother country, it was soon set apart by exposure to a different, usually hostile environment. Scots on both sides worked to maintain the bonds of blood, faith and culture, and proximity ought to have made that easy. Still, it did not manage to keep them as one people. We have marked the stages – Civil War, Restoration, Revolution – by which Ulster's distinct consciousness emerged. The process was slow, hardly noted among contemporaries, and forced no sudden wrench. It might not have been wished for on either side, but when in 1801 the Scots of Scotland and of Ulster were brought together constitutionally as one people, they had become two. This painless yet involuntary separation would mould Scotland's view of the Empire, and of herself.

CHAPTER TWO

'The key of the universe': Darien

T he 300 Scots tried to make a brave show as they marched out of their battered Fort St Andrew. They advanced holding their saltires aloft, beating their drums, bearing their arms, to mark this as an honourable surrender. Women and servants followed, laden with the colonists' mouldering possessions. Last came the sick, walking or stretchered, pale and shivering, almost as many as the healthy gone before. And the living were outnumbered by the dead buried in great pits nearby. More Scots would die even before they put to sea on the four little ships down in their narrow haven, girt by swampy jungles and on the further side by steep mountains forming the spine that joins the two Americas. Watching the straggle was Don Juan de Pimienta, Governor of Cartagena and general of the force dispatched hither to assert Spanish sovereignty. For a month, since the beginning of March 1700, he and his men had had their share of hardship too, investing the Scots' settlement from camps in the forest, pinning and wearing them down with his watchful snipers. Thrice he sent them an offer to treat. Yet they were too stubborn to yield except on their own terms, that they should be able to take away with them their guns, ships and stores. The close-fisted response from ragged starvelings astonished Pimienta but, though a punctilious, he was not a pitiless soldier. At the final parley he agreed. In drenching rain, at noon on the last day of the month, articles of capitulation drawn up in Latin were signed by him and counter-signed by two councillors of the colony, James Gibson and William Veitch. So, on April 1, this limping procession trailed to the shore. The Scots were given two weeks to load their vessels and leave. Then they hoisted sail, passed out of the bay and steered a course northwards, into the 5000 miles of ocean between the isthmus of Panama and their home. One ship leaked so badly that it had at once to return and surrender afresh. The rest reached Jamaica, where the destitute voyagers sought for a few weeks to recuperate. Setting off again, the smallest of the vessels was wrecked on the coast of Cuba, while the remaining two sank during a hurricane in the roads of Charleston. With autumn coming on, some survivors just gave up and stayed where they were. Others pressed on by what means they could find. To Scotland a mere remnant came back of the 3000 who had carried her bright hopes to Darien.

This was the last, greatest but most disastrous of the colonial undertakings by the Scots while still an independent nation. Indeed it marked one of the decisive steps towards their loss of independence. The death of so many courageous and enterprising citizens was grievous enough, but the £200,000 they took with them to their doom, perhaps one-quarter of the country's liquid capital, represented an economic disaster. It fostered a belief that the only salvation for Scotland lay in Union with England, which followed seven years later.

The only good things to say about the disaster were that it arose out of new ambitions awakened by deep changes breaking the medieval mould of the Scottish economy, most obviously in trade, and that in the long run these ambitions would not be frustrated, though indeed they had to be fulfilled in an entirely different framework. Darien in itself gave proof how Scots were turning about from their traditional traffic with European markets to the East to face westwards into the wide Atlantic Ocean and its infinitely greater opportunities. This was not their first attempt. Some had got halfway across by 1400, when their fishery off Iceland started. Commerce in the whale-oil of Greenland also began early, possibly with the fabled visit there by Henry Sinclair, Earl of Orkney, about the same time. A Dundonian merchant's papers show him trading with Newfoundland in 1600 and even before. While at the outset a clear picture eludes us because of the meagre surviving documentation, it is barely credible that the scraps of evidence tell the whole story of the Scots' first oceanic ventures.

Fresh prospects opened through the Union of the Crowns under James VI and growing exchanges with England, till then cut off by enmity. Scots (or strictly, the *post-nati* born after 1603) were soon allowed to live, work, own property, buy and sell it in all his dominions, on both sides of the border and overseas. We have evidence of an Aberdonian trader in Virginia in 1634, and of Scottish vessels visiting the River Delaware between 1638 and 1645. The earliest known cargo of tobacco from an English colony entered the Firth of Clyde in 1640, only to be seized as prize by Scots who had taken up arms against Charles I. At that stage the West Indies offered better opportunities which they also pursued, on French as well as English islands.[1]

Along with this James VI had patronised colonial undertakings. To him they were an instrument of uniting his British realms and a reward to be reaped from his pacific foreign policy. They had an economic purpose too, inside a mercantilist system of regulated foreign trade tied to monopolies at home, all under the control of the Crown. The king followed his initiative for plantation in Ireland by a series in America. To the English the New World had for some time been an object of interest, if with scant reward thus far; now, in 1607, they established a settlement at Jamestown in Virginia which proved permanent and may be taken as the true beginning of English imperialism. It is usually, but wrongly, assumed that the Scots showed no such interest, and could have shown none because of the medieval nature of their economy. For the mercantilism the state proposed to erect on it, it did offer only an immature and in the end impossible matrix. Yet in their thinking Scots were not so backward.

The first economic text they ever produced had as its subject international trade. It came from the pen of William Welwood, professor of civil law at the university of St Andrews. He published in 1613 a defence of James VI's doctrine of *mare clausum*, that the British sovereign should control the narrow seas, against the *mare liberum*, or freedom of shipping expounded by the Dutch scholar-statesman, Hugo Grotius. Welwood thus made an original contribution, the sole one that Grotius judged worthy of answer by himself, to the emerging theory of mercantilism. As an ensemble it would hold that gains from trade flowed only one way and could never be mutual, so that every nation must try to build a surplus in its balance of payments at the expense of the rest. For Scotland, which exchanged exports of raw materials for imports of finished goods, this was supposed to mean turning to manufactures, checking imports and accumulating raw materials to be processed domestically by companies established for the purpose. In 1623, Parliament set up a committee to work out a policy on these lines. It would be elaborated in fits and starts till the end of the century. Colonies could also form part of it, to exploit resources unavailable to others and widen the markets for goods produced at home. They had in any event to be tied into the domestic structure of monopoly. It was stressed specially that no great economic gain, and a positive political loss, could flow from letting strangers convey goods between a colony and the mother country.[2]

These were the principles on which Scots first set out to found colonies, not long after the English. A chartered company organised an ill-recorded migration to Newfoundland about 1620. The directors petitioned for the appointment as governor of one John Mason. He published a pamphlet showing close acquaintance with the island, so he must have been there. No trace remains of the Scots who went too, though they were certainly present. When they failed to break into the carrying trade for the abundant fish caught in those waters, they took to smuggling instead. They and others made Newfoundland one of the world's centres for illicit commerce. To that extent, the conditions soon transformed a mercantilist scheme into a more free-trading one.

William Alexander of Menstrie carried the colonising efforts forward. A laird from Stirlingshire, he was an insatiably busy fellow with an acquaintance wide enough for literary luminaries as well as transatlantic traders. Thomas Urquhart of Cromarty said he was 'born to be a poet, and aimed to be a king'. He moved indeed in royal circles in London, where he commended himself by a willingness to relieve James VI of tedious business: answers to importunities from home, repatriation of vagrants crossing the border, literary drudgery over knotty points in the British Solomon's translation of the psalms. Flattering his interest in plantation too, Alexander hoped that 'as there was a new France, a new Spain and a new England, that they might likewise have a new Scotland'. It was thus with good grace that the monarch granted him in 1621 the entire territories between New England and Newfoundland, including what has been known ever since as Nova Scotia. The tract was so large that, if successfully settled, it would have raised Scotland into the topmost rank of colonial powers.[3]

Alexander lost little time in sending out, the next year, an expedition. He waited eagerly for news of its founding a colony and planned a free port at Largs for reception of the treasures to be sent back. When news came it was brought by the aspirant settlers themselves, returning to say they had failed. They tried again in 1623 and failed again. That was already £6000 sunk without trace. James VI promised to reimburse his favourite but never did. Alexander decided that the wanting enthusiasm in their countrymen could be supplied by deployment of his own literary skills. He penned an *Encouragement to Colonies* showing that such ventures had been on the agenda of all the best nations since the ancient Hebrews: they were the Lord's work which the Scots should not shirk to follow. For any still unconvinced he added a glowing description of Nova Scotia, with its 'very delicate meadows having roses red and white growing thereon with a wild lily having a very dainty smell'. Meanwhile the canny King took a part costless to himself. He applied the idea, already tried in the plantation of Ulster, of selling baronetcies, the proceeds of which would be put towards the expense of colonisation. Normally Scots gentlemen were eager to advance in rank but this offer they showed themselves strangely slow to take up. And none fulfilled the condition attached of actually going to Nova Scotia.

Not till a new reign could more be done. In economic policy Charles I extended the mercantilist regime but in foreign policy he unwisely departed from his father's pacifism to embark again on war, notably with the French. In 1629 an English force seized Quebec. It might have been a breakthrough into Canada, whence Cardinal Richelieu had excluded foreigners in a belief that the St Lawrence River was the North-West Passage to the Orient. Though the Scots harboured no grandiose ambitions of controlling it, the fall of its citadel opened the way for settlement on the territory to the south which they claimed. This was immediately effected by a party under Alexander's son, William junior, at France's abandoned post of Port Royal, today Annapolis, on the Bay of Fundy. A second party landed on Cape Breton Island only to be promptly driven off by French forces still disputing control of the region. Port Royal, however, made a start on overcoming the problems of colonisation and briefly came to represent a major element of the European presence in North America. Half the Scottish pioneers did die in the first ferocious Canadian winter. But the rest befriended the Micmac Indians who could pass on the lore of survival in these climes; their affable chieftain, Segipt, went over to meet Charles I in 1631. Even the hovering French were placated. A modest trade in furs raised hopes for a larger settlement, perhaps peopled (shades of the future) by transports of troublesome Highlanders. Soon, however, the king sought peace. France's price included elimination of the colony, some proof how seriously it had to be taken. The expelled survivors arrived home in the spring of 1633. Charles I may not have realised this was how the French meant to interpret their treaty with him. If his further grants of charters and monopolies were anything to go by, he expected traffic with the region to be maintained somehow. In fact the Scottish Crown was now to drop out of oceanic ventures, never to resume them after the subsequent decades of political turmoil. Alexander's fertile brain identified Long Island as an alternative but stopped at that. All he finally had of his efforts was the empty title of Viscount Canada, borne by his family in addition to its earldom of Stirling till the male line failed in 1759, just as Highland soldiers were storming Quebec and closing the history of New France.

These Scottish exertions are usually scorned, but the truth was that several European nations, wishing to emulate the Spaniards or Portuguese in colonising and exploiting the New World, had as yet found no means to do so. None knew just where to look for the riches they supposed America to offer. The problems of communication and supply, let alone the risks of financing them, were formidable. Not one of those interested nations had by the early 1600s, over a century after Christopher Columbus's landfall on Hispaniola, gained better than a toehold along the North American coastline, for the good reason that it was much less hospitable than regions further south. Till the conditions should be mastered, settlement was bound to remain marginal and precarious. Nothing could be achieved except by a process of trial and error, which brought for everyone more failure than success.

Scots suffered a special handicap under the Union of Crowns. After James VI, not one of their kings really knew them and their country, or had much regard for their needs. Scotland lacked all means to conduct independent diplomacy or foreign policy, to form alliances or defend her external interests by her own arms. Subordination to England stood here at its starkest, and relief could come only at England's caprice. The first Navigation Acts, passed during the Cromwellian Union of the two countries, let in the Scots by restricting colonial commerce to domestic shipping, with a particular view to shutting out the Dutch who so far had engrossed much of the world's carrying trade. Though the advantages could scarcely be exploited in a country ravaged by war and occupation, Scotland still felt sorry to lose them after she regained her independence with the Restoration of 1660. But this also intensified English mercantilism. The next year the Parliament at Westminster passed a new Act which treated Scots as foreigners and banned their ships from the colonies too. They and their commercial partners protested; the planters of Barbados waxed especially indignant. But the Government in London would not be moved. It even tried to twist a strict interpretation out of its Act by which Scots, not being English subjects, would on English territory be debarred from business as merchants and factors; a line of attack which argues that numbers of them were already carrying it on.[4]

Still, prospects also reopened elsewhere and Scotland found other partners to supply what no longer came across the border, if a trade-war was what the English wanted. While she did not gain the full exemption she sought in France from Jean-Baptiste Colbert's hardly less mercantilist tariff of 1664, it still let Scots export French goods home at a quarter of the duty charged to the rest. An effort was made to streamline the staple in Holland. In fact England's prime target remained not the Scots but the Dutch. Towards them her ill-will did not stop at restriction but appealed to arms, and to good effect. After 1674, and the end of the third Anglo-Dutch War, Holland gave up trying to sustain a carrying trade in breach of English law. Instead Scotland became to an extent her surrogate. The colonial customs could not possibly keep out every Scottish ship. It was not easy to establish regular communication across the Atlantic but on the emergence, as now in Glasgow, of a merchant community with enough money and enterprise, other obstacles could start to be overcome. An outwardly respectable Lord Provost, Walter Gibson, just raised the cross of St George on his ships to bring sugar and similar exotic produce straight home, whence it could be forwarded to Europe. A joint-stock company of 107 merchants set the illicit commerce on a regular footing. Port Glasgow was built in 1668 to meet their needs. By the 1680s, seven ships a year on average were plying the Atlantic from the Clyde, a few more from Edinburgh and Aberdeen. Despite protests from England, the Scottish authorities turned a blind eye to this trade. While it would no doubt have been larger without the English colonial system, it was never strangled.

Scots thus followed several European peoples in opening oceanic traffic, if on a modest scale. By the best standards they achieved no shining success, but they were not left standing either. To a small nation needing trade and lacking plantations, freedom of the seas might have seemed more useful than mercantilism, yet Scots were, as so often, liable to be over-impressed by foreign example. They now wondered if they ought to fall in with the international trend towards monopoly and protection. They hit back at England with a Navigation Act of their own and slapped heavy duties on imports across the border. They formed an official council of trade which would come into its own under the Duke of Albany, later James VII, whom his brother King Charles II sent away from English controversy to rule Scotland in 1679. He chaired a meeting at Holyroodhouse in 1681 which did consider free trade as an option but in the end agreed to the opposite, a ban on manufactured imports and protection of domestic industry, exempting it from tax and duty on any foreign inputs to keep its own costs low. A rigorous mercantilism thus became the policy of the Scottish state. Yet all it did was provoke retaliation, and then the new range of products could not be sold abroad. In a regime where big markets were closing, it just did not help much to close small ones, since by herself Scotland could scarcely sustain a manufacturing base.[5]

The expedient of colonies remained. In 1684, Robert Barclay of Urie, a laird from Aberdeenshire and a Quaker, founded a settlement in East New Jersey, on land recently conquered from the Dutch. He hoped to emulate the colony along the Delaware of his co-religionist, William Penn. This one was meant partly as a refuge, for Quakers and for Covenanters too, but perhaps more as a renewed project of plantation, laid out on a plan of large estates like those in the North-East of Scotland whence many of the proprietors came. Today the area, between Perth Amboy and Elizabeth, is an industrial desert, reminiscent of Clydeside only flatter. Yet not for nothing would New Jersey be known as the Garden State: 'It is a healthful, pleasant, fruitful country, in many places of a most luxurious soil, rewarding the labour of the countryman sufficiently,' George Mackenzie wrote home to Edinburgh. James Mason sent a cheering letter to Kelso: 'The Indians are a harmless people, and very kind to us; they are not a hairy people as was said to us in Scotland'. In 1693 one of the Quakers, George Keith, wrote here the first protest against slavery to be published in America. Andrew Hamilton was the forceful leader of the settlement, and under him the Scots prospered. In 1697 he even saw off English foes trying to depose him from his offices on grounds of his nationality. He came back as governor of the whole province of New Jersey, to which the Scottish proprietors surrendered their rights in 1702, though they stayed on as a local elite.

The year of 1684 saw a second expedition set sail for South Carolina. This was primarily an initiative of Whigs in the West of Scotland, of Lord Cardross, a military commander happy to recruit Covenanters for their fighting spirit, and of William Dunlop, principal of the university of Glasgow. More distant patronage came from Gilbert Burnet in London, which he would soon think better to leave for asylum with William of Orange. Cardross led out a band of settlers to found, on Port Royal Sound down the coast from Charleston, Stewart's Town, at the time the south-ernmost British settlement. They hoped it might serve as a base to enter the Caribbean trade. But it could only be secured under protection from the English nearby. Cardross rashly went out of his way to annoy them, refusing to recognise their governor's authority. It did not compensate that the Scots again struck up friendship with the Indians. This in turn alarmed the Spanish command at St Augustine in Florida, which claimed control over the area and had a policy of harassing intrusive foreigners. In 1686, on a pretext that these were fomenting trouble among the local tribes, it sent in a raiding party. Stewart's Town, with a fighting strength reduced by sickness to a couple of dozen, could not be defended. The survivors were lucky to be allowed their escape. But here we see some transition from plantation towards the organised trading venture, though hampered by English ill-will. One of the ideas which grew into Darien had been born.[6]

A second emerged as Scots noted how other states had reduced the chance of trade embroiling them in unwelcome and expensive hostilities by passing the risk, not least the financial one, to chartered companies. The results in England and Holland had been opulent, and in 1695 Scotland set out to emulate them. Parliament passed the Act to establish the Company of Scotland Trading to Africa and the Indies. It was granted generous terms. It could found colonies in any unclaimed territory. It would enjoy free trade for many years. It was to operate under minimal legal constraints. It had a promise from the Crown, if empty in the event, to protect its interests abroad. On paper, its position excelled that of any counterpart, just what the sponsors wanted.[7]

It did seem to answer the hopes of Scots merchants active in it. James Balfour of Pilrig and Bailie Robert Blackwood of Edinburgh were keen to export textiles to Africa, where an English company had done well. The Company of Scotland set out, however, not just to serve mercantile self-interest, but to be supremely a patriotic enterprise. Perhaps it was simply too commodious and munificent, for it could never set, let alone keep, a clear order of priorities. At first its patriotism even appeared broadly British rather than narrowly Scottish. The Act named 20 members to a court of proprietors, half each in Scotland and London, the latter including seven Scots, two Englishmen and a Jew. Most looked to deploy capital in ways forbidden by the spread of monopoly and protection. In particular they had in mind to break the English East India Company. Some just sought to replace one monopoly by another, but there was also an element as genuinely free-trading as the age countenanced.

That was represented by William Paterson. Born in Dumfriesshire in 1658, he had a chequered career. After university in Glasgow he left, possibly as a refugee Covenanter, for Bristol in 1675, then the West Indies. He knocked round there for a while, and doubtless visited Darien, for soon after his return in 1681 he was extolling its potential. Nothing if not versatile, he hit while making a fortune in London on the first principles of central banking. Though he promoted the Bank of England in 1694, he was too restless to remain a director for more than months, and turned his vivid imagination back to his homeland. The merchants were meanwhile raising capital for the Company of Scotland, and collected subscriptions of £13,000. Pleased with themselves, they went to London in the autumn of 1695 to meet Paterson and discuss how to deploy the sum. They gaped in astonishment when he proposed that the company should have a capital of £600,000, half from Scotland. He urged them, too, not to footle about in Africa, but to concentrate on Darien.[8]

Paterson and his friends in the City may have acted from a variety of high and low motives, but they did want Scotland as a base to undermine their English rivals. This the rivals could see. They clamoured that the company's proprietors resident in the South were about to infringe the monopoly of the East India Company, allowing the Scots to harm England's oriental trade just as they were already harming her American trade. Her edifice of intercontinental commerce, built over a whole century, might crumble. Questions were asked in Parliament. More ominously, King William expressed his displeasure: 'I have been ill-served in Scotland but I hope some remedy may yet be found to meet the inconvenience that may arise from this Act'. The House of Commons needed no better authority to impeach the directors living under its jurisdiction. That was the last the Company of Scotland saw of them, or of the £300,000 they were supposed to stump up. British enterprise, it had become clear, was not to be promoted on Scottish but only on English terms.[9]

The episode ought to have shown Scots that, if they wanted to join up with the commercial nations, they could not too flagrantly flout the existing rules of the club. Unluckily for this new and puny recruit, the terms of membership were growing tougher. Struggles among European powers intensified. Privateers swarmed the high seas. The English, aware of the Scottish chink in their mercantilist armour, enforced their laws more aggressively and efficiently. Their navy, if unequal to full policing, began to stop and search ships in Scottish waters. Though as late as 1700 Glasgow still managed to function as a staging post between America and Europe, oceanic commerce was gravely disrupted. What could be done? One possible remedy was to take up the scheme which Paterson obsessively promoted for Darien:

> Trade will increase trade, and money will beget money, and the trading world shall need no more to want work for their hands, but will rather want hands for their work. Thus, this door of the seas and the key of the universe, with anything of a sort of reasonable management, will of course enable the proprietors to give laws to both oceans and to become arbitrators of the commercial world without being liable to the fatigues, expenses and dangers, or contracting the guilt and blood of Alexander and Caesar.

The woebegone Scots, so deserving yet so luckless, could not resist the temptation. In July 1696, the Company of Scotland committed itself to the venture. Thus the initial, if confused, mercantilist purpose resolved under its inherent difficulties into a free-trading one, at least by contemporary standards. Mercantilism was at any rate not working for Scotland, and a small country's circumstances commended a more liberal alternative. The aim now was to set up an emporium where the whole world could exchange goods. The Scots had beyond the bright idea little conception how it might actually be realised, and no better means than before to compete with larger or richer nations.

But, if we recall their general position in international commerce, they might have identified a window of opportunity. To a people of few resources, the entrepot offered the fastest way to mercantile wealth. They stood moreover poised between the English and Dutch systems of navigation, having entered into a closer but unstable relationship with the first, yet not cut loose from the second, to which by tradition they rather belonged. The English system had not been fully shut off, and probably never could be, so that some traffic between England's colonies and England's competitors seemed likely to continue. Scots were only marginally in the running as competitors, and might be able to take over the function of entrepot for that traffic. Lucrative it would doubtless prove, but it could also render the English system wholly useless, a matter unlikely to be overlooked in London.[10]

If it was fortuitous that the Scots opted for Darien, the scheme proved wonderfully able to unite them. It seemed brilliant in itself, and an answer to all their dilemmas over protection and free trade too. Thus, for example, it allied Paterson with a man sharing none of his other views, the Patriot, Andrew Fletcher of Saltoun. Both, the one by force of circumstance, the other out of conviction, now agreed it should be a purely Scottish venture. Both expected it to launch a take-off in economic growth. Both thought it would solve the political problem that Scotland, while sovereign, had no means to exercise sovereignty overseas. Both believed that, once she had thus broken her bonds, she could prosper without the costly wars and mercantile corruption by which England sustained her place among the nations. Darien therefore offered the answer to almost every Scottish difficulty. No wonder it aroused such popular enthusiasm.

But the finance still had to come from somewhere, and the notion seemed fantastic that it could come from Scotland. In their sudden confidence, the Scots did not hesitate to apply to Europe, a source anyway more familiar to them than England. Paterson led a delegation to Amsterdam and Hamburg. Its efforts in both were, however, systematically obstructed by a Huguenot friend of William of Orange and agent of his English Government, Sir Paul Rycaut. In Amsterdam he put about that 'the Scotch East India Company', as he insisted on calling it, would make the Scottish standard a flag of convenience for crooks to worm their way into oriental commerce; this was enough to deter support from the Dutch chartered companies. In Hamburg, he sent a stiff note to the senate stating that any deal with the Scots would be regarded and resented by his King as an affront to royal authority. The Hansa city, trying to keep its head above the protectionist waters too, could not afford to ignore the threat. In March 1697 Rycaut reported to London in glee that the Scots, after six months on their fruitless errand, had given up and sailed away. In desperation they turned to Armenian merchants in Amsterdam, dealers in oriental silk and gems transported by the overland route through Russia. But these too valued their connection with the English factory at Surat in India, and would not act for the Scots if it was threatened.[11]

The fatal expedient left was to raise at home the whole capital needed. So carried away were the Scots that even this idea had come to seem not all that fantastic. The appeal for subscriptions of £400,000, driven by indignant patriotism, succeeded handsomely. For the inaugural expedition, half the total was called up. That proved enough, after the endless problems and quarrels, to send a little fleet of five ships at last from the Forth in July 1698 with 1200 colonists on board. Early in November they landed at the chosen site, proudly naming the territory Caledonia, their huddle of tents and huts New Edinburgh, their makeshift citadel Fort St Andrew. High hopes could not offset the appalling conditions, with heat, hurricanes and especially sickness taking a heavy toll. Paterson was with them, and lost his own wife. The camaraderie of the departure did not last long. The governing councillors appointed from home bickered among themselves and with their subordinates. Apart from anything else, next to no trade arrived, and the colonists watched their pathetic stocks of bibles, wigs and cloth shrivel in the sun or rot in the rain. Their sole success came in striking up good relations with the Indians who, though heathens, were in the Scots' estimation rational creatures enjoying natural rights. This view had the advantage of also imputing to them authority to allow settlement on their land – something they would surely feel happy to do as they learned how much nicer to them the Scots were than the Spaniards. Still, after a few months the colonists had all just had enough. They abandoned the expedition in June 1699.[12]

Perhaps there could have been no other outcome. The King, far from guarding the rights of the Company of Scotland as its charter blithely promised, subverted them. In April 1699, he had forbidden his English subjects to offer it any aid or comfort, let alone commerce. The plain ill-temper of a cold, hard Dutchman is not to be discounted as a motive. But he had strategic aims beyond the Scots' ken. They were in fact his main preoccupation, and he could stand no domestic distractions from them. Unable to postpone the question of the Spanish succession as the ruling line of Habsburgs reached its degenerate end, he had to solve it in such a way as to stop Louis XIV of France overthrowing the balance of power. This meant partition of the Spanish realms, the diplomacy for which he conducted entirely in secret. Having no Scots in his confidence, he could never make clear to them why he was so hostile to their splendid venture: he must keep Spain sweet, and she would not tolerate a foreign colony, however well-meant, on the isthmus of Panama over which she carried her transfusions of economic lifeblood, precious metals from Peru. She anyway regarded it as her territory, which ought to have excluded the Company of Scotland by its own charter. Under protests from the Spanish ambassador, William could only send out oblique, if unmistakable, signals that the Scots must give up all idea of doing anything at Darien.[13]

They still did not take the hint. A second fleet of four ships went out, re-establishing the colony on the same site in November 1699. 'The interest of religion, the honour and the credit of the nation is now too far engaged to think of looking backward, which is the least of our thoughts,' the directors of the company declared. Yet little had been learned. English proclamations might have made no difference had the Scots carried with them goods that traders in the region wanted to buy. But a letter home complained: 'We cannot conceive for what end so much thin grey paper and so many little blue bonnets were sent here, being entirely useless and not worth their room in the ship'. Three ministers made themselves obnoxious by going round preaching that the colonists' miseries proceeded from their sins; one railed against them 'for ridiculing all that is sacred, contempt of and scorning to countenance ordinances of worship, for blasphemy, swearing, and cursing, drunkenness, lying, cheating and stealing'. The Spaniards lurking in the forests soon made their presence felt. Once, advancing on their camp at Toubacanti, the Scots did force these tormentors to an engagement and came off the better. But gradually Pimienta and his soldiers closed in. After just four months they gave the forlorn venture its quietus.

The Company of Scotland was not quite dead. A few thought it might do something in the Orient even yet. To that end it sent out four vessels. The first left in 1700 for Java and China, to be wrecked at Malacca on the way home, though her cargo was salved. In 1701 two more set sail for the same destinations. But their captains and crews tired of the journey and turned aside to Madagascar, a haven for piracy now that European states were trying to smother it in its original Caribbean nests. At St Mary's Island off the coast the buccaneers would gather their ill-gotten gains and ship them for sale in America. One Scots captain, Robert Drummond, evidently knew of this traffic: a survivor of Darien, he had kicked his heels for a while in New York. Now, to him and his men, freebooting seemed more attractive than the uncertainties awaiting them further east. But when the vessels anchored, the pirates just seized them; they were afterwards lost, though most of the crews survived and a few returned to tell the tale.

They arrived too late to halt a discreditable final episode. Lying in the tolbooth of Edinburgh at the time, awaiting execution, was an English captain, Thomas Green, with two of his officers. They and their ship had been detained at Leith in retaliation for seizure by the customs in England of the fourth Scottish vessel on its way to the East, dispatched to fetch the cargo of the first. That provocation had not even the shadow of a political pretext: it was an outrage on lawful trade. A man grown bitter against English arrogance, Roderick Mackenzie, secretary to the Company of Scotland, organised the tit-for-tat. Acting on remarks allegedly overheard from members of Green's crew, he trumped up the charge that they had engaged in piracy against the second Scottish expedition. And though everyone now knew better, Green and the officers were hanged in April 1705.

We can gauge from this injustice the depth of the Scots' frustration and enmity. A heady brew of economic ambition and patriotic enthusiasm had inspired a dramatic undertaking, and they would accept nothing but dramatic results. When none came, they had to have scapegoats. Dramatic results never came, however, because none were available. In general nations just do not make their fortunes through a great leap forward, though Scots have always found the fact singularly unpalatable. Having staked all on one throw, and lost, they tended to overlook the significance of the gain they did derive from this their greatest independent colonial enterprise: and it was more than the profit of £47,000 on the Company of Scotland's sole African voyage, which in 1700 came back from Guinea with a cargo of gold and ivory.

Despite everything, Darien had given Scots a vision of what they might achieve overseas. They had, at least in part, conceived the scheme on principles consciously different from economic policy in England or any other European country. This was unavoidable: for the scheme to get going at all it had to reflect in some sort the circumstances of a small nation, which could never aim at hegemonic commerce in the interests of a metropolitan monopoly but only offer in peace and mutual goodwill an entrepot for all. In 1700 this was premature, and did not work. But it sowed a seed for later and different times, more favourable to liberalism. With hindsight, we may view it as a not dishonourable monument to the sacrifices of a brave generation, and to the old nationhood that Scots perforce left behind at Darien.[14]

CHAPTER THREE

'Nobody wishes us well': The European Context

O n October 25, 1795, Robert Jacob Gordon blew his brains out at his house in Cape Town. He was the 52–year-old scion of a breed by his day vanishing, the Dutch Scotsmen. In every generation, males of his family joined up with the Prince of Orange's Scots Brigade. Out of it he had risen to become colonel of the garrison maintained by Holland at this crossroads of the oceans. But revolution was bursting upon the mother country. The French had invaded in January, whereupon Dutch radicals overthrew the stadholder, William V, and proclaimed the Batavian Republic. They would soon find out what it meant to be a client state of France, as they lost their colonies then their fleet to Britain. To her, in any event, the immediate and absolute priority was security of the sea-lanes to the Orient. For this she could turn to Prince William, who took refuge with his uncle, King George III, and sent an order to Cape Town to surrender itself into British hands, thus forestalling any French designs on it. The commander of the flotilla conveying the message was another Scot, George Keith Elphinstone, familiar with these waters since the outset of his maritime career when he had traded to China on the capital of his Jacobite uncle, the Earl Marischal. His arrival in False Bay in July was the first that Gordon and the rest of the colonists knew of events 5000 miles away in Europe, so they did not spring to obey a command coming at them out of the blue. Gordon might have done, but his governor and his troops were pro-French to a man, while the local population no more wanted control from London than from Amsterdam. Elphinstone's instructions were not to fight unless he had to, and he held off. As the end of September approached, however, he could afford to wait no longer. He made a show of force. Gordon's response was to run up the Union Jack and surrender. His difficult but inevitable decision outraged the settlement. Friends, comrades and subordinates abused him for a traitor. Nobody in Cape Town would talk to him, not even his wife. Elphinstone hardly helped, treating him as just another captive with no special authority. A month of humiliation was too much for him: he took a gun and finished it.[1]

Yet Gordon was more than an obtuse military man unable to cope with conflicting allegiances. He could look back over 15 years at the Cape, in a post he won by getting his well-connected father to pull strings inside the Dutch East India Company. Since its trade had long been in decline, the job seemed unlikely to stretch him, but South Africa was the summit of his ambition. He wanted to be left undisturbed so that he could explore, map and record his observations of the interior. Never stinting himself in the service of knowledge, he corresponded with European savants in Dutch,

English and French. He became, for example, the source of information for the African animals included in the Comte de Buffon's *Histoire Naturelle*. That is why we can see today what the quagga, among other extinct species, looked like. No less compelling to Gordon's spirit of inquiry was the recoil of the indigenous human population under the impact of European expansion. He tried, usually in vain, to keep the peace between the settlers advancing up-country and the natives they pushed back. On these errands he penetrated far beyond the frontier, learned the Africans' languages and sensed their despair. With a heritage of Calvinism from both Scotland and Holland he might have shared with the average Dutchman at the Cape its habitual harshness towards the heathen, yet he denied any difference between higher and lower races. In his outlook and interests, as in his divided loyalties, he remained an enlightened Scot, deserving well also of the old Dutch Republic and of the future South Africa.

But Gordon had been poised on too many cusps for his own good. Ahead of his time in intellectual inquiry and humane principle, he was behind it in serving an effete Dutch imperialism now yielding to a lustier British one. In these metahistorical collisions, Scots usually knew how to position themselves on the winning side. Since they penetrated almost all the European empires, however, the odd Scotsman was bound to find himself stranded in perplexity on some exotic shore. His woes did not necessarily go for nothing. To put a more general gloss on matters, the nation's exiguity worked to enrich national experience by making Scots open-minded, ready to take on its own terms a world which they had not made and could never make. That still did not stop them coming to cogent conclusions about its past, present and future. In other words, they made the most of their circumstances, and in the end excelled some much bigger and richer nations.

Imperialism was inaugurated by voyages of exploration which in a sense did no more than open wider to Scots the fruitful foreign fields where they had always been drawn from a bleak homeland. It was the consequent creation of global seaborne trade that made all the difference to them. The minor European nations now had a chance to compete with the major powers in economic terms, as they could never do in political terms. After all Portugal, a small, poor, peripheral country, built the first of the European empires from the fifteenth century. Scorn of her insignificance showed itself misplaced as her seamen exploited the vacuum in maritime power they found on bursting into the Indian Ocean. The ocean was in fact a pacific one, for no power round the shores possessed a navy. Arab traders monopolised the routes, and Portugal realised that she could, by way of the Cape of Good Hope, outflank them to break their hold on overland traffic between East and West too. She came with incredible speed to dominate seaborne trade, supply as well as markets, in a whole quarter of the globe. It was a huge achievement. Spain, straining to win her empire, did it at the expense of primitives; Portugal had lines of communication three times longer and fought peoples as advanced, if not more so, though never able to form contrary alliances and fend her off.[2]

For some reason Scots in their early imperial thinking always took a dimmer view of the Portuguese. These incurred the special wrath of the humanist, George Buchanan, who knew their country from a sojourn in 1547–52. He had arrived from Bordeaux, where he taught the young Michel de Montaigne; the pupil may well have absorbed his master's tenderness towards American Indians and refusal to regard them as subhuman, a theme developed in one of the *Essais*. Buchanan proceeded to the university of Coimbra, but there fell foul of the Inquisition. So he held no high opinion of his hosts, whom he thought corrupt, degenerate and priest-ridden. Worse, they carried their vices overseas. New depths were being plumbed with the sodomy practised in the all-male colonies of Brazil. The natives' cannibalism could hardly be more shameful. To Buchanan commerce itself was anyway an occasion of sin, and foreign trade better banned altogether: the sole purpose of colonies should be the erection of new Churches. Reformer as he was, his views have to be regarded as still medieval, derived from scholastic dogma rather than an empirical or scientific spirit. At any rate, we are here as yet a long way from political economy as the arena of moral sentiment.

Nor was the Scots' hostility solely intellectual. The first organised group of them to go to the New World joined a French expedition disputing control of Brazil in 1555. It was led by Nicolas de Villegagnon, the admiral who had once conducted the infant Mary Queen of Scots to marry his king. He built a fortress on an island off Rio de Janeiro and, 'knowing their fidelity', appointed the Scots his bodyguard. They indeed saved him from internal and external plots against the outpost, which he held for five years till driven off. Not that Scots can really have had so much against Portugal. When in 1589 English pirates raided her outpost of the Azores, they found Scottish ships lying at anchor. Since the islands were the great rendezvous for fleets from the Indies, the likelihood must be that the Scots had come to traffic in exotic goods.[3]

Clearly, the Portuguese were already encountering limits to a minor nation's imperialism, especially in any monopolist or mercantilist aspirations. While they saw discovery as their special mission and in the East pursued it with extraordinary ardour, they hardly penetrated the hinterland of their great fortresses doubling as entrepots. So their cultural influence remained limited. Full of religious zeal, they persecuted and forcibly converted the heathen, yet they never set themselves apart in any racial sense. On the contrary, they readily mated with local women to breed a half-caste stock, still there today, which spoke their tongue and long maintained it as the *lingua franca* of oriental commerce. In all this lay the lesson that a small, poor, peripheral country could not build an empire of settlement, its people being too few; Brazil, model of the colony of plantation, proved an exception, but in the sense that it was perforce worked by imported negroes once the Indians showed themselves useless. By the mid-sixteenth century the Portuguese had plumped for holding what they had, and making of it what it was good for, a commercial empire.

A minor imperial nation could yet exercise an influence out of proportion to its size. Portugal had altered the map of European commerce in favour of peoples along the western seaboard of the continent. The old channel for the produce of the Mediterranean or Orient ran from Venice across the Alps and up the River Rhine to the Hanseatic towns, feeding on the way great, bourgeois cultures self-confident enough to sustain the Renaissance or create the Reformation. If the Venetians thought it hardly worth the worry of what the Portuguese might be trading in as they inched their way down the coast of Africa, by the time they got to the East it was too late to stop them. And the German merchant community suffered, from the height of its prosperity, such a deep, durable collapse as history has hardly witnessed. Not even recompense in the West made up for disaster in the East. Emperor Charles V granted large concessions in Venezuela to his banker, Bartholomäus Welser of Augsburg, whose family controlled the territory for 30 years and financed the sole German conquistador, Nikolaus Federmann, in an expedition of 1539 to the plateau of Bogota in modern Colombia. But they abandoned this effort without being able to turn it to wider account for their compatriots, and a century of religious wars scotched further ventures. Germany's oceanic imperialism had been aborted.

But there was nothing secure about the achievement of the Portuguese either. They made claims to dominion as sweeping as the Spaniards', yet were so poor they could barely absorb the rewards they bore home. Their commerce actually gave them an adverse balance of payments, by exchange of gold and silver for pepper and spices. The exertion was too great to allow anything better than crude imperial government, compared to the bureaucracy of New Spain. Portugal in fact broke under the strain. After the penultimate member of the royal house of Aviz, King Sebastian, squandered her substance and his own life in a futile crusade against the Moors in 1578, she lost her independence. Two years later, she was absorbed into the Habsburgs' dominions to form with Spain a dual monarchy, much like the Union of the Crowns of Scotland and England.

This at once provoked the aggression of the Dutch, who had just launched their own struggle for freedom from the Habsburgs. They felt at liberty to grab whatever Portuguese possessions they could, first the East Indies, then the African colonies, for a time Brazil too. That was the cue for France, England and even Scotland to circle in for the kill. A short-lived Scottish Guinea Company sent out two ships in 1634 to trade for gold along the coast of West Africa, in defiance of the monopoly claimed there by the Portuguese. When one was forced to put into São Tomé, they massacred its crew. It was a symptom of Portugal's desperation. Her losses so outraged her people that at last in 1640 they rose up and threw off the Spanish yoke. They were no less aghast to find that the Dutch would hand nothing back, but on the contrary redoubled their aggression, seizing Malacca in 1641 and Colombo in 1652. Yet each had bigger enemies, and by treaties of 1661 and 1669 they made peace: Holland conceded Brazil to Portugal, and Portugal the East Indies to Holland, while in Africa they divided the spoils. Both had finally attained or retained their independence by profits from commerce and possession of colonies.[4]

Laggards in European expansion, Scots seemed so far to feel no affinity with small nations like their own. If anything they reserved their admiration for the Spaniards. That much had been clear from the response to the first voyages in the Scottish learned circles of late scholasticism and early humanism. Initial reflections on the New World came from John Mair, a son of East Lothian who rose to be professor at the university of Paris, before returning to chairs at Glasgow and St Andrews. In Paris he taught John Calvin, and was popular among Spanish students, including Ignatius Loyola. Perhaps he had in mind the enthusiasms of these young men when in 1519 he published an approving analysis of their country's imperial motives, especially in subjugating the Indians. Good schoolman, he drew from Aristotle a notion that 'some men are by nature slaves, others by nature free, and it is just that one man should be a slave and another free, and it is fitting that one man should rule and another obey'. With this, as it happened, he made a decisive intervention in a contemporary debate among Spanish jurists trying to apply canon or natural law to the American acquisitions. The debate was complicated by the juridical question whether the Emperor held the New World of the Pope, who in bulls of demarcation had commanded the conversion and instruction of the natives. In modern parlance, they were all engaged in devising a theory of empire, working through such thorny matters as rights of conquest, disposition of tribal lands and legal status of Indians. Mair's argument, brought home by his pupils, offered a grateful Spanish monarchy the handy if stark doctrine that it could justify its vast annexations on grounds derived from nature, unburdened by deeper moral perplexities.[5]

Acceptance of the doctrine in the Spanish homeland contributed there to the victory of absolutism. In the New World, however, this was never so complete. Conquistadors, not docile or biddable men, mounted expeditions at their own risk and saw little room for royal interference. They also recruited where they wished – which meant among Scots too. Francisco Vasquez de Coronado set out in 1540 to seek the fabled Seven Cities of Cibola with their gates of turquoise. He rode through Arizona and New Mexico, Texas, Oklahoma and Kansas. His soldiers discovered the Grand Canyon, but otherwise just miserable Indian villages. With them went probably the first Scot to have crossed the Atlantic Ocean since the Viking era, Thomas Blake, whom we know to have spent two decades in the Americas, in Colombia and in Mexico.[6]

It was probably through such individual opportunism that Scots also took some vicarious part in the Spanish system of navigation, closed though it was supposed to be. In fact, even the Reformation could not cut them out of it. In Europe's wars of the late sixteenth century the one that came closest to home, between England and Spain, found Scotland determinedly neutral, to the benefit of her sons who exploited openings to smuggle between the two sides. They anyway had their own ideas about who was the real enemy: in 1588, when tempests wrecked ships of the Spanish Armada on their shores, some burghs gave rescued seamen food and shelter at public expense. Philip II set seriously about wooing James VI for an alliance. Direct trade between Scotland and Spain thus grew. Having initially commended colonial absolutism on intellectual grounds, Scots began to find that economic benefits were likely to be maximised by a freer regime.[7]

Experience in the seventeenth century tended to confirm that finding. Scots under the Union of the Crowns could observe several European analogies with their own situation, especially in the dominions of the Habsburgs. These were self-conscious emulators of the Caesars whom their foes pilloried as grasping at universal monarchy over the ocean as well as the continent. If that was their ambition, it exceeded their powers, as it did of the house which at length overtook them in dynastic ascendancy, the Bourbons. These by 1700 seemed on the point of uniting through inheritance the French and Spanish monarchies. They prompted an alarmed coalition of other powers to stop them. The complex of events raised to strategic prominence the Catalans, the rich, enterprising people who dominated Aragon. They throve largely on commerce to the Mediterranean, having been forbidden direct access to America: the papal demarcation of 1494 applied only to Castile and Portugal, excluding the other Spanish kingdoms which had to send any transatlantic trade of their own through the Castilian entrepot of Seville. Scots and Catalans thus in some sort shared fates, and continued to do so. Both passed from a Union of Crowns into full Union during the War of the Spanish Succession, Scotland in 1707, Catalonia in 1714. For the latter, it came by decree of Philip V, the first Bourbon to rule Spain and in intention the restorer of the monarchy. He provoked a Catalan revolt which was aided by a British expeditionary force under John Campbell, Duke of Argyll, till he had to withdraw against overwhelming odds as the enemy closed in on Barcelona. The Bourbons' general was James Stewart, Duke of Berwick, bastard of James VII, who took the city's surrender, reversing on this distant shore the fortunes of their two houses in Scotland.

While the one people had been defeated, and the other remained undefeated, their treatment in a unified state yet showed certain resemblances. Scotland gained access to colonies and some assistance for industrial development. This second policy was pursued with more vigour in Catalonia, making up for a tardy commercial liberalisation. But in practice illegal private merchants anyway ignored the controls, even after 1756 when traffic to America was allowed under a monopolistic company. Not till 1789 did the Catalans reach equality with the Scots, by which time Spain had declined so far as to negate the benefit. Against greater odds Catalonia followed a path similar to Scotland's. In the end she profited from America not through privilege but through her traders' learning to work together and turn to account, if necessary outside the law, the secular expansion and diversification of global commerce. This also reconciled her own elite to the state where fate had placed it.[8]

While Scots came to deplore the economic restriction normally entailed by Catholic absolutism, they never swallowed the *Leyendra Negra*, the notion originally bruited abroad from Elizabethan England that the Spaniard in the New World was such a beast and bigot as to justify any reprisal against him. Rather Scots found in him, or in his country, an intellectual puzzle: why, wallowing in an endless flow of precious metals, did it suffer national decline? The most sustained reflection on this came from the pen of the Patriot, Andrew Fletcher of Saltoun, with his *Discorso delle Cose di Spagna* (1698). From a premiss that the Spanish empire was bound to change anyway, given the imminence of a new dynasty, he speculated how it might revive in terms that seemed designed to make English flesh creep. The key was for it to turn from a military into an economic empire, with religious tolerance to attract settlers who could expand agriculture, industry and trade. Thus a universal monarchy more durable than the Habsburgs' might form, in the face of which England, among other rivals, 'would become poor and of little importance'. The less anglophobe part of Fletcher's thinking carried over into John Campbell's *Account of the Spanish Settlements in America* (1747). It argued that their strict economic regulation had depressed commercial profits and robbed colonials of natural rights, though much might yet be retrieved by the introduction of free trade. Adam Smith could only shake his head over the obstinate refusal to countenance this. William Robertson, too, in his *History of America* (1777), depicted Spanish imperialism not as a monstrous aberration but as another civilising mission, excessively authoritarian to be sure, yet now improving: that would continue as the metropolis enlightened itself.

In reality, even so, it had been better to escape the Spanish yoke. The example, much closer to home, of the southern Netherlands showed how the absolutism of the Habsburgs had been the enemy of prosperity. Here they contrived to stifle an economy once no less enterprising than the liberated one of the northern provinces. From the fifteenth century, Antwerp had sent out ships to trading stations in the Azores, San Domingo, Puerto Rico and Yucatan. But the traffic was ruined by the Dutch War of Independence, and strangled after final closure of the River Scheldt in 1648. The Spanish Netherlands languished till the Treaty of Utrecht (1713), when they went to Austria. With the change of ruling line came a change of policy which at once began a revival. Scots, often exiled Jacobites, helped. In 1720, Alexander Hume served as supercargo on the first voyage from Ostend to India, and set up a factory at Bankibazar by the River Hooghly. On the advice of his countryman, John Crawford, a shady character doubling as a British spy, the Emperor Charles VI established the Ostend Company in 1723, having founded an East India Company for Austria herself in 1719. Ostend was, like the Company of Scotland, a prospective door for interlopers into the oriental trade, though the merchants there seem to have made most money from slaves. The Governments in The Hague and in London anyway viewed them with suspicion. Under diplomatic pressure, the Emperor dissolved his company in 1731.[9]

Meanwhile the Dutch Republic had gone through a cycle of imperial rise and fall. From the time of its first oceanic voyages in 1595, amid desperate struggles in self-defence against Spain, it treated them also as a way of striking back at the Catholic powers, not least at poor Portugal. Scots entered the fray too. Some had crossed to fight with their Protestant brethren almost as soon as the war of liberation broke out in 1572. They continued to do so, notably in the Scots Brigade. Scotland anyway belonged to the traditional Dutch trading network. In exchange for her own raw materials she bought manufactures through her staple at Veere in Zeeland, and soon re-exports of goods from South America, Africa and Asia, with which that port also traded.

Scots' penetration of the Dutch empire, too, thus started early. In 1614, Jan Pieterszoon Coen, the Governor-general of the Indies, commended them as willing, obedient workers 'who usually keep themselves clean'. His prim approval was more warmly reciprocated, for Scots liked and admired the Dutch more than any other foreigners – though often wondering why God, in his inscrutable purposes, did not show the same favour to their own more deserving case. At the beginning of the seventeenth century, William Alexander praised Holland's resourceful courage. At the end, William Paterson ascribed her people's success to 'generous principles of ease, freedom and security, which they have prudently opposed to the heavy impositions, restraints and impositions of others'. Ties of interest became bonds of blood in Scots-Dutch families: the chiefs of Clan Mackay, in Amsterdam the banking dynasty of Hope, the Groats settled at the northern extremity of Great Britain, the burgesses of Dysart and Flushing who called themselves Black in the one and Zwart in the other – and the Gordons who would send a scion to South Africa. There were those in 1706 who believed any Union should be with the Dutch Republic rather than with England.[10]

Holland's imperial experience thus contributed to Scotland's. Like the Portuguese, the Dutch found it hard to penetrate the lands they discovered. Not till the nineteenth century did they hold any sovereign territories. Meanwhile they contented themselves with outposts at the Cape, in Ceylon and in Java. These, enough to assure economic ascendancy, never created an exclusive monopoly: even the suppression of piracy and smuggling, let alone any more systematic defence, demanded more resources than Holland had. And as bearers of culture the Dutch lagged behind the Portuguese. Their colonialism contained no proselytising or civilising element. Calvinist doctrines of election gave them a strong sense of apartheid, reflected in the very physical surroundings they chose: Batavia made no concession to its exotic setting, being built with canals and bridges just like a town in Holland. It was not, however, meant as a colony of settlement. Dutchmen in Batavia could seldom live with Dutchwomen, who would not leave home. Many took concubines, but others preferred to contract regular marriages with Christians, which narrowed their choice to the local Indo-Portuguese. A Calvinist, European male society found itself wedded to a Catholic, oriental female society, with offspring seldom recognisable as Dutchmen, for it was the women who passed their culture on. So hardly a soul in the East could be defined as a Dutch settler. Nor was emigration possible on any scale, since Holland had no surplus of people. Even much nearer, in North America, the numbers in New Netherlands were outstripped by those in New

England, spilling over the boundary and preparing the way for the loss by the Dutch of their colony in 1664. In the East, with a dense indigenous population and a rooted economic system, colonisation was a still more chimerical idea. The death-toll anyway told its own grim story: 324,000 left Holland for the Orient in the seventeenth century, but only 113,000 returned.

Holland's situation did on the other hand prove conducive to liberal principles, starting with those of Hugo Grotius. They would serve as the best defence of a country which usually had to take diplomatic isolation as a fact of life. 'There is nobody who wishes us well in all the Indies,' a Dutchman lamented, 'yea, we are deadly hated by all nations.' Indeed they faced ceaseless competition against an array of European as well as Asiatic rivals, hardly less ferocious even when they were all supposed to be at peace. For example, Dutch success soon made an enemy of the English, who had been indispensable allies in the war of independence. Sometimes Holland could only blame herself, as when she scotched England's efforts to break into the Far East with a minatory massacre of her merchants at Amboina in the Spice Islands in 1623, organised by the steward of the Dutch factory, an Aberdonian called George Forbes. After that, Governments in London were forever trying to persuade others that they suffered from Dutch rapacity. Most, however, thought England's hegemony would be worse. Puny Holland's liberalism came to her rescue because others saw the benefit of having in her an entrepot and financial centre without the manpower or armed strength to transmute economic into political primacy. England was more to be feared because more capable of exerting the political muscle necessary to maintain the economic mastery which Holland, to her chagrin, had snatched from under her nose. She showed that muscle in 1707, when she induced Scotland to shift from the Dutch into her own sphere of economic influence, a major adjustment between the two. In any case Holland's achievement, magnificent as in its turn it was, is placed in perspective when we mark that her oriental traffic passed its peak during the last quarter of the seventeenth century. And while profitable, it was always of less real value than the routine carrying trade in western Europe. Steady sale of Holland's homely fish, cheese, wool and linen remained the prime source of her prosperity. Her influence over partners in these wide commercial networks, including Scotland, helped to preserve some room for manoeuvre in her international relations for more than a century.[11]

A second of those partners was Sweden, though she herself had looked ready to join Holland and Portugal in unlikely imperialism amid a similar unexpected outburst, during the seventeenth century, of energy and achievement. Her empire, stretching round the Baltic Sea, was a military one, sustained by her innovations in the art of war and the weakness of her neighbours. The practical Swedes dominated the commerce of their inland sea too, and shared a small nation's economic outlook. Their great Chancellor, Axel Oxenstierna, was a free trader by the standards of his time, urging all countries to lift controls on commerce. In his view the aim of policy lay not in monopoly but in a buoyant revenue, which Sweden could earn as a middleman. That was no doubt why she often felt happy to organise her own efforts in co-operation with Holland. A Dutchman, Pieter Minuit, led the expedition, in which half the capital and crews were also Dutch, to found New Sweden on the River Delaware in 1638. It was in fact acquired by Holland in 1655, before being lost to England in 1664. But Fort Kristina, renamed Wilmington, stayed Swedish-speaking till the American Revolution; its colonists are credited with the introduction of the log-cabin to America.

As Dutch influence now declined, it was Scots who took over the catalytic role. The Swedish African Company of 1647 had been an umbrella for anti-monopolist merchants in Holland; the Swedish East India Company of 1731, set up at Gothenburg with Jacobite participation, turned into a vehicle for smuggling tea to Britain. Colin Campbell, a fleeing debtor, arrived via Ostend to serve as supercargo on the first ship sent by the company to Canton. In fact a majority of the employees were Scots, the most distinguished being William Chalmers, who founded the later Technical University of Gothenburg. It all went to show that a small country maintaining its independence could even so be sure of no more than exiguous colonial rewards. Sweden did not in the long run have the economic and human resources to sustain her empire, which turned out to have been an historical aberration corrected by time.[12]

That also held for Denmark. She too was an economic satellite of the Dutch, who anyway sought good relations because of their traffic through the Sound. When Danes wanted a modern colonial commerce, however, they in turn relied a good deal on the network of Scots scattered through the northern nations. In the West Indies, Denmark took the Virgin Islands in 1665. One in ten of the planters during the eighteenth century was a Scotsman, many of them doctors who in a torrid climate soon earned enough to buy estates. The most famous scion of the community was Alexander Hamilton; born in 1755 to a settler from Ayrshire, he left as a young man for New York and his career as a founding father of the United States. In the Orient, Danish business was run by the Browns of Colstoun in East Lothian, some of whom may have emigrated because of Jacobitism. John Brown became in 1770 a director of the Danish East India Company. His brother David was governor of its factory at Tranquebar in India till 1777.

But Denmark never built up much global business. She suffered under the same constraints as Sweden, though occupying a greater number of tropical emporiums and being an older colonial power, in one sense the oldest of all. She had since the turn of the millennium peopled and ruled Iceland which, however, enjoyed a rugged if quite apolitical cultural autonomy. The poor, remote and often hungry isle was of little obvious benefit to the mother country, and some Scots felt sure they could make better use of it. John Cochrane, son of the Earl of Dundonald, came home in 1785 from sojourns in Denmark and her settlements overseas. He wrote to inform Henry Dundas, political boss of Scotland, that the Government in Copenhagen might well agree to swap Iceland for a second West Indian outpost. Scots would then acquire an economic dependency: from the slopes of Hekla they could import the sulphur needed in new industrial processes while exporting in exchange hardy sheep to breed and feed the Icelanders. As a reward for this modest proposal the house of Cochrane asked only for the earldom of Iceland to be added to its titles.[13]

Over three centuries since the first discoveries, the imperial torch had passed to the northern nations, yet not always to the biggest and richest. The Germans, for example, dawdled yet. In the Peace of Westphalia (1648) they had even lost access to the ocean. Foreigners imposed their control at the mouths of her major rivers, the Rhine, Elbe, Oder and Vistula. The land of the Hansa became in effect landlocked, its towns shrank, its wealth dwindled. No sortie would be possible till, towards the end of the seventeenth century, a modern state emerged on German soil, in the shape of Brandenburg-Prussia under the Great Elector, Frederick William. During this era of Darien, he shared some of the Scots' interests. In 1682 he founded an African Company which set up on the Gold Coast, in India and on Tobago and, needless to say, had Scots on its payroll. Yet Prussia was destined to remain a military, continental power, rather than a commercial, maritime one. Preoccupied by other things, she abandoned the colonies and suppressed the company in 1718. With a second chance gone, Germans could only look in frustration on foreigners' ventures. That was perhaps why, in a survey of European expansion published in 1720, Gottfried Zenner, a subject of the Elector of Hanover, tried to shame them by pointing out that even the Scots had done better, though they, too, suffered from disunity and subordination to foreign interests.[14]

What generalisations can be made about the experience of small nations in the European expansion? Even the Dutch never decisively overcame the basic problems, of economics any more than of politics. Every colonising nation, great and small, faced the question of how to combine the capital and labour at its disposal so as to profit from the resources opened up by exploration. The question can be analysed for any economic activity and is not primarily one of scale, since now as then most ventures start out small. In the age of discoveries a host of other imponderables, of diplomacy, geography and information, complicated matters. Their very variety and unfamiliarity admitted a range of experiment and solution.

For a century or more after the discoveries, imperialism had conformed to an old pattern, little different from the Mediterranean imperialism of the Venetians. Their profit accrued from gathering the riches of the gorgeous East, bringing them home and sending them out over Europe. They acquired an empire for that sole purpose. The traffic lay in the hands of specialists who acted on their own account without privilege, under the republic's regulation but not control. Failure of such methods when applied to oceanic imperialism led to the expedient of chartered companies, on an assumption that risk could be cut through mercantilist control over factors of production.

Sometimes it worked, sometimes not. It worked in the Indian Ocean, for the Dutch and English companies. It did not work in the Atlantic Ocean, which remained open in practice to free enterprise, so that the companies were almost bound to fail. While the Company of Scotland has had little but condescension from historians, equivalents in England never showed much staying power either. They could not keep the Atlantic, even the English Atlantic, to themselves, but had to share it with others enjoying none of their privilege. As colonisers they performed well enough, but as businesses they foundered every one, at least till the Hudson's Bay Company and the Royal African Company at the end of the seventeenth century. Both confined their ambitions to a limited region where normal commerce was hazardous, and settlement impossible because of the climate. This suggests that, in determining success or failure, the companies' targets were as important as their domestic environments. In those environments the real need was for novel types of investment, in forms of capitalism more advanced than mercantilism. Since capitalism is in principle open to everybody, there could be nothing absurd about a small, poor, peripheral country embarking on colonial enterprise. If its methods can be criticised with benefit of hindsight, they formed part of the process of trial and error which Europeans had to work through before they learned how to succeed.[15]

As for the politics, Scotland's experience differed little from that of other small European nations. However ancient, wealthy and ingenious, they could well find themselves swallowed up in a larger empire, especially the Spanish one; Scots were luckier than most in not being subjected to a crushing absolutism at the same time. The Dutch proved the exception, defying their circumstances. Their fortitude was above praise, and won its just deserts, yet did not in the long run save them from the real limitations in the size and resources of their state. By the end of their heroic age they were, in political terms, back where they had started, prosperous but barely capable of independent external action. Such weakness formed, even so, no insuperable barrier to a share in the European expansion.

Perhaps the most important consequences of the small nations' imperialism came in a third sphere. The Dutch example underlines how often it was accompanied by a cultural flowering. What proved true of the Holland of Rembrandt proved true of . the Portugal of Camões, the Denmark of Holberg, the Sweden of Queen Christina. Nor was the achievement confined to high culture. It spread among ordinary folk, in the diffusion of a popular literature of travels and wonders, in the invention of ancient and modern myths about themselves. A general explanation is again hard to find on the basis of political conditions, different in each country. Cultural universals had also fallen away with the end of religious unity in the West. Yet some such experiences remained common, the Renaissance, the Reformation (or Counter-Reformation), the discoveries: though in every instance they took a specific form and evoked an individual response. That response often proved formative of small nations. It answered a psychological need for self-assertion in a world where they were not held to be of much account, and drew on a national pride coexistent with a nagging sense of national inferiority.

All this illumines the case of Scotland, even if she lost her independence. It suggests she owed her own cultural flowering and share in the European expansion, not to speak of economic transformation, to influences more numerous and general than the Union of 1707. In other words, that arrangement was permissive, and the real reasons for much of the subsequent headlong progress lay elsewhere. At the turn of the century, Scotland seemed an unlikely candidate for it. But its engines had already been stoked by internal improvements. Scots began to exploit their resources better, stimulated by easy access to oceanic routes, but also by privation, to name just two of many forces at work. And trade became vital to them. They opened their country to foreign products, techniques and ideas, essential elements in their agricultural, then commercial, then industrial revolutions. If often hampered by discord, famine and war, they reached the point of being able to aim realistically to develop their economy. In so aiming, not least in seeking as far as circumstance allowed a share in European expansion, they were quite typical of the continent's small nations, with which a comparison has much to tell us. They also made one individual response of unique importance. They became aware of the diversity of manners among mankind, and awakened in themselves the ethical scepticism which formed a foundation of their Enlightenment.[16]

CHAPTER FOUR

'The true interest of a country':
The Scottish Debate

C aptain William Kidd was reeling drunk as his guards led him out of Newgate Prison in London on May 23, 1701. They helped him, a noose already round his neck, into an open cart draped in black, among several of his crewmen already slumped there. It moved off, led by a marshal of the Admiralty bearing the silver oar of his authority. The procession passed through festive crowds swilling beer and gin, hurling impudent or ribald jests, picking pockets, singing ballads, 'one continual fair all the way'. It made across the city to the mudflats of Wapping, where at Execution Dock a gibbet stood. Kidd had to watch while a shipmate was hanged before him. Then he mounted the scaffold, tried an address to the heedless mob and, after the usual preparations, was turned off. The gallows broke and he sprawled in the mire. On inspection, the timber proved to be rotten. The guards dragged Kidd to a tree and strung him up there. They chained his corpse to a post below the high-water mark till the tide washed over it thrice. Then they coated his head with tar, bound it in iron and fitted a cage to hold it in place while his flesh putrefied. In that state he was displayed for some years at Tilbury Point, as a deterrent to pirates.

Captain Kidd has gone down in history as one of the most notorious buccaneers. Yet he was an unlikely candidate for such a course in life, or for the scene of sordid horror that ended it. Born in 1654 in Dundee, he at length settled like many of his countrymen in New York. He married a rich widow, established himself as merchant, landowner, pillar of the community. He was in good enough standing to obtain from the governor, the Earl of Bellomont, a letter of marque for privateering on ships under the colours of France, then at war with England, and a second, special commission for suppression of piracy. Equipped for what promised to be a venture as lucrative to himself as useful to the public, Kidd embarked for Madagascar in October 1696. He found neither Frenchmen nor freebooters. His impatient seamen, some sickening, grew mutinous. To placate them, he tried to plunder the shipping he was meant to protect. He assailed passing Arabs and Portuguese, still without success. Not till February 1698 did he manage to catch a vessel owned by Indian merchants of Surat, under an English captain but on papers from the French East India Company. With misgivings, Kidd claimed her as lawful prize and brought her into St Mary's Island. His jeering sailors promptly took the chance to desert a bungler. Most turned pirate, leaving him to sail the captured ship home with a skeleton crew. Unfortunately, tales of his misdeeds carried back meanwhile had somehow been so magnified that a price was put on his head. When, after eluding pursuit, he regained Boston in 1699, he was clapped in jail. Having lost his papers along the way, he appealed for help to Bellomont. The governor coolly betrayed him, denying that he had ever issued him any commissions. Kidd and his crew were sent for trial to London, there condemned to death.[1]

His career shows how thin the line was in this era between legal and illegal seafaring, between normal business and buccaneering or smuggling. A merchant might live off peaceful commerce where and when he could, but turn without qualms to crime and violence if he could not. This was understandable among those excluded from national monopolies of trade. Yet even those included could find one monopoly clashing with the next, as the Company of Scotland did when it tried to raise capital in London. Again, letters of marque issued to privateers in their own jurisdiction would license conduct amounting in a second to piracy. Certainly it was little different from the conduct of real pirates, who acted under no authority. A man might slip from one category to another according to circumstance or convenience. Many apart from Kidd landed at times on opposite sides of the law: Henry Morgan, the Welsh rover who finished as Governor of Jamaica, Piet Heyn, the galley-slave who became the immortal, heroic commander of a Dutch fleet in a famous victory over Spain, not to mention William Paterson. Perhaps there is a pattern here of men from the European periphery who, in pursuit of commercial freedom, broke monopolies by whatever means came to hand, following more ancient marginal trading peoples, Jews and Armenians, who always ignored national or legal boundaries. A cleverer Kidd might have shown his compatriots how in the interstices of mercantilism they could still thrive, and how useless it was for European powers to distort competition in a world with trade enough for all. Monopoly instead fostered crimes such as his. The criminals were yet useful in economic history by keeping monopoly under hostile pressure, and eventually helping to force it open. Scots would do their part, in deed and thought, to bring the international commercial system at last back to its senses. Kidd may thus not have died in vain.[2]

Scots, while still an independent nation, had tried to dilute mercantilism with a more liberal impulse, though they felt concerned rather with economic growth than with free trade as such. They knew how poor they were and hoped to better themselves through planned patriotic exertion, especially commercial innovation. That effort had been doomed by Darien, or rather by the sabotage of a King William acting openly in the English interest. He taught the Scots a hard lesson about reason of state, that they could not evade the political implications of intrepid entrepreneurship. Amid the gloom of the crisis for their state which followed,-it was easy to overlook that Scotland might yet retrieve something if she persevered in efforts to improve her productive capacity and trading methods.

Only once the political crisis had been solved could Scots take realistic stock of their circumstances. Then they were able to move the debate on fruitfully, even momentously. It would prove crucial to the whole of mankind, not just to them, by shaping what they aptly called political economy. The term is significant, not least for its continental origin. Borrowed ultimately from Antoine de Montchrétien's *Traité d'économie politique* (1615), it was in general a sign of the influence in Scotland exerted by early Dutch and French economic thinkers, such as Hugo Grotius and Pierre de Boisguilbert, more liberal than Englishmen of the day. It also made explicit that economic policy could not be divorced from its political context. The rival claims of freedom and authority were as compelling to Scots in this field of inquiry as in religion and morals. And their consequent debate clearly antedated the Union of 1707: the Union was in fact one outcome of it.[3]

Still, it was a complicated debate and it divided Scots, even individual Scots, several ways. The Patriot, Andrew Fletcher of Saltoun, complained that 'this nation, of all those which possess good ports, and lie conveniently for trade and fishing, has been the only part of Europe which did not apply itself to commerce'. His trouble was that he tended to disapprove of commerce if it compromised the stern, classical values to which he gave his prime allegiance. He thus defined development as a public duty, to be promoted primarily through public works, amid drastic measures to eliminate poverty by Highland clearances, enslavement of the idle and other horrors hardly better than the evils they were meant to cure. Even if this dirigisme in one country had been feasible, it still met the problem that the country, should it be Scotland, would remain a small one vulnerable to larger, richer neighbours. Fletcher retorted with a plan for international agreement to stop some states dominating others. Sovereignty in the British Isles, for example, would be divided among a dozen or so regional centres of power, an arrangement to be replicated on a larger scale in Europe. It was all very internationalist and far-sighted, well ahead of its time, but quite impractical in the conditions of the early eighteenth century (as Fletcher no doubt saw too). Its value lay in the germ of the idea that imperial dominion was not the only aim available to European nations, which might just as well turn to some sort of federal arrangement among themselves and in their empires. For Scots, between Darien and the Union, it had a special resonance.

John Law, too, saw how the problems of a poor country were compounded in one also small. He might have had more influence on the Scottish debate by tarrying longer. He had gone as a youth to London, whence he was forced to flee for killing a man in a duel. After wandering in Europe, he only returned home in the years 1703–6. He had passed his time in originating modern ideas about credit and its distinction from capital. He did not, by today's theories, get the distinction quite right, but he saw that it was there and that money could assume some of its actual future functions, enlarging exchanges, prompting division of labour, fostering production, creating demand not only for goods but also for itself. He proposed a short cut to capital accumulation by monetising the nation's existing assets or, in practical terms, a land bank. Then, Law argued, Scots' lower costs could undercut the very Dutch: 'By a greater quantity of money and oeconomy, the Dutch monopolise the trades of carriage even from the English. Scotland has a very inconsiderable trade, because she has but a very small part of the money'. The point was that Scotland need not be condemned to poverty just because she had no gold. Law also published a plan for a new council of trade which, in co-ordinating the nation's efforts, would control credit and perhaps supervise some equitable distribution of the benefits. While Law's ideas impressed his countrymen, he had no time to follow them up. As the Union approached, he went into exile again, probably because he was a Jacobite. He at any rate disliked the English and felt more at home in France, where besides he converted to Catholicism. He won his place in history by introducing to his adopted country the chartered company, through which he promoted his schemes along the River Mississippi. At his acme he was Minister of Finance for the Regent Philip of Orléans, and the most sought-after man in Paris. Once, to close a long interview with several ladies, he excused himself to answer a call of nature. 'Oh, si ce n'est que cela,' they cried, 'cela ne fait rien. Pissez toujours, et écoutez-nous.' His crash came in 1720, but his flair had touched the imagination of the French and contributed to their tradition of grandiose public policy.[4]

Other anti-unionists registered disillusion with the idea that dramatic solutions could be imposed or inspired by the state. A contrary realism manifested itself in Glasgow's merchant community. It had not been swept off its feet by Darien. Foreign systems of navigation, notably England's, still let Glaswegians pursue that form of free trade known as smuggling, and they waxed fat on it. This would give them a reason (though their militant Presbyterianism gave a greater) to oppose the Union. Meanwhile, one of the merchants, John Spreul, already in trouble for breaking the burgh's rules, called for national trading restrictions to be relaxed. He still stressed that, with no panacea available, Scotland could expect only gradual expansion of a modest commerce. But by setting aims within her grasp, she might rid herself of dependence on England, as of its economic and political trammels. It had already, in some of its different forms, impeded progress: increased traffic was bought at the cost of greater hostility, not closer friendship, and no benefit could be derived from involuntary involvement in the eternal English wars. Spreul believed Scots might carry on a profitable trade with every nation, so restoring their European and widening their intercontinental commerce. His contention that each import could be matched by a Scottish export smacked yet of mercantilism, but contained some notion of open exchange among countries specialising in different products.

An advocate from Edinburgh and prolific pamphleteer, William Black, argued on similar lines. While Scotland needed no political union with England, commercial separation was not the stark alternative. Scotland's economic performance had been poor, yet showed signs of improving and might show more if Scots would work at it sensibly, step by step. He too still placed faith in regulated trade, but warned against expecting miracles from any political scheme: he preferred more open traffic with the English inside some federal arrangement. James Donaldson was another writer who, drawing on the existing stock of prescriptions, still wanted to move in a more liberal direction, in his case after the Dutch example. Yet another, James Hodges, even advanced free-trading grounds to reject a Union, because the stronger partner would destroy the weaker, whereas an independent Scotland could use liberalism for her own purposes. Finally the author, not yet established, of *The State of Controversy betwixt United and Separate Parliaments* (1706) went so far as to urge that Scotland, in the event of rupture with England, should declare herself a free port and negotiate commercial treaties with other countries. Such people remind us of a forgotten current of moderate opinion which did not despair of the Scottish economy, and which could regard a Union as just one, not inevitably the best, among several possible paths to plenty.

Still, a significant figure at this end of the spectrum did turn unionist. William Paterson knew violence, but almost anticipated the Victorians in idealising commerce as a pacifier and reconciler of nations. Even Darien never stopped him afterwards devising further plans for the Company of Scotland, if not always liberal ones. He too wanted a council of trade to direct economic activity towards capital accumulation for the purpose of commerce, though by fiscal rather than monetary means, under a rigorous regime of taxation. Yet he insisted that 'there is not any one part or piece of trade in the world, but might and would prosper better without, than in a monopoly'. And it does appear that, in his not very precise mind, a precocious economic individualism remained uppermost:

> In matters of trade, the interest of particular men, and that of their country, is so far from being always the same, that they are ofttimes directly opposite to one another. It is the true interest of a country, that the many should rather get every one a little, than a few should get much, because the more diffusive and universal the gain, the more it will naturally contribute to the growth and progress of industry; whereas, on the contrary, the more it is limited and restrained, the more it tends to the clogging and cramping thereof.

His schemes came to nothing, for nobody would listen to the author of a disaster, and national energies, not to mention finances, were for now exhausted. Paterson then took up the cause of Union with England: since his preference of free trade with all was impossible in a mercantilist world, Union offered the best practical prospect of extending it for Scotland. He was elected for the Dumfries Burghs in the new Parliament of the United Kingdom in 1707 but unseated on petition, after characteristic mismanagement of the poll.[5]

Such was the order of economic battle among Scots as, between Darien and the Union, they morosely contemplated the future. Much ink has been spilled on the subject in our day too, if often to little purpose, since the contours of the debate have inevitably become obscured. On the one hand there was profound ignorance of matters taken for granted now, on the other a bubbling flow of fresh ideas in a virgin field of inquiry. Modern academic historians have tended to range themselves behind one of two reductionist readings, neither of which begins to do all this justice. The first favours economic factors as the prime cause of the Union, then seen as inevitable. The other favours political factors, and so regards the outcome as rigged. The waters are further muddied by positions taken on the basis of modern opinions rather than of what may or may not have happened in 1707. Thus to pare down such complexity is a singularly silly sort of scholarly conceit, not to say a gross distortion. The economic and political considerations were as inextricably mixed as they are today, say, in the debates about Britain and Europe.

There were in fact no straightforward arguments, economic or political. On the economic side, so many of the first principles had yet to be understood. Absent from the debate, for instance, was any grasp of such an elementary concept as comparative advantage: Scotland, which could well have competed in exports of coal, instead tried vainly to compete in exports of cloth. What did come across clearly to some – notably to Spreul, who after all made his living as a merchant – was that the argument from free trade must in one way have counted against a Union, since England's commercial system was mercantilist. Other opponents denied that transatlantic commerce was necessary or even desirable. There they went too far, but the new trades were in truth less important than the old; the former might be more exotic and occasionally lucrative, yet in a workaday manner the latter always showed themselves of more lasting value. In that case the argument from free trade could not claim a Union to be unambiguously beneficial, for it also entailed penalties. It would throw barriers across tried and trusted commercial links, to France and above all to Holland; the complaints at the Union in Dutch sources attest this was no small matter. Since, incidentally, it would hurt England's main rival, the economic motivation cannot have come solely from the Scottish side.

Scots were anyway entitled, with such disruption in view, to ask recompense. What unionists had on offer was no more than the chance to revive an old trade which had been failing, that with England and her colonies, though these did form the largest zone of free trade available. But it had been failing because of unilateral action by the English themselves, and Scots might be forgiven for suspicion of liberal pleading inspired from the same quarter. The claim could not have been far-fetched that, should they want free trade, they had better stay independent and carry on as they were, legally if they could, illegally if they must. So there was nothing clear-cut about the unionist economic case. That explains why burghs dominated by commercial interests sent up petitions hostile to a Union, and why Glasgow's MP voted against it.[6]

Nor was there, however, anything clear-cut about the mercantile nationalists' case. Their policy had brought no improvement. They had to explain away the embarrassing fact that mercantilism worked better for big countries than small ones, and thus rather favoured the Union. If mercantilism was the answer, then Scotland had better attach herself to the system engrossing England and her colonies than take a chance on free trade with everyone, when there could be no guarantee of free trade with anyone. This was clearly why Fletcher felt driven to assert that the English did not mean what they said when they offered free trade. After all, Ireland's closer political relationship with them had not brought free trade for her. The line of argument was strong, and prompted the Scots commissioners negotiating the Treaty to get free trade written in from the start, at article IV. That cut the economic ground from under the feet of the mercantile nationalists, who could safely be left to split themselves politically between Presbyterian and Jacobite factions. In the event, since no case was clear-cut, no option without drawbacks, it would not be surprising if English bribery was what resolved the confusions and tipped the balance in favour of the Union.

Even then, the Scots agreed to it in some sense on their own terms. They had shown an acquaintance with contemporary economic theories, on trade and on improvement generally, though without finding effective means to put them into practice. Those theories had been the subject of debate for a century among all three great commercial nations of northern Europe: England, France and Holland. In the 1690s, Scotland suddenly became a party to that debate, and one with useful things to say. She could not yet produce a classic text worthy of international recognition, but only a flurry of pamphlets concerned with the national interest. Yet that was enough to bring her to a moment of truth, when she realised she had no future in continuing to vaunt herself as a feudal, martial nation, otherwise distinguished by her learning and her godliness. The sole way forward, as every successful European country showed, lay through commerce. What Scots then did was enter a mercantilist system on free-trading grounds. It was not the free trade they had hoped for at Darien. But it was a fair substitute: free trade with a big neighbour and its colonial system. Scots justified it with the intellectual ingenuity, perhaps Presbyterian casuistry, typical of the sort they would often devise in their complex relations with the English for the next 300 years.[7]

That also carried the debate on. The case for political intervention in trade would be most fully worked out 60 years later, fittingly by an exiled Jacobite and disciple of Law, Sir James Steuart. In the *Inquiry into the Principles of Political Oeconomy* (1767) he said that 'when a nation, which has enriched herself by a reciprocal commerce in manufactures with other nations, finds the balance of trade turn against her, it is her interest to put a stop to it altogether'. He was unmoved by the caveat that this would vitiate the international division of labour soon to be extolled by Adam Smith: 'Let such precautions be carried to a certain length on all hands, and we shall see an end to the whole system of foreign trade, so much à-la-mode, that it appears to become more and more the object of the attention as well as of the imitation of all modern statesmen'. Still, Steuart was like fellow Scots a pragmatist, trying to fathom present conditions in the light of experience from other times and places. He discerned a general pattern: trade, justifiably protected at first, could then be usefully opened up to free exchange, before reaching a final stage where it generated such riches as to render a country uncompetitive. That was when the state should again step in. His conclusions have been labelled mercantilist, but are better seen as open-minded and flexible on intervention, given that no one theory could be uniformly applied to the varied circumstances of different countries. After his return from exile he was asked to report on the economy of Bengal, and he did not hesitate to condemn the mercantilism of the East India Company, now fortified by political hegemony. It had halted free flows of funds, so that silver no longer came from Britain to buy Indian goods, while earnings from exports to third countries had fallen. Chronic monetary crisis followed. Steuart thought it might be met by note-issuing banks on the Scottish model. Later he was to agree with Smith that mercantilism lay at the root of American grievances.

The argument in principle for piecemeal intervention to correct patent ills had a long way to run in Scotland. Smith discredited mercantilism but did not explicitly repudiate it. His follower, the Earl of Lauderdale, would turn back towards it: besides calling for protection of agriculture at home, he thought the relation between Britain and India should be consciously reconstructed as a system of navigation like the former one between Britain and America. In a later generation still, the eclectic Thomas Chalmers, who was ultimately to equate economic with natural laws, at first denied that free trade could 'lead to any sensible enlargement of wealth'. By then, however, in the nineteenth century, such ideas were to most Scots merely old-fashioned. Liberalism had triumphed among them and the obsolescence of the colonial system played a large part in shaping their political economy.[8]

Yet that triumph had not always seemed certain. By 1745 the Scots, in worse odour than ever with the English after the last Jacobite rising, were also waiting still for the Union's economic benefits. It took David Hume, in his *Political Discourses* (1752), to assuage their dismay and frustration. He restated the case for free trade in a more refined era: 'Where an open communication is preserved among nations, it is impossible but the domestic industry of every one must receive an encrease from the improvements of others'. This raised living standards all round, as well as generating 'that middling rank of men who are the best and firmest basis of public liberty'. Much about the mercantilist alternative was in that light absurd, such as the concern for accumulation of specie: control of precious metals must be futile because they spread themselves according to the requirements of trade. 'I should as soon dread,' Hume wrote, 'that all our springs and rivers should be exhausted, as that money should abandon a kingdom where there are people and industry. Let us carefully preserve these latter advantages, and we need never be apprehensive of losing the former.' Here lay the real key to the development of the British Empire, especially America. Hume pointed a contrast with the Spanish colonies, which were not cultivated but exploited to the point of misery, in their turn bleeding and beggaring the mother country; empires, indeed, had always been more likely to corrupt than improve. But in an age suspecting hegemony to be impossible, and a balance of power anyway preferable, there were means to reconcile commercial progress with political stability.[9]

Adam Smith then developed and brought together these various strands of argument. For all the profundity and conviction of his case for liberalism, he was no less a pragmatist than his friends and mentors. An example is his whimsical toleration of smuggling: it remained so common as to signal to him something deeper at work than mere individual delinquency. On the contrary, he saw in it the beneficent operation of his invisible, if here nominally criminal, hand. When the smuggler exercised his individual freedom to supply others with what they wanted in defiance of unnatural restrictions, Scottish theories of moral sympathy could surreptitiously approve. On a greater scale, Smith set out to demonstrate that the Empire's political and economic arrangements had consequences which must be weighed against one another.[10]

He embarked on the theme in *The Wealth of Nations* with a declaration that a new colony 'advances more rapidly to wealth and greatness than any other human society'. This was the general case, from which he at once launched an attack on mercantilism, pointing out that colonies had been ruined by chartered companies, notably in the Dutch empire and the Danish trading stations. 'Of all the expedients that can well be contrived to stunt the natural growth of a new colony, that of an exclusive company is undoubtedly the most effectual,' he declared. By comparison, 'there are no colonies of which the progress has been more rapid than that of the English colonies in North America'. Reasons were clear: 'Plenty of good land, and liberty to manage their own affairs their own way, seem to be the two great causes of the prosperity of all new colonies'. This liberty, secured as at home by representative assemblies claiming the sole right of taxation, had been limited in just two ways. First, colonists were allowed to exploit only primary products; the duties and prohibitions shackling manufactures Smith condemned as 'a manifest violation of the most sacred rights of mankind'. Secondly, their foreign trade remained subject to the Navigation Acts. It was easy to identify the culprits, the merchants exerting undue influence on British commercial regulation: 'We must not wonder, therefore, if, in the greater part of them, their interest has been more considered than either that of the colonies or that of the mother country'.[11]

Still, Britain's policy was less oppressive than others', but she did not have a spotless record. All imperial nations were guilty to some extent of folly and injustice, 'the folly of hunting after gold and silver mines, and the injustice of coveting the possession of a country whose harmless natives, far from ever having injured the people of Europe, had received the first adventurers with every mark of kindness and hospitality'. Europeans could be proud of their achievement, yet should also recognise what had gone wrong. In particular, while the trading system seemed advantageous, the advantage was relative, not absolute. A country enjoying it did not raise its own industry and produce, but depressed industry and produce in the rest. The ensemble of the system thus could not generate wealth on the same scale as free trade. Its preference for the producers' and the merchants' interest over the consumers' interest increased colonial trade at the expense of other trade. All it had done, then, was change the direction of trade, and misallocate resources away from an optimal level of production and investment. The system might have a use on grounds of national security, and the good effects of colonial trade did exceed the bad effects of monopoly in that trade. Still, they were achieved despite monopoly, not because of it.

With his conclusion Smith obviously meant to startle his readers:

> The rulers of Great Britain have, for more than a century past, amused the people with the imagination that they possessed a great empire on the western side of the Atlantic . . . [but] if any of the provinces of the British empire cannot be made to contribute towards the support of the whole empire, it is surely time that Great Britain should free herself from the expense of defending those provinces in time of war, and of supporting any part of their civil or military establishments in time of peace, and endeavour to accommodate her future views and designs to the real mediocrity of her circumstances.

This peroration was a call to face reality and apply economic principles to the great political issue of 1776. Smith had, in exposing the results of illiberalism, built a cast-iron case against the colonial system. He completed discussion of it in fact: the system was midwife to the discipline of economics; now the discipline became undertaker to the system. Yet this did not close the matter. The political proposals he derived from his economics – commercial equality and American representation at Westminster – hardly appealed even to those of his compatriots who caught on to his general theory. That met his expectation. No chauvinist, he was yet no anti-nationalist: he never commended, for the benefit of mankind, measures harmful to particular nations, the wealth of which remained his main concern. Advocating balance between the claims of politics and economics, of authority and freedom, he appreciated how others might reach a different judgment of the right balance for given circumstances.[12]

Scots at large certainly disliked the proposition that political authority should just yield in any conflict with economic liberalism. And they took political authority seriously. In the previous century they had seen it much abused among themselves, in the present one removed from their own soil. Yet they retained a Roman sense of the majesty of natural law and of the municipal law deriving from it, one at variance with English notions of freedom, as John Wilkes and other scotophobes did not shirk to point out. Short of just abandoning it, how could they reconcile this sense with economic liberalism? Before the end of the American War, Alexander Dalrymple, father of hydrography and explorer of the South Seas, put his mind to the question and set out prescient answers nourished from a more acute sense than Smith had shown of Britain's imperial possibilities. If the old colonies aimed at independence, 'the only means of preventing these intentions, and of securing the power and prosperity of the Mother Country, must be by extending its commerce to distant nations who have no connection with those discontented colonies'. In other words, trade ought in future to be developed in places where the question of political authority simply did not figure. Dalrymple stressed the importance of discovery, 'not with a view to colonising; not with a view of conquest; but of an amicable intercourse for mutual benefit'. The spirit of Darien surely lived yet in these sentiments.[13]

Still, balance between authority and freedom had to be worked out in practice rather than in theory. Smith's friend, Henry Dundas, wanted a state strong yet limited. He at first wanted it strong in asserting sovereignty over America although, as Scottish philosophy also taught realism, he finally had no trouble accepting that if America could not be held, then America must be let go. In India he set up an authority neither so despotic as to oppress the natives nor so mild as to forfeit their respect, matching more power for government on the spot to supervision from London. In economics he was a liberal, however. He broke down barriers at home and abroad, above all undermining the East India Company. He came into public life too late to tackle the colonial system in America. But he learned the lessons, and ever after bore in mind the genesis of the United States. He agreed that mercantilism could not preserve an Empire of territorial occupation and settlement. But authority over an Empire of free trade might be upheld by keeping it empty of settlers, who would demand autonomy or independence and disrupt or arrest commerce. So he checked emigration to, and political progress in, the remaining colonies. He devised instead a maritime strategy of garrisoned outposts and secure sea-lanes, an Empire guarded by navies, not armies, commercial rather than political, where power and trade did not drain but fed one another. Here again was a concept, to be traced back to Darien, of emporium and entrepot rather than conquest and dominion.[14]

The maritime strategy proved a success, with a further result that Smith could not have imagined. By the nineteenth century the political economy inherited from him was obliged to embrace a huge change in its historical environment. Not only was mercantilism moribund, but poor Scotland vanished from the map too, or rather formed part of a British economy leading the world. Smith's continuators had to come to terms with a global commercial Empire that faced no real rival, and demanded rethinking of its political assumptions. A start was made in the *Edinburgh Review*, founded in 1802 by students of Dugald Stewart, himself a student of Smith. The lively intelligence they displayed did much to win over the rising British middle class to economic liberalism. One of them, Henry Brougham, published in 1804 an *Inquiry into the Colonial Policy of the European Powers*. He argued that colonies ought not to be regarded as distant foreign countries, but as provinces of a single large Empire: 'The commerce which a country carries on with its colonies is, in every respect, a home trade'. A further consequent change came in attitudes to the emigration which Scots had earlier deprecated for sapping a valuable national resource. As the Empire developed, however, it seemed more desirable. A second reviewer, Francis Horner, sought to fit it into political economy: though a loss to the mother country, it was 'one which accompanies the progress of general opulence', or at least had its use as a safety-valve for social distress.[15]

Such evidence might have led the continuators to reject the maritime strategy, and revert to ideas of territorial occupation and settlement. In fact, they could not hold a united front. Some saw the colonies' utility as a receptacle of emigration, but set against it their disutility as a school of bad government. James Mill found in them 'a vast system of outdoor relief for the upper classes', not worth the trouble. He acquired the habit of thus reckoning the greatest good of the greatest number after he exiled himself in London and fell in with Jeremy Bentham. During 17 years' service at the East India Company, Mill had much influence on policy. His friend, John Ramsay MacCulloch, wrote for the *Edinburgh Review* and took the first chair of political economy at the university of London in 1826. On grounds of cost, he called for the independence of all British possessions. Another of the set, Joseph Hume, the one Scots radical then in the House of Commons, amazed it by claiming colonies were a source of weakness, not strength. It was odd that he went on, like Smith, to propose their union with Britain if independence was ruled out, though logical enough if they were considered economic provinces; during passage of the Reform Act of 1832 he even moved for some of the rotten boroughs' seats to be allocated overseas. Colonies were otherwise unacceptable to him even as a refuge from hard times: 'Let every country have free trade, and the necessity of emigration as a means of relief would be done away with'. Through such southbound Scots the native tradition of political economy came together with a more doctrinaire English utilitarianism, letting it claim Smith's authority for its over-confident prescriptions. Together, they fuelled radical thinking for the rest of the century and fed into later, hostile theories of imperialism.

During the nineteenth century the Scottish debate lost, amid fulfilment of the partnership with England, its pronounced national character. Yet this survey shows how it had begun before 1707 and followed its own lines, drawn with greater intellectual clarity than in the pragmatic neighbour nation. The independence of the Scots' thinking, which usually flew in the face of London's conventional wisdom, makes it hard to see them here as victims of the Union, passive objects of English imperialism, fawning trucklers to a superior culture. We know that elsewhere, on the contrary, they continued to enjoy a high degree of cultural autonomy by reason of having saved all their institutions except the Parliament. In the distinct spheres of their religion, law and education they ceaselessly debated the rival claims of freedom and authority. In considering them under the head of political economy, they simply enlarged the debate. To be sure, this aspect of it was argued out, to a greater extent than the others, in a new context, a more rapid evolution of Scottish experience and its assimilation to a larger system. But that did not negate the native cast of the general principles applied by Scots to the particular questions arising. It was another example of how they managed to preserve a national culture after the Union, in what George Davie has defined as 'unification in politics, separation in ethics'.

Smith had perceived, and noted in terms moving for one of such sober temper, his countrymen's impulse to burst the bonds imposed on them by nature: 'It is a sort of instinctive feeling to us, that the destiny of our name and nation is not here, in this narrow island which we occupy'. When they sought that destiny, they were also fulfilling something profound in themselves. It seems unlikely that this could have been divorced by the Union from the rest of their national experience. True, the political structure of the Empire, its institutions being everywhere English, never replicated the diversity even of the narrow island. And no crude contrast can be drawn between the imperial conduct of liberal, progressive Scots and reactionary, oppressive Englishmen; we shall see how violent, destructive and extortionate Scots could become. But, preserving a vigorous social ethic at home, they could often export it. When they did, it let them meet and trade with distant peoples on equal terms, and prompted them to the study of alien cultures to do so the better. There they found their conception of a commercial Empire both practically and morally vindicated.[16]

CHAPTER FIVE

'A nation no longer': America

The rocky, wooded spur called King's Mountain, an outlier of the Appalachians, reaches along the border between North and South Carolina. Early in October 1780 a battalion of American loyalist militia occupied the summit. The 36-year-old Scot leading them, Major Patrick Ferguson, commanded for all his slightness and charm a rare devotion from these rough-hewn backwoodsmen, who called him Bulldog in token of it. He enjoyed the confidence of his superiors too, both for his social credentials, as son of a judge, Lord Pitfour, and kinsman of a philosopher, Adam Ferguson, and for his military resource: he already counted to his credit the invention of the breech-loading rifle. He had now been entrusted with a vital mission, to intercept a band of American insurgents marching across the hills bent on reviving resistance to royal authority in the low country. On the strategic plane, he was thus detailed to defend the gains from a new and so far successful phase of operations by the British in the southern colonies, where they had turned after being fought to a stalemate in the northern ones. Six months before, Lord Cornwallis had captured Charleston, together with a revolutionary army. From there he meant to secure Georgia and the Carolinas before launching an offensive against the more populous and rebellious Virginia. His hopes rested on the greater fidelity to King George III of southerners compared to Yankees. A good many were after all recent immigrants from Scotland, most faithful province of the whole Empire.

The calculation at first proved correct. With Charleston taken, Carolinians and Georgians flocked to affirm their allegiance, in such numbers that the plan of reconquest could proceed on an assumption of its being carried out by them: Ferguson was the sole British officer in his battalion. A core of resistance remained all the same. The mopping-up turned into a dirty little war. Both sides ambushed, burned, murdered. But the loyalists showed themselves the fiercer, none more than the Scots among them. William Cunningham, leader of a band called the Bloody Scouts, specialised in gouging out captives' eyes with his thumbs. Once, after trying to string two up on a tobacco rack which broke under their weight, he just hacked them to death, then shot 14 more. Such deeds only served, however, to strengthen the rebels' resolve and build their support. It brought help across the hills too, from settlements newly founded, often by Scotch-Irish, in the upper Tennessee Valley. When Ferguson heard they were stirring, he threatened to lay their country waste with fire and sword. That provoked 3000 of them to muster and come to meet him.

On the morning of October 7 they surrounded King's Mountain, shrouded in misty rain. As the sun broke through in the afternoon, they attacked. The gallant Ferguson was everywhere in the hand-to-hand fighting that followed. He had two horses shot under him while, carelessly conspicuous in a checked shirt, he directed his militiamen with a silver whistle. Though outnumbered, they repulsed several assaults. The rebels at last gained the top, however, and forced them back towards the eastern slope. Seeing them beaten, Ferguson tried to break through the enemy's line. He was hit and dragged along the ground with a foot caught in the stirrup, till halted and propped against a tree, where he died. His terrified and disordered soldiers gave up at once. But the raging rebels ran amok and massacred a quarter of them as they tried to surrender. Many were doubtless loyal Scots, falling to the blades and bullets of disloyal Scots.[1]

Far away in Edinburgh's intellectual clubs and philosophical classrooms, the greatest minds often agreed that America had a right to be free. But most Scots out in the real world, in Scotland and abroad, came to the opposite conclusion. So true-blue were they that even Englishmen remarked on it. Why should they have thought like this? Why should they not have followed their cultural elite in viewing with composure the prospect of colonial liberty? Why should even those in America, under the same conditions and pressures as everyone else there, not have reacted in the same way?

The 70 years Scots and Americans had spent together as subjects of the British Crown proved mutually enriching. Divided by distance and more, they also had some things in common. They shared the complex but fruitful status of provincials in an oceanic Empire, and consequent problems in relations with the metropolis. While proud of Britain, they felt alike abashed at the badges of their provinciality: remoteness from affairs, ignorance of the ways, even the language, at the centre. Disadvantages were, however, balanced – in modern eyes more than balanced – by advantages which accrued from moral demands on the provincial going beyond those felt by Englishmen.

Both provinces stood on the edge of civilisation, aware of barbarism in hills and forests beyond. Both felt the absence of the high aristocracy lording it in England, while they had to rest content with rulers from the minor gentry and professional class who could not vaunt themselves on blood or acres and did so instead on culture or politeness. All this loosened the hold on the provincial of traditions and habits, opened his mind to new thinking and fresh ways of regarding his inheritance. It could not make him in every case a man of genius, but it nurtured the imagination and creativity without which there would have been no general Enlightenment in Scotland or America. The product in both was a new sense of cultural identity. Up to a point, amid the interchange fostered by political unity, it strengthened ties between them. Yet Scotland and America were separate in ethics also from each other, and not just from England. This would in the end tear them apart.[2]

Recent scholarship has traced Scottish philosophy as one source of what is seen more and more as an eclectic American Revolution, child no longer of English

Lockean liberalism alone but of sundry contemporary social theories; the most advanced and germane were often found in Scotland. Francis Hutcheson, for example, was a father both of the Scottish Enlightenment and of serious British thinking on America. He addressed himself about 1740, while as yet hardly anybody else knew or cared less about opinion in the plantations, to the question 'when it is that colonies may turn independent'. His answer hinged on misgovernment by the mother country, deriving from the Calvinist doctrine of a right to resist tyrannical rulers. If administration was severe or legislation oppressive, or even if a colony felt ready for self-sufficiency, it might in justice break away.

David Hume supported colonial independence as early as 1768, before most Americans did, and continued to do so even as war polarised British opinion: 'I am American in my principles, and wish we would let them alone to govern or misgovern themselves as they think proper'. He saw England succumbing to that imperial corruption of which antiquity gave awful warning. She was a virtual republic, ruled by cliques living off global commerce and propagating a warlike nationalism destructive of culture and liberty. In October 1775, the year before his death, Hume wanted royal forces withdrawn from America: 'Let us, therefore, lay aside all anger; shake hands and part friends'. Adam Smith was never so outspoken, even in private. But he verged on the same conclusions through his critique of mercantilism. While recommending its gradual relaxation, he doubted if discord could end there. The colonies would still cause war and expense they did not pay for. There were two possible solutions, independence or imperial union. He perhaps preferred the latter, which would grant the colonies economic equality and parliamentary representation, a scheme surely suggested by the Treaty of 1707; with their continuing advance, the seat of the Empire might in time shift to America.

But it was not enough for Scots to think such thoughts: they had also to be transmitted to Americans. The richest contact between the two peoples arose out of the Presbyterian nexus of religion and education. It was present in almost all the colonies, even among the originally English population of Virginia. During Scotland's own episcopal interludes in the seventeenth century, her ministers had had no qualms about serving under Anglican auspices overseas. Still more followed after 1690, when the Presbyterian settlement ousted many at home. They often took refuge in Virginia, and found a forerunner ready to welcome and patronise them in James Blair, a cleric from Aberdeen who attained a powerful place in the colony's politics. In 1693 he became first president of the College of William and Mary, where he introduced English worship but Scottish learning. Most people in the northern colonies were English too, but their puritanism had through a shared legacy from John Calvin much in common with re-established Scottish presbytery. Under both, hard lives were lightened by hope of betterment through instruction from a learned ministry whose evangelical fervour was mixed with intolerant self-righteousness. The eighteenth century saw lively religious exchanges between Scotland and New England. But it was in the middle colonies that Scots exerted the greatest influence.

More of them settled there, along with their cousins from Ulster, and so extended the geographical spread of Calvinist values. Presbyterians were the sole sect able to form an intercolonial Church, that is, one with an American synod. An Ulsterman educated at the university of Glasgow, Francis Makemie, slave-owning planter and trader in Virginia, organised it in 1706. On the Irish analogy, it remained independent of, but preserved links with, the mother country, sending delegates to the General Assembly in Edinburgh on special errands. Not till after the independence of the United States did it set up its own General Assembly.

Of schools, many in southern and western settlements were presbyterian academies; "high school", even now the normal American term for establishments of secondary education, is Scots, not English. Of tertiary institutions, Princeton was the sole presbyterian college among nine founded in the colonial era. But all turned out closer in ethos to the Scottish universities than to the aristocratic languor of Oxford and Cambridge. It was the former's method of instruction through lectures and examinations that took hold here rather than the latter's tutorial system. Besides, many American students, unwilling or unable to attend English universities, came to Scotland. Numbers of her academics found their way to America. Thomas Jefferson, James Madison and James Monroe were all taught by one. Jefferson said his professor at the College of William and Mary, William Small, 'fixed the destinies of my life', and he extolled at large the virtues of Scottish pedagogy.[3]

The most eminent of these educators was John Witherspoon, minister of Paisley until in 1768 he accepted the call to Princeton. He transformed a school of theology into a fully-fledged university preparing its students for public affairs, not least through grounding in the Common Sense Philosophy of Scotland. One of his successors as principal, Woodrow Wilson, called it 'a seminary of statesmen'. From it there graduated 13 presidents of colleges, six delegates to the Continental Congress, 20 senators, 23 members of the House of Representatives, three justices of the Supreme Court, one vice-president, Aaron Burr, and one president of the United States, James Madison. Witherspoon's own interests were much more than academic and devoted generously to the welfare of his adopted homeland. 'A man will become an American by residing in the country for three months,' he said. He gave his Church there better organisation and discipline, with regular meetings of presbyteries and synods. He advocated rapid peopling of the colonies and urged each to form a society for Protestant emigration from Britain. In 1774 he was elected to the provincial congress of New Jersey, thence a delegate to the Continental Congress. He became the sole clergyman to sign the Declaration of Independence.

As a founding father, he could imbue the new nation with some element of his own Scottish form of political Calvinism. It was noted of him during the Congress that 'he can't bear anything which reflects on Scotland, the Dr says their history is full of their calling Kings to account and dethroning them when arbitrary and tyrannical'. He adapted the Presbyterian doctrine of a right of resistance by stressing the ends it had in view. He carried in his baggage Scottish philosophy as well as

Scottish religion, and he always, on both sides of the ocean, tried to show intellectual advance need not come at the expense of orthodoxy. His message to America was that enlightened principles pointed the way not just to political liberty but also to moral regeneration. His hopes for a 'Christian Sparta' hardly sound jocose to modern ears, but we ought not to misprize his good intentions. He wanted to show a fallen world how it could be made whole through cultivating, in educational and religious institutions reformed on republican lines, a virtue classical in its rigour yet consecrated in its charity.[4]

The second Scots-born signatory to the Declaration of Independence was James Wilson, a graduate of the university of St Andrews who set up as a lawyer in Philadelphia. The convention of 1787 held there to draft a constitution called mainly on two men for the task, him and Madison. The latter being also the product of a Scottish education, they found much to agree on, above all a preference for the federal over the imperial idea in composite governments, which in Scotland went back to Andrew Fletcher. In 1707 the imperial had overborne the federal idea in Britain but America, seceding from the Empire, could reverse the order. The government Wilson and Madison proposed was still relatively strong and popular, constitutional balance being maintained by Wilson's own great innovation, the curb of a powerful judiciary under the Supreme Court, where he later became a justice. After the convention approved the draft, it was sent to be ratified by the states. With those wishing to keep federal government weaker there followed a keen debate, one of the most fertile ever conducted on a practical political proposition. Madison's interventions, published in the *Federalist Papers*, played a major part in the successful outcome. One crucial point concerned the moral consequences of a small as opposed to a large republic, bearing on whether America should be a loose confederation or have strong central government. Against the latter it was contended, on an appeal to classical antiquity, that large republics were corrupted and destroyed by the power entrusted to rulers. Madison countered in the tenth paper that, on the contrary, since in them no single party or interest could usurp too much power, the public was better represented. The variety and size of the United States would become, by the constitution, a guarantee of stability and justice. It seems clear from internal evidence that Madison lifted this argument from Hume's discussion of an 'extended republic' in the *Idea of a Perfect Commonwealth*.

In general, Scottish philosophy bequeathed to the founding fathers the idea that social development was the most important aspect of human affairs. It reassured these bewigged paragons of prudence that sometimes an upheaval was necessary for healthy change, while letting them take immediate refuge in the most cautious revolutionary position available (except for Jefferson, with his unScottish wish to return ever and anon to nature). The rest concluded one revolution was enough: having achieved what they wanted, they should pursue stability rather than purist radicalism.[5]

Yet, despite common ground, most Scots remained hostile to the American

Revolution. Above all enlightened Scots did. If they saw themselves as liberals, their liberalism counselled not violence but moderation and reform to correct abuse. The Calvinist teaching of a right of resistance to authority had been eroded in its homeland. No philosopher but Hutcheson approved of it except as a last resort, to be tested on strict criteria, against incorrigible tyranny – and Americans were manifestly free. So this was not the theory, shared to a degree by Hutcheson with Locke, that allegiance ended when government broke a contract with the people. Not even Hume and Smith, let alone the rest, accepted that or any idea of government founded on popular consent. William Robertson, in an unfinished history of British America, argued in legitimist terms: the cure lay in more rational exercise of authority, so as to strike a balance between excess of it in a Virginia burdened with vain economic constraints and deficiency of it in a New England prey to religious fanatics.

Enlightened thought never meant to discard the inherited order, at home or abroad. Progress in the forms it extolled would long fail to shake the conservative concepts of loyalty and hierarchy rooted in the Scottish psyche, given form in a social order resting on ancient institutions with the Crown at its apex, sanctified by a tradition of natural law clad in the splendour of Roman jurisprudence stressing the majesty of the state. On such criteria, no colonial difficulties or grievances justified a repudiation of allegiance. To any paradox between the claims of authority and liberty, Scots offered the idea of sympathy as key. They saw one expression of it in the self-discipline of free trade, division of labour and unfettered exchange among economic agents. This increased the wealth of nations, then diffused it to make different ranks and orders content with their lot. The philosophers held society could thus be improved without revolutionary upheaval. They did think political change possible too, indeed necessary and desirable amid economic and social progress. But it must be controlled by and conducive to good government, in no sense transferring power to the people.

The hostility was not just intellectual, or confined to the elite, for Scotland at large shared it. Henry Dundas, her leading if not yet supreme politician, was the most hawkish of the hawks, demanding vigorous suppression of American rebels. Over the winter of 1775–6, Scottish counties and burghs sent up to London more than 70 addresses supporting armed coercion, as many as came from the whole of England with five times the population. Not one ever sent a petition for peace. Nor was the loyalty just verbal, for Scots raised many of the regiments sent over the Atlantic Ocean. Soldiers wrote home that the colonists were cowards, rascals and vermin.[6]

The hostility also prevailed among Scottish communities in America. These were not numerous or large. From the first census of the United States in 1790 it has been computed that 260,000 people, eight per cent of the total, were Scots, most in the South. Scholars are trying to revise the figures, but will not be able to raise them near the Scottish share in the contemporary population of Great Britain, twice as high. The sparsity may help to explain the hostility: Scots, unlike Englishmen, did not easily see Americans as an extension of their own nation. The link before 1707 had after all been of trade rather than settlement. While the colonies were then opened up, no rush of emigration followed. Scots just remained disinclined to sail across the Atlantic till the end of the Seven Years' War in 1763. Between then and the American revolt, however, about 40,000 did go, representing one-third of the British outflow and three per cent of all Scots. Such was the sudden demand for passages that a business could be made of them by entrepreneurs such as John Witherspoon, and even Sir James Montgomery, Lord Advocate of Scotland, nominally in charge of a policy to suppress the traffic. Otherwise, though, it worried the authorities. In 1773 they set up a general register of emigrants as the first step to controlling it.[7]

Bernard Bailyn's seminal study of this document shows how a few Scots might have found the radical environment into which they moved congenial. They included textile workers from the West, for example. Intent on shaking the dust of Scotland off their feet, they were equipped for that by their education, though national clannishness may have done as much to get them through the worst of the readjustment. It is a far cry from the helpless victims we are often asked to see in such people. Most, though young, were getting established and founding a family, in whose company they often travelled. They were quite likely to take money. Two-fifths of those on the register giving reasons for departure stated they were not in flight from the country or any intolerable conditions. Instead they appeared ambitious and enterprising, eager to exploit their opportunities. Again, there were Lowland farmers fearing to be displaced by improvement who had prepared a way out and pooled savings in friendly societies to buy American land. Here we may already descry the self-reliance which would distinguish Scots emigrants. It loosened their attachment to what they left behind, while readying them to accept and build on what lay in store on the other side. But at this stage few of their countrymen thought their hopes laudable. Emigration was oftener seen as desertion, which damaged the economy by cutting its workforce and depressed morale in the mother country.[8]

The reproaches touched especially the Highlands, whence came the biggest emigration. In 1775 Dundas, succeeding as Lord Advocate, advised the Government it could not be stopped without tackling basic problems resulting from collapse of the old social system in the North since the last Jacobite rising. The region then underwent transformation from a feudal into a commercial society. Before, chieftains had wanted on their land as many men as possible, bound in the fellow-feeling of the clan. Stripped of authority by subsequent repression, they now saw the relationship as one of landlord and tenant. Their aim was then to maximise the value of their estates by profiteering in rents. Exodus followed. Highlanders, spurned by their natural leaders, had nothing to tie them to their native soil. Dundas did not hesitate to assert that, whatever economics might dictate, it was the state's job to repair the social fabric. He stemmed the immediate outflow by using the pretext of the American War to ban emigration, all in the knowledge that this could be but a temporary cure: a more considered programme of measures culminated in 1784 with restoration of forfeited estates to previous Jacobite owners.

While Dundas was thinking what to do, a friend of his youth, James Boswell, took Dr Samuel Johnson on the Highland tour which won them literary immortality. They too were shocked at the 'epidemic disease of wandering'. The doctor thought it tragic, but found a mitigating factor. He saw how people departed with no sense of going into exile. Travelling in parties of family and neighbours, 'they carry with them their language, their opinions, their popular songs, and hereditary merriment; they change nothing but the place of their abode'. Often richer men led away their dependants, who 'if they continue the feudal scheme of polity, may establish new clans in the other hemisphere'.

Johnson identified here the middle group in the old Highland society, the tacksmen, in between peasants who worked communal holdings and chiefs who held sway over the clan's whole territory. Tacksmen had seen to practical agrarian and, if necessary, military organisation. Conversion to commercialism deprived them of their function, often of their property. They faced downward social mobility so drastic that they preferred to desert their homes, though discouraged by social superiors and political authorities. They were not to be stopped when they had the alternative in America of unlimited freehold land. There they might hope to recreate the life they left behind and so were not unwilling to seek a more hospitable setting for it. They thus fixed their sights on a Scotland of the past, not an America of the future. They went in a conservative, not progressive, frame of mind, wishing to preserve a piece of the Old World, not take part in building the New World. The settlers might manage to cling to such beguiling notions in the larger communities they formed in North Carolina and Nova Scotia. As long as they did, they remained different in outlook from others round them, as from the wretches who followed them out of the Highlands in the next century. Two received views of the earlier movement, one that it was of a helpless peasantry exiled by oppression, another that it arose from radical political aspirations, therefore have to be rejected. Eviction and the occasional accompanying unrest were just part, seldom a major part, of the complex pressures prompting emigration. At bottom lay the harsh fact that growth in the numbers of Highlanders would make social and economic tranformation inevitable.[9]

But Dr Johnson also formed from his observations a second opinion, somewhat contradicting the first. He hit on a striking metaphor of what actually awaited emigrants in the wilderness, where their material and spiritual culture would fade, leaving them and their native land alike bereft,

> for a nation scattered in the boundless regions of America resembles rays
> diverging from a focus. All the rays remain, but the heat is gone. Their power
> consisted in their concentration: when they are dispersed, they have no effect. It
> may be thought that they are happier by the change; but they are not happy as a
> nation, for they are a nation no longer.

He was to prove right about the fate of all clan-building and feudalising schemes, soon nullified by the American Revolution and the ideology of the nation it created.

Such dislike of emigration might be shared even by those Scots who did go overseas for one reason or another. For another group, not identifiable with any particular region, it meant no permanent break with the homeland, just a stage along their way in life. Like their forefathers they went because they had to, but meaning to return once their work was done. The peerage of Scotland, for example, has been most useful to the Crown. Its titles carried prestige, but its poverty inclined it to service of an unquestioningly loyal kind, not least in America. Virginia alone had the Earls of Orkney, Loudoun and Dunmore as governors. Ordinary Scots could rise to the same height. Alexander Spotswood, exotically born at Tangier in 1676, went for a soldier, fought at Blenheim, and was sent in 1710 to Virginia because it needed military organisation while the European wars went on. He gave the colony 12 years of strong, benevolent rule, the best it ever had. He finished building Williamsburg, started industrial development with manufacture of iron, and pushed the frontier to the River Shenandoah, for good measure claiming all land to the River Mississippi too.

John Stuart is a later, hardly lesser example. From Inverness he set up as a merchant at Charleston. He prospered enough to develop cultural interests, as steward of the library, and political ones, as member of the assembly of South Carolina – his springboard to becoming in 1763 Superintendent in the southern colonies, in charge of Indian relations. They were important because the Treaty of Paris had just awarded Britain the whole, vast territory east of the Mississippi. Stuart tried to keep the peace with and among the tribes, even interest them in trade. He limited expansion of white settlement by drawing western boundaries for the colonies, to the frontiersmen's fury. Transience gave him a sympathy with Indians which a permanent immigrant could not have conceived. Beside a Scots wife, at any rate, he had a Cherokee mistress and a brood of children by her, from whom all Americans bearing the surname of Bushyhead descend. He died in harness fighting the rebels in 1779.

Highlanders often thought in their encounter with Indians to find soulmates, springing like them from a tribal society founded on military prowess and oral culture. On the frontier they might almost merge. Lachlan McGillivray, an emigrant in 1736 to the settlement of Darien in Georgia, discovered in the region other men of his name, transported Jacobites living off traffic with the interior. He joined them and prospered enough to marry a Creek princess. When the Revolution came the Scots all went home, but McGillivray left behind a son, Alexander. The lad was destined, through his tribe's matrilinear descent, to succeed as its paramount chief. Amid dextrous dealings with the new authorities of the United States, he found time to transmit historical materials to Principal Robertson in Edinburgh; he also made sure to send his own son back to Scotland for an education. That Empire should not dispossess the Indians had been the consensus among Scots in these southern colonies, who were mainly merchants, men like John Gordon in Charleston or the brothers James and John Graham in Savannah. About the commercial value of political networks they knew from home: they opened channels of trade under the auspices of the tribal chiefs on the one hand and of the often Scottish imperial officials on the other. Had it not been for American independence, a native civilisation adapted to commerce could have emerged in the interior and might just have escaped inundation by white settlement. It was at any rate a pattern Scots would promote in other continents.[10]

Traffic between America and Scotland was disappointingly slow to grow after the Union, but from about 1730 it did expand markedly. A complete transformation came through tobacco. Chesapeake Bay, the low country of Virginia and Maryland, was the centre of its cultivation. Under the Navigation Acts crops had to be landed in Great Britain before going to third countries. More and more were landed in Scotland. The amount rose to eight million pounds in 1741, then shot up to 47 million pounds by 1771. It then represented half of total Scottish imports, worth £500,000, and more than half of total British traffic in tobacco. Exploiting older links, Scots responded to a surge of demand from France and clinched huge deals for delivery in bulk to her royal monopoly. Glasgow outstripped its rivals, Bristol and London. One reason was natural, that it lay nearer to America on the great circle. Its ships could cross unmolested by privateers two or three weeks faster than any from the English Channel, adding up to an advantage of a month or six weeks on a round trip. The result was quicker commercial information, lower oncosts for transport, freight and insurance, economies of scale and the chance to minimise or spread risks of a business that remained to an extent speculative. In this, Glasgow was endowed for an otherwise unlikely role of international entrepot.

The traffic, if sometimes unprofitable, proved more often spectacularly profitable. Survival of adequate records has been a matter of chance, but one full account, of a voyage in 1729, shows a rate of return of 33 per cent. In any event, the trade was managed with outstanding success by the city's merchants. A close-knit group, often related, they kept the business in their own hands by pooling resources in formal partnerships. Retained profits permitted steady growth, even across generations: much of the necessary capital accumulation came in inheritance and half the traders in tobacco were sons of traders in tobacco. By 1770 Glasgow had acquired a capital surplus, and a mentality looking out for chances to invest. Tobacco was the first big business in Scotland, generating fortunes on a scale never seen there before, and first to thrash the competition through ruthless efficiency.[11]

Merchants turned into the fabled tobacco lords when they bought estates round Glasgow and set up as gentlemen. Their quest for status, mixing and marrying with the landed class, might seem to be the reverse of dynamic and to confirm the existing social order. But their money began to work huge changes in the West of Scotland. Infusion of new blood among old lairds released land locked up in entail and other feudal archaisms. Tobacco lords were too canny to overlook the value of their estates as investments. There they could contribute to the agricultural revolution, even to the industrial revolution, by exploiting natural resources and turning them into manufactures for outward cargoes. In countless individual ways they improved the region's productive capacity, if as just one element in a complex of forces. But it was important for tobacco lords to break down barriers between their commerce and the rest of the domestic economy, as to seek out the markets their city needed to escape its historic constraints. Their acumen turned to full account its meagre comparative advantages.

Their impact on America was also great. They took over a trade the English thought to have sewn up by the time of the Union, entrenched as they were at the markets and ports of the Chesapeake. The Scots' chance arose through the spread inland of the cultivation of tobacco. They pursued new planters with package deals better than any available from the English merchant houses which, working on commission, set the highest possible price to clients in Britain and Europe. The Scots came in as resident factors, buying straight from the farmer and taking on themselves all risk, offering to final customers such bargains by comparison that the whole re-exporting business could be rapidly expanded. In exchange they imported goods from Scotland, hawked at more than 100 stores built for the purpose, whence credit could also be supplied during hard times. By the 1770s this ingenuity and calculation gave them a firm grip on the local economy. They controlled two-thirds of traffic in tobacco, and were owed enormous cumulated debts.

For grumbling Americans the superlative organisation had far-reaching consequences too. It let them embark on brisk development of their resources, transforming the social structure in Virginia and Maryland. While the English system had yoked small planters to large ones, the Scottish system freed them, even if it dunned them too. Ordinary farmers, aided also by diversification away from tobacco, could escape the paternalism of the original colonial society, with what results became clear in 1776. Grasping Glasgow middlemen who seized economic control from a genteel class of older proprietors were mere employees of masters at home with no political muscle to match, tied into what they had created. So they remained Scots, and never became Americans.

The Revolution ought to have been a catastrophe, seeing how these arrangements suited everybody somehow or other. Trade in tobacco, having just reached its peak, was disrupted. British defeat then ended the arrangements under which it had been conducted. But Scots did return after 1783 and to an extent took up where they had left off. The Americans' readiness to welcome them back suggests that they had found the business beneficial too, that it had not depended on the colonial system. Still, unprotected now from foreign competition and dogged by outstanding debts, it never attained its old vigour. Glasgow still coped well. War offered its own opportunities for speculative gain. Few bankruptcies took place. New markets and investments were found. In commerce, as in other spheres, Scots and Americans went separate ways. Some rancour remained, not only over the recent past. A political writer, John Knox, observed:

> Thus vanished, after a short possession, all the exclusive commercial privileges relative to that country [America], for which the Scots had annihilated their Parliament and their African and Indian Company, and subjected themselves to excises, taxes, duties and commercial restrictions unknown before the year 1707.

This hard-headedness may explain why Scots in America had remained unmoved by wider issues as the war spread. In any event these sojourners, if provincial in their origins and colonial in their careers, felt themselves first and foremost Britons, a feeling expressed in devotion to the Crown and the interests of the state. This state was moreover becoming, by the standards of the age, a superstate as it spread from the North Atlantic over other oceans. It must have seemed to Scots, bringing their insecurity with them from its periphery, an awesome project.[12]

A piquant variation on the theme is found even among a group of would-be permanent immigrants, the clansmen in the southern back-country who mustered forces in the King's name. Some were old enough to have been out against the House of Hanover in 1745, but times had changed. Their leader was a tacksman from Skye, Allan MacDonald of Kingsburgh, husband of Flora, the Jacobite heroine. The pair of them took their people a quarter-century later to the banks of the Cape Fear River in North Carolina, to a settlement today known as Fayetteville. In February 1776 MacDonald sent round the fiery cross. He assembled 3500 men under the royal standard in the square at the centre of the town, where they were given their envoi in sonorous Gaelic by Flora herself, mounted on a white horse. They set off to march down to the port of Wilmington, seized by revolutionaries after the royal governor sought safety on a ship offshore. But the pipes skirled in vain. Rebels ambushed and routed the force at Moore's Creek, an early sign that restoration of British authority would be at best difficult. MacDonald was held captive for over a year, until released by order of George Washington. He did not come back to Scotland till 1783, to be reunited with his wife who had been evacuated through Charleston: two of many Highlanders forced to abandon their new homes.

Nor did the allegiance of Scots traders in Virginia much waver. They were not set apart by any imported social structure. They did business with American neighbours, some intermarried, some represented their communities in colonial institutions. Yet they were distanced from Virginians by nagging economic friction, by their own dependence on imperial commerce, by their clannishness, by their conservative convictions. When they had to choose, they stayed loyal. Or else, as early as 1774, they began to leave, for the spreading unrest made them ready targets to radicals. With the outbreak of fighting in the North, latent prejudice and hostility towards them boiled up here in violent incidents. This confirmed to them, as to other non-

English colonial minorities, that for their safety they could only trust the Crown, rather than the Anglo-American majority round them. Most were anyway transients, outsiders with no desire to become Americans: the New World was not to them home, but a place to make money for a better life on return to the mother country. Everything conspired to confirm in them the values of their own nation.

Only such permanent settlers from Scotland as by design or desuetude had cast off her values might be receptive to something else. It has been proposed by one recent study that in areas where they showed durable ethnic cohesion, as in New Jersey, Scots could through the channel of Presbyterianism come to terms with the revolution. If this was true, it remained invisible to contemporaries, as to later scholars. Some such cohesion might have been maintained by transient or traditionalist Scots, but others truly intent on making a new life in the New World had to discard their ethnicity because American radicalism was incompatible with it. After 1776 these people could just become Americans, if by the change in their situation and outlook they were not so already. Those who on the other hand wanted to remain Scots could not stay in America. And they appear to have formed the majority.

They were losers from the war, many long grudging it. But at least their demonstrative loyalty helped to make their countrymen permanently welcome in the rest of the British Empire, assuring them a place in colonial development that stretched two centuries into the future. It became all the more congenial to them because this was no longer an Empire of colonisation, where Scots by reason of their meagre numbers could hardly leave their mark. Instead it turned into a commercial Empire, not least in its free trade with the United States, far exceeding the former traffic under the system of navigation. With that incubus removed, progress quickened – as Scottish philosophy had forecast.[13]

CHAPTER SIX

'The greater barbarians': The West Indies

On May 31, 1773, John Gabriel Stedman, a 29–year-old Scots mercenary, attended the funeral of his commanding officer at Fort Zeelandia, which guarded Paramaribo, capital of the Dutch colony of Surinam. He was one of a force raised by the States General of Holland to suppress troublesome bands of negroes, fugitives from slavery in the coastal plain of the territory who often raided its plantations from their hiding places in the jungles beyond. The troops' bloody and sweaty assignment was to hunt the runaways down, trap and kill them if they could, which was not all that often. Any they took prisoner were imprisoned in the fort. On this day it shocked Stedman to find some in a corner of the soldiers' cemetery 'clanking their chains and roasting plantains and yams upon their graves'. As he then looked about him,

> seven captive negroes were selected, and being led by a few soldiers to the place
> of execution, which is in the savanna where the sailors and soldiers are interred,
> six were hanged and one broken alive upon the rack; besides which in front of
> the courthouse one white man was scourged by the public executioner, who is in
> this country always a black. But what makes me take particular notice here was
> the shameful injustice of showing a partiality to the European, who ought to
> have known better, by letting him escape with a slight corporal punishment,
> while the poor African, who is destitute of precepts and laws, lost his life for the
> same crime – stealing money out of the town hall – under the most excruciating
> torments, through which he manfully went without heaving a sigh or
> complaining. Meanwhile, one of his companions with the rope round his neck
> and just going to be turned off, gave a hearty laugh of contempt at the
> magistrates who attended the execution. I ought not to omit that the negro who
> flogged the white man inflicted the punishment with the greatest marks of
> commiseration, all of which induced me to decide that, between the Europeans
> and the Africans in this colony, the first were the greater barbarians of the two.

Stedman was another Scots-Dutchman, his father an officer in the Prince of Orange's service who had settled in Holland and married a local girl. Like many expatriate offspring, their son was sent back for an education to Scotland, which claimed his first loyalty. On November 30, 1774, he wrote: 'This being the anniversary of St Andrew, and now being in excellent spirits, I roasted a whole sheep with which I entertained all the officers on the Hope [a plantation], and with a couple of gallons of good Jamaica rum in punch, which we drank to the health of all our friends on the old continent'. In 1796, home again, he published his journals. The literature of the exotic was already popular, and they proved thrilling enough to become a bestseller. Stedman appealed not just to romantic tastes, with graphic accounts of stirring campaigns and adventures, of strange creatures and landscapes, William Blake providing the illustrations. He also touched a nerve by dealing with slavery, and from the black as well as the white point of view. His prose, vivid and artless, revealed a tough young Scot with a warm heart, deeply in love with his mulatto mistress, appalled at the planters' torturing of slaves. He maintained that the races were equal, that cruelty could not be excused just to provide Europeans with their luxuries. Yet this was no abolitionist tract. Stedman defended slavery on various economic and political grounds, and thought it might have a benevolent function in raising the negro from a state of nature. But for that to operate, laws had to be passed to protect his human rights. That some such effort should be made at amelioration, in contemporary parlance, was the most frequent reaction of Scots on encountering slavery and the economies it supported in the West Indies or round the Caribbean shores.[1]

The region's riches had attracted them since the seventeenth century. Before the Union, however, the English colonial system had been more of an obstacle to them here than in North America. Nor later did anywhere in Scotland offer much competition to the established Caribbean traffic of ports in the South. Some Scots chose to enter it from there, notably the Gladstones in Liverpool. Within Scotland, Edinburgh formed the earliest closer links, largely because the West Indies offered openings for professional men. Glaswegians moved in from 1783 to offset their lost American commerce. After the independence of the United States, this was the most valuable territory in the British Empire.[2]

Two commodities specially interested the Scots. One was sugar. As long before as 1619, James VI had granted a monopoly for its manufacture, though the scheme came to nothing. It may just be that this was connected with trade: among the meagre surviving records of the Scottish customs are those for the port of Leith in 1611, which happen to list a West Indian voyage. At any rate, there was certainly a traffic by the middle of the century. By the end of it four companies, three in Glasgow and another in Leith, were refining imported sugar and distilling rum. All survived the Union too, showing that they did not subsist merely on mercantilist privilege. Indeed they continued to prosper, grow and multiply till by 1775 Scotland had ten refineries. Later the commerce and the processing were concentrated in Port Glasgow or Greenock, where sugar remained a staple of the local economy till recent times. It was in fact the oldest of Scotland's modern industries, and the ancestor of others such as chemicals.

The business in cotton was yet brisker. Glasgow seized on it as a replacement for American tobacco. The city already housed a small textile industry to build on. It had been importing raw cotton since the 1770s. It produced fine linen, so that a move into finished cotton proved relatively easy. Capital was there among the merchant dynasties, now looking for fresh outlets. Some already owned plantations in the West Indies, and had an incentive to develop means of manufacturing the produce, which the introduction of steam power in 1782 made more profitable. They commonly took up partnerships in the new ventures that soon emerged: James Finlay & Co, for example, was Scotland's largest textile company by 1801. Cotton then accounted for one-quarter of Scottish overseas trade, and the interruption of European commerce during the French wars increased concentration on it. Two decades later, it provided about half of manufacturing employment. High returns from this rapid growth could be turned to continual technological advance. Much of the yarn produced was put out for weaving into cloth, bleached, printed, dyed or embroidered in factories all over the West of Scotland. The many links to other industries completed the transformation of Glasgow from an entrepot into a great centre of production. The cotton kings, though prominent in its life, were still not as all-powerful as the tobacco lords of old, nor in the event did their turn last long. Fresh trades arose from Glasgow's ever wider connections in distant continents, with the opening of independent Latin America, the revival of North American markets and the end of the East India Company's monopoly. The cotton industry ceased to grow after 1840 and by the 1860s was in absolute, though not rapid, decline. It may have suffered, too, because there had always been a question mark over slavery, and thus over the entire economy of plantations.[3]

As a result of all this, a sporadic movement of Scots to the West Indies took place, rather unevenly spread. They numbered one in three of the whites on Jamaica, where their slaves were said to speak a 'Negro Scotch' dialect. In the course of the eighteenth century they largely took over the plantations of Tobago. After France had ceded St Kitts to Britain in 1713 the land was regranted, and half the parcels of more than 100 acres went to Scots. On Grenada, ceded in 1763, they represented one-fifth of all landowners, while dominating its dependency of Carriacou. 'Here was a whole company of Scotch people,' Janet Schaw exclaimed when she visited Antigua in 1774. This instance, being well documented, merits brief examination. The island housed 13 Scottish planter families, of which only two had been established by 1707. Their numbers surged after the Jacobite rising of 1715 with the arrival of 100 transported prisoners. Some eventually settled and set up as merchants, then brought in friends and relations. One was Walter Tullideph, who hailed from Perthshire by way of medical studies in Edinburgh. He started work in 1726 as a surgeon and as a factor for his brother's business; he would carry merchandise on his doctor's rounds. In time he could begin trading on his own account and lending to planters. By 1763 he possessed property of 500 acres with 270 slaves worth £30,000. But he had already returned and bought an estate in Scotland.

The migrants usually came from specific social milieus. Few were gentlemen. An exception proving the rule was Sir Alexander Grant of Dalvey, one of Jamaica's magnates with 2000 acres, 700 slaves and property of £70,000, which he used on his return to purchase the parliamentary seat of the Inverness Burghs. But unless, as in his case, they had Jacobite or other skeletons in their cupboards, landed Scots families saw little reason to exchange their social leadership at home for a colonial life. There was the usual flow of minor peers serving as governors, who showed here no interest in a civilising mission, being obliged to spend their time placating fractious planters or controlling restive negroes. If the Scots gentry involved itself more permanently, it was as absentee landlords of estates bought for investment, or acquired by marriage to an heiress. Tobias Smollett, novelist and scion of a family of lairds in Dumbarton, found one while in Jamaica on a military expedition in 1744. Sir Archibald Grant of Monymusk only kept going his expensive schemes of improvement by wedding rich widows, one of whom, Elizabeth Callender of Jamaica, brought him £30,000 in 1751.[4]

Resident Scots were yet often men of academic education or professional training: doctors, lawyers, factors, merchants and tradesmen, a range of occupations more varied than round the Chesapeake, the other main region of plantations, because the West Indies had few free settlers to perform skilled jobs. The purpose of going out with a profession was to make money, save up and buy an estate, from the proceeds of which a man could then live, preferably as an absentee. Most did not even marry till they got home again, but cohabited with black women. One migrant, James Gillespie, wrote: 'We all come here to improve and not spend fortunes, and of consequence, devote our whole thought and attention to the former'.

Prospects on the islands beckoned because their more fluid society offered greater upward mobility than Scotland could. This was, in an exotic setting, the usual Scottish quest for self-advancement. With the dearth of domestic opportunities, a national tradition had grown up to seek them out abroad and come back the richer for having exploited them. During earlier ages that was done in Europe; now it could be done overseas. For most, the real purpose in wandering was to move up the social ladder once they returned. Henry Brougham noted that the West Indians went out 'not to subsist in the colonies, but to prepare for shining in the mother country'. So these Scots seldom severed their connections with home, or with each other: in the islands, too, they won notoriety for their cliques and mutual self-help. Like their counterparts in North America, they were not losing or forswearing their Scottishness, but trying to keep and affirm it.[5]

Systematic emigration by free settlers to the region was at any rate rare. It could hardly have lured the ordinary Scots farmer, who knew nothing of sub-tropical agriculture in an economy of plantations. Nor was he likely to seek just a temporary refuge from his own country. If he emigrated, he would go to a colony with land to spare and opportunities for men lacking special skills, which usually meant the American frontier. That still did not stop a few trying their luck in the Caribbean. One place thought suitable for settlement was Belize. The word is itself said to be a corruption of the surname of Peter Wallace, a Scottish buccaneer who in 1638 had led a band of 80 men to found a rude colony for exploitation of the local logwood; it lasted for some decades, perhaps longer in the mixed blood of creoles who lived on there. In the early nineteenth century, these shores attracted the gaze of another colourful figure, Gregor MacGregor. A native of Breadalbane, he served in the British army then took a commission under the Liberator of Latin America, Simon Bolivar, rising to become one of his generals and marry his niece. The liberation achieved, he went in 1820 to the Mosquito Coast of Nicaragua, where the English had till 1788 had a colony. Asking nobody's leave, he styled himself His Serene Highness, Gregor I, Sovereign Prince of Poyais and Cacique of the Poyer Nation, after a local tribe. Thus dignified, he went home to promote an expensive plan for recolonisation. In Edinburgh and in London, he sold lands and raised loans. By the autumn of 1822 he had ready to sail from Leith, as the first of several parties, about 50 settlers, farmers, artisans and professional men appointed officials of his state. In the hold they carried 70,000 notes of the Bank of Poyais, adorned with a green saltire. MacGregor had promised that a civilised country awaited them. On arrival they found, of course, that there was nothing. They had to camp out and suffer the many distresses of those climes. They at once began to sicken. Before long two-thirds of them died. Luckily, Belize lay near enough for a rescue of the remnant to be mounted. The dauntless MacGregor had gone now to Paris to organise further expeditions. He was arrested there, and later in Britain as well. But nothing could be pinned on him, and he returned to live out his days in Venezuela.

Elsewhere in Latin America there was a Scots settlement at Topo, near Caracas, for which the more respectable Sir James Mackintosh recruited 200 farmers from Aberdeenshire and Inverness-shire. They arrived in 1825, but found the land not good enough for them and took refuge in alcohol. Two years later they left for Canada, where another colonising man of letters, John Galt, accommodated them at Guelph. A third group of farmers, mainly from Dumfriesshire, ventured yet further south to establish themselves in 1825 at Monte Grande, near Buenos Aires. Penury and fractiousness dispersed them within three years. But some stayed on in Argentina, to found in 1828 a congregation of the Church of Scotland, and in 1838 St Andrew's School, still there today.[6]

In the West Indies, however, permanent Scots immigrants were as a rule poor or otherwise not in control of their fate, and some came against their will. The first had arrived in the 1650s, when Oliver Cromwell transported prisoners of war, as well as 'robbers and vagabonds', to repopulate Jamaica and other islands just seized from Spain. The Scots on the shipments appeared more trusty, diligent and disciplined than the Irish. They were said indeed to be 'the chief instruments of bringing Barbados to its perfection'. The demand for them rose, since native Indians were useless for labour on plantations, and the English had not yet brought their African slave trade to its later pitch of efficiency. White men therefore started selling themselves into voluntary servitude. It was naturally not done on the same conditions as for non-whites, but in the legal form of an indenture with a term; the treatment usually proved better too. Yet it did create a continuous traffic, because replacements had to be found for those freed. An English planter recommended 'that all prudent means be used to encourage the Scots to come hither, as being very good servants' – it is clear why such people objected to the Navigation Acts. They received windfalls, for instance, when starving survivors of Darien felt forced to sell themselves. Later on more prisoners, Jacobites this time, swelled the supply. There are reports up to the last decades of the eighteenth century of youths and even children being kidnapped from the West and North of Scotland, shipped and sold into indentures 'ranged in a line like new Negroes, for the planters to pick and choose'. The latest report we have of a Scot on sale comes from Barbados in 1805.[7]

At its worst this traffic was little better than the slave trade proper. In that too some Scots joined, along with the rest of their imperial opportunities after 1707. If Glasgow merchants on the whole kept their hands clean, those from smaller ports such as Dumfries and Kirkcudbright showed less scruple. Others worked from Liverpool, Bristol and particularly London. There a free-for-all followed the collapse of the chartered Royal African Company round 1750. Among the most successful inter-lopers was a Scottish consortium under two senior partners, Grant of Dalvey and Richard Oswald, the latter hailing from Caithness by way of a commercial training in Glasgow and on the Chesapeake. In 1748 they bought a disused, ruined fort on Bance Island, near the present Freetown in Sierra Leone. They restored it to working order, and added a golf course. They set up just at the right time. With a steady rise in consumption of sugar in Europe, the economy of plantations was being rapidly expanded in the Americas, and the demand for labour with it.

The circumstances favoured innovation in the slave trade, and these Scots responded. Till now, European slavers had often culled their human wares by the direct, brutal means of raiding along the coast and simply seizing the hapless blacks. Grant, Oswald & Co introduced a system which at least had the merit of being more commercial. Its agents stayed put at their well-defended fort, or at outposts up the rivers nearby, and waited for local chiefs to bring down slaves. These were then bartered for goods shipped from Europe, America and India. Leaving the traffic in indigenous hands, the Scots asked no questions about its methods. They contented themselves with providing middlemen's jobs for their relations or friends, and business for their clients. Though newcomers to the slave trade, they thus found a way of thriving without official privilege or any aid against the competition of established English rivals. At the same time, they gave their native accomplices access to global commerce: the ensemble in effect created a free port in the eastern Atlantic. It scarcely amounted to what philosophical Scots meant by a commercial society but Oswald, in charge of it from London, did try to direct it in a manner humane by the standards of the day. If he accorded his captives no rights, he took a distant paternal interest in them while they awaited the dreaded voyage to the West Indies. He issued instructions that their health should be cared for, that families should be kept together and that individuals should wear bracelets of beads rather than be branded for identification.[8]

It would still be hard to confirm claims sometimes made about Scots, that their backwardness in entering the slave trade had to do with respect for human rights. The origins of scientific racism can, after all, plausibly be sought in the Scottish Enlightenment. David Hume wrote in his essay on *National Characters* that he suspected negroes to be inferior to whites: 'There scarcely ever was a civilised nation of that complexion, nor even any individual eminent either in action or speculation . . . Such a uniform and constant difference could not happen, in so many countries and ages, if nature had not made an original distinction between these breeds of men'. He had heard of an educated black in Jamaica, 'but it is likely he is admired for slender accomplishments, like a parrot, who speaks a few words plainly'. Lord Kames felt readier to ascribe the negroes' demerits to their degrading conditions. But his study of another race, the American Indians, persuaded him that they differed so much from Europeans, notably in lack of sexual ardour, that they must be the product of a 'local creation', not descended from Adam and Eve. Let it be pointed out in defence of these literary luminaries, however, that both condemned slavery.

At the same time, Scotland also produced apologists for it. She had done so since the age of discoveries dawned, when the schoolman John Mair restated for the modern era Aristotle's teaching that 'some men are by nature slaves, others by nature free'. In a more enlightened epoch, Andrew Fletcher of Salton and Gershom Carmichael denounced ancient Greek and Roman servitude as an attribute of despotism. Yet they took care to distinguish it from regulated economic serfdom, their own cure for sturdy beggars. This, in a feudal form, was already countenanced under Scotland's municipal law, specifically for miners, who till 1799 could be hereditarily bound to their occupation. An interesting instance occurred of how these felt for the blacks. A group of them in Fife raised money in 1770 towards the legal defence of David Spens, a slave who resisted being sent back to the West Indies whence his master had brought him home; he won his case, and spent the rest of his life working for a farmer at Wemyss. If anything, African strangers were better off than native serfs after the second, decisive case of Joseph Knight in 1778. The Court of Session then ruled that any slave setting foot in Scotland became free. In the mother country it thus abolished slavery, at least of the exotic sort.

Yet even this found an apologist in Archibald Dalzel, whose brother Andrew held the chair of Greek at the university of Edinburgh and hobnobbed with leading Moderates of the Kirk. Archibald's own aim was to get rich, so he entered the slave trade. In 1767 he became director of a West African fort where it was carried on, earning a steady £10,000 a year. He hoped to set up as a Caribbean planter, but on the way home in 1778 he was caught by an American privateer and lost everything. Declared bankrupt on arrival, he spent a few years doing odd jobs from pirate to bookseller. They included, under political and commercial patronage, hackwork in defence of slavery. Still, to an extension of these labours we owe his *History of Dahomey* (1793), one of the first scholarly books on Africa. He returned there but made no more money; at his death in 1811 he was bankrupt again. By then the writing had appeared on the wall for slavery, yet that did not stop other Scots continuing to leap to its defence. Sir John Gladstone, founder of his family's fortunes in Liverpool, paused from a busy commercial and political life to give the public the benefit of his views: emancipation should not be thought of till blacks reached some higher cultural level, and then not hastily but 'in a due and just regard to the lives, the property and the interests of their masters'. Meanwhile the squeamish could reflect that Africans were better off enslaved: 'The manumitted Negroes are idle, indolent and slothful, and too often become profligate though they possessed good characters whilst they remained slaves'. As late as 1849, Thomas Carlyle's *Discourse on Niggers* stopped little short of calling for servitude to be restored, as a cure for destitution among emancipated blacks.[9]

Yet the widest survey of records left by Scots in the West Indies concludes that on the whole they disapproved of slavery. They often thought Caribbean societies corrupt and vicious, too rich, too rootless, too repressive. This was just something they had to tolerate so long as they lived outside Scotland, to which they hoped to return. Since they had not created the form of society round them, the colony of plantations, they saw no special onus on themselves to change it, not yet anyway. In the intimacy of their own circles, nevertheless, they did not hide their disgust at the cruelty of life on the islands.

Zachary Macaulay, one of 12 children of the minister of Inveraray, was sent to Jamaica in 1784 at the age of 16. He disliked his bookkeeper's job on a plantation, but especially the fact that 'by my situation I was exposed not only to the sight but also to the practice of severities on others, the very recollection of which makes my blood run cold'. Little more than a boy, he feared protest would make him look 'foolish, childish and ridiculous', or worse, ungrateful to his parents, patrons and employers. Macaulay consoled himself by setting down the facts to a friendly minister at home, writing that he would hardly recognise the young fellow he once knew, 'were you to view me in a field of canes, amidst perhaps a hundred of the sable race, cursing and bawling, while the noise of the whip resounding on their shoulders, and the cries of the poor wretches, would make you imagine some unlucky accident had carried you to the doleful shades'.[10]

Others did speak out. James Ramsay had started as a naval surgeon before entering the Church and taking a charge on St Kitts in 1762. The island's life appalled him. He wanted to convert negroes, yet found them in a state so debased that he had no chance. He owned some in his own household, and when he treated them decently the planters ostracised him. Soon after returning home, he brought out an *Essay on the Treatment and Conversion of African Slaves in the British Sugar Colonies* (1784) which described the blacks' brutalised lives, the monotony of their work, the suffering they endured under the whip. Ramsay appealed for them to be recognised as human beings capable of reformation, indeed salvation. Bloodcurdling tales of the plantations would turn into something of a Scottish speciality. Stedman's book appeared a few years later. In 1824 came *The Horrors of Slavery* by Robert

Wedderburn, son of James Wedderburn of Inveresk and a negress. As an adult he crossed the Atlantic to visit verbal retribution on his father, who no doubt imagined he had left such worries behind, and was fêted by radicals as living proof that men of mixed race did not turn out degenerate.[11]

In Scotland, the apologetic current was anyway always weaker than its opposite, which carried the weight of enlightened opinion with it. One original feat of Francis Hutcheson was his destruction of Aristotle's teaching on slavery. He elaborated a new system of humanitarian ethics arising not out of antique canons of reason, but out of the sympathy, if anything non-rational, of every man for another. That erected a test for social institutions free of prior assumptions. They could now be judged by a sense of benevolence and thus by, among other things, the hardship they caused. Adam Smith, accepting that this deprived slavery of any moral justification, added that it was bad in economic terms too. 'The work done by slaves, though it appears to cost only their maintenance, is in the end the dearest of all', for they had no incentive to exert themselves. It gave a fine example of how misguided restraints hindered the harnessing of self-interest to the general good: slavery was at once inhumane and useless. John Millar's *Observations concerning Distinctions of Ranks in Society* added the perspective of conjectural history. On the fall of the Roman Empire, slavery in Europe could not be sustained, but the resulting division of labour fostered economic progress. To reintroduce slavery in America with men from primitive nations was to turn the clock back. Millar forecast that it would at length disappear, though he did not think immediate abolition feasible. James Beattie, professor of moral philosophy at Aberdeen, went further than the rest of the literati and became an active abolitionist, working with his friend William Wilberforce. His *Elements of Moral Science* incorporated the others' arguments against slavery into Common Sense Philosophy: 'If it be equitable, or excusable, or pardonable, it is vain to talk any longer of the eternal distinctions of right and wrong, truth and falsehood, good and evil.' His view of racial equality was essentially the modern one that

> all the inhabitants of this globe, who have reason, speech and erect figure, must be considered as one great family, and as informed with souls of the same order, whatever slight variations may appear in their bodies. So that, though there are many nations and tribes of men, it cannot be said with truth that there is more than one species.

In support of this, philosophical Scots had assembled a comprehensive critique of slavery.[12]

If we sum up the relation of Scotland and the West Indies in the eighteenth century, we can define three elements: a growing, tacit dislike of an economy based on slavery among those working in it; more open intellectual censure of it at home; increasing awareness of it among Scots at large. With the awareness grew dismay at its inhumanity. Ramsay's work helped to arouse public opinion at a crucial point, just before Wilberforce carried the abolitionist campaign into Parliament. At about the same time, Macaulay returned from Jamaica, to find one of his sisters married to Wilberforce's friend, Thomas Babington. Through this connection the young Scot rose to the forefront of abolitionism, for which he worked tirelessly till its eventual triumph, five years before his own death in 1838.

The victory of the cause came sooner in England than in Scotland, it must be said. True, Henry Dundas responded early, by drawing up in 1792 a timetable for staged abolition of the slave trade, on a plan much praised, and approved by the House of Commons, but thrown out by the House of Lords. He would try again, never to any effect. Yet while there remained hope of amelioration, in the trade or in the treatment of negroes, Scots seemed reluctant to denounce slavery for itself. At any rate, they allowed no doubts of its morality to affect the conduct of their business in the colonies dependent on production of tobacco, sugar and cotton. Ever ready to debate the theory of slavery, they apparently saw little need to do anything about it. Perhaps this was just another instance of Presbyterian hypocrisy, but there may be a better explanation.[13]

If overawed by the scale of imperial enterprise, Scots scarcely yet felt it was their Empire, to be ordered on their principles. Scotland was still the centre of their world. Even far away, they remained preoccupied with the families, communities and nation they had left behind. The contact with other cultures did of course enrich theirs, prompting them to question it, explain changes in it, reckon what price was paid for them. But in then applying the lessons, Scots showed a becoming diffidence. When they analysed different societies, they looked for more lessons to learn rather than for chances to teach their own. When they analysed less advanced ones, such as Africa, they did so in order to draw inferences about excessive liberty, here held to manifest itself in savagery. The critique of slavery was thus not meant to solve the problem of slavery. It was instead just one extreme aspect of a completely different problem, of the balance between authority and freedom, between tradition and enlightenment, the general problem with which Scots saw themselves confronted at every turn. In their philosophical speculation about it, they wished to weigh with care the conflicting claims. This could not be done by simple standards of white and black, good and bad, innocent and guilty.

There lay the difference between the way enlightened Scots thought about slavery, and the way their children came to think about it once abolition turned into a great moral cause. This happened with the rise of evangelical religion, and of the deeper social and spiritual forces beneath it. The absolute nature of its values was already by the turn of the nineteenth century discomfiting Scottish philosophers in their ethical relativism. For a time they could maintain their enlightened commentary on the phenomenon of slavery, but in the end the evangelical attack overwhelmed them. People then felt obliged not just to think about the question, but take sides on it, attack or defend their position, make it ideologically sound, force it on doubters, convert dissidents to it. Slavery was one of many matters transformed by this new mentality. The Enlightenment itself began to pass away under the ferocity of the assaults thus inspired and the rigidity of the commitments demanded. This also prompted Scots to take up roles they had previously eschewed, as moral arbiters and imperial reformers.[14]

Brougham was one of the first. He drafted, pushed through and saw to enforcement of the Felony Act (1811) which, by imposing draconian penalties on any remaining trade in slaves by British subjects, stopped it dead. He also inaugurated, with proposals put to Parliament in 1823, the final campaign for abolition of slavery in the British Empire, brought to a successful conclusion ten years later. Still, it cannot be said that at this stage Scottish opinion had otherwise developed far enough to sway matters. Little is known of West Indian Scots during the period. But John Galt, well-informed on colonial affairs, makes the hero of his novel *Bogle Corbet* (1831) a son of decayed planters, who goes out after an education in Glasgow to find that 'verily, not only the villages, but Kingston itself, showed how much the proprietors calculated, insensibly, perhaps, to themselves, that in Jamaica they had no continuing city'. In the end he gives up to try his luck in Canada. This may well have been the fate of many real people like him.

Once Scots could no longer exploit the West Indies, they were just as unsentimental in winding up their interests. Gladstone, for example, got compensation of £86,000 for his slaves in Demerara and Jamaica. And since the East India Company's monopoly was also now abolished, he used his bonanza to enter with Kirkman Finlay, the Glasgow capitalist, on oriental ventures. They brought indentured Indian coolies to the West Indies, but they also wanted to grow sugar and cotton in India, hoping to make her Britain's main source for those commodities. That would depend, however, on discrimination against producers elsewhere, and the spirit of the age favoured personal and economic liberty against forced labour and protection. The last straw came for Gladstone when in 1838 the Government suspended the system of indentures too. He sold his West Indian estates for what he could get, and went into railways at home: Scotland owes to this the ferry from Granton to Burntisland with the line on into Fife. On commercial considerations, he was of course right. The crops now grown by free, at any rate freer, labour in the West Indies or in India could never compete with the produce of slaves in Cuba, Brazil and the United States. But, in the 1840s, Sir Robert Peel's zeal for fiscal reform mastered moral scruples, and he ended tariffs on such produce. Ruin overtook the old Caribbean plantations.

The Governor of Jamaica was the young James Bruce, 8th Earl of Elgin, friend of William Gladstone. It distressed him that the blacks' problems had merely begun with their freedom. Many whites, too, were reduced 'to the lowest depths of poverty' and had to be supported from public funds. He hoped at least that racial tension was now yielding to 'more liberal and kindly sentiments', and even looked forward to a political system of popular representation, in order to blend 'into one harmonious whole a community composed of diverse races and colours'. Sheer beggary may have done more to keep the island quiet. A Glaswegian minister, David King, visited it in

1849–50 and found the negroes 'of a peaceful, unvengeful disposition. The white inhabitants are exceedingly few . . . but the blacks remain contentedly poor and submissive under their European superiors'.[15]

Yet this was not the full picture. The abandoned land on bankrupt plantations tempted the more enterprising negroes to take it over, legally or illegally. They were in fact forming a new class of peasant proprietors, who began to assert themselves politically under the encouragement of missionaries and local preachers. Moreover, Jamaica and other islands possessed their elected assemblies, dating from the earliest English occupation. Since in the old days it had been thought desirable for as many whites as possible to be represented, qualifications for the suffrage were not high. Now blacks could win it too, and choose members to defend their rights. Of these the leader was George William Gordon. Born about 1820 to a Scots lawyer and a negress, he had been well educated and brought up in the United Presbyterian Church. He married a white and inherited £10,000 from his father, which he used to buy a newspaper and found the Jamaica Mutual Life Assurance Company. He had the social standing to be nominated a magistrate, then elected to the assembly. The place he chose to take up there, however, was not pillar of the colonial establishment but tribune of the people. He mounted such fierce attacks on the administration of the island that in 1862 a new governor, Edward Eyre, took away his magistrate's warrant.

One object of Gordon's wrath was the lack of provision for blacks to gain title to land which white planters had no means to work, so that both stayed poorer than they need be. Squatters on untilled estates were driven off and harshly punished. After several such severities at Morant Bay in the east of the island, violence erupted. A mob of negroes gathered one day in October 1865 before the courthouse, set it on fire and beat the magistrates to death as they ran out. More riots and murders followed. A great black uprising was the constant fear in the West Indies. Eyre decided this was what he faced, declared martial law and sent in troops. These, according to later investigation, killed 439 negroes, flogged 600 others and burned 1000 dwellings. They met no resistance. Not one soldier was hurt. Yet the reprisals continued for a month. The governor also ordered Gordon's arrest. He, far from fomenting trouble, had stayed quietly at home in Kingston. When he heard of Eyre's order he at once, as a law-abiding citizen, surrendered himself. The governor sailed him off to Morant Bay, to place him in the zone where martial law prevailed, and hanged him from the archway of the gutted courthouse. The affair would cause an outcry in Britain and force an official inquiry which, while not condemning Eyre, scarcely exonerated him either.

But it did nothing for Jamaica, which soon surrendered its constitution, granted by the Crown in 1661. All trace of internal autonomy went with it. That seemed not such a bad thing at the outset, because it immediately brought in a governor, John Grant of Rothiemurchus, who combined strong executive powers with Scottish liberal paternalism. He duly reformed the judiciary and police, introduced schemes of economic development, gave more money to education and, by the way, disestabilish the Church of England. But after he left in 1873, the spectacle was plain to see of a poverty-stricken island worthy of nothing more than irresponsible colonial administration. Its status would not be raised till the Empire approached its end.[16]

Neither here nor elsewhere in the region did Scots leave much to show for their two centuries of continuous, if merely transient, presence. There are monuments to them in some of the big houses on the plantations, fortified like baronial castles or constructed on the strict Palladian principles of counterparts dotting the Scottish landscape. Often they bear the name of a spot in the old country. But Scots migrants had little other interest in investing here for the future. They never left behind them the usual marks of their passing, the collective institutions of churches and schools. Above all, rich or poor, they could not outlast the economy of plantations. Their traces survived only in the children of unions with negroes. Gordon's brutal judicial murder showed that, however Scottish these might manage to remain in their personal culture, they would not be accepted by new white masters as different from other descendants of slaves.

CHAPTER SEVEN

'Compassion for fallen greatness': India

D avid Wilkie, who used to depict so lovingly the detail of Scottish daily life, could rise to grander themes. The National Gallery of Scotland houses a canvas by him which shows General David Baird standing in triumph over Tipu Sahib, fallen Sultan of Mysore, whose capital, Seringapatam, he has just stormed in May 1799. While Tipu's corpse slumps in a dark corner, above him Baird, his natural stature heightened, his figure illumined, looks towards a civilised future. The radiance around is shed by a torch in the hands of a Highland soldier, himself sprung from a savage race, demonstrating what Asiatics might in their turn become under the severe but enlightened genius of the Lowland Scot.

The reality of Seringapatam was different. Baird knew the place because he had, after his capture in 1780 by Tipu's father, Hyder Ali, been held prisoner there for four years. He and his comrades in arms were kept chained in pairs. 'God help the man that's chained tae oor Davie!' said Baird's mother when she heard. In 1799 he came back with the Scotch Brigade and joined in the campaign to crush Mysore for good. Long a dangerous and resourceful enemy, it was the more so now as Tipu sought alliance with revolutionary France. The British advanced on his capital, sited on an island in the River Cauvery. They bombarded and breached its defences. The commander, Lord Harris, planned to carry them with his Highland regiments, the 73rd and 74th, so gave Baird the honour of mounting the assault. At noon on May 4 he went to the head of his columns, climbed the reverse of a trench and drew his sword. 'Men, are you ready?' he cried. 'Ready!' was the response. 'Then forward, my lads!' The general himself led 5000 soldiers under fire across the water. They took the ramparts in six minutes.

Terrible carnage followed. At first the defenders fought back, but British firepower was superior and the implacable Gaels cut grimly into the mass of Mysoreans. These wavered, then panicked, jumping from the walls to be killed in the fall, drowned in the water below or picked off from above. Baird divided his forces and sent them racing along both sides of the circular fortifications so that, when they met at the other end, Seringapatam was surrounded. The Indians' discipline broke down altogether as, mingled now with civilians, they strove to get to the citadel or escape out of the city. Herded into narrow passages and gateways, they were slain in heaps by the storming parties' murderous volleys. In one of the shambles Tipu met his death. He fell wounded at a sally-port and lay till an enemy soldier came up to seize the golden buckle of his sword-belt. When the haughty sultan resisted, the soldier shot him in cold blood. Once his body was identified, Baird went to view it. To that extent Wilkie depicted the truth. But he showed nothing of the massacre with the bayonet in the background. The following night witnessed a hellish spectacle, thunder in heaven, on earth wanton slaughter and destruction. Over 10,000 Mysoreans died, against 80 British troops killed the day before. In the heat and damp of a lurid dawn, atrocities still went on. Harris resolved to restore some sanity and superseded Baird with Colonel Arthur Wellesley, later Duke of Wellington. The general was furious but Wellesley would not argue. He told Baird to finish his breakfast and quit the fortress.[1]

Seringapatam remains today inscribed on the colours of regiments descended from those that fought there. Yet like the painting, they are a not quite fitting symbol of the Scottish Empire in India. By the turn of the nineteenth century Scots seemed omnipresent, accounting for perhaps two out of three British subjects resident on the sub-continent. Their soldiers did play a large part in conquering it, but a greater contribution came from their governors and merchants. That peaceful contact with the life of India awakened above all their rapt interest in her culture, the oldest and deepest they had yet met, the strangest with which they had ever had to come to terms.

The contact had begun long since. To the Orient, too, the Scots, so far from being imprisoned by poverty and apathy as received wisdom tells us, set out early on, a mere 10 or 20 years behind the Dutch and English. James VI again gave the envoi. In 1618 he granted Sir James Cunningham of Glengarnock, already an Irish coloniser, a patent to found a Scottish East India Company. This provoked such protests from the City of London and from the royal burghs, fearing he would directly import exotic goods, that the patent was withdrawn. Scots made their way eastwards even so, in the service of Holland or England. Perhaps the first to fire his country's imagination with the mystery of the Orient was Alexander Hamilton, who started a long career there in 1688 and published a book of travels, the *New Account of the East Indies*, full of vivid anecdote. He was intrigued by the uncorrupted body of St Francis Xavier at Goa, looking 'as fresh as new scalded pig'. He told how the Pope had ordered its right arm sent to Rome to test its authenticity: 'After a little conjuration, in full view of the sacred college, who were there present, and nobody else, the saint's hand took hold of the pen, and dipped it in ink, and fairly wrote Xavier'. He kept running into compatriots. On one Scottish ship he met super-cargoes who 'had a chest of glassware, in their own private adventure, the most obscenely shameful that ever I saw or heard among merchants. They were priapuses of a large size, with a scrotum long enough to hold an English pint of liquor'. He thought little of the captain, a Highlander who in his youth had been a drover of cattle, with no education or training in navigation but three wives in different ports. Such was the hard life, relieved only by crude pleasures, of oriental voyagers in those times.[2]

Things became easier for Scots after 1707. Now they possessed as much right as any other Briton to get on to the establishment of the English East India Company.

Hamilton's brother, William, went as surgeon with its delegation to the Moghul court in 1714. He performed sterling service by curing the Emperor of a venereal infection, and enabling him to marry. That the Union should bear such tangible results was anyway a concern of the Prime Minister, Sir Robert Walpole. He put a fair share of Indian appointments the Scots' way. Given their clannishness, it soon became better than a fair share. By 1750, they took up to 30 per cent of posts in Bengal, later under Warren Hastings sometimes more. Henry Dundas, presiding over Indian administration at the end of the century, may even out of political prudence have cut the number somewhat. As in Virginia and the West Indies, these men were transients, who went because they had to but meant to return and set up independently at home. In India they could make huge fortunes, and faster than in the New World, giving rise to an entire class of *nouveaux riches*, the nabobs. John Johnstone of Westerhall brought back £300,000 which he used to buy three estates and build up a political interest in the South-West. Even he was outdone by John Farquhar, who in his unrivalled parsimony contracted with his Indian servant to feed him for two annas a day. Worth £1.5 million on his return, he offered any Scottish university £100,000 to endow a chair of atheism, but found no taker.[3]

While the East India Company had a statutory monopoly on direct trade between Britain and all points beyond the Cape of Good Hope, it could never keep the oriental traffic to itself. Inefficiency and corruption flowered under this as under every monopoly, which its own servants colluded in breaking. The privilege anyway left other British subjects at liberty to conduct the 'country trade', the commerce along the coasts of the sub-continent or between Indian and foreign ports. A century after the Union, 14 Scots merchant houses in Calcutta (against 10 English) were engaged in it. Some flouted the law and traded illegally to Britain too. They happily worked with the East India Company's continental rivals, dealing through their own compatriots at Rouen, Ostend, Gothenburg and Copenhagen. Of great value were old Jacobite connections, sometimes stretching right to the East: John Law's son was governor at Pondicherry, the French station in India.

Dundas meanwhile whittled away from within at the East India Company's privileges. His work was crowned by his son Robert, author of the legislation which in 1813 abolished its monopoly in the sub-continent. Glasgow merchants at once began a traffic to Bengal which rapidly developed, in textiles especially; one of its gifts to the world was the Paisley shawl. This augured well for the Scots' influence in the mighty Empire emerging at the end of the Napoleonic wars, which left Britain the sole colonial power of any importance. The first, lost Empire in America had been in essence mercantilist. The second now in formation was perforce a trading rather than a colonising one, built on commercial outposts for the exploitation of resources which remained in the hands of alien peoples. The Dundases and their circle, partly through their Scottish background and partly through their daily contact with the practical problems, shook themselves free from mercantilism to embrace free trade (though in a limited sense compared to what was later taken for granted). Then they began to discern the outlines of Britain's future as the centre of an imperial system, with commodities from its outposts feeding industry and consumption at home.

In Scottish political economy, the constant counterpart to free trade was strong, paternalist government. Its blessings, too, Scots brought to India, again through the power and patronage of the elder Dundas. As soon as elected to Parliament in 1774 he started to specialise in the affairs of the sub-continent, where crisis now loomed. A few years later, having meanwhile chaired a committee to investigate abuses, he was devising reforms bold enough to impress his colleagues at Westminster. He aimed to strengthen political authority over the wayward East India Company in both London and Calcutta, though without centralising to the extent that Charles James Fox proposed in his ill-fated project of 1783, which aroused resistance so fierce as to bring the collapse of his brief coalition with Lord North. Parliament was therefore ready, when Dundas then came in under William Pitt the younger, to accept his ideas. With further revisions, he carried them into law in 1784, in what remained the primary legislation for British India till 1857.

The India Act strengthened political authority in London by creation of a new policy-making body, the Board of Control. It did so in Calcutta by various additions to the Governor-General's competences which, however, fell rather short of reducing the East India Company to a non-monopolistic trading corporation, as Dundas ultimately wished. Seeing that only gradualism would work, he felt obliged to dilute the privileges bit by bit, and continued to do so in a series of further measures themselves minor. While the directors could thus wield a residual power, temporary setbacks interrupted the process. Sacrifices had to be accepted, such as recognition of the Nawab of Arcot's corrupt debts. There were losers, the most notable Warren Hastings, who suffered an impeachment of which Dundas correctly forecast he would be acquitted. All was worth it for a higher principle: to consolidate a regime under which the old misdemeanours could not recur, in which case the controversies they represented were dead. The important changes came not just in the personnel and instruments of British rule in India, but also in its aims and attitudes.[4]

Those aims and attitudes can be better understood against the background of Scottish philosophy. Generally Scots in India adopted an attitude to local conditions familiar to us: they took them as they found them. Some assimilated – David Ochterlony, British resident at Delhi from 1803, lived like an oriental potentate in manners and dress, keeping 13 wives and parading them round the city, each on her own elephant. Making themselves at home, Scots normally shut their eyes to abuses, for no more in the Orient than in the New World could they control the conduct of Europeans. But the knowledge they transmitted home was lapped up by philosophical countrymen. These felt alarmed at the situation in India. Their disdain for the sordid gain available there was barbed by the sight of what it could buy at home. David Hume went so far as to wish for 'the expulsion of the English from the East Indies'. Adam Smith coolly applied his usual arguments against mercantilism: whatever the monopoly's original justification, it had now gone, and the East India

Company's commercial interests were incompatible with sovereign power over conquered territories. Allan Ramsay warned of corruption spreading into the sanctum of British liberty, for the nabobs grew rich enough to come back and buy seats in Parliament. George Dempster thought Indian acquisitions would do as much damage to the mother country as an Asian *imperium* had done to the Roman republic.

The last thought shows how the literati started to fit empirical observation of India into their general intellectual inquiry. They then carried European orientalism on a stage, beyond the largely missionary concern for the Far East which had informed it since the age of Xavier. With a shift of focus to the lands between Arabia and China, this stage was philosophical rather than theological, empirical rather than didactic, cognisant not only of European but also of Asiatic scholarship, thus requiring mastery of indigenous languages and literatures. Its Scottish harbinger was the translation from Persian of Firishtah's *History of Hindostan* by Alexander Dow, which he put out in 1768 while building for himself, after his return from the East, a successful career on the stage in London. As more Scots published their first-hand experiences they found grounds for reproaching other Europeans with a failure to understand or even look at the immensity and antiquity of Indian culture. They were in fact in the process of breaking with this habitual dismissive contempt, and they conveyed a growing excitement over the new perspectives they thus opened up. The *Sketches chiefly relating to the . . . Hindus* brought out in 1790 by Quentin Crawford – another busy fellow who was at the same time trying to help the French royal family to escape from revolutionary Paris – finally formulated a fresh view. India had been prosperous and peaceful, he argued, till foreign invasion overthrew her benevolent religion and liberal laws.

This intellectual odyssey represented in a sense a breathtaking act of psychological projection by the Scots literati. Enjoying a recognised status in their own hierarchical society, they felt inclined to seek and admire in others a caste like themselves. That was what they supposed Indian brahmans to be, men of enlarged minds and sympathies altruistically guiding humanity, drawing on the resources of classical language and philosophy enshrined in Sanskrit learning. With the analogy established, India could begin to take her place in conjectural history. But such history, we should recall, mirrored the broad, comparative outlook of the philosophy underlying it. In other words, it did not fully conform to what is now usually known as British orientalism, which had a primarily historiographical and linguistic focus, reflected in the work of the Asiatic Society of Bengal. Scots cared less about deriving a narrative of the sub-continent's past from reliable records. This was all to the good, because India lacked a historical discipline in the western sense: enormous stretches of her past lay in darkness, odd shafts of light serving merely to reveal further mysteries.[5]

But Scots were used to making do with what they had. One thing they did have was Hindu chronology, bizarre though perhaps capable of being reduced to sense with the help of Hindu astronomy and mathematics. On this last Colin Mackenzie, a son of Stornoway who rose to be Surveyor-General of India, was the world's greatest, if not first, expert. He arrived in the East in 1781 to be welcomed by one of the earliest and most remarkable memsahibs, Hester Johnstone, a daughter of Lord Napier married to the paymaster of Madura in the Carnatic. Here lay a famous Hindu college. She took the young Gael there, introduced him to the pandits and had him instructed in their wisdom. He followed her in acquiring and preserving their manuscripts, of which he eventually built a huge collection. Already the science they contained was being transmitted home, as we know from the paper, *Remarks on the Astronomy of the Brahmins*, read in 1789 by Professor John Playfair to the Royal Society of Edinburgh. He began by saying that the history of astronomy was usually regarded as one of linear progress from Chaldeans to Greeks to moderns, so that it might seem odd to find a body of Indian knowledge standing quite apart from that 'which has traversed and enlightened the other countries of the earth'. He tried to bring the two together by proving through inference from current observations that a conjunction of planets at the start of the *Kali yuga*, the latest Hindu epoch, must have taken place at the date stated by tradition, in 3102 BC. From this starting point he believed a system embracing everybody could be constructed, though later scholarship has not accepted his thesis.

A different method of elaborating a conjectural history for the sub-continent was to determine the relations among the enigmatic monuments, ruins and other remains abundantly littering it. Jonathan Duncan, 'brahmanised' while serving as resident at Benares in 1788–95, embarked on the task with efforts to rescue the treasures in this Athens of India. In a later generation, Alexander Cunningham's many archaeological discoveries – the Buddhist nature of the vast vestiges at Sarnath, the pre-aryan origin of Taxila, the Greek influence on the school of Gandhara – all formed crucial links in India's early history. He would see his work crowned by inauguration of the Indian Archaeological Survey. James Fergusson turned to the edifices still standing, to become the historian and classifier of Indian architecture. But it proved hard to construct a national history of stone alone, and these advances in knowledge could only take their place alongside different ones.

Advances in the science of language were to prove crucial for the Scots' understanding of India too. Here, in fact, they had a special aptitude. At home, the literati often felt keen to record and save the Scots tongue as it receded before English. They did so out of not just patriotic antiquarianism but also out of a conviction that linguistic research advanced the philosophy of mind. Adam Smith taught a connection between the histories of language and of mind. In that case philology, especially comparative philology, offered a key to the understanding of human development. Languages and links among them were indeed to yield vital evidence for assessment of India's civilisations.

An early if false start came from James Burnett, Lord Monboddo. He heard in the 1760s about the similarity with Greek that the first western scholars had found in Sanskrit, but he only used it as grist to the mill of his own argument, in voluminous writings, that all tongues descended from Egyptian. The correct thesis of a common origin for Indo-European languages is forever linked with the name of Sir William Jones, yet Alexander Murray, professor of oriental literature at the university of Edinburgh, came independently to the same conclusion. The greatest Sanskrit scholar of the age was Alexander Hamilton, who began as a cadet in the army of Bengal, resigned to devote himself to study, went home with his Indian wife and wrote for the *Edinburgh Review*. He visited Paris after the Peace of Amiens in 1801, to be stranded there by renewal of war. French intellectuals held him in such high esteem that he was not interned but allowed to live with two German exiles, Friedrich and Wilhelm August Schlegel, to whom he taught Sanskrit. Their work, *Über die Sprache und Weisheit der Inder,* inaugurated their own nation's formidable orientalism.[6]

Meanwhile, another premature yet productive attempt to sum up India's place in the narrative of civil society came from the pen of Principal William Robertson, no less. He filled out the gaps in the story by a method of his own, indicated by his title, *Historical Disquisition concerning the Knowledge which the Ancients had of India* (1791). While this knowledge, as represented in classical literature, was meagre, Robertson's task transcended it. What he rather sought was to show western readers aware of their own culture's origins that its links with the Orient were just as old. They would then be able to understand that India, quite as much as Egypt or Persia, formed part of one great story, if with a cultural continuity proper to herself. Neither Europe nor India therefore represented anything unique: the civilisations were equivalent, and admirable in themselves.

Yet readers could hardly overlook the contrast between progress in the West and decline in the East. They were entitled to note it, for if Indians resembled westerners, westerners could live among them, develop and judge them by western standards. They still ran the moral hazard of feeling superior. So Robertson counselled against conscious westernisation, or even christian proselytising. He did, however, urge the free circulation of knowledge, as good for all societies, and useful in the present case to fulfil the specific, benevolent mission of the British. This was to bring India up to the higher level of commercial society and draw her into the emergent global economy, crowning another chapter of the great story with a happy ending. Robertson's project thus had not only an intellectual but also a moral purpose, to explain why exploitation of Indians should end, and to compel respect for their rights, culture and heritage. This would let them advance in harmony with their own laws, traditions and historic achievements. In accepting such obligations, Britain would vindicate her imperial role more surely than by subjection or domination. She would do it, too, on Scottish criteria, in conservative awareness of the prerequisites for India's development towards universalist goals, in other words, towards assimilation of her experience into the narrative of human development.

Such criteria lie at the heart of what has become known today as orientalism. The modern critique of it is that it attributes to western culture knowledge about other cultures that they do not possess themselves, and so in a circular argument contains no sense of them which might test, rather than confirm, western values. Still, it did bring an advance on the belief that Indian culture was worthless, and Europeans at liberty to rape it. Robertson's disquisition had direct implications as a basis for a rational, benevolent Indian policy. Here it showed remarkable parallels with what Dundas actually did. At this distance in time we cannot be sure who was influencing whom, but the parallels strengthen the case for seeing in the Dundases, father and son, men who realised enlightened principles.[7]

At any rate, as in Scotland, so in India a fruitful exchange between scholarship and government took place. The sub-continent long remained largely under the sway of enlightened Scots who had attended university in Edinburgh and sat at the feet of Dugald Stewart. Starting at the top there came the Earl of Minto, Governor-General in 1806–11. His regime faced military necessities: he had to act the strongman in ensuring, while European wars went on, that France gained no advantage in the East, so he seized her posts, with those of the nations she had conquered. But internally he was an equable ruler. Towards the Indian states he remained pacific, especially on the North-West frontier, sending embassies to the Persians, Afghans and Sikhs. In Calcutta he held a sort of orientalist court, graced by the West's first adepts in eastern learning and dispensing patronage to any who would preserve and disseminate it. He made the College of Fort William a major intellectual centre, whence came a stream of learned works, dictionaries and grammars from a Sanskrit press, modern editions of Hindu, Persian or Arabic classics. Being far away, and having had David Hume as guardian, Minto could turn a deaf ear to demands from British evangelicals that India must be converted. As a matter of policy, he insisted on religious toleration, barred missionaries from the sub-continent and expelled the odd one who managed to enter illegally. Personally, he even refused to subscribe to a fund for translating the bible into native languages.[8]

His successor in 1811–18, Lord Moira, had been born in Ireland, but married a Scots heiress and moved to Edinburgh where, at the centre of a wide social and intellectual circle, he became steeped in enlightened culture. India let his talents flower as soldier and ruler. He waged war against Nepal in 1814, annexing Simla and other districts in the hills, besides starting the Gurkhas' tradition of service to the Crown. In 1817–18 he subdued the Marathas and seized their territories. But he also initiated a policy of improvement, reforming the revenue and judiciary, building roads and schemes of irrigation. In his time India regained a unity, in the sense that the struggles for supremacy were over, all resolved in favour of the British, who now provided the country's effective government. Under him and his consort, the Countess of Loudoun, the orientalist court blossomed yet. A stronger cultural initiative followed in the brief interregnum of John Adam of Blairadam, acting Governor-General in 1823. He set up a Committee of Public Instruction which gave grants to five colleges to promote eastern learning, and authorised reprints of more Sanskrit and Arabic literature or translations of European works into Asiatic languages. This work continued into the 1830s, till anglicists found their way on to the committee and pressed for quite different priorities.[9]

At the provincial level, especially, there flourished a generation of governors as remarkable for character as for achievement. Scots intellectuals, confident in a historicist interpretation of the present, they viewed with conservative horror any wanton destruction on speculative principles of this immemorial society, and in their policies they could give direct expression to their outlook. Their mentor was Thomas Munro, forced to seek a military career after his father, a Glasgow merchant, had been ruined by the War of American Independence. He came into his own as a very efficient civil servant, and exact scholar. For all his lucidity, there was nothing dry about him. Few other officials, at any rate, held a regular 'levee of Indian literati'. He had a deep imaginative understanding of his adopted country, and a poetic sensibility which let him transfer to the wholly different conditions of India his abiding love of a somewhat idealised Scottish countryside peopled by noble peasants. From his arrival in 1780 till 1807 he always worked in a district, so knew the everyday problems and consistently tried to solve them in favour of farmers or traders rather than of aristocrats. He crowned his career as Governor of Madras in 1819–27.[10]

A younger friend and disciple was John Malcolm, humbly born in 1769 as one of 17 children on a tenant farm in Dumfriesshire. The landlords were the nabob Johnstones, who secured him an interview for a cadetship in Bengal at the age of 13. Asked what he would do if he met Hyder Ali, he retorted, 'I'd oot with my sword and cut aff his heid'. That got him in. He was known as Boy Malcolm for his high spirits, but matched the graver Munro in his combination of military prowess, administrative ability and profound learning. After the Governor-General, Lord Wellesley, chose him as private secretary, he became the administration's great Persian expert, sent on delicate missions to Teheran in 1799–1801 and 1808–10. He took up arms again to lead the conquest of the Marathas. Then he embarked on a major reorganisation of central India: the surrendered Peshwa was exiled, the Deccan annexed to Bombay, the feudal confederacy of marauding warrior bands dissolved. Malcolm ended his career as Governor of Bombay in 1827–30. He returned home in hope of election as a Tory MP for a Scottish seat – just at the wrong moment, for the Dundas despotism was collapsing.[11]

Munro and Malcolm were outshone only by Mountstuart Elphinstone, philosopher king of the orientalists. Born in 1779, he acquired a wonderful facility in the classics, later extended to eastern languages. He would casually write in his journal at the siege of Gawilghur in December 1803: 'I breakfasted with Kennedy and talked about Hafiz, Saadi, Horace and Anacreon. At nine I left him and went to the trenches'. Slight in figure, with curly golden locks, his merry boyishness charmed all. Yet that journal, kept up over many years, was unsparing in its self-reproach, and showed the dark side of a Scot fighting to suppress his impulses in the austere mould of duty. He had gone to India at the age of 16 and won his big chance on becoming secretary to Arthur Wellesley. He was next, in 1804–8, appointed resident at Nagpur.

Minto afterwards sent him as part of his diplomacy on a mission to Kabul. Returning in 1811, he was awarded the taxing residency at Poona, where for six years he struggled to hold the Peshwa to a subsidiary alliance. The task proved impossible, so that only renewed war could solve the problem. Following British victory, Elphinstone became commissioner for the Deccan, then in 1819–27 Governor of Bombay. He declined the post of Governor-General in 1834, and died in 1859.[12]

The three were not alone in intimate knowledge of India, her peoples and languages. What as Scots they brought to bear was their philosophy, with its emphasis on morality and its understanding of environment. In India they saw a deep underlying strength, which had yielded to the British only through temporary weakness and might assert itself again at any time. They thus took caution and moderation as their watchwords. Yet nothing persuaded them that India was alien or impenetrable to men of their cast of mind, so they found little to fear or hate. Elphinstone, as versatile with the pen as with the sword, wrote his first book after the mission to Afghanistan, of which the British were then ignorant. It turned out a typically Scottish work, treating all aspects of geography, history, society, economy and politics, before coming to the verdict: 'The situation of the Afghaun country appears to me to bear a strong resemblance to that of Scotland in ancient times'. He did not think the natives unlucky in lacking European institutions. He favoured their choosing their way of life for themselves, because westernisation would rob them of the very virtues that made them a free people. The Scot in him found them a constant delight: 'I had one day been mentioning to the amazement of some visitors, that there had been no rebellion in our nation since 1745'.

But the Scottish orientalist regime was concerned with more than the traditional, curious and picturesque. It also asked questions about where it stood itself in the unfolding of history. The answer was that it represented not a consummation or a climax, but only one of the stages. Since India was hardly to be considered as a commercial society, the orientalists had little to say about free trade or her place in international commerce. They were, however, concerned that their own work should link the past and the future. Malcolm lay under no illusion that British paramountcy was permanent. Not resting on the people's affection, or ever likely to, it had to show itself invincible. But it ought still to be generous, with 'compassion for fallen greatness'. Whether the natives were reconciled or not, British authority would in the end dissolve: 'Very slow will be that dissolution, I trust, but still it is certain we are doomed, like all nations and all men who rise to wonderful, but what may be termed unnatural greatness, to perish by our own hands'. He thought the British were acquiring territory too fast and should brake their expansion. They ought instead to uphold native powers in nothing worse than a gradual decline, so that some political balance in India could be maintained. His was, beneath his zest for life, a pessimistic outlook.

Munro showed himself more positive, and somewhat more of a westerniser, in that far off he saw the prospect of a modern India with people who would have acquired moral and political qualities equal to those of Europeans. For now, however, he wanted old social forms kept, if only because the British had ruled too short a time to find new and better ones. Improving measures could not in his opinion come safely till these preservative credentials had been demonstrated to the Indians. The aim would be to leave them capable of maintaining a free, or at least a regular, government. It implied a long Raj. It implied, even so, no imposition of western ways. Munro wrote in 1818: 'It is too much regulation that ruins everything. Englishmen are as great fanatics in politics as Mahomedans in religion. They suppose that no country can be ruled without English institutions'. In 1821 he told George Canning, just appointed President of the Board of Control, how he always dreaded 'some downright Englishman . . . who will insist on making Anglo-Saxons out of the Hindoos'. Malcolm, too, found fault with younger administrators fresh to the East, not on the grounds that they despised natives, 'but that they are impatient of abuses, and too eager for reform'.

The Scottish orientalist regime was by contrast prepared to tolerate abuse, or at least anomaly, while working to restore piecemeal such native institutions as might yet be saved: only these could guarantee the country's moral independence. In central India, long a prey to anarchy, Malcolm started at the level of the villages by restoring the panchayats, customary tribunals of elders, as organs of immediate administration. He devised a system of local and accessible civil justice by giving the headmen limited powers in petty cases and appointing new grades of native judges. Elphinstone was yet more active in legal reform, exerting himself to suppress suttee, infanticide, slavery and prostitution. With the issue of a code of existing native practice in 1827 he gave the presidency of Bombay exemplary laws. Yet he was still a traditionalist. He too set great store by the panchayats. He never rigorously enforced such a western concept as equality before the law, but retained special courts for landowners and minor rulers.

The combination of philosophy and practice was seen to special advantage in Scots' concern with the land of India. They argued about it for a century, in a debate with conspicuous parallels to one at home over the respective duties of great noblemen and rights of sturdy peasants: at the meetings of the Madras Scottish Society, they explicitly linked it with the Highland clearances. Extension of the debate to the sub-continent arose out of efforts to establish a regular system of tenure in Bengal, for the sake of both order and revenue. The East India Company had never respected native property, but taxed and confiscated without restraint. Henry Dundas – and, he surmised, the gentlemen he addressed on the subject at Westminster – was ready to perceive beneath the country's impoverishment a lack of social leadership from a caste like themselves. His researches proved to his own satisfaction that India came nearest to it in a class called the zemindars, who had enjoyed analogous rights to property under the Great Moghul. Their position had meanwhile deteriorated, however, until they came to occupy a station midway between landowners and tax-farmers, a recipe for corruption among themselves and for oppression of the peasants. Dundas meant as a remedy to restore their rights. This he did by the Permanent Settlement of 1793, which declared the zemindars to be proprietors of the land. He was still disappointed in his hope that they would turn into benevolent lairds on the Scottish pattern: most lived in Calcutta and never went near their estates. In 1798, all the same, orders were sent to Madras for that presidency to adopt the Permanent Settlement.

Munro objected. He represented in India the other side of the debate, also with roots in the Enlightenment. Lord Kames had pointed to the evils of the Scots law of entail, which locked up large estates in the hands of particular families, stifled the market in land and hindered the diffusion of property, the foundation of a moral community. Munro observed the same mischief in Bengal: the zemindari system was the equivalent of entail. He believed that worse must follow if it was imposed on the peasants of southern India, in a position rendered less secure by the previous chaos of the Carnatic especially. He worked out, in conscious contrast, the ryotwari system. It vested ownership in the smallholder, and made him responsible for taxes on his land. He stood in direct relationship to the colonial government, which assessed him in detailed, regular and temporary settlements to take account of his improving efforts. Honest, efficient collectors gathered what was owed, subject to the ruling of the panchayats on any dispute. This strong, simple structure dispensed with landlords or other intermediaries. Munro hoped the virtue it would foster might remain proof against both oriental and European corruptions. When Elphinstone was charged 20 years later with revising the system of tenure in the presidency of Bombay, he adopted it too. His instructions to his collectors were typical of him: 'Maintain the native system; levy the revenue according to the actual cultivation; make the assessments light; impose no new taxes, and do away with none unless obviously unjust; above all, make no innovations'.

Perhaps the truest mark of Scottish orientalism was a belief that education could reverse Indian decline. That begged the question how far traditional education had caused the decline, and so how far it should be modified. Elphinstone rejoiced that Scots patronised oriental learning, but thought this hardly enough while British expansion was still ousting native authorities, the only ones interested in sustaining Indian pedagogy. For his part, he founded a Hindu college staffed by Sanskrit scholars at Poona in 1821. He too provided more and better-paid teachers for mathematics and law, as well as setting up a technical school in Bombay with instruction in Marathi and Gujerati, besides English. He quoted Adam Smith on the state's duty to educate the poor, interpreted as a need for aid to native schools and teachers in the villages. When the directors of the East India Company rejoined that education offered on its territories ought to be in English, Elphinstone answered that there was no demand for it outside the circles of business and administration in Bombay. To serve a useful purpose, education must be for the whole people, and should aim at augmenting Indian knowledge with what could be conveyed from the West in the vernacular. Elphinstone held, too, that attempts at christian instruction would put the natives off; the books provided in his schools were Hindu in character, with no reference to sensitive matters of religion or morality.

The opposing points of view in this debate, soon labelled orientalist and anglicist, cloaked deeper issues. Education in the vernacular could impede westernisation, but might equally create an India capable of ruling herself. Education in English might reconcile an Indian elite to European values; the elite could then, however, hardly be denied positions of responsibility. Elphinstone offered no cut-and-dried answers to these problems, but did stress that the suppression of ability and ambition must eventually cause an explosion. If education encouraged Indian political demands, there was not another policy that could deter them; at least it should permit, in the long run, a peaceful transfer of power. He wrote to Malcolm:

> The acquisition of knowledge by their subjects may have lost the French Haiti and the Spaniards South America, but it preserved half the world to the Romans, gave them a hold on the manners and opinions of their subjects and left them a kind of moral empire long after their physical power was destroyed.

These Scots were thus not perturbed at the prospect of losing power as Indians began to take charge of their destiny again and become their own moral arbiters. In reality, progress towards that goal was to be violently cut off and drastically diverted. The orientalists' principles and methods in India gave way to different and ultimately much uglier ones: which makes it unreasonable for modern critics to tar them with the same brush as high imperialists. The Scots had in fact been able to cushion the sub-continent against the impact of the West, exposing in the reformers latent authoritarian tendencies that might vitiate their ostensible liberal benevolence. The warnings proved right, but only in the sense that the Scots' mediation came to nothing.[13]

CHAPTER EIGHT

'In true highland style': Canada

On June 19, 1816, a band of men was observed moving over the prairie near the banks of the Red River, in an area today covered by the city of Winnipeg and then marking the extreme western edge of settlement in British North America. They were not themselves settlers, but Métis, hunters of mixed Indian, Scots and French blood, able to communicate in Gaelic or half-a-dozen other tongues, famed for their recklessness, valour and endurance, pure products of the frontier. Such supremely was their commander, Cuthbert Grant, born 23 years before in what is now Saskatchewan, son of a Scottish fur-trader and a half-caste woman. His parents took him for baptism to the Presbyterian church in Montreal and may later have sent him back to Scotland for an education, as they certainly did his brother James. These Canadian Grants still counted themselves members of a group of intermarried families in the North-East which regularly dispatched their offspring across the Atlantic to make a fortune. By 1812, young Cuthbert was ready to start his career as a dealer in furs. He belonged fully to two worlds. On the one hand he was a sober, intelligent, hard-working, God-fearing, calculating, judicious Scot. On the other, he was brimful of the turbulent spirit of the prairies. His Indian kin loved him. His huntsman's prowess became legendary. The untamable Sioux, far out in the West, feared and respected him as a warrior. Soon he was the recognised leader of the Métis.

On that afternoon in 1816, they were trying to pass unseen by the armed post of Fort Douglas, strategically sited at the confluence of the Red and Assiniboine Rivers. It took its name from Thomas Douglas, Earl of Selkirk, a peer of Scotland but also something of a tycoon, at least the largest shareholder in the Hudson's Bay Company. He regarded himself as proprietor of all this territory. On it he was settling Highlanders systematically, to vindicate his thesis that emigration could cure the overcrowding and privation of their glens; about 100 were living at the fort and in cabins nearby. He had also resolved to stop the wild men of the plains using them as just a hunting ground, since this was incompatible with agriculture. He instructed his agents to enforce his feudal conception of property over any primitive tribal rights the Métis thought themselves to enjoy. In command of the fort was Robert Semple, like Selkirk an enlightened Scot, a humane and cultured man, a contributor to the *Edinburgh Review*. He felt frustrated at being unable to follow those orders and impose his master's authority. He had been powerless to stop dusky strangers who turned up out of nowhere, befriended the colonists, then terrified them with stories of cruel Indian tribes, while assuring them that they

96

would fare better if they moved back east – and all in Gaelic, a language Semple did not speak. It was the settlers, rather than the hunters and traders, who seemed the likelier to be scared away.[1]

So Semple was provoked when his look-out spotted Grant's men from the tower of the fort. He called together about 30 of his own people and, advancing along the Colonial Road, nowadays the main street of Winnipeg, went out to challenge the intruders. He intercepted them near a spot where a circle of seven oaks broke the endless vista of the prairie. The confrontation at once turned tense. Grant riposted by deploying his band in a half-circle round the settlers. A Frenchman, François Boucher, rode out from it and, in broken English, picked a quarrel with Semple who, showing incredible rashness, tried to seize his rifle. As they grappled, it went off, and at once the two sides opened fire on each other. The Métis went berserk. Howling their battle-cries, they blasted away at the colonists, then fell on them with knives and tomahawks, killing all but a few, before stripping and scalping them. Semple, lying wounded in the leg, was shot through the heart. Grant claimed afterwards that 'the melancholy catastrophe was entirely the result of the imprudent attack made upon them by Mr Semple's party, and once the Indian blood was raised his utmost efforts could not arrest the savage revenge of his associates'. When they did cool down he went over to the fort and offered his protection to the rest of the terrified settlers. These had no choice, and let him escort them to the shores of Lake Superior, where they might hope for rescue.[2]

The Battle of Seven Oaks, a bloody clash of Scot and Scot, or half-Scot, at civilisation's limit, can also be taken as a collision of two ideas, the Empire of trade and the Empire of settlement. One was a Scottish idea, conceived before 1707 out of the circumstances of a small nation with no power to rule distant lands and no surplus of people. The other was in origin an English idea, if now of growing appeal to Scots, for the Union had removed the political constraint on their activity overseas and, more than a century later, was beginning to bring the two nations into genuine partnership.

We can see how that gradual process started immediately after 1707, for example, in the change the Union wrought to the outlook of Samuel Veitch, survivor of Darien, brother of the man who signed the capitulation to the Spaniards. He escaped to New York, where he rebounded from his ordeal and prospered amid a network of compatriots engaged in smuggling, the national pastime of Scots on English territory. Veitch specialised in runs from Massachusetts to France, with which England was at war. Yet by 1708 he felt fully loyal to Great Britain. He then submitted to the Government in London a memorandum, *Canada Survey'd*, urging acquisition of that country. It would 'infinitely advance the commerce of the British over all America, and particularly make them sole masters of the fur, fish and naval stores trade over all the Continent'. Canada could also be settled, however, and become 'a noble colony, exactly calculate for the constitutions and genius of the most northern of the North Britons'. At his prompting an expedition went to retake Nova Scotia in 1710. He was present at the surrender of Port Royal, soon renamed Annapolis, the trading post which Charles I had forced the Scots to abandon to the French three-quarters of a century before. Later he was governor of the territory, the first that Scotland and England had conquered together.[3]

This marked just the start of renewed Scottish interest in Canada. The ruse which captured Quebec in 1759 was largely owed to Donald Macdonald, a Jacobite reconciled to Hanover after a sobering exile; he fooled the French guards with his command of their language on the night that Highland troops crept towards the doomed city. Its first British governor was James Murray of Elibank. He issued a proclamation telling the French that he proposed to rule with the help of an assembly of the people, and to tolerate their religion. But the instructions he afterwards received from London told him in no uncertain terms to anglicise the province. This he could not stomach. He replied that the Canadians 'are perhaps the bravest and the best race upon the globe' who, 'could they be indulged with a few privileges which the laws of England deny to Roman Catholics at home, would soon get the better of every national antipathy to their conquerors and become the most faithful and most useful set of men in this American empire'. He admired their pastoral way of life under their seigneurs, so much more virtuous than the shady businessmen brought in by the British. He threatened to resign unless the French were well treated. The response was to recall him, despite protests from the seigneurs, who wrote to George III saying that Murray's good deeds to them amid the miseries of war 'nous ont forcés de l'admirer et de le respecter'. Luckily, wiser counsels soon prevailed, and the Quebec Act (1774) granted religious toleration.[4]

With the conquest meanwhile confirmed at the end of the Seven Years' War, more Scots had arrived, for it remained the Government's aim to secure this northern half of the continent by introducing a British population. Veterans were rewarded with land and stayed on. Organised immigration followed, notably under schemes to deal with demographic pressure in the Scottish Highlands. The first consignment of 200 settlers from there landed at Pictou Harbour, Nova Scotia, in 1773. The Maritime Provinces, the nearest transatlantic landfall and largely a wilderness, offered a superficially lucrative proposition to entrepreneurs, such as Lord Advocate Montgomery and Principal Witherspoon, who made a business of emigration. But it needed large amounts of capital on which returns proved slow, for the proprietors could only gradually fill up the tracts they acquired. The system was besides essentially feudal, as in Scotland. Since colonists could not become outright owners, few showed any interest. In truth, these schemes were relatively unattractive to both parties. Yet their failure, by and large, did not deter further attempts. The romantic reverie of somehow rebuilding clans in the New World flourished rather than faded. Selkirk was himself inspired by it. As late as 1825, a real chieftain, Archibald McNab, the imperious last of his line, led a group of clansmen to the upper reaches of the Ottawa River and tried to secure a feudal system by legal contract, under which they gave services in kind for their holdings. The result was constant quarrels between him and them, so fierce that in 1840 the Government stepped in to cancel the arrangement.

The most contented and therefore lasting colonies were founded on unqualified grants to individuals. One such concentration of Scots built up in Glengarry County, at the eastern extremity of what soon became Upper Canada, between the Ottawa and St Lawrence Rivers; it remained Gaelic-speaking till the twentieth century. By the end of the eighteenth it was already almost a Highland preserve, with whole communities settled under their tacksmen, attracted by a supply of land no longer available at home. The Scottish population, here and elsewhere in Canada, swelled with the flight of loyalists from the American Revolution. Later, about 700 Catholics who had been evicted in 1794 from homes in the Great Glen at length took refuge in the district. They had initially gone to Glasgow where their priest, Father Alexander Macdonnell, formed them into the regiment of Glengarry Fencibles, the first military corps of their religion ever constituted in the British army. On disbandment after the Peace of Amiens in 1801 they crossed in a body.[5]

All these could be classed as more or less voluntary colonists. Certain groups had of course come against their will, the worst case being the Catholics driven from South Uist by the persecution of a Protestant landlord. But most emigrant Highlanders were not victims, neither dispossessed nor forced out by destitution. Rather, they wanted to leave to avoid the modernisation, and its threat to their cultural identity, which all sensible Scots thought vital if the Highlands were ever to prosper. That needed the benevolent economic planning and social engineering of which a later age might have approved had they been carried out by the state rather than by the only agency available at the time, the landed magnates. The idea among them, fully in accord with the best expert advice, was to develop a Highland economy in which natives would want to remain. Against this philanthropic vision of their future the emigrants in effect mounted a reactionary and intransigent resistance: if they could not hold what they had by staying, then they went. Here and there they did manage to reproduce in the Canadian wilderness many features of their old, independent, pastoral life, free now of economic, religious or any other pressures from landlords. The great example was Cape Breton Island. The Gaels, by the first quarter of the nineteenth century disembarking at an average rate of 1000 a year, set its character. Their community afterwards dispersed somewhat in consequence of natural and economic misfortunes, but as late as 1914 it was recorded that 'they still live much as their ancestors did in Scotland, retaining their language and much of their customs to the present day'. These have decisively declined only in the most recent times: testimony, surely, to an extraordinary resilience. It was not the sole region where Highlanders refused to conform to good intentions for them. John Galt, in his novel *Bogle Corbet*, satirises colonists in Upper Canada 'who sit all day in the sun, groaning to each other, Thank Got we are true clansmen, though we pe in Canada, och hon, umph!'[6]

Emigration appealed to Lowlanders too, as much from their inborn self-reliance as from external pressures on them. Friendly societies where families of slender means could pool the necessary resources had long existed. They attained a new vogue after the Napoleonic Wars, to become more common in the West of Scotland than anywhere else in Britain. They even received some modest encouragement from on high. In 1820, several in Lanarkshire and Renfrewshire won the support of their MPs for a petition to Parliament which requested grants of Canadian land and enough material assistance to last till the colonists could raise their first crop. The Treasury took a dim view of this importunity, replying that it was a matter for local magistrates and heritors. But the Cabinet overruled that advice and agreed to meet part of the costs. In addition, the Duke of Hamilton promised to pay for the building of schools in the emigrants' new home. They still had to find from their own pockets the money for transporting themselves and any goods they took with them, but 2000 crossed to settle in Lanark County, Ontario.

This and other instances showed a change in attitudes among Scotland's ruling elite. It had always deplored any loss of the nation's resources of manpower. Thus far, it had been readier to stop Scots leaving than drive them out. Henry Dundas, who fully represented the views of his class, once made a specific point about Canada. In 1792, amid a wave of emigration, he stressed that he wanted her to prosper, though not by taking people from home. 'An ingrafted population', he wrote, would bring 'a want of that regularity and stability which all, but particularly colonial, governments require.' His wariness was a product of reflection on the history of territorial occupation and settlement in the first British Empire. Ever since the 1770s, when emigration to the 13 rebellious colonies had raised it as a problem in his mind, he had toyed with various forms of legal restraint, even if he was averse from imposing any direct ban on movement to territories under the Crown. Experience demonstrated, then and later, that such restraint would prove in the end unworkable. Especially once Britain entered after 1815 on a century in which no wars directly impeded shifts of population, or offered pretexts for official measures to stem them, the floodgates opened. The first years of peace were moreover a time of terrible economic depression, of unemployment and social degradation, of great political tension in consequence. To countenance emigration as an expedient for defusing the unrest seemed only sensible.

Some still noted with regret that the more hard-working and law-abiding workers were often the ones to go. James Hogg, the Ettrick Shepherd, wrote: 'I know of nothing in the world so distressing as the last sight of a fine industrious independent peasantry taking the last look of their native country never to behold it more'. But he already sounded old-fashioned and sentimental. Galt, another Tory literary luminary, was also an enthusiast for emigration. He promoted the Canada Company, chartered in 1826, of which the main settlement, round Guelph, Ontario, has prospered ever since. His motives were hardly progressive: he saw 'too much of the intelligence and capital of the community being directed to trade and manufactures'.

He hoped colonisation would cure this, and so sought for his schemes men of culture and breeding, younger sons of good family to build an agricultural society more durable than Scotland's by now seemed likely to prove. The cultural loss to the mother country bothered him not one whit: 'The troubles of the emigrant chiefly proceed from his habitual feelings. If with our native country we could throw off former habits, there is no such difference, I suspect, between countries, as to make the change from one to another a matter of much importance'. With that as an example of conservative thinking, one may judge how easily Whigs could inscribe emigration in the holy writ of political economy once they entered on their Scottish hegemony after 1832.[7]

Under the same rubric, settlers were useful to their countrymen at home in stimulating demand for the growing volume of domestic manufactures. To Scots generally, Canada long remained first a field for trade. Unlike India, this nearest territory in the Americas was fully open to them right from the conquest. Nor did they have to carve out a place for themselves among earlier English arrivals. By its size and resources, too, it was territory ideal for the practice of their liberal and flexible commercial principles, free of the mercantile pretensions of England or the domination of London in particular. Their experience of defying economic regulation stood them in good stead, though it exacted its price. Contrabandism had frequently worked through cliques and clans, and this tradition the Scots carried to Canada. They usually traded with their home ports, often showing great generosity to one another but an utter lack of scruple towards outsiders. At their most successful, which could mean their most ruthless, they sometimes revealed in their methods the same tendency to monopoly as they were wont – again hypocritically, it must be said – to deplore in Englishmen.

Merchants of Glasgow, Greenock, Kilmarnock and Leith established Canadian agencies soon after 1763. During the next 60 years, 275 Scots trading houses and shipowners, on both sides, took part in this transatlantic traffic. In the early history of Canada the wealth of these usually temporary residents made them more important than the peasants who had found a permanent abode on her land: it was a country which lived rather off the appropriation and shipping of its natural resources than off the domestic production of its inhabitants. This had more than economic consequences. From 1791 to 1812 even long-settled Lower Canada, the present province of Quebec, was politically dominated by 'the Scotch party', the merchants of Montreal. At first they enjoyed excellent relations with the French. But as, in running things, they showed themselves typical Scottish improvers, they began to alarm the highly conservative indigenous community, which feared that rapid development would attract more English-speaking colonists. It need not have worried. Canada in fact filled up slowly, for these Scots wanted to keep the country empty. Their trade, principally in furs, could indeed only continue as long as it remained empty, since tilled land yielded no furs. The merchants therefore aimed, by whatever means were necessary, to bar colonists from the vast stretches to the north and west of the narrow strip already populated along the St Lawrence and the shores of the lower Great Lakes.

At the centre of the mercantile interests stood a group of related, originally Jacobite, families from the Great Glen, though many other individual Scots joined them, such as James Dunlop, who came in 1776 by way of Virginia from Glasgow, later the McGills, also from Glasgow, and the Mackenzies from Stornoway. The instrument of their dominance was the North West Company, actually a kind of syndicate. Several existing partnerships formed it on trial in 1779, with an accord for one year only. This proved successful enough to be renewed annually, from 1784 for five years at a time. Its driving force was Simon McTavish, known as 'the Marquis', a lover of fine wine, fat oysters and pretty girls. Born in 1750, apprenticed in New York from 1763, he set up on his own at Albany and moved to Montreal as the American War loomed.

He knew just what the needs of the business were, and the North West Company let him fulfil them. They had to combine the efforts of the 'wintering partners', who lived in the West, manned the trading posts and gathered furs, with those of the 'business partners', who financed the exports and the returning imports. Every year delegates from the two sides met to discuss prospects and carry out the exchanges. Since the wintering partners had in some cases to travel thousands of miles, the rendezvous took place as far out in the wilds as was feasible, originally at Grand Portage, the extremity of Lake Superior, later at Fort William on its northern shore. McTavish saw that the business partners could to a large extent command the traffic. His own aim was to dominate these partners and through them the whole trade. Controlled skulduggery marked the syndicate's operations from the start. One big Scottish firm, Gregory, McLeod & Co, initially held aloof, but a senior partner was murdered under mysterious circumstances in Athabaska during the winter of 1786–7. To avoid a feud it promptly merged with the North West Company, thus uniting all Canada's biggest traders. They could then realistically aim to create a monopoly of furs on British territory. They even had the gall to make official application for it. It was refused, but before long they began to look as if they could win it by their own efforts. With profits running in the 1790s at £70,000 a year, this was one of the first big businesses in the New World, dealing in manufactured goods as well as natural resources, trafficking not just to Britain but also to Europe and Asia.

Like many enterprising Scots, the Nor'Westers were often educated men from good families, a cut above the mercantile class of other nations. Alexander Mackenzie, the explorer, made a living with his brother Roderick at a depot on Lake Athabaska, right on the edge of the Arctic. It was dubbed the Athens of the North, because in that howling wilderness they set up a library. They were equally Scottish in their tenacity, bravado and readiness to seize what pleasure they could from lives of hardship and danger. They thought little of walking 600 miles on snowshoes to pass Hogmanay with a friend, dining on roast beaver and boiled suet pudding, washed down with their favourite 'eggnog', rum laced with caviare. Here is the account of a

1   The Scots' first experience of Empire: the Antonine Wall which stretched across the middle of their country from Kinneil on the Firth of Forth to Old Kilpatrick on the River Clyde. The major fortification of Rough Castle (above), probably built at the beginning of the first century AD, is near present-day Falkirk. From the first, Scots were both insiders and outsiders, for it is unlikely that life on either side of this makeshift and porous frontier differed much. (Royal Commission on the Ancient and Historical Monuments of Scotland)

2 James VI of Scotland (1567–1625) and I of England (from 1603) styled himself King of Great Britain, but was almost the only person to regard his two realms as one. A way of promoting the premature idea of Britishness was to encourage both Scots and English to found colonies, which they did together in Ireland but then separately in North America. (Scottish National Portrait Gallery – hereafter SNPG)

3–6 William Alexander of Menstrie (c1567–1640) was a Scotsman on the make who advanced himself, like many later examples of the type, through obsequiousness to his master, King James VI. Encouraged to found a colony, he promptly did so, encouraging others to help him in their turn – though largely in vain. At a hefty cost in money and lives, a Scottish settlement was briefly established in Nova Scotia (New Scotland). On its abandonment in 1632, it left behind an elaborate coat-of-arms, and a name on the map which survives to this day. (Left: SNPG; opposite – top and bottom left: Trustees of the National Library of Scotland; bottom right: National Archives of Scotland)

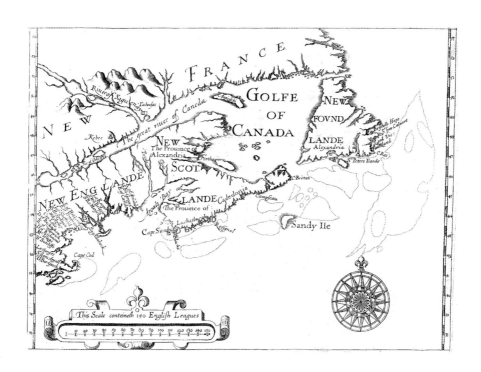

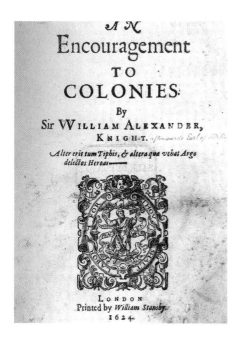

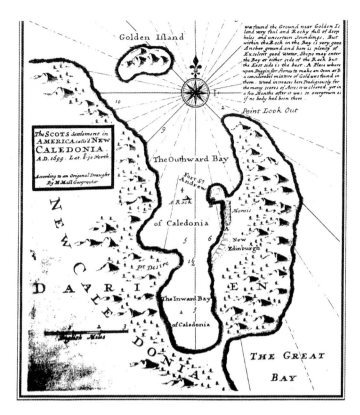

Golden Island

we found the Ground near Golden Island very foul and Rocky full of deep holes and uncertain Soundings. But within the Rock in the Bay is very good Anchor ground and here is plenty of Excelent good Water. Ships may enter the Bay at either side of the Rock but the East side is the best. A Place where upon Diggin for Stones to make an Oven at B a considerabl mixture of Gold was found in them. Wood increases here Prodigiously for the many scores of Acres we cleared, yet in a few Months after it was so overgrown as if no body had been there.

Point Look Out

The SCOTS Settlement in AMERICA call'd NEW CALEDONIA A.D. 1699. Lat. 8.30 North.

According to an Original Draught By H. Moll Geographer

The Outward Bay

Fort St Andrew

A Rock of Caledonia

Morass

New Edinburgh

Pt Desire

The Inward Bay of Caledonia

Z E W   C A L E D O N I A

D A R I E N

English Miles

THE GREAT BAY

PANDITUR
QUA   ORBIS

VIS UNITA FORTIOR

7–8 The final effort by the independent Scottish state to found a colony was the most disastrous of all, and Darien remains a byword for failure to be evoked when Scots are feeling sorry for themselves. In two expeditions between 1698 and 1700 more than 3000 lives were lost, along with one-quarter of the nation's working capital. Again, only a coat-of-arms and a name on the map – by H.Moll, 1699 – survive. (Above: Trustees of the National Library of Scotland; below: Royal Bank of Scotland)

9   Andrew Fletcher of Saltoun (1653–1716) was nicknamed simply 'The Patriot' for his uncompromising opposition to the Union with England in 1707. But his support for continued Scottish independence yielded to his interest in an international system of states able to accommodate the emerging pressures of global trade. In conducting his research, he spent more time in the fleshpots of Amsterdam and London than at rustic Saltoun, in East Lothian. (SNPG)

10 To William Paterson (1658–1710) (below), born in Dumfriesshire, the world owes the first principles of central banking. He was instrumental in founding both the Bank of England and the Bank of Scotland. He also went on the expedition to Darien, barely escaping with his life. Scotland owes him more through his conception of banking without gold. A poor country, Scotland had no gold, yet was able to finance the enormous economic advances of the eighteenth century. (Bank of England)

11 The third Scottish forefather of political economy was John Law of Lauriston, Edinburgh (1671–1729) (below right), who developed the theory of the distinction of money and credit, and might have done great things for his own country except that he could not stomach the Union of 1707. He went to France, where he founded the Mississippi Company and eventually became Minister of Finance. In that capacity he created one of the greatest of all great inflations, but the French admired his style. (SNPG)

12 John Campbell, 2nd Duke of Argyll (1678–1743), came to dominate Scottish politics in the early decades of the Union. He did so partly because of his reputation as a fierce, auburn-haired Highland warrior – 'Red John of the Battles'. As well as clearing Scotland of Jacobites, he campaigned in Europe, defending Catalan independence against the Bourbons and conquering for Britain the island of Minorca, foundation of a Mediterranean Empire. (SNPG)

13 Scots played a large part in the capture of Quebec, 1759. Repentant Jacobites thinking better of French exile had joined up to serve King George; they fooled Canadian sentries by replying to challenges in their own language as the British army crept by night towards the doomed city. In the battle at daybreak before the walls, the charge by Simon Fraser's Highlanders, swinging their claymores, broke the defending forces. (Trustees of the National Museums of Scotland)

14 David Hume (1711–1776) remains a central figure in modern philosophy but this, to his chagrin, was not something which interested his contemporaries. He made a living off his histories and his essays on current affairs, where he advocated both political and economic liberalism. 'I am American in my principles,' he declared just before his death at the outbreak of the War of Independence. (SNPG)

15 Adam Smith (1723–1790) is arguably the Scot who has had most influence on the world we live in. The father of political economy systematised the liberalism which he shared with his friend and mentor, David Hume, to produce in *The Wealth of Nations* the classic statement of why markets should be open rather than closed. A major focus of his thesis is the colonial system which restricted the economic activities of Americans – who reacted by breaking away from the British Empire. (SNPG)

16 William Robertson (1721–1790) was a wily politician in Church and University, central institutions of the Scottish Enlightenment. But he could also raise his sights above skulduggery, and in his histories created the picture of a world in which a benevolent providence and the progress of mankind were combined. He felt sure there would one day be a single civilisation uniting Europeans with Chinese, Indians and, at length, more primitive peoples too. Perhaps he was right. (SNPG)

17 John Witherspoon (1723–1794) was an evangelical minister who gave up preaching hellfire in Paisley to become principal of the College of New Jersey (now Princeton). Espousing the causes of his new home, he became one of two native Scots to sign the American Declaration of Independence. He hoped the 13 colonies could be transformed into a 'Christian Sparta', but fortunately was disappointed. (SNPG)

18 Flora Macdonald (1722–1790), the Jacobite heroine who rowed the Prince over the sea to Skye, faced the end of the Highland way of life after the rebellion of 1745 failed. For her and her husband, Allan Macdonald of Kingsburgh, this entailed eventual emigration to North Carolina. They took arms a second time in 1776 against the American enemies of King George III. Though they had changed sides, they still chose the wrong one: and ended up back on Skye. (SNPG)

19 James Bruce of Kinnaird (1730–1794) opened the classical age of African exploration with his journeys to discover the source of the Blue Nile in Abyssinia. A huge, fierce man, he needed all his courage and resolution for the perils he faced. So terrible were they that, when he wrote them up on his return, many refused to believe him. Dr Samuel Johnson called him a liar for writing that he had lived off blood drawn from live cattle, in native fashion. Today we know these tales were true. (SNPG)

20 Sir Ralph Abercromby (1734–1801), from Menstrie, Clackmannanshire, was among the first of the long line of Scotland's war-heroes. He led armies in the West Indies and in Ireland during the French Revolutionary Wars. After Napoleon invaded Egypt, Abercromby was sent to deal with the situation. He captured Malta on the way, but met his death in winning a great victory at the Battle of Alexandria. (Trustees of the National Museums of Scotland)

21 James Boswell (1720–1795) wrote the finest biography in the English language, but had many other interests. After a tyrannised childhood, he sought more satisfactory father-figures. Besides Dr Johnson, he tried General Paoli, who fought for the independence of Corsica from the French – a cause Boswell also supported, not least by appearing publicly in the native costume of the island. In 1794, Corsica entered into a Union with Great Britain, though unlike Scotland's it did not last. (National Portrait Gallery, London)

22 Admiral George Keith Elphinstone (1746–1823) came of Jacobite family which made a smooth transition from rebellion to Empire. With money from his uncle the Earl Marischal, in exile at the court of Frederick the Great of Prussia, he voyaged to China. Eventually he got into the Royal Navy, and in 1795 had the honour of taking the surrender of Cape Town from his brother Scot, Robert Jacob Gordon, commander of its Dutch garrison. (Trustees of the National Museums of Scotland)

23 'God help the man that's chained tae oor Davie,' said the mother of David Baird (1757–1829) when she heard that British prisoners taken by Hyder Ali of Mysore were shackled in pairs. Baird at length got his revenge and brought about the downfall of the state of Mysore with his capture of Seringapatam in 1799, personally leading his Highland troops in the assault. During the ensuing rout, Sultan Tipu was killed. (SNPG)

24 Henry Dundas (1742–1811) was Scotland's greatest imperial statesman. For brother Scots, he was head of the Scottish mafia which took charge in so many far-flung outposts, above all in India, which he administered from the London end for two decades. Over and beyond the favours to friends, Dundas was a man of vision who saw the importance of intercontinental trade and conceived of an imperial system in which the produce of the colonies would feed manufactures at home. (SNPG)

25 'King Tom' Maitland (1759?–1824) was the sort of Scot who got drunk every night but had beneath his daunting exterior a heart of gold. A radical in his youth, he was cured by soldiering. Promoted a colonial governor, he ran an enlightened regime in Ceylon, before being transferred to Malta, where he established the permanent British regime at the end of the Napoleonic Wars, notable for its panache but also for its honesty. (Trustees of the National Museums of Scotland)

26 Gilbert Elliot (1751–1814), born in Edinburgh and a pupil of the philosopher Dugald Stewart at the University there, carried the heritage of the Enlightenment with him to India when he went there as Governor-general in 1807, as well as a shipload of brother Scots. In Calcutta he set up a sort of orientalist court, where he patronised eastern learning and encouraged contacts between Scottish and Indian scholars. On his return he was created Earl of Minto. (National Portrait Gallery, London)

27 Thomas Munro (1761–1827) was the senior of the Scottish philosopher-kings who ruled the subordinate presidencies of India in the early nineteenth century. A Glaswegian, he spent most of his career in Madras. As a warmly romantic admirer of the stalwart Indian peasant, he exerted himself to ease the lot of those who lived off the land, with measures which might have been envied by the Highlanders he had left behind at home. (National Portrait Gallery, London)

28 John Malcolm (1769–1833), from Burnfoot, near Langholm, Dumfriesshire, won his cadetship in India by promising to 'cut aff the heid' of Tipu, but was soon refined as a diplomat and spent much of his career at the court of the Shah of Persia. Towards the end he became Governor of Bombay. He believed British supremacy maintained by force necessary to keep order in India, but counselled against westernisation. (SNPG)

29 The suave and handsome but gloomy and self-doubting Mountstuart Elphinstone (1779–1859) was brilliant scholar and brave warrior at once. He started his Indian career in Afghanistan, where he amazed the natives by telling them there had not been a rebellion in his country since 1745. He ended as Governor of Bombay, where he applied enlightened principles to strengthening Indian culture. 'Make no innovation!' he told his officers. (National Portrait Gallery, London)

30 Lachlan Macquarie (1762–1824), from Ulva, off Mull, and Governor of New South Wales, was a benevolent despot who began the long process of turning Australia from a penal settlement into a civilised colony. A military officer, he brooked no insubordination from his colleagues or from the convicts, but planned development carefully so that the latter could settle down to normal life in a new continent once they had served their time. (Mitchell Library, State Library of New South Wales)

31 A Lewisman whose character combined bravado and melancholy, Alexander Mackenzie (c1755–1820) found ample scope for both in opening up the wilderness of Canada. On a journey of exploration in 1789 he discovered the river, now bearing his name, which leads to the Arctic Sea. On another in 1793, he was the first to cross North America overland. (Glenbow (Calgary) Museum and Archives)

32 Alexander Mackenzie's worthy successor in the tradition of Scottish Arctic exploration was Admiral John Ross (1777–1856), born at Inch near Stranraer. He undertook three arduous expeditions in search of a North-West Passage from Europe to the Orient round the top of North America. He could not find a practicable route, but greatly extended geographical knowledge of the Arctic region. (SNPG)

33 As well as being a novelist and acutely conservative observer of contemporary Scotland, John Galt (1779–1839), from Ayrshire, was a pioneer of systematic colonisation, which he saw as a safety-valve for the problems of industrialisation in the mother country. The Canada Company which he helped to found sent settlers to Guelph in Ontario, which retains a Scottish character to this day. (SNPG)

dinner laid on by Alexander Mackenzie and William McGillivray, McTavish's nephew:

> We dined at four o'clock, and after taking a satisfactory quantity of wine, perhaps a bottle each, the married men . . . retired, leaving about a dozen to drink their health. We now began in earnest and in true highland style, and by four o'clock in the morning the whole of us had reached such a state of perfection that we could all give the war whoop as well as Mackenzie and McGillivray, we could all sing admirably, we could all drink like fishes, and we all thought we could dance on the table without disturbing a single decanter, glass or plate by which it was profusely covered.

The party ended like this:

> Mackenzie now proposed to drink a toast to our memory and then give the war whoop over us fallen foes or friends all nevertheless on the floor, and on attempting to push the bottle to McGillivray at the opposite end of the table he slid off his chair and could not recover his seat, while McGillivray in extending himself over the table in the hope of seizing the bottle fell hopelessly to the floor.

The partners of the North West Company pushed ever further into the interior, because in order to expand it had to explore. They hoped that their efforts, which might be tied to extensions of British sovereignty, would win support and concessions from the Government in London. This was why Mackenzie went on his journeys. The first, in 1788, followed the river which now bears his name, twelfth largest in the world, to its mouth in the Arctic Sea. He covered 3000 miles in three months, travelling up to 16 hours a day. The company at once turned his discoveries to account by establishing a chain of outposts from the Great Slave Lake down to the delta of the Mackenzie. In 1798 it already had more than 250 men working in this basin, where the Indians became reliant on supplies of trade-goods. But Mackenzie aimed above all to seek a practicable commercial communication between the Atlantic and Pacific Oceans: the old dream of a short cut to the Orient. For this his river was unsuitable. So in 1793 he set off on another expedition to look for an overland route through the western mountains. It demanded great physical exertion, and the skill to overcome constant perils. Mackenzie was a tower of strength, meeting every test with restraint and courage, cheering his men on when they reached the brink of exhaustion and despair, finally bringing them all safe home. Yet his journals reveal an obsessive, highly strung character given to black depressions. He did find a westward route, though one again impossible for normal traffic. Still, he had made the first crossing of America north of Mexico. His published chronicle of it immortalised him, and brought him a knighthood from George III.[8]

With this triumph, the Nor'Westers ought to have seen an overwhelming interest in holding together, if they were to win the reward of the privileges they hoped for. Instead, being Scots, they fell out. Mackenzie himself was the major defector, though he may have felt forced to go by McTavish's arrogance. He anyway left in 1800 to join with a competitor, the XY Company, which renamed itself the New North West Company. The stubborn individualism, relentless rancour and all too ready resort to violence of the men on either side brought a disastrous conflict. Duncan McGillivray, brother of William, thought nothing, when he chanced upon a rival trader camped by Lake Superior, of slashing the man's tent to shreds, while his companion Archie McLeod kicked into the water the goods which their victim had doubtless worked hard to acquire. Both companies were soon making losses, indeed came near to ruin as they outbid one another for the furs harvested by the Indians. Only McTavish's death in 1804 calmed things down. William McGillivray took charge of the North West Company and, since he had remained a friend of Mackenzie's, was able to arrange a fresh merger.

The new outfit did well up to the outbreak of war with the United States in 1812 and beyond, despite disruption of traffic across the Great Lakes. It was rich, if also interested, enough to underwrite a military expedition in 1813 to the furthest American outpost, John Jacob Astor's trading station of Astoria at the mouth of the Columbia River on the Pacific Ocean. This was captured by a combination of British and Canadian forces, the first under John McDonald, McGillivray's brother-in-law, the second under John George McTavish, his cousin. From Fort George, as they renamed it, the Nor'Westers now commanded the main outlet from the interior of the continent on this coast. They could perhaps even control the Spanish, Russian and other traffic starting to pass along it. Their hopes were kept alive by the terms of the peace in 1814, which let them lease the fort for another ten years (though in the event it would be restored to the obdurate Americans). Despite the North West Company's financial problems, this coup could be taken as its climacteric.[9]

With it, Lake Winnipeg became the hub of a great network of communication, along which a man might travel by canoe all over North America with never more than a day's portage. Yet on this very spot the Nor'Westers faced an intolerable intrusion, for it was there that Selkirk had chosen to settle his Highland colony. They feared that at the least the Hudson's Bay Company, grantor of the land to the Earl, would start to compete with them in regions they were used to having to themselves. They had only ever known it slumber at its posts. According to Selkirk, 'the Canadians in the interior were in the common habit of ridiculing the officers of the Hudson's Bay Company as old women who had not the courage even to defend the furs which they had obtained'. Yet it always refused to let the Nor'Westers carry goods over its own chartered territory, which would have been their shortest route to the sea. It insisted instead on their following the long route through the Great Lakes and the St Lawrence. If it was now to impose the same ban along the Red River, the interior of the continent would be cut off from Montreal. The Nor'Westers had opened up the wilderness, befriended the Indians and exploited the natural resources. Now they looked forward to reaping the reward of their toil and hardship, Selkirk threatened to ruin their livelihood.

It made an especially piquant circumstance that, while the Hudson's Bay Company was English, Scots had infiltrated it almost from its foundation in 1670. One of its first governors, John Nixon in 1679–83, seems to have been a Scot. He anyway preferred to recruit Scots, while warning that they must be 'encouraged with drams'. After 1707 the company systematically engaged young men from Orkney, for convenience, since Stromness was its ships' last port of call before the open Atlantic. The Orcadians had a trait in common with the wild Highlanders, that they mated readily with Indians, but were otherwise quite different: dour, loyal, persistent, industrious. An English manager expressed himself baffled: 'They are the slyest set of men under the sun; and their universal propensity to smuggling, and clandestine dealings of every kind, added to their clannish attachment to each other, puts it out of the power of any one Englishman to detect them'. This quiet toughness came out, for example, when one of the company's depots, Eagle Lake, received a visitation in September 1809 from a Nor'Wester, Aeneas Macdonell. He terrorised the poor Indians he came upon in the compound, seizing their furs, wounding them and chasing them into the woods. The Orkneyman in charge, John Mowat, shot him dead. Captured by other Nor'Westers and sent to Montreal for trial, he refused to accept a pardon on the grounds that he should never have been accused.[10]

The North West Company had qualms not just about the competition but also about the ideology which underlay Selkirk's schemes. His aristocratic Scottish Whiggery stood not quite in the political vanguard of the age, in fact still owed much to earlier conceptions of the public good. His *Observations on the Present State of the Highlands of Scotland* (1806), though advocating emigration, also stressed that the traditional Highland character was anti-modern. He maintained that the surest guarantee of its survival was a better setting for it. That lay in Canada, where it would besides form a useful bulwark against American republicanism. Selkirk even recommended entails on the larger grants of land to ensure the transfer of an aristocracy. While he thought Highlanders had a right to flee progress, progress there must nevertheless be. As a Whig who hobnobbed with the reviewers of Edinburgh and held history to be on his side, he espoused political economy in its most logically implacable form. Application of it to the Highlands of course meant shifting the people to make way for sheep. This regimen he urged on the houses of Sutherland, Argyll and Breadalbane, with results sufficiently well known. The slightly defensive references in contemporary literature to unscrupulous promoters deluding the foolish people with outrageous promises of North American lands were often to him, but he could feel compensated by rave reviews from his fellow Whigs. Francis Horner wrote: 'It appears that in the subversion of the feudal economy, and the gradual extension of the commercial system over [the Highlands], emigration forms a necessary part of the general change'.[11]

Such an enthusiast was Selkirk that he personally founded three colonies. He led a group of pioneers to Prince Edward Island in 1803. He sent a second in 1804 to

Baldoon in Upper Canada between Lakes Huron and Erie, to form 'an exclusive National Settlement for people speaking the Gaelic language'. He became fatefully involved in the West because his second marriage, to an heiress, brought him a shareholding in the Hudson's Bay Company, which he set about expanding. For a while he was in friendly contact with Sir Alexander Mackenzie, who had long advocated its union with the Nor'Westers in order to meet the heavy long-term capital demands which both faced. The pair mounted a joint assault on the existing proprietors of the company, which was being visibly trounced by the merchants of Montreal and which in 1809 failed to pay a dividend. Selkirk and Mackenzie gained control, but the next year abruptly broke with one another. The latter had come to see that the Earl was uninterested in the current commerce. He wanted rather to colonise and transform the West, an idea anathema to Mackenzie as to all traders.

Selkirk pressed on. For the nominal sum of ten shillings, he had the company grant him a tract, covering what is now a large part of Manitoba and of North Dakota, five times the size of Scotland. He undertook in return to supply 200 servants a year to the agricultural colony to be developed on it. He appointed as its governor Miles Macdonell, a Catholic from Glengarry County, under whom the first party of settlers left Scotland in 1811. They took a year to reach the Red River, spending the winter in much discomfort on Hudson's Bay. Selkirk commanded that on arrival they should destroy all buildings in the area belonging to the North West Company, and stop its men exploiting the natural resources: 'We are so fully advised of the unimpeachable validity of these rights of property, that there can be no scruple in enforcing them whenever you have physical means'. But the disorientated crofters, *jardiniers* to the derisive Métis, were hopelessly unequal to their mission. By the autumn of 1814 they were starving. Macdonell issued a proclamation ordering the Nor'Westers to quit the posts they persisted in occupying. That might have seemed a strange priority, but was meant to prevent them exporting from the region the foodstuffs his settlement needed. Obedience, however, would at once have halted their traffic to Montreal. The North West Company defiantly turned the tables on Selkirk by sending a band to the Red River to destroy his buildings, though on this occasion without causing any casualties.[12]

The furious Earl now showed himself not only an impulsive idealist and arrogant aristocrat, but also an extremely stubborn Scotsman. He went doggedly at retrieving the situation. At home when he heard the news, he immediately took ship. On arrival in Upper Canada he made the strongest representations to the Government, though he soon realised it was in the North West Company's pocket. So he tackled the company head-on. He found no meeting of minds with William McGillivray, who insulted 'this piddling lord'. He had arranged meanwhile for a second colonising expedition, recruited round Helmsdale in Sutherland and placed under Semple's direction. After the usual wretched journey, it reached the Red River in November 1815, with barely time to establish itself before the Canadian winter closed in. If the settlers could survive that in their makeshift cabins they could survive anything. By the spring, their colony had a permanent air about it. That was why the Nor'Westers, in a fraught meeting at Fort William, authorised Grant to gather his Métis and make some demonstration to frighten the settlers away. The result, no doubt unintended, was the massacre at Seven Oaks. McGillivray, recognising that his stratagems had gone too far, blustered: 'The madness, for it cannot well be considered in any other light, that could have induced Mr Semple to attack a party of armed men who were passing quietly by his fort and studiously avoiding him, is unaccountable'. Selkirk was not to be so casually placated. He journeyed straight to Fort William, where the survivors had now arrived too. At this 'rendezvous of robbers and murderers and the receptacle of their plunder', he displayed his authority as justice of the peace for the Indian territories, then arrested McGillivray and several of his partners. At least the armed battles now gave way to legal ones, but Selkirk still underrated the North West Company. When McGillivray arrived under guard in Montreal, he got himself at once freed on bail. Rather he persuaded the magistrates to issue a warrant for Selkirk's arrest and institute proceedings against him. It took sharp orders from London, prompted by a shocked Prince Regent, to bring this mutual retribution to a halt.[13]

While both sides expended energy in fruitless litigation, their businesses went to rack and ruin. Selkirk left Canada a broken man in 1818, to die two years later with his fortune exhausted and debts of £120,000. Yet if this was victory for the Nor'Westers, it proved pyrrhic. Their trade was fatally disrupted, not least because the Earl had despite everything made his company a real competitor, with the crucial advantage of lower costs because it could ship furs out through Hudson's Bay. By 1825 the McGillivrays and McTavishes were bankrupt too. In both Britain and Canada the political authorities had weighed the situation and been pressing for a union of the two companies. These were propelled into an agreement in 1821 under which each would provide an equal amount of capital and share the profits for 21 years. But the reality of the deal was that the Hudson's Bay Company absorbed the North West Company and established a monopoly. Even so, it borrowed its subsequent commercial policy from the Nor'Westers rather than from Selkirk: to keep the West empty. That policy was autocratically enforced by the man chosen head of the joint enterprise, a Scot from the Hudson's Bay Company, George Simpson. Emperor of the Plains to his awestruck underlings, he would preserve this strangest yet most characteristic province of the Scottish Empire for another half-century.[14]

CHAPTER NINE

'Thriving in the produce of flocks': Australia

One day in July 1842 Angus McMillan found the mutilated body of his friend Ronald Macalister by a track leading to Port Albert, the main settlement in the coastal district of Gippsland, just to the south of the later border between New South Wales and Victoria. The corpse lay near a paddock belonging to Macalister's uncle Lachlan, where he gathered his cattle ready to ship them out to distant markets. He made a living here on the other side of the world in much the same way as the generations of Highlanders before him who had raised stock amid his native mountains. Born on Skye in 1797, he came to Australia as a young soldier and stayed on after the end of his service to establish a farm at Clifton, not far from Sydney. From this base he personally explored Gippsland, 300 miles further south, saw its possibilities for pastoral agriculture and opened it up. He did so on the system known as squatting, that is to say, he simply occupied virgin territory in the nominal possession of the Crown, as the vast unsettled portions of Australia were legally held to be. Since the continent lay empty, such informal disposition of the land perturbed nobody, except the aborigines. With them the elder Macalister nevertheless stayed on good terms. This made it all the more shocking that they had murdered Ronald, as was evident from the nature of his wounds. They had speared him, knocked him about the head till he was unrecognisable, then opened his body and removed the fat round his kidneys for some nameless purpose of their own.

It was a smiling country, hilly, well-watered and fertile, surely with room enough for the small numbers of either race wanting to dwell there. The aborigines' primitive way of life kept their population low, while the immigrants, most of them Scots, were scattered thinly on their huge stations. But both still coveted the land for their own use, so that they could not remain at peace. During the previous year five white men had met a fate like young Macalister's. Now their compatriots decided enough was enough. McMillan called out every Scotsman who had a gun and a horse, and they rode off to exact retribution. 'It was, of course, impossible to identify any blackfellow concerned in the outrage,' one said, 'and therefore atonement must be made by the tribe.' The Highland Brigade, as they vaunted themselves, sought out a particular band of aborigines known to be truculent. They found them, more than 100 men, women and children, camped by a waterhole on the Warrigal Creek. The Scots galloped up, surrounded them, then without warning began to shoot them down. The terrified people ran defencelessly hither and thither, some jumping into the water to try and hide under it. The Scots made great sport of picking them off as they had to come up for air.

The creek ran red with their blood. The avengers, pausing only to cover the heaps of bodies with sand from the banks, cantered away in grim satisfaction.[1]

Knowledge of the massacre long remained confined to this Scots community, for Macalister was powerful enough to keep his henchmen's deeds quiet outside it. Already a man of substance, he would continue to prosper. He remained a pillar of the Presbyterian Church. He would be elected to the legislative assembly as soon as Victoria gained responsible government in 1851. He even became an official protector of the aborigines. So the silence over the slaughter was no wonder. While Scots, conscious that their own national progress had robbed them of old, rude virtues, admired the noble savage on other continents, with the aborigines they never felt any fellowship. Only recently have historians of Australia preoccupied with the nemesis of her native peoples rediscovered cryptic references to the bloodbath in pious local histories. Now they reckon it may have been the worst incident ever seen on the antipodean frontier. If so, its concealment was especially sinister. For within a few years, the several thousand aborigines of Gippsland virtually disappeared. Nothing but systematic action by the intruding Highlanders can have fully accounted for such a holocaust. It makes what their forefathers had suffered at Hanoverian hands seem by comparison merciful and mild.[2]

Here Scots certainly left their usual disproportionate mark, but they did so in other and more commendable respects during Australia's pioneering days. Not all that many came to this primarily penal colony. Scotland was a law-abiding country, with a system of justice less repressive than the English one. It resorted little to transportation, or banishment in Scots legal terminology. The normal place of banishment was actually England, which had led David Hume to suggest that the idea was conceived out of hostility to the neighbour nation. Be that as it may, Scots comprised only three per cent of the early convicts in Australia, a quarter of their share in the population of the British Isles. The figure did start to climb after 1830, but never equalled that share before transportation was abolished in 1852. In absolute terms, nearly 8000 Scots had by then been transported, out of a total of 150,000 from the United Kingdom as a whole. To an extent they made up in quality what they lacked in quantity, for the mere 100 Scots who arrived before 1810 included particularly prominent personages, the radical martyrs of 1793. Thomas Muir and four others, condemned as the authorities tried to stamp out democratic agitation, were treated more generously at the end of their journey, allowed to occupy farms and even keep convict servants. Muir took the liberty of escaping in 1796 and after many adventures reached France, where he was designated a leader of the future Scottish Republic. But he died an alcoholic death within a couple of years.[3]

Scots exerted their major influence over the young colony through its administration. They brought to it some degree of retributive Calvinism. Patrick Logan served as commander of the penal settlement that became Queensland. In one period of eight months he handed down sentences of corporal punishment for an astounding total of 11,000 strokes; this only ceased when a prisoner sentenced to

350 died under the lash. Logan was eventually killed by aborigines while exploring the interior. But other Scots felt offended at the degradation and waste of the convicts' lives. They proposed humanitarian remedies instead. Alexander Maconochie, scion of legal Edinburgh, was Australia's earliest penal reformer. He had travelled in the Pacific Ocean before becoming the first secretary of the Royal Geographical Society in 1830, then professor of geography at the new university of London. In 1836 his career took a different turn on his appointment as secretary to the Governor of Tasmania. He wrote a report on convict discipline which damned it as 'cruel, uncertain, prodigal, ineffectual either for reform or example'. He suffered dismissal for his pains, or rather was mocked by being shifted sideways to become Governor of Norfolk Island, 900 miles out from Sydney. There the worst offenders lived in isolation under a regime of relentless brutality. But he humanised it, devising a system by which they could earn 'marks of commendation' and start to better themselves.[4]

In more widely helping to transform the Australia of penal establishments into a normal colony, Scots would play a still greater part. As in the other continents, their explorations opened up the interior, while their scientists revealed its natural resources. Among those who did most to civilise the slowly expanding settled region were two successive Governors of New South Wales, Lachlan Macquarie and Thomas Brisbane. Macquarie was born on the island of Ulva off Mull, son of a tacksman. He soldiered in America, India and Egypt before coming to Australia in 1809. His irascible Presbyterianism frowned on every form of worldly corruption. This he detected not only among the convicts but also among their custodians, the New South Wales Corps. Its officers spent much of their time running rackets: speculation in land, control of the market in grain, a profitable monopoly on imports of rum, manipulation of the Treasury Bills which were the only means to pay for expensive imports. Macquarie disbanded the corps, and replaced it with trusty men from his own Highland regiment.

That freed him to set up a benevolent despotism. First, he turned against drink. He cut the number of pubs in Sydney from 75 to 20, ordered them to close during the hours of divine service, raised a duty on spirits and banned illicit stills. He was no less zealous against sexual misdemeanour: he issued an edict to prohibit cohabitation and shut down the brothels. He reinforced public morality with sabbatarianism. He forbade trading on Sundays, made church compulsory for convicts and set up Sunday schools for their children. But his moral severity was well-meant. He furnished the colony with institutions it had lacked: a judiciary, a coinage, a banking system, a post office. He promoted public works in the belief that physical surroundings influenced the condition of the people. He drew up a plan to embellish Sydney with official, military and civic buildings. The cost worried the Government at home and exposed him to scorn in the *Edinburgh Review*, under the heading 'Ornamental architecture in Botany Bay!' That did not stop him. He also laid down roads to the interior and founded planned villages like the ones in Scotland, each with its square and bridge, school and police station, where prisoners could settle at the end of their sentences. He insisted that they should then enjoy full civil rights, and caused a furore when he made one a magistrate. He hoped they would acquire a propertied stake in society, by buying smallholdings from the Crown and turning themselves into sturdy peasants, not unlike the ryots of India. He was just as keen for convicts still serving their time to begin reforming themselves, and liberally rewarded good behaviour with pardons. He looked beyond the bounds of the colony too. He was firm towards the aborigines, forbidding any with arms to enter the towns or gather in large numbers. But he also embarked on the work of civilisation, endowing an educational institute for them at Parramatta, encouraging their conversion to Christianity.

Macquarie left in 1817, in dispute with the Government at home over his leniency to the prisoners. The population of New South Wales now stood at 40,000, against 12,000 when he had arrived eight years before. Its stocklands carried 100,000 cattle, against 12,000 then, and 300,000 sheep, against 25,000. The cultivated area had grown from 8000 to 30,000 acres. This was an economic revolution, for agriculture had previously been rather unsuccessful and life consequently hard. He wrote that 'he found New South Wales a gaol, and left it a colony; he found Sydney a village, and left it a city; he found a population of idle prisoners, and left a large free community, thriving in the produce of flocks and the labour of convicts'.[5]

Brisbane succeeded him. Born to a family of lairds at Largs, he was philosophically inclined and thought New South Wales a perfect environment for application of the principles of political economy. In the event, as a benign and sensitive man, at times taken aback by the rawness of colonial society, he found for its problems some sensible, pragmatic and usually liberal solutions. He showed himself in his turn generous with pardons, and sparing of capital or corporal punishment. It was for being too liberal that the Colonial Office would recall him too in 1825. He had just given the colony a legislative council, if one on which unofficial members were only nominated, but still a check to his own autocracy. He had granted freedom of the press. He had mounted the sort of drive against waste and corruption, with a purge of responsible officials, favoured by reformers at home. He saw it as his great achievement to have cut the cost of government and made the colony pay its way. The results came to more than cheese-paring. Particular benefit derived from his introducing as the local currency, in place of a pound sterling in short supply, the Spanish silver dollar used generally in commerce all over the Far East. It ended the local swindles in Treasury bills, but more to the point brought an effective devaluation. Trade, in wool and the by-products of whaling and sealing, rapidly expanded as a result, for Australians had now to export if they wanted to consume foreign goods.

Brisbane also gave his official patronage to agriculture. As it developed, demand for land and labour rose. The governor used that, too, to enhance the economic efficiency of the penal regime. Prisoners had been hired out cheap to toil in the fields of free settlers, but he ruled that a proper rate for their work must be reckoned. In case the farmers did not like it, he made further grants of land conditional on their co-operation. He wanted anyway to liberalise the market in land. He believed that while the Crown just granted it there would be no extensive improvement, because improvers could never compete with people who had their farms for nothing. In 1824 he began to sell ungranted lands at five shillings an acre. By the time of his departure he had disposed of more than 500,000 acres. He thereby exhibited a typically Scottish concern that Australia should become, like all civilised countries, one where regular rights of property were recognised and respected; otherwise there would only be confusion, especially on account of the squatting. This was now so customary that squatters blithely carried out transactions in their assets, with never a legal title to tracts transferred among themselves or any adequate procedure to define boundaries. That way chaos lay, and Brisbane meant by this moderate measure to avert it.[6]

He had, despite a personal diffidence, governed decisively, yet his term of office marked the point where development ceased to be the prerogative of the colonial administration. It was increasingly to be entrusted to private interests, with Scots again in the lead. Australian trade remained modest, but not so modest as to be overlooked in Scotland. It drew the particular attention of commercial circles in Edinburgh, worried that their rivals in Glasgow were outstripping them in oceanic traffic. The capital still mainly traded with northern Europe or coastwise round Scotland, and bold initiatives seemed necessary for Leith to regain its former place as the country's leading port. One of them, in 1820, was to dispatch a ship to Australia; to India none would be sent for another five years. After that trial the Australian Company of Edinburgh and Leith was formed in 1822. Under its aegis 13 more voyages followed during the next decade, though for no great reward, because of trouble in finding freights to return.

The commerce had also attracted Scottish houses in Calcutta. Well ahead of the rest was Campbell & Clarke, run by John and Robert Campbell, sons of the town clerk of Greenock. Hardly had Robert arrived to join his brother in 1797 than he left again for New South Wales, where John was already sending cattle, sugar and spirits. But since his ships had found at that time even less to bring back, he just ran up credit in Sydney. Robert was given the job of realising it. His appearance caused consternation to the officers of the garrison, who wanted nothing less than free trade. Still, in 1800 he got permission to take up residence. Like canny Scots elsewhere he spotted that intoxicants made the most profitable cargoes, and rum became his largest import too. The administration limited his shipments to 4000 gallons on any single voyage, but he was once caught carrying 14,000 gallons in a vessel supposed to be full of cattle. The scarcity of rum and the demand for it among convicts soon gave it the function of a currency. After complaints, the Government of India forbade the Campbells to send any more.

Yet they often brushed boldly with the authorities. The best commodities to return from Australia were the by-products of whaling and sealing. These the

Campbells wanted to take to London and sell to the lucrative British market. Their first load was seized on the grounds that it infringed the East India Company's monopoly. Long litigation ensued. It was at last Macquarie who solved the problem, by declaring Sydney a free port in 1815. After that Australian trade stood open. Robert Campbell became a rich man and a pillar of the community, an agent for the London Missionary Society, a member of the legislative council and finally Treasurer of New South Wales. He had earned it from his tenacious efforts to turn an honest penny. And he deserves it that Australia should remember him to this day as Merchant Campbell.[7]

He may deserve to be remembered still better for his astute perception of the need for investment, not just for trade, if the economy of Australia was to become more productive. He spent, for 20 years till his death in 1846, large sums on pastoral properties which he took over on the squatting system, his own covering the future Australian Capital Territory. They were indeed the colony's greatest potential resource. They had the advantage of requiring little by way of the factor of production it most lacked, namely labour. A proprietor, with a few herdsmen or shepherds, could run a large station by himself. The conditions promised, in a wholly different setting, the same sort of Empire as in Canada, the exploitation of an immense country empty of settlers. The only barrier might be presented by the aborigines, but much of the country was emptied of them as well.

Still, as in Canada, the Scots fulfilled that promise. Commercial enterprise was their prime contribution to imperial expansion. To date, it had often taken the form of companies created in distant outposts, by the country traders of Calcutta and Canton or the merchants of Montreal, with capital generated locally. But Australia had next to no local capital, and little that could generate it. Scotland herself was now, however, beginning to build her own capital surplus from the continuous boom in domestic industry and foreign commerce. It only needed people with enough ingenuity to match Australia's demand to Scotland's supply. This brought about a major innovation, in the shape of the Scottish investment houses. It also accounted for the otherwise curious fact that they often looked first to the Antipodes. The early leader was the Clyde Company, founded in 1836 to make loans for the development of pastoral agriculture in the district of Port Phillip, later Melbourne. As its name suggests, it originated in Glasgow, in close connection with the merchant dynasty of Dennistoun, though it had a wide range of investors reaching far down the social scale. Soundly managed, it realised after 20 years highly satisfactory profits. It found several imitators, especially in Aberdeen. In 1839 a group of businessmen there set up the North British Australasian Company. A second house, the Aberdeen Australian Company, remained in existence for more than a century. A third, the Scottish Australian Investment Company, was established in 1840 and would become one of the country's great commercial institutions.[8]

They dealt effectively with novel risks. Vital to success was their readiness to wait on long-term returns, and ability to persuade shareholders to do the same. These did complain, but their distance from the locus of investment and ignorance of its environment made them sufficiently patient. The companies also had to face unpopularity in Australia, where their managers were accused by turns of leeching on local labour, squandering money in hopeless speculations or remitting profits better reinvested on the spot. Calls came for a law against usury to limit the earnings of financiers from overseas, and inevitably Scottish companies were charged with being the most usurious. Still, they generally flourished and by the 1850s were doing extremely well, especially on sheep, for in that decade leases over vast tracts of grazing land could be easily obtained and fat profits made from the high price of wool. The managers if anything steered clear of promoting cultivation of crops for domestic consumption. Again as in Canada, they preferred a simpler system of exploiting natural resources for export to the sort of agriculture that might have required and fostered settlement. What grain Australia needed could be bought from Asia or South America on the proceeds of wool, hides and tallow, all sent rather on the long journey to northern markets. But she was being integrated into the global trading system. By productive deployment of capital and consequent attraction of capable management, the companies developed a viable economy, making good use of a country both new and bountiful. Altogether, they opened up a rich field for agrarian enterprise.[9]

Because the companies were Scottish, so were many of the squatters they brought in and financed. Scots made shrewd, hard-working and successful pastoralists. Their outlook, shaped by a national tradition of regarding agriculture as a business, worked even better in Australia. There land and profits beckoned on a scale they could only dream of at home. The most important Australian Scots of the era were thus not the convicts or their captors, but those lured by just such opportunities. They were often men of means, wishing to found or retrieve the fortunes of a family. A fair number sprang from that middle stratum of Highland society, the tacksmen, who had been so active in the New World. Officers on half-pay after the Napoleonic Wars, taking up farming of necessity, were also prominent. Typically, a youngster from one of these backgrounds, but with no great prospects, would come and work on another's station before branching out independently. Angus McMillan, whom we left at Warrigal Creek, had arrived from Skye in 1837 and, after seven years under the Macalisters, moved on to his own 16,000 acres, with a grazing capacity of 800 cattle and 5000 sheep. He had no title, but paid £10 for an annual licence, plus £2.10s. for every thousand sheep and the same again for his herd of cattle. Colin Campbell of Lochbuie, Angus Maclaine of Ardtornish, John Macleod of Raasay, Neil Malcolm of Portalloch and many others became Australian pioneers in the same way.[10]

To call them squatters gives, in its modern connotation, a misleading impression of what was in effect a landed elite, though rather rougher than its cousins in Scotland. If some brought capital with them, more were in hock to the companies. Whatever the case, they worked with the dedication of all Scottish improvers to develop their estates, clearing the bush, building houses, putting up fences. Perhaps because they tended to come from the same class at home and share its social confidence, they seemed unworried by their doubtful status, which in strict legal terms made them no more than temporary tenants liable to lose the tract they occupied as soon as a purchaser came along for it. Still, the insecurity remained negligible in practice, and found ample compensation in the system's cheapness and flexibility. In 1842 Robert Dundas Murray, visiting Port Phillip, wondered at this and decided that the chance of being dislodged was too small to bother about: 'So distant, indeed, is such a prospect under the present circumstances of the colony, that I have no hesitation in affirming, that the squatter is as secure in the occupation of his land, as if he had purchased it'. He, like everybody else, could see that Australia was mostly desert, incapable of settlement. He thought she would remain empty. Thus she could reproduce the spatial pattern of Canada, with a core of colonisation and a Scottish Empire beyond.[11]

An administration often run by sensible, practical Scots had, if with reluctance, recognised this reality too. But they wanted even reality to be ordered. In 1822, Brisbane set a limit to his jurisdiction by making a division between two regions, the 19 settled counties, with defined boundaries, 150 miles or so round Sydney, and the unsettled region beyond, about which he did not propose to concern himself further. Squatters still had the right to move into it, but were not encouraged to; if they did, it was at their own risk. A similar arrangement for the district of Port Phillip came into force in 1834. At first the squatters, dependent on imported supplies and anxious about the aborigines, tended to stay near the coast. But later, as the Crown tried harder to sell land, they penetrated the interior and formed much bigger holdings. Grazing stock over any ground they fancied and fixing boundaries by neighbourly agreement, they stayed in effect beyond the reach of their rulers. They could anyway count on friends in high places. Especially helpful was Edward Deas Thomson, born and brought up in the Tory circles of Edinburgh. He joined the administration of New South Wales in 1828 and served as Colonial Secretary, that is to say, as the Governor's chief Minister, then as member of the Legislative Council once responsible government was granted. He saw in the squatters the kernel of a ruling landed interest, such as was coming under threat in the Scotland of his time. He always exerted his influence in their favour, while resisting the civic equality for ex-prisoners or the wide electoral franchise which might open the door to democracy.

But there were others, in the colonial administration and in the Government at home, who disapproved of squatters. This caused some conflict in policy. Bureaucratic cavils at unauthorised squatting brought in 1837 a rule that pastoral runs must be held under official licence or ticket of occupation. In 1839, broader control was asserted in an ordinance for delineation of pastoral districts beyond the settled counties, with a protector of aborigines in each of them. The authors of such measures aimed in the end to convert squatting into ownership. They saw a chance when agricultural depression in the early 1840s crippled many pastoralists. Westminster was induced to legislate for the first time on the sale of Australian land, but only showed ignorance of local conditions: the price set of £1 an acre made it the dearest in the world. Few bought, and the squatters' position hardly changed. So in 1847, largely at Thomson's instance, policy went into reverse. A new regulation protected squatters in the unsettled regions by excluding from public sale the areas they held. Instead it offered them leases of 14 years, with the option of purchase at the end. It was hoped such a generous condition would make them grateful enough to take up the option. It certainly gave them more or less complete security at minimal cost. With huge tracts locked up in their hands, the squatters must have seen in this the consummation of their pastoral paradise, or at least a just reward for the slog of reclaiming the wilderness. And in the next decade or so, they did prosper as never before; it has even been called Australia's 'squatting age'. Official encouragement for free settlers scarcely seemed to matter. When Francis Jeffrey Cockburn, son of Edinburgh's great memorialist, came out to visit his brother's estate, he noted that 'squatters who went in for vast tracts and thousands of sheep despised the people generally who stratched the surface and planted seed, and called them cockatoos'.

In fact the end was nigh. Many runs excluded from the market could have been as well, perhaps better, turned over to crops, for which the price was rising. A virulent epidemic of scab among sheep underlined the point. The human irruption in the gold rush of 1852 carried away with it herdsmen and shepherds ready to swap a dull life in the outback for a chance to get rich quick, and not to be replaced except at a cost the squatters could now hardly afford. This flash-flood of immigration was followed by a steady stream of free settlers who usually came expecting to set up as farmers. So they dramatically raised demand for land and were often ready to pay, on the good prospects for cultivation, the sort of money that could persuade squatters to forgo their privileges. Apart from all that, 1852 brought an end to transportation of criminals. The way now lay open for Australia to develop into a modern society. In it, the squatters could never be more than a tiny minority, submerged in a population with quite different interests. If they wanted security, it looked as if they would have to buy it along with everybody else.[12]

The concessions wrung by squatters from an unaccountable colonial administration could anyway not last once responsible government was granted. The landed class managed for a while to limit the suffrage and ensure that elected representatives were drawn from itself. The very existence of Queensland is owed to this. It separated from New South Wales in 1859 at the behest of a local squatting oligarchy intent on defending its monopoly of the best land. Till 1870, it succeeded in controlling the government of the new colony and bend laws in its own favour. But then it too was swamped by immigrants, who returned the compliment. The more populous New South Wales had already set an example. There an Act of 1861 gave anyone ready to occupy and cultivate his farm the right to select it within areas so far held as pastoral runs. In effect it threw open to crops all leased land in the colony. Victoria followed. The squatters lost their special status, and some left Australia altogether. The Clyde Company, among others, was wound up in a few years. Cut loose from its legal and financial lifelines, the squatting community as such disappeared. There was no stopping what was bound to happen as Australia filled up, largely with the English and Irish proletariat. Once it took over colonial politics, it had the power to discriminate against pastoralism in favour of more diverse and small-scale agriculture created for and supported by a numerous class of owner-occupiers. The consciously progressive spirit of the legislation often took after ideas for radical agrarian reform in the mother countries. It was hallowed in retrospect by Australia's own version of Whig history, which reckoned that this had all along been in line with the country's needs.[13]

Still, till the process was complete, pastoralism remained a rational use of resources rather than the forced product of privilege. In the 1870s, despite the changed legal position, Australian land again became a fertile field for Scottish finance. A decade later, sales of it were booming. At this point Scots owned, after half a century of investment, perhaps one-third of the various types of pastoral security. They took much of the blame after the boom collapsed in a financial crisis of 1893, when 14 of the 25 Australian banks had to suspend payment. But the Scots were soon back. Since the country could not as yet do without foreign capital, the crisis was resolved at the expense of depositors rather than shareholders. That gave Scottish investment houses the confidence to buy up stricken securities with a view to holding them till maturity, in a gamble on recovery which turned out a good one. So the flow of funds continued, if at a less torrential pace, and only ebbed as Australia grew capable of financing herself.[14]

The end of the squatters' story had thus not been universally unhappy. Those in Victoria survived best, most contriving to preserve their lands as freeholdings. A register drawn up for the purpose of taxation in 1879, and recording places of birth, showed that 59 Scots families possessed nearly two million acres, an average of 33,000 acres, in other words an area for each about the size of Clackmannanshire. Numbers of these landowners lived in comfort as leaders of society in Melbourne, where they set the tone till the end of the century. The roster of 'Port Phillip gentlemen' revealed a Cockburn of Cockpen, an Erskine of Mar, a Macdonell of Glengarry, a Mackenzie of Flowerdale, a Macleod of Talisker, a McNeill of Barra, a Murray of Elibank, scions of the noble houses of Cassillis and Stair, and many more. Most had been linked with the Clyde Company. Its local principal, George Russell, survived its demise by 30 years as the patriarch of a wide network of cousins and relations by marriage, with connections stretching all the way to Queensland. They spent their time on the boards of banks and other financial institutions, sitting in the Legislative Council, supporting the religious and educational works of the Presbyterian Church, deploring the impudence of democrats.[15]

The democrats at last gained the upper hand all the same, and the commercial Empire of the Australian Scots proved in its turn short-lived. Yet it had again demonstrated the utility of Scottish principles for the relevant circumstances, in which development had to be efficiently carried forward on limited resources. It even devised a new instrument, the investment house, for supporting such enterprise at extremely long range. Funds were readily transferred on terms which brought gratifying rewards for Presbyterian thrift, not just to capitalists but also to small Scots savers. Here was one of the commercial Empire's accustomed moral benefits. On the other hand a second, of fostering fellow feeling for the native peoples, never figured. But then, if Australia was bereft of an indigenous culture to respect, Scots had no excuse for impeding entry by all the immigrants who wanted to come. Since anyway she turned out more hospitable than she looked at first sight, systematic colonisation could not in the long run be averted. And because from the middle of the century the British Government started to encourage it, on the emerging formularies of high imperialism, the matter was clinched.

Unlike many transients in Canada, the Scots in Australia settled down too. At length they became, except on occasions of sentimental conviviality, citizens of a new country much like the rest, comfortably reconciling themselves to a dispensation not of their making. The commercial Empire had served them well. Yet it had not formed the character of this colony, nor diverted general imperial policy from a course set by its masters in London. Perhaps that only went to show once again that, *tout court*, Scots could not determine the nature of the Empire. Or perhaps it showed that, in order to do so, they would have to harness a force mightier than commerce.[16]

CHAPTER TEN

'Occasional scenes of the broadest farce':
The Mediterranean

J anuary 12, 1859, saw the most famous tableau in the modern history of the Ionian Islands. William Gladstone, High Commissioner Extraordinary of Her Britannic Majesty's Government, was visiting them one by one to gauge the opinion of the people about their political future. Two choices lay open to them: continuation of the British protectorate under which they had lived since the end of the Napoleonic wars; or, as most seemed to wish, *enosis*, union with a Greece now in the third decade of her independence. One official, Viscount Kirkwall, recounted what happened when Gladstone called on the Bishop of Paxos. As everywhere else, he 'showed the most unbounded respect for the dignitaries of the Greek Church'. He disconcerted this one, a simple man from a tiny island:

> Mr Gladstone, having taken and respectfully kissed the Bishop's hand, leaned forward to receive the orthodox blessing. The Bishop hesitated, not knowing what was expected of him; and not imagining, perhaps, that a member of the Anglican Church could require his benediction. At last, however, he perceived the truth, and, bending forward, he hastened to comply with the flattering desire of the Representative of the British Crown. But at this moment, unfortunately, Mr Gladstone, imagining that the deferred blessing was not forthcoming, suddenly raised his head and struck the episcopal chin. The Resident and other spectators had considerable difficulty in maintaining the gravity befitting so solemn an occasion.[1]

There was indeed serious business afoot because Britain, as she grew into the greatest naval power, had found need of Mediterranean stations. From Gibraltar, seized in 1704, she proceeded to occupy Minorca in 1708–82, Corsica in 1794–6, Malta in 1799, Sicily in 1806–14, the Ionian Islands in 1813; the sequence would end with Cyprus in 1878. Before she left off a continental strategy, they offered forward positions against her rivals – Spain, above all France, later Russia – as well as springboards for incursions on the mainland or props for weak allies like the Italians and Turks. Later, when she switched to a maritime strategy, they served as bases for blockades or in peacetime as commercial outposts and as stepping- stones along the main sea-lane to India. They were therefore grist to the mill of the Scots' debate on Empire.

In the case of the less permanent occupations, the effect proved fitful. The first regular Governor of Minorca in 1711 was John Campbell, Duke of Argyll. He seized the island in order to retreat there from Barcelona, where in a sideshow to the War of the Spanish Succession his British expeditionary force had been trying in vain to defend Catalan autonomy. In the same spirit, he assured the Minorcans of his 'intentions to do everything that may tend to the making you a happy and flourishing people'. He freed their trade but found time for little else. Not till 1774 did Minorca enjoy a second spell of Scottish rule, under James Murray of Elibank, previously benefactor of the Canadians. Here, too, he looked beyond military tasks to the people's welfare. He encouraged their seafaring, only to find they wanted from him nothing but letters of marque to cover their depredations as privateers. Still, he granted the letters, turning them at a crucial point in a European war from being supine and treacherous to being loyal and enthusiastic. Within the island he wished to end oppressive monopolies and, so that he no longer had to live off emoluments from them, demanded from home a regular salary. These measures were the germs of more durable Scottish traits.[2]

About Corsica the Scots' imagination had already been fired by James Boswell's *Account* (1768) of the island. It was his homage, after a visit, to the people's proud, independent spirit which in his view made them, if a bit uncouth, morally superior to others. This showed the influence of his mentor Jean-Jacques Rousseau, who had given him a letter of introduction to the Corsican chief, General Pasquale Paoli. He entranced the young Scot, who was overjoyed to welcome him back to Edinburgh in 1771. When in 1793 he appealed to the British to annexe the island and protect it from French revolutionaries, Boswell begged to be sent out to arrange matters. Instead the job went to Sir Gilbert Elliot, later Lord Minto, who was in his turn delighted by the place, 'just like Scotland with a fine climate'. Paoli summoned an assembly of the people and tendered the Crown of Corsica to George III, represented by Elliot as Minister Plenipotentiary. The pair then appointed a committee to prepare articles of Union with Great Britain. The philosopher in Elliot found the task beguiling as, under the old constitution, 'nothing could be more democratic than the forms, nothing more autocratic than the result. The Corsicans used their rights to invest with supreme authority the man who had won their affections and their confidence'. He set out to adapt these forms to a new situation, but his work came to an abrupt halt with Britain's abandonment of the Mediterranean theatre in 1796. He had to leave the Corsicans to their fate under Napoleon Bonaparte.

Soon Britain was back in the Mediterranean, though, in the course of a now global struggle which allowed Scots to conceive of these insular conquests in a wider context. George Leckie profited from the occupation of Sicily in 1806 to acquire estates there, and published two years later his *Historical Survey of the Foreign Relations of Great Britain*. He took the correctness of maritime strategy as axiomatic, since 'the Empire of the sea will always balance that of the land'. But, as was all too obvious at the time, conflicts between the two types of empire often led to long wars. The British, fewer than their foes, could not fight these long wars and remain a prosperous trading people: the strain on resources would prove too much, and set off a decline. The answer was to match imperial expansion with 'conquest or adoption of European nations', not through futile military intervention on the Continent, but by building an 'insular empire' in the Mediterranean. Therefore, 'we must Britannize every part of insular Europe which suits our purpose'. He added for good measure, though without quite explaining what he meant, that such dominion should be constructed as an 'abstract principle', expressing a 'great and philosophical view' in contradiction of French republican imperialism.[3]

To take the liberty of placing Leckie explicitly in the Scottish debate, we see that he shows some transition from the older concepts of a commercial Empire, not yet towards an Empire of settlement, but certainly towards one of territorial occupation, with a degree of cultural imperialism. Other Mediterranean Scots found his precepts useful, if on more pragmatic grounds. It seemed advisable, however the matter was rationalised, for Britain to hang on to the captured islands. That meant they had to be regularly governed. But they made atypical colonies. They were neither advanced nor primitive societies, but European ones mostly founded on the Catholic and absolutist tradition. Their histories had yet been disrupted and bloody, for Britain was not the first to perceive their strategic value. Over two millennia, great powers had come and gone, ruling and misruling them. It was a miracle that established institutions had survived, yet they often had. Scots were, in the light of their own stormy past, equipped to deal with that experience, to guarantee the islanders what these most valued in their way of life, while insinuating rational improvements into the social structure and opening it to the transformatory power of commerce. This, we shall see, is what Scots did. It was fitting for their work to be rounded off at length by Gladstone, whose father had migrated from Leith to Liverpool, whose mother had been born to a provost of Dingwall: as he prided himself, every drop of his blood was Scottish.

Two archipelagoes in particular came to bear that impress. One was the Ionian Islands, the other Malta and Gozo. Malta showed vivid evidences of her turbulent history. But for his death, they would have inspired Walter Scott to write a great work on the fall of chivalry. He visited the island on his last journey in 1831 and found Valletta 'a city of gentlemen built by gentlemen'. There remained from the remote past a Punic populace, still speaking a Semitic language, but Roman Catholic, having lived from 1530 under the religious and military order, the Knights of St John, who held this as a bastion against Islam. Napoleon threw them out on his way to Egypt in 1798. The native notables preferred, however, even the Protestant British to the godless French. When the Royal Navy passed by the next year, they asked for protection.

The request was seized on since a base here would also serve to cut off the enemy in the East. General Sir Ralph Abercromby of Tullibody laid down principles for a provisional occupation, including a guarantee of 'all the rights, privileges and immunities in Church and State'. Malta also proved her worth as a safe haven from which to keep up trade to southern Europe in defiance of Napoleon's continental system. To John Galt, who stopped by on his way to Turkey in 1809, the boom seemed a threat to a traditional society of which the people 'have reached a Chinese state of self-sufficient perfection'. He did not doubt, all the same, the value of measures to promote commerce, even while 'those things which regard the law and the administration of justice should be examined with care, and proceeded in with caution'. The British were still not sure they wanted to stay but, when peace approached, they could descry no other power to which they might with comfort hand the island over. They proclaimed it a Crown colony in 1813.[4]

The first governor was Thomas Maitland, soon known as King Tom. He turned out the right man for the job, though not cast in the conventional proconsul's mould. He was 'particularly dirty in his person', or 'constantly drunk and surrounded by sycophants'. Notorious for abrupt rudeness, he asked one recruit to his staff, 'Who the devil are you? I hope you are not such a damned scoundrel as your predecessor'. Waking each day with a huge hangover, he stayed in bed while receiving his tremulous subalterns. If he did not like what they said, he would just roll over and groan. One recorded how he felt proper to reach forward and tweak the cover across the bare gubernatorial bottom before proceeding. Maitland was a brother of the Earl of Lauderdale, an acute but eccentric political economist in the process of swinging from radicalism to reaction; at this time he stood halfway. Maitland himself had as a young man joined the Friends of the People, the democratic movement of the 1790s, and opposed the war against revolutionary France. But a few years' soldiering, culminating in the governorship of San Domingo in 1797, cured him of youthful indiscretion. He was considered sound enough to serve as Governor of Ceylon in 1804–11. By the time he got to Malta he too had become more of a Scots Tory than a Scots Whig: inclined to despotism, dismissive of any idea that his lieges could bear political responsibility, yet anxious for their welfare and respectful of their sensibilities.[5]

He still put imperial interests first. Some Maltese dared to hope that Britain, home of ordered liberty, might grant a little of it to them. They recalled that their traditional institutions included an assembly, the *Consiglio Popolare*. Though reduced to a nullity by the Knights of St John, it had once contained delegates from the villages and been able to legislate. Maitland favoured traditions, but not this one. His aim was rather to render his power 'free and unfettered'. Citing 'the King's service' whenever his actions were questioned, he set up an autocratic government. It proved effective enough to outlast him. Not till 1835 did the Maltese gain the right to choose even an advisory council. A constitution would be granted in 1849, yet the administration remained British in personnel right till 1887.[6]

One imperial obligation on Malta, not a fertile or productive island, was that like all colonies she should pay her way. Scots taught, however, that prudent liberalisation rather than grinding exaction was the best means of seeing to a buoyant revenue. The Knights of St John had presided over a feudal system, binding the peasants to render servitudes, in labour and in kind, to them and to other proprietors, usually absentees represented by local headmen. All these privileges Maitland ended. He got rid of the headmen too, choosing in their stead trusty landlords who, nominated as *luogotenenti* to himself, would visit their estates, regulate rustic life, administer petty justice and keep order. Thus he set out to control the populace through a modern landowning class, such as he knew from Scotland, tractable and responsible at once. By emancipation on the one hand and patronage on the other, he succeeded.

He undermined other outworn institutions, notably the *università*. It had nothing to do with higher learning, but bought foodstuffs which Malta could not supply for herself, grain, beef, pasta and oil, then sold them to the people at inflated prices. It was, according to the governor, 'the most troublesome den of corruption I ever met with'. By freeing the market in grain, he made a start on dismantling its monopolies. To get rid of any need for them, he sought to pay for necessary imports by promoting exports, if with limited success; apart from the general agricultural depression now setting in all over Europe, there was in particular little beyond local demand for Mediterranean products. Maitland came up with a further familiar Scottish solution for an island that could not live of its own, that it should function as an emporium. It had already prospered in that role during the wars. They, while disrupting its older trades, yet established it as an entrepot for British and colonial goods brought in by, among others, the Glasgow merchant house of James Finlay. Though these birds of passage left once peace came, the governor understood how valuable they had been. He lured levantine types in their place, sharp Jews and Greeks likely to look for fresh commercial outlets. To them he offered protection while he made life difficult for French, Spanish and Portuguese competitors trying to resume their former privileged traffic. So if he manipulated Malta's markets, it was with a view to finding some comparative advantage for her.[7]

Maitland wanted her not just materially but spiritually content. There was a political problem here, as in other colonies with a Catholic population. The United Kingdom remained in principle a confessional state, imposing disabilities on papists applicable in all its dominions. In practice, in Canada and Ireland for example, the disabilities had been lifted when likely to cause too much trouble. The governor was not himself burdened by any deep religious convictions. William Wilberforce had berated him as a pagan for his deference to Buddhist cults in Ceylon. There, he also relieved the native Catholics of the previous Dutch regime's penal laws. The old Scots Toryism had a soft spot for their Church, not on any theological grounds, rather because it looked kindly on ecclesiastical establishments of every sort. The two had indeed been allies against the French atheists: we may recall that Henry, the last Jacobite pretender and a Roman cardinal, died in receipt of a pension from George III, arranged at Scottish behest.

In Malta, Maitland commended the people's piety, which made them obedient and bound their society together. He renewed the guarantee for their religion, or rather for 'the free exercise of worship to all persons who inhabit and frequent the islands'. He did not in the event carry this out to the letter, for he was if anything intolerant of Protestantism. He restricted evangelical missions eager to convert the Maltese. When it was proposed that a single one of the many churches might be appropriated for the use of Protestants, he refused. He thus pleased the native priests, fearful lest their flock stray under the rule of heretics. In return he required of them, however, subservience in everything touching his civil jurisdiction. This was again a ticklish point, not only in reformed countries. The Vatican had been for centuries in dispute with Catholic monarchs over rights of presentation. Here the rights belonged to the King of the Two Sicilies, the see being suffragan to Palermo. The British had helped him to regain his throne, and for the governor that went quite far enough: no foreign potentate was going to interfere on Malta any more. But a change in the old arrangement needed consent from Rome. Having won the goodwill of the local hierarchy, Maitland was in a position to get it. The Pope agreed to separate the see and, when it should become vacant, to permit a new candidate to be presented to him for approval by the King of Great Britain.

The governor found a fitting symbol of his ideal relations between Church and state. The first thing he had had to deal with on his arrival was an outbreak of plague. Once it passed, he proclaimed a day of prayer and ordered a Te Deum sung in the cathedral of Valletta. The bishop asked him whether he would attend and, if so, whether he would occupy the throne. Maitland did not understand. The prelate explained that the Vatican had long ago authorised Grand-Masters of the Order of St John to place a throne beside the high altar and sit there during the office. The governor said that thrones were not for him, but observed that the island now possessed an undoubted sovereign in George III: the throne should stay, and be left vacant to signify his sovereignty.[8]

Ingenious yet forceful methods won Maitland promotion as commander-in-chief of the whole Mediterranean, except Gibraltar, in 1816. In that capacity he also became Lord High Commissioner to the nominally independent Septinsular Republic, the Ionian Islands of Corfu, Paxos, Leucas, Ithaca, Cephalonia, Zante and Cythera. During the war the French had occupied them, after seizing them from the Venetians, their overlords since 1386, before which date they had been Byzantine. Now secure from further invasion, they remained almost the only part of the Greek world free of the Turks. Again a chequered history still left some native institutions intact. Venice had allowed a Roman Catholic see to be erected on Corfu, but never tried to suppress the Orthodox Church. The islands even boasted a senate, composed of local noblemen, which had gained power during the last century as the authority of the Signoria languished.

The British arrived in 1814, with an expedition under General Sir James Campbell of Inverneil sent to mop up the last pockets of French resistance in these parts. In reporting his success, he urged annexation of the islands: 'There is not a possession in Europe so admirably adapted to uphold British power'. Though instructed to act with caution, he imposed, over the senate's head, a harsh regime of occupation, with censorship, martial law and a ban on public assembly. He knew the Ionians sensed a chance for self-determination in the new order that must now be established in Europe. The sentiment was not liberal here, as in some similar cases, and so not very friendly to Britain. The nobles were on the contrary conservatives, Orthodox in religion and intent on preserving feudalism. They thus looked rather to Russia, and kept in touch with Czar Alexander I through a compatriot, John Capodistrias, who had as a youth entered his service and had now risen to be one of his chief Ministers. When he went to the Congress of Vienna, Capodistrias went with him. The senate asked leave to send a delegation, but Campbell refused. Capodistrias took up the islands' case all the same, and drew from Britain a promise to turn them into a 'free and independent state'. In return she was confirmed as the protecting power, which rendered the promise meaningless. The last thing the British wanted was a Russian presence in the Mediterranean. They preferred to hold on to the islands themselves.[9]

Again, Maitland matched local politics with global strategy. Here, though, he had also to respect the obligations accepted by Britain in Vienna. He was bound, for instance, to call a constituent assembly and submit proposals to it. He softened the people up by spending the rest of 1816 on tour round the islands, redressing their grievances and wooing their worthies. This scrutiny gave him no higher opinion of the Greeks than of the Maltese: they ought not to be abused or brutalised but were unfit for constitutional government in the British sense. If he had to grant them some semblance of it, he was determined to stop them 'running wild'. Like the architect of the Scottish Empire, Henry Dundas, and like many other Scots proconsuls, the Lord High Commissioner had a deep distaste for representation: 'Any man who has seen much of them would agree with me that colonial assemblies are injurious to the people, and disadvantageous to good government'. It would be better to hold in his own hands a 'definite power, however extensive' than to hand over to legislators a 'power alike uncontrolled and undefined'.

He might have simply nominated the constituent assembly, but thought that would be going too far. He could, however, pack it. He kicked off by dismissing the sitting senators, on the grounds of their russophile sympathies. Having sought out on his tour the most reliable of the Ionians, he named eleven of them to form what he called his primary council. 'Maitland's Magnificoes' would be assured of seats in the assembly themselves, and meanwhile recommend how to choose the rest of its 40 members. The means they devised was, by some strange chance, a sort of amalgam of the electoral systems in the Scottish counties and burghs. They drew up a list of 58 candidates, of whom the general body of voters, kept small by a narrow franchise, would pick half. The result was the same as in Scotland: to exclude any significant opposition. When the assembly met in the spring of 1817, it managed within a mere two weeks to approve the draft constitution presented by Maitland. That done, it sent a delegation all the way to the Brighton Pavilion to get the Prince Regent's ratification. By the next year the system was running, and would last till 1849.

It was an 'artful, but complete despotism'. It preserved the trappings of an independent republic, even gilded them. The Lord High Commissioner left one lasting legacy to British history by his foundation in 1818 of the Order of St Michael and St George as a cheap reward for his dependable Ionians. He guessed they would love nothing so much as to succeed to lost Venetian glories, to dress up and swagger around in gorgeous regalia. It seemed such a splendid wheeze that he let the Maltese in on it too, allowing them to pretend they were just like the Knights of St John. The local order was suspended in 1864 but, as an idea too good to waste, would be refounded in Britain to inflate in like manner the *amour propre* of the great and good in Whitehall, which it still does today. Maitland understood the value of human vanity as a distraction from reality.[10]

The constitutionalism of his regime was, in reality, a sham. It vested all effective power in him. He was free even from London except in the control of military establishments and the conduct of foreign relations. Otherwise, Ionian legislation did not require Westminster's sanction, while the Colonial Office seldom interfered and the Treasury stayed happy so long as the republic cost it nothing. Internally, Maitland could do more or less as he liked. He had immediate charge of public order, posts and sanitation. Various legal devices gave him ample scope to curb or dismiss officers of state responsible for other things, appointed by the legislature though they were. While a reformed judiciary under a supreme court assured impartial justice, he revived, with this time a surely mocking deference to tradition, the Venetian powers of High Police. They let him declare an emergency, silence the press or arrest, imprison and exile individuals without trial. To be sure, he seldom used these powers: it was enough to set up gallows in various public places ready, so he said, for the execution of pirates.

Again, however, Maitland's despotism did not lack benevolence, at least to loyal subjects who merited it. As on Malta, he dismantled feudalism, abolished servitudes and broke entails in order to open hereditary estates to a free market. He ended the oppressive farming of the Church's tithes. He forbade usurious advances from landlords to tenants. He suppressed monopolies and created a more prosperous commerce. Revenue from the customs rose so much that he could do away with direct taxes. He used to laugh that he had 'the richest treasury in Europe'. But he spent the money too. His elaborate establishment was anyway expensive: at home the radical Joseph Hume, MP for the Montrose Burghs, denounced his extravagance, while Ionian aristocrats grumbled at their position being usurped by his British officials, 'well-born young gentlemen, whose sole duty seems to be to loll on verandahs'. Yet with his appointments he also 'bribed a vast number of influential, though needy, families'. To the people he showed himself, in true Scottish fashion, both an improver and an educator. He undertook a range of public works, many still serviceable to this day, and gave the islands their exquisite neo-classical architecture. On every one he endowed at official expense an elementary and a secondary school. The Septinsular Republic became, for the time being, the centre of Greek culture.[11]

On each of the outer islands the Lord High Commissioner was represented by a resident. One showed the regime at its very best. Charles Napier, appointed to

Cephalonia in 1822, was a man of boundless energy and confidence. He had odd looks, with a great hawk's nose and long hair sprouting from chin and pate. They suited the air of insubordination he carried about with him. By instinct he sided with the underdog. A Napier of Merchiston, he had as a boy followed his soldier father to Ireland, where he learned how oppressive British rule could be. The Ionians struck him as a sunnier sort of Irishmen: 'The merry Greeks are worth all other nations put together. I like to see them, to hear them; I like their fun, their good humour, their paddy ways'. He had in his turn pursued a military career, and been six times wounded while serving in the Peninsula, in America and in Belgium during Napoleon's 100 days. A younger son, he had no money or prospects outside the army. Put on half-pay once the wars were over, he found himself broke and frustrated. Cephalonia offered him release: 'My predecessor is going home half-dead from the labour, but to me it is health, spirit, everything! I live for some use now'. The experience would enchant him: 'What pleasure it gives me to do good to this delightful island; with those dear to me I could spend my whole life here without wish to leave'. This he may have meant to do, for he acquired property, took a Greek mistress and had two daughters by her, one of whom he christened Cephalonia.[12]

But his was not a blind enchantment. He saw how history had ruined the Greeks who 'have, from bad government, come to that strange state, that the instant they are treated justly they conclude it is a humbug and try to be beforehand: to deal with them demands caution and care in finding out what ought to be done, and then bullying all who resist'. On his arrival Cephalonia still lay under martial law, plagued by feuds among its clans and villages. He lost no time in imposing order. Within three months he set up a regular system of justice, though making sure to administer it himself: 'The people are much to my liking, but the greatest liars in the world'. That essential preliminary complete, he embarked on improvement, and worked his fingers to the bone for it. The island was not rich, though not poor either. It may have looked arid and mountainous, but its 60,000 souls could live well enough – they sent to Britain, for example, almost her entire supply of currants – and it was more populated than the neighbouring parts of Greece. Napier felt sure they could all live better by toiling harder. He instituted a corvée, one day's unpaid labour for every able-bodied man, and did not hesitate to use the whip if he found any slacking. With these hands at his disposal, he built roads, bridges, lighthouses and prisons, repaired houses and widened streets, drained swamps and extended the area of cultivation.

Yet he did not mean to make helots of the islanders. On the contrary, he sought to elevate them morally too. He could look for little help to the sole moral authority among them, their Church, though he did restore it: 'Meanwhile to bless us we have got a bishop appointed; an excellent pious man, who formerly lived by sheep-stealing, which he now calls his *pastoral life*'. But once kept out of mischief, the Cephalonians would anyway enlarge their peaceful intercourse with one another.

The resident wanted them above all to develop a spirit of independence, proud especially of the land. He brought from his Irish upbringing a dislike of landlordism and its oppressions. A healthy society would, he believed, rest on a sturdy class of smallholders: an idea much in vogue among Scots, at home, in India and elsewhere. He curbed the power of local proprietors and bettered the peasants' lot by means of loans, of a model farm for instruction, of easier access to markets. He felt so pleased with the results that he would expound his methods in a book, *Colonisation* (1835), intended as a manual for the rest of the British Empire.[13]

Nor did Napier confine his attentions to the Empire. He hoped to awaken the same spirit of independence in the whole Greek people, now engaged in its struggle for freedom from the Turks. The patriots were also, and scarcely less often, fighting each other, in the savage Balkan manner. Maitland, till his death in January 1824, allowed no official of his any deviation from a neutral policy. He himself sympathised with the Sublime Porte: at least it stood for established order, while Greeks were unlikely to settle down under any sort of regular government. Still, philhellenism ran strong in Scots. In London, Hume was prominent in the Greek Committee which raised money to aid the rebels. George Finlay, scion of the Glasgow mercantile dynasty, gave up his studies to join in the war of liberation. So did David Urquhart from Caithness, who later went to Constantinople, learned rather to love the Turks and became the great British expert on the Eastern question. So again did Thomas Gordon of Cairness in Buchan, who would write a *History of the Greek Revolution* and end his career as chief of staff to the army of the free nation.

One man, though, stood out above all. On August 10, 1823, Napier announced to his journal: 'Lord Byron is here, and I like him very much.' Perhaps it was a matter of nationality, for Byron, George Gordon by name, had been brought up in Aberdeen:

> But I am half a Scot by birth, and bred
> A whole one, and my heart flies to my head . . .
> I 'scotched not killed' the Scotsman in my blood
> And love the land of mountain and the flood.

He had made a first journey to the East in 1811, and then had written his *Turkish Tales*. He depicted a luxurious and passionate world, shot through with violence, revenge and cruelty. But he did not mean, by drawing it in poetic contrast to the mundane reality of the West, to give it any political seal of approval: he hated Ottoman, like all other, tyranny. Still, he traced this blemish not so much to the character of the Turks as to the Asiatic despotism under which they and their subject peoples lived. That was why he wanted to liberate the Greeks, though entertaining few illusions about them either. He would tell Finlay that 'you are young and enthusiastic and therefore bound to be disappointed when you know the Greeks as well as I do'. Napier remarked that, of the many westerners who helped them, only Byron, along with Gordon, knew what he was about: 'All came expecting to find the Peloponessus filled with Plutarch's men, and all returned thinking the inhabitants of

Newgate more moral'. Those two proceeded, however, 'not thinking them good, but hoping to make them better'.[14]

Having embarked at Genoa with a few volunteers, Byron would halt on Cephalonia for four months, while he received emissaries from the mainland and tried to fathom what was going on there. The resident's friendship and military experience proved of great use to him. Only after much prompting did he cross to Missolonghi, 20 miles away. As Napier noted, 'it is hard to get there, harder to get back; and if the Turks catch him off goes his poetical nob'. Before any such thing could happen, he died the following April of an epileptic fit and overbleeding, though perhaps even more of disillusion at the ceaseless quarrels in his camp. His example inspired others with an ambition to join the struggle, including Napier. Byron had written: 'A better or braver man is not to be found. *He* is our man to lead a regular force, or to organise a national one for the Greeks'. But when he asked leave from London to reconnoitre among the patriots, he was refused. In 1825 the Greek Committee thought to offer him a command, to be taken aback at the stiff conditions he set: a straight fee of £12,000 for himself, with a guarantee of 10,000 muskets and £150,000 to pay his forces, which would include 'at least 500 Englishmen, Irishmen or Scotsmen, equipped and armed like British soldiers'. When his demands were referred to the Greeks, they found his price far too high and decided they would rather spend what money they had on naval operations.

They then gave it to yet another Scottish wellwisher, Admiral Thomas Cochrane, just returned from liberating the Chileans and Peruvians. He took charge of the Greek flotilla in 1826. It consisted of three steamers, two of them American, and thereby became the world's first steam-driven navy. If they could not defeat, they bemused the Turkish fleet, which the western powers in any event destroyed at the Battle of Navarino the next year. With that Cochrane, having tired of the Greeks, departed. So did Finlay, though he would come back three years later after completing his education. Gordon stayed on, to organise the war almost single-handed. Soon the Greeks' squabbles grew so bad that he threatened to leave as well. Then they at last took western reproaches seriously. They united long enough to choose a president, the evergreen Capodistrias, by now back in Russia. He arrived, in no great hurry, in 1828, to face the all but impossible task of imposing order on a land of devastation and anarchy. One day in October 1831, as he entered church, he was assassinated, shot and stabbed by the chiefs of a clan who held him to have insulted them. His republic failed, but at least Greece was now free.[15]

This, though few realised the fact, was also a decisive step towards the end of the British protectorate on the Ionian Islands. It passed its peak when Maitland was followed as Lord High Commissioner by his deputy and military commander, another Scot, Frederick Adam of Blair Adam. Adam's character is hard to assess through the stream of invective with which Napier later doused him. If pompous in manner, he had proved a gallant soldier, serving with distinction in Sicily and at Waterloo. He was a friend of Scott's, who but for growing frailty during that last journey would have gone on from Malta to visit him. He appears to have been a man of liberal outlook. He felt at home on the islands. He patronised Greek culture, with particular generosity to the romantic poet, Dionysios Solomos. He even married a Corfiote rejoicing in the name of Diamantina Palatianos, 'the beard on whose upper lip would ornament a hussar'. She belonged to the aristocracy, which no doubt explained Adam's eagerness to ingratiate himself with it. The fault was compounded by his fiscal incompetence, gross enough to bring a threat of parliamentary investigation. Public works continued, but now exhausted the treasury. The Lord High Commissioner raised taxes so steeply as to threaten the entire economy of islands.

That set him at odds with Napier. Adam's petulance came out in niggling impositions on this meritorious officer. He even commanded him to shave off his moustaches: 'the order was obeyed to a hair', and the results sent to Corfu. The quarrel came to a head in 1828 when the Lord High Commissioner, prompted by Greek cronies, ordained that residents should no longer have charge of public works on the outer islands, and for good measure abolished the corvée on Cephalonia. Kirkwall would date from this point the decay of the Septinsular Republic's political system: the institution of resident gave way to local intrigues and injustices, so that 'British Government fell into contempt'. Napier was due a furlough in 1830. A touching scene took place on the quay as he prepared to sail away. His mistress brought their daughters down to bid him farewell. Just at the last moment, she decided they would be better off with him and sent them out to him in a little boat. It was lucky for them, because he cherished them all his life, even after he regularly married. He would never see Cephalonia again. Adam gave him an unctuous envoi, but once he was away forbade him to return, claiming the landowners nursed such grievances against him that they would revolt if he did. Napier retorted that 'the howling of the wolves had been mistaken for the bleating of the sheep'.[16]

Adam was at length promoted Governor of Madras. A third Scot, Howard Douglas of Carr, succeeded as Lord High Commissioner in 1835–41. Under him, the despotism remained benevolent enough in improving the educational and legal systems. But he had also to deal with the first popular stirrings in favour of *enosis*. He countered with diversionary tactics. He encouraged trade to the mainland. He showed favour to the Orthodox Church and frustrated an attempt by the Pope to restore a Catholic see in the islands by throwing out the bishop sent from Rome. But he could not stop the electors choosing nationalists to represent them. Nor, inside the legislature, could he silence calls for reform, for some political control of the executive, for a free press and so on. Outside the legislature, he often resorted to the powers of High Police to lock up agitators, prevent circulation of petitions and ban newspapers from the mainland. All this disquieted the Whig Government in London, as it never would have disquieted an old Tory one, and he only just managed to fend off an inquiry into the state of the islands.

The Whigs, before they went out of office in 1841, appointed a new Lord High

Commissioner more congenial to them, though also giving him the contradictory instruction 'not to introduce change of any kind'. James Stewart Mackenzie came from their own ranks, as a former MP for Ross and Cromarty and meanwhile Governor of Ceylon; his wife, chieftainess in her own right of Clan Mackenzie, had been another friend of Scott's. Their colonial experience and stately manner failed to placate the restive Ionians. A crisis developed which in 1843 prompted Mackenzie to the unprecedented step of dismissing the president of the senate. The Colonial Office baulked at ratifying his decision. Disgusted with the lack of support, he resigned. That led straight to the constitutional reform of 1849 which deprived the Lord High Commissioner of his absolute power. Yet it did little to satisfy opponents of British rule.

So things continued up to Gladstone's arrival as trouble-shooter. His brief was to solve the problem, but for once a task defeated him. His private secretary, Arthur Gordon, son of the Earl of Aberdeen, described the episode as 'a political drama alternately tragical and comic, not unmixed with occasional scenes of the broadest farce, but always picturesque'. Gladstone set to with his usual energy, conducted wide consultations, visited the islands and Athens as well. Gordon was still not impressed. He objected to his chief's 'kissing the pudgy hand of every bishop he could get hold of', to his cavalier treatment of the British officials in post, to his fawning on Greek nationalists, to his verbose dispatches. Most wayward of all, and inexplicable to everyone, was his decision in January 1859 to replace the existing Lord High Commissioner with himself. His term lasted a few days. Its climax came in a high-flown oration to the Ionian legislature, setting out elaborate proposals acceptable neither to it, since they did not offer *enosis*, nor to London, which wanted a quiet life. He then left in high dudgeon. Deadlock continued for four more years, till Britain decided that the simplest thing would be just to cede the islands to Greece. It was the sole voluntary abandonment of organised imperial government during the whole century – and the end of an eccentric but engaging outpost of the Scottish Empire.[17]

Part Two

A Christian Empire

CHAPTER ELEVEN

'Scattering the seeds of civilisation': South Africa

O ne night in late September 1802, gunfire and whooping suddenly shattered the silence round the missionary station of Botha's Place, on the shores of Algoa Bay about 350 miles east of the Cape of Good Hope. Inside the compound uproar instantly reigned, men shouting the alarm, women screaming, children crying. They had dreaded some attack since eight days before, when they said farewell to the last British troops at Fort Frederick nearby. The garrison was being evacuated under the Treaty of Amiens which required, as part of the price for peace in Europe, the Cape to be returned into the hands of Holland. The British had gone, but the Dutch were not expected back for weeks or months. Meanwhile, lurking bands of black warriors would have the scattered colonists of this remote district at their mercy.

Amid the commotion appeared the head of the mission, John Theodore Vanderkemp. He had hoped against hope that no harm would come to his flock, most of them inoffensive natives cut off from their tribes, rescued by him from a life of racking toil for white farmers. He had tried to fool himself that his goodwill to these and to all the people roundabout would keep the peace. He had declined to move away even when urged to by the outgoing British governor, General Francis Dundas, nephew of Scotland's great imperial statesman, Henry Dundas. The governor had always taken a friendly interest in the mission. He it was that granted the land at Botha's Place. Before leaving he sent supplies, then came to pay a final visit in person. He urged Vanderkemp to take refuge in Fort Frederick, as the local Dutch were doing, or even sail back to Cape Town with his official party: till fresh European forces arrived, life along the frontier would be just too dangerous.

Sure enough, hostile tribesmen had wasted no time in stirring. The station's crude stockade could not hold up their assault. They drove its bellowing cattle before them, as a screen from any counter-attack. Vanderkemp still thought he could make them see reason. He dashed about gibbering in Dutch, Hottentot and Xhosa, ordering his people to use their weapons only in self-defence. He ventured out himself into the darkness in an effort to win the enemy with friendly words, but only their bullets answered him. One of his close helpers tried too, till they saw him and cried: 'Look, there comes a peace-maker, kill him, shoot him!' The poor fellow staggered back with blood streaming from a wound in the leg. Suddenly, when all seemed lost, the cattle ran up against a pile of planks between two huts. Unable to advance, the terrified beasts bolted to one side. That left a free field of fire to the defenders, who now understood that resistance was their only chance. They let off two volleys, and one luckily hit the chieftain leading the onslaught. His men fled. They would come back the next night, and again a couple of nights later with a yet bigger force. But now the mission was ready for them, and easily beat them off. Vanderkemp saw, though, that this could not go on. He sent to Fort Frederick. He had never been popular with his neighbours, who thought he encouraged idleness. Yet they did not refuse him help in his extremity. An armed detachment of them came out and escorted everybody to safety. Some returned later and burned the mission down to make sure it could not be used again. No doubt they grumbled that the idea had been mad from the start, and wondered how Dundas could have been foolish enough to encourage it. The answer lay in Vanderkemp's standing as a minister of the Church of Scotland.[1]

Just as there were Dutch Scotsmen, a Robert Jacob Gordon or a John Gabriel Stedman, so there were Scots Dutchmen, one of them being Vanderkemp. Born in 1747, the son of a professor in Rotterdam, he had followed a military career before attending the university of Edinburgh to study medicine. His intellectual interests were wide, extending especially to natural theology and above all to the pre-socratic philosophy of Parmenides. On that he published a book in Latin which won him high respect from the city's literati. He decided to return to Holland, however, only to suffer a horrible tragedy: he saw his wife and daughter drowned before his eyes in the River Rhine. Previously lukewarm in religion, he now became a devoutly orthodox Christian and dedicated the rest of his life to missions. In order to fulfil that vow, he was in 1797 ordained a minister at the kirk of Crown Court in London.

Zeal for conversion of the heathen at home and abroad was among the first signs of evangelical revival in Scotland. Though it got a cool welcome from the established Church, the country did not lack a missionary tradition. The ministers at Darien had been enjoined to instruct the natives. In 1709, others set up the Society in Scotland for the Propagation of Christian Knowledge, to save the Highlands from popery but also to proselytise in foreign parts, primarily North America, where they would send 'messengers of joy to the bewildered Indians'. Principal William Robertson commended missions, if in terms which explained the general laodicean attitude towards them. He did so in a sermon of 1755, the first work he ever published, *The Situation of the World at the Time of Christ's Appearance*. He called on the authority of St Augustine to assert that the divine word had only been revealed when some portion of mankind was ready to receive it. Reformed religion had enlarged the revelation and, with the progress of society, that was bound to happen again. By the same token, the revelation was clearly wasted on those not ready for it. Robertson then applied this argument to missions. The most determined proselytisation of modern times had taken place in the Spanish Empire, yet by means as absurd as they were cruel. Not only had Spaniards devoted themselves to the extraction of bullion rather than the development of commerce, but they had also forcibly converted Indians who, as a matter of fact, were incapable of receiving the abstract propositions of

Christianity. Instead of progress towards toleration and civil liberty, therefore, had come regress into superstition and slavery. With his thesis, Robertson unified the Protestant doctrine of providence and the Scottish theory of conjectural history.[2]

The thesis, in effect the official policy of the Kirk, survived his death in 1793. Soon afterwards, missions again became a practical proposition through the activities of James and Robert Haldane of Airthrey. Scots lairds enjoyed little reputation for piety, but these two brothers experienced personal conversions which filled them with a burning desire to preach the gospel. They wanted above all to witness in Bengal, but Henry Dundas told them firmly they could not. For want of anything better they travelled their own country, especially the Highlands, spreading their good news. This enthusiasm impressed the Evangelicals in the Church of Scotland, who regretted it was only being put to use outside the framework of established religion. They felt the Kirk should emulate the Haldanes, certainly at home and even abroad. In 1796 the question was brought before the General Assembly.

There the Moderates, Robertson's old party, opposed any fresh initiative. The Rev George Hamilton, his successor in his first parish of Gladsmuir, gave out the lofty counsel 'to leave our fellow creatures to the protection of the common father of mankind, and to such glimmerings as the lights he vouchsafes them by nature afford . . . Men must be polished and refined in their manners, before they can be properly enlightened in religious truths'. Such haughtiness provoked a forthright response from the venerable and couthy Evangelical leader, the Rev John Erskine, who drew himself up with the famous line, 'Moderator, rax me that bible.' Then he read out Matthew xxviii, 19, 'Go ye therefore, and teach all nations, baptizing them in the name of the Father, and of the Son, and of the Holy Ghost'. His intervention still failed. The assembly resolved that 'to spread abroad the knowledge of the Gospel among barbarous and heathen nations seems to be highly preposterous, in so far as philosophy and learning must in the nature of things take precedence'. So the official policy did not alter. In 1815 the Rev Thomas Chalmers was complaining still that 'in this corner of the empire there is an imperious and overbearing contempt for everything connected with the name of missionary'. There would be no real change till the Disruption of the Church of Scotland in 1843 when, after ten years of constitutional struggle with the British state, most Evangelicals marched out to form the Free Church. At once they embarked with the greatest ardour on missions, and left the rump of the Kirk labouring to keep up.[3]

Despite clerical indifference, evangelical revival meanwhile burgeoned in the country at large, and interest in missions with it. Even as the General Assembly of 1796 met, groups of enthusiasts set about forming missionary societies in Glasgow, Edinburgh and elsewhere. They were prompted by the establishment of the London Missionary Society, itself largely the creation of two Scots ministers in English nonconformist charges, David Bogue in Gosport and John Love in London. Love would soon return home and serve for 20 years as secretary of the Glasgow Missionary Society. These Scottish voluntary bodies could hardly call on the resources for sustained effort overseas and often acted rather as auxiliary committees for their friends in the South. But the Glasgow society did at length send out on its own account the most renowned of early Scottish missions, to Lovedale in the eastern Cape.[4]

Named after Love, who had just died, it was set up in 1824 by the Revs John Bennie and John Ross. The society had made careful inquiries, found a choice, fertile region and prepared the ground thoroughly. Over the previous three years it had dispatched in advance four other ministers, who already counted to their credit the foundation of King William's Town and the reduction to writing of the Xhosa language, so that they could translate the Bible. Such ambition reflected the parent city's boisterous enterprise and technical efficiency. Still, in seeking support the society preferred to dwell on its fidelity to the Presbyterianism of yore. Glaswegians were asked to see in Lovedale an exotic variant 'of those simple and venerable institutions for which your fathers bled and died. Its labourers continue to look to this city as their cradle. All their associations are towards the religion of a Scotsman's hearth and the variegated scenery of their fathers' land'. Odd as the language sounds, it was to be taken seriously. Lovedale assumed the specifically Scottish task of ensuring that conversion was rooted and made fast in education. To that extent it responded to Robertson, if in a more democratic spirit. Beside their evangelism, the missionaries taught agriculture and other useful arts, later industrial skills, finally for girls as well as boys. They aimed to make the negroes Christians, indeed, but also literate and useful. These were potent concepts on the frontier of civilisation, but the work did not prove easy: war from time to time even forced evacuation. The future only became secure when in 1841 Lovedale was able to set up a native seminary and start producing its own missionary personnel. Its first African minister, Tiyo Soga, went to finish his education in Glasgow and to be ordained by the United Presbyterian Church; later he married a Scotswoman and returned to South Africa, where he died in 1871. Lovedale had meanwhile strengthened itself by adherence after 1843 to the Free Church.[5]

The change of ownership underlined, though, Lovedale's exceptional nature. It was actually just easier for Scots to go through the London Missionary Society, to which they made a great contribution: of 1800 missionaries it would send out during the next 150 years, nearly 300 came from Scotland. Vanderkemp had been one of its pioneers. His entry into the ministry of the Kirk indicated no wish to seek a charge in Scotland, but was simply the quickest way for him to witness in South Africa. After the British captured Cape Town in 1795, the society saw the chance to establish a foothold and urgently sought the personnel to do so. Vanderkemp heard about that in Holland and came over to offer himself. With his evangelical faith and Dutch tongue, he exactly fitted the bill, needing otherwise only formal ordination. As for the Church of Scotland, it felt happy to oblige a man already familiar with it and commended by some of its leading lights in Edinburgh.

Vanderkemp would go on to inaugurate not just one sort of mission but two. He arrived at the Cape in 1798 to be placed in the parish of Graaff-Reinet, about 300 miles away in the interior. His advent, toiling across the veld in an ox-cart, improbably set off a refreshment of the Genevan heritage common to Scottish Presbyterianism and to the Dutch Reformed Church in South Africa. That Church suffered from the country's mixed fortunes in war. Holland, after reoccupying it under the Treaty of Amiens, held it for only three years. In 1806, David Baird, the Scots hero of Seringapatam, retook it. Under military rule, no decision about the political future, or about much else, was made. By the time Britain decided to hang on to the colony and received its formal cession in 1815, the neglected Church lay at a low ebb, with a mere seven isolated congregations.

But now that the sovereignty was settled, the new owners felt eager to sustain the established religion. They needed Calvinist ministers, and Scotland was the nearest place to find them. Two sponsored by the London Missionary Society, the Revs George Thom and John Taylor, were placed in Afrikaner parishes in 1818. Three years later, Thom went home to find more among his fellow Evangelicals, as well as schoolmasters. The authorities hoped to use them to anglicise the Boers; in fact they all went to Holland to learn the language before taking up their posts. As a result of this recruitment, 18 of the 25 ministers were Scots when the Church reached the position of being able to form a South African synod in 1824. At the clerical level, a Dutch Church had been transformed into a Scottish one. The ministers marked it with traits they brought from home, with evangelical fervour, with some degree of puritan intolerance and with a taste for theological disputation: the Church would even suffer its own disruption, between liberals and orthodox, in 1862.[6]

Yet Vanderkemp himself, despite his nationality, had had little time for his Boer parishioners. Rather, to their anger, he ministered to the blacks. They struck this good-hearted man as the truer objects of his compassion: the Hottentots especially were an exploited people, robbed of their land and pride, even of the right to choose where, when and for whom they worked. He tried in vain to persuade Francis Dundas to guarantee them equality with the whites, to set aside land for their use and free them from forced labour. He did at least get possession of Botha's Place, as his society's first official station in Africa. When, too late to save it, officials from Holland reappeared at the Cape early in 1803, he persuaded them to grant him a new site. Here, at Bethelsdorp, this ever more otherworldly figure stayed for the rest of his life, steadily going native. He married Sarah, a Malagasy he redeemed from slavery. He shambled round shirtless and barefoot. He housed his people in rickety huts and let them lounge about all day. He apparently meant to train their minds first, but found he could never teach them anything useful, till finally forced to admit that he had 'started at the wrong end'. Meanwhile he went on regardless even when the authorities called him in to Cape Town to explain himself. The London Missionary Society could not have been well-informed when in 1811 it asked him to be superintendent of the eight stations it now had in South Africa. He died before any arrangement was confirmed.

The society decided that, for this missionary field of such pregnant importance, it must have a superintendent all the same. The post was to be manned by a line of Scots, of whom Vanderkemp may at a pinch be counted the first. The next was John Campbell, a son of Edinburgh from good merchant stock, a contemporary of Walter Scott at the High School, then a goldsmith's apprentice. But a religious conversion made him abandon commerce for the dissenting ministry. He went about with the Haldanes, and helped to found the Religious Tract Society of Scotland. His good works included voluntary support of missions, which was why the society called on him. It did not require him to stay in South Africa. Rather his duties took the form of two extended journeys, in 1812–4 and in 1818–21. He travelled far into the interior, across the Orange River and up to the Kalahari Desert, collecting information on peoples about whom next to nothing was known.

In several subsequent books he showed himself a keen, intelligent observer. He disapproved of the white settlers, who 'ought to be considered savages by the Africans'. Yet he took no romantic view of the blacks. He was much more concerned to find out, as a prelude to the work of conversion, what they actually believed. Though it did not add up to much, he took pains to record it accurately. One chieftain replied to his questioning 'that they knew nothing of God, but when they saw waggons, and the things in them, and the tents, etc., they thought that the men who could make such things must be a kind of gods, but now that we had told them otherwise, they knew we were men like themselves'. Asked then if he knew he had a soul, 'he said he did not, nor did he know any difference between men and beasts; but that they had always known there was a God, and that he was near them, and killed them; but they never knew why he was angry'.[7]

On the second visit Campbell took along John Philip, who would contribute not just to missions but to the whole of South African society. Born in a weaver's cottage at Kirkcaldy in 1775, he was destined for his father's trade till he too found a vocation as a dissenting minister. After training, he was called to a church in Aberdeen in 1804. He interested himself in the London Missionary Society as well. At length he decided to continue his career in its service. It was at the society's request that he went out with Campbell, who would introduce him to South Africa then leave him as resident superintendent. He succeeded admirably in setting the struggling missions on their feet at last. By reorganising the workers, paying them better, giving them and their families greater personal security, as well as attracting new recruits, he was able to expand the network to 26 stations. These he kept up to scratch by monitoring them himself; he would spend months at a time touring them by ox-cart. On his journeys he also got to know the indigenous peoples, probably better than any other white man of the time.[8]

He became a pioneer not only in a physical but also in an intellectual sense. He fathered the tradition among Scots working in Africa of giving their moral sanction to defence of the indigenous peoples. In him, the tradition drew as much on the philosophy as on the religion of Scotland. He himself was an evangelical Christian of radical political commitment, a man of the nineteenth rather than the eighteenth century; indeed he had a thoroughly modern feel for public relations. Yet the record of his labours, *Researches in South Africa* (1828), deserves to be considered a work of the Enlightenment, and reminds us how deeply the thinking of its great minds had permeated the broader strata of literate Scots. As he wrote, 'The aggregate of the virtue or vice, happiness or misery, in a nation is not to be established by the habits, sentiments and pursuits of a few literary or scientific men, but by the features distinguishable in the great mass of society'.

The book started out from Lord Kames's condemnation of slavery and went on with citations from David Hume and Adam Smith. Philips' basic premiss was this, that 'so far as my observation extends, it appears to me that the natural capacity of the African is nothing inferior to that of the European'. The tyranny of one over the other could thus only store up perils. For instance, legal tolerance at the Cape of forced labour subjected the blacks to humiliation and suffering which offered no cure for savagery: 'The vices of the Hottentots are the vices of their condition; and they are generated and perpetuated by the very system which is pleaded as necessary for their cure'. It was anyway unworthy of the Crown to permit discrimination against peoples in its care: 'If the British government would contribute effectually to the prosperity of South Africa, let them at last do justice to the aborigines of the country, by imparting to them liberal institutions, and just and equal laws'. Special measures were not needed: 'We simply ask that the colonists, and the different classes of the natives, should have the same civil rights granted to them'. Then they would soon acquire what a Scot thought the marks of civilisation – property and personal respectability – as the answer to those who deemed them inferior.

Philip naturally believed the missionaries, the only whites prepared to defend Africans, had a vital part to play. It went beyond humanitarianism, however. Critics often pointed out how missions attracted idle blacks who would have been better put to work on European farms, but in riposte Philip contrasted the Cape with India under the orientalist regime. There the natives owned the land, while Europeans were by and large barred from doing so. In South Africa the reverse held true. Since the blacks formed and must form a large part of the population, their systematic abasement depressed the industry and morals of the whole colony. There had to be a radical change of attitude, an acceptance that they might acquire and hold property on equal terms, then set about constructing a virtuous, productive society.[9]

Still, Philip's book cleverly played on feelings other than tender ones by stressing the political utility of its arguments: 'While our missionaries, beyond the borders of the colony of the Cape of Good Hope, are everywhere scattering the seeds of civilisation, social order and happiness, they are, by the most unexceptionable means, extending British interests, British influence and the British empire'. This was no imperialist tract, however. On the contrary, it set out a classic case for the Scottish Empire, one respecting indigenous culture and rights because not reliant on territorial occupation and settlement. It opposed schemes of immigration, the promoters of which, it said, 'wish to see these countries we are now evangelising emptied of their inhabitants and in the possession of white men'. Instead Philip called for settlers to be confined within the colony's existing bounds, and only missionaries to be allowed across them. Like the Canadian traders or Australian squatters, they would dot the wilds with outposts but leave the land's essential character intact. Here in small compass, but with expert detail and penetrating analysis, lay an imperial credo for a complex emerging society.[10]

Philips's strong mind and manner were enough even in remote Cape Town to attract an enlightened circle round him. It was not large but in its way it mirrored, say, the earlier Enlightenment of Calcutta or of American outposts of civilisation. At the Cape, too, Scots stood in the forefront. One was Philip's son-in-law, John Fairbairn, a journalist from Berwickshire. Another was Thomas Pringle, an engaging young man who had worked in the Scottish Record Office and contributed to *Blackwood's Edinburgh Magazine*, where he won Scott's favourable notice. He arrived under one of the schemes of emigration now being sponsored by the British Government with assisted passages. In 1819–20 three groups arrived in South Africa from Scotland. For Pringle this was an opportunity 'to collect again into one social circle, and establish in rural independence, my father's family, which untoward circumstances had broken up and begun to scatter over the world'. They were so kind-hearted, however, that uncomfortably large numbers of natives, uprooted by war, gathered round them in hope of protection and work. This strained their tight resources, and their venture soon failed.[11]

Pringle now had to find fresh means of supporting himself. As he was lame, it did not prove easy in a rough country. He set up house in Cape Town and was put in charge of the public library. There he got to know Philip and Fairbairn, whose intellectual interests he shared. But they all ran foul of the autocratic governor, Lord Charles Somerset, or Muckle Sumph, as they called him. He highly disapproved when Pringle and Fairbairn started to publish a liberal newspaper in English and Dutch, because the spread of modish opinions among the unreliable Boers might be dangerous. When they tried to launch a magazine as well, the governor first censored, then suppressed it. As soon as they sought to set up a Literary and Scientific Society, Somerset declared it illegal. There he went too far, though, and prompted a ruling from London in 1828 that the Cape must enjoy freedom of the press. Having established a progressive reputation, Pringle then returned to Britain to head the Anti-Slavery Society. He was himself a man of gentle idealism: 'Let us subdue savage Africa by justice, by kindness, by the talisman of Christian truth,' he begged. Yet with half his mind he had a more rugged vision of the way for a true Scot to live, shared with his mentor at Abbotsford. Thither he now wrote: 'I consider myself a sort of Cape patriarch in my way – having still a flock of big-tailed sheep and some thousand acres of rock and forest belonging to me there'. The Caledonian antisyzygy emerged again in the volume of poetry, *African Sketches*, which he brought out just before his death in 1834. It paid lip-service to the prospect of converting and civilising the blacks, yet could not conceal a delight in their fierce customs. Perhaps the fighting tradition in his native Borders, or some of Scott's fellow feeling for Highland cattle-raiders, made Pringle identify with the Xhosa. He has been called the father of South African poetry, but its spirit belonged just as much to Scotland.[12]

Fairbairn stayed on in Cape Town. He made journalism a central part of intellectual life there, just as it was in Edinburgh. He used it to promote causes dear to Scots and so attracted more enlightened men to his circle, including Afrikaners. In 1827, Presbyterianism was officially constituted in South Africa with the arrival of the Rev James Adamson as minister of St Andrew's church, Cape Town. It built up a congregation not only of white settlers but also of coloured people and of former slaves, for it took on all the Kirk's duties, relief of the poor, medical advice, biblical instruction and above all education. Adamson befriended the Rev Abraham Faure, a son of the colony who had returned after being trained by Bogue in England. The pair agreed that young Boers, especially those destined for the Church, needed a broad intellectual background, not just theological book-learning. They organised enough support to found, within a couple of years, the South African College, later the University of Cape Town.

They also joined Philip and Fairbairn in campaigning for rational reform of the colony's rudimentary but chaotic system of schooling: when a new one got going in 1839, it neatly offered bilingual instruction in Dutch or English at 12 primary and 12 secondary schools. The old system had been largely voluntary, though the Government provided a few free schools, and a sluggish quango to preside over them all. Fairbairn had this transformed into an official department, to include a professional superintendent of teaching. For that post the best candidate turned out, needless to say, to be another Scotsman. James Rose Innes, born in Banffshire, educated in Aberdeen, had been one of the schoolmasters recruited by Thom. Posted to the veld, he refused to teach, as he was told, only in English: he used Dutch as well, besides becoming a deacon of the Dutch Reformed Church. In 1830 he had been promoted professor of mathematics at the South African College and in his turn joined the enlightened circle of his compatriots in the capital. Now promoted again, as an educationist rather than a politician or civil servant, he ran the Cape's schools under a structure which in that sense was more completely professional than any in Europe or America.

Altogether, the Enlightenment here partook, for all its modesty, of the character of its Scottish counterpart in the later stages, with literature submitting to the judgment of journalism, with social science taking a practical, above all educational, turn and with religion resurgent over scepticism. This Enlightenment drew its local character from its strong political commitments, something owed in part to an earlier generation of Afrikaners, to Willem Boers and Adriaan van Jaarsveld who had quoted Hugo Grotius and John Locke to assert rights against the Dutch East India Company. Philip, in the unfolding of a long career, revealed not only a powerful personality and intellect but also the skills of a formidable reformer. Like many just men, he was tough, touchy and tactless. So he made enemies. One was Somerset, who had no other idea than to run the Cape under strict discipline, with the blacks as a reservoir of exploitable labour in a state little better than slavery. Still, for three years after Philip arrived his relations with the governor remained cordial enough. By then the missions had more personnel in the country than its administration had, and Somerset appreciated the services rendered in promoting good order and keeping him well-informed. Disagreement started when he rejected Philip's request for missionaries to be allowed beyond the boundaries of the colony. He would not have them working free of official control, suspecting that their aims would turn out incompatible with his. How right he was may be gauged from the issue over which relations broke down in 1821, concerning an abuse of natives by local authorities. Philip secured an official investigation, but it found there was no case to answer. So he pursued his own inquiries and came to the opposite conclusion. The governor refused to act.[13]

With no further recourse in South Africa, Philip outflanked him by turning to the powerful evangelical network in Britain, now well-versed in arousing public opinion. As a result the House of Commons appointed a committee of inquiry in 1823 to visit the Cape and look into the conduct of the administration, with particular reference to conditions of work for the blacks. Philip himself went to London in 1825 to press his views on the Colonial Office. He took the opportunity to meet sympathetic parliamentarians such as Charles Grant the younger and Sir James Mackintosh. At a time of growing concern about the state of the colonies, he ensured that there would remain, after his return to the Cape, a permanent lobby favourable to his inter-pretation of its interests. In the event, Somerset preferred to resign in 1826 rather than face a report from the committee which seemed sure to damn him. Then in 1828 the Commons passed a resolution that the indigenous peoples at the Cape should enjoy the same rights as white settlers. Such pressure the colonial administration could not ignore.

The result was the first humanitarian measure promulgated in British Africa, the 50th Ordinance. It had the purpose of 'improving the conditions of the Hottentots and the other free persons of colour', and specifically forbidding forced labour. Philip could not yet bring himself to trust the authorities in Cape Town and made sure the provisions were reinforced by an Order-in-Council from London to prevent bureau-cratic evasion on the spot. But in fact a great change was taking place, and public policy became officially humanitarian. Philip had the satisfaction of seeing further measures. The Master and Servant Law (1842) removed in the system of justice all discrimination between blacks and whites. Even the franchise was given to coloureds, thought at first not to negroes. On the constitution of the Province of the Cape of Good Hope with responsible government in 1853, however, the electoral roll turned colour-blind, in that Africans could qualify for it on the same terms as everybody else. Philip was by then dead, but Fairbairn played a large part in winning support among whites for this, arguing that it would prompt the blacks to educate and improve themselves, promote racial harmony and in time bring an integrated society. It was the triumph of what became known as the Cape policy, which lasted till the imposition of apartheid.

The policy was also encouraged from home, during one of the few periods which found the Colonial Office in Scottish hands. Lord Aberdeen held it in the Conservative Government of 1834–5, when unpacified tribes invaded the eastern Cape. Their repulse, he instructed, was to be tempered 'by all those considerations of humanity which it becomes the servants of a civilised nation to bear in mind in avenging the assaults of ignorant savages'. He was followed in a Whig Ministry by Grant, now Lord Glenelg. He believed the Africans had been provoked to violence by the encroachments of European settlers. He contrasted the conduct of missions, which harboured no thoughts of aggrandisement and had proved peaceful coexistence perfectly possible. He pointedly added that 'in our relations with those tribes, it yet remains to try the efficacy of a systematic and persevering adherence to justice, conciliation, forbearance and the honest arts by which civilisation may be advanced, and Christianity diffused among them'. He ordered the colonists, to their fury, to hand back all the land east of the Fish River seized from the Africans.[14]

That in itself indicated how the change wrought by Philip in official attitudes yet had unforeseen and to him unwelcome results. Among them was the acceleration of European advance into the interior, notably by the Great Trek of the Boers. They wanted, among other things, to escape laws against ill-treatment of blacks. They had good reason to see a foe in Philip, though he was not as hard on them as others of his countrymen. He even preached in Dutch himself in order to meet their objection to the use of English as a language of instruction. He fully appreciated why they felt embattled against savagery, and angry or fearful at the thought of ever treating the indigenous peoples as equals. The way forward, he argued, was not repression but civilisation. The Boers well understood, however, that he would force them to mend their ways if he could not win that argument.

Philip was at any rate deeply troubled by the Great Trek. It generated chronic warfare as it confronted more distant native tribes, while the brief periods of peace only lured the Boers onwards. He would follow them on a journey of his own in 1841–2 to satisfy himself that they were not reinstituting slavery in their new homes. His persistent fears on this score made him an advocate of what he had previously opposed, the formal extension of British sovereignty. He encouraged African chiefs to enter into treaties with the Crown, by which the colonial administration would arbitrate in disputes over land. His real purpose, never fulfilled in the event, was to create for the different peoples inalienable reserves ringing the area of white settlement. But Fairbairn wrote to his father-in-law that, on the contrary, 'I feel convinced that there is a design for handing over the best part of the country between the Colony and Natal to the colonists, with the final destruction of the natives from sea to sea'. At the end of a further war in 1846–7 the British did annex more of the eastern Cape with the apparent intention of creating such a continuous tract. Philip died before the Government decided what exactly it wanted to do. In 1854 it relinquished the territory, mainly because of the expense of any other expedient, and recognised on it the independence of the Orange Free State. This left the indigenous people once again at the Boers' mercy.[15]

Loathing was the usual Scottish reaction to their incorrigible racialism. Yet we have seen how some Scots, through their willingness and ability to adapt to alien surroundings, managed to conceive a certain fellow feeling for the brave but misguided Afrikaners. It was already there by the time the Voortrekkers left Cape Colony when, rather to their surprise, several of their Scottish ministers and schoolmasters chose to share the hazards of a journey into the interior. So did some settlers: Alexander Biggar and his two sons, George and Robert, were to die fighting bravely against the Zulus in Natal. The choice, however, was not really so surprising. The ministers' reformed tradition, like the Dutch one, justified resistance to tyranny, even in petty colonial guise. These educated, capable and idealistic pastors obviously found in the embattled religion and culture of the Boers an allegiance worthier than any to an English aristocrat. They would help to preserve for posterity both the Church and the Afrikaans tongue.

They made their mark especially in the Orange Free State, run though it was by stern Boers. Two Scots clans, Frasers and Murrays, played a large part in its public life through the years of its independence and beyond. Both sprang from the company of Thom's recruits. The Rev Colin Fraser came from Ross to be a minister in the eastern Cape, where he sired nine children and sent the sons back to be educated in Scotland. The eldest, also Colin and also a minister, would serve five times as Moderator of the Dutch Reformed Church. At the age of 63, in the middle of the Boer War, he was put in a British concentration camp, probably because his daughter had married President Martinus Steyn. The second son, John, followed a political career himself. In 1880 he was elected to the *Volksraad* for the capital of the republic, Bloemfontein. He championed liberal reforms of both a moral and a practical kind, from temperance to the construction of railways. When his countryman, James Bryce, the imperial statesman, came on a visit, he declared this to be a model state. In foreign policy Fraser took a pro-British line, favouring links with the Cape rather than with the Transvaal. In 1896, by then chairman of the legislature, he stood against Steyn in the presidential election. As a Briton by blood, he had no chance in the tense atmosphere following the Jameson Raid. In 1900 he surrendered his city to Lord Roberts, but had 20 more years of public service ahead of him as leader of the moderate opposition in provincial politics.

Andrew Murray from Aberdeenshire also reproduced a clan of Dutch Scotsmen on African soil. He sent his sons, John, born in 1826, and Andrew, born in 1828, to school and university in Aberdeen, then to study at Utrecht, before they came back as ministers to South Africa. John was appointed in 1857 head of the Dutch Reformed Church's theological school, later the university of Stellenbosch, which he would lead for a quarter of a century. Andrew junior really turned into an Afrikaner after settling in the Orange Free State, and later condemned British aggression. Their Scottish combination of educational and evangelical endeavour informed their contributions to the development of Afrikanerdom. One was linguistic. Both wrote numbers of religious books and tracts in the vernacular, at a time when Boers were still reading their bible in High Dutch. They helped to render Afrikaans capable of elevated discourse, as a properly literary language. They also built into the Boers' religion a definition of piety essentially Scottish – stern morality, knowledge of scripture, simplicity of worship, strict observance – which would go to make up an integral part of Afrikaner nationalism.

Perhaps it was the source, too, of another tenet shared with Scottish evangelism, that faith could change reality. Andrew Murray lived till 1917, to become in John Buchan's words 'a great Pope among the devout Afrikanders'. He appeared in public almost for the last time at the consecration of a memorial in Pretoria to the women who had died for their country. The patriotic oratory proper to the occasion gave way at certain moments to the Boers' penchant, shared with the Scots, for open discord. A younger minister, D.F. Malan, paid tribute to the preceptor of his people but declared that to survive it must go further than Murray had ever counselled. What he meant became clear when in 1948 Malan, the first Nationalist Prime Minister of South Africa, introduced apartheid.[16]

CHAPTER TWELVE

'Commerce and Christianity': David Livingstone

'D r Livingstone, I presume.'
'Yes, that is my name.'
The most famous conversation of the century, on November 10, 1871, was so stilted as to have soon turned into an overworked gag in the music-halls. Certainly, to catch the popular imagination, no better set could have been designed than the meeting place under a mango-tree at Ujiji by Lake Tanganyika, amid a babbling crowd of Africans and Arabs. Striding onstage came the stylishly intrepid explorer, Henry Morton Stanley, dressed for the occasion in smart white flannels over shiny Wellington boots, topped off by a well-chalked solar topee with newly folded puggaree. Waiting in the spotlight stood the rugged old hero, David Livingstone, in his favourite consular cap, his workaday red woollen jersey and trousers of grey tweed, and his ill-fitting shoes. Their exchange seemed to symbolise the civility which Europeans held to mark themselves out even in the depths of the dark continent. The double act retired from the shade of the tree to the verandah of Livingstone's house and continued the strained dialogue, till Stanley recalled that he had some champagne with him. He gave a toast: 'Dr Livingstone, to your good health, sir'. The conversation flowed more easily after that, and they chatted late into the night. Livingstone still refrained from asking just why Stanley had arrived here out of the blue. 'It was not my business,' he later said, in another display of Victorian reticence little less remarkable than Stanley's greeting. Yet they could each hardly have been more atypical of the genteel norms in the western society from which they sprang: the gauche, gruff, though now – at 58 – somewhat mellowed Scots proletarian, always easier with black men than with his own race; and the wild Welsh orphan of uncertain identity, personal and national, so hard to love or trust. They were men from the margins, yet by that fact exemplars of a modern age with different conceptions of heroism from any celebrated in the past.

Livingstone was not born to his destiny, nor had he had it thrust upon him. On the contrary, he had climbed out from the submerged masses of industrial society, one of the first to prove capable of doing so, even though the fate he chose instead was no less hard than theirs. Stanley could have shown him how much easier it might have been. He, had Livingstone asked, would have had to admit that he came, champagne and all, as ace reporter of the *New York Herald*, paradigm of the yellow press, created by a failed Roman Catholic seminarist from Aberdeen, James Gordon Bennett, than which nothing was more redolent of modernity. If, while stuck at

Ujiji, the ageing pioneer had possessed the power to scan Africa from the centre to the western side, he would have seen a party expecting him to reappear there out of the jungle. It had been sent by his friend and brother Scot, Roderick Murchison, president of the Royal Geographical Society, ever ready to set science at the service of Empire. He surmised that Livingstone had meanwhile crossed the continent through unknown regions, and was eager to learn just what he had espied. Another compatriot, John Kirk, consul-general at Zanzibar and *éminence grise* of British imperialism on the eastern side, perhaps knew or guessed his true whereabouts. Having known him since their journey up the River Zambesi in 1858, but somewhat parted company from this 'ungrateful and slippery mortal', Kirk appeared in no hurry to save him now. Finally, an expedition under his son Oswell had recently passed through the Suez Canal on a mission to find him. The modern world was mobilised to rescue Livingstone. Stanley should have counted himself lucky to beat so many Scots and get to Ujiji first.

On this broader scene the forsaken, steadfast Livingstone comes to look more like a Livingstone in the van of imperialism. That was the Livingstone whom Britain would exalt after his death nearly 18 months later; it took place on April 30, 1873, at Ilala, in a district south of Lake Tanganyika where he had set off to search for the source of the River Nile on taking leave of Stanley. Another year after that his country, stirred to boot by the story of faithful black servants carrying his corpse hundreds of miles to the coast for transport home, gave him a funeral in Westminster Abbey. It struck a note of intense patriotic emotion not heard since Admiral Nelson was brought back from Trafalgar. It was also interesting that the English by now regarded him as one of their own. There seemed at the time no question but that he should be buried according to the rites of their Church, which he never adhered to. It had been a long road for the poor boy from Blantyre. or even for the young man, awkward and by his own admission rather simple, who landed at Cape Town in 1841. Between the canonised, legendary figure and the odd details of his sometimes almost pointless wanderings, the reality is hard to grasp.

But a start can be made with deconstruction of the mythology, ably performed in recent works by John Mackenzie. Thrilling tales of exploration had long been popular, yet Livingstone's did not generate themselves. His legend was consciously composed, by imperialists and particularly by missionaries, a novel combination which it had taken him to bring together from previously antagonistic positions. They wrote in hagiographical style, editing out the odder aspects of his angularity. The image they aimed to create, of a Protestant saint, would vindicate to their public the causes of the age: free trade, rule of law, abolition of slavery, defeat of barbarism, diffusion of Christianity, global distribution of the British stock, reconciliation of scientific and religious truth in progress practical and moral. In the end, therefore, this became not just a personal story but an epic of Britain's greatness and an apologia for her imperial state. The package was powerful, resistant to the ravages of time, adaptable even to the circumstances of a declining Empire. When people wanted to show there had been more than glory to British expansion, Livingstone was on hand again, having pioneered the civilisation of the dark continent and given power over it to whites only in trust for future generations of the indigenous peoples. He came at last to be seen as a father of African nationalism. He in any event remains the one imperial figure of the nineteenth century to be honoured in the independent Africa of today.

In the legends, all the same, his life was as exemplary as his work. From among the millions of the industrial working class, with none of an imperial idol's usual advantages of birth or schooling, he rose through self-improvement and sacrifice to abundant genius, not just functional but imbued with unmistakable moral grandeur. Beyond doubt it inspired many who shared his origins and faith, who could then assimilate imperialism into their popular culture. The example was equally comforting to Victorians higher in the social scale, who liked to see such ideals among the masses. Livingstone reassured the bourgeoisie that the proletariat might advance by means other than politics, rather by religion and respectability. He could thus be venerated among people of all stations in life.

Moreover, this marginal figure became a true citizen of the United Kingdom, so uplifted even the phlegmatic English that they found him a resting place in their national shrine. He served not only God but also the Queen, not only religion but also the Foreign Office and the Royal Geographical Society. Altogether, he affirmed an order both British and imperial, both liberal and hierarchical. Still, he was never lost to Scotland. He did not deny his Scottishness, rather played on it, as in returning in 1864 to visit his ancestral home on the island of Ulva off Mull. To Scots of the time, he was if anything living proof of the moral superiority they owed to their religion. This sentiment, too, proved resilient enough to flower in new forms amid more trying circumstances. Most Scots sensed, for example, that the First World War marked a turning point for them, though in what direction remained unclear. One symptom of uncertainty could be found in incipient nationalism, and a mark of that was the completion, after a start as long before as 1877, of the Livingstone National Memorial at Blantyre in 1929.

Mackenzie has shown, too, that biographies of this period made more and more of Livingstone's Scottishness. They came to portray him as the absolutely typical Scot, an amalgam of the nation's classic virtues, interested in and capable of every intellectual and practical task, undeterred by obstacles spiritual, conceptual or factual. He also reconciled, in a synthesis second only to Walter Scott's, the Highlander and the Lowlander, whose blood was mixed in his own veins. He demonstrated how the contrary qualities of each were yet complementary. From the North he had his impulsive generosity, his keen imagination, his burning passion, his chivalry and mysticism, from the South his dour determination, his sense of justice, his pragmatic self-reliance, his stern faith. To his own people his greatest appeal may, just like Scott's, have lain in a supposition that he could carry their old virtues forward into a new age. It would go once more to prove Scotland's protean ability to refashion herself against the odds in succeeding generations, the imperial being just one among many.

The same qualities were held to have aroused his sympathy for blacks, and theirs for him. A son of Scotland, he could readily appreciate their oral traditions, historical or didactic tales, respect for ancestors and heroic exploits. Sprung from a dispersed clan himself, he could as easily understand the bonds, the mutual obligations between them and their chiefs, that formed a durable community of the African tribe in its hostile environment. If he could not quite approve, he could at least make out the mixture of motives, partly political, partly economic and partly sportive, that channelled so much energy into the reiving of cattle, time-honoured among Scottish Borderers and Highlanders too, in the latter case till barely a century before his birth. Such insights escaped men who came to Africa simply as from civilisation to barbarism, especially if they happened to be stolid Englishmen as well. Livingstone was in sum both nationalist and internationalist, a figure of global importance by dint of his very Scottishness.[1]

So much for the legendary Livingstone. The legend looks threadbare now after a twentieth century which saw the Empire dissolve, the United Kingdom come under question and Scotland largely forsake, as useless for the modern world, her Calvinist values. What remains of Livingstone? We might for an answer start where he did, with his missionary activity. Here, if anywhere, is the place to seek the depth and coherence in his career so obvious to contemporaries but somehow lost from our view under the mythological accretions. Amid the deconstruction, it may be easy to miss his giant status in the history of missions, which he transformed. But he did so in a way that tended to obscure the nature of his contribution because it let that history be integrated into the general history of imperialism. For better understanding, we may recall that he was all the same no solitary giant. Two other men of stature merit mention as his forerunners.

One was John Philip, who gave him lodging in Cape Town for his first month in Africa. Even this brief encounter – such was the force of the older man's views – proved without doubt deeply formative of Livingstone's own. They already had fertile common ground between them, in their Calvinism. It came of that austere strain which had lived on through the Enlightenment among the Scots people, often as the religious dissent on which both were brought up. Since it instructed a man to expect little of the world, he could never be surprised at the corruption of humanity. By the same token, it excluded any concept of racial superiority or inferiority. Livingstone, like Philip, saw the degradation of Africa as different only in degree rather than in kind from that in other places. In this sense, God had created all men equal. That the godly were commanded to take such equality seriously Livingstone never doubted even in the privacy of his journal: 'I have no prejudice against their colour. Indeed anyone who lives long among them forgets they are black and feels they are just fellow men'. After Philip's death, Livingstone assumed the role of humanitarian advocate for indigenous peoples against aggression on the frontier. But the demands of practical evangelism took him beyond his mentor. If, during their talks in Cape Town, he accepted that civilisation and Christianity went together, that improvement in the natives' condition would prepare them for conversion, he sensed greater obstacles than the injustice done to them by colonists.[2]

That he could still absorb so much from Philip was singular, given that he arrived prejudiced against the man. The reason was the yet earlier influence on him of another missionary. He had met Robert Moffat in 1839, while still training with the London Missionary Society. Moffat, then home on furlough, had gone in 1816, aged just 21, to run its mission to the Bechuanas at Kuruman in the northern Cape. His work there won much praise at headquarters. Livingstone, too, was so impressed that, disappointed of a posting to China, he asked to be sent to Kuruman himself. Moffat agreed, having in his turn been taken with the youngster. So firm was their personal bond that in 1845 he would marry his daughter Mary to Livingstone. Moffat had on the other hand disliked Philip since meeting him on his inaugural tour of the Cape and disliked him even more as, energetic and domineering, he attained the status of a missionary leader consulted by civil authorities in South Africa and at home.

Moffat, shy and touchy but absolutely single-minded in his purpose of converting the heathen, felt appalled at Philip's suggestion that general compassion for suffering humanity could substitute in some sort for unsparing inquisitions into the state of individual souls. To Moffat nothing mattered but the fact or otherwise of faith, made manifest by submission to the inerrancy of scripture. So deeply did he deplore Philip's influence that during his furlough he wrote a book, *Missionary Labours and Scenes in Southern Africa* (1842), evidently conceived as a riposte to the *Researches in South Africa* and its argument for a broad approach to evangelism, including secular reforms. He countered with his own experience among the Bechuanas, a people so unspiritual that they assumed every mission was an agent of the colonial administration in Cape Town, thus to be dealt with politically; they could only be disabused of such notions if the missionaries' conduct and language showed an exclusive religious purpose and a complete indifference to worldly matters.[3]

His misunderstandings with the blacks were often simply the product of a rigid and unimaginative personality. Yet it gave him the advantage of Philip by shocking him at every turn with the difference in the way their minds worked, so that he knew there must be more to preparing them for conversion than enforcement in their favour of a scheme of abstract rights. Progressive laws on land and labour could do, whatever else, little for their spiritual state. For the darkness of their souls Moffat offered a ready explanation: the influence of Satan. The archfiend had worked in other times and places by implanting polytheism, but here 'he has employed his agency, with fatal success, in erasing away every vestige of religious impression from the minds of the Bechuanas, Hottentots and Bushmen'. Quite apart from Philip's political diversions, there would thus always remain a basic problem in putting across what the missionaries had come for. However much instruction the natives received, they never appeared to reflect on or even remember it, and answered questions with what they thought the missionary wanted to hear. Moffat used the Bechuana word Morimo for God, yet 'they could not describe who or what Morimo was, except something cunning or malicious; and some who had a purpose to serve, ascribed to him power, but it was such as a Bushman doctor or quack could grunt out of the bowels or afflicted part of the human body'. So he just could not tell whether they had any real concept of deity (a matter which would still be exercising his successors in the middle of the twentieth century).[4]

Moffat clearly had his missionary deficiencies too. Every tribute must be paid him for his pioneering endeavours, as the man who took Christianity north first of the Orange then of the Limpopo River, as explorer of the Kalahari Desert and recorder of native life, as linguist and translator. By any standards his is an honoured place in African history. Still it may be doubted if, at the end of 60 years' labour, he understood the blacks better than at the start. He was impervious to their culture, to the social function of such customs as polygamy or ceremonies of initiation, to a system of values which saw nothing much wrong with nudity, stealing, gluttony, witchcraft and so on. He conceived it as his business only to go about in disapproval of such things, to denounce and censure them till they stopped.[5]

This was the man whose mission Livingstone, after taking leave of Philip, came to join at Kuruman towards the end of 1841. Moffat was not yet back from furlough, but his presence proved unnecessary to show his apprentice too how far, even in a setting free of social barriers to evangelism, the indigenous people's leap to faith must all the same be. Livingstone realised that missionaries were not like the apostles, could expect no prompt acceptance by whole communities of their good news. In fact they could hardly expect to encounter the faintest inkling what was good or new about it.

But discovery of this spiritual void worked in him different reactions from Moffat's, whose simple, biblical faith excluded any notion of cultural relativism. Livingstone was not just open to the experience of Africa but enchanted by it. He found here the Lord's handiwork, rather than Satan's, in the very physical aspect of the continent. The people won his heart. He did sometimes follow Moffat and single them out as 'sunk into the very lowest state of mental and moral degradation'. Yet he seldom echoed his father-in-law's tone of incredulous horror at the everyday sights and sounds of Africa. He could view with detachment scenes, such as the mirth provoked by Christian religious rites, that only outraged Moffat. He thought worth recording as matter for reflection rather than reproof a native's words to him: 'To be plain with you, we should like you much better if you traded with us and then went away without forever boring us with preaching that word of God of yours'. Livingstone deplored such sentiments, of course, but saw them as human, not satanic. And he found African humanity responsive to a spirit of kindness and conciliation once it came from a white man. The undoubted spiritual deficiencies could not to that extent be irredeemable. Livingstone concluded, on the contrary, that in the native mind 'we can gather fragments which seem to point to a primitive faith and worship'.[6]

The novice thus soon identified defects in the method of southern Africa's two most expert missionaries. He agreed with Philip that blacks were equal, but accepted that they were also different; he agreed with Moffat how great the difference was, yet did not accept that it damned them. These insights let him look afresh at the obstacles which dismayed all those evangelists avid for quick results. The reason why their tidings met with no eager reception, or even understanding, might lie as much in them as in the souls they sought to save. He questioned especially the standard practice of establishing a missionary station in one place with the purpose of converting the natives around. Kuruman gave proof enough of the point, lying in semi-arid territory with a scattered population of 1000 or so supposedly awaiting conversion. There, in a privileged position because of his relation to the often absent Moffat, Livingstone could do much as he pleased. What pleased him was to get away and see authentic Africa. After visits to other stations, he set up independently in 1847 at Kolobeng, 270 miles to the north, among the Bakwena. He would stay four years, and win his first convert (also his last) in their chief, Sechele. This sojourn came to a close when the Boers waged war on the tribe, vindictively looting Livingstone's house during a raid. He abandoned it, thus making for himself an end of sedentary missions. No doubt his inborn restlessness reinforced his professional judgment, or rather, the excitement of exploring at least matched his Christian zeal. He anyway ceased to be a missionary of the conventional sort; resignation in 1857 from his society, for a position as roving consul in the employ of his Government, conceded as much. He had already, with a traverse of the continent, begun his great journeys. He devoted the rest of his life almost entirely to them.[7]

'The end of the geographical feat is but the beginning of the missionary enterprise,' Livingstone wrote. It is a statement that several biographers have found hard to take seriously, because he never again appeared to get beyond the beginning. He posed the same problem to his missionary brethren. They thought it bizarre of him to treat so lightly the preaching of the word, to busy himself rather with introducing civilised arts and sciences, sometimes scarcely that, as he pressed on into unknown regions and left behind people who had by no means fully accepted the gospel. It cut clear across the conventional view that evangelism must be the key to improving indigenous society, not the other way round.[8]

In Livingstone's practice it was certainly implicit that missions ought to accommodate themselves, within the limits of Christian ethics, to the realities of African society. There was no other way if, as he found, the blacks resisted conversion because they believed missionaries had the aim of 'reducing them and their much-loved domestic institutions'. As his knowledge of them grew, he saw more clearly the formidable depth of this mental block: it was not just a fortuitous matter of, say, the natives' perplexity at Moffat's difficult character. For example, many tribes, being only semi-sedentary, had no means to improve their condition because they just moved on after the resources of their abode became exhausted, to another where in the long run they were no better off. And, whether nomadic or not, they often maintained a hermetic existence, broken only by fighting with other tribes. The dark superstitions born of an insecurity which could never be stilled belonged not just to a state of the soul, but to a way of life. In other words, the Africans' spiritual deficiencies were bound up with their material ones. It was a connection that had escaped Moffat and in a crucial sense even Philip. Moffat would never have entertained the thought of a mere material bar to reception of the gospel. Philip underestimated, amid his efforts to break the material bar, what a spiritual gulf yet yawned beyond.

Put another way, Livingstone's view of missions rested on an understanding that development, spiritual or material, arises from complex interactions, not from such a simple chain of cause and effect as replacing heathenism by Christianity. Where had he got it? There was perhaps little in his own upbringing, of grinding toil in the mills of Blantyre relieved only by a dour religion, to dispose him to the ideas of enlightened Scotland. Yet we know that as a young man he avidly read such works of popular enlightenment as Thomas Dick's *Philosophy of a Future State*. His urge for self-improvement then took him to Anderson's College in Glasgow, an institution of popular enlightenment if ever there was one. In any event, we find him equipped to reason in the categories of conjectural history. 'Our own elevation,' he wrote, 'has been the work of centuries, and . . . we should not indulge in overwrought expectation as to the elevation, which those who have inherited the degradation of ages, may attain in our own day.' It was likewise of a piece with Scottish teachings to conclude that 'no permanent elevation of a people can be effected without commerce'. Above all, Livingstone discovered a vital link with his own vocation, and the error of conceiving it in narrowly evangelical terms: 'Wherever a missionary lives, traders are sure to come, and if they had European goods to exchange, they would not have to deal in slaves'.[9]

Here lay one thread to unravel the tangle of spiritual and material deficiencies. The slave trade was the greatest material evil in Africa. It caused untold suffering, and it kept the continent primitive. Since it was one of the few contacts that peoples in the interior had with the outside world, they could form little idea what civilisation was, and no aspirations towards it. The trade induced them rather to expend their energies in war. The aggressive and powerful preyed on the peaceable and weak, their accumulation of riches being unredeemed by any notion of charity. This destructive cycle was thus a spiritual evil too. It stopped Africans seeing themselves as members of one human family. Since, on the contrary, it treated them as commodities, it suppressed every sense of their worth as individuals in need of salvation. If, however, they could start to work towards the kind of commercial society which the Scots had posited, they would forge different relations with one another: 'Commerce has the effect of speedily letting the tribes see their mutual dependence. It breaks up the sullen isolations of heathenism'. It might even launch them towards the greater, universalist goal of the Scottish Enlightenment: 'My observations on this subject make me extremely desirous to promote a preparation of the raw materials of European manufactures in Africa for by that means we may . . . introduce the negro family into the body corporate of nations'.[10]

Like Principal Robertson, who had a programme with the same purpose for India, Livingstone believed that British influence, properly used, could hurry a backward society through its necessary development. So, even more, could the Christian religion, a point on which he was fully at one with the Evangelicals in the Church of Scotland. He also agreed with their critique of the Enlightenment's cultural caution: 'I consider that we made a great mistake, when we carried commerce into India, in being ashamed of our Christianity'. When he returned home in 1856, therefore, he put a more arduous imperial task to his country, of spreading its faith as well as its power. And he found it, now as much evangelist as expansionist in spirit, ready to respond. Indeed, it proved never more receptive than to him as he lobbied the great and good while generating on national tours the first wave of popular missionary fervour. He spoke thousands of words geared to particular audiences. But if we sum up in Scottish terms what he had to say, he placed a Christian gloss on the teaching that individual pursuit of enlightened self-interest could have an unintended altruistic effect. At the Senate House in Cambridge, he hit on a formulation of it so instantly grasped as to become a byword overnight: 'I go back to make an open path for commerce and Christianity'. It can stand as the rubric of a new Christian Empire, with a greater moral purpose and a broader British appeal than any framed in the old commercial Empire of the Scots.

This was thus a crux not only for British imperialism, but for the Scottish Empire too. It had largely contented itself with trade, with exchanges among distant countries involving no dislocation on one side or the other, except insofar as trade caused all of them to advance; in each the laws of development were yet subject to particular moral and environmental influences, which exacted respect. It had been Philip who first adapted these concepts to a missionary purpose. He had the idea of stations scattered across territory still occupied by peoples continuing their organic development, though he reached, in the peculiar circumstances of South Africa, the final position that only imperial sovereignty could safeguard the network. That was, however, impractical on any more general level. Governments of the time thought it an absurd notion that they should hold sway over lands empty or peopled by savages. How, then, could missions raise those blacks beyond the bounds of civilisation, the ones in most need of it?

An answer needed to identify what was fundamental to Africa that impeded its assimilation into the great narrative of humanity. Here again conjectural history helped, since it predicated for each phase of development a certain social super-structure. Robertson's analysis of India, for example, drew comfort from the long existence there of civilised, though in his century corrupted, political authority which was, if native, amenable to control and, if British, capable of reform. But in the

African interior the only political authority showed just another face of savagery. Resting on the tribal structure, sustained by the economy of raiding and slaving, it generated the collective allegiances, loyalty to chieftains, heroic values, cults of ancestors and so on, which closed the blacks' minds to enlightened self-interest, let alone to Christian truth. It would all have to change, and nobody but Livingstone, who knew and in his heart even loved it, realised how far it would have to change.

He had decided that missionary stations could not themselves effect the change. He was working towards the idea that outposts of western civilisation could. It was not an easy idea to formulate. Up to the mid-1850s, he seemed to assume that European traders would come into the interior, cut out the slavers and start to dilute tribalism, which accompanying missionaries would finish off. He gave no thought to the co-ordination of all this: it was no doubt to be the work of philanthropic businessmen with time and capital enough. But his triumphant tour of Britain, assuring him of popular support, political backing and, not least, money, opened up a more dramatic chance of forcing the pace. It also brought to the forefront of his mind an idea which had so far lain only at the back of it, to settle 'Christian families' in Africa as the catalyst. With such notions, he soon appeared carried away towards high imperialism: it was now Britain's calling 'to plant her Christianity with her sons on the broad earth which the Lord has given to the children of men'. He even wrote of a 'superior race' with a divine vocation 'to elevate the more degraded portions of the human family'.[11]

Yet we should take care to distinguish his programme from that of systematic territorial occupation by emigrants, adopted or soon to be adopted among high imperialists as a conscious policy in every suitable region of the world. Livingstone did not want to displace the blacks. He foresaw instead European enclaves to take the lead in economic and social improvement without exercising more than a moral domination of their hinterland. If the indigenous peoples were not to be asked whether they welcomed the encroachment, they would at least be treated with respect and consideration. Above all there was to be no racialism. Livingstone viewed with equanimity the prospect, in the settlers' train, of 'a fusion or mixture of the black and white races in this continent'. His programme stood somewhere between that of his forerunner, Philip, and that of his successors. He was a precursor of high imperialism, rather than the real thing.[12]

At Cambridge, he had told his audience that he would leave these greater tasks to people like themselves while he, the pioneer errant, disappeared again into the wilderness, forging paths through it to find places for outposts. So great, however, was his impact that his countrymen looked to him for leadership of the civilising enterprise which ensued. The Government gave him £5000 to spend as he wished. He used it for an expedition to follow the course of the Zambesi from its mouth in Mozambique. He had during earlier travels on its upper reaches identified it as God's highway into Central Africa. Its huge basin seemed to offer every prospect of healthy areas for missions, fertile lands for agriculture, markets for British goods, colonies of settlers living peacefully with their black brethren. He suffered a shattering blow when in December 1858 the expedition found the river to be unnavigable, blocked by a fearsome gorge at Cabora Bassa. Though in reporting back he tried to pretend otherwise, it spoke volumes that he himself turned aside into the tributary River Shire. At its sources he did discover the highlands bordering Lake Nyasa which he seized on as his promised land: 'I think 20 or 30 good Christian Scotch families with their minister and elders would produce an impression in ten years that would rejoice the hearts of all lovers of our race'. But even to imperial enthusiasts the notion looked premature.[13]

What Livingstone then fell back on was nothing other than a project for a sedentary mission of the kind he had himself long rejected. Yet he had no choice, if he was to take at the flood the tide of British missionary enthusiasm. Out of it, and out of the meeting at the Senate House in particular, had sprung the Universities' Mission to Central Africa. It called forth such a response from the young, muscular Christians of Oxford and Cambridge that in a couple of years it felt ready to found a station. Not for the first or last time inconsistent, Livingstone persuaded himself that this would be the very thing to spark off the civilising process. He even offered to guide the expedition himself. He thus clinched the organisers' decision to send it out in 1861, but they had not reckoned with his eternal yen to make away into the bush alone. He did so as soon as he discovered a suitable spot for the nine pioneers to settle, at Magomero near Lake Nyasa.

He left in charge another Scot, Charles Mackenzie, who had graduated brilliantly at Cambridge, taken Anglican orders and served in Natal, before being now consecrated the Church of England's first missionary bishop. He was 35 years old, tall, balding, genial, but quite lacking in foresight or common sense, and possessed of a bottomless capacity to offend the blacks. Apart from that, the selected spot proved wholly unsuitable. The district around was being overrun by a fierce tribe, the Yao, who ruthlessly massacred and enslaved the indigenous Manganja. Mackenzie felt so outraged at their sufferings that he girded his own loins to strike back at the invaders, on a memorable occasion striding towards them with a crozier in his left hand and a rifle in his right. He freed prisoners and gave them a safe haven, aiming to form them into the nucleus of a Christian community; his congregation sought him, as Livingstone remarked, rather than the other way about. But Mackenzie then stumbled on one of the greatest missionary problems: how to look after detribalised Africans amid a tribal society. In peace the job would have been hard enough. In a setting of chronic combat, meagre supplies and tenuous communications it proved impossible. In fact, he could give his charges no permanent security, hardly even a bare livelihood, while the local peoples treated him as just another warlord. His conduct actually doomed the mission. In 1862, he sickened and died. His fellow missionaries bolted.[14]

Livingstone, if indifferent to the practical running of the station, had still carried high hopes of its method of applying intense commitment to a crucial spot. Now he had proof that this would not suffice either to diffuse commerce and Christianity among tribes with no concept of them. He had squandered his missionary capital. Worse, he left for himself, after all his toil and hardship, no other obvious way forward. He made one more trip home, his last, to recuperate in 1864–5. Then he launched himself into the final stage of his career. This created the real riddle about an always opaque character, since its missionary content was at best nominal. Forgetting the Shire Highlands, Livingstone spent the decade to his death in obsessive searches for, among other things, the sources of the Nile, while American newspapers made money out of him. It might be best read as a defiantly Scottish reaction to failure. It revealed an old man daring beyond all reason, ruthless in his disregard of others' interests or reputations, driven against the odds by a self-centred ambition to open up Africa and to be the first in every region he explored. Perhaps he just wanted to make sure of being remembered for something. Even on these subjective criteria, however, the achievement remained less than impressive. At the end he still had to his credit only one real discovery, of Lake Bangweulu, to match the one convert of an earlier stage in his career. And he was losing friends, or making enemies, too fast to go on. Dramatic images evoked by Stanley and others cloaked that truth, while Livingstone brought enough aplomb to his role to avoid facing it. But with a life's work crowned by this, his canonisation was more than he might have expected.

Of course, the canonisation ensured, and was meant to ensure, that his work continued beyond the grave, if now in ways defined by his disciples. Soon missionaries were back along Lake Nyasa, to start a sustained Scottish evangelical effort which goes on even yet. By the turn of the century the British did control Central Africa. Whether Livingstone would have approved of the kind of political authority they exercised there is best left in the realms of conjecture, because he did not foresee and could not have foreseen it. At any rate, it was never to the taste of his missionary epigones. The point illustrates how modern views of him are distorted through the prism of the high imperialism which divides his era from ours. High imperialism created the legend, yet Livingstone acted on the beliefs of a pre-imperialist, or at least proto-imperialist, age. By looking backwards from him, rather than backwards to him, we may better define his place in history. That may also show us how Scottish he was, though Scottish in a spirit different from the legendary one: in many respects an old Scot, from the times when Scotland still lived for herself, with her own intellect and values, before she took up those British and imperial ideals which, for good or ill, she came to regard as superior.

Mackenzie's revisionist work also touches on this. He depicts Livingstone as representing, defining and disseminating the independent Scottish social ethos, that expounded by George Davie, in relation to the Empire, to England and to his own country. Yet the ethos was not static. Davie himself stresses that Scotland cannot live in the past, but to survive must constantly remake herself, carrying forward what she can but discarding what she cannot, a choice which circumstance usually imposes on her. Livingstone, a man of the nineteenth century and of its religious revival, saw the Scot as particularly called to impart his Christianity to the world. The commerce was vital, and bound up with Christianity. But global commerce existed already. The task was to supplement it with Christianity. In the process, some commercial assumptions had to be cast off; for instance, that it was unnecessary to take more than a scientific, as opposed to a moral, interest in the societies with which trade went on, that it sufficed to meet them sympathetically rather than change or rule them.[15]

So Livingstone was in other respects a new Scot. On his analysis, a satisfactory commerce could not be constructed unless Africa was converted. Africa had to be changed and if Africa had to be ruled too – then, perhaps he would have conceded, so be it. Here we see the Scottish ethos not standing as a fixed point in the stream of history, but advancing and adapting, as must any ethos with life in it. But we may also see a reason why it was at length fragmented and enfeebled. If in Livingstone it still evolved in line with its antecedents, it also moved towards union with a different ethos. A mission on his ambitious scale could scarcely be fulfilled within the bounds imposed by nature on a small nation. In a material sense, it had since 1707 broken those bounds through access to an international commercial system, a process not entailing any obvious sacrifice of Scottishness. Livingstone broke those bounds in a spiritual sense too. He consummated a moral purpose for the nation. Yet when he wanted to find a name for it, he most often called it not Scotland but England. Doubtless he never meant the term literally, since England was already, at home and abroad, among Scots too, common shorthand for the British Empire. But the implication stood out clearly. In fulfilling her moral purpose, Scotland was to be transcended by something greater than herself.

CHAPTER THIRTEEN

'The voice of Scotland': Central Africa

O n February 20, 1879, at Blantyre, the missionary station in the Shire Highlands not far from Lake Nyasa, named by the Church of Scotland after David
Livingstone's birthplace, an African was led blindfolded and pinioned to the edge of a
grave dug for him. With him came the Rev Duff Macdonald, for the last 18 months
head of the station, where he had been called from his chilly northern charge of
Pulteneytown at Wick. The minister told the condemned prisoner he was about to
be shot, not from any feeling of vindictiveness but because the white man's God
ordained that killers should themselves be killed. The wretch had been convicted, on
flimsy evidence, of a woman's murder. Even now he protested his innocence. A
contemporary report of the ensuing scene was composed from the evidence of eye-
witnesses:

> Eight natives were then told off to perform the duty of executioners, and ranged
> in line at twelve paces. At the word of command the volley was fired and when
> the smoke cleared the poor fellow appeared to have received the shots in every
> part of his body but the vital spot, as he still stood upright but quivering in
> agony. There he stood while the guns were again loaded, and some firing again
> one of the shots went clean through his right lung, and yet he stood there
> bleeding and maimed, a sight too sickening for the whites, one of whom,
> stepping forward, pulled him back by the head into the grave. Further
> description would disgust, but the man did not die until one of the chiefs of a
> neighbouring village ended the tragedy by taking the breech-loading rifle of Mr
> Robert Henderson, an engineer of the Livingstonia Trading Company, who was
> standing by, and stepping up to the writhing form in the grave blew the man's
> brains out, at the muzzle of his gun.[1]

Such was one aspect of Scottish missionary activity only six years after the death of
Livingstone, proof how hard it might be to practise what he preached. The novices to
Africa following in his footsteps could have been forgiven for ignorance of the
conditions they met there. But at least those who sent them out might have sought
evidence in the recruits of desirable qualities other than piety: for example, some
elementary sense of justice. As things stood, their authority over the blacks seemed to
be descending into culpable mismanagement and gratuitous cruelty. Henderson,
thoroughly ashamed, blamed it on Macdonald: 'I always thought him soft, and that
he hid his softness by sticking through thick and thin to whatever he had once agreed

to'. He showed himself at the least temperamentally ill-suited for his responsibilities. His talents were not executive but pastoral and literary; he would publish on his return to Scotland a rather charming collection of *Africana*. What on earth, then, was he doing dealing death in the jungle?

Blantyre was a direct result of the wave of evangelical fervour unleashed in Scotland by Livingstone's obsequies. In order to continue his work and launch missions into the regions he had explored, the Church of Scotland and the Free Church, divided on all else since the Disruption of 1843, even agreed to some wary co-operation. By their nature, these projects were hasty. They took slight heed of the practical problems involved in bringing civilisation to a country which lacked the social structure to support it; on this the departed hero had left them little guidance either. As usual, the Free Church was to the fore, awakening in its members enthusiasm sufficient to overcome at least the initial difficulties. Its expedition arrived in the Shire Highlands and founded the station of Livingstonia in 1875. Not till the next year did the Kirk follow at Blantyre, and then with just a party of laymen, since no minister could be found to accompany them. It was in effect a tiny Scottish colony, and survived mainly on help from its sister mission. Later Macdonald came, but this did not greatly improve matters. He brought with him no material aid and only vague instructions from his Foreign Missions Committee, evidently as clueless as himself. He was, for instance, expected to stop the slave trade, yet given no means to do so. Because the district lay exposed to it, Blantyre soon attracted fugitives, enough to people seven villages nearby. Looking for protection to Macdonald, they raised him more or less to the position of a native chief, treating him with the same dignity and according him the same prerogatives. In European terms, he was exercising civil jurisdiction. Still, if it led to him killing Africans without due process, something was obviously wrong.[2]

He ought to have been warned, for this was the same problem as Charles Mackenzie had once encountered on the same ground: how to look after detribalised blacks amid a tribal society. Macdonald bungled it too, but was not left with it long. Travelling in the region came Andrew Chirnside, Fellow of the Royal Geographical Society, and he was appalled at what he found. On returning to Scotland, he sat straight down to write a furious pamphlet, including the account given above of the execution. For that and other incidents brought to his notice, he hit on the stinging tag of the Blantyre Atrocities. His revelations caused a furore. The Scottish press and public were up in arms. The Government in London expressed its concern. The Kirk, deeply embarrassed, ordered an inquiry, which found that Macdonald should never have exercised civil jurisdiction but yielded it, in some undefined fashion, to the local chiefs. This did not satisfy the General Assembly. It recalled almost all the staff from Blantyre. For a while the mission was in effect closed.

A man of greater mettle, the Rev David Clement Scott, refounded Blantyre at the end of 1881. The chastened General Assembly of the Church of Scotland this time told him exactly what to do. The mission was to be above all evangelistic. While, in the Scottish manner, it might offer literary and technical education, it must take care to limit the cultural impact; the best thing would be for the natives just to learn the gospel in their vernacular. The question whether Livingstone's legacy could be fulfilled by thus leaving negro culture and society alone was passed over in silence. Scott anyway took no notice. He satisfied his superiors at home by being always sufficiently master of the practical matters, of running schools, printing books and promoting Africans. That still left him plenty of time to pursue his ideals. They were high ones, and set a goal more ambitious than for any other Presbyterian mission. He aimed at nothing less than the production of 'new men' to regenerate indigenous society. What he seemed to mean by this was the creation of African forms of modern religion and culture. A future African Church would be catholic in rising above all racial or sectarian division, while a future African society would have absorbed what it needed from the West without being overwhelmed. Scott accordingly neither wanted to destroy, nor officiously to preserve, indigenous traditions. To the horror of some colleagues, he countenanced dancing by moonlight at Blantyre, yet invited natives to tea-parties in his manse in order to teach them manners. But he seemed able to pursue his designs with little serious opposition and interference either from home or from those around him, perhaps because, according to a colleague, he habitually used language so lofty as to be unintelligible to Europeans, let alone to negroes. Certainly, undaunted by the scale of this self-appointed task, he assumed he had a better idea than anybody else how much the natives could get out of the Scottish tandem of education and evangelism, once granted free access to it at Blantyre and assured of equality as the result. This assumption proved rather unrealistic.[3]

The Free Church's mission at Livingstonia prided itself in its early days rather on its down-to-earth Scottish competence, diverted by neither blunders nor visions. There was no question here of sending out missionaries armed only with good intentions to teach Calvinist theology to bemused blacks and hope for the best. There was yet no lack of high aspirations, but they were more bound up with what could actually be offered. The offer proved in any event generous. The Free Church could always call on some of Scotland's most vigorous talents, who responded with the confidence that came from having triumphed against the odds during the 30 years since the Disruption.

In this case, it could call on James Stewart. He had been fired with missionary ambitions, largely by the example of Livingstone, while still a medical student at the University of Edinburgh. Indeed in 1862 he accompanied Mrs Mary Livingstone when, after several years' separation, she went back to Africa to rejoin her husband. Already in poor health, she was exhausted by the journey and died soon afterwards. So Stewart, rapidly disillusioned by Livingstone's personality and plans, set off to explore alone. He adjusted without trouble to life in the wilderness: 'a man with a good sound appetite would enjoy a roast sirloin of hippopotamus'. Returning then to Scotland, he tendered this precocious experience to the Free Church, which he urged to send out an official mission under himself. Turned down there, he took the idea to businessmen in Glasgow, a city where commercial acumen and evangelical zeal were often mixed. When nothing came of that either, Stewart applied for and got a job at the college of Lovedale in the eastern Cape. Arriving in 1867, he so quickly demonstrated his abilities that only three years later he became the principal. Again in Britain for Livingstone's funeral, he set once more about badgering the Free Church: it was he who stood up at the General Assembly of 1874 to propose establishment of a commemorative missionary station 'in a carefully selected and commanding spot in Central Africa'. To general acclaim, he easily carried his point this time.[4]

Stewart went out himself as soon as he could and ran Livingstonia for the first couple of years. Through him it owed much to Lovedale. In other words, it had beside its evangelical purposes a practical commitment to education and justice for the blacks, with a view to their eventual political equality as literate, productive citizens of an integrated society. It had, on the other hand, no imperialist purpose: Stewart denied that there need be any connection between territorial expansion and missionary work. But it did have a national purpose for Scots. The Disruption had divided them and shattered the historic structure of their institutions. Stewart saw external endeavour as a way of overcoming the painful legacy. That was why he so readily aided the Kirk's mission at Blantyre in its tribulations. To his mind the intense domestic rivalries could be transcended in a great missionary task. All Scots might find a common aim of passing on to Africans their peerless educational inheritance and with it the values of Christian Scotland, so helping to bring an end to tribal society and its corruptions, slavery in particular. They could then build in the midst of the dark continent a community as far as possible resembling themselves, which in generations to come would naturally link itself to the civilisation of the mother country.[5]

After Stewart went back to resume his position at Lovedale in 1877, he entrusted these duties at Livingstonia to Dr Robert Laws. Laws had been with the Free Church's mission from the start and would serve as its head till 1929. He was a thorough and capable man, bent on laying solid foundations, unworried about quick results, confident as Livingstone had been that Africans would respond to their opportunities in time. The Scots, he remarked, 'are here like so many stamps and dies, impressing the natives with our characters'; more chillingly, a colleague said he 'cut into the lazy lotus life of the Nyasaland negro, and made him honour hard work'. At any rate, he set sensibly about exploiting Livingstonia's real expertise in its schools and hospitals. He was himself a medical missionary, who carried out the first operation with chloroform in Central Africa, while also readily handing out Victorian placebos such as epsom salts and rhubarb pills. In education, he laid the Scottish stress on a broad grounding; he taught his pupils about William Wallace and Robert Bruce but also about their own history and culture. As for evangelism, he cautioned his Church not to send out missionaries who would arrive expecting conversions *en masse*. Setting himself more modest aims, he felt reasonably satisfied at the progress. Under him the mission extended itself in a physical rather than spiritual sense, developing a network of subsidiaries right up the shores of Lake Nyasa and into the neighbouring region that would become Northern Rhodesia. He thought the inaugural site in the Shire Highlands too far away from this field of activity, and in 1881 he moved his headquarters to a more convenient spot at Bandawe, 250 miles away on the north-western side of the lake. There Livingstonia soon seemed securely established.[6]

It was thus not only the consolations of religion but also the advances of civilisation that the Free Church's mission hoped to bring, and for the latter purpose the political environment of the new site did present difficulties. Livingstonia came up against the same problems as the Kirk's mission at Blantyre had faced, though it tackled them with more forethought and charity. They were problems of temporal responsibility, exercised under no clear jurisdiction, in a restless region of fragmenting tribal structure. In such conditions new chieftaincies could carve out a place for themselves. Again, the mission itself, with a population of 600 round its main station, was in effect one of them, and it entered into relations with others. It had, of course, different purposes from theirs. They were out to aggrandise and enrich themselves by what means came to hand, usually by slaving. This Livingstonia meant to suppress. Most of its dependants were fugitives from Arab slavers and African invaders. Indeed the mission won a welcome and wide support among the indigenous peoples, not just for the educational or economic opportunities it offered but also as a humanitarian agency and safe haven. On all these counts it attained great influence. The natives hailing it as saviour and benefactor, however, were by definition those of no political standing. For that very reason many chiefs viewed its activities as suspicious, provocative or threatening. The mission reciprocated the ill-feeling, at least towards the slavers among them, whose authority it refused to recognise. It was a situation that might turn nasty at any moment. Livingstonia learned the lessons of the failed expedients at Blantyre and sought a surer solution by asking for a British consul to be appointed to the region; the General Assembly of the Free Church officially backed the request in 1880. Three years later one was sent to reside in the Shire Highlands, a harbinger of imperial sovereignty.

Missionary questions were complicated by political questions because both were complicated by economic questions. At the outset of the Free Church's mission, Stewart had meant to follow the precept that commerce and Christianity should come in together, that missionaries and traders should support each other. But Livingstone, its formulator, had never really managed to explain how it was to work. He seemed to assume that the negroes of the Shire Highlands would naturally start cultivation once a mission gave them an opportunity and an example. British merchants could then purchase their produce and bring them into the international trading system, by which fact slavers would be driven out. In effect he trusted to the invisible hand of political economy. Stewart, not impelled by the same ideological credulity, knew enough about Africa to see that the change might not run so smoothly, a reservation which experience confirmed. In his view there ought to be some special agency, independent of the mission, to act as economic catalyst.

To set it going, Stewart could appeal to the commercial middle class of Scotland, the driving force in the Free Church. During his visit home in 1874, he also looked up his contacts in Glasgow. Promising them to bring to Africa 'the blessings of Industry, Civilisation and Religious Truth', he managed to range several of the city's moguls, men doubtless not easily persuaded, behind the trading venture he had in mind. His biggest catch was William Mackinnon. This devout son of Campbeltown owned the British India Steam Navigation Company, which had started regular runs from Britain through the new Suez Canal to East Africa in 1872, so he wanted to build up business along that route. Not far behind him in capital and clout came two manufacturers, James White and James Young, the latter Livingstone's old professor of chemistry, inventor of paraffin, founder of the modern petrochemical industry and president of Anderson's College besides. They raised £10 million, religious offering and commercial investment at once.

With this, in 1878, the firm was set up which became known as the African Lakes Company from 1881. It was managed by two godly young men of Edinburgh with a mercantile education, James and Frederick Moir. From its headquarters at Mandalo near Blantyre, it spread its own network of posts up Lake Nyasa. It promoted cultivation of such crops as cotton and sugar which it was to transport and exchange, so supplying the missions' every want as well. In fact, the Moirs succeeded in hardly any of the plans. They did contrive to start some growing of coffee, which yielded high returns and was easy to haul. But they had no chance of dealing profitably in general agricultural produce: their capital and labour were too limited, and they lay too far from their markets. They had to concentrate instead on hunting elephants and buying ivory. Even this they could not export at a price undercutting the Arab merchants who had so far monopolised the traffic, and who used slaves as porters. Otherwise the prospects were exaggerated. The company proved not very successful, and erected no new economic structure.[7]

What it did do, however, was in effect determine the political future of the region. Its activities involved it in constant disputes. The Arabs, incensed at the competition, stirred up trouble among the peoples on the routes to the Indian Ocean. The company countered by seeking allies of its own. In 1885 it offered protection to the Tonga, a tribe prey to the slavers. It hoped this might represent a step towards being itself recognised as a civil power by the British Government, which would equally solve the missionaries' problem of jurisdiction. It certainly sharpened the tension, and by 1887 virtual war had broken out between the company and its Arab or African enemies. These, in the worst incidents, kidnapped two missionaries from Blantyre and raided a trading station. The company recruited mercenaries and struck back at the Arabs' outposts. Trouble smouldered on till 1889, when a formula for peace was agreed, though not before 1896 could slaving finally be stamped out. The Moirs found that their extraordinary expenditures had brought the business to the brink of bankruptcy. But political salvation was at hand.[8]

The British Empire came to the rescue in the scramble for Africa set off among the European powers during the 1880s. It often meant that small clashes generated big consequences. Preoccupied with the bedlam among the blacks, the Scots had paid little attention to this broader background, or in particular to the nearest Europeans, the Portuguese. Their colony of Mozambique straddled one of the major routes from Lake Nyasa to the sea, by way of the River Shire and the lower Zambesi. Contacts were made, friendly enough, but not such as to give the Scots a high opinion of their neighbours. Livingstone had long ago dismissed them as degenerate and incompetent. In fact when in 1884 the indigenous peoples down the Shire rose against their rule, Frederick Moir led his own force to suppress the revolt as the only way of making sure that trade on the river would not be disrupted. Portugal was indeed a poor, exhausted country, but still fancied she might restore her empire and rise again. One of her quixotic hopes lay in forming a territorial link between her settlements here on the eastern coast of Africa and those on the western coast, in Angola. To this the Scots were clearly an obstacle. The Portuguese began to harass them. They declared sovereignty over a huge region including the Shire Highlands, levied tariffs and restricted traffic on the waterways, hindered drives against the Arab slavers and finally planned an expedition to assert control.

The missionaries felt deeply alarmed. The question of sovereignty had forced itself on them willy-nilly, and the last thing they wanted was for it to be resolved, *faute de mieux*, in favour of a Catholic power so lacking in moral fibre. To them, British assumption of sovereignty offered the sole acceptable alternative. In 1888 they sent to London asking for the declaration of a protectorate over the Shire Highlands. This was not a welcome request. On the whole, the Government deplored the scramble for Africa as likely to impose unnecessary and expensive additional commitments. Here was a fine example of one which would be taken on simply to foil another country's schemes. The Conservative Prime Minister, Lord Salisbury, disapproved of them, but not so much as to block them. He hit on the strange policy of accepting them with an open display of pique. As its instrument he chose Harry Johnston, his consul in Mozambique, who happened to be home on leave. He was sent first to Lisbon with the draft of a treaty offering the Portuguese much of what they wanted, but in a surly spirit. Then he went to Edinburgh, apparently to present it to the Scottish Churches as a *fait accompli*, adding only the assurance that missions happening to fall within Portugal's jurisdiction would have nothing to fear. He was wasting his time. The clerics would not hear of it. Scotland at large rose in wrath, denouncing the treaty in public meetings and petitions.

One of the Kirk's best friends, conveniently a Tory to boot, Lord Balfour of Burleigh, buttonholed Salisbury at Westminster. 'My Lord,' he began, 'my Scottish friends don't like the Portuguese terms.'

The Prime Minister came back: 'Neither do I. I don't want your Scottish friends to accept them. I want the Portuguese to know that I, too, have a strong public opinion behind me and I am sending their Government a warning that they must not go too far.' This may reveal a machiavellian Salisbury, seeking to mollify the Portuguese, with Johnston as his stooge, while evading gratuitous commitments to a country with no means of advancing its claims. Or else it may be that he miscalculated the Scots' reaction. Whatever the case, they were not going to let him off the hook. When Dr Archibald Scott, convener of the Kirk's Foreign Missions Committee, brought him a petition signed by 11,000 ministers and elders, he looked the English aristocrat straight in the eye and said: 'This, my Lord, is the voice of Scotland'. The Prime Minister made known to Portugal that the deal was off. She, completely humiliated, had no choice but to climb down. Johnston imperturbably returned to Central Africa and conveyed the glad tidings to the Portuguese on the spot. In August 1889, John Buchanan, one of the lay missionaries and acting vice-consul in the Shire Highlands, raised the Union Flag for the first time. Shortly afterwards, the British Government declared a protectorate. Scotland seemed by herself to have swung its foreign policy.[9]

In that sense the missions got what they wanted, but they had not reckoned with all the consequences. The protectorate became a reality in 1891 when Johnston himself arrived as its administrator. He was an Englishman, and his relations with the Presbyterian missionaries remained poor: they had not forgiven his concessions to Portugal, any more than he had forgotten his roasting in Edinburgh. There were other matters over which they could all fall out. With a proper civil government instituted, the missions lost even unofficial vestiges of their former jurisdiction. They hoped that the protectorate would amount to something like British suzerainty of the Indian princely states, which left domestic affairs to the indigenous authorities. Instead they found Johnston intent on subjugation of the territory. He brought recalcitrant tribes to heel by war if necessary. He replaced African governing structures with colonial bureaucracy. He covered its costs out of taxation, notably by a severe levy on huts. He regulated ownership of land so as to reduce many blacks to serfdom under white planters.[10]

The missions took an especially dim view of Johnston's plans to make a ruthless capitalist outfit of the vaguely philanthropic African Lakes Company. Not far away in South Africa, the economy, as well as the political climate, was being transformed by mineral wealth. That raised hopes of the same further north. The company set up a subsidiary for exploration in 1889 but, never having been very profitable itself, lacked the capital for serious effort. Johnston was scathing: 'The riff-raff of Glasgow is not the best material with which to develop the commerce of British Central Africa'. He turned instead to the great white hope of imperialism, Cecil Rhodes, who in 1893 offered what the company needed, but at the price of taking it over. This opened the possibility that his own British South Africa Company, already holding as a fief the future Southern Rhodesia, would extend its control to Lake Nyasa. The fear was well-founded at a time when the Government in London, reluctantly joining in the scramble for Africa, did so on the cheap by resorting to the old expedient of chartered companies.

The Kirk especially went all out to stop Rhodes. Scott declared: 'Africa for the Africans has been our policy from the first . . . Central Africa in no way can be regarded as a dwelling place for the white races; it is the home of the black man and of the black man alone. He alone can develop its resources under the guidance of the European'. In case that might seem to leave a loophole for imperialists, he specified his aim 'to see in this land native power established in thorough sympathy with superior civilisation and permeated by it', the reverse of what Rhodes had in mind. From Edinburgh, the Church of Scotland's journal, *Life and Work*, chimed in: 'A chartered company is not a government and never can be. To be ruled by such is to be ruled for commercial ends by absentee directors and shareholders whose real interests are only served by tangible dividends'.[11]

Johnston accused the missions of meddling in politics and intriguing with negroes, not without reason; they even managed to win over some white settlers to their side. He at last conceded: 'The bringing of the Protectorate under the British South Africa Company is almost impossible. These detestable Blantyre missionaries and almost all the now numerous band of planters out here are dead against it'. Rhodes's commercial takeover stood, but he got none of the chartered concessions which further south gave him an economic and political free hand. The African Lakes Company ceased to be an auxiliary of the missions and became a business like any other; in this guise it would actually do quite well. Its history has been called a 'replay of Darien', now successful because the weight of an Empire was thrown behind it. But the truth is almost the reverse. From the moment the weight of an Empire was thrown behind it, it lost its distinctive Scottish purposes.

The Empire was in any event well on the way to assuming full political responsibility. This did not in itself represent a defeat for the missions. The freedom of the Free Church was from temporal powers, and for Livingstonia it seemed only logical, after deliberately getting rid of them, to accommodate itself to an administration called in to exercise them; the powers were in any case defined as protective, which might imply some degree of black political responsibility. Blantyre proved more awkward – or rather Scott did, so much so that in 1898 the Kirk thought it better to send him elsewhere. Yet his successor, Alexander Hetherwick, proved no less firm in defence of indigenous rights and in a conviction that British rule risked being founded on injustice. Neither mission affected the course of that rule, however. The territory was sucked inexorably into the imperial maw. Until 1904, the Foreign Office held responsibility for it. Then it was put under the Colonial Office, which formalised the regime in 1908, bestowing the name of Nyasaland and setting up the normal apparatus of governor and legislative council. Missionaries, while valuing their security under this regime, refused to act as its spiritual arm. On the contrary, they consistently brought a critical spirit to bear on it. Especially Hetherwick, who was appointed to the legislative council, assumed there the role of leader of the opposition, though of a loyal one. As Nyasaland remained more or less a Scottish colony – nearly half its British residents were recorded as Scots in a census of

1911 – her affairs could always come under independent scrutiny in the General Assemblies of the Churches too. Even so, this was an imperialist polity, not the native Christian civilisation for which the missions had worked.

Only on a longer view might the missions be said not to have worked in vain. It was noteworthy that Johnston's remonstrance over the African Lakes Company had singled out the attitude of the Church of Scotland at Blantyre. In that affair it did adopt a more radical stance and exert a greater influence than the Free Church at Livingstonia, for the first time since the pair were founded. For all its faults Blantyre came to show a greater faith in the indigenous peoples, even to the point of espousing the goal of self-government for them. Clearly the goal lay a long way off, but the mission did whatever was possible in its own sphere to bring it nearer. In 1903 it formed a presbytery, allowing native elders to make a contribution to its work. In 1911 it ordained its first negro minister.

The difference in local practice of the two missions had its origin in Scotland, in the doctrines born out of the Disruption. Just as the Free Church had been in large measure produced by industrial society, so Livingstonia was the readier to propagate the values of that society. These had severely tested traditional morality, yet never shaken the conviction of Free Churchmen that it was fully applicable to a new age. They brought the same conviction to a new land, to the villages round Lake Nyasa. Many came after serving with the Home Mission in Scotland, often in industrial parishes. There they had developed a plan owed to the social teaching of Thomas Chalmers, which deprecated general or permanent aid to paupers as sapping their capacity to help themselves. Laws wrote in the same spirit of the blacks: 'The missionaries greatly object to do anything, which might tend to pauperise the native, and seek to inculcate the benefit of honest labour'. As in Scotland since 1843, this honest labour was meant to break the slack links of traditional society and forge fresh ones. Again as in Scotland, global economic interdependence would help to shape a new structure. So the missionaries expected a class of negro artisans to emerge who, impelled by the same aspirations and subject to the same forces, would turn out as near as possible like their Scots brothers. Livingstonia's major domestic initiative of the 1890s was accordingly the foundation of the Overtoun Institute, financed by and named after a Scottish tycoon, which aimed at a higher level of industrial education. As the best historian of the missions observes: 'Houses that were square rather than round, funerals conducted without signs of visible emotion, marriages blessed with a festival of tea and scones and culminating in the singing of Auld Lang Syne in Chinyanja were all symbols of progress as defined by presbyterian Scots'.[12]

Yet this remained mere symbolism when Livingstonia was not in reality transforming the economy as it sought to do. Indeed it set off a process of change, but with mainly unintended consequences. The missions did not so much recreate Scotland by the Shire as smooth the path for a colonial economic regime. The tribal trade in slaves and ivory never gave way to the commerce of craftsmen, rather to the toil of growing cash-crops. In some respects this did represent an advance: the

Africans were paid wages and as a workforce became more mobile. Yet both their local and their distant markets remained limited. Their economy became self-sufficient neither in supplying their own major needs, nor in contributing as an independent unit to a wider international network. There its only real role lay in providing a pool of labour for the mines of the Rand. That wasted the talents of blacks who in growing numbers seized the missions' offer of educational opportunity; nothing beckoned them on but a few jobs in the plantations or the administration.[13]

If their secular schooling thus left indigenous peoples with a sense of frustration, their religious instruction gave them means to vent it. From the 1890s intense popular devotion developed in Nyasaland, expressed in evangelical conventions attended by thousands impatiently demanding baptism: in vain, for the missions trod warily with communal conversions, fearing they might be superficial. In retrospect it must be asked if the preference for individual conversions was really consistent with the aim of regenerating, materially and spiritually, a society of which the whole history and tradition had been communal. Be that as it may, in response to the excitement the missions actually raised the standards of observance and of education required for acceptance as a convert.

At least, for the Kirk's mission at Blantyre, such stringency may then have been offset by granting religious responsibility to natives who met its standards. For the Free Church's mission at Livingstonia that act was hard to follow, since it still did not really envisage giving negroes any say in the mission as such. These misgivings, no doubt felt in good faith, were all the same coming to look like mistrust of Africans, as of their tribal institutions and customs. In consequence Livingstonia began to lose control of the people. It happened, for example, at the subsidiary station amid the Ngoni of northern Nyasaland, one of the last tribes to be evangelised, by the unconventional labours of the Rev Donald Fraser. In the process he effectively created a Ngoni Church, still in connection with Livingstonia, but deeply marked by the tribe's social, religious and musical traditions; the most striking outward signs were huge celebrations of the sacrament with massed singing of vernacular hymns. The tendency went still further elsewhere. Independent native religion appeared in the so-called Ethiopian Churches, founded by negroes for negroes. The earliest was the Watch Tower Society, which sprang up in 1908 under a young migrant worker, Elliot Kamwana, returning to his tribe, the Tonga, after seven years, during which he had become a Jehovah's Witness. Within a few months, he baptised more than 9000 people. Then he was deported as too dangerous. Still no great exodus took place from Presbyterianism, which remained the colony's dominant confession. What did occur was significant, however, and would shortly produce the first crisis for white rule, a true portent of things to come.[14]

CHAPTER FOURTEEN

'An incipient civilisation': West Africa

What sort of woman I expected to see I hardly know; certainly not what I did. A little frail lady with a lace or lace-like shawl over her head and shoulders . . . swaying herself in a rocking-chair and crooning to a black baby in her arms. I remember being struck – most unreasonably – by the very strong Scottish accent. Suddenly she jumped up with an angry growl: her shawl fell off, the baby was hurriedly transferred to some one qualified to hold it, and with a few trenchant words she made for the door where a hulking, overdressed native stood. In a moment she seized him by the scruff of the neck, boxed his ears and hustled him into the yard, telling him quite explicitly what he might expect if he came back again without her consent . . . The man was a local monarch of sorts, who had been impudent to her, and she had forbidden him to come near her house again until he had not only apologised but done some prescribed penance.[1]

Such was the open-mouthed reaction of a polite, well-bred colonial official to his first display of Scottish proletarian matriarchy, with its warm heart and sharp tongue. Mary Slessor had started life in the tenements of Dundee, complete with ne'er-do-well cobbler for a father, drinking himself to death. Her earliest experience of the great world came with the grinding, unhealthy toil of twelve-hour days in the weaving mills. But she made the most of the few consolations available: she bettered herself through reading at night and devoted her spare time to the Secession Church, a sect of austere dissenters. It had an interest in foreign missions, especially the one at Calabar, on the sluggish estuary of the Cross River in what is now eastern Nigeria. Stirred like many others by David Livingstone's death, she offered herself as a missionary and was accepted to go out there. In 1876, after a year's training in Edinburgh, this strapping, plain, bony lass of 28, who had never even crossed the Tweed, found herself amid steaming, tropical swamps four degrees above the Equator. She would stay till she died in harness in 1915. By that time she was also an official of the British Government, as a vice-consul with 25 years' service behind her, an official of the colonial administration too, as vice-president of the native court. She integrated, to an extent never matched by her colleagues in Central Africa, her missionary endeavour with imperial expansion. Yet she remained very much a product of Scotland, instantly recognisable by Scots as one of their own.[2]

There were some general reasons for the way her work took shape. For 500 years the coast of West Africa had known Europeans, including Scots, who arrived in the seventeenth century not far behind the rest of the northern nations. Most of these white men came to traffic in black men. Even so, a certain degree of cultural interchange occurred, at any rate more than was possible in the remote interior of the continent. It included evangelism. In that sense, there was less need here to force the combination of commerce and Christianity. The obstacle lay in the nature of the prevalent trade: at once to enslave the indigenous peoples and try to convert them was, to say the least, incongruous. On the whole, however, Scots' consciences did not have to bear this burden. The Scottish Guinea Company of 1634–9 traded crude, home-made goods for gold. More than 60 years later the Company of Scotland, had it not thrown everything away on the opposite side of the ocean, might have followed up its sole African voyage. This returned in 1700 with another cargo of the precious metal out of which the Darien pistoles were fashioned, the last gold coins ever struck at the old Scots mint.

As for the slaving, if a few Scotsmen later took part in it, many more made a mark in the agitation against it. Zachary Macaulay, whom we have seen so shocked by his experiences as a youth in Jamaica, as a man offered his services to the Sierra Leone Company. Incorporated by abolitionists in 1791, it had the purpose of settling freed blacks in the continent of their origin. In 1794 it sent out Macaulay as governor to Freetown. He guided the colony through hard times, including a devastating French raid. In 1797 he received the inaugural expedition of the Glasgow Missionary Society, a pair of pious laymen named Duncan Campbell and Robert Henderson. Six more joined them, but most soon died in the terrible climate. Of the survivors, one stayed on to engage in slaving, while another came back to Scotland and 'turned infidel'. A third, Henry Brunton, published a grammar of Susu, the earliest study of a West African tongue, this spoken on the coast north of Freetown. It pioneered a striking aspect of the missionary movement, the modernisation of hundreds of extra-European vernaculars. We may ascribe that precedent, too, to the interests of the Scottish Enlightenment.[3]

Abolition of the slave trade in 1807 might have sent all these Scots home again. Since it could be enforced only gradually, policing it gave them cause to linger. That was what, even 20 years later, brought out George Maclean, a son of the manse from Keith who chose a military career. He went down as far as the Gold Coast, where he was given the task of winding up British involvement. It had consisted entirely in slaving, run by chartered companies from a dozen forts, all now redundant. Disengagement from this turbulent littoral proved tricky, though. The big problem was to leave some guarantee for the small peoples round the forts, friendly and helpful to the whites, against the powerful, aggressive inland kingdom of the Ashanti. The Colonial Office hoped to draw up a treaty before pulling out, but was getting nowhere. So it pulled out anyway, and banked on Maclean to retrieve what he could.

Afterwards, the sole vestige of administration relied on British traders who wanted to stay behind and use the forts as bases for new business. From them, in 1830, a council was constituted, the so-called Merchant Government. Maclean became its president. Within a year he discharged the task which had defeated the Crown's official representatives. He negotiated and signed an agreement with the Ashanti recognising the independence of the menaced tribes while setting up procedures to maintain order and resolve disputes. He then brought into it the Danes, also still trafficking in these parts, and other tribes which might benefit. Having thus constructed, so far as he could, a system of security for the region, Maclean applied himself to the work of civilisation. He was keen to develop agriculture and trade in palm-oil, which had been found useful for industrial processes at home. He brought in missionaries, and tried to enlist the aid of his local allies to suppress the human sacrifice still practised on the deaths of African chiefs. This won the support of the humanitarian Colonial Secretary, Lord Glenelg, who authorised Maclean to use armed force for the purpose if need be.[4]

Though doubtless in an emergency he could have called in a gunboat, Maclean was not in any formal sense the agent of British power. At bottom he owed his influence to his imperturbable native qualities. He attained in real life something like the mythical status of those figures who flit across the pages of John Buchan or Rudyard Kipling, downright Scotsmen able to cast a spell on alien peoples. One of his gambits was to train an orchestra of black bandsmen who, according to a visitor from home, 'play all the old Jacobite airs with good taste and precision'. He built up his prestige by dispensing justice, at first in its least august form, as an arbiter trying to make sure that his merchant colleagues were paid and their indigenous customers satisfied. He went on to devise broader arrangements for commercial law. By now fluent in Fanti, he was glad to help when chiefs began to refer to him disputes among themselves, so that he acquired a peacemaking role. Before long they were using him almost as a court of appeal from their own tribal authorities, with the acquiescence of their peoples because he handed down less severe sentences; he was especially in demand for capital cases. Altogether he extended a sort of irregular civil and criminal jurisdiction over the coastal peoples, then inland too. The following description may have been culled from someone who knew him: 'Maclean was calm and deliberate in forming a judgment. He was a typical Scotsman. His caution in coming to a conclusion appeared to the superficial observer to amount to timidity. In proportion to the strength of his convictions was the decision which he displayed in carrying out his resolutions'. In the event the Merchant Government as such did not prove durable amid the continuing threats to the Gold Coast, which brought the declaration of a British protectorate over it in 1843. But, in its ordinary internal affairs, Maclean carried on as before, now with the title of judicial assessor. On his early death in 1847, he was succeeded in his duties by his friend and countryman, just as shrewd and sage, Brodie Cruickshank. No firmer imperial administration proved necessary until, after another Ashanti invasion, the British took full control in 1874.[5]

Scots also penetrated the interior. From the northern coast they had indeed inaugurated the classical era of African discovery with the journeys of James Bruce of Kinnaird, who in 1770 found the source of the Blue Nile in Abyssinia. From the western coast Mungo Park, a cottar's son from near Selkirk, set himself the yet more arduous task of tracing the course of the River Niger on two expeditions in 1795–7 and 1806. On the second he meant to follow it to its mouth and settle the contemporary dispute over the direction of its flow, some thinking it might also issue into the Nile. Having crossed from Freetown to its upper reaches, he sailed downriver for over 2000 miles. On the eve of reaching his destination he lost his life when tribesmen attacked his boat. So his achievement long remained unknown, and brother Scots persisted in efforts to unlock the same secrets. Alexander Laing, another resourceful military officer who could strike up instant rapport with primitive peoples, reached Timbuktu in 1826. His observations proved that Nile and Niger must flow in different directions. He was murdered soon afterwards. Meanwhile, Hugh Clapperton from Annan and Walter Oudney, an Orcadian, died in an attempt to ascend the Niger from its delta.[6]

This fatal Scottish obsession with the river was fuelled by its commercial possibilities. Macgregor Laird from Greenock, a member of the shipbuilding family which set up at Birkenhead, formed a company for exploiting them in 1830. Two years later, he led an expedition on the pride of his yards, the *Alburkah*, the first iron ship to make an oceanic voyage. He travelled 250 miles along the Niger to its confluence with an eastern tributary, the Benue. There he was forced to halt. Of his original party of 48, all but nine were dead, most from malaria. Fortunately, Laird survived. On reaching home, he wrote up and published his experiences, in the forlorn hope that they would encourage others to traffic with the region. Not for 20 years did even he feel ready for a fresh effort. At his own cost, though with the approval of the British Government, he sent out a second expedition in 1854. Its surgeon and naturalist, William Baikie from Kirkwall, took charge after the designated leader died at sea. It had the geographical object of pushing on up the Benue, thought to rise in Lake Chad at the very heart of the continent. The river did prove to be navigable for another 250 miles, at least in the rainy season, but not to go in the right direction. Baikie also had an object of his own, to demonstrate the prophylactic use of quinine. This succeeded triumphantly. No more of the explorers perished, and one key to European penetration had been found. The venture was promising enough to persuade the Government to sign contracts for annual voyages by steamer to various trading posts on the Niger.

Baikie himself returned in 1857, now with the dignity of consul, to establish a post on what he had identified as the most promising spot, Lokoja, overlooking the confluence of Niger and Benue. He won the trust of the local emir, bought a site from him, cleared it, built houses and enclosures: in his mind's eye he saw a great city of the future. The blacks' eager response seemed to bear out his vision, for they came flocking to use the market-place he offered, to exchange produce among themselves and to gaze in wonder at the shipments coming up the river, often from Glasgow. To the motley settlement which then gathered Baikie, usually dressed in gaudy local costume, acted as ruler, doctor, teacher and pastor; the last function did not stop him taking also to drink and women, on whom he fathered a small clan of African Scots. Still, he translated portions of the Bible into Hausa, as well as collecting vocabularies of 50 languages. One of them still bears witness to the impression he made. In Ibo, *beke* is the normal word for white man, used also as a suffix to denote things introduced by him. Thus *ewi-beke* is a rabbit, *ezi-beke* a pig, *asusu-beke* the English language, *akwukwo-beke* a book, and *manya-beke* are bottled drinks. Not just Baikie himself, but his material and cultural legacy are perpetuated here. Even so, in the long term the commerce did not match his expectations, and the Government, embarrassed at his having gone native, ended support after his death in 1864.

The excuse given was that the region remained too barbaric to benefit from European contacts. Cruickshank, observing from the Gold Coast, thought this nonsense. The traders had not done enough to prepare the ground for success, through ignorance of the society into which they were moving (though that seems a severe verdict on Baikie). 'Precept and example were considered sufficient to eradicate evil and substitute good among whole tribes of people,' Cruickshank judged. The fault lay not with them, but with the means of approaching them; with better means, more prudently applied, greater progress should be possible. This sounds rather like the conclusion Livingstone reached about the failings of missions, but Cruickshank's direct comparison was with the Gold Coast, where 'little is now required for the more perfect development of an incipient civilisation'. It had a government with enough moral or physical power to repress any sudden outbreak by the Africans, an efficient judiciary suited to the social conditions, even the makings of an educational system. Cruickshank concluded on an orthodox Scottish note that with 'the employment of a moderate amount of capital in the country, the work of improvement may be safely left to time'.[7]

A similar situation, if unblessed by any official presence, obtained at Calabar, further along the coastline. It flourished on a brisk traffic due to its strategic position, at the convergence of routes from the interior on a point where shipping could depart either west or south. The local Efik people, once fishermen and farmers, had thus come into precocious contact with international commerce. They exploited with skill the potential of their port. It had been the busiest in West Africa for slaving, but once they saw the trade's days were numbered they switched to traffic in palm-oil. With economic advance came an evolution of their tribal system. They developed a stable confederacy out of their cluster of settlements round a broad estuary, each under a chief whom Europeans styled a king. While this small trading empire was something of a power to reckon with, it did not evoke the admiration of white visitors. Laird had called in and found it the most uncivilised place in the region: 'I was much struck by the demoralisation and barbarism of the inhabitants in comparison with the natives of the interior. The human skulls seen in every direction and that are actually kicking about the streets attest the depravity of feeling among the people'. For that and the other reasons, Calabar ought to have offered a fine site for a mission. But one was quite a long time in arriving.[8]

When it did, it was not sent by missionaries already in Africa, nor from Scotland, but from the Jamaican Presbyterians, a striking piece of colonial cross-fertilisation. Their ability to sustain it proved remarkable too. It was not as if they looked back on a tranquil history or enjoyed a secure present. On Jamaica, Presbyterianism had been segregated. The Kirk maintained two places of worship and two schools, for Scots planters and their sons. The Scottish Missionary Society, the mainly dissenting group formed in Edinburgh in 1796, chose Jamaica for its first venture. It aimed to convert the slaves, to whom it sent the Rev George Bethune in 1800. He needed the acquiescence of their masters, but not even his own countrymen welcomed him, and his efforts foundered amid the general hostility of the whites. A quarter-century later the atmosphere had changed, though, at home with greater commitment to missions and in the West Indies with emancipation in prospect. In 1824, it was the Scots planters who asked the society for someone to come and imbue the blacks with religion while time remained. The Rev George Blyth accepted the call, and made a success of it. As the hour of freedom struck in 1833, the island housed eight Scottish missions and six large congregations of the United Secession Church. There were now enough missionaries and ministers to form a presbytery. By 1847, when in Scotland most of the small sects gathered in the United Presbyterian Church, to which this presbytery acceded, it boasted a clergy of 20.[9]

Yet the period of emancipation was also a time of trial. These dissenting ministers counted as members of the ruling race. But they had appointed themselves friends and leaders of the negroes. The growth of their flocks therefore worried the whites, who sought means to discipline or even get rid of them. The established Church in Jamaica had, of course, always been Anglican. A plan was concocted to coestablish the Kirk, to constitute then a Colonial Church Union with the English clergymen. The Government would have the option of expelling ministers who did not conform to it. The plan would have entailed building Presbyterian places of worship in every parish, an expense worth it to some if it could drive the dissenters into the Kirk, where they might be better controlled. Nothing came of it, for it reckoned without the dour Calvinist individualism which had made them dissent in the first place.

Typical of them was the Rev Hope Waddell, born in Ulster in 1804, accepted as a student by the Scottish Missionary Society and ordained into the United Secession Church in 1829. He set off at once for Jamaica, and was there not two years when he played a useful part in stilling a revolt by the slaves. Yet he refused to join up with the militia, because its purpose was to use violence against them; for less than this, other missionaries had their churches burned down, were tarred and feathered or threatened with charges of sedition. After emancipation, they continued to preach peace and harmony, and to condemn rebellion against the social order. But it was the message of spiritual equality that struck home among the blacks, inspiring those who rose to the challenge of fending for themselves, for example, by squatting on the land which ruined planters abandoned. It was not something the missionaries felt they should sanction, yet it lay beyond their or anyone's control. All they could do was try to bring some order to the process. They themselves bought several of the large estates now available at knockdown prices, established free villages on them and parcelled up the land to members of their congregations. They also paid fair wages: that completed their estrangement from the last, struggling planters, since no negro would work for less.

When all this tension issued in the revolt of 1865, missionaries reproached themselves for having gone beyond their religious calling. Yet their sorrow was perhaps the inevitable outcome of the singular place they had chosen to take up in the old Jamaican society, where they were never in fact fully accepted by the blacks, yet rejected as traitors and enemies by the whites. The sequel proved happier, for their Church flourished despite the island's economic decline. We may before proceeding round off the history of Jamaican Presbyterianism. By the 1880s it was self-supporting, and able to send more missionaries to Calabar, as well as to India. By 1900, one-third of the ordained ministers were negroes. They served 50 congregations, a number which continued to grow in the twentieth century, till a union with other Protestants ended the Church's independent existence in 1928.[10]

One of Calabar's purposes had been to give a fresh sense of purpose to liberated slaves. The most able and intelligent could be sent to bring Christian enlightenment back to the very place whence some of their hapless forefathers had started the journey into bondage. The presbytery of Jamaica wrote to the kings at Calabar asking whether they would welcome such a venture, and received a favourable reply. In 1841, Blyth went home to put the plan to the Scottish Missionary Society. Once it gave approval in 1844, Waddell was nominated head of the mission. He had now to return to Scotland as well in order to complete the preparations. He took with him a party of five, including three blacks. In fact Calabar would always rely on Jamaicans, 40 of whom served there, though Scots led and financed the station. During the outward voyage Waddell was shipwrecked on the Cayman Islands. While waiting to be picked up, he spent his enforced leisure converting the people to Calvinism; they afterwards joined the Jamaican presbytery.

This was the measure of the man who reached Calabar in 1846. Its veneer of civilisation looked thin to him and his colleagues. Closer inspection confirmed as much. For their station they were allotted a hill outside one township which they found littered with skeletons and rotting corpses; here the dead poor were left to the leopards, since only the rich merited burial. They shuddered to hear of cannibalism, and see signs of witchcraft everywhere. They were horrified by the screams of people dragged off to be strangled or buried alive as sacrifices on the death of a king. Now and again they rescued the anguished mother of twins from the destruction that awaited them, since to the Efik these were taboo. The place swarmed with slaves, disciplined by casual killing, flogging and mutilation, so cheap that they were used to settle debts or pay fines for infringements of native laws. Often, too, the Efik sold them to traders, despite British interdiction of the traffic. No less heinous to prudish Scots eyes were the concubinage, polygamy and miscegenation with European sailors, not to mention the universal disregard of the sabbath. When Waddell once preached on the text, 'Thou shalt not steal', his congregation burst into laughter. It was as thriving a little haven as could be found on the five continents, yet to the missionaries a heart of darkness.[11]

How to save so many lost souls? Evangelical Christians in Scotland might have a straight answer. In 1850, an editorial in the *Record* of the United Presbyterian Church gave one. It declared that, now the station was established, the negroes need only acquaint themselves with the Bible, and 'they would not allow themselves to be held in the fetters of a dark and degrading mental bondage or submit to those senseless rites that ruled the feelings of their ancestors'. The trouble was that the missionaries felt obliged to impose strict standards for conversion, unlike in Jamaica, where they welcomed a whole population of negroes. But Calabar still formed a cohesive unchristian community, its chiefly tyranny bound up with cruel religion, so they did not feel they could take chances. In fact Waddell accepted no converts at all until 1853, and then expected those he did accept to observe the grimmest Calvinist austerity, enforced with threats. The first African minister was ordained in 1872, yet even by the time of Mary Slessor's arrival four years later the full members of the Church numbered just 178, and included no Efik leader.

The missionaries thus found their situation more complex than could be imagined by the devout at home. Not just preachers of the gospel, they ran schools, a hospital and a vernacular press. They came into contact with every level of a vigorous and successful African polity. It led them towards the conclusion which Livingstone reached, brooding alone, that salvation must go together with social change. Of course, from the start they abominated every aspect of heathenism, even if it was not necessarily incompatible with Christianity. Inside the precincts of the mission, they forbade all drumming, dancing and singing, traditional negro expressions of joy. But they found the people eager to adopt at least some superficial alien customs, forms of marriage, funeral rites, observance of the sabbath and European dress. This nerved them to denounce the more offensive ways of the Efik and demand their abolition. By 1850, Waddell managed to persuade the kings to forbid the habitual slaughter on their deaths. Again there was a popular response: the slaves made so bold as to band together and defend themselves when, nevertheless, they were threatened with another bloodbath the next year.

The inveteracy of the custom prompted Waddell to several trials of strength with Eyo, king of the town where the mission stood. They almost went horribly wrong. After yet more killings in 1855, British traders on the river had their consul at Fernando Poo send a gunboat to bombard the town. Punishment of barbarism was the pretext, but the affair seemed to have more to do with a dispute over debts. The missionaries could not see much morality on either side. But they did worry that their efforts to link ethical with economic progress, in the same way as Livingstone, might instead result in the crushing of native authority by imperial power. The answer they hit upon was collusion with the kings. A jittery Eyo saw to it that the sacrifices ceased, while Waddell worked to avoid further confrontations. To do this he had also to compromise and, in the interim at least, accept domestic servitude. Anyway he knew by now that slavery could not be quickly abolished because it was built into the social and economic structure: an Efik reckoned his status by the number of slaves he had. All Waddell could do was lay down rules for humane treatment, and deny membership of the Church to owners who would not promise to work towards freedom for their chattels.

Otherwise he turned to the Scottish cure-all of education. 'It is here in the schools,' he avowed, 'that the high fabric of superstition that has stood untouched for centuries is to be undermined and the way prepared for its final overthrow.' At Calabar too, he hoped to form not only Christians but also citizens, valuing themselves as individuals and so respecting others. He opened the schools to everyone, to both sexes and all classes, with the children of slaves sitting alongside the children of their masters; nor did he ever stipulate that they should become converts. He aimed to bring them up nevertheless in a Calvinist ethos, instilled by strict discipline and high standards. He did so through a practical rather than philosophical curriculum, supplementing biblical and literary instruction with the usual Scottish range of vocational subjects. He had more success in offering opportunities than in recruiting for Presbyterian dissent, to the chagrin of himself and of those at home supporting him. But it was this broad approach to education, rather than a narrow religiosity, that did most to undermine the iniquities of Efik society. Waddell already had to his credit some impressive results by the time of his retiral in 1858. In the same year, the Scots marked the permanence of their presence in the wonted manner, and formed a presbytery.[12]

Still, modernising pressure just as decisive came from the kings of Calabar. They were amenable to economic and social change, which they often pushed through against the conservative resistance of their own subjects. The jovial and astute Eyo, for example, sought genuine good relations with foreigners, while avoiding the pressure from Waddell to become a Christian himself. And he did manage this balancing act, apart from the one lapse involving the gunboat. His prime aim was to educate his subjects for the new commerce which must follow from the end of the slave trade. He in effect asked the Scots for the skills to exploit different resources with a ready market in Britain. He and the other kings encouraged the missions with generous gifts of land and materials. Waddell noted continual rivalry among them to construct the most impressive schools, which then often had to be enlarged because enrolments grew so fast. In education, at least, the kings did not need to force the pace; the people's demand for it outran the missionaries' capacity to supply it.[13]

In sum, a special relationship formed between the Efik and the mission over a range of mutual interests. It did not turn out a relationship of white master and black servant. The missionaries were, after all, Scots of lowly origin or Jamaicans just out of servitude, sent by the smallest of the three main Scottish Churches and hardly its first concern either. They could expect no more than occasional political support, for the region's climate made colonial administration difficult and white colonisation impossible. So what the missionaries in the event brought to an alien soil, like many ordinary Scots who left home under the immeasurable impact of modernisation, was themselves, their humble version of the best in their culture, above all its aspiration towards an equitable society, with which they set out to renew the moral foundations of this one. Dissenters, after a distinct ecclesiastical and educational history, had an especially strong sense of it.

The kings were by contrast despots, manoeuvring to maintain their economic and political position. They saw that the mission might threaten it. Hence Eyo's refusal to convert, and his insistence that his people should only abandon their traditions when ready to. Otherwise the Efik realm might descend into chaos, which would help neither him nor the missionaries. Yet pressure from the missionaries did produce a momentous change in the internal condition of Calabar, by persuading the kings to accept moral constraints on their absolutism. Since the missionaries wanted to work by moral means, further reforms would of necessity be slower. That, at least, was the position more or less openly accepted by Waddell's successor as head of the mission, the Rev William Anderson. He led it for 30 years, relying for his purposes on friendship with the kings, by which he even attained a position in local politics himself. The special relationship thus consolidated was to last over a century, till the Republic of Nigeria secularised the schools in 1965, because each side believed it was getting the better of the bargain. It proved one of the happiest episodes in Scottish missionary history.[14]

Yet the relationship was never stable, and the equilibrium reached in the third quarter of the century did not survive. At home, missionary enthusiasm mounted. If there was no direct link, it went hand in hand with the advance of formal imperialism. While at Calabar the older generation of missionaries came to acquiesce in much of native culture, the evangelical character of their enterprise was renewed by younger workers fresh from the fervour at home, and charier of the special relationship. One, the Rev Alexander Ross, wrote back to denounce his elders' tolerance of barbarism as well as their hobnobbing with cruel, tyrannical and – worst of all – unconverted chiefs. He caused so much trouble that Anderson had him recalled. But he refused to leave and seceded to run, for two years before he died, a schismatic station. Mary Slessor, just as impetuous, yet kept within the fold and used her talents to breathe life into the mission's methods. She attained new heights of ingenuity in running it on a shoestring, and applying its stretched resources to the backward hinterland. This work would give her a status in Scottish evangelical literature second only to Livingstone's. Still, she was not a pioneer like him. She took her place in an already established enterprise, achieving slow but steady advance. This is not to deny her genuine contribution. But it would have been impossible without the foundation long laid.[15]

The legends yet depict, from the start, a woman penetrating the heart of darkness. Her biographer, William Livingstone, introduces her mission thus: 'The first sight she saw on entering her new sphere was a human skull hung on a pole at the entrance to the town'. He continues in such bloodcurdling vein. Perhaps some of the old customs had not yet quite died out, but they were no longer openly practised or encouraged. The viciousness of the kings' rule in this later period is being exaggerated for effect. If their polity was still largely pagan, that must be put down to the mission's stringent policy on conversion: it had not stopped social improvement. In fact, Calabar was now a relatively sophisticated and respectable port, where kings lived in harmony with missionaries. The stark opposition between Mary Slessor's Christian rectitude and the heathen darkness round her existed only in the literature: compare, too, what we know of the kings with the contempt for a 'local monarch of sorts' in the epigraph to this chapter. No doubt it all pandered to a popular audience's taste for exotic tales of heroism, especially about a woman, and swelled the flow of funds. It also obscured the nature of the special relationship, in terms belittling the accomplishments of the missionaries and the needs of the indigenous peoples alike. Even where the missionary movement had succeeded in bringing on an incipient civilisation, if not to the peak of Christian perfection, its propagandists now refused to admit as much. The deracinated and impoverished society of Jamaica could be acknowledged as belonging, however tenuously, to the civilised world. The society of Calabar thriving on a symbiosis of Scottish democracy and negro aspiration had still to be defined as savage.

Mary Slessor herself grew disillusioned. Perhaps she could not feel content till she came face to face with real barbarism. She got permission anyway to leave for a place, and amid a tribe, called Okoyong, well up-country, in surroundings much more primitive and not so far evangelised. Even here she found that the great obstacle to Christian truth and progress lay not in human sacrifice or cannibalism but (just as among Dundonians) in alcohol. It was consumed by old and young, noon and night, and by her own account most of Okoyong went to bed drunk. She had to start education from scratch, but made it widely available through training teenaged teachers to pass on the rudiments of learning. She managed also to give her pupils, the girls included, some degree of civic and industrial training. She prided herself on the numbers of makeshift schools she founded, though her staid seniors worried about standards in them.[16]

But the legend also misrepresented the real reasons for her status in the interior. We have noted how evangelical fervour at home went with formal imperialism abroad. To Calabar a British consul came in 1878 to set a seal on the moral progress made, by signing a treaty under which the kings undertook to desist for ever from their bad old ways. They merely confirmed what was in most respects an accomplished fact. Yet from there it took but a step for them to defer to superior external power. At any rate, they put up little resistance to the occupation of Calabar in 1889 when, amid the scramble for Africa, Britain proclaimed a Niger Coast Protectorate. It became necessary to appoint a depute consul to Okoyong. Mary Slessor was the obvious person. The missionary then passed over into the colonial official, though she fulfilled both roles with deepening sympathy for blacks now beset by bewildering changes. They flocked to find out from her how they might conform their customs to the demands of their new masters, while these came to sip at the spring of her couthy wisdom; or, as her biographer delicately puts it, to be 'charmed with her original qualities'. She was to be seen at her best presiding for hours in the native court, knitting her way through the palavers to stop the litigants getting excited. She did worry at the diversion from her true purpose: 'Where is the time and strength for comprehensive and consecutive work of a more directly evangelistic and teaching type? – specially when the latter is manned year by year by the magnificent total of one individual. Is it fair to expect results under such circumstances?' Since oversight of public affairs took up most of her time, her main achievement was indeed finally imperial: by bringing the Okoyong into commerce so far monopolised by the coastal tribes, she contributed largely to the extension inland of British control.[17]

Imperial authority as it afterwards evolved could allow none but a passive role to blacks, though a few of its servants might have wished otherwise. The most liberal proconsul in West Africa, William Macgregor, was a Presbyterian of the sternest and a patron of missions. He had risen from the rural poverty of Strathdon, labouring on a farm to pay his fees at the university of Aberdeen, before going out as a medical officer to the Pacific. His administrative abilities won recognition, and in 1899 he was appointed Governor of Lagos. Here too, in a pestiferous colony, he applied his professional expertise. 'I have an invincible, selfish, irrational objection to being buried in these swamps,' he said. He drained the swamps, sank healthy wells instead, then set about introducing modern medicine. He built hospitals, recruited doctors, enforced quarantines, introduced vaccination. Even this humane work ran up against political obstacles. He caused a storm when he denied that whites caught their diseases from negroes, and refused to segregate them in different wards. He did so again when he employed Africans as medical officers: 'It would be most unwise to cause political dissent in the population of a country like this simply to comply with and nourish the racial prejudice of a mere handful of Europeans, the prejudice that exists in inverse ratio to liberal education'.

He approached his political tasks in the same spirit, and met the same reaction. He adopted the system of indirect rule pioneered by Lord Lugard in Northern Nigeria. He perhaps practised it more consistently, for he never resorted to coercion when it went wrong, as it was sometimes bound to do, and Lugard thought him soft. Privately, indeed, Macgregor condemned policy towards negroes, and reformed his own colony so as to give them a semblance of responsibility. He appointed the first African assistant to the Colonial Secretary. He constituted native councils to deal with some judicial and administrative matters. He made equitable treaties with chiefs in the interior. But other ideas, for negroes on his legislative council, for a council of chiefs, for a board to draw up native regulations, met with a veto from the Colonial Office. It found in him 'a curious streak of sentimentalism . . . which made him object to the segregation of Europeans and natives', and judged that this attitude 'must tend to make the native arrogant, and may lead to trouble in the future'. After his retiral, Macgregor had his own rejoinder: 'I have given a new trend to government there, and I have met with great, almost virulent opposition to my policy . . . I had shed not a drop of blood in Africa. That is considered phenomenal but is it not a sad and woeful commentary on British rule?' It ought to have sobered the missionaries he befriended that, for all their goodwill towards Calabar and other native polities, they had helped to make British rule absolute.[18]

CHAPTER FIFTEEN

'Into the Stygian pool': India, the Religious Mission

The Punjab sweltered in the heat of May 1857, but it was one of the safer places in India for Europeans. To the south-east, down the plain of the Ganges, the Mutiny flared among the sepoys. They turned on and massacred their white masters, the women and children too. But up here the natives were relatively quiet. The province had been taken under the Raj only in 1846, after a war honourably fought which called forth from conqueror and conquered alike their highest respect for each other. The British had meanwhile been eagerly recruiting from what they called the martial races, the virile peasantry of this fruitful farmland. In return, they sent to govern it the wisest of their senior officials and the brightest of their juniors. When the Mutiny broke out they yet felt themselves poised here too on a knife-edge: such a vast country, so few to hold it. The merely necessary had to be sacrificed to the inescapable, and into the former category fell the security of Europeans on the smaller Punjabi stations. One was Sialkot, a bustling if decrepit market-town, built round an ancient fort. Nearly all the British residents, when they heard of the mayhem further off, decided to seek safety with the garrison at Lahore, 70 miles away. One who refused was the Rev Thomas Hunter, minister at the mission recently established by the Church of Scotland, a young man of 30 from Aberdeen, with a wife and a new baby. He ranked his faith and what he conceived as his duty higher than love for them. But his courage turned out to be foolhardiness. His nerve anyway cracked when, after his countrymen had fled, mutineers seized the place, one of very few in the province that they were able to take over. Panicking now, he made a dash with his family for the fort, where he believed the last Europeans to have sought refuge. As he drove through the deserted streets, a sepoy stepped forward and fired. The bullet passed through Hunter's cheek and into his wife's neck. He reeled under the impact, giving the sepoy the chance to stop the horse, then step up into the carriage with sword drawn. Perhaps the last sight the Hunters saw was that sword plunged into their innocent child, before it descended on them.[1]

Scottish evangelical interest in India had been continuous since the turn of the nineteenth century, despite the rejection of missions by the General Assembly of 1796. That was a decision of the majority, the Moderate party, taken out of posthumous respect for Principal Robertson and of deference to the Dundases' policy. It accorded with Scottish orientalism, represented eminently in the party's ranks by the Rev Alexander Murray, minister of Urr and later professor of oriental literature in the university of Edinburgh. Men of the Enlightenment, whether of a

185

sacred or a secular profession, whether at home or in the East, wished India to find her own way along the path of progress that Scotland had already traversed. Meanwhile they were tolerant of her exotic culture, descrying in it the variant of a universal history awaiting fulfilment, which would come through leadership by the most cultivated and benevolent natives. Thus they held the brahmin caste and its Sanskrit learning in high regard.

But the Enlightenment had also produced a reaction on the part of Calvinist orthodoxy, now quickened by a broad evangelical revival, one mark of it being that motion in favour of missions before the General Assembly of 1796. After its defeat, with ministers debarred from any initiative, a layman took the lead. Recently returned from long service in Bengal, Charles Grant the elder published the very next year his *Observations on the State of Society among the Asiatic Subjects of Great Britain, particularly with respect to morals; and on the means of improving it*. Its title indicates its tenor: 'It has suited the views of some philosophers,' he noted pointedly, 'to represent that people [the Hindus] as amiable and respectable', yet old hands in India knew they were 'exceedingly depraved'. For himself, he felt shocked that his own Christian nation should decline to transmit God's truth to a heathen one sunk in superstition, idolatry and vice, a morass of depravity created by Hindu government, laws and religion. Its causes were in other words moral, and the cure had to be moral too: the introduction of Christianity.

Grant would bang this drum for years. Another opportunity arose in the case of the Rev Claudius Buchanan, one of the few clergymen to have made their way to India, as vice-provost of the College of Fort William. The country horrified him. This was his opinion of Indians: 'Their general character is imbecility. Their moral powers are and have been for ages in a profound stupor'. He published opinions so violently abusive of Hinduism as to alarm Robert Dundas and Lord Minto. They agreed that it was dangerous to public order and in any event simply impractical to introduce an alien creed into a deeply spiritual land, and they suppressed Buchanan's ravings. He solaced himself by instituting an annual prize at his old university of Glasgow for essays on the best means of civilising India, which could evidently be carried off by writing what he wanted to read. The Rev John Mitchell, minister of Anderston, won it in 1805 by declaring: 'Let every factory, which the British may possess in different countries, become an evangelical depot'. Meanwhile Grant took up the cudgels for Buchanan and told the Dundases that the religious impartiality of their Indian regime flew so obviously in the face of the divine providence which had created the Empire 'that I tremble at the thought of it and the consequences it would be likely to produce'. He could not be silenced, for he was powerful enough in the East India Company to hold its chair for three terms, continuing to press his view that British dominion offered the chance to convert and westernise the natives. Being also an MP, and a leader of the faction known for its devout enthusiasm as the Saints, he was in a position to do more. When renewal of the East India Company's charter came up in 1813, he proposed to maintain its monopoly of trade but allow missionaries to enter under its aegis. In the event, he had to exchange the first aim for the second. It was a sign of the times that, while monopolists could no longer find a majority in Parliament, evangelicals could. These inserted into the legislation the 'pious clause' which unlocked British territory to missions.[2]

As India housed so many Scots, the controversy at home found a reflection there. Those of Calcutta were making it into a fair copy of a city of Enlightenment, in the way Scottish cities had long been. Much was done through official patronage, but this enlightened culture also attained a life of its own. Proof lay in the fertile educational scene, enriched by Scotsmen making their living as teachers. David Drummond from Fife ran a private school where he offered instruction in the philosophy of David Hume. His compatriot, David Hare, himself a declared atheist and secular rationalist, devoted the fortune he had earned as a watchmaker to philanthropic ends, for publication of books in Bengali and English and for support of the preparatory department at the Hindu College, or *Vidyalaya*, the city's latest cultural innovation. It was founded in 1817 by Bengalis to provide western education in English and soon became, again with aid from the Government, the major school in Calcutta. One of Drummond's pupils, a Eurasian, Henry Derozio, was the principal master. He taught Scottish philosophy too, and formed a debating society, the Academic Association, where his pupils could discuss it for themselves. Out of these ventures arose the Young Bengal movement, a westernised group trained at the college and sceptical of all religion, of Hinduism especially.[3]

The legislation of 1813 did not at once, from the Christian point of view, improve matters. It merely authorised the Kirk to send out three chaplains to the Scottish communities in India. In Calcutta, Moira's wife, the Countess of Loudoun, inaugurated St Andrew's church in November 1815, after fending off an absurd effort by the Anglican bishop to keep its steeple lower than that of his cathedral. The three Scots ministers had no brief to make contact with the natives, but that was what one of them, the Rev James Bryce, at once did by befriending Rammohun Roy, the guru of enlightened Hinduism.

Roy has, with Rabindranath Tagore, been integrated into the cultural identity of Bengalis in much the same way as Robert Burns and Walter Scott are integrated into the identity of Scots. Beyond that, he has today been canonised as the "father of modern India". He was the first native who could stand comparison with cultivated minds elsewhere. He mastered ten languages, studied four religions and applied his learning to a restoration of intellectual and moral self-respect among his own people, so that they might give to, as well as take from, the outside world. The most distinguished of his personal scholarly labours was a translation out of Sanskrit into Bengali of the Vedanta, the philosophical system derived from the four most ancient and sacred Hindu scriptures. He had much more than scholarly intentions. Sanskrit being a closed book to all but the brahmins, he meant to make a purified Indian spirituality available to the masses, as the basis for a reformed religion. He wanted to show that, in a Vedic golden age, Hinduism had been free of the gross superstitions disfiguring its modern practice. He discerned in the Rig Veda a progression from lower to higher religious ideas, out of animism through naturalistic polytheism and syncretism to a sort of monotheism, leading then into the more formal philosophy of the Upanishads. The Vedanta could in his view further help to demonstrate that all the great religions had a similar essence despite their diversity of form. In his interpretation, it would be India's own contribution to enlightened, universalist theism.

Roy had friends among Calcutta's Scots of all persuasions: not only Bryce but also Hare, then others such as James Sutherland, editor of the *Calcutta Journal*, and George Gordon, who gave the guru financial advice. In the local intellectual climate, they took his line of argument seriously. The cultural transmission thus did not flow all one way. This Enlightenment married East and West. To the Scots it seemed a development of the highest importance. It vindicated the orientalist confidence that within a decadent India lay the seeds of rebirth, and proved Robertson's proposition that, under western encouragement but by her own efforts, she could join the comity of nations. Admittedly Roy and other Indian literati did rather cut themselves off from the true representatives of contemporary Hinduism, the orthodox pundits who had neither the refinement, nor the linguistic ability, nor apparently any great inclination to defend their system. Across a yet deeper gulf lay the mass of Bengalis, the peasants and their priests who knew nothing, and cared less, of what went on in their sophisticated capital. Even so, it had the final purpose of influencing them. That was why, believing that Hinduism could be cleansed, Roy deplored the 'godless atmosphere of intellectual life' in the city, where the Young Bengalis were putting theism on the defensive. His counter-attack had by 1828 awakened a wide enough response for him to found, with help from the wealthy family of Tagore, a society dedicated to the propagation of his ideas, the Brahmo Sabha. He died in 1833, but Debendranath Tagore refounded the society in 1843 as the Brahmo Samaj. This tried to give Roy's universalism a more definitely Hindu character, as the answer to the Bengalis' quest for a new identity under the impact of the West; the analogy with the dilemmas of Scots intellectuals after the Union is conspicuous. The Brahmo Samaj took firm root, and out of it grew various other liberal Hindu associations, most of which were to send delegates to the constituent session of the Indian National Congress in 1885.[4]

Roy had given an especially warm welcome to Bryce as emissary of the Kirk because he was already impressed, if to some extent negatively, by what he knew of Scottish education. This official presence offered him the chance to draw on its tradition in a form more orthodox and congenial to him than its sons' bolder experiments in Calcutta. Soon Bryce and Roy devised plans for a Scots college in the city. This would need the approval of the General Assembly, which had in its wisdom declared missionary work to be 'highly preposterous'. But did not the situation in Calcutta answer the objections raised in 1796? Here were Indians able to receive the abstract propositions which Calvinist theology would present to them. If that was put across at home, the Church of Scotland could surely not hold back from a work of enlightenment commended by Robertson himself, even while it still left Africa and other barbarous regions to mere dissenters. Crucially, the idea found a friend in a prominent member of the Moderate party, the Rev John Inglis. It was to him that Bryce and Roy addressed their proposal. He passed it forward to the General Assembly of 1824, which asked him to report back the next year. He did so favourably, deploying the argument that in Bengal ministers would have the opportunity to mix with the aristocracy and intelligentsia, so exerting the same influence as they enjoyed in Scotland. On the strength of that, the General Assembly gave its consent. To inaugurate the Indian mission, the Kirk chose two of its brightest young men, Alexander Duff and John Wilson. They formed a striking contrast.

Wilson, born at Lauder in 1804 and educated at the university of Edinburgh, was destined for Bombay. He remained there for the rest of his life and saw it rise from backwater to metropolis, after the opening of its hinterland at the dissolution of the Maratha confederacy. Landing when Mountstuart Elphinstone had been gone only two years, he imbibed the orientalism of its cultural elite and himself took to linguistic scholarship. He soon became fluent in the city's vernaculars, taking care not to be 'too frequently inclined to speak on the folly of idolatry, and to neglect the preaching of the unsearchable riches of Christ'. He immersed himself in local life, forming a native church then a school where Marathi was the language of instruction. He advocated 'general education of the natives *through the medium of their own tongues*, which form the readiest key to their hearts'. He did not neglect higher studies. He held public disputations with Hindu, Moslem, Parsee and Jewish doctors. As president of the Literary Society of Bombay, he collected Sanskrit manuscripts, attempted to decipher the edicts of Ashoka and became the first European scholar of Zend, the liturgical language of the Parsees, of whose religion he published a study in 1841. In 1843 he went into the Free Church, and during a furlough in 1870 would serve as Moderator of the General Assembly. On foundation of the university of Bombay in 1857, he was the natural choice for vice-chancellor. One reason for the city's rapid progress lay in its educational system, owed in no small measure to him: the college founded in his memory, 15 years after his death in 1874, still shows off its saltires to the Arabian Sea. 'What is it that Scotland intends to do by this college?' asked the Governor of Bombay, Lord Reay, on opening it. 'The professors wish to ennoble your hearts by imparting that moral fibre which is the mainspring of the Scottish character.'

The origins of Bombay's cultural blossoming can be traced back a bit further than Wilson's arrival, to the first decade of the century. Then Jonathan Duncan had come as governor after years as resident at Benares, to be joined by James Mackintosh, who founded the local branch of the Asiatic Society, and by William Erskine, a scholar of Persian and a historian, Duncan's secretary and later son-in-law. By the time of Elphinstone's governorship, Bombay was catching up with Calcutta in the central intellectual endeavour of linguistics. It was then, in 1823, that John Stevenson arrived, sent out by the Scottish Missionary Society. He stayed more than three decades, served as president of the Asiatic Society and made himself an accomplished Sanskritist, editing several Vedic texts. But his most original contribution came as grammarian of Marathi. He proved it to be Indo-European despite features, arising from a position at one of the family's geographical extremities, leaving room for doubt. That also set the northern boundary of the separate Dravidian family, and began to free its philology of an assumption that it must be descended from Sanskrit too. This new branch of the discipline, largely a Scottish creation, dated back little further than Alexander Campbell's Telugu grammar of 1817. Three decades later it had reached into the recesses of aboriginal linguistics, thanks to Stephen Hislop, a phenomenal polymath who in 1844 founded the Free Church's mission at Nagpur; in his spare time he ascertained that the Himalayas dated from the same era as the Alps and posited the existence, now generally accepted, of a prehistoric continent of Gondwana. After his and others' work, southern Indian philology reached in 1856 a triumphant summation with the Rev Robert Caldwell's comparative grammar of the Dravidian tongues. This was a contribution also of the first importance to Indian history. It lit up a huge area of darkness with convincing evidence that Aryan or Sanskrit culture had irrupted over a surviving older substratum. It thus heavily modified the earlier view of India formed by Scottish conjectural history. The classical language of the sub-continent, Sanskrit, no longer seemed to bear the relation to its civilisation that Greek and Latin did to the West's. Perhaps, after all, the brahmins had been overrated.

Estimable as Wilson and his circle were, however, Duff overshadowed them. This second of the Kirk's inaugural missionaries, born in Perthshire in 1806, went to the university of St Andrews to become the most brilliant pupil of Thomas Chalmers, absorbing his synthesis of evangelical religion, scientific confidence and social conservatism. Duff landed in Calcutta, despite two shipwrecks on the way, early in 1830. And as we know, he arrived amid a cultural ferment. He set out to direct it along new, Christian channels by bringing the Scottish educational tradition to bear on it. In so doing he made himself an intellectual leader of the city, a status he retained till the foundation of its university prompted development in a new direction. So devoted to the place was he that he declined the Free Church's supreme honour, elevation on Chalmers' death in 1847 to his chair of theology at New College, Edinburgh; it almost went without saying that, when Duff returned to Scotland in 1851 to raise funds, he became Moderator of the General Assembly, the first missionary to be thus distinguished. After he left India for good in 1864, he continued to exert an indirect influence, as convener of the Free Church's Foreign Missions Committee. And even when he retired from all official responsibilities, he remained the world's greatest authority on missionary education right up to his death in 1878.

Duff started instruction in what became known as the General Assembly's

Institution, now the Scottish Church College, in July 1830. Charging no fees, he had 200 boys enrolled in no time. In one respect, he complemented Calcutta's existing facilities, for he shared the orientalist aim of fostering an Indian intellectual aristocracy. His institution did have an elementary department, but at the upper levels it aimed at depth rather than breadth of education, at thorough training on a high mental plane. He wrote: 'It was our studied endeavour to court the society of those natives belonging to the more wealthy, influential and learned classes, who had already received a liberal education'. But Duff explicitly sought to counter the influence of the Hindu College, in his view pernicious because infidelity was as bad as idolatry: the era of revolutions in Europe proved the danger that lurked in an advance of learning without Christianity. Here, in the struggle against secularism, was the basis of a brief but firm friendship with Roy, cut short by the guru's death, but not before he had personally persuaded some apprehensive brahmans to send their sons to Duff. Where he went beyond Roy was, of course, in meaning to make out of them not purified Hindus but Christians. Duff was absolutely anti-orientalist, unable to see anything good in Indian religion:

> In that vast realm is the most stupendous fortress and citadel of ancient error and idolatry now in the world. Its foundations pierce down into the Stygian pool; its walls and battlements, crusted over with the hoar of untold centuries, start upwards into the clouds. It is defended by three hundred and thirty millions of gods and goddesses – the personations of evil – of types and forms to be paralleled only by the spirits of Pandemonium. Within are congregated a hundred and fifty millions of human captives, the willing victims of the most egregious falsities and lies that have ever been hatched by the Prince of Darkness.[5]

Duff knew, though, that pupils came to him not for Christian dogmatics but for useful knowledge. Yet to him this was a distinction without a difference. He followed Chalmers in the conviction that truth formed a unity: science and philosophy accorded with the Bible; ancient and modern learning were alike fulfilled in revelation; laws of nature reflected the divine wisdom and gave an assurance of ultimate moral order. If this ensemble could be cogently presented, it was bound to discredit and supersede Hinduism. Duff told the General Assembly of 1835, while in Scotland on furlough: 'Every branch of sound general knowledge which you inculcate becomes the destroyer of some corresponding part of the Hindu system. It is this that gives to the dissemination of mere human knowledge, in the present state of India, such awful importance'. If in Scottish terms Duff was a typical Evangelical of the new school, in Indian terms he was a modernist and rationalist, the keenest in Bengal.[6]

Duff thus offered a wide western curriculum, of religion, science, history and political economy, with the notable omission of secular literature. He set out to integrate the different subjects into a coherent whole, centred not on moral philosophy, as in the universities at home, but on evangelical Christianity. Beyond that, his great innovation was to give instruction in English, whereas other missionaries used Bengali. It was interesting that he himself had been brought up to speak Gaelic, still the vernacular in his part of Perthshire. English, however, had long been the medium of Protestantism and social advance there, so that he could readily associate it also with the culture he meant to impart to his pupils, and through them to India. He compared them to the young Highlanders who completed their education at the English-speaking universities of Scotland. Duff never even learned Bengali, though he still felt sure it was 'but a poor language, like English before Chaucer, and had in it, neither by translation nor original composition, no works embodying any subjects of study beyond the merest elements'. Acceptable for everyday use and for elementary schooling, it would never do for higher studies. He wrote:

> In the very act of acquiring English, the mind, in grasping the import of new terms, is perpetually brought into contact with the *new ideas*, the *new truths* . . . so that, by the time the language has been mastered, the student must be *tenfold* less the child of pantheism, idolatry and superstition than before.[7]

Such was his confidence about the superiority of English that he even used it to teach oriental subjects – Sanskrit, Persian, Indian history; one of his extramural interests was the printing of Arabic and of Indian languages in Roman script. So much for philology, but the times were changing. Duff's first years in Calcutta coincided with the climax of the debate over Indian education between orientalists and anglicists, in which he himself took part. It brought total victory for the anglicists. In 1835 the Governor-General, Lord William Bentinck, decreed that public funds should be devoted only to the teaching of European literature and science. The officially patronised revival of classical eastern learning ended. Duff's institution then became all the more a magnet to the ambitious youngsters of Calcutta.

With them Duff adopted the methods of the dominie, sturdy and uncompromising. Yet indoctrination was not his method. In teaching he used the socratic question and answer, and allowed no notes to be taken in case they were used for cramming. He thus transplanted the Scottish democratic intellect, with its sanctioning of arguments between teacher and students and its acceptance of common sense as the standard of reference. And while he vehemently denounced Hinduism in books and public lectures, he did not do so in the classroom. Intending, for example, to explode the cosmologies of India's venerated scriptures, he felt content for each pupil to come by his own process of thought to a realisation that they could not be true. In other words, his students would best be prepared for acceptance of an alien faith by the liberation of their minds.

He took these techniques outside the walls of the institution too. At his open lectures on natural and revealed religion, he invited his boys to come and debate before and with others; ructions followed when conservative Hindus tried to ban their attendance. Conversion was Duff's ultimate goal, and progress there remained frustratingly slow. But by 1848 a Bengali congregation, mainly of well-born intellectuals, could be formed. One member, Lal Behari Day, atypical only in that he went the length of becoming an ordained minister, also won literary prominence as editor of periodicals and novelist of peasant life. This was just what Duff wanted: through education the replacement of the old Indian elite by a new one ready to reform the country and act as a channel for Christianity and western learning to the Indian masses.[8]

Where Duff left a greater mark, however, was on the hearts, minds and deeds of Scots. It was striking, for example, that almost at the outset the Kirk accepted missions as part of the institutional Church – another idea ultimately owed to Chalmers – rather than leaving them to missionary societies on the usual pattern of other countries. The Scottish societies, never very lusty, now went into decline, and within two decades consigned every one of their stations to the Churches. It was true that by then the old Kirk had been disrupted, and that afterwards Scots wasted too much energy on sectarian strife. Yet the events of 1843 also strengthened their cultural identity and spurred them to release their talents outwards. They had through their philosophy understood the world; now in the confidence kindled by their revived religion, they believed that they might, after all, be able to change it. The institutional crisis in itself scarcely punctured their confidence. Both the successor Churches still held with the principle of Establishment and conceived of themselves as true representatives of the nation. This made the difference that, while the individual practice of Scots missionaries could seldom claim originality, it was much more the product of an integrated philosophy than the work of others. They did not merely rely on the example to pagans of their own piety which, rightly or wrongly, was taken for granted. Rather they sought to make positive use of education as a weapon against heathenism, inculcating godliness and a sense of human equality together. This might be readily formulated as an expression of national values, exploiting something that Scotland had, exceptionally, in abundant surplus, her trained minds. So Scots could claim their contribution to be unique, as indeed it was. And Duff was an exemplar of it.[9]

At the Disruption, he and the 14 other Scottish missionaries now in India had no doubt about their response. To a man they went into the Free Church, leaving to the Kirk only the East India Company's three chaplains and one lay woman helper. By the time that Duff and his colleagues in Calcutta acquired a new place of worship in August 1843, and called a meeting to reconstitute themselves as a religious body, nearly all the elders and a majority of the congregation of St Andrew's church had followed them. He took it on himself to give public lectures about the reasons for the separation, and was able to fill the hall. The aftermath proved rancorous. The Kirk decided to eject him from his institution, though he had personally collected the money for it and got it built. A policeman arrived one morning in March 1844 and threw everybody out. The scene was repeated at the premises in Bombay and Madras (where a mission had been founded in 1837 by the Rev John Anderson). But the missionaries just started again elsewhere, taking their 2000 pupils with them, and soon had the schools running normally again. Each Indian presidency now found itself with two Scottish missions instead of one, but the resources available to them grew rather than shrank. In the year before the Disruption the Church of Scotland had collected £20,000 for missions. Six years later the Free Church alone was collecting an annual £50,000. This financial product of the evangelical revival, by no means confined to the Free Church, allowed a steady increase in the number of missionary stations of all sects. The unfortunate Hunter's presence at remote Sialkot was one result.[10]

The missions tried to take the Mutiny in their stride too. But it clearly called Duff's policies into question. Returning from furlough just in time for it, he still refused to accept there was much wrong: 'I have a secret, confident persuasion that, though this crisis has been permitted to humble and warn us, our work in India has not yet been accomplished – and that until it be accomplished, our tenure of empire, however brittle, is secure'. He urged that it was not enough for the new imperial administration, set up in place of the East India Company, to confine itself to secular affairs. It should be explicitly Christian and squarely combat idolatry. But, to say the least, a relationship between Church and state which had broken down some time since in Scotland could hardly be recreated here. The Government of India remained set on the policies it felt to be imposed by the Mutiny, a mix of military rule, economic development and political immobility. The Raj would change, if at all, only gradually. The missions, balked of more support, also resigned themselves to gradualism.[11]

Once Duff left, however, his colleagues could put salient questions more pointedly. They had actually begotten a class of Indians able to express themselves in English, acquainted with western culture and willing to assume leadership. But these otherwise scarcely acted as they were meant to. They did not thank their rulers, but abused them. They did not bolster British power, but competed with it for command of the masses. They did not mix with European officials and merchants, but condemned their racial prejudice and cried 'India for the Indians'. They did not faithfully serve the Empire, but denounced it. Indeed, as they started to build political organisations more solid than the remnants of the old, princely India swept away by the Mutiny, some of this westernised elite turned revolutionary. At any rate, they would not see the goodwill of their missionary teachers as anything better than paternalism, or the missions themselves as more than another artifice of a foreign ruling caste.

Faced with such sobering facts, it was hard for missionaries to discount the possibility that they had been wasting their time. They reflected ruefully on the meagre numbers of converts, relative to the effort of winning them. The total between 1830 and 1880 was reckoned at 3359. Missionaries might reproach themselves, but they also had to answer to superior authorities. The Free Church was a populist evangelical body, which raised amazing amounts of finance. Its members, seeing the clamant need at home for churches and schools, wanted to know that money sent overseas was well spent. They liked to hear of souls saved by the preaching of the gospel, not of brahmans who read the Waverley novels but hatched sedition. There was thus a great gap between what the faithful expected missionaries to do, and what the missionaries in fact did; the poor results seemed to prove that it was the missionaries who had things wrong. From the time of the Mutiny, they were therefore impelled away from western education of an elite towards direct vernacular evangelism among the masses. The change received official sanction from a delegation of the Free Church which came out on a fact-finding tour in 1887–9; the Kirk followed in its own missions. Clearly, the Churches had at all levels lost confidence that they would ever see enough educated Hindus to lead Christian communities.

At the end of the century the missions thus pressed out from the cities, to which most of their work had so far been confined. They switched from the ingrate brahmans to the most degraded people on the sub-continent, the aboriginal tribes and untouchable castes, the Parganas of Santal in Bihar, the Pariahs of Madras and the Chuhras of the Punjab, expanding also their medical missions, notably for the care of lepers. James Peattie, secretary of the Mission Council in Madras, wrote: 'The true solution of the caste-question lies here. Raise the non-castes: give them brain-power enough to take their place in the battle of life with the caste-man; infuse Christian principles into their lives, and soon a change will be perceptible in Hindu society'. The shaping of Christian communities at this level did prove much less costly in time and money. The Presbyterian missions grew faster than before, and faster than others. Up to 1914, the number of converts rose tenfold to more than 30,000. It was still a drop in the ocean of India's millions, and hardly enough to generate the native ministry needed for an autonomous Church. Other denominations found the same problem, which they could only at length solve by unions among themselves. The Kirk's congregations would merge with the Churches of South India and North India on their respective formation in 1947 and 1970. They were meant to bring together all respectable Protestant sects, but the condition laid down by Anglicans for their adherence was acceptance of episcopacy by the rest. Thus presbytery as such ceased to exist in the sub-continent.[12]

Still, Presbyterians never abandoned their educational effort: enrolment in their schools remained higher than in the schools of all non-Scottish missionary societies together. But it occurred to realistic Scots that, given the improbability of communal conversions, they should settle for a second best of aiding reform of Hinduism. The change of mind came in the guise of educational innovation, led by the Rev William Miller, whom the Free Church sent in 1862 to its institution in Madras. He would transform it in 15 years into the Madras Christian College, a constituent of the university, and head it till 1907. The example was followed, so that by the turn of the century several Indian universities had Christian colleges attached. They were not there, though, to convert the Hindus of the upper castes who filled their classes. Their function was in Miller's word 'preparatory', with any conversions a 'side product'. He stressed rather his principle of diffusion, of insinuating Christian influence into the moral outlook of India. He proposed the concept of *Christus Consummator* – after Matthew v, xvii, 'I came not to destroy but to fulfil' – for missions to offer as a final expression of the higher aspects of all religion. Then the heathen need abandon nothing they held important as they were educated towards a new form of belief. The Madras Christian College is the *alma mater* of many intellectuals, the most eminent being the philosopher, Sarvepalli Radhakrishnan, who has counted among his distinctions a chair at the university of Oxford and the presidency of India. Like most of his fellow students, he remained a Hindu.

Miller claimed to be only modifying rather than negating Duff's work. Both meant to propagate the faith, but while Duff had defined this in terms of souls saved, Miller was content to see Hindus thinking and acting more like Christians. Otherwise, if converts remained the aim and converts were not coming, missionaries might as well give up. Still, he by no means persuaded them all. Dugald Mackichan, Wilson's successor in Bombay, insisted on conversion as the prime task: Hinduism had to be regarded as in essence intolerable unless the missions were to be reduced to an educational charity. Miller's own successor in Madras, Alfred Hogg, recalled his college to orthodoxy by demonstrating how the Hindu concept of karma, implying eternal moral improvement, differed absolutely from the Christian act of redemption once and for all.

Yet the flagging of evangelical energy, the rise of ecumenism, the realisation that religion was rooted in culture, the consequent shift of focus from the individual to the social: all these were signs of the times in Scotland too. They gradually sapped her interest in and help for the missions as thus far conceived. Meanwhile in India the nationalist movement gained more neophytes than western Churches. Evangelical work carried on regardless, and at an apolitical level the native elite did seem more receptive to Christian influence in the way Miller sought. A further development in enlightened Hinduism was the emergence of socio-religious societies intent on healing India's age-old rifts, and easing the plight of the untouchables in particular. Everyone had anyway to face the reality of the country, that its transformation was bound to be slow, and could only start off with obeisance to its ancient traditions. There, perhaps, the orientalists gained a posthumous revenge.[13]

CHAPTER SIXTEEN

'I have sinned': India, the Secular Mission

Each miscreant, after sentence of death is pronounced upon him, will be taken down to the house in question, under a guard, and will be forced into cleaning up a small portion of the blood-stains; the task will be made as revolting to his feelings as possible, and the Provost-Marshal will use the lash in forcing anyone objecting to completing his task. After properly cleaning up his portion the culprit is to be immediately hanged, and for this purpose a gallows will be erected close at hand.

So ran the order issued by Colonel John Neill in July 1857 soon after the 78th and 84th Highland regiments recaptured Cawnpore during the Indian Mutiny. Neill, born at Ayr in 1810, educated at the university of Glasgow and with service in the army of Madras dating from 1827, was according to a friend 'the finest-looking man I ever saw, great shaggy moustaches and eyebrows, and he feared nobody . . . He was the sternest and, at the same time, kindest and best-hearted of men'. He had been moved beyond measure, to both grief and rage, by the sight that awaited him when he led his men to the Bibighur. This was the scene of the massacre, only the day before relief came, of the families of British soldiers taken when the rebellious sepoys had overwhelmed the garrison. Neill described it himself:

I saw that house when I first came in. Ladies' and children's bloody torn dresses and shoes were lying about, and locks of hair torn from their heads. The floor of the room they were all dragged into and killed was saturated with blood. One cannot control one's feelings. Who could be merciful to one concerned? Severity at the first is mercy in the end. I wish to show the natives of India that the punishment inflicted by us for such deeds will be the heaviest, the most revolting to their feelings, and what they must ever remember.[1]

In fact, the sepoys of Cawnpore had refused to have anything to do with the butchery, which was carried out by men from elsewhere. That saved none of them now. The revolting punishment Neill had in mind was to hale the Indians into the fouled room and force them in turn to lick up some of the gore. Since this had congealed and hardened on the floor, to resemble red leather it was said, the job would be physically difficult, apart from loathsome, and soldiers stood ready to flog anyone who flagged. A few prisoners did what they had to do with an air of sullen defiance. Neill and his troops better relished dealing with others who gibbered for mercy, gagged at the task and howled as the whip cut into their bowed backs. The idea of a gallows outside was that the Hindus would have lost caste by polluting themselves, and be launched into their next, presumably miserable, incarnation before they had a chance to purify themselves. But in his lust for revenge Neill was none too scrupulous in dealing with the evidence for or against those he doomed. He sent down fat subahdars and solemn civil officers along with the sepoys. 'The Word of God gives no authority to the modern tenderness for human life,' he said grimly, and it seems clear that he did condemn some innocent men. If a doubt occurred to any of the soldiers, it never deterred them. One, William Munro, recalled: 'I had never seen a human being hanged before, and, though at any other time I would have avoided such a sight, on that occasion I remained to look on without the least feeling of pity or compassion'.[2]

The Scots exacted a terrible retribution, but it did not lack apologists. The Rev Alexander Duff himself wrote that Neill, 'though naturally a mild, gentle, quiet, inoffensive man, seems to have irresistibly felt that an exhibition of stern justice was imperatively demanded. His Scottish Bible-training had taught him that justice was as absolute an attribute of Deity as mercy'. James, a nephew of Thomas Chalmers in the service of the East India Company, figured among the many whose rumour-mongering excited high emotions: 'Thousands of Europeans have been murdered in cold blood; European ladies violated, publicly exposed, and then tortured to death. Soldiers have amused themselves by pitching European children from bayonette to bayonette'.

His colleague George Campbell was one of the few to keep a cool head:

Afterwards Neill did things almost more than the massacre, putting to death with deliberate torture in a way that has never been proved against the natives . . . If these people had been really guilty of the massacre it would have been disgusting enough, but Neill does not say that they were found guilty of the murders. He executes vengeance for the massacre of 'all who had taken an active part in the Mutiny', and when we know how these things work we may well doubt if there was any proof of that . . . I can never forgive Neill for his very bloody work.

Of the other stories, Campbell remarked: 'I think it was eventually admitted that no mutilated person has ever been found, and most people will admit that no case of the dishonour of a European woman has been proved'.[3]

Neill went on to the relief of Lucknow, where he was killed leading forces into the city at the end of September. In the fierce fighting here the 93rd regiment, the Sutherland Highlanders, played a major part. Their landing in Calcutta, straight from the Crimean War, had caused according to Munro 'quite a sensation in the city of palaces, for a kilted soldier had never been seen there before. The natives gazed in silent awe at the peculiar dress and the stalwart figures of the new sahibs, or gagra wallahs (petticoat men) as they called them'. The corps was a stronghold of the Free Church. Once, while stationed in Canada, it had refused orders to parade on a

Sunday when the service was to be conducted by a chaplain of the Establishment. The men did not share, however, the usual Evangelical views on temperance. Complaining that the climate of Calcutta made them 'gey an' drouthy', they let the many Scots residents ply them with beer. Lady Canning, wife of the Governor-General, disapprovingly noted the drunkenness of the troops arriving in heavy reinforcements, and observed that 'the Highlanders have been by far the worst'. This led to unfortunate incidents with peaceable Indians. When some soldiers ran into a naked fakir bedecked with shells, teeth and empty soda-water bottles, they threw him in the river.

At Lucknow, Colin Campbell, Glaswegian commander of the relieving force, had to start by taking the Secunderabagh, an enclosed garden with strong walls held by the sepoys as an improvised bastion outside the city. He told his Highlanders how to do it:

> When we make an attack you must come to close quarters as quickly as possible. Keep well together and use the bayonet. Remember that the cowardly sepoys, who are eager to murder women and children, cannot look a European soldier in the face when it is accompanied by cold steel. 93rd! You are my own lads. I rely on you to do the work.

Cannonades battered a hole in the rampart, but the first soldiers to attempt entry, from the Punjab Rifles, were shot down. Campbell turned to John Ewart, colonel of the 93rd, and cried: 'Bring on the tartan!' With superb skill, his troops infiltrated the narrow breach. One by one, they forced their way in, each holding the defenders at bay while he let the next one through. When enough of them had managed it, they set about the grim task entrusted to them by their general. In four hours, and for a loss of 76 officers and men, they destroyed about 2000 of the enemy, most in systematic slaughter to yells of 'Cawnpore!' A silent, well-read Highlander known to his mates as Quaker Wallace was reported to have bayoneted 20, reciting verses of the 116th psalm as he drove his blade into their bodies. The Scots were astonished to find themselves up against female negro slaves who 'fought like wild cats', but these they cut down along with the rest. Ewart at length emerged from the carnage, covered in blood and powder, to report proudly to his commander: 'I have killed the last two of the enemy with my own hands, and here is one of their colours'.

'Damn your colours, sir!' snarled Campbell. 'It is not your place to be taking colours. Go back to your regiment this instant!' But when it was all over, and they surveyed the corpses piled five feet high, they felt immensely proud of themselves. 'We had done *something* to avenge Cawnpore!' wrote one trooper, William Alexander. They struck up *The Campbells are Coming* on the pipes to hearten the besieged defenders of the British residency only a mile or two away.[4]

How had it come to this, in a land which Scots knew and loved like none save their own? Not so many years before some of their best sons had been writing of India as of a sacred trust, to be cherished and preserved for posterity. Now others were engaged in wanton killing and destruction. The contrast might be taken as proof that orientalism had been a sham, a mere foreword to imperialism. Even orientalists admittedly condescended to Indian civilisation, as decayed and even degenerate; however genuine their wish to restore it, they inevitably brought some European preconceptions to the task. Still, they embarked on it not only in all the deference to native sensibilities they could muster, but with a positive desire to exclude innovation as well, especially that inspired from the West. If this too is to be dismissed as imperialistic or proto-imperialistic, then we must find some other name for the exactly contemporary current of thought which held that Indian culture was despicable, that ignorant Indian opinion could be laughed off, and that it were the sooner the better for this alien, barbaric country to be subjugated and transformed by Europeans. The one current did yield in time to the other, but this does not prove their essential continuity. It is surely more convincing to accept that they were distinct, and that they were at odds.

There is a Scottish analogy which shows how this may be so. Thirty years before many Scots had still wanted to preserve the old Scotland. These were swept aside in the national quest for progress by rivals oblivious of tradition except in sentimental, domesticated form; it can hardly be argued just from their consecutive ascendancy that the two views were much the same. To be sure, once the battle had been lost and won, the protagonists saw less need to maintain rigidly the distinctions between them. The Disruption of the Church of Scotland in 1843 was in many respects a curiously reactionary event, but more obviously it hallowed the quest for progress, since it also represented an effort to meet and solve the problems of industrial society. For that purpose, it demanded a counterpart in secular action. The religious mission to an India defined by evangelicals as corrupt and degraded implied in the same way a secular mission. Scots equipped by their faith to change the world would in practice fulfil that aim by applying their scientific knowledge and their technical skill, driving India – for her own good, of course – along the road they had traversed at home. The respective missions were two sides of the same coin, espousing the same aim: to wipe out one culture and replace it by another.

A Scotsman had formulated this antithesis of orientalism. James Mill was among the original great publicists of the modern age: comprehensive Liberal and utilitarian ideas, on a firm factual and theoretical basis, start with him. His role in the history of Scottish philosophy, in which he had been trained, was to transport it in his own person to London and there cross it with the utilitarianism of his friend and mentor, Jeremy Bentham. As a result, political economy gained in logical consistency what it lost in empirical open-mindedness. Mill's job as a senior official of the East India Company, for nearly 20 years till his death in 1836, allowed him to apply the hybrid doctrine to Britain's Empire in the East.

Its textbook was the six volumes of his *History of India* (1817), the first complete treatment of the subject. Rabidly utilitarian in spirit, it rejected every claim of Scottish orientalism and demolished Principal Robertson's *Disquisition* in remorseless detail. Mill posited rather that all defects of the past could be swept away by mechanical application of the principles, universally valid, on which modern European civilisation had reached a peak of perfection. He depicted Indians as labouring under the burdens of superstition, tyranny, privilege and caste, which kept their religion, government, law and learning in a primitive state. Their future lay in westernisation, in reforms just like those which Mill and the philosophical radicals sought at home. For Britain, that would garner the true benefit of her oriental connection. It lay not in domination or exploitation, since these were quite unnecessary for the truly transforming power of commerce to work, but rather in opening up India to free trade and capitalist enterprise. Mill anyway did not suppose that the British would govern the sub-continent long. But while they did, he wanted to dispel the orientalists' silly, sentimental admiration of despotism, benevolent or otherwise, which only held things back.

Yet in many ways Mill's was a typically Scottish book, indeed about the last, but also the most elaborate and detailed philosophical history. It applied to India the laws of natural science, taken besides as general laws of society, by means of much detailed evidence about the interplay of different causes in gradual change. It had, too, the formulaic manner of ascribing particular phenomena to particular stages, defined by the mode of subsistence. On the standard scales of conjectural history it placed India low, well behind modern Europe or even classical antiquity. For example, the usual Indian form of government was despotism, in the ancient world the crudest level of political organisation; the East had not progressed beyond it. The only relief from these comparisons to India's relentless disadvantage came from an implicit, tendentious undercurrent drawing on a second aspect of conjectural history, which sought a deeper understanding of the more advanced societies by inquiring what they owed to the less advanced. To Mill the conditions in India and Britain, outwardly so different, illuminated each other, because the latter still had her political or religious castes and privileges too. That is to say, the British would have to reform themselves before they could sensibly reform India.

In other ways also, this was hardly an empirical work. Mill had no personal experience of India, and knew no Indian language. That bothered him not a whit, rather to his mind it made him all the more disinterested, objective and severe. Had he gone out there, he might never have seen enough and have fallen victim to the partial misconceptions of his contemporaries. His consciousness of having written a didactic and scientific study encouraged in him a special dogmatism about European superiority. There was here a new note of cultural arrogance towards any and all of the non-western peoples, a total rejection of their civilisation never found in Robertson or the orientalists, who on the contrary tried to redress any such tendency. To Mill, however, it represented the supreme utilitarian value of his work: if the British thought India had a high culture, when in fact she had a low one, they would misgovern her.[5]

Mill gave decisive intellectual inspiration and political impetus to the westernisers.

Within 20 years, they routed the orientalists. The Whig governments at Westminster in the 1830s crowned the process, by preferring men from the new school of thinking for the most senior positions in India. A Scot among them was Alexander Ross, placed on the Governor-General's council in Calcutta. He had a special interest in legal reform, significantly so because utilitarians took law, not social evolution, to be the main intrument of change. He wrote a Minute in 1833 advocating extensive codification of Indian law, but in order to alter rather than merely state it. As it stood, it generally rested on concepts of communal ownership and management, which Ross proposed to replace by others favourable to individualist capitalism. As in Britain, the doctrine of *laissez-faire* would be the touchstone of progress.[6]

By comparison, Thomas Macaulay's more famous Minute on education of 1835, holding eastern learning up to scorn, was almost a moderate document. His belief that Asians could achieve a higher quality of civilisation in the manner of Europeans bespoke yet the cosmopolitan spirit of the eighteenth century. It certainly separated him from the cruder racial prejudice apparent even in his own day. Nor, since his programme was secular rather than religious, did he have much in common with evangelical zealots. His prime target was orientalism, of the kind espoused by the old Scots Tories who had ruled India. Macaulay was, or at least would become, a Scots Whig, using his ancestry to claim a parliamentary seat in Edinburgh after he returned in 1839. Scots Whigs proved particularly fanatical in their admiration of English institutions, as not only India but also Scotland found to her cost.[7]

Yet the rout of the orientalists could hardly have come so soon had Mill's utilitarianism not been somehow in tune with the times, articulating the pressure of deep forces which affected the reality of relations between Britain and India. Westernisers felt history was on their side; orientalists sensed it no longer was. Among those at Lord Minto's court in Calcutta had been John Crawford. He later went to Penang and Java to become the West's first expert on Malay culture. But he also continued writing about India, and with growing commitment to westernisation. His works reflected the ever wider disparity between the levels of technology in traditional economies and the much more advanced ones being attained in Europe. The previous century had not shown any great awareness of western superiority in this respect: Adam Smith condemned the government of Bengal, yet thought the province possessed otherwise all it needed to prosper. But by now, Europeans had no doubt that their organisation and methods far surpassed others. According to Crawford, Indian economic institutions were so backward that they exerted a real depressing effect on income and consumption. He proposed to reform the currency and the monetary system, to lower taxes and inject funds from Britain, together with the skills of her entrepreneurs. The best way of achieving all this, he went on, might be not only through the 'unlimited and unshackled application of British capital and intelligence', but also through 'free settlement', that is to say, white colonisation of India. He denied this could take her the way of the United States, because of the indigenous population: 'The Indians know not what freedom is: they are, for the most part, a timid, often an effeminate, and, as a nation, a feeble race of semi-barbarians'.

Crawford would win his greatest renown as the inaugural president, in 1841, of the Ethnological Society of London, and as the champion of the theory of polygeny. This held mankind to be not a single species but a group of allied ones, some higher, some lower. Crawford drew from Indian data much of his teaching that a necessary, permanent link existed between race, revealed by physical appearance, and other human variables, notably intelligence. So he also took issue with the empirical finding of the earlier philology that peoples settled right from Ceylon to the Outer Hebrides had some common origin, manifested in Indo-European languages. Altogether he proposed a project of intellectual progress quite different from the orientalists', a quest for discrete races in place of the diffusion of enlightened universalism. In the era of the Indian Mutiny, he struck lucky. Orientalists rapidly retreated before the general British revulsion and outrage. That much is clear from the scholarship of George Campbell, the official we saw horrified by Neill's 'very bloody work' at Cawnpore. In 1866 he would publish what became the standard volume on the ethnology of India. For all its author's liberal outlook, he here shares one basic assumption of scientific racism, that race must point to something deeper; the problem lay in defining and classifying it. In Scottish thought, ethnology was dethroning philology.[8]

The decay of orientalism was not just intellectual. At its best it had been for Scots a practical programme too; an example of how compromised the rump of such people now was appeared in the struggle between James Outram and Charles Napier over Sind in 1843. Outram was among those now called the Old Indians. Born in 1803, he was patronised by Henry Dundas and like many hard-up Scots went for a soldier. In India he became a champion pig-sticker and tiger-hunter, indeed a god, worshipped by the Bhils, aborigines of the Deccan, out of whom he formed a military corps. During the 1830s he was on the North-West Frontier, by then the main focus of British strategy because of its turbulence and of Russian designs on it. He spent much time dashing round on secret missions disguised as a *pir*, or holy warrior. Then in 1839 he was appointed political agent in Sind, a highly sensitive posting. The behaviour of its scheming Amirs could never be predicted. Besides, it straddled the River Indus, which the British hoped to use as a military and economic highway. Outram on principle wanted the state to remain independent, which he knew could only be if the fractiously incompetent princely regime was reformed. He undertook the task in person, setting up proper administrative procedures, ordering external relations and arranging suitable education for the rulers' heirs. He expected little in return, no more than that regard should be paid to British interests, something he could see to himself. It was work which in time might have borne fruit, and stabilised the country under an improved native system. But time was not given to Outram. The phase of British strategy in which he played his part came to a climax with the First Afghan War of 1841. An army tried to occupy Kabul but was driven back in disastrous retreat. London then decided to convert the North-West Frontier into a military one, so there would be no further need of political agents. Outram found his job abolished, and received orders to wind his business up by negotiating a subsidiary treaty with the Amirs. In case they required persuasion, he was sent a force under Charles Napier, whom we last saw setting sail for home at the end of his residency on Cephalonia.

The man on the spot still fending off imperial coercion and the newcomer there to impose it soon found themselves at loggerheads. For several months the two Scots manoeuvred against each other to determine the future of the state. Outram insisted that a settlement with its rulers was possible, and desirable for the purpose of bolstering patriarchal government: 'I say *patriarchal* for however we may despise the Amirs as inferior to ourselves, either in morality or expansion of intellect, each chief certainly lives *with* and *for* his portion of the people.' Hardly any of the Sindhis, he argued, could be shown to prefer a British administration to their own; it was enough that anyone wanting protection could come to him. As he sensed control of the situation slipping nevertheless away from him, he wrote: 'It grieves me to say that my heart, and the judgment God has given men, unite in condemning the measures we are carrying out'. They were criminal, robbery with menaces, and for what? 'The sudden revolution we seek is as little called for by necessity, as unjustifiable in fact.'

Not that Napier was a hard-hearted utilitarian, but on the contrary maintained his eccentricities against the conventional wisdom of the age. Since his departure from the Ionian Islands he had usually been unemployed, but just before coming out to India was posted with forces assigned to overawe the Chartist agitation in Yorkshire. Here the suffering of industrial workers deeply distressed him. He hated what he called the shopocracy of England – 'a more base and cruel tyranny never wielded the power of a great nation'. So the principles he carried to the East were the same as he had upheld in Europe. He put the moral condition of the people first, and judged by that priority whether British or native rule was preferable in a particular case. His criteria may have looked utilitarian, except that he did not connect them with economic dogma or with contempt for the natives. He connected them rather with a greater question, whether the British, besides bringing Indians justice and prosperity, could 'give them a share of all things until we blend with them and become one nation. When a half-caste or a full native can become Governor-general we shall not hold India as a colony or conquest but be part of it and hold it for our own'. The rest struck him as cant, on the orientalist side too. He once received a delegation of brahmins complaining of the prohibition of *sati*. They protested that it was a national custom. He replied: 'My nation also has a custom. When men burn women alive, we hang them . . . Let us all act according to national customs'.[9]

In Sind's case, he had no doubt that it would be better off under British rule. Its economy was hampered by its rulers' greed: 'I am not an admirer of commerce, God knows . . . but here our interest and that of the Scindian people are on this point one'. And from a political point of view the Amirs 'are such atrocious tyrants that it is virtuous to roll them over like ninepins'. As Outram fussed about an agreement with rulers probably incapable of making or keeping one, Napier coolly built up military tension till various incidents brought an outbreak of hostilities. Outram then abjectly fled his residency in the capital city of Hyderabad, while Napier set off on a brisk little war. After victory at Miani in the spring of 1843, he proclaimed annexation of the province. 'Peccavi' (I have sinned), he telegraphed the Governor-General. He created an administration which at once embarked on legal and economic reforms, suppressed slavery, built roads, canals, schemes of irrigation. Outram went home humiliated. For some years he engaged in public controversy with Napier about the affair. It turned out that his own career had not, as he feared, been ruined. He was recalled to the East, if at first only to the minor residencies at Baroda and Aden. But this series culminated in Lucknow, capital of Oudh, the largest remaining independent Indian kingdom. By now his experiences, and doubtless the march of history, had changed his own outlook. It was in any case he that recommended the state's annexation from an 'effete and incapable dynasty'. This followed in 1856, an event which directly precipitated the Mutiny.[10]

The annexation was part of a radical Indian policy adopted at the highest level, by the Governor-General himself. This might have seemed unlikely, since James Ramsay, 10th Earl of Dalhousie, was a Conservative in British politics, a scion of the Scots Tory nobility which had stuck with the Dundas despotism to the end. Born in 1812, son of a Governor-General of Canada, Dalhousie made an early political mark. As Lord Ramsay, he was briefly MP for East Lothian until succeeding to the title in 1838. When Sir Robert Peel became Prime Minister in 1841, he appointed Dalhousie a vice-president of the Board of Trade under William Gladstone, whom he followed as president in 1845. He tried to cool down the railway mania of the time, proposing that the state might undertake to provide such a wonderful new means of transport. Peel rejected that out of hand, and Dalhousie had to get to India before he could try it. With the break-up of the Ministry on repeal of the Corn Laws, the Whigs angled to recruit this rising star. It was the new Prime Minister, Lord John Russell, who appointed him to India, as the youngest Governor-General ever. Dalhousie's position in Scottish domestic affairs was likewise ambiguous. A friend of Thomas Chalmers, he had come out against lay patronage in the Church of Scotland. All the same he preferred the maintenance of a religious Establishment, and did not secede in 1843.

Dalhousie combined an inexhaustible appetite for work with an almost perfect intolerance of opposition. This did him very well at Westminster, but stored up trouble in a land as ancient and slow as India. He received plenty of advice from old hands, most of which he ignored. To Napier, now his Commander-in-Chief, he said: 'I have been warned, Sir Charles, not to let you encroach on my authority, and I will take good care that you don't'. Napier only stood him for a year or two, then resigned, with the parting shot that the Governor-General was 'as vain as a pretty woman or an ugly man'. Dalhousie's sheer strength of character, however, sufficed to carry him through all present difficulties, leaving his successor to reap the whirlwind. He himself was broken by his exertions and died, aged only 48, four years after he retired in 1856.[11]

At his arrival, the British already held more or less complete political and military power over India, as much at any rate as they could reasonably need. Yet Dalhousie sought to amass more. In particular, he followed a policy of annexation on a scale not seen since early in the century. He came just at the end of the Sikh War, which the British had won. But the splendid fight put up by the hardy warrior race dominating the Punjab awakened their deep admiration. Wishing to treat the vanquished leniently, the British at first preserved a puppet state under a boy maharajah, Duleep Singh. Many Sikhs would still not admit defeat, however, and in 1848 they rose in revolt. Dalhousie crushed them, then determined that all remnants of their sovereignty should be swept away. He sent its symbol, the Koh-i-noor, to Queen Victoria. He refused to countenance even the role of figurehead for Duleep Singh, who was carried off to Scotland and installed at Castle Menzies in Perthshire to learn the ways of a gentleman; the local lairds held the Black Prince, as they called him, in great regard. Meanwhile, Dalhousie set up an administration for the Punjab under the two brothers from Ulster, Henry and John Lawrence, whose beneficent regime became the pride of the Raj. Never sparing themselves, they established new systems of defence, revenue and justice which brought to the province an unexampled prosperity.

Here Dalhousie discharged inherited responsibilities, but soon made clear that he meant to assume new ones towards the native states. First he struck beyond the borders of India. He provoked war with Burma in 1852 after complaints from British merchants about their treatment at Rangoon, though it amounted to no more than the routine difficulties encountered at any number of exotic ports. Dalhousie dispatched an army, took the city and annexed the surrounding province of Pegu. He would not allow that the people had a grievance at seeing their capital confiscated: 'I swear solemnly that if the Burmese nation renews war on us, I shall hold myself free to utterly destroy the Burman Kingdom, and to hunt down the race that rules it, till I make them beggars on the face of the earth'.[12]

To the Indians themselves, his most controversial policy arose under what he called the doctrine of lapse. He expounded it as

> the policy of taking advantage of every just opportunity which presents itself for consolidating the territories which already belong to us . . . for thus getting rid of those petty intervening principalities which may be made a means of annoyance but which can never, I venture to think, be a source of strength.

At least lip service had always been paid to the principle of independence for native states in their internal affairs. Dalhousie insisted rather that Britain's interests, as determined by herself, must be absolutely paramount. Even in the protected states where he chose not to interfere, he still held that protection might be terminated by

annexation. Misrule certainly incurred his severe retribution. Dalhousie forced the
Nizam of Hyderabad, in hock to the British, to cede lands yielding enough revenue
to clear the debts. He suppressed nominal sovereignties, those of the Nawab of the
Carnatic, the Rajah of Tanjore and the Peshwa of the Marathas, though he spared the
Moghul Emperor at Delhi. A lapsed state he regarded as one in which the prince had
no heir. Customary Hindu law coped with failure of the ruling line by permitting
adoption, but he would not hear of it. As a result, he made seven states disappear
from the map. It was hard to see what limit, in terms of territory or revenue, might be
set to British interests thus defined. They seemed to imply the future extinction of
the native states.

Meanwhile Dalhousie pursued in British India a programme of intense westernisation. At the bottom of it lay, as befitted a pupil of Peel, comprehensive fiscal
reform. 'I am a Scot,' he remarked, 'and prefer to do what I have to do cannily as well
as boldly.' The reform enabled him to create a unified department of public works,
which set about giving India systems of railways, canals, posts and telegraphs in
advance of most European countries. He restored the Moghuls' Grand Trunk Road
from Calcutta to Peshawar. He launched industrialisation by developing resources of
coal and iron. He improved agriculture by schemes of irrigation, with encouragement for the cultivation of tea and for forestry. All ports were made free, and internal
barriers to trade removed. Education formed another major part of the programme.
The Governor-General's dispatch on the subject was anglicist, speaking of 'the
acquisition by the higher classes of a liberal European education, the effects of which
may be expected slowly to pervade the rest of their fellow-countrymen, and to raise,
in the end, the educational tone of the whole country'. He accordingly founded
India's first three universities, gave grants to multiply the number of private
institutions and set up an engineering college to service the new economic structure.
In truth Dalhousie appeared to traditional India to be turning the world upside
down, and by all accounts his success impressed the people with a sense of defeat.
Thus were the fires stoked which broke out with such fury in 1857.[13]

The Mutiny, apart from everything else, buried political orientalism. Its Scottish
cadre had already received a mortal blow under the legislation which, for the last time
in 1853, renewed the East India Company's charter. Among other reforms, it brought
in public competitive examinations for administrative posts. At a stroke, that ended
the prospects which generations of Scots landed and professional families had
enjoyed, because they relied on patronage to get the plum jobs. Worse still, the
first examinations turned out a national disaster. The _Edinburgh Review_ wailed that
'Scotland failed egregiously'. Of 20 places offered, only one went to a Scot, Charles
Aitchison, the university of Edinburgh's most brilliant student of philosophy, but
otherwise, as a Cameronian dissenter, hardly of the old stamp. Still, the country had a
just complaint that the examination tested subjects, notably classical versification,
not taught at its universities. Parliament asked Macaulay himself to report on the
matter. He recommended a revised syllabus to reduce the bias in favour of English

candidates. Yet Scots were never again to win the share of official Indian positions which had been theirs for a century.

There was also a domestic effect. This painful revelation of inadequacy brought to a head the debate about reform of the universities which had been going on for 30 years. Now it seemed a sheer necessity if Scots were to compete on equal terms with graduates south of the Border. That produced the first retreat from the Scottish academic philosophy of generalism, and a shift towards the English one of specialisation. The affair gave in other respects, too, a salutary warning. It showed how easily, in an emerging global system, a small country could lose a position carefully built up. It also showed that, while the Scots might have a lot to teach the world, the world was likely to answer back. Their eager response to imperial opportunities had wrought great changes in their commerce and industry, altering in turn the balance of their social forces, an alteration already transmitted to the level of national institutions. The process had by and large taken place, if not quite by the will of the Scots, at least on their own initiative. Here, in the universities, came the first case of an institutional reform at the same time unwanted and in effect imposed from outside.[14]

It was an ill portent, not least in giving rise to a prototype of the modern Scottish whinge. But one Scot refused to stand passively by. Perhaps the last of the Presbyterian orientalists was John Muir, a wealthy retired Indian official. He employed his leisure to become a philologist of the first rank, in the five volumes of *Original Sanskrit Texts* (1868–70), which showed that Scottish surmises about Indian history could be corroborated from the written record. Any spare time he devoted to missions, applying his scholarship here too. He wrote a series of pamphlets on aspects of Christianity in Sanskrit verse. In his deep respect for Indian culture, he tried in *An Essay on Conciliation* to persuade missionaries to make the acquaintance of orthodox Hindus, who believed some things that a Christian could not reject. On the contrary, 'there is much in their learning which we can honestly admire and praise'. He feared that the dissolution of the East India Company after the Mutiny would spell the end not only of Scottish opportunity but also of Scottish orientalism: the grounding in languages given as a matter of course to lads setting out eastwards would no longer be available. So, in 1862, he endowed the chair of Sanskrit at the university of Edinburgh. In fact, it only underlined that an era was over. Two successive professors owed something to Scottish antecedents, if we trace them back through the Schlegels to Alexander Hamilton. But they were Germans: Theodor Aufrecht and Julius Eggeling.[15]

CHAPTER SEVENTEEN

'We are too Scotch': Canada

On the afternoon of April 25, 1849, the Governor-General of Canada, James Bruce, 8th Earl of Elgin, drove from his residence to Parliament House in Montreal in order to give royal assent to Bills passed in the session just ending. The ceremony was usually a formality: while Elgin sat silent on his throne, a clerk would read aloud each title, another would signify his assent. The Governor-General did, however, have the power to withhold it and refer a measure to London. One coming up this day, the Rebellion Losses Bill, had proved so controversial that many thought that was what Elgin would do. The Tories in Parliament were convinced he would. When it received assent along with the rest, they groaned and stamped. Some walked out in indignation, and as soon as they were in the open air began to yell and hoot their displeasure. A crowd gathered. In Montreal it was easy to get up a Tory crowd, because most Scots in the city supported the Tories. When the Governor-General left an hour later, they were ready for him. In the 100 yards he had to walk from the portals of the Parliament to the street, they pelted him with eggs. They let out a cheer when one hit him in the face. As he gained his carriage and raced away, they followed him with curses, mud and stones. Nor did their excitement abate. They ran through the streets ringing bells and calling a public meeting on the Champ de Mars for eight o'clock. The authorities thought the trouble would burn itself out there, and left the maintenance of order to the police; but of these there were only 72 for the 50,000 people of Montreal. Large numbers did assemble. Under no effective control or guidance, they marched back on Parliament House, where a late sitting continued. The tall, brilliantly lit windows offered too tempting a target. The members found rocks crashing through, and fled. Now there was nobody to stop the mob entering. One man removed the mace. Another, with a broken nose, sat in the Speaker's chair and pronounced in mock solemnity, 'I dissolve this House'. Somewhere within, somebody set fire to something. Inside a quarter of an hour the whole building went up. With two libraries and a mass of public records, it was completely destroyed. Wags dubbed the ruins the Elgin Marbles, because it resembled the Athenian Parthenon as left by the Governor-General's father.[1]

Too late, Elgin called up troops. A highly cultured, painfully moral man, he wanted no more trouble, however. He was a friend of Lord Dalhousie, and one can just imagine how the Governor-General of India would have dealt with such an incident, but the Governor-General of Canada allowed himself only a symbolic retribution. He deprived Montreal of its status as capital of the Canadas: in future he would reside, and the Parliament would meet, alternately in Quebec and Toronto. Five days later he returned to hear an address from the members expressing abhorrence of the late events. Still the mob was not sated. Elgin again drove off through a hail of stones, his escort of volunteer dragoons trying vainly to shield him. On his way home, rioters hired cabs to pursue him and only the skill of his postillions kept him ahead of them. Afterwards he picked up 216 missiles from the floor of his carriage. In the streets and taverns, there was wild talk of assassinating him. At any rate the St Andrew's Society of Montreal, not to mention the Thistle Curling Club, indignantly deposed him as honorary president. 'I confess I did not know before how thin is the crust of order which covers the anarchical elements that boil and toss beneath our feet,' he wrote. But he might have been reassured by a second address, a loyal one from Glengarry County, and others that followed. Before long he ascertained that they did more fully represent public opinion. Three months later he would record: 'Truly if ever rebellion stood upon a rickety pretence, it is the Canadian Tory rebellion of 1849'.[2]

He was in a position to know, for he had been brought up an old Scots Tory himself. Like Dalhousie, he drifted towards the Whigs after his party collapsed under the impact of the Disruption and the repeal of the Corn Laws. What remained of it anyway held to one hoary principle, that Her Majesty's Government ought ordinarily to be supported. But when Elgin accepted appointment to Canada in 1847, also from the Liberal Prime Minister, Lord John Russell, he found a country which was still ruled by Tories, which for that matter had always been ruled by Tories, usually by Scots Tories. He, however, carried instructions to conduct his administration on the advice of Ministers commanding a majority in Parliament, in effect, to introduce responsible government. To start with a clean sheet, he no sooner arrived than he called fresh elections. He sought not just constitutional advance, but also some reliable answer to the problem of holding the hotchpotch of Canada together, otherwise she might fall into the hands of the United States.

The problem still lay in reconciling the French, whom some British officials regarded as traitors. But Elgin invited their leader, Louis Joseph Papineau, to dinner, and talked to him in his own language: 'I found him a very well-bred, intelligent man'. All the same, the Governor-General was not disarmed. He concluded that Papineau occupied a position far too radical and anti-clerical for most of his people, so that, if only their grievances were redressed, their conservatism could come out. Among the British, especially the growing population of Upper Canada, flourished another reforming party, which Elgin assessed as constitutional and so probably ready for reconciliation too. He felt less sure of its radical offshoot, known as the Clear Grits, headed by the Scots editor of the *Toronto Globe*, George Brown. If tainted with American ideas of republican democracy, it seemed to get more excited about religion, the menace of Roman Catholicism and the evils of ecclesiastical establishments. Anyway, all these parties together clearly outweighed the Tories, under two Scotsmen of different generations, wicked old Allan McNab, son of a

Highland soldier settled by the River Niagara, and clever young John Macdonald, an immigrant from Dornoch. The polls proved as much. The new Parliament had a majority of French Canadians and English-speaking reformers. From them, Elgin formed the first responsible Ministry in March 1848. This at last implemented the most important recommendation of Lord Durham's report after the rebellion of 1837, in the country's greatest political step forward between the Canada Act of 1791 and the confederation of 1867. For the Empire as a whole, Elgin launched the idea that it should be founded where possible on local autonomy.[3]

The Tories, angry at being forced out of office, tried to regain the initiative by stirring up trouble over the Rebellion Losses Bill. This centrepiece of the incoming administration's programme was meant to settle the claims for damages, still outstanding after a decade, against the destruction wrought in 1837. The previous Tory Government had agreed in principle to a global sum of £100,000 for them. The question remained what share ought to be allocated to Lower Canada and its Frenchmen, among whom victims and rebels were not easy to distinguish. The Tories declared it outrageous that they should have anything. McNab said: 'If we don't make a disturbance about this, we shall never get in'. Elgin himself thought the Bill premature, and would have preferred some prior agreement on distributing the money. When Parliament passed it all the same, he dutifully followed the principle of responsible government and gave assent, with the results we have seen. Still, the riot in Montreal vindicated him and his constitutional reform, because it discredited the Tories. Some of them even began to murmur that American annexation might be better than surrender to sedition.

Canadian Toryism was a chip off the old Scottish block, perhaps indeed more robust, to judge from the fact that it lasted in office two decades longer. It rested on economic power, which in Canada was mercantile rather than landed, concentrated among the fur-traders and other plutocrats of Montreal. They could exercise their power in a number of ways: by manipulating elections, by distributing patronage, by manning the institutions of the country, such as they were. This being the New World, they also had to make themselves reasonably popular, and here they outdid the Scots Tories. They controlled most of the press. They could count on the ultraloyalism of places like Glengarry County, peopled by Highlanders. Elsewhere in the social fabric, they operated through the networks of the St Andrew's Societies and, latterly, of the Orange lodges springing up in reaction to the first wave of Irish immigration. The whole structure was directed towards upholding royal government, which in return upheld the Tories, at least till Elgin came along. It had easily checked the liberal forces. These attached the abusive epithet of the Family Compact to their rulers.[4]

The obvious difference between this and Scotland's *ancien régime* lay in the absence, or rather very pallid presence, of the Kirk. In Canada, as in other colonies, the Establishment was Anglican. The practical benefit of that status accrued from the Church of England's income out of the "clergy reserves", the one-seventh of

Canadian soil set aside under the Act of 1791 to provide it. With the Scottish population growing, the Church of Scotland wanted to secure some share as well: it was after all co-established under the 1707 Treaty of Union. The principle of official support for colonial Presbyterianism had already been conceded in Nova Scotia since 1791. The problem with that line of argument was where to stop it. The Roman Catholic Church, too, had been established in Quebec before the conquest. Its bishop in Glengarry County, Alexander Macdonell, pressed for it to get its own share of the reserves, not least in reward for the conservative principles he instilled in his flock. All the same, in Canada the establishment of Anglicanism alone had so far been taken for granted.

The great champion of this state of affairs was a Scot, one of the type who, having done nicely elsewhere, delights in needling his countrymen. John Strachan, born in 1778 the son of a quarryman on upper Donside, had risen far from his humble origins, as pupil of James Beattie at the university of Aberdeen and friend of Thomas Chalmers at St Andrews. Emigration to Canada was not an obvious option for him but, having taken Anglican orders there, he married well, into the clan of James McGill, the Glaswegian fur-trader who endowed the university named after him. McGill was besides a politician, a member of the assembly of Lower Canada, so one of the Family Compact, which Strachan thus joined as well. It opened all doors. He himself was elected to the assembly in 1815, became then archdeacon of Toronto and first bishop of Upper Canada on foundation of the diocese in 1839. If he turned out more Anglican than the Anglicans, he stayed on good terms with Chalmers, who had him awarded a doctorate of laws from St Andrews. Perhaps he owed to this link the strength of his belief in religious establishments, in order to educate and morally improve the people. In Canada's case he argued that, since Anglicanism was already established, members of other denominations would over time conform to it so long as their own Churches were not encouraged. Certainly it was unheard of anywhere for there to be two establishments on one territory. He claimed he would rather see the Roman Catholics triumph than the clergy reserves be taken away. As a matter of fact, Canada was eventually to have four establishments, a manifest absurdity which led to the reserves being secularised, in other words, to disestablishment of all Churches. To that extent, Strachan proved right.[5]

Unfortunately, his Church was not content to justify itself by logic alone. Its behaviour in Canada did it no credit at all: it showed itself greedy and aggressive in defence of its privileges, stubborn and perverse in obstruction of other denominations. For example, it tried to assert a monopoly of solemnising marriages, and impose religious tests on teachers to keep every school and college under its control. Strachan, in the front-line of these battles, remained a Scotsman in his sectarianism, at least. If he sought to goad his compatriots, he succeeded. John Rae, the emigrant political economist, protested: 'We leave our native land to come to a British, not an English, Province . . . But we find here a party, a powerful and hitherto an all prevailing party, who tell us a very different tale, who tell us we must submit to bear the burden, and wear the badge of inferiority and subjection'. Robert Gourlay, a touchy laird from Fife, whose progressive views were unwelcome at home during the repression after the Napoleonic Wars, caused even more offence when he moved to Canada. For his attacks on the clergy reserves he was actually charged with sedition and banished back to Scotland. Scots at large grew indignant too. With more Christian zeal than the English in Canada, they also aspired, not unreasonably, to have their religion wear the same face in their new as in their old abode, under a robust parochial structure seeing to their education, welfare and morals.[6]

Since this worthy aim was conducive to public order and happiness rather than the reverse, the Canadian Government could hardly stop its ears. It did begin to respond with modest aid to the petitions of individual ministers. These took care to stress not only their genuine need, but also their respectability and political soundness. What else was an establishment for? It took not much more for Presbyterians to claim stipends as of right, that is to say, on the grounds of co-establishment under the Treaty of Union. Pressure from the Scottish community persuaded the legislatures of both Upper and Lower Canada to pass resolutions in that sense, requesting either a share of the clergy reserves or else a separate endowment. Fortunately Canada had at this time, in the 1820s, a Scot as Governor-General, the 9th Earl of Dalhousie, father of the Indian Governor-General and founder of the university named after him in Halifax, Nova Scotia. His was not in general a happy term, being marked by a feud with Papineau that won him an anti-French reputation. Yet this conscientious, if apolitical, proconsul felt anxious to build durable social and cultural institutions on Canadian soil. He could see nothing better for the purpose than the Kirk. With his support, the legislatures sent petitions in its favour to London, and secured a ruling in principle that the Church of England had no right to monopolise the reserves.[7]

That was only a first step, however. In order to sustain its claims, Presbyterianism had to surround itself in a new country with the panoply of establishment. As things stood, it consisted of little more than isolated congregations, to all intents and purposes voluntary. Most were anyway connected with dissenting Churches at home, which in British North America as elsewhere had been more active than mother Kirk. The Secession Church sent its first ministers to Nova Scotia in 1766, and formed a synod there in 1795. The sect then penetrated Upper and Lower Canada, where it set up a presbytery in 1817. To date, this was the most advanced local form of the normal territorial hierarchy of Scottish Churches. But since it represented one avowedly dissenting, many immigrant Scots would not join it.

To such confusion the Kirk had to bring some order. It first chose to work through a sort of missionary society, the Glasgow Colonial Society, founded in 1825 with Dalhousie as its patron, in which the moving spirit was the secretary, the Rev William Burns of Paisley. It drew its funds partly from private sources, the evangelical generosity of the parent city, and partly from a public one, some grudging assistance by the Colonial Office. Its purpose was to send ministers, schoolmasters and similar useful personnel to Canada. Groups of settlers wishing to employ one or another could apply to it for a grant. They were expected, however, to make a contribution of their own, and soon found they had a further price to pay. The missionaries dispatched in response arrived asserting that they alone represented true, loyal Presbyterianism, while any deviation from their instructions and procedures represented the opposite. This sometimes split the host congregations, or made them decide they would be better off continuing to govern themselves. When clergymen already serving in Canada welcomed these brethren, they were thanked but told they would be regarded as schismatic unless they rendered complete obedience to the decrees of the General Assembly. Some again felt put off by such arrogance. The Church of Scotland did embark on negotiations with the existing bodies of Canadian Presbyterians for a union. But they collapsed in 1832, because it insisted on its own terms. Yet great numbers of colonists also welcomed the official presence of the orthodox Kirk, and were eager to help get it organised to the point where it would qualify for support from the clergy reserves.[8]

There followed a faintly unseemly competition for the allegiance of the faithful, which did not go all the Church of Scotland's way. By the mid-1830s there existed in the Maritime Provinces 56 presbyterian congregations, of which 23 had entered into connection with the Kirk, but they were still outnumbered by the 31 in the Secession Church's synod. Upper and Lower Canada housed 73 congregations, with 38 adhering to the Kirk, which here had been able to set up a regular structure of synod and presbyteries. That was another step forward. At home the General Assembly appointed a Colonial Committee in 1836, to bring these efforts fully under the wing of the institutional Church and to lobby in London for a share of the reserves. In Canada it renewed the negotiations for a union in 1839. This time it managed to win over 17 secessionist ministers, and the next year formed a new synod embracing them all. No word fell of any autonomy for it, or otherwise of its relationship with the parent Kirk: for the time being it was, though unrepresented in the General Assembly, apparently bound to order its affairs according to Scottish usage.

The Church of Scotland now believed it could proceed with co-establishment in the full sense, and the Canadian authorities agreed. They distributed the reserves among four Churches, the Kirk, Methodists and Roman Catholics, in addition to the Church of England. The last was still the most generously treated. It contained about one-fifth of the population, yet got more than two-fifths of the income. The Church of Scotland's allocation was proportional to its size, also one-fifth of the population. The remaining three-fifths shared two-fifths of the reserves. Still, Canadian Presbyterianism felt that it had reached a real turning point, and that there was nothing it could not now achieve in extending a network of churches and schools under a learned clergy. But all this happened just in time for the Disruption.[9]

There was little reason for it to spread to the colonies. They had no system of lay patronage and a weaker connection of Church and state. Canadian Presbyterians, the question of their autonomy left open, were anyway unlikely to stand for permanent subordination to the Scottish Establishment, so its future could hardly determine their own. Still, the Disruption aroused strong emotions among them. It struck at the heart of Scotland's greatest national institution, and their recent experiences probably gave them a special interest in institutional matters. The organised Canadian Kirk being of recent growth, nearly all its ministers had been born and educated in Scotland. Not only did they stay in touch, but many were also Evangelicals who had crossed the Atlantic because they could find no patronage at home. They and their flocks certainly followed the final stages of the Ten Years' Struggle with intense interest. When the break came, the partisans of the Free Church felt they could not but emulate their friends in the mother country. The feeling was reciprocated. Burns of the Glasgow Colonial Society, having joined the Free Church, sailed across in 1843 and again the next year to travel around urging sympathisers to declare open support. During the Canadian synod of 1844 most commissioners still argued that the matters at issue in Scotland were irrelevant here. But a strong minority would not agree, and in the end they disrupted this synod too. One quarter of the ministers in Upper and Lower Canada, together with almost the whole synod of Nova Scotia, and other ministers in the Maritime Provinces, came out and formed a Free Church of their own. It startlingly attested the strength of emigrant Scots' attachment to the homeland and its domestic concerns. One scholar has called it a 'triumph of Scottishness over Canadianisation'.[10]

To begin with, most laymen remained in the Kirk, yet this was the start of its slow death in Canada. Not before 1845 did it vie with the Free Church, with Burns in particular, in rallying its Canadian adherents, meanwhile the object of aggressive recruitment by its adversary. It suffered when numbers of its ministers abandoned their flocks to join in a scramble for the 400 pulpits suddenly vacant in Scotland. Those congregations often switched sides. The Kirk made another mistake in standing out from the general Protestant reaction during the 1840s against the clergy reserves. It needed the money more than ever, but other denominations were deciding on reflection that public subsidy of Roman Catholics had been a bad idea. After 1848 responsible government, by giving greater weight to public opinion, anyway rendered it impossible to sustain this relic of an oligarchical Canada. The Kirk's attitude lent it the air of a conservative and alien influence from the Old World, especially compared to a Free Church looking more like a genuine Canadian form of Presbyterianism. Defence of the reserves was now a lost cause. In 1854, the Government abolished them, bringing to an end the curious Canadian experiment in co-establishment. Nobody regretted it, for it had simply become an irritant between the Churches and the state, as among the Churches themselves. But in consequence of all this the Kirk shrank, while the Free Church grew. By 1861 they had 100,000 and 150,000 members respectively.[11]

As in Scotland, so in Canada, the emergence of the Free Church was a religious revival too, the more fervent because riding the crest, it believed, of an international evangelical wave. Its leaders in the mother country took care to keep up this spirit.

Burns settled in Canada and sustained contacts with them. Alexander Duff came on a tour to boost morale, and for a long time to come Canadian clergymen would complete their training in Scotland. Such vigour suited the pioneering spirit of a new country. Here too, it could count on some of the most enterprising elements in the commercial middle class, and with backing from Brown and the *Globe* it had no trouble making its views heard. Here too, it set out, undaunted by scant resources, on the titanic task of providing a minister and a place of worship for every congregation needing one. It was usually the loudest and most insistent, the most articulate and intellectual voice in the chorus of Canadian Evangelicals denouncing popery, intemperance and desecration of the sabbath. It became in fact the driving force of Canadian Presbyterianism.

We need only compare its conduct over the clergy reserves with that of the Canadian Kirk. On this question it initially faced a dilemma like one which taxed the Free Church of Scotland. Its ideology upheld the principle of establishment, the duty of a Christian state to support the Church in the freedom it chose for itself. Since the Kirk had won a share of the reserves in 1840, the Free Church felt entitled on that principle to apply for some continuation of the arrangement; this was refused. So in practice it found that, again as at home, it had placed itself in a voluntarist position. Several decades passed before the Free Church of Scotland could bring itself to accept this reality. But, within four years, the Canadian one made a virtue of it. In a last attempt to save the system, the outgoing Tory Government announced early in 1848 that it was making available for division among any interested denominations an accumulated surplus in the fund from the reserves. The Free Church answered that it wanted nothing. Rather than touch pelf from such hands, it would abandon its claims for support and in future rely, with a little help from Scotland, on its own flock.[12]

This brought it into line with the canons of the Secession Church, comprising the synods and congregations which the Kirk had failed to rope in before 1840. They enjoyed modest growth, and in 1847 joined other minor sects, once more in parallel with a Scottish development, to form the United Presbyterians, numbering about 50,000. They identified strongly with Canada. Their leader, the Rev William Proudfoot, declared that, because Canadians were creating their own nationality, 'it has been a great hindrance to our success that we have kept up the Scotch character. We are too Scotch – our habits, our brogue, our mode of sermonising are all too Scotch. The thistle is everywhere seen; we have effected no lodgement in the public mind'. In those sentiments, perhaps, he differed from the Free Church, but in precious little else. It seemed a natural step for the two to seek a union. The negotiations still got captiously bogged down for a time in the theory of establishment. But by 1861 they were successfully concluded, 40 years ahead of a similar union in Scotland. The Canada Presbyterian Church, as it called itself, had about 200,000 members and more than 200 ministers. By 1875 even the Kirk gave up the unequal struggle and threw in its lot with this rival. Canadian Presbyterians, gathered in one

Church, then made up the country's largest body of Protestants. They again anticipated the final Scottish reunion by more than half a century. But by contrast with the Kirk, which won formal concession of its spiritual independence from Westminster, the Canadians did not attempt to define their relationship with the state. Still, the silence was eloquent. It meant in effect that the ethos of the Free Church prevailed, an ethos now voluntarist and Canadianised.[13]

Canadianised voluntarism had secular implications too. In journalism and politics, as both dissenter and nationalist, Brown of the Clear Grits and the *Globe* embodied the link. He was a tall, beefy, lantern-jawed Scotsman, the son of a radical town councillor in Edinburgh who became involved in financial scandal and thought better to emigrate with his family in 1838, first to New York. There the father began publishing a newspaper for Scots in North America, the *British Chronicle*. In the prelude to the Disruption it took the Evangelical side. Young Brown, employed as a reporter, went to look at the situation in Canada and grew so fascinated that he decided to stay. The rest of the Browns came after, closing down the *Chronicle* and setting up the *Banner* in Toronto, which underwent a further metamorphosis into the *Globe* in 1844.

It made Brown's reputation. It presented itself as sturdily Canadian, urging its readers to cast off any colonial inferiority complex, never ceasing to preach the virtues of life in the new country. A part of its heart all the same stayed in the Old World, in Scotland especially. It followed events there with unflagging attention to detail, presumably reflecting its readers' interests. At the Disruption, it championed democratic Presbyterianism against episcopacy and monarchy. It urged the liberation of all religion from the trammels of the state, not least because this would have the effect in Lower Canada of disestablishing Roman Catholicism again; Brown's antagonism to the French verged on the fanatical. Naturally he also wanted the clergy reserves secularised, and did much to bring an at first uncertain Free Church round to this view. Responsible government was on his agenda too. Shrewdly, he perceived in Elgin, who otherwise stood for everything he hated, one of the few statesmen of the time believing that colonies could enjoy economic independence and political equality without separation from the mother country. So Brown gave the Governor-General all the support he could. The *Globe* might have been expected to denounce the Rebellion Losses Bill as a sell-out to the French. Yet it commended the measure as equitable for all concerned. In the aftermath, the Tory talk of joining the United States could be heard in radical circles too, but Brown would have none of that either. Responsible government for Canada was what he wanted, and responsible government was what Elgin brought.

Brown himself had a long political career in front of him. In 1852 he was elected to Parliament, and pursued his nationalist line. He called for the incorporation into Canada of the vast western territories. They could then be systematically settled, so tipping the balance of population against the French and their entrenched, corrupting position in a system of two equal provinces. This cause also led him into direct opposition to the country's other main conservative force, the financiers of Montreal, with their liking for the politics of patronage and need to keep the West empty. He opposed, in other words, the old Scottish Empire, and wanted to change the world sustaining it. His own constituency lay in the people of Upper Canada, the farmers especially. But he mellowed with time and came to see confederation as the key to the future, in which all the country's disparate sections could claim legitimate influence. He played a useful part in bringing that about in 1867. His odyssey, from Scottish radicalism by way of religious then secular voluntarism to the establishment of a new nation, was a significant one. Since he spent his whole life in the heat of battle, his tragic end had a strange aptness. In the history of Canada's notably decent public life, only one leading politician has ever been assassinated. This was Brown, shot dead in 1880 at the age of 62, by a disgruntled employee whom he had sacked for drinking.[14]

CHAPTER EIGHTEEN

'Bothwell Brig faces': Australasia

I n 1848 Cape Breton Island off Nova Scotia suffered a harvest so disastrous that
many of its colonists decided to leave. Among them were the people of St Ann's
Bay, a group of Scots, most originally from Assynt, a few from Applecross, who had
so far made a success of new lives in this remote spot, under the leadership of their
minister, the Rev Norman Macleod. They all worked hard, he for them and they for
him. In the early days, when they scarcely ever saw money, he accepted no stipend
but took his recompense in the form of manual labour from both men and women,
rendering his own plot the most productive of all. It was an example of the discipline,
stern even by Scottish standards, that he exercised over them.

They were simple, crofting Gaels who had left for the New World in 1817 under
threat of clearance. They had also become estranged from the Kirk, and needed a
preacher. They opted to follow Macleod, though he was then no more than a
schoolmaster employed at Ullapool by the Society in Scotland for Propagating
Christian Knowledge. Indeed, he may never his whole life long have been regularly
ordained: he merely returned from a certain missionary journey to the United States
all of a sudden wearing clerical garb. He did not, at any rate, spare his fellows of the
cloth. He abused one of them – and this a friend from their days together at the
university of Aberdeen – for his 'false conversion, scraps of philosophy, fragments of
divinity, painted parlour, dainty table, sable surtout, curled cravat, ponderous purse,
big belly, poised pulpit, soft and silly spouse'. Macleod would relate with special
distaste, as exhibiting the degeneracy of the modern clergy, his experience of a manse
where 'after dinner, on a Lord's day, the samplers of his Reverence's daughters were
brought forward round the table for inspection'. He was himself, of course, a strict
sabbatarian, insisting that the potatoes for Sunday had to be peeled on a Saturday.
On the sabbath he would preach two long sermons, first in English and then
immediately afterwards in Gaelic, the whole performance taking three hours.

In this and in almost every other respect his ranting, domineering, charismatic
figure controlled the emigrants' existence. He tolerated no deviation, and enforced
his will through a network of informants. One, after a theft in the village, cast
suspicion on a young boy. The elders interrogated him, refusing to accept his denials
and urging him to confess. At length they threatened that, unless he did so, they
would lock him overnight in the graveyard. The poor mite broke down in terror and
admitted his guilt. Macleod, who acted not only as minister but also as judge, at once
passed sentence: part of the culprit's ear was to be cut off. He proceeded to perform

the operation himself. The lad turned out to be completely innocent, and Macleod was lucky to escape prosecution by the civil authorities. But within the settlement he met at most a silent opposition. One of his sons organised dances in the attic of the manse whenever he was away on some evangelical errand, and 'the votaries of the festivities banded together into a secret society'. The rest, too devout or too cowed, had only the odd, presumably tame, ceilidh as relief from their austere lives. Macleod's psychological hold over them remained otherwise complete: when he resolved that, staring famine in the face, they should all go to Australia, to Australia they went.[1]

Macleod made this choice on the good reports of another son already out there. But he had been given a false impression of the country. When his party of 140, including 40 children, arrived by way of Cape Town at Adelaide in 1852, he descried nothing like what he expected, never a place roundabout to gather a community of the elect. Other Highland emigrants in the colony offered scant encouragement. Landing weak and sickly from the long voyage, and recuperating only slowly in the irksome climate, they found no ready means to make a living. Some despaired, took to drink, became a social problem. With that example before their eyes, Macleod's people departed again. But they had little more joy when they moved on to reconnoitre the district of Melbourne; being in the middle of the gold rush, the town looked to them more like an outer circle of hell. Their leader faced, according to his biographer, 'for the first time since his youth the possibility that the glory of Norman Macleod could be in conflict with the glory of God'.

Australia was anyway not a land in which Presbyterianism had found it easy to take hold. There was a dearth of Scots settlers, and those who did come had tended to scatter across the vast spaces of the outback. It was easier for the Church of Scotland to cope with missions to the heathen than with this territorial untidiness. It did not actually bother to try for some time, in Australia any more than in other colonies. A group of Presbyterians who organised themselves as early as 1809 and went the length of building a place of worship by the Hawkesbury River, near Sydney, had waited in vain for a minister. Not till 1822 did the first arrive, Archibald MacArthur, and he was a dissenter who settled at Hobart in Tasmania. Another year passed until one came duly representing the Kirk. John Dunmore Lang, born at Greenock in 1799 and educated at the university of Glasgow, had like many young Evangelicals had difficulty in getting a regular charge in Scotland. He endured several years of frustration, till he heard from a friend on military service in New South Wales about its lack of provision for Presbyterian worship. Intrepidly, he determined in 1826 to go out and found a kirk in Sydney himself. He would minister there for 52 years. So, when Macleod turned up in Australia, Lang's career was still in midflight. They never met, perhaps fortunately, since they would have found little to agree about. For instance, Lang welcomed the gold rush because 'the ascendancy of the squatters will cease', and new immigrants 'will employ their power to achieve the country's entire freedom and independence'. These were indeed unusual opinions for a Scots minister to hold.[2]

Lang was one of nature's heretics, but his experience of a new country certainly brought out in him that trait of Presbyterianism which found in mere reality no bar to the visions of the righteous. He ought not to have been taken aback, though he seemed deeply offended, by the fact that convicts made up a majority of the population. For them he could conceive no sympathy at all, even after they had served their time. Under an increasingly liberal administration, they came to be treated the same as free settlers. Indeed they formed a political interest, known as emancipist, to press for remaining anomalies to be ironed out. Lang bitterly opposed it at every turn. He waxed especially furious, for example, that many ex-convicts earned their bread as journalists: 'It was absolutely disgraceful to the colony to have so powerful an engine as the Press notoriously is in the hands of men who had been transported for their crimes, and whose limbs were still blue with the marks of the double irons'. This rancour arose partly out of professional rivalry. Lang ran a newspaper, *The Colonist*, highly moral in tone but so outspoken that it brought several charges of libel on his head. He was twice convicted too, and so knew the inside of Australian jails at first hand.

It offended Lang still more that many of the convicts were Irish Catholics. He never shrank from battle with the Scarlet Woman. Called on once to act as chaplain at the execution of an aborigine, he discovered to his horror that the man proposed for his last act to be baptised by a popish priest. He burst out in an unseemly wrangle on the scaffold, shouting that the wretch had no idea what he was doing and that mere rituals saved no souls. He felt in general alarmed at the moral character of the community, with its drinking, whoring and recidivism, which the administration was unthinkingly creating. Moreover the Irish, as foot soldiers of papal aggression, threatened the civil liberties of all other Australians. So in his view it was vital to reduce their share of the population. Instead he found the stupid British Government allowing it to rise. It let official schemes of immigration fall unsupervised into the self-serving hands of merchants in Sydney and brokers in London: 'They had merely to send out so many statute adults to enable them to claim their regular bounty; and, like all mercantile men, they endeavoured to find these adults in the cheapest market. That market was the South and West of Ireland'. Lang eventually worked his way round to being a repealer, an advocate for dissolution of the Union between Great Britain and Ireland, simply on the grounds that an Irish republic would have no right to send settlers to Australia. It cannot be said either that he was satisfied with England's contribution to the country, whither she dispatched the dregs of her society.[3]

To Lang the remedy was clear: Australia should be peopled not by Irish and English criminals, but by sober, thrifty, hard-working, God-fearing Scots. He became obsessed with the idea. To promote it, he made nine voyages back to Britain. They would take up alone in sailing time 13 of his 79 years. But he used the enforced leisure to effect by writing accounts, or rather eulogies, of the opportunities in New South Wales for the right sort of colonist. The obsession accounted for many of his political attitudes. He hated the squatters because they wanted no systematic immigration, at most a trickle of shepherds and labourers. He, by contrast, already espoused the ideology which would eventually triumph in Australia, that immigration, while balanced as to age and social station, should be directed towards forming a class of small, independent farmers. In his time the British Government still thought the notion half-baked. Lang, not content merely to abuse it for impolicy, found in this a justification for the independence of Australia: she would then be able to make rational choices about her future without reference to a contemptible English ruling class. He extolled the democratic, republican model of the United States, with weak central government and strong, therefore good, local government. He showed even more strikingly than George Brown in Canada an organic progression from evangelical Presbyterianism, through a commitment to colonisation, to espousal of autonomy for the emigrant community; and to the transformation, along the way, of a commercial Empire into a Christian one.[4]

Still, Lang could be satisfied with the results of his first voyage home in 1830, before people tired of his importunities. He hawked in Edinburgh and London a plan for the migration of 'Scotch mechanics', an object to his mind fully worthy of some official inducement. For their passage he reckoned he needed £6000, which he had hopes of securing as an interest-free loan to be gradually paid off out of their wages once they started earning their living on the other side of the globe. The idea came at a good moment, because the Government now wished to sell Australian land by encouraging settlers who might buy it. Lang got more than half the money from that source, and easily raised the rest. So he returned with a party of 60, the first body of skilled workers to reach the colony. As such, according to him, they wrought a revolution. Before they came, the only tradesmen available in Sydney had been ex-convicts, 'working in a very inferior style so many days in the week, and drinking the rest'. They had to give way to 'superior tradesmen, who husbanded their earnings to purchase allotments, and build houses for themselves, insomuch that the change for the better in the moral aspect of the city was very soon evident to all'. What happened to the now unemployed ex-convicts, except that they were 'self-exiled', Lang did not say.[5]

While pleading his cause in Britain, Lang had stressed that Scots would not emigrate unless they had a structure of familiar institutions waiting for them. They needed, for example, to be certain of good schooling for their children. Indeed the specific project on which his mechanics went to work was the building of an educational institution in Sydney, the Australian College, duly completed in 1832. It was to follow the precepts of Scottish pedagogy, this to be assured by having the professors and clergy of Edinburgh appoint its six masters, under Lang himself as principal. He was not ideally suited for a collegiate foundation, however. While it proved useful enough, it did not establish itself permanently and closed down in 1854. But at least he introduced the concept of higher education to a people who knew scarcely anything of it. A legacy of his influence may have been that, when the

Australian universities were erected later, they followed the Scottish rather than the English model.

Lang also stressed that Scots settlers would want to be sure of practising their religion. Indeed, to implant Presbyterianism in Australia was the chief object of all his labours. He found them thankless, as he recorded bitterly in his memoirs: 'Thus, for the greatest services possible, I have been repaid for 40 years past with the basest ingratitude, and thus have the foundations of our Presbyterian Church been laid, with much individual hardship and suffering, in this colony'. He ran up first against his own Kirk, which showed a 'cold-blooded and unnatural indifference'. Its only response to him was to ask where the money would come from, and to demand of emigrant congregations a bond for payment of their ministers' stipends. In Australia he met obstruction too. Thomas Brisbane he described airily as 'a brave, but unfortunately a very weak man, totally unfit for the office he held as the Civil Governor of a British Colony'. His offence was that he would not squeeze a grant out of his tight budgets for a Presbyterian place of worship, parsimony all the more heinous to Lang because Brisbane was a Presbyterian himself. 'The Scots' civil and religious liberties,' he informed the governor, 'were won for them by the valour of their forefathers, and . . . they were a degenerate race, if, in every situation, they did not vindicate their right to both.' On his visit of 1830, he appealed to Scottish presbyteries to seek ministers willing to serve in Australia, but was fobbed off with a couple of drunkards. Later recruits proved more suitable, however, and in 1832 it was possible to form a presbytery for New South Wales; another followed for Victoria in 1842. It might have been a step forward when the Church of Scotland appointed the Colonial Committee in 1836, to deal with these growing problems of organisation in distant territories. But any good it could have done in Australia was vitiated by Lang's constantly picking quarrels with it.[6]

So far it had been taken for granted there, as in Canada, that the establishment should be Anglican. This struck Lang as the sort of effrontery to be expected from a mincing and petty outfit like the Church of England, which had nothing in its history to compare to the 'glorious memories of the Church of his forefathers'. No good could come of it in Australia either. He needed only to look once again to the United States to see how miserably Episcopalians had fared, despite having formed the establishment for 150 years before the Revolution; this was without doubt owed to the unscriptural nature of their ecclesiastical government. He simply refused to comply, as a 'humiliating subjection', with an Act in New South Wales requiring him to notify Presbyterian births, deaths and marriages to an Anglican clergyman. He was outraged when the Parliament at Westminster followed a second colonial precedent and set apart one-seventh of Australian lands as clergy reserves.[7]

In Australia too, the Kirk adopted a policy of building itself up step by step till it could plausibly claim co-establishment. Since the situation here was less complex, it got on faster. A further Act of 1837 in New South Wales gave it a small share of the reserves and so raised it from voluntary to official status. Lang reacted by withdrawing from the presbytery. Perhaps he was already coming round towards support for the voluntary principle, though what he said was that he believed several of the clergy unworthy of such favour. He set up a rival synod of those he deemed meet for it, which put in its own bid for some of the money. This failed, so in 1840 he came back into the fold, if only briefly. He shot off on a completely new, wholly voluntary tangent as a result of the visit he now made to America, which had always fascinated him. He found the Churches there flourishing with no aid from the state and providing, to his mind, superior pastoral care. When he returned to Australia in 1842, he immediately urged his synod to turn voluntary. When it refused, he renounced for himself all connection with the state and with established Churches. He was then deposed from the ministry. But his own congregation backed him and refused to let the synod retain ownership of its church. Lang thus continued as an independent till 1850 when, after persuading the Scottish dissenters to send out more clergymen, he managed to form another synod of New South Wales.

Such was the tangled background against which news of the Disruption reached Australia. It was the last thing her ministers wanted to hear. They felt they had done well so far in establishing a Presbyterian community. For that reason they could not afford to antagonise anyone at home, because it was from there they drew all their personnel, and much of their finance even yet, so a false move might ruin everything. In 1844 the local synod expressed sympathy for the principles which the Free Church was defending, but agreed to remain in communion with both sides in the mother country. Neutrality proved impossible, however. In Scotland, established and seceding clerics alike mocked it. They finally forced an unwelcome Disruption on the Australians too. At the synod of 1846, these were called on to make their choice. A majority resolved to remain in the Kirk, but four ministers left.

As in Canada, it was the seceding faction that grew faster. Free Churches formed in every Australian colony. But the general result was to fragment the Scottish community in its religious allegiance, amid a profusion of unattached presbyteries and congregations. Nobody could dispassionately see this is as good for the true reformed faith in a new land. In 1859 all Presbyterians in Victoria reunited, and in 1865 so did all those in New South Wales. In the latter case, Lang absented himself from the negotiations, probably the main reason why they ended in an agreement. But he conformed to it, and devoted his last years to combating the growing moral turpitude of Australians, manifest in their frivolous taste for cricket, horse-racing and regattas. He had a public platform for this because, apart from everything else, he served as a member of the legislative council of New South Wales, on and off, from 1842 to 1869. He and others of like mind gave Australian public life in the later decades of the century a singularly sanctimonious tone.[8]

How much Macleod and his Highlanders knew of these ructions as they approached from Nova Scotia is unclear. At any rate, they finally decided Australia was not for them. What, having come halfway round the world, could they do now? They had one last resort, to go on to New Zealand. She was still in the early stages of settlement, so perhaps free of worldly corruption. It happened, too, that she housed one of the main schemes of systematic Scottish emigration, at Dunedin in the province of Otago, on the South Island. It was planned, and for some time functioned, as a colony of the Free Church specifically.[9]

British exploitation of the country had started, with no great success, under the chartered New Zealand Company. By the early 1840s the directors were desperate for new ideas, and got one from George Rennie of Phantassie, a Scotsman sitting as Liberal MP for an English seat and later Governor of the Falkland Islands. He had an associate, William Cargill, another man convinced that Presbyterians made the best emigrants. The pair proposed in 1842 the establishment on the company's territories of a New Edinburgh. The response was dilatory. But the Disruption quickened the enterprise, by calling forth from the projectors a fresh surge of enthusiasm. It also brought into play the institutional Free Church, at first in the person of the Rev Thomas Burns of Portobello. A nephew of Robert Burns, he had been born at Mossgiel in 1796 just after the bard's death. It cannot be said that he bore a strong resemblance to his uncle. He was a fanatic in the cause of temperance, in the cause of the Free Church – he preached for a while in a tent – indeed in all the causes he took up. Zealous and energetic, he found it hard to indulge human failings.

As we have seen in the case of Canada, the Free Church prided itself on standing at the forefront of an international evangelical movement. In token of that, it early on appointed a Committee of Colonial Schemes. This took over negotiations with the New Zealand Company. Now, however, the project lost Rennie: he had quickly come to the conclusion that in these new hands it was turning a little too holier-than-thou. That left matters entirely with Cargill and Burns, on behalf of the Free Church. Under the agreement then reached, the company would acquire and survey a suitable tract of land, while they would select the emigrants, supervise the sale of farms to them, and provide them with churches and schools. In this form, the General Assembly of 1845 approved the scheme, and designated Burns as minister of the future settlement. All he finally needed was settlers, whom he sought through a campaign of lectures and pamphlets. He met no overwhelming response, but at length he and Cargill, as the company's agent, led out a party which arrived in the spring of 1848 and founded Dunedin.[10]

Burns now came into his kingdom. He had drawn up elaborate plans for it and set about implementing them with vigour. They yet contained a basic flaw, for he had not realised his hope of filling every available place with the faithful of the Free Church. In fact a good third of the colonists, who numbered 1700 after staged emigration over several years, were not members of it, or even Scots. He still meant to subject them all to a regime organised entirely round labour and worship. One rule was that they should toil ten hours a day. That broke down at once, because they just refused. In other respects, though, Burns got his way. The settlement ignored Christmas and Easter. Every schoolchild had to learn by heart the Shorter Catechism. Funeral services were forbidden. But opposition to such austerity arose among the

English people who had been brave enough to come along, dubbed 'the little enemy' by Burns. Within a few months they formed a religious association, the Friends of the Established Church of England. They were told they could meet in the jail. On the first anniversary of the landing, Burns wanted 'a day of public thanksgiving and humiliation before God'. An Englishman suggested a sports day. And so it went on, in endless petty strife, which clearly retarded the progress of the colony compared to others in New Zealand.[11]

It was not even as if the emigrants had the usual advantages of pioneers, in land and living that were cheap, at least in terms of money. Burns also strictly regulated the disposition of their holdings. Every one was to be bought, not granted. Of the proceeds, three-eighths would go to covering the costs of the passage, one-quarter to surveys and roads, one-quarter to the New Zealand Company and one-eighth to religious and educational purposes. Of the 2400 properties into which the tract was divided, 100 would be reserved for the public authorities, another 100 for religious and educational endowment and 200 for the company. This left 2000 for purchase. It all looked very rational. But the land cost £2 an acre, twice as much as the dearest in the rest of Australasia, or anywhere else for that matter. It made the settlers, most from the respectable working class, feel that the price had been set at a level to stop them becoming proprietors. Cargill, as agent for the company, yet refused to bargain. After seven years he had sold only 450 lots, and put no more than 3600 acres under cultivation.

Even so, for a while everything seemed to go well enough. The New Zealand Company surrendered its charter in 1850 but, since it had never really got off the ground, its exit from Otago was not unwelcome. The price of land promptly fell at a time when, with the introduction of sheep, the revenue from it was rising. Nothing could better suit a thrifty Scots farming community, which now testified to the value of carefully selecting colonists. Their prosperity allowed fulfilment of the plans for ample provision in religion and education. Churches, schools, libraries abounded, while Dunedin had a university by 1869. Otago even looked Scottish. The settlers left it treeless, unlike the neighbouring province of Canterbury, occupied by the English and extensively afforested. The main feature of the manmade landscape here was the universal but-and-ben. Yet events would demonstrate what had been proved in other regions of the world: how hard it was to establish little Scotlands beyond the seas and maintain their integrity without the strong, deep roots of the mother country.

Here the roots were too weak and shallow. With the New Zealand Company vanished also any legal guarantee of Burns's pernickety regulations. Some form of self-government had to follow. An Otago Settlers' Association was set up to seek it. Demands rose for other changes in the pharisaical regime. Still, its grip did not at once slacken. By the constitution granted to New Zealand in 1852, each province came under an elected superintendent. Cargill, who had of course ceased to be the company's agent, topped the first poll and so found himself still in a similar position. But some things he could not superintend. This early pastoral paradise gave way, as in Australia, to a gold rush in 1861. Hordes of prospectors, few from Scotland, arrived to swamp the original colonists. At least, however, the growth of Otago caught up with and overtook other provinces of New Zealand. That was encouragement enough for a steady flow of new Scots immigrants, attracted besides by what they assumed would be familiar surroundings, so that the balance of the population later somewhat redressed itself. When the Rev James Begg of Edinburgh came on a tour in 1874, he remarked that he 'never addressed more thoroughly Scottish congregations, I think, than in New Zealand . . . I saw a great many people with what I would call Bothwell Brig faces – real true-blue, staunch, sterling presbyterians'.[12]

But for Macleod and his Highlanders, sailing across the Tasman Sea in 1853, Dunedin would not do either. He had grown to detest organised religion, including that of the Free Church, and Burns was nothing if not organised. So the question whether any settlement would have been big enough for both of them never arose. It seemed almost deliberate that Macleod went instead to the opposite end of New Zealand, to the peninsula beyond Auckland on North Island, and chose for his colony a spot called Waipu. To be sure, the terms he got here were specially favourable. The provincial authorities gave free grants of land up to a certain size, and offered credit for larger purchases. In his approaches to them, Macleod laid great stress on the wish of his people to keep themselves separate, just as on Cape Breton Island, in isolation from the sins of the world. On this point, too, the province obliged him. It agreed that his followers should have an exclusive right to acquire land in the block covering Waipu, a right legally entrenched in 1860. Macleod was now able to organise the transfer of the rest from Nova Scotia. By 1858 nearly all had come. By 1865, they owned virtually the whole district, to form a settlement of frugal Scots farmers living off the export of their produce.[13]

Perhaps because they wanted nothing else, it never progressed beyond that. Lacking an adequate harbour which might allow more diverse economic activity, Waipu remained a rustic backwater, its character determined by its natural environment. In that form, it did survive as a little Scotland beyond the seas. Till he died in 1866, Macleod continued to reign as both minister and magistrate. His regime, if fierce, was the means of preserving social cohesion in a people apart, and that cohesion proved durable. They used Gaelic at home till the 1880s, and many still understood it till the 1920s. According to a survey in 1986, some yet living had spoken nothing but Gaelic before they started school. They maintained other customs dating back to the Highlands of the early nineteenth century, notably marriages between cousins or between pairs of brothers and sisters. In the end, groups of kin became so intertwined that nearly every descendant of the colonists from Cape Breton Island could trace a relationship to any other. To this day they believe their exclusiveness has served them well, especially in care of the sick, of the young and of the old. They have as yet, they say, 'no inclination to mix with strangers'.[14]

The religiously inspired emigration to the Antipodes, the filling of empty or cleared territory by Presbyterian settlers, plainly contradicted the older Scottish concept of a commercial Empire. Whether this had consisted in the exploitation of natural resources in undeveloped regions, or else in trade on equal terms (at least as defined by Scots) with developed regions, colonisation cut across it. The constraints on their endeavours overseas which Scots had once accepted as inescapable here fell before their awakened urge to change the world. If it could inspire for the developed regions a scheme of emigration as quixotic as John Crawford's in India, there was nothing to stop it in the undeveloped regions. For the time being its evangelical motive instilled in the settlers a loyal and religious frame of mind, apparently guarantee enough for the future moral character of their communities.

Yet that reckoned without the Presbyterian tendency to schism. Colonial Churches soon struck away from the parent Establishment, while dissenters became the first to conceive of autonomy or independence for their new countries. So here, too, there was a secular consequence. These Scots began to fulfil the prophecy of their philosophical countrymen after the American Revolution, that emigration spelled autonomy and at last probably independence for the territories settled. Perhaps the only way to halt that progression would have been through trying to recreate not just the moral character of the old Scotland, but also something of her institutional and social balance, in order to hold Calvinist individualism in bounds. That had proved impossible, however: the institutions of the Empire remained English. Otherwise, any little Scotland beyond the seas was thrown back on its own means of maintaining discipline, which had to be ferocious if they were to work at all. This could turn out to be self-defeating, and seal off the colonists from opportunities as well as from worldly temptations. Perhaps it all went to show that a Christian Empire, in the emigrant sense, was a contradiction in terms.

CHAPTER NINETEEN

'The true art of the missionary': Oceania

E arly in the morning of Easter Monday, April 8, 1901, the Rev James Chalmers took the decision that would make him a Christian martyr. He had been working in the South Seas for more than 30 years, and was greatly admired by those who knew him, native and European alike. Robert Louis Stevenson, self-exiled on Samoa, described him as 'the most attractive, simple, brave and interesting man in the whole Pacific', and called him by his vernacular name, 'Tamate, a man I love'. But now Chalmers faced a problem not amenable to his benignity. He and some Papuan missionary helpers were on a ship, the *Niue*, anchored near the island of Goaribari, off the southern coast of New Guinea. A crowd of tribesmen occupied the deck, so many that the crew found no room to move. They had come on board, armed to the teeth, soon after sunrise. And the indigenous people hereabouts were reputed especially savage, though so far these had shown no hostility. Chalmers was unable to fathom just what they wanted, since theirs was not among the local languages he commanded. But, so far as he could tell through one of his Papuans, they had two things in mind. They were interested in the trade-goods the vessel carried. And they were anxious that somebody from it should go to their village with them. After two hours of their awkward, menacing presence Chalmers said that was what he would do, in hope of inducing them to leave. He and his party, a dozen or so all told, set off in a whaleboat. He assured the captain he would be back in time for breakfast, after which they could depart for a more agreeable spot. Half the islanders did clamber into their canoes and follow him, but half stayed on the *Niue*.

Her sailors watched the missionaries row ashore, then up a creek to the village, where a large crowd had gathered. They saw Chalmers leave the rest and advance into a long-house; he came out briefly, then went in again. They had no leisure to observe what followed, since the natives still on the ship started looting it, before themselves making away in high excitement. The captain, relieved that nothing worse had befallen, weighed anchor immediately, in order to sail about and wait for the missionaries to return. They never did. In the village, Chalmers had been enticed with every sign of hospitality into the long-house, which was newly built. He walked up its open central passage, lined on either side by partitions or cubicles, some full of weapons, others containing carved and painted idols with piles of human skulls before them. What he did not grasp was that he had been designated the human sacrifice customary on completion of such a work. At the far end, somebody brought a great club of stone crashing down on the back of his skull. A slash to the gullet finished him off, and his head was severed. The men standing round at once cut up the still quivering flesh and handed over the bits to their women, who added them to a stew of sago. Others slaughtered Chalmers's companions outside. They were all eaten up in the great feast which now began. The tribesmen would, if they could, have supplemented it by returning to kill the crew of the *Niue* as well, but her captain had unwittingly foiled them. He tarried a couple of days offshore till forced to conclude that Chalmers was dead. Then he took the news to the colonial authorities in Port Moresby. They sent in a force to burn the island's villages, and learned the full story from one of the natives they captured.[1]

Chalmers, born at Ardrishaig in 1841, was the best-known figure in one of the least-known episodes of missionary history, the evangelisation of the South Seas. It carried great risks, because of the vast distances, the isolation of the stations and the diversity of the indigenous peoples. A stranger could never be sure if he would meet with bounteous friendliness or murderous enmity, and political protection of such faraway places was all but impossible. Still, the London Missionary Society, undaunted as ever, had early set to. The very first expedition it planned was bound for Tahiti, though the party did not arrive till 1801; this included two Scots, James Elder and William Scott, recruited through the Edinburgh Missionary Society. David Cargill, an Aberdonian, was sent to Tonga in 1834 and on to Fiji in 1835; he devised the Fijian alphabet but left his translation of the bible unfinished when in 1843 he died of drink, a common fate even of evangelists in these parts. Archibald Murray from Jedburgh and George Turner from Glasgow went to Samoa in 1836. Other Scots followed, making a steady and in the end huge contribution to the society's work in Oceania. The no less intrepid United Presbyterians actually preceded it in the New Hebrides, drawing on their strength in Canada as well as in Scotland. John Geddie, a son of Banff brought up in Nova Scotia, landed in 1848. He was followed by John Paton in 1852, in which year a minister of the Free Church of Scotland, John Inglis, also arrived.

Here as elsewhere, the Disruption caused both rapid growth and a change of emphasis in Scottish missionary activity. It was one of the fields in which the various forms of Presbyterianism competed, so keenly that they tended to elbow the societies aside. With more Scots came firmer Scottish purposes. Their aim was to convert but also to educate the indigenous peoples up to a point where they could regularly constitute their own Kirks. With that foremost in mind, the evangelists took little time to consider even the obvious signs of their cultural impact. Paton had to be recalled when threatened by natives convinced he was causing epidemics and hurricanes. He returned to a different site in the New Hebrides, but the mental gulf he still had to bridge might be gauged from comments of his wife Maggie: 'John was unfeignedly grateful to get them to hear the Gospel, in almost any condition; but I maintained that we too had a right to Church privileges, as well as the natives; and that I could not worship the Lord in his Sanctuary, with practically naked people sitting right in front of us'. She was glad to move her sewing and singing classes for

34 The rugged peasant features of Mungo Park (1771–1806) bespeak his origins in the Ettrick Valley of the Scottish Borders. He needed all his inherited toughness for the gruelling journeys in West Africa during which he unlocked the secret of the course of the River Niger. Having at last descended almost to its mouth in 1806, he was killed by natives. (National Portrait Gallery, London)

35 John Philip (1775–1851), from Kirkcaldy, went to South Africa as superintendent of the London Missionary Society's stations, taking with him the ideas of the Scottish Enlightenment. He had a simple teaching: that Africans possessed the same rights as all other human beings. It was not one readily accepted in his time or later, yet Philip was instrumental in getting Cape Colony to adopt relatively liberal policies towards the indigenous peoples. (Private collection)

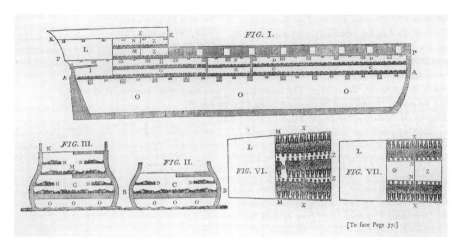

FIG. I.

[To face Page 37.]

FIG. III.

FIG. II.

FIG. VI.

FIG. VII.

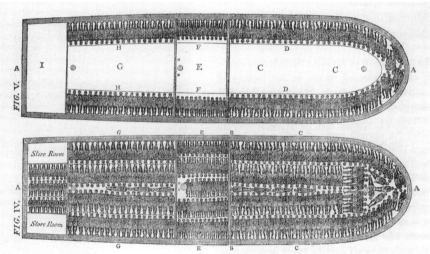

FIG. V.

FIG. IV.

Store Room

Store Room

36 Scots took a leading part in campaigns against slavery, circulating pamphlets – this one was published in Edinburgh in 1791 – which stressed the horrors of the trade and its individual human effects. Even so, they had a practical concern with the economic consequences of abolition. John Gabriel Stedman (1734–1797), who hunted escaped slaves in Dutch Surinam, was one of many who argued that the unfortunate blacks should be civilised before being emancipated. The illustration opposite is from Stedman's *Narrative of a Five Years Expedition against the Revolted Negroes of Surinam* (1790).

37 The romantic novelist appears as classical hero in Bertel Thorvaldsen's bust of Sir Walter Scott (1771–1832), for which he sat during his last journey to Rome: he was in fact almost on his last legs at the time. But nobody has been more successful in the generation of Scottish images. The unionist, imperial Scotland born as he was dying borrowed liberally from his creative genius. (SNPG)

38 *Peace – Burial at Sea* was J.M.W. Turner's commemoration of his friend and brother artist David Wilkie (1785–1841), who had died off Gibraltar while sailing home from a journey to Palestine. Wilkie's much-loved portrayals of everyday Scottish life found a reflection in his Palestinian canvases, depicting a people and their civilisation as yet untouched by the impact of modernity. (Tate Britain)

39 In advocating emigration from the Highlands, Thomas Douglas, Earl of Selkirk (1771–1820) (top), braved the censure of many Scots – of those in Scotland who wanted to keep the people on the land, and of those in Canada who wanted to keep the people off the land, which if tilled would yield no furs. His persistence in promoting the settlement on the Red River, now in Manitoba, brought him failure, ruin and broken health. (National Library of Canada)

40 James McGill (1744–1813) (lower left) was among the Glaswegians who first developed transatlantic trade to Scotland. He crossed in the 1770s, not on the face of it a good time, but he and others quickly diverted the traffic in furs from its old depots in the rebellious colonies to new ones in Canada. Scots established Montreal as a major commercial centre. More philanthropic than most, McGill left his fortune to found the university named after him there. (McCord Museum of Canadian History, Montreal)

41 'Soul of Ice' was one of several awed sobriquets applied by his subjects to the imperious George Simpson (1792–1860) (lower right), from Wester Ross. As Governor of the Hudson's Bay Company, he ruled one of the largest territories in the world, covering the entire Canadian West and Arctic, together with Oregon. It was run entirely for the sake of the lucrative fur trade. (National Archives of Canada)

42 That part of the Scottish Empire ruled by the Hudson's Bay Company in the mid-nineteenth century was the largest but emptiest realm in the world, occupied by only a few thousand Indians and a few hundred Scots controlling the fur trade. Their relations were most amicable. Here the Governor of Red River listens to the Red Lake Chief making a speech at Fort Douglas in 1825. (National Archives of Canada)

43 At the confluence of the Red and Assiniboine Rivers lay Fort Garry, unofficial capital of the Hudson's Bay Company's strange realm. Here its last drama was played out in 1870 when Donald Smith, the company's representative, held a five-hour meeting in sub-zero temperatures at which he persuaded the people to abandon their support for Louis Riel's rebellion and join the Confederation of Canada. (National Archives of Canada)

44 The anglophone population of Victorian Montreal was largely Scottish, and its politics largely Tory. Scots Tories showed themselves, however, brasher in the New World than in the Old. In 1852 they burned down the Canadian Parliament, which then stood in the city, provoked by the even-handed liberalism towards religious minorities of the Governor-general, the Earl of Elgin. (McCord Museum of Canadian History, Montreal)

45 John Rae (1813–1893), from Orkney, was another hero of Scottish Arctic exploration. An employee of the Hudson's Bay Company, he covered thousands of miles in his journeys by land and sea, during which he discovered the Magnetic Pole. The secret of survival, he learned, was to live like the Eskimos. He ascertained the loss of Sir John Franklin's expedition, which had tried to live like Englishmen. (SNPG)

46 Two Scots having a fling in the big city pose in the height of Arctic fashion in James Inglis' studio, about 1860. Montreal, a major centre of Scottish economic power, remained the metropolis for those sent out to the West. Snowshoes were essential for any sort of social life in the wilderness, and there are records of Scots walking hundreds of miles on them to celebrate Hogmanay together. (Trustees of the National Library of Scotland)

47 By the late nineteenth century it was possible to get on a train at more or less any station on Clydeside and end up in New York or points west. The advent of cheap, fast transport created something of a common market in labour for the North Atlantic region. Seasonal or cyclical traffic in workers between Scotland and the United States or Canada remained familiar till after the First World War. (National Archives of Scotland)

48 Photograph, taken in 1888 by William Notman & Sons, of James Croil and family. It was intended to recreate the arrival of the Croils in Canada in the 1840s. Croil became editor of the *Presbyterian Record*. (McCord Museum of Canadian History, Montreal)

49 The early political life of the Canadian Confederation, formed in 1867, was dominated by Scots – here, left, the Liberal leader, Alexander Mackenzie (1822–92) and, right, the Tory Prime Minister, Sir John Macdonald (1815–91), in a cartoon of 1873 (*The Mail*, 26 September) about scandals relating to the Canadian Pacific Railway. The financial foundations of a vast, new, sprawling country were shaky, but practised Scottish methods allowed them to be shored up. (National Archives of Canada)

50 On November 7, 1885, Donald Smith, formerly of the Hudson's Bay Company (see Plate 43), now of the Canadian Pacific Railway, drives in the last spike to the track connecting the Atlantic and Pacific Oceans at a place named after Craigellachie, not far from his birthplace of Forres. The railway was one of the most prodigious feats of Victorian engineering, but also needed men of Smith's financial genius to be started at all. (Glenbow (Calgary) Museum and Archives)

51 As British consul-general at Zanzibar, John Kirk (1832–1922), from Barry, near Dundee, sought to bolster the Arab dynasty which ruled in some sort over the island and the adjacent mainland, while making these territories less economically dependent on slave labour. Like other Scots, he wanted to preserve native forms of government, but his efforts were ruined by the scramble for Africa of the European powers. (Trustees of the National Library of Scotland)

52 The view from the consulate over the old city of Zanzibar, taken by John Kirk himself, a keen photographer. The dhows in the harbour brought ivory from the interior, whence it was carried by Africans then put to forced labour on the island's plantations of cloves. As an economy Zanzibar worked, but as a polity it could not survive imperial rivalry and became a British protectorate in 1890. (Trustees of the National Library of Scotland)

53 The dapper but colourless Highlander, William Mackinnon (1813–1893) (right), devoted alike to God and to profit, was probably the richest Victorian Scot. His vast commercial interests sprawled from his native Kintyre to the East Indies. His native canniness did not stop him being fleeced by King Leopold II of Belgium or sinking money into the bottomless pit of developing East Africa. (Trustees of the National Library of Scotland)

54 The African sun has etched out the tough, gnarled features of Blantyre's most famous son, on his first visit home in 1856–8 after sixteen years of exploration and missionary work. David Livingstone (1813–1873), pictured here by Thomas Annan, was the greatest figure of the Scottish empire, though much misunderstood: besides converting Africans to Christianity, he wanted to equip them for facing the demands of the modern world without subjecting them to European power. (SNPG)

55 Less adapted to local conditions was Robert Moffat (1795–1883), from Ormiston in East Lothian, the missionary whose daughter married David Livingstone. He believed the Gospel was all Africans needed to turn them from tribesmen leading a traditional way of life into the imitations of Europeans kneeling at his feet. Other missionaries found no such simple equation of Christianity and westernisation. (SNPG)

56 There is no winning smile for the camera but a take-it-or-leave-it simplicity from Mary Slessor (1849–1914), the plain, bony Dundonian lass who worked as a missionary in West Africa. She merged into native life as readily as David Livingstone did, but could not stop herself being used by westernising missionary propaganda or by the imperial power of the British Government. (SNPG)

57 The cold, imperious stare of James Ramsay, Marquis of Dalhousie, Governor-general of India (1812–1860), was calculated to make the proudest maharaja quail. Dalhousie directed a drive for helter-skelter modernisation of the sub-continent amid the utter subjection of native states. His ruthlessness only brought on the Mutiny of 1857, but he had already returned home broken in health. (SNPG)

58 In unmistakable profile, Charles Napier (1782–1853) looks out on a world which often dismayed him with its needless inhumanity. He enjoyed two imperial episodes, as resident on Cephalonia, where he loved the people, 'the greatest liars in the world', and as military commander in India, where he succinctly celebrated a conquest with the word *Peccavi*, 'I have Sind'. (SNPG)

59 Lieutenant F.C. Farquharson of the 42nd Royal Highlanders, part of the Black Watch, leads an attack on mutineers' guns at Lucknow in March 1858, in an action for which he was awarded the Victoria Cross. The three weeks' siege of the city which then followed was more or less the mutineers' last stand, and all resistance to the British had been mopped up by the end of the year. (The Black Watch Regimental Museum)

the women from the schoolroom to her verandah, 'there being a constant current of air, which wafts away the odour of Ethiopia'. No wonder that in this region too the missionaries often felt dismayed by the lack of response to their good news. William Gunn, sent by the Free Church to Futuna, wrote that progress there was so slow because 'confined within the narrow limits of a rocky island, the nature of the people seemed to resemble it. They were eminently dilatory, had little decision of character. They were slippery and unreliable. They were unemotional, unimpressable, undemonstrative'.[2]

Repugnance at the condition of indigenous peoples was, of course, common among missionaries. But in Oceania they came to terms with it in a way different from what we have observed in India or Africa. In India in the social stratum they first sought to evangelise, they ran up against an ancient civilisation and a rooted heathen religion which they could not defeat, so they turned elsewhere. In Africa, they combatted savagery by consciously introducing secular western influences, at least those they held to be morally justifiable. In the Pacific they encountered savagery too, notably the widespread practice of cannibalism. Yet the islands often housed well-organised and stable societies, conducting trade, living by customs that struck Europeans as generous or even noble. Stevenson's mother, who had done voluntary work for missions at home in Edinburgh, doubted their value after she joined his menage on Samoa and got to know islanders whose 'conduct to each other and to strangers, so far as kindliness and courtesy are concerned, is much more Christ-like than that of many professing Christians'.

Such realisations affected the Christian response too. Stevenson himself, addressing the Women's Missionary Association of Sydney in 1893, noted how evangelistic practice was changing, so much so that he had cast off his newcomer's prejudice against it. Of late, the missions 'incline to think that it is best to proceed little by little, and not much by much. They are inclined to spare so far as it is possible native opinions, and set native habits of morality . . . to proceed rather by confirmation and extension than by iconoclasm'. They had once tried to break tribal taboos, but 'I am pleased to think that these days are over, that no missionary will go among a primitive people with the idea of mere revolution'. Rather he sought out what was good, or could be made good, which appealed to Stevenson the romantic, 'because we are, one and all, and in every rank of life, and in every race of mankind, the children of our fathers. We shall never do well, we shall certainly never do nobly, except upon the lines marked out for us by our fathers' footprints'. He concluded that 'the true art of the missionary . . . is to profit by the great – I ought really to say vast – amount of moral force reservoired in every race, and to expand and to change and to fit that power to new ideas and to new possibilities of advancement'.[3]

Through Stevenson the romantic there also spoke, as in other contexts, an old Scots Tory. And it was more widely true that something about the indigenous peoples irresistibly reminded his countrymen of themselves, or at least of their forefathers. In 1876 the Governor of Fiji, Arthur Gordon, wrote to William

Gladstone that the islanders over whom he ruled 'are in much the same state that our Scotch rural ancestors were 400 years ago. Like those Scotch they are eminently improvable, and the problem is . . . how to get them from the 15th century to the 19th'. He doubted whether they would be given the chance, yet wanted to offer it. They otherwise faced extinction, but 'if they can get some 25 years for their present civilisation to grow and root itself firmly, they will hold their own without need of further adventitious help'. The same response awoke in Donald Maclean, an emigrant from Tiree to New Zealand, who learned the Maoris' language and compared them to the Highlanders of yore. In his new home he made a political career, and rose to be Native Minister in 1877–80. He was the first to take the job seriously, trying to ensure that white colonists always regularly purchased their land from the chiefs, and that these sold it of their own free will. The Maoris would thus not be driven to the margins of society, but could choose how much of their country to keep as reserves for themselves, while acquiring the capital to develop their own agriculture. Unfortunately, the officials succeeding him proved readier to respond to the settlers' demands, and to dishonour promises he had made.[4]

In Oceania, Scots often felt aware, like Livingstone in Africa, of their own nation's place at the edge of European civilisation where survival was a struggle. They might thus see into the untutored mind as other westerners could not. If we try to pin Stevenson down from the generalities he addressed to a non-Scottish audience, it turns out that the Highland analogy impressed him most. He wrote to J.M. Barrie in 1892: 'The natives are the next thing conceivable to the Highlanders before the Forty-five'. His little book, *In the South Seas*, elaborated on the theme, as he described how easily he struck up friendships during his travels:

> It was perhaps yet more important that I have enjoyed in my youth some knowledge of our Scots folk of the Highlands and the Islands. Not much beyond a century has passed since these were in the same convulsive and transitionary state as the Marquesas of today. In both cases an alien authority enforced, the clans disarmed, the chiefs deposed, new customs introduced, and chiefly that fashion of regarding money as the means and object of existence. The commercial age, in each, succeeding at a bound to an age of war abroad and patriarchal communism at home . . . The grumbling, the secret ferment, the fears and resentments, the alarms and sudden councils of Marquesan chiefs, reminded me continually of the days of Lovat and Struan. Hospitality, tact, natural fine manners, and a touchy punctilio, are common to both races.

He had no doubt that the affinity he felt was peculiarly Scottish. Recalling how he had played on a mutual sense of kinship to get on at once with a group of tribesmen strange to him, he added that 'the presence of one Cockney titterer will cause a whole party to walk in clouds of darkness'. His biographers have observed how he lived on Samoa like a Highland chief, gathering relations and dependants round him in a kind of clan, even dressing his servants in lava-lavas of Royal Stewart tartan. To his community at Vailima he acted self-consciously as provider, mentor and judge. The Samoans could themselves then recognise in him the familiar figure of a tribal patriarch. They esteemed him as they did their own chiefs, so that he was even able to take part in local politics. A receptive mind could still make the same connections in the middle of the twentieth century. When Eric Linklater visited New Zealand, he came across a half-caste by the name of Stewart, and remarked that 'the Maoris and the Highlanders, indeed, have much in common. Both exercise a solemn repect and a considerable talent for genealogy, and neither use to attach much importance to the workaday side of life'.[5]

Since Scots discovered so much to admire, they realised what a threat the West posed to it. The missionaries, beside their tasks of evangelism and education, often found themselves defending the tribesmen against economic exploitation. A big difference from their approach in India, or especially in Africa, was that here they almost came to see commerce as an enemy rather than an ally. Of course they wanted to change this part of the world as well, in the sense of converting it. But they often decided that the rest of modern civilisation ought to be kept out. In the conditions of the nineteenth century, they set themselves an impossible task. Even Stevenson cautioned them against being too hard on traders. These, he noted, often settled among the islanders, while the missionary might only pass through on a flying visit from a distant station. 'The trader is therefore, at once by experience and influence, the superior of the missionary. He is a person marked out to be made use of by the intelligent missionary,' he declared to the ladies of Sydney, doubtless to provoke, since the two were usually at odds. In his story, *The Beach of Falesa*, he has the hero, John Wiltshire, say of the evangelists: 'I didn't like the lot – no trader does; they look down on us, and make no concealment'.

Many traders were themselves Scots, though the sources remain maddeningly silent on their names or their employers. A resident magistrate on New Guinea mentioned 'a good old Scotch firm of trade grabbers . . . sending their ships, in spite of any risk, wherever a possible bawbee was to be made, and taking their hundred per cent of profit with the same dour front they take their frequently trebled loss'. There seems no obvious reason why they should have acted better than others. But in 1866 Archie Murray had found in a remote spot of Samoa that slaving, or something very like it, was going on. He recorded: 'Only a few days before our visit, a genuine slaver had been to Nintao, and . . . but for the adroit management of a canny Scotchman residing on the island as an oil agent, some 50 or 60 or more of the natives would have been carried off'. While nothing else is said of the canny Scotchman, his intervention confirms that not all traders were vicious.[6]

Murray identified the culprits of Nintao as Australians. Their 'labour vessel' was doing its dirty business off the beaten track so as to avoid any district where missionaries might be expected. Such strong-arm methods of recruiting a workforce were the frequent resort of planters in Queensland, growing sugar and other semi-tropical crops. The colony still suffered a shortage of manpower, and anyway no white settler would volunteer for the backbreaking toil involved. The solution seemed simple: to sail off among the Pacific islands, to which, unlike to the recesses of Africa, the approach was easy, and enlist the necessary hands by fair means or foul. Sometimes they did go willingly, either for the wages or even because their chiefs, enlisted as agents, bid them go. But the kidnapping of tribesmen became commonplace in the 1860s. It went too far in one case on the New Hebrides when the delinquents also threatened Scots ministers trying to interfere. These reported an especially shocking incident at a place called Latona to Arthur Kinnaird, MP for Perth. He raised the matter in the House of Commons, and in particular with his friend Gladstone. Evidence of an illicit slave trade always nettled the British Government. From now on it took an interest in the South Seas, which it had so far ignored.[7]

As things stood, exploiters need not even abduct defenceless islanders, but could easily abuse them on their own soil. Here we know that Scots did seek to join in. Those who had come to Australia as squatters by now saw the writing on the wall for their own province of the Scottish Empire. It occurred to some that they might preserve their pastoral licence in more far-flung reaches of Oceania. William Macleay, for example, who hailed from Caithness, had emigrated as a youth with a good scientific and medical education. He prospered in the wonted way, acquired his own sheep-station and was at length elected to the legislative assembly of New South Wales. He cast covetous eyes on New Guinea, which he thought the Australians might annex. It was vital to get there before many missionaries did, and in 1875 he led an expedition to explore the island's potential. But he found it unsuitable for anything he had in mind, and contented himself with collecting specimens of its flora and fauna.

There was no such luck for Easter Island, though here the Scots brought pastoralism with them from the opposite direction, from South America. The island appeared ideal for rearing sheep. To that end it was taken over in 1868 by a joint venture of Frenchmen from Tahiti, and a Scots merchant family of the name of Branders also settled there. The business did not flourish, for the two sides quarrelled and involved themselves in a complex legal dispute. When it was finally settled in 1893, they sold out to Balfour, Williamson & Co, traders who from modest beginnings at Anstruther had drummed up business all over Latin America. Under the firm's branch at Valparaiso in Chile, it set up a subsidiary to exploit the island for wool. The regime lasted till 1952, when the Chileans asserted their sovereignty and sent a ship to take possession. Yet for almost a century Easter Island existed as a pastoral holding, with 40,000 Australian sheep yielding up to 100 tons of fine wool a year. It most resembled a cleared and improved Highland estate. The factors allowed no more than 200 natives to remain, and obliged these to live in a walled village with what amounted to a croft for the subsistence of each family. Their employment was casual: they would be called up to work on the sheep-station only when needed, although this irregular life seemed to suit them. Easter Island even looked as if it had been set down in the Minch. It was covered with rough grazing, regularly burned to bring on fresh growth, dissected by walks and fanks built round with drystane dykes, presenting a bleak appearance scarcely relieved by scanty clumps of planted trees. Only the giant monoliths, carved with enigmatic faces by some ancient folk, would have struck any passing Scot as outlandish. All this the Chileans now preserve as a national park.[8]

That Scottish ways might have brought a better outcome is proved by the example of Niihau, smallest of the inhabited Hawaiian Islands. In the nineteenth century they formed an independent kingdom, where the royal house unwarily fostered the contacts with Europeans and Americans that would bring it down in the end. But wandering Scots helped to preserve this precarious autonomy as long as it lasted. Alexander Adams was made commander of the Hawaiian navy and helped to repel a Russian annexation. Archibald Cleghorn married into the ruling dynasty and pioneered social reforms. Robert Wyllie served as Foreign Minister and concluded the delicate treaties that kept Hawaii free. In 1863, Mrs Elizabeth Sinclair arrived. She was a Glaswegian with seven children who had earlier settled with her husband in New Zealand. When he was lost at sea, she decided to try her luck in British Columbia and loaded a schooner with her cattle, sheep, chickens and household goods. She was forced to winter on Niihau, but found it so delightful she decided to stay. She offered King Kamehameha IV the sum of $10,000 for it, with her piano thrown in. The same family still owns the island today and runs it on three happily compatible principles. It is a pastoral estate, carrying 15,000 cattle, 7000 sheep and a stud of Arabian horses. It is a Calvinist community, with the sabbath strictly observed, drinking forbidden and smoking discouraged. It otherwise consciously preserves Hawaii's traditional way of life, obliterated elsewhere. The people, 12 families numbering more than 200, farm and fish as their ancestors did. Their language is Hawaiian. Tourists are banned.[9]

These were examples of islands too small to resist exploitation, for good or ill. Others, larger and better organised, could do so and found Scots to help. One eventual outcome of Kinnaird's parliamentary protests was the first move in what would turn into a scramble for Oceania, when Britain annexed Fiji in 1874. She felt prompted to it not by the prevalence of kidnapping, since brawny Fijians were quite capable of defending themselves, but by an influx to these islands too of planters or pastoralists, mainly from Australia, who already made up two per cent of the population. Gladstone, Prime Minister at the time, was not in principle a colonialist, least of all here, where Britain had no vital interests. But annexation seemed to him the only way to serve warning that disorder and displacement of the natives would not be tolerated. By and large, the missionaries could henceforth work hand in glove with the imperial authorities. It was Gladstone who appointed Gordon, formerly his private secretary in the Ionian Islands, as first Governor of Fiji.

Gordon thus advanced in a proconsular career for which he was not all that suited, being a shy and lonely figure with an old Scots Tory dislike of territorial occupation and colonial autonomy. He had already ruled New Brunswick, Trinidad and Mauritius, with little liking for any of them. Though he disapproved of the annexation of Fiji, he faithfully did his duty. In this more exotic and primitive setting, he uncannily echoed the sentiments of the Indian orientalists. He stressed that while the Fijian moral sense differed from the European, it was no less real. He therefore took it as his aim 'to seize, if possible, the spirit in which native institutions have been framed, and endeavour to work with them as to develop to the utmost possible extent the latent capacities of the people for management of their own affairs, without exciting their suspicion or destroying their self-respect'. The first task was to impose law and order. Gordon pacified the fierce tribes in the hills, and protected their peaceable lowland cousins by regulating conditions of labour. In setting up an administration, he also bolstered the indigenous political structure, guaranteed the chiefs their powers and created a permanent council of them. He warned white settlers to take care in a country where the people felt the peasant's true love of the land. In the end he restricted European immigration. His solution for the social disruption it had caused was to import Indian coolies who would work for the planters in the islanders' place: an unfortunate solution in the long run, because it created the different racial problem afflicting Fiji today.

In four years Gordon established peace and good government. As a result, he was promoted High Commissioner for the Western Pacific, with general responsibility over the whole area for British subjects and their activities, especially the traffic in labour. Contrary to the wishes of the Foreign Office, he was authorised to act extraterritorially. He would intervene with native rulers on Samoa and Tonga, but had the special pleasure of foiling the Australians' ambitions in New Guinea. He was sure they would treat the inhabitants badly: 'In no case do I think the rule of a vast native population can be safely entrusted to a small and, for the most part, ignorant and selfish oligarchy of another race, having interests opposed to those of the natives themselves'. He thought the autocracy of a governor, directly responsible to London, far preferable. On that basis, the missionaries joined forces with him. Chalmers himself went to Brisbane to lobby the Premier of Queensland, Thomas McIlwraith, a son of Ayr: 'I found him a stubborn, good, honest Scotchman, anxious that justice should be done, and willing, if coolies could be obtained, that the labour traffic in natives should be stopped'. As a result, all talk of annexing New Guinea ceased. The British Government would anyway take the matter in hand by declaring a protectorate over the territory in 1884.

Gordon again did a fine job, but it all went wrong after 1889 when he became, in addition to everything else, Governor of New Zealand. He accepted the move against his paternalist's better judgment, having vowed never to take a self-governing colony again. It was unfortunate that he approached this one, where whites now formed a clear majority, from posts where he had primarily been required to protect the indigenous peoples. He found in office a Government blatantly hostile to them. Efforts to maintain a balance between the races were breaking down. Gordon believed the Maoris to be threatened with extinction, and set out to save them. But he was then working at cross-purposes with his Ministers. In 1881, while he made an official visit to Fiji, they turned a blind eye to a particularly outrageous legalised confiscation of some Maori land. On his return he at once determined to resign. He was persuaded to stay on for a year, to get a General Election out of the way, but then went. 'I have been profoundly disgusted by the treatment of the Maoris,' he protested to Gladstone. Democracy, he declared, made a governor's job a waste of time. In fact, however, he alerted London to the injustices still being done to natives by Australians and New Zealanders, so to that extent his personal mission did not entirely fail.[10]

While his own career ended in disillusion, he left a successor regime in protected New Guinea. It could hardly be called Tory; its character showed rather how in this region the older concepts of the Scottish Empire might for once come together with more radical ideas, of the missionaries especially. During the crucial early stage of British control, the island was ruled by another Scot, William Macgregor, a self-made man of high moral principle, incredible industry and heroic determination. He had previously been chief medical officer of Fiji, where he won Gordon's confidence and assumed responsibilities far beyond his formal duties. On the strength of that, he was appointed administrator of the protectorate in 1887, then Governor of New Guinea after it became a colony in 1888. He would occupy the post for ten years till he left for Africa, where we have already seen him at work as Governor of Lagos. He relied on missionary help, and enjoyed warm relations with Chalmers. He encouraged the founding of new stations, of which there were soon 20. Only Roman Catholics found no favour with him; he scornfully dubbed them 'the bloodless brothers' and disliked seeing their churches adorned with pictures 'of the rather repulsive crucifix type'. In 1889 one French monk, Father Louis Navarre, reported in apparent panic that by now all the island's officials and traders were Scots, presbyterians and freemasons of the Scottish rite, the most frenzied enemies of Rome. He expected persecution to break out at any moment. Macgregor held his fire for blacker sinners, however. He continued to keep the Australians at bay. He imposed draconian penalties on anyone supplying the Papuans with firearms, liquor or opium, in 'what was probably the most severe act of its kind in the world . . . When he said that the natives should not have liquor, he left no loophole of escape for the person found guilty of supplying it'.[11]

Macgregor's main task was to stamp his authority on the island's warring tribes. He did not hesitate to use force: 'I looked on it as my first duty to impress on the natives that white men are not to be robbed and murdered and I was determined to teach them by an awful lesson that killing is murder and the punishment for it death'. Yet from his own first-hand experience of fighting them, he came to admire their martial qualities. They were, he grew sure, men whose confidence he could win. One missionary wrote: 'His whole life is spent in studying the natives and endeavouring to understand their peculiarities. Already he has gained a marvellous influence over them and they recognise him as the "Big Chief of New Guinea" '. It was not the conventional mind of a colonial official that, in such primitive surroundings, conceived of its charge as trusteeship. He had no romantic desire to preserve the Papuans' culture intact. But he did believe he could show them how to make use of their resources and join as partners with Europeans in development, rather than merely suffer exploitation. Though it would, of course, be a long job, that made it all the more vital to start in the right way. At the end of his term he said that he and his officers 'have not worked day and night for the past 10 years simply to put down inter-tribal warfare and to reduce the natives to control. They have been trained to treat natives justly and fairly, and to see that they are so dealt with by others'. The Colonial Office, soon to change its mind about him, agreed that here he had done a 'wonderful ten years' work'.[12]

While Macgregor was, we may assume, an old-fashioned Liberal, Stevenson loved to play the old-fashioned Tory. It could even make him, in his aspirations for the tribesmen, somewhat the more radical. On Samoa, he settled outside the bounds of British sovereignty, on territory that would in fact soon be recognised as German. The Second Reich paid special attention to the Pacific as a region so far uncluttered by others' colonial ventures. A latecomer to imperialism, it might there win exclusive advantages. To that end it applied its growing economic strength, acquiring plantations, which it harshly exploited, while subsidising the shipping to and from them. Norddeutscher Lloyd, according to one report, quickly saw off the veteran Scots traders. It was indeed the Germans' aim to build up as far as possible a commercial monopoly in the South Seas. Other interested parties, the British and Americans, looked on uneasily, having no real means to stop them. Samoa, a productive island in a strategic position, saw these tensions come to a head, not least because, as Stevenson noticed on arrival in 1890, the Germans had made themselves thoroughly unpopular. While theirs was the strongest presence, the other two powers had a footing. All jockeyed for position through surrogates, indigenous contenders for dominance, contending by the only means they knew, by war. After a serious outbreak of violence in 1888, the powers decided on a treaty to pacify Samoa. It gave the islands a system of justice and a commission to suppress fraudulent dealings in land. But by installing a German at the head of this apparatus, it left no doubt who had really taken charge. European faces were to be saved by vesting nominal sovereignty in a native kingship. This clause of the treaty, however, caused as many problems as it solved. It did not specify who should hold the kingship, leaving that for subsequent negotiation. The Germans had in mind a puppet of their own, one Malietoa. The British and Americans preferred his rival Mataafa, though their missionaries objected to him as a Roman Catholic. Into this delicate situation Stevenson stepped, none too lightly. He was himself a supporter of Mataafa, and helped him so openly as to jeopardise British relations with everyone else involved. Her Majesty's irate consul actually tried to have Stevenson deported: it took a brother Scot, the Foreign Secretary, Lord Rosebery, to countermand the order. The situation continued to deteriorate, till fighting broke out again. The Germans gave Malietoa enough aid to defeat Mataafa. He and his supporters were rounded up. Stevenson paid a consoling visit to them in their detention. Out of gratitude, they afterwards built the road from his home to the main town of Apia.[13]

Stevenson reported the affair to the *Times* of London and wrote it up in his tract, *A Footnote to History*. He presented his own part as an attempt to reconcile the chiefs, in the belief that Samoa belonged to the Samoans and that the powers should stand aside. He felt certain that these had in effect stirred up the conflict, sacrificing the tribesmen to resolve an impasse among themselves. But he wanted to do more than dwell on details of an obscure struggle already lost and won. He told his readers rather that, while the Germans were the cruellest colonialists, the British and the Americans had nothing to be proud of. He explained how the islanders' cast of mind was communistic, so that they could not understand the economy of plantations, and felt at a loss confronted with the sort of administration foisted on them: 'the law to be enforced, causes of dispute between brown and white eliminated, taxes to be raised, a central power created, a country opened up, the native race taught industry: all these were detestable to the natives'. As for missionaries, they had not matched the hopes he entertained before the ladies of Sydney. They meddled in politics, yet in a narrowly sectarian spirit, not realising that 'the missionary in such as land as Samoa is something else besides a minister of mere religion; he represents civilisation, he is condemned to be an organ of reform, he could scarce evade (even if he desired) a certain influence in political affairs'.[14]

Whatever the conditions on Samoa, that judgment was too harsh in any more general way. As in much of the African interior, missions pioneered European penetration of Oceania, and here too proved to be harbingers of imperialism. For Scots, this formed no part of the original intention. But it emerged as the best way of pursuing their other purposes, and saving the islands from depredations likely to defeat those purposes, including a few carried out by their own countrymen. Enormous change followed, but also some success in the work of salvation. The culture of certain islands suffered irreparable damage, yet on others it survived, if in altered form. Since the natives had become Christian, often devoutly so, they voluntarily cast off their barbarous customs. Decolonisation brought them no traumas. When the westerners eventually departed from the Eden they had ravaged, they left its denizens not entirely disinherited.

CHAPTER TWENTY

'Fitted to pollute public sentiment': The Scottish Debate

I n preparation for the General Assembly of the Free Church of Scotland in May 1881, one of its committees delivered this judgment on an article, "Animal Tribes in the Old Testament", published a year before by the Rev Professor William Robertson Smith in the *Journal of Philology*:

> First, concerning marriage and the marriage laws in Israel, the views expressed are so gross and so fitted to pollute the moral sentiments of the community that they cannot be considered except within the closed doors of any court of this Church. Secondly, concerning animal worship in Israel, the views expressed by the Professor are not only contrary to the facts recorded and the statements made in Holy Scripture, but they are gross and sensual, fitted to pollute and debase public sentiment.

Smith held the chair of Hebrew and Old Testament at Free Church College, Aberdeen. He had won it in 1869, aged 23, after amazing accomplishments as a student at New College, Edinburgh, under Andrew Davidson, father of modern biblical analysis in Britain. Smith built on his mentor's teachings to earn international repute as a pioneer of comparative religion, in particular as an authority on scripture through precise understanding of the text with its background in the beliefs and practices of ancient peoples in the Middle East. He set an example to all scholars of how to see past civilisations from within and understand them as totalities. He thus brought to a peak a great intellectual endeavour of his age, the attempt to construct a genealogy of languages, races and cultures.

But it was already too much for some of his clerical brethren that he returned from tours of German and Dutch universities to apply to sacred texts the latest in the higher criticism practised there. To their horror he went on to prove that the Old Testament, so far from being dictated by God, had been transmitted through the hands of many human editors. In their eyes this amounted to heresy, a charge on which they tried him before the courts of the Church in a series of actions from 1878 to 1880. His small stature and spry demeanour belied his lion-hearted courage, and his integrity would not let him recant. He anyway had the better of the altercations. His foes might have preferred to burn him at the stake, but the General Assembly, always managed with care, struck a balance: it admonished yet, in a half-hearted way, absolved him. The price he paid was a promise not to publish any more questionable work unless he cleared it with his superiors.

So honours were even, but this latest philological offence gave fundamentalists the chance they were awaiting to finish Smith off. At the least he could be held to have broken his word, though he had written up his findings before he gave it, and the unhappy timing of the article's appearance was the publisher's fault, not his. The substance of the text anyway swept aside consideration of such niceties. It argued that Abraham, Judah and David had contracted marriages incestuous within the degrees of Leviticus, indicating survival in Israel of a pre-Judaic system of matrilineal kinship. Smith also showed that many persons and place-names in genealogies of the Old Testament represented animal totems, evidence that God's chosen people had worshipped them. That sealed his fate. On May 26, 1881, he was deposed from his chair.[1]

History has vindicated Smith against his accusers, and this was not an episode casting Scotland in a good light. He himself had no future there. He moved to Cambridge, where he continued to produce work of high distinction till his death in 1894, aged just 48; he was buried in his family's lair at Keig on Donside. He can be seen as victim not just of small-minded bigotry, but also of a clash of great ideas. It found acute expression in his own country. European expansion had opened Scots' eyes to the diversity of customs among the nations, a powerful stimulus to the Enlightenment. In elaborating the first social sciences, the philosophers recognised exotic civilisations as fellow members of one human family, equal or even superior in some respects to the West. But then the advance of physical sciences, which offered means to conquer nature, equally gave rise to a conviction that men could sweep away what was bad or backward in the world about them. That these two fields of knowledge, one concerning man and the other concerning nature, might require different methodology did not for the present appear clear. Exact procedures and commitment to stating what was true and what was false seemed enough. Nor did the commitment, and its underlying ethos, conflict with moral philosophy, even when conceived in theological terms, or even when the terms were tightened by the evangelical revival.

The vulgar modern view of the evangelical revival as obscurantist is wrong. It could accommodate in its aim of saving souls the idea of planned social improvement, an idea soon extended to encompass the spread of civilisation across the globe. The Free Church of Scotland in particular accepted the laws of political economy as scientific, at the same time consonant with the will of God. All society needed for their beneficent working was personal moral regeneration of sinners through faith. It adapted the same concepts to missions. That produced a robust, even inspiring, system of thought, which pointed beyond the horrors of industrialisation, and beyond the discovered degradation of non-European peoples, to an intrinsic harmony in creation. There could then be no bar to scientific investigation of religion, rather every incentive to it as revealing deeper facets of the harmony.

The last point was new, though. In the previous age enlightened Scots, many themselves ministers of the Kirk, had been circumspect about such a task. The salient exception was the great sceptic, David Hume. He had lived under French absolute monarchy which, in the religious sphere, gave rise to more atheism than his own liberal society. He brought something of the freethinkers' resulting intellectual truculence home, where it did him no good at all. Hume was addressing, however, an audience much wider than Scots in his *Natural History of Religion* (1757), a title which would have been unexceptionable to the nineteenth century but looked provocative to his own. Here, for the first time, he envisaged religion as a manmade construct open to analysis. It arose neither, as on the conventional Christian view, out of an innate idea of God in human beings, nor yet, as was held in contemporary deism, out of their remote ancestors' contemplation of the harmonious universe. To Hume religion was indeed a product of primitive minds, but that meant of minds uninstructed, unable to use the reason they were endowed with. In real life they could have had no time for contemplation, their mental energy being taken up with a struggle for survival. If visited by earthquake or storm or dearth, they thought only of appeasing the natural forces behind it. In this, in fear, lay the origin of religion. Hume would not allow that the emergence of monotheism affected his thesis. It just showed men persuading themselves that beneath the multiple causes of their misfortunes lay one great cause. It was a mere act of generalisation, of preferring one god over others, and did not differ in origin or motive from the fear veiled by polytheism.

Many tried to refute Hume, not least brother Scots, who in the process elaborated Common Sense Philosophy. But, in the particular matter of comparative religion, there the case rested till the middle of the next century. This was no surprise. The subject had been pursued to the extent it could be through conjecture. While the Scottish Enlightenment furnished a framework for ordering, rather than romanticising or dismissing, knowledge of primitive societies, not enough knowledge was available at the time to beget a scientific discipline. It was only to be won at random by the curious, including numbers of missionaries, in the course of further European expansion.[2]

Scots carried on their intellectual inquiry meanwhile. The apostolic succession led from David Hume by way of Adam Smith to Dugald Stewart and his pupils, precocious youngsters who set up the *Edinburgh Review* and popularised Scottish ideas all over Britain. The native tradition of philosophy continued to develop on distinctive lines at least till the time of William Hamilton, who died in 1856. But diffusion fragmented it. Marriage with English utilitarianism produced its lustiest offspring, whether in the school of philosophical radicals or the more moderate school of scientific Whigs. The overall character of the breed came out most obviously in James Mill and his son, John Stuart Mill. Their programme was progressive, secular, evolutionary, positivist: they set off from, though they did modify in the light of experience, Jeremy Bentham's dream of a science of society, through which its structures could be analysed and reformed on rational grounds. There was also, notably in Thomas Carlyle, a recoil from the whole movement, romantic, organicist, reactionary and often religious, though for various reasons it never became political; English Tories were indifferent to ideas, and Scots Tories all but extinct. It saw the human ideal as lying in the past, not the future, as embodied in great individuals, not in groups. With empirical evidence gathered meanwhile, these tensions gave fresh impetus to comparative study of religion.

Among propagators of Scottish philosophy in utilitarian guise was John Ramsay MacCulloch. For years he wrote as economic commentator in the *Edinburgh Review*. Then, refused an academic post under the Dundas despotism, he decamped to Bentham's University College in London. MacCulloch had a daughter who married a young Invernesian of vigorous and combative intellect, John McLennan. He made a successful career at the Scots bar, to become in due course parliamentary draftsman for Scotland, that is to say, charged with writing texts of Scottish Bills. A paid-up member, therefore, of the northern kingdom's new Whig elite, he was also one of the last in a line of fine minds, stretching back over two centuries, which had made the Faculty of Advocates an intellectual institution, rather than just the closed professional cartel it soon turned into. Among contemporary philosophers, he was almost unique in declining to internalise his Scotticism, lest he put off metropolitan readers. On the contrary, he regarded Scottish material as significant, even exemplary, and made ample use of it. He seems to have been a Gaelic speaker; at any rate, he corrected misconstruction of an Irish source by Sir Henry Maine. It was a pity that his revelation of the role of sex in history cost him his advocate's practice in straitlaced Edinburgh. But it won him a place among the ancestors of modernist thought.

The focus of McLennan's intellectual activity was prehistoric religion. He began sending articles on it to the reviews, later amplified in two books, *Primitive Marriage* (1875) and *Studies in Ancient History* (1876). He rejected the by now standard utilitarianism to revive, on the authority of Lord Kames and Dugald Stewart, the Scottish apparatus of conjectural history. He thus saw humanity passing through various stages of development, features of which could be reconstructed, where direct evidence was wanting, from their survivals in later eras. Though he had the national love of dialectics, his work did not rest at a general, speculative level, but concentrated on thorough analysis of the most striking phenomena. Chief among them was the strange practice of marriage by collusive abduction, as in the Romans' rape of the Sabine women. McLennan found many more examples of it, not just in the classics; he was indeed never Eurocentric, but studied a vast range of material from all five continents. Out of it he deduced that human society must once have organised itself in hordes. They recognised no kinship but were sexually promiscuous and practised female infanticide, so had to prey on each other for women. That laid down a custom of having sex only with women outside the horde, of exogamy, which was in time elevated into religious principle. Over time, however, kinship did come to be recognised in its uterine form, that is, among children of the same mother regardless of the father. Two survivals tended to confirm the theory. One was what

McLennan called Nair polyandry, after its practice by a caste in Kerala, among whom the family formed round a woman who had any number of unrelated mates. A later stage was Tibetan polyandry, in which several brothers shared a wife. At all events, kinship had a matrilinear origin, evolution of which was connected with passage from primitive communism to the beginnings of private property.

In a sense this was a breathtaking act of psychological projection by a Victorian male, meaning to prove the primitive world the opposite of his own, with its securities of sexuality, property and class. He could then show that things had advanced, and done so through the agency of groups and institutions. However subjective in motivation, McLennan's account left a permanent legacy to the emerging sciences of anthropology and ethnology. A second major theory of his concerned totemism. From, among others, Greek myths of gods turning themselves into bulls or swans, he concluded that the primitive hordes had worshipped animals, round which they erected taboos.[3]

Under the same progressive banner, Andrew Lang mounted a different offensive. Born at Selkirk, son of a sheriff clerk who had worked for Walter Scott, he carried the legacy of the Borders through a literary career covering everything from Homeric scholarship to journalistic hackwork. He wrote too much to leave many enduring marks, but he thought he gave of his best to anthropology, where he interested himself in relations of myth to folklore. The second was reckoned a degeneration of the first by most scholars, still in awe of classical antiquity. They devoted much philological ingenuity to proving it. Lang swept all that aside by pointing out that peoples the world over, many in no kind of contact, yet told tales exhibiting the same motifs. Since names in them differed, the philological account was nonsense. Lang proposed instead a Scottish explanation, based on stages of human development: one of them must have been characterised by myth-making. Literary mythology therefore proceeded out of folklore, not the other way about. It was a persuasive empirical demonstration of Hume's conjectural history of religion. A single detail troubled Lang. This was the discovery that Australian aborigines, regarded as the most backward race on earth, yet knew a high god, the All-Father, who had made the world and given moral commandments to his human creatures. If this, the most primitive religion, had a monotheistic origin, marred over aeons by mumbo-jumbo, then the degenerative rather than the progressive hypothesis must hold. Lang wrestled with that for two decades, stirring up in the process an international academic debate. In the end he changed his mind and denounced his previous progressivism. His death, however, forestalled elaboration of any new general theory.[4]

But others had been trying to fashion one. It was in the natural rather than spiritual world that they thought to have found data pointing in the right direction, to scientific racism, which thus became another of Scotland's gifts to the world. It had its ultimate origins in speculations of Hume and Kames, elaborated after the turn of the century by James Hunter, John Pinkerton and George Combe, then given wider currency by John Crawford under the rubric of polygeny. Robert Knox took it as his life's work to complete the edifice built on these foundations. He had won early fame in Edinburgh for his advances in anatomy. He owed them also to the help of William Burke and William Hare, procurers of corpses he dissected. Amid public outcry over their trial in 1828, he had to flee. He went to London, where years of observation and reflection supplied him with material to write *The Races of Man* (1850).

This book offered an all-embracing intellectual system, grounded in deductive reasoning out of objective evidence, with race at its centre. It took laws applied to other organisms and applied them to man himself in his natural and social environment. It began with comparative anatomy, to define the relation of shape to structure and the influence of interior mechanism over exterior function. It went on to the varieties of psychology and behaviour. It then explained aesthetic, intellectual and moral qualities. In this scientific continuum it established a total physical, geographical and cultural account of man, who thus emerged understood, with the secrets of his development unlocked. Knox avowed: 'In human history race is everything'. Yet, by odd contrast with Crawford, his logic led him to condemn colonialism. This 'premeditated robbery glossed over with a religious purpose' was immoral, useless and bound to fail through degeneration of settlers in surroundings for which they were unfit, especially if they indulged in miscegenation with natives. Even where this did not happen, but one race replaced another as in North America and the Antipodes, evil would follow. Amid his paradoxes, however, Knox lost track of history's purpose and continuity. He was left at the end of a long life contemplating the destructive forces unleashed by the clashing ambitions of different cultures. Before his death in 1878 he at last admitted to himself that his project of a universal racial science was impossible.[5]

All these fresh avenues of inquiry were being opened up in Robertson Smith's lifetime, but on the whole his own work lay well away from them. He had been brought up in the older tradition of philology, and never strayed far from it. This is not to deny his startling originality, of which the earliest sign came in his application of scientific techniques to Semitic religion. It had not been done before, out of that Scottish circumspection in the face of orthodoxy. Philosophers who were besides Christians on this account held Semitic religion to be true, a product of direct divine revelation. So they could not employ comparative method in any strict sense lest they fall into sacrilege and futility. It was the first and greatest taboo that Smith broke; in fact he paid no attention to any other race than Semites. Perhaps his position as minister of the Free Church gave him more leeway. In the end, however, it was not enough.

Smith did owe a real debt to McLennan, his senior by 20 years. Linked through an education in Aberdeen, they became good friends and philosophical soulmates. The younger man saw no problem in placing within a Christian framework the elder's application of Scottish principles to comparative religion. History of religion was to him stadial, though in a particular sense. He conceded that it had started in superstition, magic and taboo, stained by demonic, polluting and irrational elements. But they were just lower forms of belief and morality to be expected in lower stages of society. That in no way touched Smith's faith as a Christian, which required intellectual assent to an absolute rising above all reality, and all society, because rooted in the true God. It yet did not mean that Christianity stood apart from history. On the contrary, it had caused progress towards higher forms of belief and morality. It improved on Judaism, just as Presbyterianism improved on Roman Catholicism. Among Presbyterians themselves improvement could continue through returning to the Bible armed with advancing scholarly technique.[6]

This was why Smith looked up to McLennan. His work set aside the Presbyterian, indeed Protestant, assumption that the vital relation was the one between individual and God. Taking instead the horde as the earliest stage of society, it implied the group as the basic unit of religion. In Smith's development of the theory, members of the group were linked by blood, but included within it their deities and totemic animals from which they thought themselves descended. They accepted as a religious duty the performance of rites needed to sustain the order of things in their world, that is, to preserve the group and affirm their identity as its members. What they therefore really worshipped, Smith believed, was that order of things, their own society idealised and deified. They gave it religious sanction just because it seemed to their uninstructed minds natural and inevitable, so divinely ordained. Thus the source of symbolic behaviour lay in the group. Beliefs had a social origin. Among Semites the main rite was sacrifice. Smith's great work, *The Religion of the Semites* (1889), analyses many types of sacrifice mentioned in ancient records, biblical and non-biblical. In its highest form, at important points of the year or in time of danger, members of the group killed their totemic animal, otherwise taboo to them, and devoured it as their brother-god.

The weight Smith gave to this ceremony may have been a distortion, though. Since he focused on Semites to the exclusion of other races, he left rival forms of symbolic behaviour out of account. Even within his purview, he may have had a bias towards the idea of sacrifice, a tendency to regard it as central, since for him the greatest fact of history was the sacrifice of Christ. Tracing the idea back, in *The Prophets of Israel* (1882), through the Old Testament to yet earlier sources, then tracing forward the sanctification of savage rites as God revealed his purposes to man, in his view gave proof of a divine plan. By any standards he thus demythologised Semites, and he did so, too, because his evident grasp of primitive categories and his revelation of general truths behind empirical vagaries of human behaviour carried overwhelming conviction. Yet it is easy to see how others in the Free Church feared this might appear in a different light to those of weak or questioning faith or of none. Why should these regard the culmination Smith found in Christ as symbolism qualitatively separate from its primitive forms? Why should they not conclude that when Christians took communion they were acting out a modern survival of totemic bloodletting? Why should they not see Christianity as just another product of primeval confusion and error?[7]

A trial for heresy did not get rid of such disturbing questions. It caused Smith years of strain and may have hastened his early death, but never prompted him to retract what he had written. Prosecution was forced by a Highland clique of fanatical Calvinists, who if anything aroused distaste among Scots at large: the presbytery of Edinburgh made rather a point of choosing Smith a commissioner to a subsequent General Assembly. In any event he persisted in his work. One way in which he afterwards earned his living was as editor of the ninth edition of *Encyclopaedia Britannica*, the "scholar's encyclopaedia", so called because it featured essays by a distinguished international range of authorities. It was the first to incorporate the century's intellectual advances and set them before a broad public. So his condemnation and exile neither limited his influence nor halted evolution of his ideas.

Among Smith's feats was to refresh a project of the Enlightenment, the linking of language and mind. In the Scottish intellect this was being neglected as philology yielded pride of place to ethnology and anthropology. Not that Smith isolated himself in an ivory tower from these new subjects, for he found it worthwhile to visit peoples of whose ancestral culture he wrote. He travelled in the Middle East, delighting as much in the warrens of the old cities as in the grandeur of the desert. He had good Arabic, liked to don traditional dress and ride by camel; with his slight figure and swarthy face he could often pass for a native. In 1881 he published a fair-minded account of the Hejaz, neither besotted by the romance of Arab life nor repelled by its strange and uncouth customs. But he never fell for ethnology and anthropology in the sense of adopting their principles for his own work. He perhaps caught about them a whiff of pseudo-science, which they have carried down to very recent days. At the least, he avoided the temptation of their modish racist pitfalls.

That is a reason why, in Scotland, Smith stands near the end, rather than at the beginning, of a tradition. At home the sole worthy continuator of religious studies was George Adam Smith, a scholar as versatile in language, theology and history, if not so profound. His career shadowed the older man's in more than one way, as pupil of Andrew Davidson at New College, as successor in the vacated chair at Aberdeen and as quarry of heresy-hunters, after he gave offence in visiting lectures at Yale university by treating of polytheism in ancient Israel, the relation of Genesis to Babylonian myth and the fanciful nature of patriarchal narratives. He was a traveller as well, who after roaming Palestine on a mule produced a splendid *Historical Geography of the Holy Land* which showed the Bible still to be the best guide to it; so well had he come to know it that the Foreign Office appointed him an official adviser on its affairs during the First World War, when he was also Moderator of the General Assembly. So in the end he joined the great and good, doubtless a sign of acceptance for his essential teaching that we should not be shocked to find behind the God of Israel a tribal deity, since he was God of the whole of history too, and history, like religion, developed. Thus had the Free Church, most evangelical of all, transformed traditional exegesis through labours by a trinity of its sons, Davidson and the two Smiths. But there was nobody much to follow them.

To Robertson Smith in anthropological studies the sole Scottish successor was James Frazer, son of a Glaswegian pharmacist and author of *The Golden Bough.* A populariser and an agnostic, he spread ideas in the way most dreaded by Christian fundamentalists. He dissolved the contrasts among religions, including that between Christianity and paganism, in a paradigm where all formed just one stage in human progress from magic to rationality; though his own faith in reason would be today regarded as little less delusory than the bizarre beliefs he uncovered in antiquity. His influence lies rather in the way he managed to keep in perspective a growing chasm between cognition and imagination, science and letters. More valuable in the event than his anthropology was his symbolist or stylistic legacy to modernism, linking our epoch's fractured mentality with the age-old contest of civilised and savage: T.S. Eliot, Ezra Pound, James Joyce, D.H. Lawrence and Joseph Conrad all owed something to him. At a yet more profound level he helped to persuade Ludwig Wittgenstein of the need to take man's social behaviour through the ages and interpret it like a text, not define it in the manner of natural science. Wittgenstein was therefore able to propose, in place of deductive method and theoretical explanation, to formulate for any significant activity a synoptic picture revealing its rules: the rites of the priest at Nemi offered the archetype.[8]

Smith himself had been the first to leap straight from philology to those deepest layers of human mind and consciousness that obsess the twentieth century. Whether by reason of the hostility in his own country or the lesser quality of epigones there, the work was carried forward outside Scotland. Not just burghers of Edinburgh but also a growing band of European socialists had been provoked by McLennan's findings. On him Friedrich Engels launched a violent attack in the fourth edition of *The Origin of the Family,* for denial of Karl Marx's dogma that there had been primitive equality between men and women. Lang, showing how mythology interpreted social reality, raised it into an object of scientific study for scholars down to our own day, culminating in Claude Lévi-Strauss. Smith himself opened the eyes of the sociologist Emile Durkheim to how common ends were served by religious ritual, which thus had to be probed not for the beliefs it contained but for the community it promoted. At the moral core of a community stood the prophet, the innovative individual, preserving its best qualities and realising them in higher values: even if rejected and persecuted, great men of this sort were altruistic. Smith unlocked a dimension of the subconscious also to Sigmund Freud. He, however, changed sacrifice from a cathartic confession and affirmation of social bonds into a guilty, secret and hostile ceremony of expiation, in which the swallowed animal taboo sublimated aggression against the father.[9]

By such channels, the creative exploits of the late Scottish Enlightenment entered the common fund of western thinking. From there they passed into attitudes towards the non-western world, to affect the quality of encounter with it. The theories owed little to Empire as such, but European expansion offered direct access to empirical raw material they needed, even if much of it was at first rationalised in naive pseudoscience.

For missionaries, in any event, Smith's heresy remained the real worry. Alexander Duff had identified him as a threat to his own life's work. Whereas the one never doubted the superiority of his culture, the other set it in its place alongside different cultures. There was immediate relevance to missions in Smith's demonstration that, among primitive religions, the rite took the place of the creed, almost in inverse proportion to the importance bestowed on each by Protestantism, and by the Free Church especially. That meant missionaries deceived themselves to look, as they did by instinct, for the creed of peoples among whom they went: we saw it being done in Africa by John Campbell, inquiring what blacks knew of God and the soul, by Robert Moffat, when he tried to puzzle out what Bechuanas meant by Morimo, and by David Livingstone, when he thought to perceive among them fragments of some primitive faith. Missionaries found no creed, because there was none to be found. So they fell back on a second best, myths of the gods. And in India it foxed Duff and his colleagues how any sane person could believe such a jumble of rubbish, inconsistent and often sordid. Hence, they concluded, nothing existed here worthy of the name of religion. Unless versed in comparative method, they could not have appreciated that myths were a secondary development, and that the significant acts of a religious community lay in its rites.[10]

Few missionaries were intellectuals: they needed more or less unquestioning faith to stand the thankless drudgery of the work. But in Africa, their experience might have confirmed whatever they could absorb from changes in the cultural climate at home. Workers at Livingstonia or Calabar never lost confidence in Victorian achievement, though they at length understood that blacks could not assimilate it soon. It then became harder to see Christianity and western civilisation as inseparable. In fact, there was a choice: either to maintain that even converted natives remained backward, so unequal, and risk loss of spiritual influence over them; or else to acquiesce in the stubbornness of their difference, with its offensive pagan elements, and abandon westernisation. Above all it dawned on missionaries that primitive peoples did not conceive of themselves as autonomous individuals. Their self-consciousness merged with a sense of belonging to extended families, clans, tribes and peoples, including ancestors. The hope that they would come one by one to Jesus was bound to be frustrated. They would either come together with their group or they would turn into isolated and deformed misfits. That was true even of higher civilisations, such as India, where it enabled indigenous religions to defy missionary blandishments.

William Miller of Madras drew logical conclusions from all this, in the face of Dugald Mackichan's and Alfred Hogg's outrage. Miller's own powers were failing after the turn of the twentieth century, but that could not diminish the force of his arguments. He had a disciple in John Nicol Farquhar who, armed with degrees from

Aberdeen and Oxford, had gone out in 1891 to work in Calcutta for the London Missionary Society. He found its focus on conversion too narrow, and resigned to pursue broader purposes in the Young Men's Christian Association. His spare time he gave to scholarship, as a liberal critic of the Bible and of Hindu scriptures. In his *Christianity in India* (1908) he set a seal on the latter-day policy of vernacular evangelism. And in his *Crown of Hinduism* (1913) he wrote of Christian society as the 'evolutionary goal' for every other one, putting forward Christ as the true answer to the Hindu's quests and needs.

Through his influential writings, Farquhar emerged as the leading figure at the first World Missionary Conference in 1910. Protestants from all Churches and continents, including a few non-whites, met to plan a universal strategy which today is recognised as blueprint of the ecumenical movement. It paid homage to Scotland's Christian exertions – 'le dynamisme de l'Eglise presbytérienne d'Ecosse se fait sentir dans toutes les régions à évangéliser' was a French comment on the occasion – that Edinburgh should have been chosen as venue. With Lord Balfour of Burleigh in the chair, 1200 delegates reached agreement on various practical points: that the advance of Islam presented the greatest threat in Africa; that they must remedy their relative neglect of China; that they should co-ordinate their efforts in an International Missionary Council.

Intellectually the conference was less coherent: no surprise, given its eclectic character. Lutherans, led by a missionary historian, Gustav Warneck, most readily advocated tolerance of indigenous traditions. They looked to the emergence of national Churches outside Europe matching those erected at the Reformation inside Europe, which would similarly preserve and develop the culture of converted communities. A Danish delegate, the Rev Henry Ussing, spoke of 'greater facility in obtaining a true understanding with the natives on more equal terms, because we are without any pretension to be the ruling race or nation'. This was a remark pointed at English and North American missionaries. Their evangelical or humanitarian work was linked with introduction of legitimate commerce and western ways advancing in step with imperial power. The Scots' experience encompassed both outlooks. They came from a small country overshadowed by a big one, with an ethos instilling sympathy for native peoples. It was perhaps a consequent need to prove themselves and vindicate national pride that drove them to tackle the toughest challenges on the furthest missionary frontiers: in the heart of Africa, among the untouchables of India, across the far South Seas. But missionary heroism, even unto martyrdom, made them ambitious to transform indigenous societies too. Sometimes it also made them ready, where such societies proved intractable, to call on resources available to Scotland as a constituent of the world's greatest Empire.[11]

Even so, the missionary movement in general felt baffled by now at its meagre progress. That was why Farquhar's paper to the conference on fulfilment made the deepest intellectual impression. He reiterated the principles that while every religion was human, only Christianity satisfied at once humanity's religious instincts and the critical spirit of the modern age. He wanted, however, to discard the concept of contrast between different faiths and, by skilful work in the relevant committee against Mackichan and Hogg, got this view across in its report back to the main conference. On to the official record therefore went the conclusion that the accepted, orthodox missionary attitude, holding Christianity to be true and all other religions to be false, was no longer tenable. The missions' practical contact with these others, and on a different plane the elaboration of a science of comparative religion, showed that they all contained some kernel of truth. This will serve very well as marking the end of the evangelical revival, and of the hope that it could change the world.[12]

Part Three

A Contested Empire

CHAPTER TWENTY-ONE

'Using the safe and small': Imperial Economics

On March 5, 1875, John Downie, the 56–year-old Glaswegian general manager of the British Dynamite Company, was engaged in dirty and dangerous work on a quay at Crookhaven, County Cork. A damaged consignment of explosives had been landed there, and he thought it his personal duty to render them secure. He proceeded to do so by breaking open the cases, taking out single cartridges and throwing them, from a distance of six feet, on to a fire. Scots managers were doubtless made of sterner stuff in those days, but this did appear an extraordinary way of proving the point. After a quarter of an hour there was a large explosion, blasting and burning Downie and hurling him into the sea. Hauled out, he survived for five agonising weeks before succumbing to his terrible injuries. It seems a suitable metaphor for the eventual fate of Scotland's imperial economy.

Downie's firm held the patent rights in the United Kingdom and British Empire for the inventions of Alfred Nobel, Swedish originator of modern explosives. He, wishing to move into that vast imperial market, had first tried to find partners in London, but got nowhere. So he turned to Glasgow. Its acumen and enterprise were obvious to the merest glance. Besides, it already housed the world's greatest concentration of chemical companies, run by a circle of plutocrats whose interests intertwined not only there but in all the heavy industries and generally throughout the city's commerce. In 1868 Nobel made contact with Downie, who introduced him to these people. They understood instantly, as mercantile Londoners had not, the possibilities of dynamite.

Negotiations for some kind of partnership then began. An unwelcome interruption came from Westminster. In 1869 Parliament passed the Nitro-Glycerine Act, which banned the import or manufacture of the substance except under licence from the Home Secretary. Downie applied for one, to be told that, since dynamite was dangerous to transport, none could be issued except for producing it at the place where it would be used. This was a piece of nonsense, and the reason why Downie had to go all the way to County Cork to set up a local plant and at length to meet his maker. But it meant that Scotland too would have to manufacture dynamite and so develop a new industry of her own owing nothing to England in finance or technology. The negotiations in Glasgow reached a successful conclusion in 1871. The deal reflected the novelty of the risks. A joint-stock company was to be formed of which, in return for transferring his rights, Nobel would hold half the capital. The other three directors were Glaswegians, under the chairmanship of Charles Randolph, a distinguished engineer who had started his career as an apprentice with Robert Napier, the pioneer of steamships. The board, however, was non-executive. It entrusted the management entirely to Downie, as a salaried professional. The enterprise would be a modern one not only in its know-how but also in its corporate structure. It built a factory at Ardeer, between Stevenston and Irvine in Ayrshire, amid barren dunes to muffle any blast. This would establish and sustain a position as one of the Empire's biggest centres for production of explosives till well into the twentieth century. It was an example of how, for a few more decades, Scotland remained among the leading economies, often at the technical forefront, able to call on superbly skilled labour, wallowing in more capital than she knew what to do with.[1]

On accomplishing the second phase of the industrial revolution about 1870, this economy matured. It had switched away from its earlier base, which lay largely in textiles. Instead it passed through the exploitation of local coal and iron to establish heavy industries where, in certain cases, it would win a global dominance. That also changed the nature of the Scottish Empire. So far, Scots had been above all conscious of their scarcity of resources. They were spurred to compensate through intelligence and initiative, by getting to know foreign countries and making use instead of their resources, often bringing back the proceeds to enrich the mother country. But now Scotland had an abundance of resources.

One lay in labour. Between 1801 and 1901 the population almost tripled, to 4.5 million, though not uniformly. Rather it crowded into the central belt, while outlying regions, left behind in the economic race, suffered a decline. Scots thus clearly became a mobile people, at least internally. To begin with they could find scope for their talents and energies in the progress of their own economy. It grew so fast as to absorb nearly all of them. And for the first three decades Scotland had a political regime, the Dundas despotism, which discountenanced emigration as tending to weaken the social bonds. It was still anxious for Scots to seize their opportunities overseas, but not through territorial occupation and settlement. Even in the destitute Highlands, whence an outflow could never be stemmed, the Dundases yet hoped that policies of development might keep most of the people on the land. They fed that hope with aid from the state, but the century was not far advanced when the policies revealed themselves as bankrupt, resting as they did on a false analogy with the achievements of the Lowlands, and taking little account of a rise in numbers that was just too fast. After the potato famine of the 1840s, the advocates of development had to admit defeat. Shortly, in 1852, policy went into reverse with the formation of a Highlands and Islands Emigration Society. Its director trusted it could offer the '*final* measure of relief'. By the time another crisis of subsistence came in the 1880s, emigration was regarded as the natural cure.

There had been a broader change of mind among Scotland's rulers. The Whigs who felled the Dundas despotism positively advocated migration, as a utilitarian dogma: if labour was in surplus, it should move elsewhere. John Hill Burton, chronicler of the Scot abroad and member of Edinburgh's leading philosophical circle, gave in his *Political and Social Economy* (1849) the now standard view. Britain ought to see the world as a source of commerce, and not bother about other countries' culture or politics. What mattered was 'their energy and activity', since these determined the extent of their trade. Scots did good by emigrating, for they possessed such qualities and could seed distant nations with them. Though they often seemed rather to stick together and in the end return home, he was not dissuaded. 'To go abroad merely for the purpose of dealing with one's countrymen dispersed in foreign lands' might seem an 'egregious instance of nationality'. But it looked better when one conceived of Scots in their new homes as 'to all economical ends . . . an extension of the home territory'. If there was free, productive land in Canada, it 'is an estate as valuable to the emigrant as if it were situated in one of these islands forming an immediate limit of the British Empire'. Burton was obviously focusing on colonisation rather than transience. Scots Whigs had on this point fully adjusted to English imperial assumptions.[2]

The distinction Burton drew reflected, among other things, the surplus for settlement now available among Lowlanders too, from a rising population, but also from an environment and upbringing which fitted them for life in the wider world. Most of these emigrants departed not because they had to but because they wanted to. The difference may be appreciated by looking at the behaviour of foreign peoples, such as the Irish and the Norwegians, who showed a similar propensity to leave and who, just like the hapless Highlanders, really were pushed out of backward agricultural economies. The rest of the Scots moved off just as their country, having accomplished the second phase of the industrial revolution, could give them higher living standards and more jobs. From 1870 to 1900, real incomes rose by about half in a workforce which itself increased by more than 600,000, to nearly two million, yet net emigration was of the same order. If opportunities abounded abroad, they did not lack at home.

The answer to the paradox lies in the very maturing of the economy, which was also a process of integration into an international system. This had gone furthest, largely through improved transport, in the region of the North Atlantic. On its western side, rich in resources but underpopulated, it held out limitless prospects to those with education and skills. At times the region seemed almost to constitute a single labour market. Emigration increased sharply when North America boomed, and levelled off when it slowed down. Employers and their connections abroad doubtless played a part. Scottish labour went chiefly to the countries where Scottish capital went; it usually rose when foreign investment was active, usually fell when foreign investment was depressed. Even yet, the migration did not always prove permanent. A seasonal flow became common, a reverse flow more common still, leavening the domestic workforce with men who knew conditions overseas and could keep up the continual to-and-fro. The point is that emigration from the Lowlands reached such levels not because of misfortune and victimisation, but because skilled,

258 THE SCOTTISH EMPIRE

educated Scots workers were of a calibre to benefit from international mobility, and because the economic structure developed in their country fostered it. In domestic terms, they merely vacated the lower end of the labour market, which could be filled with Irish immigrants. That was another reason why in the 1890s, for example, net emigration amounted to only one-quarter of gross emigration. Seldom, in any case, has the annual number of emigrants surpassed one per cent of Scotland's total population, for which the rate of natural increase exceeded the outflow into the twentieth century. Except amid the uniquely awful circumstances of the Depression after the First World War, the population continued to grow till the 1970s when, as in several other western countries, it stabilised.[3]

Since most of the emigrants embarked in confidence rather than in dejection, sometimes in hope of an ultimate and affluent return, we may well wonder why they have become such an object of lamentation in modern Scotland. Contemporaries could take a quite different view. In 1841, a parliamentary select committee heard that 'the Scotch are the best and most successful of emigrants. Come they with or without money, come they with great working sons, or with only little useless girls, it is all the same, the Scotchman is sure to better his condition, and this very silently and almost without complaint'. But before the end of the century, an elegiac note was being struck. Robert Louis Stevenson observed with dismay those who crossed with him to America. He had supposed they would be youthful, yet they looked past their prime. He thought they 'should offer to the eye some bold type of humanity', yet he found them 'a company of the rejected; the drunken, the incompetent, the weak, the prodigal, all who had been unable to prevail against circumstances in the one land, were now fleeing pitifully to another'. Perhaps it was just an old Scots Tory who felt affronted at a boatload of working men setting out to better themselves in a humdrum way. But his opinion would become general. Especially the Highland experience, arising in the one region of the country suffering still from chronic scarcity, created in the Scottish mind an entirely negative image of emigration, as an absolute loss to the mother country with no redeeming features. Stevenson's sentiments may also have been among the first signs of disillusion at what the new, internationalised, thus denatured Scotland might be coming to, one of the grounds on which the Empire was to be contested.[4]

This novel imperial order, marked among other things by a permanent Scottish diaspora, still did not efface overnight the former one. They might be compatible: the least the settlers could do for their homeland was to buy wares from transient brother Scots. And the commercial Empire would be seen for some time to come at work in the wonted way, in the great emporiums of Montreal, Calcutta, Hong Kong and the rest. It was the Scottish version of the informal Empire, to use the term now standard in the literature of imperialism, as opposed to the formal Empire of lands annexed under colonial administration. When John Gallagher and Ronald Robinson wrote their seminal article on that distinction, they did so partly in answer to the question why territorial expansion seemed to slow in the middle of the nineteenth century, the heyday of the doctrine of free trade. They concluded that British trading power was enough to reduce distant lands to dependence without any assertion of sovereignty. While rejecting a Marxist line on imperialism, they all the same left economic forces paramount. Controversy over this thesis has nowadays lost its edge, because of problems in defining such broad concepts. Here we can dilute it further: since Scotland exercised no sovereignty which might reach overseas, the Scottish Empire had always been informal, but seldom implied dependence. It still remained commercial rather than political, more intent on trade and development than on dominion over what marginal regions of the world had yet to be subjugated by Europeans. But it also changed.[5]

In its outposts, Scots continued to exhibit a vigorous commercial mentality, honed in Calvinist education and hardened in the sort of fight against the greater resources of other nations that they loved, yet not averse from clannish rigging of markets, nor even latterly from receiving discreet official subsidy. The networks operated best through some typical institutions. The original imperial expansion of English trade had taken place largely by means of mercantilist chartered companies. Individual Scots managed to infiltrate them, and had no qualms about exploiting their privileges. But Scotland as such possessed nothing comparable, a lack which Clydeside, for example, distinctly felt by the turn of the nineteenth century. Scots did, however, find different means of achieving the same ends. During their commercial and industrial revolutions, they learned to foster enterprise from scarce resources in novel ways, notably through the private partnership. It was often formed of people personally associated by place of birth or some other circumstance, even of members of a single family. Scots law conferred peculiar advantages on the usage. Recognising every combination of individuals as a distinct persona, it gave the partnership a legal standing of its own. Within it, the partners' contract, while renewable, was normally entered into under a definite limit of time, allowing frequent withdrawals of capital and replacement of old by new talents. Thus, in effect, shares could be transferred, by holders enjoying limited liability. Altogether, the arrangement provided the chief benefits of incorporation in advance of statutory provision for it. It was certainly more flexible and serviceable than anything to be had at the time under English law. The consequent reliance on the 'safe and small' may in economic practice have reinforced Scotland's concentration on a narrow range of specialisms, though a country of her size could hardly be expected to produce everything. But it did not exclude the attainment of large scale and complexity in organisation, which helped assimilate this pint-sized economy to a British and global system.

The practice also proved exportable, even to an Empire under English law. One derivative of it was the agency houses of India and China, to be dealt with in their proper place. They, though, were strictly expatriate enterprises with little direct effect on the economy of Scotland, save through the personal fortunes borne home by the partners at the end of their careers. A richer network of connections grew through the shipping lines. Those originating in Scottish private partnerships – and there were many – showed an almost complete adaptability, opening the way into every new field of business offered by the age.

There had been no need of shipping lines in the mercantilist Empire of the English. Chartered companies arranged their own convoys, leaving all else to haphazard sailings of individual ships' masters. This would not do in the new era of free trade and proliferating global links. It was replaced with regular transport by specialist shipowners between colonial ports and the metropolis. Glaswegians figured among the first to start the transformation, the firm of Pollok, Gilmour & Co leading the way. Originally a grocery, of which for two generations every single partner came from the parish of Mearns in Renfrewshire, it went into the import of timber from Canada, then into the construction of its own vessels in Nova Scotia. By 1824, with 78 vessels, it was probably the largest owner in the world.

As the transformation proceeded, it brought out the best in Scots. It demanded continuous adaptation to markets and bold application of new technology. A maritime revolution took place through steam, then through the opening of the Suez Canal in 1869, which cut 4000 miles off the route round the Cape of Good Hope. Together they confirmed the superiority of shipping lines over other means of organising the carrying trade. For anything that required rapid transit and predictable arrival, like tea or meat, for valuable freights, bulky commodities or mixed cargoes, steamers showed a clear advantage over sailing ships, though these survived on marginal business for another 30 years. Steamers also earned more profits because they could charge higher rates. Yet their technology was expensive, and exacted huge investment to gain economies of scale. Unfortunately, banks were at the outset reluctant to lend to shippers, supposing their securities to be too precarious. Internal finance did play its part in expansion, but the lines' need for capital outran it. Since their business could be represented as beneficial not just to themselves but to the Empire as a whole, they at first often found official help in the form of subsidies for conveyance of the mails. In time, however, they had little choice but to resort to the developing capital markets, by turning themselves into public companies and abandoning the system of partnership. This deeply affected their future.

The most precocious and at length most prestigious line was Peninsular & Orient, founded by a Shetlander, Arthur Anderson. Born in 1795, he joined the navy while a boy, then worked as a shipbroker in London. He entered a mercantile world still, in the decades after the Napoleonic Wars, sceptical of steamers, which were used just for coastal traffic. Anderson foresaw their greater destiny on the high seas. In 1837 he established the Peninsular Steam Company and won the contract to carry the mails to Gibraltar, along which route his vessels could also stop at Spanish and Portuguese ports. In 1840, on picking up the similar contract for India by way of Alexandria, he formed P & O. Subsidy did not guarantee security. The company suffered several bouts of financial stress, the first after repeal of the Navigation Acts in 1849. That threw wide the colonial runs to foreign competition, which came from Americans especially. By 1854, P & O had to undergo a reconstruction taking Anderson out of its day-to-day management; by now he had other concerns anyway as MP for Orkney and Shetland. A second crisis followed the opening of the Suez Canal. That wiped out the company's investment in the old route by rendering most of its fleet obsolete; thus far, ships for European waters had had a different design from those for the tropics, and now new ones were needed to sail all the way through. To the rescue came an Aberdonian, Thomas Sutherland, previously head of operations in Hong Kong. He had made them profitable through the transport of opium, but the company could conveniently forget that as he extended its runs all over the Far East and Australasia, to make it the greatest and grandest imperial shipping line. Though by now its Scottish ownership was greatly diluted, Sutherland kept the connections strong. About half its fleet was registered at Greenock, which he happened to represent in Parliament from 1884 to 1900.[6]

Its counterpart in the western oceans was Cunard, founded in 1840. With the subsidy on the mails, it opened the first regular service from Liverpool to Halifax and Boston, afterwards extended to New York and the West Indies; later it moved into the Mediterranean. Samuel Cunard himself came from Nova Scotia, but his managing partners were Glaswegians, George and James Burns and David and Charles MacIver. While the three families controlled the company through its first 40 years, their partnership was a typically loose one. The Burns and MacIvers actually competed on the run from Glasgow to Liverpool, till they agreed to amalgamate their services in 1853. Cunard died in 1865, and various redeployments of capital led to the Burns being virtually bought out for a while. The whole company was then reorganised in 1880. Within it the interests of the founding families remained strong, but by now the second generation of Glaswegians were losing their commercial links with their native city. In any event, the reconstructed line definitely based itself in Liverpool, reflecting an ascendancy which that port gradually gained over Glasgow in the Atlantic traffic.[7]

It was the East that found room for the third major Scottish line, the British India Steam Navigation Company, established in 1862. This grew out of a firm in Calcutta set up in the 1840s by Robert Mackenzie, later lost at sea, by William Mackinnon and by James Hall. They dealt in textiles between Scotland and India, and in general goods to Australia. It was also a shipping business and, after Mackenzie's death, Mackinnon returned home to concentrate on that. With his own fortune he bought himself on to the board of the City of Glasgow Bank, which he helped to save from a crisis in 1857; luckily for him, he had got out of it by the time of its collapse in 1878. With its support meanwhile, and with the contract for the mails to Calcutta and Burma, he launched his new company.

He was a shrewd and dapper yet colourless and puritanical Highlander: he made all his enterprises observe the sabbath, and would join the Wee Frees, the Free Presbyterian Church of Scotland, when they split off from the excessively liberal Free Church in 1892. Still, he might lay claim to being the greatest Scottish tycoon of all time. He judged the generality of his countrymen far too cautious, and declared he would invest in anything, however slow the return, so long as he sensed one would come in the end. Usually he did not have to wait. He at once made huge profits from the boom in Indian cotton during the American Civil War. He expanded rapidly after the Suez Canal was built, as the first to transfer the technology of iron-hulled steamers to the East. In the 1880s, British India dominated seaborne traffic there. It then had paid-up capital of £500,000 and 60 ships, but Mackinnon owned four associated companies with triple that number of vessels altogether. He had stakes in an arresting array of further enterprises, in finance and industry too, co-ordinated from Calcutta, London and above all Glasgow. Without a single parent or holding company, linked by no more than his own slight figure, it developed into a vast, sprawling commercial empire.

Yet Mackinnon had less trouble holding it together than more specialised rivals. He stood amid a large clan of family and friends, itself the nucleus of a clan of private firms and partnerships, purposefully trading on its great name but keeping its internal operations hidden from public view. The easiest way into membership of the clan was to have been born in Kintyre, Mackinnon's native heath. Its denizens bought thousands of shares in his companies. On his ships he served only the malt whisky of Campbeltown. From there to Tarbert, any willing lad could be sure of a job from him, with the prospect after seafaring adventures of a snug berth among the network of agents which British India maintained in every port of call. Just once was Mackinnon repaid with ingratitude, when he stood as Liberal candidate in Argyll at the General Election of 1885, to be beaten by the Crofters' party. But he made generally sure to serve brother Scots well. He cultivated the shipbuilders of the Clyde, notably William Denny & Bros of Dumbarton, placing orders himself and negotiating on their behalf for joint contracts with governments at home and in the colonies. In this and other ways his shipping line functioned also as an agency house, a combination crucial to its success. Mackinnon became a vital link between Scotland and the global economy.[8]

These were only the shipping lines of the first rank. Others flourished, even from a base confined to Scotland. That was no bar to the concentration of ownership combined with diversification of trade which proved to be the keys to survival. Concentration also took place in a geographical sense, as more and more business emanated from Glasgow. The exception proving the rule was the Ben Line, founded in 1839 by Alexander and William Thomson of Leith, which started in a small way on the run to Leghorn in Italy, then went into the Atlantic traffic but also expanded eastwards after the opening of the Suez Canal, drumming up business enough in grain and sugar for its sailing ships right till the 1890s. Otherwise Glaswegians dominated Scottish shipping, from among whom four major companies emerged. The Anchor Line, established by the brothers Handyside for the Baltic commerce in 1838, branched out to America when the family of Thomas Henderson came into the partnership in 1852, then turned to the Orient and had the honour of sending the first merchant vessel through the Suez Canal. The Glen Line emerged in the 1840s from the shipbroking business of James McGregor and Leonard Gow to specialise in imports of Chinese tea, often winning the race to get each season's new crop home. In 1861, Glaswegian interest in palm-oil prompted formation of the British and African Steam Navigation Company, later merged into the Elder-Dempster Line. Charles Cayzer, a Londoner who had set up in Liverpool, migrated further north in the 1870s, to go into partnership with Alexander Stephen, shipbuilder at Govan, and with John Muir, head of the merchant firm of James Finlay & Co, in the Clan Line.

Glasgow was also a magnet to ambitious Scots from elsewhere. Paddy Henderson, starting as insurance brokers at Pittenweem, moved there and built a complex network of joint ventures. One, the Albion Line, pioneered a shipping service for New Zealand, whence it dispatched the first refrigerated mutton in 1882. Three others did business with Burma, including the Irrawaddy Flotilla. Fondly regarded in its day as an exercise in sheer romance – its 'paddles clunkin'' from Rangoon to Mandalay' were to be immortalised by Rudyard Kipling – it yet burgeoned into a far-flung agency house. As such, it fathered the Burmah Oil Company, itself the parent of British Petroleum. The original Rangoon Oil Company was registered in Scotland in 1871 by James Galbraith, head of Paddy Henderson in Glasgow, and T.D. Findlay of the Irrawaddy Flotilla. They wanted a product to fill up ships returning from the East. But since their prime markets lay in India, they had no great success and put the company into liquidation in 1876. It was then taken over by David Cargill, of William Milne & Co, traders between Glasgow and Ceylon. He too struggled with it till the annexation of Upper Burma, which made all the difference. In 1886, the Burmah Oil Company was incorporated, with a wholly Scottish board. By 1913, the Burmese territories formed the Empire's largest source of oil, though their output of a million tons a year amounted to only 2 per cent of the world's production. On those grounds, even so, the company was often the trusted recipient of contracts from the Government. It moved again on to a higher plane through another unpromising venture, the purchase in 1906 of a business which had been vainly prospecting in the Middle East. Three years later, Burmah struck oil there. With mainly its own capital, it established the Anglo-Persian Oil Company, which despite the name had a majority of Scots as directors. When the Government acquired a large stake in 1914, the foundation was laid for BP. Till that point, Burmah Oil remained in its basic structure merely one branch of a Scottish agency house.[9]

In the Lyle Shipping Company, originally a partnership set up in 1827 by Abram Lyle of Greenock, diversification took a form just as unlikely. His business was cooperage, and he found a big market for barrels in sugar and molasses. The line acquired its own interests in them, minor till removal of duties in the 1840s brought a sharp rise in their consumption. It now multiplied its runs to the West Indies, Mauritius and India, taking Scottish coal, iron and, in the last case, railway sleepers in exchange for sugar. It grew so profitable that it branched out with a processing subsidiary, soon a major industry in its hometown. But during the 1870s competition from beet and from sugar refined in Europe forced it to look beyond a traffic primarily between Scotland and the colonies. In 1891 it built a factory in London, where cheap imports were landing and a bigger market beckoned. This formed a prelude to merger with the business of a rival family, the Tates of Liverpool, to become Tate & Lyle. The shipping line remained separate, but really as a plaything for Alexander Lyle, son of the founder, who disliked the drift south and wanted something to occupy him in Scotland. Unhappily, he also preferred sailing ships because he thought them nobler. This was not a formula for success. By 1906, the line had had to be reconstructed, to move to Glasgow as a limited company dominated by external capital, and to set out in search of new, modest but sensible trade for a fleet of tramping steamers, which in the long run secured its independence.[10]

Shipping lines and agency houses still made ideal careers for transient Scots in exotic climes, letting them stick together, but slip back to Scotland when, in their modest and cautious way, they had made enough. We have seen these institutions showing their worth in changing circumstances as well, offering scope for invention and enterprise, for financial networks and for solid investment in production at home and abroad. They pleased the imperial authorities, while bringing the blessings of commerce to alien peoples. There was little here to prick a Scottish conscience. To that extent, the old commercial Empire proved adaptable to the mature economy at home. But we have also seen how the increasingly global scale of business could operate in reverse, and impinge on the cosy clannishness of the Scots. There were fewer successors to the senior generations of partners, with their closeness and parsimony, enterprise and ruthlessness, quickness and versatility. Integration into the wider world, in Britain, the Empire and elsewhere, thus carried a price. It had been transforming the internal structures of Scotland too, to produce an economy more integrated and complex. Some businesses, like some of the social institutions facing similar historical forces, adapted. But others failed to, and fell behind, yielding the initiative to others. In the economic sphere too, that could mean in the end a loss of Scottish autonomy.[11]

The process was in part bound up with the accumulation and distribution of capital. Up to 1870 or so, Scotland did not on the whole export capital, any more than labour. Scots of the commercial Empire made what they needed on the spot, or passed it among themselves without calling on domestic resources. The case could hardly have been otherwise. Few channels for transmission of money existed. Heavy capital demands at home during the second phase of the industrial revolution anyway ate up Scottish savings. But the fresh capital generated in a mature economy would mount on a scale never seen before, or since. There were limits to what it could itself absorb. It had little incentive to substitute capital for labour because wages stayed lower than in England. This kept Scotland competitive and maintained jobs even while capital flowed out. But it did not encourage diverse investment into fresh fields. Instead, a few heavy industries, achieving economies of scale from enlarged and consolidated markets, flourished on larger volumes of specialised products. In other words, they exploited comparative advantage. They then shed their marginal activities. That was why manufacture of cotton declined in Scotland, yielding a clear lead to Lancashire by the 1860s. Even production of pig-iron, another Scottish staple, was at the same time starting to grow faster elsewhere. This must not be equated with a general trend. On the contrary, Scotland boomed, amid the rise of shipbuilding and its ancillaries. Clydeside especially had early on an almost self-sufficient economic base. It imported foodstuffs, and the cotton now usually brought in coastwise from Liverpool; that, however, was the sole major manufacturing commodity dependent on an external source. Otherwise, the heavy industries supplied themselves with local raw materials from their own smelters and refiners. Glasgow's economic task had completely changed since its development began. Once it had been forced to find means of importing resources to develop its own industries. Now it had to expand foreign markets so that those industries could grow faster. It evolved from an entrepot into a great manufacturing centre precisely because it built up trade so strongly in the products of the city itself and of its hinterland. As other countries set out on their own industrialisation, the prospects looked buoyant.[12]

One way of feeding foreign demand was financial, out of the exportable surplus of capital that Scotland soon enjoyed. We wonder today whether the funds had to leave, when there was such poverty in Scotland and, in retrospect, a lack of domestic investment for the future. The question did not go unasked at the time. In 1884, *Blackwood's Edinburgh Magazine* ran an article on foreign investment from Scotland which noted that 'in proportion to her size and the number of her population, she furnishes far more of it than either of the sister kingdoms'. Three-quarters of the companies formed for investment overseas were said to be of Scottish origin: 'If not actually located in Scotland, they have been hatched by Scotchmen and work on Scottish models'. The article set out not just to boast. It also doubted if the outflow would be good for the country in the long run.

This was not, however, a question that bothered many Scots. With money at home plentiful and cheap, they had every incentive to seek a better return on it elsewhere. They saw maximisation of the return as morally and economically right. While it enriched individuals, it brought benefits to the whole nation by stimulating output of commodities for international trade. It was in a sense investment in a primary sector for Scotland herself, because it raised demand for the secondary goods and services in which her mature economy specialised. These thus remained the best things to specialise in, and rendered innovation to that extent unnecessary. How strongly Scots felt all this was demonstrated by what they actually did with their money. Capital exports may have equalled ten per cent of net national product in the period 1870–1900, much greater than the English counterpart. In absolute terms, the amount invested overseas grew from £60 million in 1870 to at least £500 million in 1914. According to *Blackwood's*, the return on it was 6 per cent gross and 4 per cent net: which squares well enough with a modern finding that Australian investments, for example, paid an average 4 to 5 per cent, compared to the average 2.3 per cent available from Scottish banks.[13]

That last fact casts light from a different direction on the flood of capital exports. Scotland housed financial institutions of her own, which now had the chance to adapt to an international economy. Again, some did not. Central to the structure were the banks. Wholly of native origin and scarcely regulated from London, they had by a miraculous combination of sound practice and continual innovation worked out for themselves the principles of a successful and stable free banking system, based on the private issue of money. It had carried the country through all the strains of the first industrial revolution without severe financial disturbance: not something that could be said of English banks. But, after the English banks alleged unfair competition from Scotland, Sir Robert Peel imposed in 1845 an Act of Parliament which ended her independence in this respect. Afterwards there could in effect be no new entrants to the business, while the existing banks were encouraged to sacrifice profitable flexibility to the security of a protected and cartelised domestic market, where their growing reluctance to compete for deposits was reflected in a steadily declining rate of interest.

Two major commercial effects followed. The first, fully intended by Peel, was to make London the financial centre for Scotland. Under the new dispensation the Scottish banks remained unsure of their precise relationship to the Bank of England, in particular whether it would act as their lender of last resort. They therefore kept a large part of their assets on call in the City. This was unique in its market for short-term credit, forming the vast reserve that kept global commerce on the move. Like many foreigners, Scots traders often found it easier to operate from there and use the accessible credits. For the Scottish banks in turn, that made London the best place to deploy spare resources, which remained both near-liquid and profitable. In the 1870s their encroachments raised fresh protests from English competitors and brought down on their heads a parliamentary inquiry. They were more careful after that, but still seemed to prefer this mercantile business to long-term industrial lending at home, where their caution in the face of legitimate demand verged on the churlish.

The second effect was that in general the banks developed no interest in direct business overseas, unlike almost every other commercial entity in Scotland. Two of those that did, the Western Bank and the City of Glasgow Bank, set the discouraging example of going bankrupt, if through fraud at home rather than the nature of their foreign portfolios. This glaring omission was all the more extraordinary in that the traditional principles of Scottish banking, the sound issue of notes through a network of branches uncontrolled by a central bank, mirrored exactly what was required in distant colonies with no link between political and monetary authority. Still, if the banks missed their chance, the bankers did not. At least the brighter sparks among them knew their skills were exportable and put them to use in colonial banks. These sprang up to meet the demand for trading credit in the Empire, and diffused British economic influence beyond it. They raised their capital in London and their deposits as a rule locally but, being often run by Scotsmen, some turned to Scotland too. Of many examples, two merit special mention because they have now grown into major global institutions. The Hongkong and Shanghai Bank was founded in 1864 at the instance of Sutherland of P & O, conscious of the need to finance the burgeoning commerce of the Far East. Just because there was no means of regulating it, Sutherland explicitly chose 'Scottish principles' of self-regulation. Its notes became in time the preferred currency not only in Hong Kong but also in neighbouring Chinese provinces and in cities further north. Later it made the running in the issue in London of loans for the Manchu regime. In other words, it became the prop of the entire British informal Empire in the Orient. Meanwhile in India the Chartered Bank had been established in 1853. It too was largely a creation of Scots, who gave it most of its inaugural directors and its first chairman, James Wilson. Born at Hawick and apprenticed to a hatmaker, he went as a youth to seek his fortune in London. There indeed he found it, and used it to set up *The Economist* in 1843. He entered Parliament, held various official posts, then went out to Calcutta in 1859 as finance member of the Viceroy's council; but he died in a few months. Even without him, the Chartered Bank soon dominated the Indian market. It was joint ancestor of today's Standard Chartered Bank. As for the banks inside Scotland, nobody even proposed till 1919 that they might jointly venture abroad. By then they were too set in their ways to risk it.

That a financial institution straining for respectability need not be tied down to Scotland was clear from the example of the Standard Life Assurance Company. Its business required a different type of portfolio from banking, but scarcely less regard to security. In this case it brought no complacent assumption that foreign business was inherently suspect, or that high rates of interest signified unacceptable risk. The company, founded in Edinburgh in 1825, expanded steadily. Half a century later it was transacting the largest amount in Britain of new annual life business. In 1866 it took over a colonial firm, and so acquired staff in Canada and India. Up to the First World War it grew still more profitable, largely from imperial investments. In the 1880s it concentrated on the securities of Indian and colonial Governments, in which it typically held 10 per cent of assets. By 1910 it preferred their bonds, in which it held up to 16 per cent of assets. The company played the market, switching rapidly from one bond to another, subject only to ceilings for each country. But in addition to the vital matter of fluctuations in yields, the directors had to consider the different economic prospects, and they looked for stability and security. They were criteria that the banks also had to respect, but here they did not induce the same sterility.[14]

The times favoured financial innovation. Still, it could not have proceeded so briskly without a parallel process of corporate innovation, which was also the start of corporate integration, inside Scotland and with England. A common market in securities began to emerge as soon as stock exchanges were founded in Edinburgh and Glasgow in 1843, and Aberdeen in 1845. Their foundation may itself have been a form of integration. In Scotland, stockbroking had been a preserve of solicitors, and this created a new business on an imported pattern. When Glasgow and London then became linked by telegraph in 1847, the markets in securities moved much closer together. At that date, the prices of shares in the Grand Trunk Railway of Canada, for example, matched or overlapped about one-third of the time. By 1860, the proportion rose to more than three-quarters. Though the two exchanges influenced each other, London's influence was bound to be the greater, because a single market responded to national rather than local conditions of supply and demand.

It would do so all the more as Scottish and English companies acquired a common legal basis and structure. Scotland's predominant system of private partnership had served her well, better than any equivalent in England, but it was England that furnished the corporate model for the future. There, with the increasing scale of industry, something clearly needed to be done about the juristic principle holding every company to be the personal property of its directors, who bore unlimited liability for its operations; this quite apart from the problem of mobilising larger and more permanent capital than private individuals could provide. The answer was the limited joint-stock company, authorised by Act of Parliament in 1856. In order to meet the same problems, Scotland imported the concept ten years later, though under a separate system of registration. By 1870, 200 such companies had been formed. There followed in 1872–4 a sudden surge of new formations, in those two years alone exceeding the previous total. By the end of the century, the joint-stock company dominated most branches of the economy.[15]

A feature of that surge was formation of companies for foreign investment. Not strictly an innovation in Scotland, they had, however, emerged before primarily in response to external demand. Such were the pioneers in Australia, meeting the needs of a country without funds. Even among this first generation of investment houses, some were lost to London, with its more plentiful capital: the Scottish Australian Company, founded in Aberdeen in 1840, went south a dozen years later. Two-thirds of its original partners, many of them small investors, came from its parent city or the hinterland, with only a handful from outside Scotland. There was sporadic tension between them, wary of committing their money unless guaranteed high dividends, and their agent in Australia, who above all needed capital as the vast opportunities of a new country opened before him. The gold rush of 1851 made the difference. Many more people in London bought the shares, and soon the agent was preferring to work with these incoming interests. They gradually gained control, forcing the resignation of the old directors in 1853. Events vindicated the coup. The capital was doubled in 1855 and quickly subscribed. The company could then expand smoothly.[16]

The next generation of investment houses arose, however, as much in response to internal supply, to the Scots' wish to deploy the capital surplus they were accumulating. Though these new companies were public ones, they still displayed a Scots clannishness. Most were organised from the offices of solicitors and accountants, especially in Edinburgh, city of the professions *par excellence*. Solicitors had plenty of financial expertise from stockbroking, the administration of large estates and so on. In the close-knit world of Scots law, many kept up contacts with colleagues in remote countries, while sitting amid a frugal populace which might own large sums left idle or deposited in the banks at low returns. The professional men, members of the ubiquitous Scottish bourgeoisie, were quite likely to have cousins and acquaintances in imperial outposts as well. All these brother Scots felt happiest dealing with each other, as they would not have felt dealing with some outsider, and the solicitors were uniquely placed to draw their networks together. England, of course, possessed her provincial markets, but it is hard to see how they could have worked in quite the same way. At any rate, Scots did set up their own channels for capital export. Nor were they negligible: they invested about £5 million a year at their peak in the late 1880s. The market was by then so well-developed and so replete with funds that the activities of Scottish solicitors almost seemed to determine the ability of certain companies overseas to borrow in Britain. Especially those considered risky, such as the Australians, raised capital successfully in Scotland when it is far from clear that they could have done the same in London.

All this created a new investing public. In the period up to the First World War, the number of Scots holding foreign assets reached 80,000. They included not only the wealthy but also many small savers: professionals, merchants, shopkeepers, artisans, women. Just as impressive was the sheer number of companies that their funds begot. A survey has shown 853 formed for investment overseas in Scotland by 1914, of which 315 then remained active and 40 survive today. Most came in the mining sector, which accounted for 376, with plantations and ranches the next most numerous, though well behind. Up to half the capital was destined specifically for the Empire, in which Scottish investment per head ran at 60 per cent above the British average. Every discovery of a new colonial resource seemed to spark off a burst of Scottish speculation. The Indian gold mania of 1879–81 prompted the formation of 33 Scottish companies with paid-up capital of £2 million, but most of it went into the pockets of the promoters. The so-called Kaffir boom of 1895, in the companies of the Transvaal, mounted on such a scale that it enabled a separate market in mining shares to be set up in Glasgow. In 1909–10 there followed a rage for rubber, caused by shortage of the natural product and the opportunity to finance plantations in Malaya which could assure supply. Scotland floated 38 companies for the purpose. In the exploitation of Australian minerals alone, she had 77 companies by 1920.[17]

If Scots borrowed a new corporate structure from England, they soon adapted it to their own purposes. It was, of course, no guarantee against failure. A number of those 853 ventures produced little, and some went bust. But 87 were investment trusts, the first vehicles of collective capitalism. Under professional management they deployed shareholders' funds across a diverse portfolio, when soundly conducted often to a level above the paid-up capital, returning a dividend based on the average yield. In practice they cut risk and so expanded the whole scale of the business, to a level which might truly be called popular. Investment trusts were not strictly a Scottish innovation, having been pioneered in Belgium. But the financial genius who imported them, Robert Fleming, established their principles of operation and must really count as the father of this new financial institution. The son of a shopkeeper in Dundee, he went to work aged 13 in the offices of one of its textile dynasties, the Baxters. He rose to be private clerk to the senior partner, proving astute and reliable enough to be entrusted with management of the family's shareholdings. With this experience, he launched the Scottish American Investment Trust in 1873. It caught on at once, and he soon had £500,000 deployed, especially in the railways being built across the United States, but also in selected mortgages, official securities and much else besides, with never more than 10 per cent of assets staked on a single enterprise. His inspiration was at once copied in the Scottish American Investment Company, improbably set up by William J. Menzies, a firm of ecclesiastical lawyers in Edinburgh, perhaps to enliven an otherwise stagnant practice. It specialised in transatlantic stocks, while the Scottish American Mortgage Company, coming hard on its heels, concentrated on real estate.

They launched a Scottish craze. The trusts quickly outstripped in importance the companies founded for a single purpose. Within a couple of years, 15 of them appeared and a steady flow of new formations followed: the Canada North West Land Company, the North British Canadian Investment Company, the Australian Mortgage and Agency Company, the Scottish and New Zealand Investment Company and so on. Edinburgh, with Dundee just behind, remained the principal centres for them. Glasgow, preferring to deploy its money in other ways, created its first trust only in 1907, Aberdeen in 1908. A further boom ensued up to, then after, the First World War. These years saw 17 new trusts established, most again in Edinburgh, where they were now the largest single component of the financial sector. Each of the cities tended, if not exclusively, to specialise in a different locus of investment, Edinburgh in Australia, Glasgow in South Africa, Dundee in the United States, usually dealing through its own sons on the spot. Their cosy clannishness thus stretched across the globe. The Scottish connection could at the same time be tremendously important for a new country: Australia, for example, drew one-third of her external capital from it.[18]

In this, as in so much, the economic edifice of the Scottish Empire was truly awesome: there can have been few places or industries in Scotland that lacked some link with it. No less amazing than its extent was its creation out of a small country's resources, with little participation from anywhere else, except perhaps Liverpool. Internal industrialisation promoted external expansion in exports of labour and capital, and worldwide exploitation of Scottish expertise and technology. Scotland also had her own financial and legal institutions, an educational system capable of supplying all the trained personnel for commerce or the services supporting it, and trade across the oceans conducted directly, without recourse to ports in the South. So up to the First World War she could still exercise a high degree of economic autonomy, and creatively develop fresh connections to the outside world. Doing it without the English was beyond doubt a matter of deep satisfaction.

What happened to it? Certainly little enough survives today, when instead external capital dominates Scotland. The account conventionally constructed with the benefit of hindsight rests on the national failure to foresee what different investments might have been required for a remote future. Scotland clearly did not diversify enough from the capital goods needed by an industrialising world. The export of her own funds, coupled with sustained demand from overseas, especially the Empire, reinforced technological conservatism. The ensemble posed by 1914 a formidable barrier to change. But, because at the time it reflected comparative advantage, it was rational behaviour. If Scots suspected anything amiss, they took it as no more than another item on the inevitable balance-sheet of profit and loss in the operation of free markets, the net benefits of which remained patently overwhelming. In fact many of the imperial developments where they put their money did show great promise, and often fulfilled it. Even so, the foundations amply laid for a home-based, yet international economy have not been built on.[19]

Scots' calculation of net benefit would surely have produced the same over-whelming verdict in favour of their existing political status, especially as members of the world's greatest Empire. That it might entail some economic drawbacks struck scarcely anyone. Yet, with the same hindsight, it cannot be gainsaid that they were there. We may again instructively compare Scotland with other small European countries. The Dutch, for example, also possessed an improbable Empire. Out of it they have been able to endow themselves with an economic base hospitable to multinational companies, and so equip themselves to hold their own amid the principal evolution of capitalism during the twentieth century. More multinational companies were born in Scotland than ever existed in Holland. Yet hardly any have stayed. It might seem extravagant to suggest that Scottish political autonomy, or some degree of it, would have been good or even possible in the late nineteenth century. But as a second lesson from hindsight it is no better or worse than the first. The political unit to which Scotland was attached, the United Kingdom, housed in London the greatest financial centre of the day, and its metropolitan pull mounted steadily. If it could do business for the continental nations, it could obviously do business for Scotland, where there were no frontiers to cross, no barriers to concentration. In that sense, some attrition of established and successful Scottish business took place even while in new activities it continued to expand. In this sphere too, Scotland was starting to turn into a province.

Nothing illustrates it better than the evolution of the shipping lines, even though their founders, attached to their roots, often resisted the pull. An early victim of it was the one eventually known as the Castle Line, set up by Donald Currie, a son of Greenock who had started his career with Cunard before striking out on his own over the run from Leith to Hamburg. By the 1870s he had already transferred almost his entire business to London. Thence he pioneered, with the usual subsidy on the mails, regular services to South Africa, where he also acquired interests in diamonds and gold. As some recompense for commercial abandonment of his homeland, he bought an estate in Perthshire and served as the county's MP.

Then before the century ended, with Scotland's economy still dynamic and growing, she was taken aback by the decision of British India to move its head-quarters from Glasgow to London. This happened as soon as Mackinnon died in 1893. He and his fellow patriarchs had wanted to stay in Glasgow to reinforce their clannish control, and had even transferred northwards the management of compa-nies they acquired in England. Yet through their spiralling operations they had also drawn metropolitan capital into the group. They were in fact conducting more and more business from the South. One reason lay in the failure of the City of Glasgow Bank, which had aggressively, and at last fraudulently, tried to meet demands for credit which stuffier bankers refused. It provided funds for much of British India's earlier expansion. Afterwards, the group did its big financial deals in London. The pattern of its trade changed anyway. Scottish textile manufacture declined, and with it the main export carried from Glasgow. No longer did the line sell consumer goods through merchants so much as capital goods to final users without intermediaries, and thus had less use for snug commercial networks. London besides offered the largest markets for the returning commodities. Then the Suez Canal brought some concentration of traffic in the Thames. New services, at any rate, seldom emanated from the Clyde or the Mersey. Altogether, British India embedded itself in the commercial establishment of the City, and it just became easier to do everything from there. The grounds for the move from Glasgow looked in the end simple, and to younger directors of the company, most themselves Scots, commercially unim-peachable: it was a matter of which place held out more convenient facilities for growing international trade and investment.[20]

One contribution to its growth came from carving up business, by written agreement from 1869, with P & O. This other big subsidised line in the East had been founded by a Scotsman and was still run by a Scotsman, if no longer under any larger degree of Scottish ownership. The two would be united by a third Scotsman, James Mackay. Born at Arbroath in 1852, the bastard of a shipowner, himself the bastard of the 9th Earl of Dalhousie, Mackay inherited brains, energy and ambition. He used them to become one of the great capitalists of his time, and die with the dignity of Lord Inchcape. After apprenticeship in London he went in 1874 to work for Mackinnon in India, and soon showed his mettle. Put in charge of operations in Bombay, he picked up partnerships in other concerns he dealt with. They included Indian ones, for Mackay strongly believed that development should benefit the natives, whom he liked; how much better if they, he said on a visit to Australia, could replace her 'by no means attractive' British settlers. In 1884 he moved to Calcutta, and leadership of its commercial community. The viceroy chose him for his council in 1891. Here Mackay defended local interests in disputes over British trading regulations, and became a scourge of bureaucratic interference with business. In 1894 he returned home. For British India, Mackinnon's death, amid rising competition and protectionist moves by foreign countries, brought an ominous fall in turnover and profits. Mackay put it back on an even keel. With the feather of its restored fortunes in his cap, he took on a wide range of public tasks, notably negotiation of a new commercial treaty with China in 1901. He would have become Viceroy of India, except that the Prime Minister, Herbert Asquith, refused to appoint a businessman. His peerage in 1911 was meant as compensation.[21]

This career brought him into ample contact with Sutherland of P & O. They admired each other, and it was part of a peculiarly Scottish way of doing things that the friendship should have determined their companies' future. Sutherland picked Mackay to succeed him, just as he himself had been picked by Anderson years before. The only obstacle lay in Mackay's position as chairman of a competitor, though the competition was by now fairly nominal. It could not have been hard to hit on the solution of a merger, which they started discussing as early as 1901. P & O was now distinctly the worse off of the two, short of capital and in need of further reconstruction, but Sutherland still felt proud of it and of his life's work for it. The terms of the prize he dangled before Mackay were that the younger man should head a merged company under P & O's name. In other words, British India must appear to sell out to its rival. Mackay just agreed. It was not in truth a sell-out but the biggest and shrewdest deal of his life. For £15 million, he gained control of P & O and left far behind any conceivable competition in the eastern seas. The whole shipping operation then formed in 1914 became a subsidiary of the Inchcape Group. Tracing back to their origins all its previous component enterprises reveals that, of the 56 founders in the period 1796–1874, 34 were Scots. But only tenuous Scottish connections survive in the major multinational corporation it has turned into today.[22]

If this was a unique case, the pressures for concentration in the shipping industry had become general, because of violent fluctuations in its trade cycle. Since the 1860s, when the three leading Scottish lines were already established, there had followed first a rapid expansion, then depression in the 1870s, recovery in the 1880s and another depression in the first decade of the twentieth century. The shipping moguls were unable to control any of this. All they could do was make incessant efforts to cut costs, largely through technological advance. This in turn only intensified competition, especially on runs to the Far East. By 1900 the Germans and Japanese had expanded their fleets, while Greeks and Scandinavians were entering the tramping business. The British just about kept ahead on imperial routes. But the competition had long got too much for everybody, as they appeared to agree. The remedy for its evils was obviously to remove it.

The lines achieved that by so-called shipping conferences, cartels which set minimum prices for freight, binding on customers, for the regular long runs. They may have been another of Scotland's gifts to the world. The earliest can be traced to an arrangement among the Burns and McIvers for the route from Glasgow and

Liverpool as early as 1832. By 1850 it had spread to the transatlantic level, when Cunard and an American rival agreed to fix rates and pool earnings. The four major companies operating from Liverpool, carrying 96 per cent of the passenger traffic across the Atlantic, concluded a still wider and more explicit accord in 1879. By now there was also a conference for traffic to Calcutta, and in the same year five British lines established one for China and Japan. Since it could scarcely succeed while confined to them, they later admitted German and American competitors who, however, often worked together against them. Conferences still proved their utility, if only in their durability. By the Second World War the Far Eastern conference, based on geographical delimitation of business, had grown to 18 members, six of them British.

With profits allocated by agreement, shipping lines could only grow through planned reconstruction. In the West, Cunard in effect went into partnership with the Government. While the founding families no longer held control, from among their ranks John Burns, later Lord Inverclyde, had succeeded to the chairmanship. In his last years the company was making losses. After he died in 1909, J. Pierpont Morgan, the American financiers, sought to take it over. The horrified 2nd Lord Inverclyde preferred to call on Whitehall. Help came in loans and subsidies for new ships, and kept Cunard afloat. In the East, Mackay's creation of the new P & O left operating only four British groups of any size, three of which could boast a Scottish origin. The Glen Line had likewise evolved away from it. The partnership moved its head-quarters to London as early as 1873 in response to the opening of the Suez Canal. Close links with the fabulously wealthy Chinese agency house, Jardine Matheson, might have proved its salvation from rising problems, except that the partners refused to give up command for an infusion of capital, and utterly rejected reconstitution as a joint-stock company. But a younger generation showed no such scruples and in 1911 sold out to external interests, which formed the Glen-Shire Line. Ben Line, the third and most doggedly Scottish partnership active in the Orient, survived by settling for the tramping trade. This was what the older, individualistic system of shipping, predating scheduled traffic, had turned into. In other words, it sailed no fixed routes, but accepted any type of contract or cargo, often in markets with which nobody else now bothered. Yet that suited the cautious, conservative partners of the Ben Line, who deliberately limited its exposure by never over-extending operations and never seeking finance from outside. It also benefited from the failure before 1914 to establish any conference for trampers, which could meanwhile undermine more powerful outfits with lower rates. So the line still grew. With further adaptation it has up to the present held its own as a private partnership of the old sort, though its complex structure also includes, since 1919, a company with limited liability. A similar, if slower, solution followed in different waters for the Lyle Line, once wrested from the grasp of its founding family.[23]

Shipping is an atypical industry, but offers an especially well-documented example of concentration in an activity favoured by Scots which became global in scale, and which through reverse operation of global pressures largely lost its Scottish character. For a small country, it proved impossible to hold the lead in a business expanding over the long term, yet subject to dizzying swings over the short term, with no chance of excluding new entrants. That not only doomed private partnership, but also soon rationalised the public companies emerging from it.

One atypical example may not readily illuminate the rest. Still, during the nineteenth century other industries clearly suffered analogous structural pressures. Some did resist better. In Scotland, even more than in the rest of Britain, formal concentration was confined before 1914 to a relatively limited range of businesses, at least compared to, say, the United States. While joint-stock organisation had become dominant, Scots families still ran numerous enterprises. Only one in five of the country's commercial and industrial leaders were professional managers, the rest all being either founders or inheritors of their firms. This state of affairs was preserved by new legal status for the private company under an Act of 1907, giving it the same limited liability as other corporations. But the resistance had its price too. If one of the main purposes was to avoid takeover, that also reduced the drive to innovate. Instead of spending on internal efficiency, Scottish companies were as likely to extend their defensive screen by acquiring equity in others, or by temporary co-operation with rivals.

In this sense, Scottish business did not repel the pressures, but met them with a characteristic riposte. Its expedients were reinforced by the national taste for interlocking interests, for having directors from different companies sit on each other's boards. Perhaps that revealed a commercial and industrial community hidebound in its clannishness. On the other hand, it could have been a path to the greater integration of financiers, merchants and manufacturers which conditions anyway called for. The limited company, with its option of non-executive directors, actually encouraged the interlocking of interests. They became common not only and most obviously in the financial sector, where they persist in strength to this day, but also in a major industry such as shipbuilding. The yards competed fiercely, yet held each other's shares, and those of their customers. Denny's, for example, linked itself with 19 shipping lines. To 15 of them, between 1880 and 1913, it sold 770 ships, for more than £20 million. The investments seldom aimed at vertical integration or control of assets. They never succeeded in countering the trade cycle. Nor were the capital gains impressive. But they did generate sales and profits, and allow Denny's to develop specialisms, often in advanced technology. The practice was in one way a strength of the Scottish industry, guaranteeing long series of orders, and elsewhere saving on overheads by giving greater scope for standardised designs. In another way it was a weakness, maintaining an already apparent over-capacity.[24]

More comfortable surrogates for formal concentration could therefore be found, by this and by other devices. They spread among several industries, though few have been adequately studied. The Scottish coalmasters were constantly making, if also breaking, accords on prices. The ironmasters did the same, to greater effect, among themselves and with competitors in the North of England. In one salient case the surrogate brought a longer step towards industrial integration with the neighbour nation. The great Glasgow engineering firm of Beardmore arranged in 1902 for an exchange of shares with its English rival Vickers, as the prelude to building a new works for new technology. Formal concentration did occur too, but in significant instances by mutual agreement. The Distillers Company was created as a combination of six firms in 1877. The North British Locomotive Company, builder of the Empire's steam trains, established itself out of three existing businesses in 1902. Predation was rarer. But J & P Coats, which had started as a manufacturer of thread at Paisley in 1826 and survived nearly all the rest of the textile industry on Clydeside, grew into a giant, the largest in Scotland, third largest in Britain and one of the earliest truly multinational corporations, simply by buying up any conceivable competitor.[25]

So we have to conclude not just by acknowledging one conventional account of the nation's modern industrial failure, that its very success in the nineteenth century made it slow to innovate. We must also stress the effect at the dawn of the twentieth century from problems of scale created by business which was becoming global, in Scotland's case largely through the Empire. Within it her industry faced as yet little invincible competition. But these markets would remain secure only as long as the Empire lasted. They did not in fact solve the problems of scale, because those problems were inherent to the Scottish way of doing business, 'using the safe and small', as George Douglas Brown called it in *The House with the Green Shutters* (1901). The Scots' every tradition and instinct spoke for it. It had so far served them well in the whole fabric of society, not just in business. Leaders of business showed in their patronage and philanthropy an intense commitment to their local communities, working together where they otherwise competed. In this complex of Scottish circumstances, however, lay a basic disjunction with the emergence of global capitalism. Many private partnerships had already had to go public for the sake of limited liability and access to capital markets. Expansion could follow, but often brought with it a steady divorce of ownership from control. The company then stood exposed to outsiders wielding superior financial power or commercial expertise. The way opened to the formation of much larger corporations, internally as a matter of industrial logic to gain economies of scale, and externally in response to the competition as other countries caught up with Britain. The consequence was in almost every case the dilution or loss of a company's Scottish character. The commercial Empire had given a small country access to the great world. Now the world turned the tables, and brought that country's smallness home to it again.

A further refinement of the process could be seen in the eventual fate of Downie's British Dynamite. This technological and corporate pioneer prospered mightily into the twentieth century on ceaselessly growing demand for its product. Somewhere or other, discoveries of minerals were always there to be exploited, or new roads and railways to be built. Somewhere or other, wars always went on. By 1918 the Nobel

Company, as it now was, had grown bigger than ever under the leadership of a Glaswegian from a younger generation, Harry McGowan. Still, peace was bound to reduce demand for explosives. In consequence of a rationalisation overseen by the Government, Nobel swallowed a lot of minnows in the business. For reasons which would carry little weight today, the combine then moved its main office from Glasgow to London, to be reincorporated as Imperial Chemical Industries in 1926. By administrative fiat, in effect, the headquarters of another major company, and a titan of the future, were lost to Scotland.

It was a foretaste of the still more decisive assault on Scottish economic autonomy to come, as the twentieth century proceeded, from intervention by the British state. The later story lies outside the scope of this chapter, but we may pause to note one coincidence: the advent of big government, during and after the First World War, helped to produce almost at once the modern Nationalist movement, if at first only on the fringe of politics. Hitherto, it must be said, Scotland's constitutional status had been a matter of relative indifference to her people. In fact, as we shall see below, they had already looked at, swithered over, then cast aside or lost the chance of reorganising the formal Empire in a way that might have set up a different, more satisfactory framework for meeting the imminent crisis of the informal Empire. As things now stood, it was no longer a matter of moving forward politically, but of struggling, in growing weariness and despair, to cling on to the economic ground that the nation had in its vigour so intrepidly conquered.

CHAPTER TWENTY-TWO

'Les peuples de second rang': The European Context

T he House of Commons could always tell when James Ramsay MacDonald had a bee in his bonnet. The earnest young Scot, already obviously destined to take over moral leadership of the Labour movement from his older compatriot Keir Hardie, would bang on and on, undeterred by a whispering chamber or a restive Speaker. On February 25, 1909, he was giving them the benefit of his views about recent changes in the Congo, by which it ceased to be the personal property of Leopold II, King of the Belgians, and became a regular colony of his state. MacDonald complained at length how little the Government in Brussels was doing to improve the infamous regime inherited from the king. It had neither sacked his guilty officials nor amended his oppressive regulations. On the contrary, it had just proposed a Congolese budget clearly assuming the continuance of forced labour for public works. Finally he got to his point:

> I want to make perfectly clear that this country has not surrendered what it has always maintained to be its right to interfere in the administration of the Congo. The mere transference of the Congo to the Belgian Government did not set this country's responsibilities aside. When this country is satisfied that everything is right then it will surrender its responsibility. Until that does happen this country must assert its right to interfere and see that the Congo is adequately administered.[1]

The British Left had been in uproar over the Congo since 1904, when the Foreign Office made available to Parliament a report on conditions there from its consul at Boma, one Roger Casement. He told in harrowing detail how Leopold II had set about destroying a traditional society. In its place he had created a submissive class of helots with which to exploit the rich resources of the territory and extract his huge profits. This was virtually a slave state, the hapless natives, men, women and children, being made to work under a reign of terror, of flogging, mutilation and murder. If in desperation they resisted, soldiers went out and massacred them, cutting off their ears and stringing them on cords to prove the number of kills. It was perhaps a curious proceeding for an official of one Government to investigate the conduct of another. Yet the consequences vindicated it. It aroused a fierce outcry in Britain, then across Europe. The king, forced to answer at the bar of international public opinion, and running into trouble with his own Ministers, finally caved in and surrendered his domain. He died a year later in 1909, still seeing himself as a benefactor of his country, but to everyone else revealed naked in his greed and wickedness. Posterity has seen no need to alter that judgment. The outcome was satisfying above all to a British Empire still at the height of its prestige, and still ready to use its power for moral ends.

That was what MacDonald meant by its right of interference. He did not seem to be aware that some of his own countrymen had been interfering in the opposite sense, in enabling Leopold II to erect his Congolese charnel-house. Many Scots were now committed to a greater Britain, but that never stopped others lending their services to her rivals. Scotland's own commercial Empire, built from the slender resources of a marginal trading people, had been almost by definition indifferent to political boundaries. It had not posited British territorial expansion, but happily allowed that commercial partners might remain under their native authorities, so long as these could effectively guarantee the conduct of business. By the same token, Scots had seldom much cared under whose flag they sailed from the European end either. Even when they later espoused the cause of a Christian Empire, which usually meant a westernising one, it did not to their way of thinking necessarily imply any British political hegemony. Livingstone himself took no such view, while his successors in Central Africa often dissented from colonial policies not conducive to eventual native self-government. Scots never let themselves be completely swept away by the British chauvinism of the high imperialist era. For most this was a matter of morality; some just had their eye on the main chance.[2]

One of Leopold II's associates was William Mackinnon, shipping magnate and favourite son of Kintyre. He had returned from India a wealthy man, to achieve the commercial and social eminence that wealth warranted in Victorian Britain. He aimed at greater things still, at lending his name to some splendid and lasting imperial enterprise, British or no. Not unmindful of his country's interests, he never felt bound by them either. Through the middle decades of the century, its rulers remained stingily wary of overloading it with foreign commitments, so a self-styled man of vision could feel entitled to turn elsewhere. At any early stage Mackinnon's interests spilled across the bounds of the British Empire, into the Brazilian, Dutch and Ottoman ones. He owned enough shares in the Suez Canal Company to get on its board, an empyrean of international high finance. In these spheres it was natural to hobnob with royalty. Mackinnon came to know the King of the Belgians through a shared fixation on Africa as one of the last regions of the world to be opened up. Sober and devout he was, yet it tickled his fancy to machinate with a monarch over dividing the spoils of the dark continent. Leopold II found use not only for the money but also for the demeanour of the staid and God-fearing Mackinnon, the better to clothe his own schemes, essentially of annexation, in a mantle of international co-operation for humanitarian and scientific ends. But there were further good reasons why the Scotsman and the Belgian should be friends. Both came from small countries where industry and trade had been controlled by private partnerships, now seeking means to operate on a greater scale, at home and abroad.

Each of those small countries felt conscious of the political handicaps imposed on it amid the grand strategies of European powers. While for Scots the handicaps were also spurs to find and exploit riches on a scale that others would be compelled to respect, Belgians long appeared indifferent to their King's dreams of greatness for them. He had to give them an empire whether they wanted it or not, often against their opposition, at least till he could show how the proceeds might embellish the mother country. He also assured them that 'c'est en servant la cause de l'humanité et du progrès que les peuples de second rang apparaissent comme les membres utiles de la grande famille de nations'. If the Belgian never took that seriously, the Scotsman did. At any rate they were, in their personal co-operation across the frontiers, in effect compensating for the handicaps.

They first met when Mackinnon turned up at the conference for the geographical societies of Europe summoned by the king to Brussels in 1876. His agenda was to define the best ways of developing Africa. The delegates agreed that the continent must be systematically explored with a view to establishing lines of communication, perhaps first by a chain of stations between the eastern and the western coasts. These could collect the scientific and commercial information needed for further advance, and provide bases for suppression of the slave trade. To set about creating them, a national committee was to be formed in each European country, drawing on the energy and expertise of geographers, philanthropists and entrepreneurs alike. The work would be co-ordinated by an International African Association, the presidency of which Leopold II graciously accepted. The project looked disinterested, but was pointedly ignored in the chancelleries of Europe. The only people who involved themselves at all were Belgians and Scots. Mackinnon, though disappointed at the response elsewhere, kept in close touch with the association, went regularly to Brussels and entertained the king's emissaries in London. Brooding at home in Argyll he decided that, if nobody else was going to help, he ought to do so himself, with his own fortune and influence.

The association's initial target was East Africa, whence the interior could be penetrated along the rivers and the slavers' routes. This the Scots were already doing in the Shire Highlands, so it suited the King to woo them. On a visit to Balmoral, he told Queen Victoria how much he admired their pioneering mission. As a contribution of his own, he proposed to build an international highway across Africa, starting from the Indian Ocean. That required two things. The first was a large investment, which Mackinnon would supply, though it could be only gradually recouped from tolls. The second was the good graces of the British Government, which directed the external relations of the Sultan of Zanzibar, the sovereign, at least nominally, of the lands to be traversed. Mackinnon lobbied hard in London, but the Foreign Secretary of the time, Lord Salisbury, thought development less important than keeping other powers out of Africa. In 1879 he in effect vetoed the scheme. The failure, however, strengthened Mackinnon's attachment to the king as a man ahead of his time.

They turned instead to the western coast. In this region the practical problem was easier, since the River Congo led straight into a vast basin which, in the following years, Leopold II sent H.M. Stanley to explore. The political problem looked harder. Who, if anyone, was sovereign here? The Portuguese had discovered the river in 1483 and maintained some presence on the adjacent littoral ever since. No longer strong enough to hold on by themselves, however, they needed co-operation and tolerance from London especially. In the nineteenth century their country had become a British satellite, an adjunct of the informal Empire. They were allowed to occupy strategic points, but only as Britain's proxy, and only as long as they remained amenable to her interests. So, if it suited Britain for Brazil to win independence, Brazil won independence. If Britain wanted the slave trade ended, Portugal, though dragging her heels, ended it. The Portuguese acquiesced in their subordination for external and internal reasons. They thought they could rely on the mistress of the seas to protect their meagre place in the existing scheme of imperialism. They were also grateful that, when necessary, she intervened in their politics on the liberal side. The big and the little country had thus worked out a *modus vivendi*.

The British accordingly held an answer ready to the question of the Congo: to recognise Portuguese sovereignty over at least the lower reaches of the river. By 1884, concerned to maintain peace and order in European expansion, they wanted to sign a treaty with Lisbon to that effect. Leopold II had to stop it. He set about doing so with skill and resource. He stirred up opposition from France and Germany, both of which already had their own interests in the region. The combination against her of two powers otherwise hostile to one another was something Britain could not ignore. Then the king put Mackinnon to work in London. In his character of astute businessman, he impressed on the City what commercial opportunities were about to be lost by ceding a huge territory into feeble foreign hands. In his persona of pious Presbyterian, he reminded the humanitarian societies how remiss the Portuguese had been in dealing with the slave trade. As a result, enough voices of protest were raised in Parliament to kill off the treaty. But the Government's retreat did not stop there.

With the needs of business and philanthropy met to his own satisfaction, Mackinnon was too limited to see the political consequences for Britain, and perhaps too much of a Scotsman to worry about them. In fact he helped to set off a chain of events by which her global strategy of half a century and more – of informal Empire in principle eschewing sovereignty for herself and others – was to crash down in ruins. William Gladstone had come back into office in 1880 determined to halt the adventurism of Benjamin Disraeli and restore that strategy. He failed. Imperial commitments rather multiplied. Before long resources were stretched to the limit, with war on the North-West Frontier of India and an unwanted military occupation of Egypt. Rivals saw their chance. The most vigorous, Germany, called a conference of European powers to Berlin in the autumn of 1884 to seek settlement of their colonial differences. It ended in carving out spheres of influence for each of them and sanctioning the scramble for Africa. That meant for

London a diplomatic defeat of the first order. Leopold II, however, was one of the winners. Having disposed of Portugal, he now also outwitted his erstwhile ally, France. She had designs on the Congo too, but the conference decided they should be confined to the northern banks. It awarded the larger and more productive southern side of the basin to the King, on his promise to establish there a neutral zone of free trade, with suppression of slavery. This was not to be Belgian territory, but to be administered by an *Association Internationale du Congo*, again under himself. It simply turned out, of course, to be a new Trojan horse for his own schemes. He would in fact use it to keep other countries off this private domain. Such a victory could scarcely have been foreseen when he first presented himself on the global stage eight years before. He had realised his ambitions.

The settlement paved the way for a third phase of co-operation between the king and Mackinnon. By the early 1890s, each had personal control of large tracts of Africa. Leopold II was consolidating in the Congo his so-called free state, and closing it to any but his own exploration, occupation and exploitation. Mackinnon had become chairman of the Imperial British East Africa Company, a venture to be discussed in a later chapter. Under royal charter, it was entrusted with opening up what is now Kenya and Uganda. As in effect African sovereigns, then, the pair entered into a treaty delineating spheres of influence where their interests met in the centre of the continent. The King took the Bahr-al-Ghazal on the western bank of the upper Nile in exchange for donating to Mackinnon a strip of land over Congolese territory which he might offer, to his own profit, for Cecil Rhodes's project of a railway from the Cape to Cairo. Neat as the deal was, it cut across plans of both the British and the French governments, which forced the two parties to cancel this piece of impudence. They yet remained ardent advocates of each other's interests till Mackinnon's death in 1893. For his part, it was a matter of giving economic development priority over any more specific national interest. In this era, the most forward-looking Scots thought it right for Scotland to be transcended in the imperial mission; it was but a step for them to accept that the British Empire might be transcended too in the service of humanity.[3]

In his counsels, Leopold II soon replaced Mackinnon with another Scotsman, Robert Williams. Son of an Aberdonian distiller, trained as an engineer, he emigrated to South Africa to work at the mines of Kimberley. There he met Rhodes, who took a shine to him and admitted him to the circle of cronies which brought together some of the continent's great swashbucklers, including a brother Scot, Dr Leander Starr Jameson, later to lead his infamous raid on the Transvaal. Williams became Rhodes's geological expert, adept at discovering gold and diamonds, then ran two of his corporations, the Zambesia Exploring Company, which went into the future Southern Rhodesia, and "Tanks", Tanganyika Concessions Ltd. He would also involve himself in imperialist politics at home, standing as Unionist candidate in North Aberdeen in 1900, on a platform of colonial expansion and multinational enterprise. All these men waxed fabulously rich, and most set their wealth at Britain's service too. But Williams was an individualist who preferred to strike out on his own. In doing so he made the acquaintance of the King of the Belgians.

Williams knew what stupendous mineral wealth lay beneath the Congolese province of Katanga. In 1900 he went to Brussels to tell Leopold II about it. The king needed convincing, but his avarice got the better of his mistrust. It might have been easiest for him to call on British adventurers to help him exploit the resources. They were already prospecting immediately to the south, in what is today Zambia, so that the personnel and technology were on hand. But Leopold II feared that if they came in he would be unable to control them, and might even lose the province. Williams, seeing his problem, switched camps: he undertook to place himself entirely at the king's service, and keep his old companions out. In 1901 the pair entered into partnership, and Leopold II appointed Williams vice-president of the *Union Minière du Haut Katanga*. It was not enough just to work the minerals. They also had to be exported, preferably without touching any of the areas newly coloured pink on the map. The British possessed in Central Africa, in order to ship its produce and mobilise its workforce, a natural interest in creating an integrated system of transport, which might be linked to Rhodes's projected railway from the Cape to Cairo. Here again Leopold II saw danger. Since navigation of the Congo was impeded by rapids, he would himself have to lay a railway, but that could scarcely be done through the steaming jungles of his free state either. The resourceful Williams proposed instead to carry it across Portuguese territory, from Benguela on the Atlantic coast to the border with Katanga.

It was therefore necessary to woo Portugal. Since 1884 her position as a colonial power had gone from bad to worse. Following the humiliation of that year, she again came off the loser from the dispute in 1889 with Britain over the Shire Highlands, when the Scottish Churches forced abandonment of a second treaty. A third one actually concluded in 1891 still left the Portuguese mortified, because it obliged them to give up all claims in the interior and set boundaries for Angola and Mozambique depriving them of a hinterland. In Lisbon there was wild talk of war with the British bullies and hypocrites before the Government could bring itself to sign. If they were to treat their oldest ally like this, then surely she should seek new and better friends. Poor, indeed almost bankrupt, Portugal could not easily find them. Both the British and the Germans thought her plainly unfit for imperial responsibility, and sounded each other out on repartitioning her colonies between themselves.

Williams himself was privy to these palavers in London. But he shrewdly foresaw that the plan would prove too drastic, and that leaving Portugal alone was likely to stand as everybody's least bad solution. He could then step in as her only true friend and offer a helping hand, or rather two, his own and Leopold II's. He set himself up in Lisbon and spent so freely on wining and dining important people that he became known as 'O Millionario'. At length he obtained what he was looking for, the concession for the railway from Benguela. Though he sought to keep the British Foreign Office in the dark, its Minister to Portugal got wind of his dealings, reporting back that he was 'a bit of a bounder'. Without doubt his behaviour too ran counter to the interests of his country, or at least of those fellow imperialists operating loosely under its sovereignty.[4]

Still, with difficulty, the railway was built. Begun in 1903, it ran into big problems across the difficult terrain. The British Government, then the South African one with its more direct economic and strategic interest, did what they could to halt it. It was not to be completed for a quarter-century. But, once linked to the Copperbelt, it made a major contribution to the economies of Katanga and Angola, all the result of Williams's flair and tenacity. He kept his eye on the main chance. As far as he was concerned, Leopold II's grand designs went with him into the grave, and he did not hesitate to construct afterwards a spur to the system of Southern Rhodesia, with the blessing of his pal Jameson, by then her Prime Minister. The idea was to lay a lateral railway across the continent which could connect nicely with a line from the Cape to Cairo. These greater plans were never realised, but they show the breadth of Williams's ambitions for 'a civilised and industrialised Africa'. He believed European governments should act as trustees for the blacks, yet clearly he never regarded British rule in itself as essential: he worked better with the Belgians and Portuguese. Like Mackinnon, if without the philanthropic bent, he saw nationalism as secondary to economic development.[5]

Leopold II had had, amid his crimes, at least one benevolent purpose. It was to give Belgium a substitute for access to the Dutch Empire lost by the fact of her independence in 1830. He saw what a market his industrialised country could have won in the East Indies. An influence on his own policies, if carried by him to extremes, was the "culture system" which the Dutch ran there, an updated version of mercantilism planning colonial exploitation in detail. Holland offered in some ways, however, not an altogether apposite model for Belgium. Historically she was, along with Britain and Portugal, one of the three maritime nations to have established themselves overseas long before the rise of modern imperialism. While the other pair decayed, Britain flourished, from her trade, industry and conquests: the Treaty of Vienna (1815) left her the only important colonial power. Like Portugal, Holland then turned into a satellite, relations with the British being governed by a treaty of 1824. Dictated on their terms, it did not look much of a guarantee. After division of the united Kingdom of the Netherlands, breaking up the buffer state against France created at Vienna, the Dutch feared they were too weak for Britain to continue tolerating them as colonialists. They therefore took great care, till well on into the century, to do nothing likely to cause her deep offence. They accepted, for example, that their status imposed on them the humanitarian obligation of abolishing the slave trade. But later, while Portugal remained a satellite, Holland recovered some independence, largely by inventing the culture system and making an economic success of it. And because she had no part in the scramble for Africa, she could quietly intensify her control of the East Indies.[6]

Her colonial policy accordingly underwent a series of metamorphoses, in one of which Scots again played a part. By decree of the Batavian Republic, a French client, the Dutch East India Company was dissolved in 1802, though its monopolistic regime continued. Then in 1811 the Governor-General of India, the Earl of Minto, conquered Java to keep it out of Napoleon's hands. He wanted Britain to hold on to it for good, along with other Dutch possessions she had captured, the Cape and Ceylon. He therefore set about reforming the colony on lines of his own, at once orientalist and free-trading, as 'an establishment which while it afforded to the British Government all the commercial advantages of the islands, shall restore to the several chiefs the exercise of their independent authority, and bestow upon the inhabitants the beneficial use of their own soil and labour'. Minto took with him to Java the inevitable train of compatriots. One was John Leyden, whom he dubbed a 'perfect Malay' for his knowledge of the native peoples' language, literature and history. A second was a 'tolerable Dutchman', Hugh Hope, related to the Hopes of Amsterdam, put in charge of liaison with the Dutch officials on whom this military occupation still relied.

Other Scots who came along at once took the chance to begin trading. They carried on after the British tossed Java back to Holland in 1816, considering that her possession of it made no difference to them; she did indeed maintain free trade for the time being. The Maclaines of Lochbuie in particular established a long association with the Dutch East Indies. A scion of the clan, Gillean Maclaine, landed at Batavia in 1820 with his friend Edward Watson, each with £500 in his pocket. They rapidly built up business and in 1827 went into formal partnership. Another firm, McNeill & Co, set up at Semarang, then a third, Fraser Eaton & Co, at Surabaya, both further along the northern coast of Java. All three, in the usual Scottish way, held shares in one another. All three ran into difficulty when Maclaine decided to retire in 1840, and sailed off with his wife, two children, mother-in-law and other dependants. They were never heard of again. Gillean's brother Angus went out to claim their assets, reckoned at over £30,000, but the rest of the Scots would hand over nothing till the deaths were proved. The Dutch authorities had to step in to make an equitable arrangement. The family's affairs were not finally set in order till Donald Maclaine became head of it in 1852. With the profits from his plantations in Java, where he served besides as a British consul, and from his dealings in coffee in London and Rotterdam, he was also able to rescue the ancestral acres on Mull.[7]

A different type of Scottish connection came in the person of Donald Mackay, chief of his clan and 11th Lord Reay, He was born in Holland, where his family had lived for 80 years, in 1839. At the university of Leiden he wrote his doctoral thesis on the administration of Java, which qualified him for a post in the Dutch Colonial Office. Afterwards he entered the States General as a Liberal. But he kept in touch with the old country, and in 1875 decided to settle there. He was naturalised, succeeded to his title and in 1881 was created a British peer. Cutting a figure at Westminster, he moved into the circle of Lord Rosebery, who recommended him as Governor of Bombay in 1885. On his return he became President of the Royal Asiatic

Society and, in 1894, Under-Secretary for India in Rosebery's Government. A man of such academic and political distinction made a fine choice for the rectorship of the university of St Andrews, to which he was elected the same year. At his inauguration he gave a stirring call for the Scottish universities to aspire again to the international eminence they had once enjoyed, to emulate the German ones in producing 'men of general culture, of professional merit and of original research'. And he thought a Scottish Parliament the means of arresting their decline under anglicising pressures: 'This is not a question of local importance. It concerns the greatness of the Empire'. In him, attachment to a small nation remained fully compatible with big ideas. But it had to be a small nation with an outlook broader than Holland's. After his death in 1921, his friend James Bryce, another of Scotland's imperial statesmen, recorded the reason for his change of allegiance: 'He saw that the movements in the larger country were on a grander scale, and were destined to exert a much more powerful influence on the future of mankind'.[8]

That gives a clue why the Scottish-Dutch relationship never flourished in the age of high imperialism quite as might have been expected from the long contact and friendship between the two nations, or even by comparison with the Scots' role in the Belgian and Portuguese empires. The East Indies could have offered another broad field for Scottish enterprise, except that Holland in time reversed the liberalisation and began again to close her colony to outsiders. Free trade had not brought any great prosperity to Java. The indigenous peoples were restive: a revolt broke out in 1825 which it took five years of savage repression to crush. Later Holland was to fight for three decades one of the bloodiest, certainly the longest, of the colonial wars, against the native state of Acheh on Sumatra. On both economic and political grounds, isolation seemed desirable.

The Governor-General in 1830–3, Johannes van den Bosch, who had been interned by Minto and come to hate all he stood for, instituted the culture system. Under it, the administration in Batavia organised through an official trading agency the global sale of the colony's produce. Internally, it imposed contracts on the Javanese chieftains binding them to yield up from their lands fixed quantities of crops, mainly sugar, for export. They in turn made the peasants devote a portion of their plots to cultivation of the crops, which were paid over in lieu of rent. The system thus transferred the great mass of natives into an economy of plantations where, if not enslaved, they lost their freedom. Still, the results were spectacular: exports sextupled in ten years, and Holland's colonial revenue rose from an annual average of 93 million gulden in the 1830s to 267 million gulden by the 1850s. It paid off most of her national debt and financed her system of railways.[9]

But the profits soon passed their peak. New regulations of 1856 lessened the system's rigours. In 1860 Holland elected a Liberal Government pledged to reform it. Among other measures, the East Indies were reopened to foreign commerce. Incomers still had to register their companies, however, and registration could be refused, a fate which befell Mackinnon's effort to move in. He was unwelcome because, after construction of the Suez Canal, Dutch shipping greatly expanded, eating into the virtual monopoly that British lines had thus far enjoyed in the Orient. Holland wanted to keep things going that way, and was ready to intervene to make sure they did. Her new liberality had in fact less to do with trade than with the progressive idealism towards the natives of scholars and statesmen, notably of Christiaan Snouck Hurgronje and Abraham Kuyper. Kuyper would when Prime Minister in 1901 adopt as the official philosophy of Dutch colonialism what had meanwhile been dignified by the name of the ethical policy. Snouck Hurgronje, its author, was a famous orientalist. He lived in disguise at Mecca for three years, passing off a heavy accent in Arabic as one from a far corner of the Maghreb. Later he chose the less perilous career of professor at Leiden. The ethical policy in his formulation would westernise the East Indies by educating a native elite as equal partner with the Dutch. There were analogies with Alexander Duff's programme in India, yet differences too. The policy would have no Christian purpose. Snouck Hurgronje denied any need to rob the elite of its Islamic culture, because this was not founded on religious fanaticism. He had to stress the point to his countrymen, whose patriotic myths held memories of the menace of bigoted papists honouring no pact with the infidel. He argued that, by contrast, Moslems accepted legitimate authority. With their faith tolerated, they would stay politically docile. Then, public instruction should be given in the vernacular, to avoid a situation where the elite might cut itself off from the people by speaking Dutch; it was taught, but only to the brightest and best. This in turn caused social problems, however. In practice, it severely limited indigenous access to higher education. It ran schools in the colony on a different principle from the one in the mother country which encouraged linguistic proficiency, as it still does. In sum, contact between the Dutch and the natives was minimised.

Execution of the ethical policy raised political problems too. The Governors-General of the East Indies, usually from a military background, presided over a colonial civil service almost wholly educated at Leiden, where it acquired, along with a firm grasp of the conditions it would face on the ground, a high moral purpose and a consciousness of its country's imperial past. This created an *esprit de corps* with strong nationalist overtones, looking to restore the glory of the seventeenth century. In any event the Dutch, having seldom bothered with anywhere but Java, could only make the policy work by imposing dominion over all 1000 islands and 300 native rulers of the archipelago. That generated great changes in indigenous society, which had in turn to be controlled. The administration in Batavia often accomplished the task by force of arms. During the first decade of the twentieth century it transformed the East Indies into a single, centralised state. In this respect the ethical policy did not look all that ethical. The security of the colony in fact always took first place over the wish to act with enlightened paternalism towards its peoples.[10]

Yet the Dutch continued to display typical traits of a small nation's imperialism. They never expected to make the East Indies a white man's country under the permanent rule of expatriates. Rather they went as transients, and did not foist western language, religion or customs on the natives. They still had a Calvinist conscience which could be pricked. Even so, in the commercial calculation that went with it, they would not let the Scots, or anybody else, take up the same auxiliary roles as in the Belgian and Portuguese empires. Despite the paucity of individual links we can, however, see in this mixture of motives an enduring affinity between Holland and Scotland.

Scotland would try to resolve the tension in higher ideals of imperialism. Holland, however, had been forced to examine her conscience in true Calvinist fashion by a literary bombshell, *Max Havelaar*, the novel published in 1860 by E.D. Dekker under the pseudonym Multatuli. He was a former colonial official who had resigned in disgust at the culture system, not a pleasant man but a humourless egotist. Those traits yet endowed him with a single-minded resolve to help the Javanese and smash the system. The book was his implement. It centred on an odious character called Batavus Droogstoppel, butt of a biting satire against the complacent, provincial and sentimental Dutch. Interwoven with the depiction of his bourgeois world, pointing up its inward and outward corruption, came a grim catalogue of Holland's misdeeds in the East Indies, which was what made the tale a bestseller and gave it a real impact on public opinion. The Dutch had had nothing to prepare their minds for such a merciless portrayal of themselves. It was in a sense the worse that this, of all novels, should have figured among the few in their canon to gain an international readership. There were in several countries intellectuals already criticising the conventional imperial wisdom. Dekker's work gave them for the first time, and at first hand, graphic images of the realities which that wisdom hid.[11]

Perceptive Scots readers could hardly fail to register the resemblances to their own country: 'Holland has remained *Holland* because our old folk attended to their business; and because they had the true faith,' Droogstoppel declared. It was the kailyard in clogs. The same Calvinist hypocrisy, the same small-minded parochialism are satirised, to offer a salient example, in George Douglas Brown's *House with the Green Shutters*. Strikingly, he touches too, if more briefly, on their relation to the ebullient imperial enterprise which accompanies them. While this needs vision, it is not such as would be found in a more imaginative society. Rather it is a 'lower faculty', possessed by the Scot in full degree: 'his *perfervidum ingenium* is quick to attempt the realising of his dreams. That is why he makes the best of colonists'. His vision may even carry him away till it

> sends native caution by the board, and a man's really fine idea becomes an
> empty balloon, to carry him off to the limbo of vanities. There is a
> megalomaniac in every parish of Scotland. Well, not so much as that; they're
> owre canny for that to be said of them. But in every district, almost, you may
> find a poor creature who for 30 years has cherished a great scheme by which he
> means to revolutionise the world's commerce, and amass fortune in monstrous

degree. He is generally to be seen shivering at the Cross, and (if you are a nippy man) you shout carelessly in going by 'Good morning, Tamson; how's the scheme?'

In adversity, the type cannot turn to creative sublimation, but retreats: 'Common sense, indeed, so far from being wanting, is in most cases too much in evidence, perhaps, crippling the soaring mind and robbing the idea of its early radiance; in quieter language, she makes the average Scotsman to be over-cautious'. Brown puts his finger on a paradox between material success and lack of the communal cultural achievement that might have been fed by a higher faculty of imagination, in other words, by deeper human sympathies. As in Scotland, so in Holland.[12]

Here was a forceful literary expression of the affinity which, before its deformation, had often made the pair partners and friends in the European expansion. Clear till 1707 and surviving for some time afterwards, it was not fully dispelled even in the era of high imperialism, despite political destinies otherwise radically different. What most obviously maintained the link was the common mentality of two small nations, in this case strengthened by a common fund of Calvinist and commercial traditions. In both this brought a shift away from the idea that Europeans should just trade with indigenous peoples then leave, having no business in territorial occupation and settlement. It moved instead towards high-minded acceptance of a duty to improve the condition of those peoples, in Scotland largely religious in inspiration, in Holland almost entirely secular. Each therefore adopted different methods of fulfilling its duty, though neither would succeed in creating a native elite ready to acquiesce in some sort of partnership between East and West. It is easy then to see how the methods, frustrated in their purpose, in time gave way to coercion, so that they came together in the era of high imperialism with other methods which were, now and in the past, the natural resort of larger and more powerful countries. The Dutch, however, had what the Scots had not and never could have, some independent political discretion, and the means to agree on a national policy. The mental conflict in Scotland was thus deeper, as we shall see in what follows.

CHAPTER TWENTY-THREE

'The most proper persons for this country': Canada

E arly in February 1870 an irregular armed band of Canadians camped on the
icebound banks of the Red River round the kirk of Kildonan, named after the
strath in Sutherland whence many of Lord Selkirk's original colonists came. Those
who had survived the massacre at Seven Oaks in 1817 reoccupied the land and lived
on there. The peace of their descendants was now disturbed as a result of the
Canadian confederation, and the new dominion's effort to absorb the huge territory
to the west. The French-speaking part of its population resisted. Few as they were,
their resistance looked formidable because it arose in such a remote region. It found
an inspiring leader in Louis Riel, whose passionate nature could speak for the fears of
his wild, half-breed race, the Métis. He told them they stood to lose their language,
their religion and the vast, waste country which was their source of livelihood. He
urged them to fight back, and they followed him. Two months before, he had led 120
of them to seize Fort Garry, on the site of modern Winnipeg, which housed the local
administration of the Hudson's Bay Company.

Neither the company nor the Canadian Government had means to expel them.
That was why irregulars took it into their heads to do the job instead. They planned
to use Kildonan as a base for attacking the fort, a mile or two away. While they
prepared, they found a Frenchman, Norbert Parisien, skulking round their camp.
They accused him of spying, locked him up under the pulpit of the kirk and left him
there overnight. The next morning he was let out with a guard. He spotted a gun
lying nearby, darted over and grabbed it, then ran off towards the frozen river. Just
then, an unlucky young Scot, Hugh Sutherland, came riding across on some errand.
Parisien, seeing his escape barred, shot him. The Frenchman was caught, beaten up
and imprisoned again; when he tried the same trick the next day, the Canadians
killed him. Sutherland had already succumbed to his wound. Theirs was the first
blood to be shed for a united Canada.[1]

The company had previously, ever since the agreement which ended its struggle
with the Nor'Westers half a century before, governed these territories almost as an
independent state. Stretching from the limit of settlement in Ontario to the Pacific
Ocean, and from the frontier with the United States to the Arctic Sea, it was among
the largest states in the world, and the only one designed to remain so far as possible
unpeopled. The inhabitants carried on a little agriculture. Otherwise, the economy
was wholly geared to the export of furs, with which further colonisation would have
been incompatible. The governor of the reconstructed company from 1821, George

Simpson, rigidly maintained this state of affairs. Born in 1796 in Easter Ross, he was a great-grandson of Duncan Forbes of Culloden, the Lord Advocate of Scotland who had tempered the rigours of repression after the Jacobite rising of 1745. Simpson inherited Forbes's appetite for business, but not his humanity. Underlings regarded their chief, on the contrary, as inhuman; the French called him *âme de glace*. It served his exalted conception of his calling. He resided at Lachine, near Montreal, but spent much time travelling his domain, sitting in a top-hat and immaculate tail-coat on a grand *canot de maître*, whence he would step ashore, on reaching a trading post or Indian village, to the tunes of his own pipers.

Humanity may not have been at a premium when he had so few humans to deal with. His territory contained scattered tribes of Indians, in numbers never counted but hardly high. While for the sake of the furs they brought in he sought friendly relations, he ruled them with a rod of iron. He saw little point in educating them or converting them to Christianity: 'I have always remarked that an enlightened Indian is good for nothing'. Yet he did not mind the mixed marriages or concubinage of his men, though he declared such temptations beneath his own dignity. 'Had I a good pimp in my suite,' he said with Scots bluntness, 'I might have been inclined to deposit a little of my spawn, but have become so vastly tenacious of my reputation that no one can say to me black is the white of your eye.' This was hypocrisy: he had several illegitimate children.

He reigned besides over a sparse European population, some French and some Scots, many with Indian blood, about 12,000 in all. In the course of time the French element was apparently coming to predominate. One Scot, Alexander Ross, complained of his own folk that 'they often imitate the French, but the French never imitate them'. Especially the youth of the community seemed susceptible to Latin insouciance: 'The fine horse and gay cabriole may be seen gliding over the ice on a sabbath morning, not going moderately, much less in that solemn and devout manner befitting the day or the occasion, but driving like Jehu of old, contesting the honour of arriving first at the church'. And, horror of horrors, 'it is not uncommon for "young Scotland" to enter the church whip in hand, and his tobacco-pipe stuck up in his pocket'. Of Simpson, too, the old-timers had plenty to complain. It was years before he would let them have a minister. He left them to farm their plots, but never allowed them to market their produce in case they grew rich and attracted others. He meant in other words to make clear that their settlement was no harbinger of civilisation. Its sole function lay in supplying food for itself and for the company.[2]

Not that Simpson showed himself more generous towards what might be called the ruling class of his territory, the company's officers. They were most of them Scots, 171 of the 263 commissioned in the half-century after 1821. Their governor kept wages at that year's level for the remaining four decades of his life, and few especially of the French would work for them. Rather than recruit on the ground, then, the company continued to draw its manpower from poorer regions of Scotland, no longer so much from Orkney, where youngsters preferred the navy or the army, rather from the northern counties of the mainland, from Shetland and from Lewis. While some stayed on with Indian wives and families, many were still transients. The company guaranteed them passage home at the end of their service, as an additional incentive to enter it. For promoted posts particularly, Simpson followed his compatriots' time-honoured practice of preferring one another. He entrusted day-to-day administration inside the territory to a man with the grand title of Governor of Rupert's Land, which amounted to being chief factor for the company. A line of Scots held the office. Donald Mackenzie, 1825–33, was a veteran trader who did sterling work reoccupying stations abandoned in the earlier troubles, notably along the Mackenzie River, and restoring contact with distant tribes of Indian and Eskimo hunters. Alexander Christie, 1833–9, imposed what internal political control was needed, setting up a Council of Assiniboia, naturally nominated rather than elected, and building Fort Garry as a permanent seat of government. He delivered himself of the remarkably objective sentiment that 'without any partiality to my countrymen, really in my humble opinion they will ever be found the most proper persons for this country'. He was followed by Duncan Finlayson, then a couple of English interlopers. The line finished with William McTavish, of the Nor'Wester clan. We may note in passing how the regime delighted in sonorous sobriquets: Cuthbert Grant, perpetrator of the massacre at Seven Oaks, became Warden of the Plains, of which the duties seemed to be hunting the buffalo and fighting the Sioux.[3]

Simpson, on coming into his kingdom, had appreciated that it could not endure unless it made profits. His first priority was to ensure there would be no more disorder, for trade had suffered greatly during the contest with the Nor'Westers. His rancour against these 'lawless marauders' was undiminished by peace with them. He regretted having now no chance to thrash them in commercial competition. Since they stood on the verge of bankruptcy anyway, he was able to ease them out in a further reconstruction of the company in 1824. His second step was to seal the West off once more from undesirables. As the Indians again grew reliant on the trade-goods they exchanged for furs, he excluded every influence that might wean them away from hunting and trapping for a livelihood. The company even tried, with some success, to make the basin of the Mackenzie self-sufficient. Hardy Scottish crops such as potatoes, turnips and barley proved cultivable at least in the south of the region. Fisheries were set up on the lakes, and the Indians encouraged to vend the rabbits, caribou and moose they killed. Climate and geography kept the territory empty anyway, but efficient management ensured that nobody who did live there need starve. The third job was to reorganise the traffic in furs. Simpson abandoned the route through the Great Lakes and the St Lawrence. He saved time and money by directing everything to York Factory on Hudson's Bay, where the trade-goods could also be more easily brought in. The routes to the interior presented a greater problem. Simpson tackled it with the ingenuity of a Scottish improver by replacing, where possible, the fragile canoes of birch-bark with the capacious, flat-bottomed York Boat, ideal for the transport of light but bulky wares.

With those tasks accomplished, Simpson could embark on territorial aggrandisement. It offered the only way, if the balance of nature was to remain undisturbed, of
increasing the harvest of furs and opening fresh avenues of trade. The effort started
with renewed exploration of unmapped regions. One target was the Arctic, still in
hope of finding a practicable North-West passage. The company sent out John Ross,
son of a Scottish manse, who discovered the Magnetic Pole in 1831. For later ventures,
Simpson selected a young Orcadian, John Rae, who between 1846 and 1854 led four
groups, travelling 6000 miles on foot and another 6000 by boat. On the first
journey, in charge of a dozen men, he actually wintered in the Arctic, a feat unheard
of. But he demonstrated that a party of such size, living like the Eskimos, could
support itself in the frozen wastes. On the final journey, he ascertained that the lost
expedition of Sir John Franklin dispatched from Britain had, by ignoring this lesson,
starved to death.[4]

As a practical proposition, though, Simpson was more intent on striking
westwards to the Pacific Ocean, across country abounding in wild animals and
furnishing on the further side prospects of lucrative trade to the Orient. The
strategy would tax his political skills, for it meant competition with the Americans.
He dealt with them by maintaining outwardly cordial relations but actually
undermining their commercial position. He was not content to direct the strategy
from his desk. In 1824–5 he himself made the first of several journeys to the
Columbia River, which he reached from York Factory in 84 days, 20 days faster
than anyone before. He saw the river's importance, for it issued from the greatest
basin on the Pacific seaboard into a fine harbour. Control of it was already disputed
between Britain and the United States. Simpson claimed it on the grounds that his
traders had led in its exploration.

For a time it looked as if, by his own exertions, he might make good that claim.
His great ploy was alliance with the Russians who had come across the Bering Strait.
He went in person to St Petersburg in 1838, on what can only be called a state visit,
and triumphantly concluded an accord leasing the Alaskan panhandle from the Czar
in return for supplying provisions to his outposts beyond. They agreed on further co-
operation aimed at keeping Americans away from the whole northern Pacific littoral.
The company's aggrandisement did not stop there. It put down a marker for the
future by setting up at San Francisco, in the Mexican territory to the south of its
existing stations. In the interior of California a botanist under its patronage, David
Douglas, former gardener at Scone Palace, tramped about ostensibly collecting
specimens; the Douglas fir is named after him. He went on the same errand to
Hawaii, where in 1834 he was killed by a bull. That year, by some chance, the
company founded an agency at Honolulu. There Simpson called by *en route* to
Russia, with friendly advice for King Kamehameha III about foiling other foreigners'
designs on the islands. In 1848, he sent Ranald MacDonald, son of his secretary and a
Chinook princess, on a secret voyage to Japan, six years before the celebrated visit of
the American, Commander Perry. MacDonald was detained for some months at

Nagasaki, where he learned Japanese and taught English to official interpreters. These were the company's halcyon days, and hugely profitable ones.[5]

They did not last. A decisive reverse came with the war in 1846 between the United States and Mexico, the American victory and annexation of California, followed in the gold rush by hordes of settlers. The company shut up shop in San Francisco. It was then high time to resolve the grumbling discord over the British-American border on the Pacific. The Oregon Treaty set it at the 49th parallel, north of the mouth of the Columbia. While the Foreign Secretary, Lord Aberdeen, ignored Simpson's advice on the matter, he did salvage a continued right of navigation along the river for the company. But it could not now expand in these parts. Simpson had long before taken out insurance against such a turn of events by developing an alternative route down the Fraser River, north again from the parallel. Soon, as Britain moved to retrieve her straitened position in the region, he lost that too. The company held a post at the terminus of this trail, Victoria on Vancouver Island, founded by one of its officers, James Douglas, half-caste son of a Scots planter in Guyana. To transfer him to the official pay-roll seemed the cheapest way of asserting British sovereignty. He was made governor of the island in 1851, which then became a Crown colony in 1856. Its jurisdiction did not yet extend to the mainland. But another gold rush, on the Fraser itself, brought in 30,000 prospectors, including many Americans. Douglas, trusting in the majesty of the state now behind him, simply proclaimed his authority over the area. The state concurred, luckily for the future Canada, and the Queen herself chose the name of British Columbia for this latest addition to her realms.

But for the company the outcome was dire. Its trade all but ceased hereabouts. It found its second transcontinental passage cut off, and the vital link in any chain of stations to Asia broken. The Hawaiian agency had no more use. There were even fears of the territory on the Red River being overrun by American squatters. Before his death in 1860, Simpson saw the writing on the wall. He himself invested in enterprises, such as railways and mining, sure to encourage colonisation. He and his officers, he wrote, could no longer 'conceal from ourselves the fact that we are in a certain degree overawed and dictated to'.[6]

The confederation of Canada in 1867 gave the *coup de grâce*. In 1869, after two centuries all but a year, the company surrendered its charter for the trading monopoly in Rupert's Land. The Canadian Government let it keep its posts and 45,000 acres round them, with more to be selected later, and promised compensation in cash of £300,000. The deal in fact guaranteed the company's future, for it would end up in possession of much productive country and of rich mineral deposits. The price to Canada, on the other hand, turned out dear. The problem was that the West now drifted into anarchy. Though Governor McTavish remained in residence at Fort Garry, his authority was gone, and no new one established. That did not save him and his officers from being blamed by the Prime Minister, Sir John Macdonald. He, not having the compensation to hand anyway, refused to pay it till they restored law and order; he would at length be let off the hook by a loan from Britain. But there was little anyone could do when the trouble came from the people of the West. Outraged at their destiny being decided over their heads, they found in Riel a man to match the hour. That autumn he formed a National Committee of the Métis, which began *de facto* to rule the western territories. It first ordained the expulsion of the lieutenant-governor appointed by Canada, William McDougall, a move hardly necessary because he only stepped across the boundary long enough to proclaim the province of Manitoba. When Riel went on to seize the fort, he set up a provisional government under himself as president. He was later to arrest McTavish, only, with a Gallic sense of protocol, to present to him a constitution meanwhile drawn up by the committee. The governor, considering himself under duress, signed it. The Métis now held themselves sovereign, the company's legitimate successors.

Riel invited the Canadians to enter into negotiations. While they could not accept him as an interlocutor, they had to do something. For one last time, the company stepped in. On a mission of mediation it dispatched Donald Smith, born at Forres in 1830, its senior official in Canada. Once at the fort, he held a joint public meeting with Riel. They addressed a crowd of 1000 for five hours in the open air with the temperature at minus 20 degrees. This seemed to still the people's fears, and pave the way for a peaceful solution. But everything was upset yet again by the march of that irregular band on Kildonan. It had not got round to attacking the fort before it was easily rounded up by the Métis. Riel then executed one of his captives, Thomas Scott, a fiery young Orangeman, for rebellion against his provisional government. This caused uproar in Canada. Ontarians wanted Riel's head, while Quebeckers hailed him as a hero. The dominion, scarcely formed, threatened to burst apart. Macdonald kept cool, however, and mixed firmness with conciliation. In July 1870, a royal proclamation annexed to Canada the whole of North America above the 49th parallel between Ontario and British Columbia. The Prime Minister then received delegates from the Red River to draw up terms of entry into the confederation. He gave the Métis the guarantees they wanted for their religion and language. At the same time, he got together an expeditionary force of militiamen and a few British regular troops, which in August occupied Fort Garry. The logistical difficulty of doing so had been the one real strength in Riel's position. Seeing the game was up, he did not stand and fight but fled into the United States. His rebellion collapsed, yet he had vindicated his people's rights.

On January 1, 1871, Manitoba joined the confederation. The Canadian Government launched, within the decade, policies for settlement of this and the entire West. In 30 years the fertile belt 200 miles deep along the American border was colonised. That still left empty everything beyond, the desolate North-West territories. Here no real change took place till the 1920s. Its administration had always been rudimentary, and Canada did little to augment it. So the company carried on much as before. Smith was its governor in 1889–1914, doubling up from 1896 as Canadian High Commissioner in London, with the dignity of Lord Strathcona. From that distance, he ran the region to general satisfaction. He too drew most of his officers from the thrifty, hard-working sons of northern Scotland, who continued to be recruited by the company right through the twentieth century.[7]

Otherwise this province of the Scottish Empire, with which in duration and success only the orientalists' India compared, came to an end. The new Canada displaced it with an Empire different in conception, an Empire of territorial occupation and settlement, essentially an English Empire. Realistic Scots nursed few regrets. They just set about tackling the novel conditions. Their imperial mentality was anyway changing, as reflected not least in their rulers' policies. True, not many policies could be formulated in the stunted apparatus of Scottish government left by the Whigs' work of 1832. But emigration was one. Quasi-official agencies offered assisted passages overseas from the 1850s. On establishment of the Scottish Office in 1885, it took up emigration to Canada among its first initiatives. This was another attempt at a final solution for the problems of the Highlands, where violence had just erupted among the crofters. With a population falling since 1841, demographic disaster loomed. But that threat was itself one cause of a Gaelic revival, in religion, literature and social protest. Some Gaels, after generations under siege from modernity, decided it was time to take their fate in their own hands. They rekindled an old dream for their society's salvation, of transferring it to a kinder setting in the New World. Donald Macleod, author of *Gloomy Memories of the Highlands of Scotland*, himself took refuge in Canada when cleared from Strathnaver. Other literary men, Angus Nicolson, Alexander Mackenzie and John Murdoch, had been across and come back impressed with the strength of transatlantic Gaelic communities. They found a friend in official circles, Malcolm McNeill, a son of Barra sitting on the Board of Supervision, which ran the Scottish Poor Law. He could count it part of his responsibility to draw up in 1886 an ambitious scheme of emigration, which he put to two successive Scottish Secretaries, A.J. Balfour and Lord Lothian. They liked it because it appeared to obviate any need for more drastic reforms. But the Cabinet would not authorise the expenditure, and it had to assume a more modest shape. Under it, in the end, fewer than 500 people settled in Manitoba, where they complained of finding nothing ready. The project was cancelled in 1893, and the old dream faded at last.

That served to underline how Canadian destiny was now being forged in Canada, never again to be determined by the wishes of people in the mother country. This maturing society had long been on the way, as the philosophers of enlightened Scotland once predicted that any such would, to autonomy and independence. But while the American colonies, the only ones to have followed the same course, had been in essence outposts of England, the population of Canada contained a large proportion of Scots. Even if a minority of the whole, they stamped their character on her evolution. They did so through, as much as anything, their extraordinary dominance of her politics, whether as settler statesmen or as proconsuls sent from home.[8]

Their contribution to Canadian nationhood can be traced back to William Lyon Mackenzie. The hot-headed young Dundonian shopkeeper, self-taught in the literature of liberty, had emigrated in 1820 with Scottish radicalism in his baggage. As a strident activist in local reforming circles, he was persecuted by Scotland's most reactionary town council. But whereas at home he only ever advocated moral force as the means of progress, in Canada he would move over to physical force. He took to journalism as a fierce critic of the Family Compact, extolling American democracy instead. He was elected to the assembly of Upper Canada, and became mayor of Toronto in 1834. For his trouble, Tory blades hurled his presses into the lake, while their elders, the tame majority in the assembly, repeatedly expelled him from it. Each time his constituents returned him. It was frustration at refusal to Canada of the reforms now won in Britain that led him to leadership of the Canadian rebellion in 1837. Defeated, he took refuge in the United States, with the empty gesture of declaring himself chairman of a provisional government. Its aim, however, was to bring about American annexation of Canada, a cause not without support among her people. To head it off, London dispatched Lord Durham to report on their grievances. In 1840 he recommended a transition to responsible government, which was to be accomplished during the next decade. At the end of it, Mackenzie felt safe enough to return. He was re-elected to Parliament, no longer as the firebrand he had been in his youth, but reconciled to a Canada under the Crown.[9]

Responsible government came not only to Canada but soon also to every sizeable British community round the globe. It coincided with, and was a logical consequence of, the mother country's adoption of free trade, to which it would for some decades rigorously adhere. Lord Elgin, Canadian Governor-General at the time, saw here an imperial crux. Britain, he said, had to choose between being an Empire and being a country. She made her choice: in a sense, she declared independence of the Empire, though the ruling elite in London carried on regardless. The fact remained that, as still the leading industrial power, she needed cheap food for a burgeoning population and henceforth sought it where she could, with no favour for colonial producers. The old mercantilist control of them then became redundant.

If desire for democracy drove Canadian radicals to look to the United States, this commercial contingency did the same at the opposite end of the political spectrum, among the plutocrats of Montreal. They had lost control both of Canada's executive government and of assured markets for her produce: they could hardly fare worse even if they were annexed. After the riot and arson which in 1849 made the city's feelings plain to Elgin, 300 leading citizens signed a manifesto calling for 'friendly and peaceful separation from [the] British connection'. For the many Scots among them, it also reflected a changing relationship with their homeland. Nowadays often from Glasgow, they had maintained links with that booming centre of industry and commerce, applying some of its abundant resources to development of a Canada much more backward than Scotland. But lately Glasgow, even while coming to dominate the domestic economy, had been yielding its place in Atlantic trade to

English ports, Liverpool above all, where indeed many Scotsmen followed their business and settled. As direct connections to Scotland slackened, Canadian Scots naturally adopted a more local outlook. Economic autonomy was evolving anyway, if also being thrust upon them; should political autonomy follow, Britain would have only herself to blame.

The key was Canadian nationhood, whether it existed and in what it consisted. Elgin was the first British statesman to acknowledge the emergence of something of the sort, and took the basic decision to trust it. He wrote in a dispatch to London in 1850: 'You must renounce the habit of telling the colonies that the colonial is a provisional existence'. In other words, Canada now housed a population in no sense transient, but permanent. Its development could never be fully controlled from beyond the ocean. Its loyalty must be secured in the first place by conceding the liberties to which 'organised communities of free men have a right to aspire'. David Hume or Adam Smith could scarcely have put it better. But, unlike them, Elgin did not believe that the residual bonds need be severed, at least not soon: Canada was still a young country, to which Britain's diplomatic talents and influence might continue to be of use. He showed he could use them to get the commercial benefits of American annexation without putting Canadians to the trouble of changing their allegiance. In 1854, he himself went to Washington to negotiate a treaty of trading reciprocity with the United States. He knew no less how to butter up his hosts. His secretary, Laurence Oliphant, famously described the treaty as 'floated through on champagne'. It rounded off Elgin's programme: he offered Canada a self-governing place in a free-trading Empire.[10]

The Americans were, only twelve years later, to abrogate the treaty, after the protectionist northern states won the Civil War. That also forged out of them a military power quite capable of conquering Canada. Yet responsible government was already beckoning Canadians towards an independent future. In both theory and practice, Scots helped them to make up their minds. Another John Rae, the emigrant political economist, outlined ideas for substitution of imports and transfer of technology that would become standard nostrums in former colonies during the post-imperial age. Curiously, the practical limits of the new dispensation were first probed by primitive Australia and New Zealand. With freedom to fix their own fiscal policies, they carried it the length of raising tariffs on British imports. These struck the Colonial Office as such an outrageous perversion of the proper relationship to imperial authority that it disallowed them. But Canadians were thinking along the same lines, and they could not be put in their place so easily. Alexander, son of John Galt, grasped the nettle. After a Scottish boyhood he had joined his father in Canada, and proved rather better at making money from land, as from railways. He was one of the Montrealers to sign the annexationist manifesto of 1849. Then he entered politics, to become Minister of Finance in 1858. He wanted to balance the budget. He proposed a duty on manufactures, mainly cotton, with the support of his friends in Montreal, now organised by the Glaswegian Isaac Buchanan in the protectionist

Association for the Promotion of Canadian Industry. The Colonial Office again demurred. It had never before been asked to go beyond anything recommended in Durham's report, its Bible on Canada. Now it was called on besides to dilute the sacred doctrine of free trade, against opposition not only from British business but also from Canadian liberals. Galt retorted in a memorandum which, after various placebos, declared that he could not 'in any manner waive or diminish the right of the people of Canada to decide for themselves both as to the mode and extent to which taxation shall be imposed'. After some soul-searching, London decided not to disallow the tariff. The Canadian Government, establishing that it owed its first duty to its country rather than to Westminster, had in turn declared economic independence.[11]

The logical next step was political independence, or at least confederation in the Dominion of Canada. A major factor in its achievement was the co-operation, again from opposite ends of the political spectrum, between George Brown and Sir John Macdonald. Brown's motives have already been examined: they too sprang out of the imported Scottish radicalism which followed its own path towards colonial autonomy. Macdonald was the true architect of the confederation. Till his death in 1891, he dominated its politics with ingenuity and charm, as a pragmatic conservative burdened by no great weight of principles but intent on giving all his disparate country's leading interests a stake in it. There lay one debt to the old Scots Toryism also imported to Canada, which had long outgrown mere defence of privilege. On the contrary, Macdonald called his the National Policy, and not without justice. If Galt and the moneyed men of Montreal set his protectionist economic agenda, it still had broader purposes. It expressed fiscal freedom, and more especially would allow infant Canadian industries to grow till they could compete fully in a global system of free trade. Macdonald did not stand alone among the world's statesmen of his day in sensing that pure economic liberalism was probably past its peak. His version of the old Scots Toryism also showed its wonted passion for economic improvement, infinitely heightened by the technological capabilities of the Victorian era. Perhaps the most prodigious of all feats by the Scots who exploited them would be the Canadian Pacific Railway, finished in 1885, four years late, against formidable financial and physical odds. Smith of the Hudson's Bay Company, meanwhile risen into Canada's financial elite, drove in the last spike at a place in the Rocky Mountains named Craigellachie. While he had formed the syndicate to construct the railway, it was actually the brainchild of his cousin, George Stephen, who had exchanged his dreary life as a draper's apprentice in Aberdeen for the promise of the New World and made the fortune that would raise him to the House of Lords as Lord Mount Stephen, and to the chairmanship of the Canadian Pacific Railway Company *en route*. It did almost go bankrupt at one stage, to be saved by an official subsidy but more by lavish grants of land along the line, 25 million acres in all. These were sold to settlers while the directors awaited the slow returns. Here, the Scots' commercial Empire modernised itself into an agent of colonisation. The greater task was the one set it by Macdonald of building a nation.[12]

As a Scot, however, Macdonald also knew the concept of nationality was not clear-cut. Scots of his time had concentric loyalties, to Scotland, Britain and the Empire. The sense of concentric loyalty helped him in his own tortuous task of bringing together the scattered provinces of British North America. In his federal system he gave guarantees for their local interests, on the whole effectively, though the French still felt themselves under pressure from the English-speaking majority, not least from rancorous Scots whose horror of Romanism too easily spilled over into racialist invective. But Macdonald, while elaborately deferring to Quebec's sensibilities, also recognised in the Britishness of the provinces one basic element of any conceivable common identity. It was not just a matter of foiling the United States to preserve imperial authority. Thus far disaffection in Canada had taken on an anti-British colour. Macdonald stressed that an equal if not greater risk to her interests came from the Americans, and must be countered by unity and by a concerted effort to develop the West before they seized it. This could be, and has been, defined as negative nationalism: British Canadians were to build, along with the French, a more ordered and stable society than the liberal experiment in the United States. Negative or not, Canada would grow increasingly conscious of it.

That, however, formed only one side of the equation. It was also necessary to determine the dominion's working relationship to the Empire, to find authentic expression for that allegiance explicitly retained. Trusting to its firmness, Macdonald could on this side go quite far. For example, he was no longer content to leave even Canadian external affairs entirely to the Governor-General or the Colonial Office. He wanted some diplomatic independence too. Since that would be a sticking point at Westminster, he took the matter into his own hands by sending John Rose, a son of Turriff and his Minister of Finance, as informal High Commissioner to Britain in 1869. Rose got a frosty reception, but Canada gained her point and was able to designate Galt her first official High Commissioner ten years later.

In 1884 Macdonald himself turned up in London, at the inaugural meeting of the Imperial Federation League. This might be taken as opening the era of high imperialism in the mother country. Schemes of union with the self-governing colonies were to be one of its perennial fruits. Macdonald remained cautious, resting on what colonial opinion would accept, in the first place co-operation over trade and defence. He advised imperialists to tackle only what was feasible and set out bluntly what was not, a supreme Parliament in London. After 1886, the crisis over Irish Home Rule made many wonder whether it might be resolved in an imperial framework, under just such a Parliament charged with the care of joint interests, but leaving the domestic affairs of the different British territories under subordinate legislatures in them. Macdonald again rejected it. Ireland, he said, should be content with the same status as Scotland, though pointing out how much better the latter was being treated. This may seem inconsistent with his claims for Canada. But he was indeed a pragmatist, who saw that any worldwide commonwealth must allow scope for gradations in the relationship of the dispersed parts to the whole, as he had allowed it inside his own confederation. The Canadian was different from the Scottish case because needs and aspirations were different in each, even while one particular aspiration, of preserving allegiance to the Crown, remained common to both.[13]

The test of Macdonald's work was that it survived him. The decade following his death proved trying for Canada. One Goldwin Smith now arrived from the regius chair of history at the university of Oxford to edit a newspaper in Toronto. In his writings, he told English-speaking Canadians to accept the facts of geography and history, scrap the confederation and join with the Anglo-Saxon elements in the United States to become the Scotland of a grand North American union. This fate Canada, not least her Scots, rejected. She did so despite internal political turmoil and sharpening racial tension, which brought the virtual collapse of Macdonald's Conservative party. It gave way to the Liberals under Wilfrid Laurier, the first French, indeed the first non-Scottish, Prime Minister of the confederation. That was in itself a victory for ordered pluralism.

Just about the turn of the century Canada's growing maturity and stability demonstrated themselves in an imperial context as well. The Governor-General at the time was the 4th Earl of Minto, latest in an almost equally continuous line of Scots to hold the office. He brought with him some older Scottish attitudes to Empire: he lamented desecration of the prairies and the 'passing of the red man'. But he brought new attitudes too, notably a wish to strengthen links with the mother country. While aware of Canadian reservations, he believed his status as an imperial officer gave him such a mandate where common interests were clearly at stake. It led him, however, into a sharp constitutional controversy which proved to be a decisive point defining Canada's working relationship to the Empire. Minto was no intellectual, and the contradictions in his outlook at first made it hard for him to perceive the reality of Canada. 'I suspect that he dreams of Canadian independence in some future age,' he said of Laurier. He soon learned that the age might be at hand. The Governor-General had two functions, as constitutional monarch of Canada and representative of the Ministry at Westminster, neither with much power. In purely domestic affairs, he was happy to act on Laurier's advice. But he did not regard defence, for example, as a purely domestic affair. He intervened when the Cabinet was deliberating whether to turn the militia into a national army. Neither in London nor in Ottawa did anyone want this argument, though, and he had to concede that it was entirely a matter for the Canadians.

He felt himself on stronger ground at the outbreak of the Boer War in 1899. He was keen for Canada to play her part. But public opinion split, between the English-speakers mostly for it and the French mostly against it. Canada just could not afford to have her two races again at daggers drawn. Minto tried to butt in and order soldiers to South Africa on his own authority, but Laurier put his foot down. The Governor-General persisted, with heavy hints that if Britain could rely on no support in this, she should not necessarily be expected to back Canada in disputes with the

United States. Laurier resolved the impasse with an obvious compromise of his own. He announced that the situation was serious enough to entitle him, without referring to Parliament, to recruit, equip and dispatch an initial force of 1000 volunteers under imperial command. Eventually 7000 Canadians served in South Africa, and with distinction, in contrast to the blundering British. An inglorious war not only exposed their military disorganisation but also raised questions about their whole way of life under an aristocratic ruling class. Canadians, like many indeed in the mother country, began to doubt its capacity for leadership. To that extent their anti-imperial sentiment strengthened. Laurier certainly grew more conscious of risks in the British connection, and warier of future efforts to reinforce it.

Minto had still performed a useful role. He brought areas of dispute, formerly potential, to resolution, and all were resolved in favour of Canada. If his relations with the Ministry turned difficult, he gained a more realistic estimate of the nature and extent of Canadian attachment to Britain, and a new respect for it. He almost became a Canadian himself in his view of the Empire, as a defence against American influences to be sure, but capable of only the limited unity allowed by self-interest and sentiment. When he left in 1904, he was praising Canada for her combination of American utility and British tradition, as a country which in her own way gave her people, as she had given this by no means wealthy or brilliant scion of the Scots nobility, their chance to prove themselves. The nature of the Empire had been contested here, not least in Minto's own mind. A Scottish vision of it had won.[14]

CHAPTER TWENTY-FOUR

'Our principal reliance is on opium': China

On October 18, 1860, British troops under two Scotsmen, James Bruce, 8th Earl of Elgin, and General Hope Grant, burned down the Yuen-ming-yuen, the Summer Palace of the Chinese Emperor. It lay on the fringe of Peking in a huge park seven miles square. Here, amid one of the world's loveliest manmade landscapes, more than 200 exquisite pavilions and kiosks beckoned along shady walks or noble terraces, with views over splendid gardens, lakes and woods, where dainty deer tossed their antlered heads. It was the favourite residence of the ruling Manchus. In it they preserved the tablets, or muniments, of the dynasty. By popular association that made it sacred, a repository of the mandate of heaven. It was a centre of power too. For the business of the court, lords and ladies of the Middle Kingdom came in constant attendance. The Emperor received them sitting on an intricately carved throne in his great hall, paved with marble and decorated in brilliant gold, blue and red; even the little wash-hand basin and jug from which he refreshed himself between audiences were fashioned of precious metals and jewels. The palace was altogether a treasure-house of priceless works of art, of porcelain, jade, silk, and of what the Emperor chose to regard as foreign tribute: from Louis XIV of France, classical paintings and a service of Sèvres china; from George III of Great Britain, a state-coach and two howitzers. The Chinese thought the last mere curiosities, and had shown no interest in learning how they worked or in using them for their own defences.

Some must by now have rued it. For three years they had been fighting the Second Opium War with Britain, then with France as well. It would end in forcing them to open wide their commerce, and for the first time to enter into diplomatic relations with western countries. Elgin, former Governor-General of Canada and now High Commissioner to China, had arrived at the end of 1857 to resolve a number of outstanding disputes. To demonstrate that he meant business, he brought 2000 soldiers with him. But he had only accepted the command because he felt someone of high moral standards and stable disposition should temper the pugnacity of the Foreign Secretary, Lord Palmerston, as of the British merchants in the East egging him on. The feeling was shared by Laurence Oliphant, who had served as the Earl's private secretary since the Canadian years, and abandoned his own prospects as Liberal candidate in the Stirling Burghs to come along now. He looked around at an 'active, industrious and enterprising race', at heart like his own, and found 'every reason to hope that a better acquaintance with us would remove their old existing prejudices'.[1]

In truth, there was no reason to hope any such thing. The Emperor did not even deign to notice them, so nobody came to negotiate when Elgin arrived before Canton. To make his presence felt, he had to order an attack. It carried the city, but still the expected Chinese emissaries failed to appear. The force therefore moved north towards Peking. It assaulted and took the forts guarding the mouth of the River Peiho, the imperial capital's gateway to the sea. Then it pushed inland. The Emperor, lest worse befall, at last sent commissioners to ask for terms. The Uncontrollably Fierce Barbarian, as Chinese dispatches called the Earl, deputed his brother, Frederick Bruce, to impose them: among others, a British Minister resident in Peking and unhindered travel for British subjects inside China. Meanwhile, Elgin sailed in July 1858 for Japan, to sign a commercial accord with her too. Then, satisfied that all was well, he went home.

But all was not well. Ratifications of the treaty were meant to be exchanged in Peking a year later. When Bruce approached for the purpose, he found his way barred, and the Chinese resolved not to honour what had been extracted from them under duress. There was no choice but to mount a second and more intimidating expedition of the 12,000 British troops led by Elgin and Grant, with a French contingent of 8000. They landed in August 1860 and advanced once more towards the imperial capital, fighting and negotiating by turns. It was not an ideal way to proceed. During October it had a dire consequence. In revenge for some incident, the Chinese detained an allied delegation with its escort of Sikh soldiers, executed several and so mistreated the rest that some died. Henry Loch, son of the Duke of Sutherland's factor and another of the well-connected compatriots with whom the Earl surrounded himself, survived to report this gruesome sequel. An appalled Elgin decided to teach the Chinese a lesson they would never forget.

The Summer Palace was already desecrated. A short while before, French cavalry reconnoitring nearby had found it deserted by the terrified court, and occupied it. Other troops arrived and wrecked the interior. The Earl went to inspect the damage: 'Alas! such a scene of desolation'. He came, of course, of a family of connoisseurs. His father had removed the marbles from the Athenian Parthenon and sold them to the British Museum. The son could not now find in himself the same finesse. On his own responsibility (the French refused to co-operate) he ordered the palace razed. With this, long recalled by the Chinese as the most despicable western crime of all, a set of enlightened, aristocratic Scotsmen consummated an oriental encounter now two centuries old.[2]

It is odd, for a people supposed to have been sunk in impoverished torpor until the Union, how early and how often we keep coming across Scots in faraway places. Before 1611, William Carmichael, serving in the government of Portuguese India, had visited Macao. In 1632, William Campbell, formerly in the Dutch service, had brought to the attention of the English East India Company the trading potential of Formosa. His detailed account of the island avoided the religious or political afflatus usual in colonising documents of the era, sticking to the facts and the opportunities.

He proposed this as the base for a concerted effort to open up traffic with China, and himself as the best man to be put in charge of it. The company paid him £5 for his trouble, but regretted it had not enough resources for a new station. That was no wonder, given the difficulty the English experienced during the seventeenth century in sustaining any position beyond India. Besides, the Celestial Empire, on which Campbell had gazed across the Strait of Formosa, maintained a haughty indifference to European approaches. True, the importunities of the Portuguese had in 1557 won them use of the tiny peninsula at Macao for their commerce. But Dutch pleas for a similar privilege were brushed aside. Not till 1685 did the Emperor K'ang Hsi, an open-minded liberal by mandarin standards, grant general permission for Europeans to trade at Canton, under strict precautions. They were not to be allowed anywhere else in the country, not even into the city itself. A strange, cramped settlement grew up between its walls and the banks of the Pearl River. Cheek by jowl along the waterfront, in hot, crowded discomfort, European merchants built their factories. The English one soon became, as Dutch and Portuguese enterprise ebbed, the most important.

From here, too, the East India Company enjoyed a nominal monopoly on direct traffic home. But again no constraint was placed on the country trade, a standing invitation to break the monopoly. Scots appeared at Canton in the 1720s, first in the company's service, then outside it. William Chambers, of a family which had decamped to Gothenburg, was apprenticed to the Swedish East India Company, in effect a smuggling outfit. He voyaged to China as a teenage trader to finance his real ambition, a grand tour of the monuments in Italy and France. Then he settled back in Britain, to become one of her great architects. He wrote two seminal treatises on chinoiserie showing off the stylistic innovations with which he would relieve the severity of Scottish classicism at the noble seats of Hopetoun, Penicuik and Yester. He had bidden farewell to China in 1748, just as fresh recruits to the Scots fraternity were arriving there, hotfoot after the Battle of Culloden. From one Jacobite family in Dumfriesshire, the Herries of Halldykes, William fled to Ostend while his brother Charles, who had kept himself clean, made his way to London and opened a business which struck subversive deals under the noses of the Hanoverian authorities. The pair did well enough out of smuggling from the Orient to buy the family's passage back to political respectability in the next generation. During the 1760s, William and George Keith Elphinstone travelled to Canton with capital from their great-uncle, the Earl Marischal, exiled in Prussia since 1745.[3]

If these people wanted to import their wares to Scotland, they needed only to go by way of a continental port or a Dutch colony, whence they brought the cargoes to the Isle of Man and ran them in overnight. The contraband consisted mainly of huge quantities of tea, openly delivered inland. With cheaper prices, the smugglers even seized part of the market across the border. The defiance of English economic regulation was an old Scottish sport which the Union had done little to stop. It gave if anything a stimulus, for it generated a wider diaspora, whether voluntarily through access to the colonies or involuntarily through exile in Europe. Several Scots in Canton prospered nominally by obtaining the commissions of foreign governments, but actually by performing a vital economic function in the liberation of the commerce.

Their compatriot in the highest British counsels, Henry Dundas, came to see that. He wanted to find an answer to what was now the biggest problem in the balance of payments, the mounting deficit, paid in bullion, against imports of Chinese tea. One answer might have been for the East India Company to convey a larger volume of direct exports. In order to promote it, Dundas dispatched three embassies, the first to Canton in 1786–7 to improve local commercial conditions, a second under one of his Scots MPs, Charles Cathcart, who died on the way to Peking in 1788. The third, under Lord Macartney in 1791–2, did reach the imperial capital, but failed to establish diplomatic relations. An increase in traffic could, therefore, only come through private merchants. Dundas set out to enlist them in a triangular trade. He believed Britain could sell more manufactures, again displacing the customary specie, to India. Onward development of commerce from there to China needed a wider range of native merchandise, textiles, pepper, sandalwood. Then, with some financial juggling, the tea could be paid for in goods rather than gold. In the process Britain would turn herself into the pivot of quickening exchanges between East and West.

But it was to be opium, the perfect export, imperishable, easily carried, in great demand, that really set the triangular trade going. By 1800 traffic in it had grown so fast that the Manchu Government imposed a ban. Some had been transported by the East India Company. For the sake of good relations, it stopped. That just drove the shipments into the hands of private merchants, who made far more of them than the company ever had. Production and sales of opium accelerated until this became probably the largest commerce of the time in any single commodity. The flood of cheap drugs was to subvert the ancient Chinese Empire. It undermined the ethos of an industrious and obedient race. It corrupted the machinery of government. Above all, it unleashed economic forces from the West, in a ferment which would stop short only of destroying the country's independence. But the company had no part in this. Though it held on to its Chinese monopoly in 1813, when it lost the Indian one, the privileges meant little. It had to defend them again in 1833 and, with no economic arguments to deploy, could for once take the moral high ground. The most venerable of nabobs, John Malcolm, warned a court of proprietors crammed with Scots that the liberal agenda was always apt to turn political, in a 'pretension to be above the laws and usages of other countries'. Charles Forbes saw a greater danger: 'So wild an idea as the conquest of China never could have entered the mind of any person in the court, or in the British dominions, although it appeared to have been entertained by some of the wise men in Canton'. The new Whig Ministry refused to listen and took away the residue of the monopoly too. The old commercial Empire had after its fashion respected this exotic civilisation. A new utilitarian one would revile and torment it.

In the forefront stood two younger Scotsmen, William Jardine and James Matheson. Jardine, born at Lochmaben in 1784, signed on as a ship's surgeon with the East India Company at the age of 18. Later he went into the country trade with a Parsee of Bombay, a shipper of opium, as whose agent he arrived in China in 1819. Jardine was a formidable man, stern to the point of frigidity, much more feared than liked. In his office he kept a single chair: those granted an interview had to stand. But his daunting self-possession won him the admiration of the Chinese. They called him Iron-Headed Old Rat, a compliment, because of an incident once when he was on his way to present a petition at the gates of Canton, the usual way of dealing with the authorities there; a heavy bar fell, or was thrown, on his head from a scaffold, yet he walked on as if nothing had happened. The fortitude pointed to his deeper and more admirable qualities, his devout Christianity, his sagacity and shrewdness, his intuitive if cynical grasp of politics, his fast friendships more than a match for his implacable enmities.

Matheson was born at Lairg in 1796, the illegitimate son of a Highland gentleman who gave him a good start in life, sending him to university in Edinburgh, then into business under distant relations in an Indian trading house. On its behalf he too had made his way to Canton in 1819, arriving on a Danish passport. But he soon branched out by himself. His first couple of trips up the Strait of Formosa grossed him over 200,000 silver dollars in illegal profits from opium. In contrast to Jardine, the suave and handsome Matheson was well-bred, but no fop, for he proved himself sharper to sense opportunities and quicker to seize them than any rival in sight. Yet he had a genuine human warmth. There was some intellectual depth to him too; he had been trained in political economy and was impelled by the belief that its application would be a boon to China. He was a cut well above the seedy characters otherwise found in the country trade. Still, he and Jardine were also utter rascals, who distinguished themselves by a ruthlessness bordering on infamy. In 1832, under a saltire flag, they entered into a registered partnership. They aimed to seize commercial leadership in Canton now the East India Company was on the way out. Jardine Matheson, the "princely hong" to awed orientals, would grow into the greatest enterprise of the East.[4]

Once free trade came the next year, however, its effect was chaos. Under the novel conditions, the private partnerships descended into confusion. Newcomers trying to force an entry added to it; the Gladstones, for example, despite their wealth and acumen, got their fingers burned and soon withdrew. Almost alone, Jardine Matheson came through unscathed. The two Scots kept cool, spread their risks and wriggled out of every danger, while never letting others escape the consequences of misjudgment; this grim spirit of retribution was, though, tempered by their readiness with personal help for the bankrupt. They were just better at their business than anybody else. They proved themselves adept at stepping in to pick out and carry on with the money-making bits of their fallen rivals' inventories. They produced a flow of brilliant little coups, no doubt the fruit of native intellectual daring.[5]

They cast, for example, an avid eye on the Rev Dr Karl Gützlaff, a squat, plucky Prussian running a medical mission from Macao. He travelled in all conditions up and down the coast, to a universal welcome from ordinary Chinese, who humoured him by taking his bibles and tracts along with his pills and ointments. Master of their language as of its dialects, he talked to them with untiring vehemence of the really good news he had brought, far surpassing his cures for aches, pains or agues. Alas for this solemn, busy, garrulous, good-hearted man: he fell into the Scots' clutches. Like every missionary, he stood short of funds for his journeys. He could hardly refuse if offered free passage on one of the princely hong's ships, in return for acting as interpreter in selling the cargo. Jardine sent in October 1832 to make him an offer. The letter continued:

> But as the expenses of the voyage cannot be defrayed from this source, we have no hesitation in stating to you openly that our principal reliance is on opium. Though it is our earnest wish that you should not in any way injure the grand object you have in view by appearing interested in what by many is considered an immoral traffic, yet such traffic is so absolutely necessary to give any vessel a reasonable chance of defraying her expenses, that we trust you will have no objection to interpret on every occasion when your services may be required. The more profitable the expedition, the better we shall be able to place at your disposal a sum that may hereafter be employed in furthering your mission, and for your success in which we feel deeply interested.

Gützlaff knew the ship would be spreading among the Chinese a double evil, physical and moral. He agonised, but Jardine's casuistry persuaded him that the evangelical benefit outweighed both. So during the voyage it often happened that, having struck a bargain with dealers in drugs on one side of the vessel, he would cross the deck and hand out religious tracts on the other. From the undoubted best of motives, he became complicit in a business ethically indefensible and in China actually criminal. As good Presbyterians, Jardine and Matheson averred that they too sought China's conversion, but this was inseparable from her subversion through opium. How else could a sealed realm be prised open to commerce, and to the blessings of western civilisation it would bring in its train?[6]

Soon they were handling 6000 chests of opium a year, one-third of Canton's trade, and making 100,000 silver dollars on them. To Jardine it was 'the safest and most gentlemanlike speculation I am aware of'; Matheson chortled at 'the snug way' in which 'income comes to you without asking'. Commercial success gave them political standing. They took a lead in calling for normal relations between China and the West, as a practical necessity rather than a diplomatic nicety. Merchants incurred heavy costs from the time and effort spent on evasion of the authorities, affecting to despise them and refusing them legal rights outside Canton. Or rather, mandarins milked the restrictions for all they were worth by taking bribes to get round them. This inhibited development of established commercial practice, let alone of enforceable law in case of disputes. In other words, the system asked for political trouble.

The merchants had travelled up and down the Celestial Empire and seen how weak it was, its coasts defenceless, its decrees impotent, its rulers unwilling and probably unable to reform it. Who doubted that the edifice would topple under western pressure? And Britain, commercial leader of the world, mistress of its oceans, could hardly ignore appeals from her own subjects intent, as they put it, on peaceful trade yet persecuted for their pains. Bombarding the Government in London with their grievances and enlisting partners in business to agitate for them, from 10,000 miles away they could easily depict themselves as the victims. Hypocritical they indeed were, though one may add that they felt thoroughly fed up of Chinese hypocrisy; Presbyterian hypocrisy must have seemed footling in comparison.

The first official response was nevertheless cautious: dispatch of a superintendent for trade at Canton who would seek, on a low initial level, the diplomatic relations which China spurned. The man chosen was Lord Napier of Merchiston, retired naval officer of 48, veteran of Trafalgar, fellow of the Royal Society of Edinburgh and model landlord in the Borders. On his staff he had a neighbour, Captain Charles Elliot, nephew of the Earl of Minto and sometime official protector of slaves in British Guiana.

They arrived in 1834 with two frigates. Solid and reliable as Napier seemed, he turned out brusque and indecisive by turns. He stood on the rights of an envoy of the Crown and, without permission, made straight for Canton. This gave offence. The mandarins would not receive or otherwise deal with him, writing his name in ideographs meaning Laboriously Vile. When he defied an order to leave, they halted British trade: a fine outcome for a mission to promote it. Jardine advised sending for the frigates. They fired on forts at the mouth of the Pearl River, then got stuck amid obstructions sunk in the watercourse. Napier had no choice but to retire to Macao, where he soon sickened and died. The mortifying "Napier Fizzle" appeared to prove that China could not be persuaded to enter by normal channels into relations with the West. Jardine thought as much, which was why he had urged Napier to provoke a crisis and force the British Government's hand. Now he left for London to press the case in person. In Whitehall they still did not want to know. When Elliot took over responsibility on the spot, he was left almost without instructions. The best he could do was respect Chinese rules and stay at Macao while he got the trade going again in the old way, hoping that some new arrangement might evolve.[7]

On the contrary, chaos grew. After one of the Emperor's sons died of an overdose, the authorities moved to suppress the traffic in opium. A new governor, Lin Tse-hu, arrived with a free hand in Canton. He ordered stocks of the drug to be handed over and trade in it to be halted. The merchants refused, so he shut them up in their factories for 48 days, innocent and guilty alike, on the Chinese axiom that groups tainted by crime were collectively responsible for it. Elliot came from Macao to mediate. His compromise was to surrender 20,000 chests of opium on a promise to the merchants of compensation from Britain. They happily complied, for now they would get money they might have lost. But Lin was not appeased. He also required, on pain of expulsion, a bond that they would deal no more in opium or answer to the law of China if they did. Matheson signed, sure of its futility: he forecast revolt by a population deprived of drugs, and beyond that war, for British property had been seized and British subjects detained, a matter unlikely to be overlooked when news of it reached Palmerston. Matheson and several other delinquents were expelled all the same. So he broke his bond. He went to Manila to arrange its use as entrepot for the vast quantities of opium he now ordered from India. It was brought into the delta of the Pearl River, where he set up business on a ship: 'Whatever happens, our firm will endeavour to maintain a floating position in this vicinity'. Elliot thought better to leave again too, taking the rest of the merchants and forbidding any British ship to come up to Canton while he awaited instructions. They retreated to Macao, but found it unsuitable for trade and feared it was not quite safe. So they transferred to Hong Kong: this flitting, on August 26, 1840, marked in effect the foundation of the colony.[8]

The First Opium War broke out. Frigates again tried to force the approaches to Canton, and worsted a flotilla of junks. After them came 16 ships and 400 troops to impose a blockade if the Chinese would not at once make concessions. During a truce, Elliot seized the chance to make them cede Hong Kong, subject to ratification in a subsequent treaty. He took formal possession of the island in January 1841. In eight months as its administrator, he set about making a regular colony of it. He declared that the inhabitants, found by a census to number 6000, were subjects of the Crown. He announced that the port would be a free one. He sold the land off in lots, mainly to British firms. Jardine Matheson at once shifted its headquarters here and erected the first permanent European building, its godown for storing opium. Yet Elliot was to be recalled in disgrace, for not having extracted more from the Chinese. He was afterwards relegated to a series of minor postings, as consul-general in Texas, governor successively of Bermuda, Trinidad and St Helena. Still, he deserves remembrance as founder of Hong Kong.[9]

Negotiations had meanwhile proceeded, till it grew clear that the Chinese were in no mind to conclude them, rather to play for time. Britain again sent reinforcements. On arrival late in 1841, they captured the forts at the mouth of the Pearl River. The Cantonese mob retaliated by destroying the European factories: a barren gesture, for they were no longer needed. The expedition went on to occupy various crucial posts along the coast. Wherever it did, the trade in opium at once started up again. The irrepressible Matheson even managed to run the blockade of Canton with foreign ships. Since he was Danish consul, he could change their names and colours at will, and pounced on this novel means of commercial advantage. By the summer of 1842 there were 10,000 British troops in China, and her resistance crumbled. She signed the Treaty of Nanking, ceding sovereignty over Hong Kong and admitting foreign commerce to five ports. The Middle Kingdom had been closed: now it was open, and the princely hong moved straight in. Its branch in Shanghai, set up in 1844, would do much to develop the city into the great emporium of the Far East. The Manchu dynasty had still yielded unwillingly, and was far from reconciling itself to the humiliation. Only the Second Opium War and Elgin's more devastating punishment were to cow it.[10]

Hong Kong embarked on its own glittering commercial career with Jardine Matheson its leading enterprise. Of the founders, Jardine never returned to China. Instead he set up and developed in London a banking business to handle his lion's share of the expanding oriental trade. He had besides made such a favourable political impression that the ruling Whig party arranged to get him into Parliament. It then lost the General Election of 1841, so he remained in opposition till his death two years later. In 1844 Matheson came back as well. For £500,000 he bought the island of Lewis, where he built Stornoway Castle. He earned a baronetcy in 1852 for work on relief of the Highland famine, but was also an improving landlord in the modern style who cleared more than 500 ne'er-do-well families and packed them off to Canada. The estate was his springboard into the House of Commons, where he sat as Whig MP for Ross and Cromarty in 1847–62. Benjamin Disraeli described him in *Sybil*: 'Oh, a dreadful man. A Scotchman richer than Croesus, one Mr Macdrug, fresh from Canton, with a million in opium in each pocket, denouncing corruption and bellowing free trade'.

In China, the princely hong was being run by three of Matheson's nephews. Alexander, the taipan or senior partner, stuck to business. But James earned gratitude with good works, including construction of Hong Kong's first permanent church. The equally devout Donald kept company with missionaries, who filled him with guilt about opium. Alexander warned him that, unless he overcame his scruples, he must resign his partnership. When he did in 1848, it marked a turning point in the relations of the two clans. The Mathesons ended participation in a common management; others went out to China but never became partners. Their interest centred rather on Matheson & Co, established separately in London and built up into one of its leading merchant houses. But this too the Jardines would acquire. When Alexander Matheson retired in 1852, he was followed as taipan by three Jardines, all nephews of the founder William: David in 1852–6, Joseph in 1856–60 and Robert in 1860–82.[11]

They were less swashbuckling than the founders, and more convinced that Christianity offered a key to the Middle Kingdom. To embark on the huge task of evangelisation they patronised a compatriot, James Legge of Huntly. Under the London Missionary Society he had first come out to Malacca, succeeding as principal of an evangelical college for the sizeable community of Chinese living there. In 1841 he at once moved it to Hong Kong. In this missionary field Scots faced the same dilemmas as in others. The Rev David Sandeman, who arrived in the service of the Presbyterian Church of England, found his contact with heathenism 'benumbing' and dismissed the civilisation of the Celestial Empire with scorn. By contrast Legge,

312 THE SCOTTISH EMPIRE

while declining to follow Gützlaff and live like a Chinese, did cultivate a scholarly orientalism: 'The idea that a man need spend no time in studying the native religions, but has only, as the phrase is, to "preach the gospel" is one which can only make missionaries and mission work contemptible and inefficient'.

As elsewhere, the contrast also came out in educational method. Legge gave instruction in Chinese except when his pupils were actually learning English, which some did well enough to go to Britain and study at his Aberdonian alma mater. Of course he gave instruction in Chinese to the trainee mandarins sent him by the Manchu regime for acquaintance with western ways. He even gave instruction in Chinese to junior British officials, who in Hong Kong had to serve a cadetship, and gen up on the culture, before assuming any responsibilities. Some of his native pupils became pioneers of modernisation. Ho Tsun-shin, in 1846 the earliest Chinese pastor to be ordained, had a son, Ho Kai, who founded a medical college, and a son-in-law, Ng Choy, who was the first of his race to qualify as a barrister, going on to an eminent career in diplomacy and politics. Wang Tao, who returned with Legge in 1867 to study for three years in Scotland, inaugurated the Chinese daily press. Hung Jen-kan was among the leaders of the Taiping rebellion, the popular uprising against the Manchus on a millenarian political programme mixing Christian with classical Chinese concepts, and suffered execution in 1864.

Meanwhile Legge's own career was disturbed by nothing more than differences over the nature of public schooling for Hong Kong and its growing population. The Central School, origin of its modern educational system, came into being in 1862. The first head was a young colleague of Legge's, like him a product of both the grammar school and university of Aberdeen, Frederick Stewart. His method deviated somewhat from his mentor's. He made the school secular, if only to keep the aggressive local Anglicans at bay. He soon also decided English had to become the medium of instruction, as more attractive to students. That did not mean it was right or possible to eradicate the ancient culture of which Hong Kong formed part. Instead the system combined Chinese and Scottish forms of education. Nothing like it was available elsewhere in the Orient, as proved by the numbers flocking in from mainland China, Japan and Korea. Success enabled Stewart to foil an English governor, Sir John Pope Hennessy, who wanted to impose a western curriculum. Once this enemy left in 1882, Stewart moved from one influential position to another till by the time he died, aged only 53, he was acting governor.

Legge meanwhile cultivated his cultural interests. Financed by Joseph and Robert Jardine, he became the first, tireless translator of the corpus of Chinese classical literature, parts of it into Scots poetry. This life's work took him in 1873 to a chair at the university of Oxford where, till his death in 1897, he was the father of British sinology. That never distracted him from missions altogether. But his studies made him revise his evangelistic attitudes much as did, in his turn, William Robertson Smith's. The texts on which each laboured were, however, different in nature. The Chinese classics contained nothing like the mythology of other ancient peoples, let alone religion in any western sense. This was an agnostic civilisation's prosy literature of moral philosophy. Legge saw that the Chinese felt no sense of sin or need of salvation. But he satisfied himself that the true God, who had chosen Israel and revealed himself in the Bible, could be detected in their books. The presence persisted, if in debased ritual form, through the imperial tradition. So when Legge had to invent a term for a true God now obscured, he sought one which bore some meaning within Chinese culture. He rejected *shen*, the normal word for the sprite-like deities of popular belief, on the grounds that African missionaries rejected such words, as not august enough. Instead he used *shang ti*, "supreme emperor". To certain colleagues this seemed suspect: did it not after all concede a degree of divinity to the *ti*, the Emperor in Peking? They grew more anxious as Legge in copious writings drew closer parallels between Confucianism and Christianity. After surveying all Confucius had to say on God, the destiny of man and moral or social duties, he found the sage to be not wholly in error; the *Analects*, if syncretic rather than monotheistic, might contain material useful for evangelism. A paper on these lines which Legge sent to a conference of missionaries in Shanghai in 1877 so alarmed his critics that they had it excluded as heretical from the published proceedings.

If the exotic again fomented heresy among Presbyterians, it did not stop them becoming a force in Chinese Christianity. The Scots Churches proper took time to follow the missionary societies. The United Presbyterians, as ever in the forefront, did not arrive till 1862, the Kirk not till 1878. Irish, American and Australian sisters seconded their efforts, all working, for Presbyterians, in unwonted harmony. By the turn of the century they were able to form a Presbyterian Church of China; its inaugural General Assembly met in 1914. The harvest from these exertions remained nevertheless small compared to the size of the field. Barriers to the interior of the country came down before the Churches had much inkling what it might take to convert a people who, if pagan, were civilised. In any event, merchants rather than missionaries rushed in, and the latter disposed neither of the men nor the money to keep pace. Here, commerce and Christianity never really went together.[12]

But perhaps morality did modify commercial practice in the princely hong of William Keswick. This great-nephew of William Jardine took over in the East in 1855, rose to be head of the whole house and stayed in charge till 1912; from him all later taipans were descended. At his hands the firm matured and consolidated itself in a far wider range of interests. They had often already been there. Jardine Matheson early on built a fleet of clippers for regular runs to India, pioneered new routes inside China and developed lines other than opium. It had at once in 1833 sent to London the first free cargo of tea, later linking up with Glasgow and other ports. It went into textiles, notably silk, dealing with manufacturers in the West of Scotland and elsewhere. It branched out into more specialised exotic commodities: teak from Siam, ebony from Mauritius, rice from Siam. It opened up markets in America and Australia. It was the driving force behind the expansion of British commerce with the Orient. While opium had once been indispensable, by the time Keswick arrived the direct profits from that and the other main commodities of traditional trade were stagnating. Those failing to take note of the trend faced chronic financial crisis, and in many cases bankruptcy. The princely hong again weathered storms which sank weaker ones.[13]

At any rate Keswick withdrew from opium. Even Legge had felt able to defend the trade, on the proceeds of which his own work relied: he maintained that God made use even of evil things, and thought opium no worse than alcohol. For Jardine Matheson, profit was doubtless a stronger motive. As a trading concern, it could move into such lucrative fields as shipping, docks, wharves and warehouses. Amid the growing commerce of the Treaty ports, money was to be made from property and utilities, or services such as banking and insurance. Beyond that, China offered absurdly cheap factors of production. Untapped mineral resources could be opened up with modern mining methods. In 1870, the taipan went directly into the manufacture of silk, building a filature in Shanghai.

Not everything ran smooth: in 1876 Keswick started building China her first railway, on the 12 miles from Shanghai to the outport of Wusung. Ignoring bottomless official suspicion, he bought land on the pretence of planning a road, then laid a track. Once opened, the line proved an instant success and carried 200,000 passengers during its short existence. That ended after two months, along with the life of a local man run over by an engine and killed. Hostile mandarins orchestrated an outcry so huge that they forced the princely hong to sell the line to the Chinese Government. It at once ordered the rails torn up and shipped with the rolling stock to Formosa, where the whole lot was dumped and left to rot on a beach. The age of railways did not dawn on the Middle Kingdom for another ten years. Undaunted, Jardine Matheson was meanwhile setting up in everything from beer to guns, as an investor and entrepreneur, a supplier of the capital, technology and skills that a modern China would need. By 1900 it employed over 100,000 people in Asia. It made so bold as to adopt the Confucian name of Ewo, "righteous harmony", for many of its subsidiaries, in order to follow the local custom of trading under a propitious precept.

The expansion did not take place in a vacuum, however. If humbled politically, the Middle Kingdom grew quite buoyant economically. That showed up in livelier domestic commerce, as well as in direct exchanges with the outside world. Into these, so far monopolised by Europeans, locals began to move, eager to learn western methods, extend their skills, gain experience to compete with foreign devils. This was how Chinese capitalism started, with the so-called compradores: middlemen between European and Chinese businesses who often built up firms of their own, a sort of indigenous counterpart to the agency houses. The princely hong did not make these people unwelcome. The founders themselves had worked with native merchants or mandarins, and Keswick's chief compradore, Robert Ho Tung, was held in high enough esteem to win the hand of Clara Maclean, daughter of another partner in Jardine Matheson. The couple founded a commercial dynasty which lives on in

Hong Kong to this day.

To Keswick joint ventures seemed an obvious next step, combining the expertise from without and capital from within alike necessary to transform the Celestial Empire. But the process also depended on the resilience or otherwise of the Manchu regime, which had several decades to run yet. Mandarins too were being converted to the idea of development, though not for the same reasons as the taipan. At most they sought a controlled capitalism in order to filter from the West what the Middle Kingdom wanted; the policy has been resurrected in our own time. So, in their external relations, they used a repertoire of ancient wiles to play off against one another the foreign firms now crowding in and the governments behind them. In internal relations, they understood the rising importance of the mercantile class and the social threat of economic changes not restrained by themselves. They dealt with the new rich by offering them imperial honours, superior status rather than just filthy lucre. And the merchants, however wealthy, however esteemed by the foreign devils, still rated such rewards higher. In other words, degeneration in the state by no means went hand in hand with degeneration in the society or the mentalities built into it.

If decadent and corrupt, the regime yet kept a hold of the country and the commerce. Jardine Matheson, having itself felt the blunting of the western challenge, accepted that and adapted. Till the end of the century everything seemed to go on, if in slow and halting fashion, well enough. Not for any incompetence of the hongs or impolicy of the British Government, at any rate, did the process fail to cause sufficient change within the time left to the Celestial Empire. Even the most eager missionaries, too, were brought up short by a civilisation so ancient, so devious, so set in its ways. It continued to follow its own complex evolution, as it continues yet. In that the foreigners played a large, disruptive but in the end subordinate part. Scottish philosophy would not have expected anything else.[14]

CHAPTER TWENTY-FIVE

'A huge military despotism': India

O n October 20, 1897, in one of the most glorious feats of Scottish arms, the
Gordon Highlanders stormed the heights of Dargai on the North-West
Frontier. They formed part of the punitive expedition sent out to suppress a revolt
sparked off among the Pathan people of the mountains by the Mad Mullah of Swat.
The force was seeking to penetrate the Tirah Maidan, the innermost sanctum of the
Afridi tribe, never before seen by a white man. At the approach to it, the troops faced
fanatical warriors occupying the heights, their holy banners silhouetted against the
sky. Unless they could be dislodged, no advance was possible. English and Indian
regiments assaulted the sheer slopes. Each failed, their soldiers mown down by
sharpshooters. Finally the Scots went in. At first it seemed that they too must fail.
But they refused to be beaten. George McGunn, a young soldier who would rise to
become a general, recalled how their commander

> ordered officers and pipers to the front. The swagger with which the pipe major
> threw his plaid and his drones well over his shoulder was magnificent. The
> colonel strode out in front, and the pipes set up "Cock of the North". And out
> on to the narrow ridge scrambled a mass of some 600 cheering Highlanders. The
> artillery redoubled their supporting fire, and though many men fell, the mass, as
> the colonel expected, got over, and in their train came Gurkhas, Sikhs and the
> men of the Dorset and Derby. Piper Findlater, lying wounded in the neck,
> played his pipes as the men rushed on . . . The companies set themselves in
> some confusion to scramble upwards along the slopes and goat paths and among
> rocks and crevices. It was a matter of at least 300 difficult feet, and everyone
> thought it would be the worst, but no! the heavy rifle fire soon died away, and
> the leading files gained the top at various parts almost unmolested. The
> tribesmen had seized their standards and gone.

Casualties were heavy all the same: the Gordons lost half their muster. Perhaps, in
their elation, few of them paused to recall how unnecessary that cost ought to have
been. With great dash they had once already, a couple of days before, captured the
heights. But then it was found that, because of feeble staff-work, they could not be
supplied, so they had to descend again. This was not the last time that valiant
Scottish soldiers felt let down by effete superiors.[1]

Their retribution fell on the Afridis. When they went on to the maidan, they
found a hidden haven. Every inch was tended, with neat homesteads and groves of

fruit-trees in between the tiny fields. The tribe, since arriving perhaps 900 years before in these arid, lofty mountains, had by dint of ceaseless labour turned a desert into a garden. Now nobody was to be seen. The warriors had fled with their families and animals into the hills. The expedition waited for a day or two to see if their leaders would come to parley. Then the soldiers began to burn the houses, and chop down the trees to add to the blaze. A hundred columns of smoke rose into the chill air, blotting out the sun. This had the desired effect. The ragged chieftains appeared, some wearing medals from service as young men in the Indian Army. They agreed to surrender weapons and money, but so sullenly as to make clear that they by no means repented of their marauding ways. They knew the British would have to withdraw as winter closed in over the next few weeks. The Afridis themselves suffered greatly during that winter, yet the spring of 1898 found them as defiant as ever. The Government of India announced a fresh offensive. This, however, was an empty threat.[2]

In fact the episode cost everyone dear. The British had been trying to pacify the region by a rather confused, inconsistent policy of subduing the foothills piecemeal and slowly extending the area of direct rule. But even while civilisation in theory advanced, the tribesmen beyond remained untamed, inciting disarmed cousins lower down to slip across the cordon and join them. The policy had anyway failed to stop the frontier going up in flames, and thus turned out to have been a waste of time, offering no security at all. Worse, these were years of crisis all over the sub-continent, of earthquake, floods, plague, famine, riots, assassinations. They raised again the spectre which ever and anon haunted the British, of anarchy one day making India too hot to hold. That would sound the death-knell of the Empire. The Raj had therefore since 1857 been a military regime. It did continue, if at a less frenetic pace, Lord Dalhousie's secular mission, of westernising through economic development. Otherwise it relied on repression to keep the dusky millions quiet, along the lines of the military administration of Ireland or of the European autocracies.

In this regime the Scots' presence still loomed large. It also set them thinking, and gave scope to their bent for strategic speculation. India posed the Empire its major military problem, in the matter of internal security, and then because she contained on the North-West Frontier the sole colonial territory defended by an army, rather than by a fleet. The threat came from wild men of the hills but more, or so it was thought, from Russia. In retrospect, fears of the Czar exploiting tribal unrest to send his divisions across the Hindu Kush seem overdone. When his successors at last did, in 1979, their conquests proved little more durable than British ones of an earlier era. Still, the menace had long been taken seriously. It gave rise to the Great Game, as irresistible to the bravado and individualism of the Scots as to their penchant for analysis. Henry Dundas, pondering the consequences of Napoleon's invasion of Egypt in 1798, had been the first to warn of the peril if Russia supplanted Turkey and Persia as the dominant power in Central Asia. A line of his compatriots, from John Malcolm and Mountstuart Elphinstone onwards, then scouted these debatable lands:

John Kinneir, Alexander Burnes, William Lockhart, Andrew Dalgleish, George Robertson. Some paid for arduous and lonely work with horrible deaths.[3]

Another in that line, and the foremost military theorist among them, was Charles MacGregor. Brought up in Perthshire, he joined the Indian Army just in time to see service during the Mutiny. Then this young man sat down to think out the strategic implications. His response was the so-called forward policy, of a systematic defence in depth also capable of offence. It first saw light in his treatise *Mountain Warfare* (1866), based on his own experience meanwhile in Bhutan. As a result, he was appointed to the North-West Frontier, where he set himself to put the policy into practice. He sent out a network of secret agents. He called for a single commissioner to oversee the whole region. He urged a diplomatic initiative in the native states, especially Afghanistan, where he travelled in person. Finally, he proposed a thorough reform of the whole Indian Army, to turn it into a professional force on European lines with, in one sense, a European purpose, to take and hold territory on the frontiers. Its existing primary task of controlling the internal population it would then pass on; MacGregor thought that could be left to irregular cavalry. Instead, the conditions here dictated that Britain should adopt a continental strategy, in contrast to the maritime strategy by which she had been accustomed to defend her Empire. It was a good Scottish thesis, of realistic deduction from first principles.

MacGregor had made little progress in getting his ideas across by the time of the next big test of British arms, the Second Afghan War of 1878–80. He served with distinction in the war, then wrote, in six volumes, its official history. He used this chance to demonstrate how defeat could have been turned into victory if he had been listened to. In Calcutta the viceroy was now ready to listen, but not his political masters in London. They suppressed MacGregor's history, which only appeared as an uncontroversial condensation in 1924. At least his career did not suffer, for he was appointed quartermaster-general of the Indian Army, also in charge of military intelligence. He was still set on telling his superiors what they did not want to hear. With the help of brother Scots, including his commander-in-chief, Donald Stewart, and his friends James Grierson, George Napier and Robert Sandeman, he wrote a still more exhaustive but this time confidential report, *Defence of India*.[4]

Its message was stark. It assumed an advance by the Russians into Afghanistan to be likely, rather than merely possible, and showed in detail how they could build up a strength which the Indian Army would be unable to defeat. The answer put forward was, first, to expand that army on the lines Macgregor had already set out. It should then occupy strongholds as far west as Herat and Kandahar. Afterwards, the territories of the extended frontier should be bound to India with roads and railways, while certain tribes were paid to remain amenable, or in effect to represent the British in their wars with the rest, while being converted into peaceful tillers of the soil. It was to Sandeman, who like him had long personal experience of spying out the Himalayan fastnesses, that MacGregor owed this concept: though perhaps both were indebted to a piece of common knowledge among Scots, the role of Clan Campbell in the Highlands of old. MacGregor meant not only to keep the Russians out of Afghanistan but also, by in time enlarging the system, to drive them from Turkestan and the Caucasus as well. Secret though it was meant to be, he circulated his report, even in London. But there he merely provoked outrage in the Liberal Cabinet that a mere soldier should meddle in matters proper to high diplomacy. His hawkish tone came across as offensive. Perhaps more suspect still was his stress on an Indian nation-in-arms as the sole way to maintain its own security, a sort of military orientalism. That seemed to imply, somewhere along the road, national autonomy.

There indeed existed a logical link between professionalism in the Indian Army, as something separate and distinct from the British one, and the germ of a conviction that the obligations of defence were inseparable from nationhood. MacGregor recognised India's strategy to be necessarily different from Britain's, and in this sense prepared for a consciousness of Indian independence. But his new work never saw the light of day either. He himself fell ill and died in Egypt while travelling home on leave in 1887, mourned as an officer of the highest courage, tenacity and intellect. Nobody else would bring the same coherence to military policy in the sub-continent, as the endless problems on the frontier showed. Whitehall continued to regard the Indian Army as an auxiliary of the British one.[5]

An analogous germ of conviction could be found among Scots in quite different walks of Indian life. They maintained their role in the economy. When Charles Dilke came on a visit in the 1860s, he wrote: 'Englishmen could not long survive the work, but the Bombay merchants are all Scotch . . . For every Englishman who has worked himself up to wealth from small beginnings without external aid, you find ten Scotsmen. It is strange, indeed, that Scotland has not become the popular name for the United Kingdom'. This prominence could be traced back for a century or more, to the free merchants who, on the system of private partnership, had run the country trade under the nose of the East India Company. Well before it went into terminal decline, they took over most of the sub-continent's foreign commerce. They did so with the collusion of their many countrymen serving in the company, which granted licences to chosen traders for traffic which it could not itself handle. They therefore had an oligopoly of their own. The system came largely to an end in 1813, when the company lost its Indian monopoly, and entirely in 1833, when it ceased to be a commercial operation. Then an age of unfettered free trade ostensibly dawned in the sub-continent. It was a paradox that soon an age of officially promoted development dawned too, under Dalhousie and his successors. In a general sense they believed in political economy. But this, imprecise on crucial points, could mean many things to many people. When it seemed not to be working, and when reference was made to the classical texts, they were found far from rigid on the matter of promoting development. Besides, the Scottish intellectual tradition stressed comprehensiveness at the expense of logical rigour. If supreme political power in India offered economic advantages, Scots were not the ones to spurn them. Their own clannishness tempted them, here as elsewhere, towards the manipulation of markets.

That was consistent with a certain degree of official *dirigisme*, as long as it benefited themselves, of course, but as long as it also brought actual economic advance. Keeping India backward formed no part of the Scottish agenda.

The liberalisation of the 1830s had one immediate and startling effect, in causing many of the free merchants' partnerships to fail. Still, those that survived built up very big business indeed. With all constraints on their traditional middleman's function fallen away, they took over the trade between Britain and India. Out of that a more complex role evolved. The merchants dealt with individual buyers at home and producers in the sub-continent, or *vice versa*, but lay under no obligation to restrict their favour to single customers. On the contrary, they had every incentive to assume multiple agencies and construct from them intricate trading networks. Thus they positioned themselves to offer their principals a range of commercial facilities. They themselves began to move into agricultural production, especially of tea and jute. Before long, advanced technology arrived from Britain, to be put to use in mining coal and ore. These in turn required the latest means of transport, in railways and shipping. A more advanced economy needed banking and the issue of bank-notes, finance and insurance, and investment in urban property. In all these fields the partnerships established a powerful presence.[6]

Their expansion was often sustained by links with the homeland. The Gladstones, for instance, deploying some of the fortune they made in Liverpool, had entered India in 1818 with a company, successively known as Gillanders, Arbuthnot & Co and Ogilvy, Gillanders & Co, composed of country cousins from the North of Scotland. These brought it through the crisis of the 1830s, and for the rest of the century could provide a well-feathered oriental nest to any member of the clan; the Prime Minister, William Gladstone, did not disdain to send out one of his own sons. The firm had a special line in finance, with several of its partners serving also on the board of the Bank of Bengal. Here Steuart Gladstone distinguished himself enough to be appointed Governor of the Bank of England in 1899.

Glasgow had especially strong connections with the sub-continent. Of many examples perhaps the best was James Finlay & Co, established back in 1745 as a West Indian merchant. The son of the founder, Kirkman Finlay, became the greatest cotton king, indeed, on the booty from blockade-busting in Napoleonic Europe, the leading capitalist in Scotland. It was he, by then MP for his native city, who sent its first ship to Bengal in 1813, as soon as the East India Company's monopoly ended. Before long he was trading to all the continents, out of Manchester and Liverpool as well. But from the 1860s the firm moved eastwards, prompted by a quest for new supplies of cotton when the American Civil War cut old ones off. The Scottish textile industry continued to decline all the same, and Finlay's got out of it, turning instead to Indian tea and jute. Though several partners disliked the shift, the head of the house in this era, John Muir, pushed it through with triumphant results. They carried him to the highest honour his hometown could bestow, the Lord Provost-ship. He more than repaid that debt in turn, by organising the Great Exhibition of

1888, the declaration to the world that it had a new cosmopolis. He promoted the Act of Parliament in 1891 extending its boundaries to make it indeed the second city of the Empire. For good measure he gave it the bridge by which the Great Western Road crosses the River Kelvin, the St Andrew's Halls, the Mitchell Library and electric lighting. In his hands, the progress of India and of Glasgow went together.[7]

Today such links are seen rather as exploitative, the means of transferring to the wealthy mother country the product of primitive native labour. But the Scots often felt happy to work with the Indians, happier perhaps than to work with the English. Wallace Bros, founded in Bombay in 1842, brought in Parsees to a house exchanging piece-goods from Manchester for Burmese teak, in which they developed the international market. Still under-capitalised, they opted in 1862 to transform themselves into one of the first limited companies, the Bombay Burmah Trading Corporation, again with Scots and Indian directors. That kind of activity in a sense continued the country trade, widening exchanges between India and third countries. A similar example was the Glaswegian partnership of W.R. Paterson & Co, which had set up in Manila, Batavia and Singapore. In 1856 it won a concession from the white Rajah of Borneo, James Brooke, who wanted to promote his free port of Kuching. This was the start of the Borneo Company. It channelled proceeds from the island's gold and other metals to a branch in Calcutta which invested and traded in its turn. India became a magnet for mobile Scots and their money: they allowed, in these and other cases, developments that she might not have been able to manage for herself.[8]

The extraction of profit often required large investment first. Scots showed a striking tendency to set up essentially Indian companies, unconnected with the homeland except in senior personnel. At any rate, their contribution to the Scottish economy was no more than marginal and, if they remained private partnerships, they did not even distribute their dividends very widely. In the course of time, they put down Indian roots. Two of the sub-continent's biggest corporations were Burn & Co and Andrew Yule & Co. The first could trace its origin back to the previous century, but was refounded in the 1830s. It grew into the East's major producer of iron and steel, with a wide range of interests in railways, shipbuilding and general engineering. In 1895 it became a public limited company, one of the few expatriate firms to do so, not least because it wanted to attract Indian capital. The second also arose from long-standing links with Calcutta, and was refounded by Andrew Yule of Stonehaven, who went out, not yet aged 30, in 1863. He dealt in all the staples of the sub-continent, at first tea and coal, later jute and cotton, acquiring large stakes in their production, diversifying also into finance and insurance. After a quarter-century, he handed over to his brother George, as notable for his political as for his economic activities. In that same year of 1888 he was elected president of the Indian National Congress.

Despite the similarity in corporate structure, we may distinguish all these from the free merchants, men of the old commercial Empire with no aims beyond trade in the traditional staples. Their successors, soon known as the agency houses, were rather instruments of the Victorian secular mission, the drive to transform and modernise India. Their diverse interests introduced a range of western technologies. Above all, they brought capitalism and its institutions into the country. Once, after starting as merchants, they came to act for many different customers together, it was easy for them to move over into management, then production. People from home keen to invest, but unfamiliar with local conditions, turned to the houses with their established teams and proven records, for the mere 10 per cent of turnover that these charged in commission. At a certain stage, the roles of middleman and entrepreneur reversed, and agents became principals. Success, experience and creditworthiness let the houses float new firms themselves, typically holding only a small share of the equity, since they needed no more for control. By the end of the century, they could offer a package deal of everything that India otherwise lacked: capital, modern technical and managerial expertise, international commercial information, exporting networks. They spanned all the links from the peasant producers in the countryside to the final markets in the outside world.

Indian nationalist historiography, with its western hangers-on, has taken a dim view of these Scottish activities. The charge is that the agency houses produced not general economic advance, but restricted enclaves of it, notably in mercantile eastern India. There only the agencies connected the plantations, mines and factories. These did not deal with one another, or lay down their own economic linkages to the hinterland. So, for example, a house running a coalmine and a jute mill would not use the association to provide cheap energy for manufacture. On the contrary, it sold coal to the mill at a fixed price well above the going rate: the mine had a captive market and earned monopolistic profits at the expense of the mill's shareholders. The agencies may also have found easier access to credit than others. The board of the Bank of Bengal, for instance, always drew several of its directors from their ranks. Between its foundation and its winding up, 16 houses were thus represented, five of them continuously. All this is held to have been typical of the way that their restrictive practices kept investors at their mercy and barred competition from new entrants. In sum, under the manipulations of Scottish capital especially, India never saw the technological innovation or bold investment that might have changed hers into an industrial economy on European lines. Instead she remained a primarily agricultural client, a supplier of raw materials to Britain, and a market for British goods.[9]

The Government of India is accused of colluding in all this. An example came in the 1890s when a Scot, the 9th Earl of Elgin, was Viceroy. A dynastic preference often prevailed in appointments to this supreme office; his father, the Governor-General of Canada and High Commissioner to China, had himself been promoted Viceroy in 1861 but died worn-out within 18 months. The son proved nothing like so adept a ruler. Rather he presided over a stifling bureaucracy more intent on its own procedures, and on causing no offence to London, than on tackling the country's problems. Hence Elgin's treatment of competition between British and Indian textiles. Competitive advantage had swung to and fro between the two. During the eighteenth century, India was a net exporter of textiles to Britain. The rise of mechanised production at home reversed this. The Government of India then encouraged cultivation of cotton, to make her an exporter of the raw commodity. But soon the profits allowed industrial mills owned and run by natives to be set up on the spot, notably in Bombay, putting India once again in a position to compete. Elgin's intervention arose not so much from that as from the deficit in his budget. He proposed to cover it by a tax on imports of British cotton. London objected, on grounds of free trade. When Elgin imposed a tariff all the same, it was vetoed. Despite support from Indian opinion, the Viceroy backed down, exempting cotton from the impost and reducing it for other materials. Evidently the fiscal freedom claimed by the colonies of British settlement could not be permitted to India, though her economy was more important than theirs, and her people poorer. In a contest between Lancashire and Bombay, the authorities took Lancashire's side.[10]

But there were more complex and on the whole happier stories. In jute, a similar contest took place between Dundee and Calcutta, the industry being as important to the one as to the other. The raw material was grown in Bengal. Its manufacture in Scotland for baling and the like started during the 1830s. It was originally processed along with other coarse materials, but in the end, as the cheapest, it displaced the rest. Out of this process of substitution arose one of the world's great textile industries, employing up to 30,000 people in Dundee's mills. It first boomed during the Crimean War, which at once raised demand for jute, because of the need for sandbags, while cutting off supply of a major alternative, Russian flax. The demand afterwards sustained itself since war was always going on somewhere, though much jute would also be used for packing agricultural produce in India, and be exported for that purpose elsewhere. In fact Dundee found it hard to cope with the demand. Rather than ship more raw jute to Scotland, it seemed easier to start production in Calcutta. Scots, including essential workers from Dundee, opened a mill at Serampore in 1855, by that fact also introducing mechanisation to India. Soon more and more mills were being built on an ever larger scale, prompted by the huge profits. Nearly all the capital came from Scotland: Thomas Duff alone founded three mills after 1874 with an outlay of £1.3 million, one-eighth of total investment in the industry. Calcutta achieved a breakthrough by the 1880s, when it had 23 mills employing 48,000 hands.[11]

The position of jute was now similar to that of cotton, in that Britain and India could compete with each other, but different in that jute was manufactured at both ends by Scots. The conduct of Indian Scots under these circumstances proved interesting. In 1884 they organised themselves in the Indian Jute Mill Association, a cartel like those that companies at home in Scotland were starting to form. This had powers to enforce on its members measures to counter the trade cycle, to shorten working time or seal looms if prices came under threat. One aim was to keep native rivals out, and this succeeded, to judge from the fact that existing firms built most new mills. They also worked with the agency houses, which often held shares in them, because markets for jute, by contrast with the finer cotton, had to be sought out, and international contacts were vital. The mill-owners pressed the Government, too, for incentives to increase the area of cultivation and the yield of raw jute. The total effect was to keep prices up, costs down and production growing. From the 1890s the Indian industry enjoyed an unbroken record of prosperity, expanding in America and even capturing some segments of the British market. By the First World War, Calcutta housed 38 mills and 184,000 workers, including 1000 Scots.

But all this cloaked another purpose, of competing against the Scots of Scotland: an odd compulsion, since some had interests at both ends and Scottish machines kept the Indian industry running. The Dundonians, under pressure, ascribed Calcutta's success to conditions of virtual slavery in the mills there. Their senior MP, Sir John Leng, went out in 1894 to investigate and get the Government of India to do something. To his surprise he found the workers in certain respects better off than those at home, with medical attendants and superior latrines. So there was no magic wand to wave and turn the pressure down. Rather it built up. By 1908 Calcutta's production outstripped Dundee's. The latter then always had to struggle to hold its position and in the long run could not. In 1914, it was producing the same volume of jute as 30 years before, while Europe was consuming four times and India six times as much, or half the total crop; the relative Scottish share of expanding markets was thus plummeting, with no remedy in sight. By efficiency, and by shifting from common sacking to finer specialities, Dundee did maintain its absolute level of output. Yet from Calcutta, too, exports of finished products were now only a little lower than those of the raw material. Indian Scots would switch to a higher grade of product, and encroach even on Dundee's innovations. At least, however, the industry in India remained under Scottish direction till the independence of the country in 1947.

Jute offers a rare example of a great industry which emerged in the Empire and trounced its rival back home, standing on its head the theory of imperial exploitation. If we recall also how jute, along with other sectors favoured by Scots, played a big part in transforming Calcutta from a trading and financial into a manufacturing centre, it seems doubtful whether the city's story can be captured by the single, simple line of post-colonial conventional wisdom.

While the situation varied from sector to sector, seldom were capital and management entirely appropriated by foreigners. Indians on the whole controlled cotton and steel, though there also employing Scottish technicians. The British controlled the coalmines and plantations, and won most of the contracts on public works. As for transport, the agency houses did seem to block the emergence of Indian steam-shipping companies, yet they could not prevent the rise of Chinese rivalry in the eastern seas, so the reason must have lain in something other than imperialist manipulation. It may be conceded that the India Office in London did not always play fair with natives who sought to compete. But the Government of India showed itself more sympathetic, if not consistently so. And the expatriate commercial community was committed to economic development. It would be a calumny on William Mackinnon or James Mackay to say they had no interest in the future of the country which enriched them, but simply feathered their Scottish nests. They did bring money home, as well as investing elsewhere in the Empire. But their role in capitalising the sub-continent's infrastructure and future industries, then helping these to grow through the economies of scale in management offered by the agency houses, should not be underestimated. The system, if peculiar to India, was a means by which from an existing low base she could enter the global economy. It is true that she would never become much of an industrial power under the Raj, or even in the first half-century of her independence. But if one day she does, the origins of that status will have to be traced back, in some part, to these enterprising Scots.[12]

Wherever they were, Scots seldom ignored the political implications of economic development. Nor did they in India. Yule marked his election as president of the Indian National Congress with a stirring declaration of liberalism. Britain and India would be united 'not by the hard and brittle bonds of arbitrary rule which may snap at any moment, but by the flexible and more enduring ligaments of common interests promoted and common duties discharged'. For a businessman, he held unusual opinions. For a Scot, they were not so unusual. Yet Scots could no longer exert much direct political influence on the Raj. They did provide the odd Viceroy. But they had never got over the introduction of competitive examinations for the Indian Civil Service in 1853, which permanently and drastically cut the numbers of them in positions of authority. Even now, they won on average just three or four of the 30 annual appointments. Among the lucky few was John Wilson, a son of the manse from Perth, who told the rest that 'interest is of almost no avail in India, and it is very seldom that one hears of anything like favouritism or jobbery in the distribution of posts'. This news was liable, if anything, to put them off, but he assured them they would do better if more of them applied: 'It is a mistake to suppose, as some have done, that the examinations are so conducted as to favour lads educated under the English public-school system'. His wife Anne was meanwhile writing home with complaints of its tyranny: 'I think I deserve some pity for being an inaccurate Celt, without any bump for officialdom or ability to remember anyone's official position or title'. Even her interest in Indian music, she added, raised eyebrows.[13]

The fact was that the administration had been anglicised. James Bryce, MP for Aberdeen South and imperial statesman in waiting, arrived on a tour in 1888. He found the Indian Civil Service 'rather wanting in imagination and sympathy, less inspired by the extraordinary and unprecedented phenomena of the country than might have been expected . . . too conventionally English.' He and other Scots of course remained, out of sentiment, interest and conviction, loyal to the Crown and to the Empire. If they were reluctant to cause trouble, it might still be legitimate to look for a Scottish accent in their commentaries, for nuances that reveal a different mentality.

It may be discovered, for example, in a few liberal paternalists surviving from the old days. George Campbell was, even beyond the Mutiny, capable of an enlightened comparative approach to this alien society: he thought the Hindus looked after their poor better than the British, and worked harder than the Celts. In the civil administration of Oudh he tempered the severity of repression after 1857. Then he devoted the rest of his career to improving the lot of the ryot. This now grew worse, for the decision was taken to extend the zemindari system to regions which had never known it, because of its supposed virtue in maintaining order. Instead, as Campbell remarked, 'Oudh threatened to become another Ireland'. At the close of his service, in 1871–4, he was promoted Governor of Bengal. There he did what he could to reform the Permanent Settlement of 1793, still the main source of revenue in the province, and to dispone the land on its cultivators under fixed and secure tenure: 'Our *raison d'être* in India is the failure of the native rulers and upper classes, and . . . our main function is to look to the interests and happiness of the masses'. But he could achieve little before he went home, to become MP for Kirkcaldy.[14]

Like-minded Scots of a younger generation tended in the end to fall foul of a harsher Raj. Allan Octavian Hume was the son of Joseph Hume, the sole Scottish radical to have reached the House of Commons under the Dundas despotism. A many-sided man, he befriended one of the first natives to get into the Indian Civil Service, Surendranath Banerji, who recalled that 'with the shrewdness and practical sense of the Scotsman he combined the generous warmth and the fiery impulsiveness of the Oriental'. Late in life he fell under the spell of Madame Blavatsky and the teachings of theosophy. But he had started as a paragon of administrative efficiency, had served in a district of Bengal, fought in the Mutiny, then had risen to become Secretary to the Government of India. From this height he was, however, dismissed in 1879 on grounds of insubordination. The Viceroy, to whom he had expressed his progressive views too freely, kicked him downstairs to the revenue board at Allahabad. There he sensibly spent his time on his own hobbies: he edited an ornithological journal, *Stray Feathers*, and wrote the standard work on *The Game Birds of India*. Soon he quit the service altogether.[15]

He left behind a younger friend, William Wedderburn, one of the few scions of an Old Indian family to spring the hurdle of the examinations. He too had a distinguished career, finishing as Chief Secretary to the Government of Bombay. He took over from Campbell as champion of the ryots. The worst aspect of their new situation was the standard assessment. It did not, like the previous tax on them, vary with the crop, so it hit them hard in a bad year. Since it also had to be paid in cash, it spawned moneylending and extortion. Conditions in the Deccan grew bad enough to prompt a virtual revolt by the peasants in 1875. Wedderburn proposed a package of remedies: a permanent settlement by which they would pay an annual sixteenth of their gross produce; agricultural banks to provide capital at moderate rates;

THE ADVANCE OF SIR COLIN CAMPBELL.

WITH THE
BRAVEST OF THE BRAVE.
DESCRIPTIVE OF THE
FALL OF LUCKNOW.
ARRANGED FOR THE PIANOFORTE
BY
JOHN PRIDHAM.

Pr. 2.6

60 The grizzled Glaswegian, Colin Campbell (1792–1863), leads his troops towards Lucknow, all in full Highland dress under the Indian sun. The British community in the city was besieged in the Residency, and a long period of street-fighting was needed to break through to them. The pipers played 'The Campbells are Coming' to buoy their hopes. This is the cover of the sheet music for 'The Advance of Sir Colin Campbell'. (Trustees of the National Museums of Scotland)

61 James Bruce, Earl of Elgin (1811–1863), had a long, versatile and arduous career as imperial pronconsul, serving in Jamaica, in Canada (where he witnessed the Parliament being burned down (Plate 44)), in China (where he burned down the Summer Palace) and finally as Viceroy of India, where he died exhausted at the beginning of his term of office. (Fife Council)

62 The Earl of Elgin chastises the Emperor of China. Among the Chinese, he is remembered as the most barbarous of barbarians, his name written in ideographs which mean 'Uncontrollably Fierce'. Yet he was a humane and cultured man, just more exasperated than others at the deliberately obstructive diplomacy of the Celestial Empire. (*Punch*, 4 November 1860)

63 In splendid accoutrement, General James Hope Grant (1808–1875), of Kilgraston House, Bridge of Earn, surveys a tropic field, wearing his family's tartan with ostrich feathers on a helmet designed by himself. Grant accompanied the Earl of Elgin on his expedition to China and directed operations which brought the allied forces, British and French, to the gates of Peking. It was Chinese intransigence, even in these desperate straits, which prompted them to destroy the Summer Palace. (SNPG)

64 Alexander Duff (1806–1878), from Moulin, Perthshire, faced as a missionary in India not a primitive society but an ancient civilisation. He judged it to be as irredeemable as Africa, though easier to westernise because more open to the values which could be disseminated by Scottish schooling. What he created was not a Christian India, but an educated elite which would in due course demand political power from its imperial masters. (SNPG)

65 The greatest Scottish mind of the nineteenth century, William Robertson Smith (1846–1894), by apparently arid labours in Semitic philology unlocked the key to understanding the role of religion in society. This was far too strong meat for Scotland, where he was charged with heresy and deposed from his academic chair at Aberdeen. (SNPG)

66 What caused all the trouble in China. Indian opium was imported by western traders in order to finance their exports of Chinese tea. The drug soon caused severe social problems. But these were thought to be outweighed by the benefits of opening the Celestial Empire to free trade. It led to the Opium Wars and the foundation of Hong Kong. The illustration, 'Opium Smoking', is taken from John Thomson's *The Land and the People of China* (1876). Like John Kirk (Plates 51–2), Thomson was a photographer. The picture below, of a temple in the grounds of the Summer Palace, is from his *Through China with a Camera*. (Trustees of the National Library of Scotland)

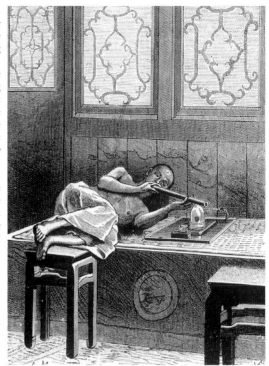

67 William Jardine (1784–1843), born near Lochmaben, was the more tough-minded of the two Scots who founded in 1832 the greatest of the Chinese trading houses, Jardine Matheson. Its basic business was drug-running and its activities led to the Opium Wars. The Bible-reading Jardine urged an aggressive policy on the British Government, as a result of which it won the cession of Hong Kong in 1842. (Private collection)

68 The suave and handsome Highlander, Alexander Matheson (1796–1878), was Jardine's partner. A man of brilliant commercial flair, he also prided himself on being an intellectual acquainted with the canonic texts of political economy. He was convinced that China would benefit from being prised open to free trade, even by means of drugs. With his fortune he bought the Island of Lewis, where he followed a policy of clearance and development. (Private collection)

69 The *Cutty Sark* (above) and her rival the *Thermopylae* (both from Scottish yards) were the most famous of the clippers which brought tea from China to Britain. They were the finest development of sailing ships, built for high speed on the high seas. Since the freshness of each year's harvest was a great selling point, they raced one another along the 10,000 miles home. Scottish firms dominated the trade: Cutty Sark means short shirt, or vest, in Scots. (Above: private collection; below: Aberdeen Maritime Museum)

70 Thomas Brisbane (1773–1860), from Ayrshire, succeeded Lachlan Macquarie as Governor of New South Wales but, while also a military man himself, presented a mild and pleasant contrast with his martinet of a predecessor. He introduced further reforms for the benefit of convicts who had completed their sentences, allowing a united community to be eventually formed with the free settlers arriving in increasing numbers. (Trustees of the National Library of Scotland)

71 The irascible John Dunmore Lang (1799–1878), from Greenock, introduced Presbyterianism, as a formal structure, to Australia. In his adopted country he is more widely remembered as the earliest advocate of national independence, though it is sometimes conveniently forgotten that his motive was to stop the population becoming too Irish. He thought a colony peopled by Scots would be far preferable. (Trustees of the National Library of Scotland)

72 John Leyden (1775–1811) was a poet from the Scottish Borders, beloved of Sir Walter Scott. For a living he had to rely on his medical training, which allowed him to go and practise in India. But his deepest interests were philological, and he became the first European expert on the Malay languages. He died while delving into the archives of Batavia in the Dutch East Indies, captured by a Scottish-led expedition in 1811. (SNPG)

FIRST SCOTTISH
COLONY for
New Zealand

That Fine **TEAK-BUILT**

FAST

SAILING **SHIP**

BENGAL MERCHANT,

501 Tons Register---JOHN HEMERY, COMMANDER,

WILL POSITIVELY

SAIL FROM PORT-GLASGOW

For NEW ZEALAND,

With the first Body of Settlers

FROM SCOTLAND,

On FRIDAY, Oct. 25.

SINGLE WOMEN, going out as Servants to Cabin Passengers, or in charge of Married Emigrants, will receive a *Free Passage* on board of this Ship.

All Goods and Luggage must be forwarded by the **20th** instant *at latest*, on which day the Ship will clear out.

For *Freight* (having room for dead Weight and Measurement Goods) and *Passage*, apply to

JOHN CRAWFORD,
24, QUEEN STREET.

NEW ZEALAND LAND CO.'s OFFICE,
GLASGOW, 5th Oct. 1839.

J. Clark, Printer, Argus Office.

73 The first Scottish party of colonists which left for Port Nicholson (Wellington), New Zealand in 1839 on the *Bengal Merchant* was soon followed by several more: the city of Dunedin in South Island, given the Gaelic name for Edinburgh, would be founded in 1843. This new country was thought especially desirable by members of the Free Church of Scotland, though in the event it proved impossible to maintain there the strict moral and social standards they brought with them. (Glasgow Museums: The People's Palace)

NOTICE TO SHIPPERS.
HAS ROOM FOR EIGHTY TONS CARGO.

AT GLASGOW—FOR SAN FRANCISCO DIRECT.

THE well-known British-built Brig MAR-THA, 197 tons register, (No. 334 in book,) A 1 at Lloyd's, is now actively Loading.
For freight or passage, apply, in Liverpool, to Messrs. Muller & Co. ; here, to
ORR & DAVIE,
20 St. Enoch Square.
Glasgow, 15th March, 1853.

** All former Advertisements withdrawn.

NOTICE TO SHIPPERS.

AT GLASGOW—FOR MELBOURNE, PORT-PHILIP.

THE well-known A 1 at Lloyd's Aberdeen Clipper-Barque ELIZA LEISHMAN, 298 tons register, is now in Port, and will be despatched instanter.
This fine Ship is well and favourably known in the Indian trade from the rapidity of its passages.
For freight or passage, apply to the owners, Messrs. Neilson & M'Intosh, 129 Stockwell Street ; or to
POTTER, WILSON & CO.,
28 St. Enoch Square ; or
ORR & DAVIE, Brokers,
20 St. Enoch Square.
Glasgow, 19th March, 1853.

A REGULAR TRADER.

AT GLASGOW—FOR QUEBEC,

THE very fine fast-sailing first-class Barque ACADIA, 364 tons per register, JOHN YOUNGER, Commander, now loading, and will be despatched 28th March.
For freight or passage, apply to
WILSON BROTHERS,
125 Buchanan Street.

TO SUCCEED THE ACADIA.

AT GLASGOW—FOR QUEBEC.

THE well-known very fast-sailing Barque HEROINE, 374 tons per register, *Æ 1 (in red), and coppered, JOHN MELDRUM, Commander, now in port, and having the principal portion of her cargo engaged, will be despatched 1st April.
For freight or passage, apply to
WILSON BROTHERS,
125 Buchanan Street.

AT GLASGOW—FOR LISBON.

THE remarkably fast-sailing, Clipper-built Schooner "VICTORIA," 112 tons, A 1, and coppered, Captain JAMES SMITH, will be despatched on Thursday, 24th March.
Apply to

WILSON BROTHERS,
125 Buchanan Street.
To be succeeded by the A 1 Clipper "CINTRA."

NOTICE TO PASSENGERS PER SHIP "ABDALLA," FOR MELBOURNE.

PASSENGERS per *"Abdalla"* are respectfully requested to have that portion of their Luggage which is not wanted on the voyage put alongside the Ship at Lancefield Quay, Broomielaw, on Thursday and Friday, 24th and 25th inst. The above to be distinctly marked with the words "Not wanted on the Voyage."
MACCALLUM & GRAHAM,
110 Buchanan Street.

CLYDE LINE OF PACKETS TO THE GOLD REGIONS.

Now Loading at Lancefield Quay, North Side of the River.

AT GLASGOW—FOR MELBOURNE, PORT-PHILIP, DIRECT.

THE magnificent new Three-decked Frigate-built Ship CATHERINE GLEN, 1327 tons register, 2100 tons burthen, A 1 at Lloyd's, J. H. WALKER, Commander, who has great experience in the Australian Trade.
As a Passenger Ship, this Vessel stands unrivalled, and her Commander's ability and kindness to his Passengers, are well known. The number of Passengers will be restricted to two-thirds what the Law would allow her to carry, thus affording a most select, agreeable, and comfortable conveyance.

FARES.

	Guineas.		Guineas.
First-Class Cabin,	40	Intermediate	20
Second Do	24	Steerage, a few in 'twixt decks,	18

Including a most liberal scale of Provisions of the very best quality.
Carries an Experienced Surgeon.
This Vessel will be fitted out under the personal inspection of Captain Keele, R.N., her Majesty's Emigration Surveyor.
For freight or passage, apply to the undersigned, who are despatching a succession of first-class Regular Packets.
PETER & THOMSON AIKMAN,
110 Buchanan Street.
Glasgow, March 15, 1853.

Is proceeding rapidly with her loading at Shed No. 12 South Side, and will be despatched in a few days.

AT GLASGOW—FOR MELBOURNE, DIRECT,
LANDING CARGO ON THE WHARF THERE.

THE very fast-sailing A 1 Schooner ELIZA-BETH, 110 tons register, Captain SHARPE, has still room for a small quantity of Light Freight.
This Vessel has excellent accommodation for 8 Cabin Passengers. Fare, 25 Guineas each. No berths secured till half the passage money is paid.
For freight or passage, immediate application for which is necessary, apply to Messrs. James Mackenzie & Co., National Bank Buildings ; or to
O'HALLORAN & BROWN,
91 Buchanan Street.

Is now in Port, will be at a loading berth immediately, and sail in about Ten days.

AT GLASGOW—FOR GEELONG, DIRECT.

THE fine fast-sailing Brig VIGILANT, 134 tons register.
For freight or passage, apply to Messrs. M'Keand, Smith, & Co., Dixon Street ; or to
O'HALLORAN & BROWN,
91 Buchanan Street.
Glasgow, 14th March, 1853.

AT THE BROOMIELAW—FOR SYDNEY, N.S.W.

THE very fast-sailing A 1 coppered Barque RE-PEATER, 296 tons register, JOHN WILSON, Commander, is now rapidly proceeding with her loading at Shed No. 22 South Side, and will sail pointedly 28th instant.
Apply to

JOHN & WALTER SCOTT,
17 Gordon Street ; or
PATRICK HENDERSON & CO.,
4 Bothwell Street.
Glasgow, 19th March, 1853.

74 Here is a sample of the destinations available by sea from Glasgow in 1853, when the city was reaching its height as a centre of shipping. Australia, where the gold rush was on, is heavily represented, but North America and Europe figure too. There were as yet few ships designed with passengers in mind, and the advertisements stress that the notoriously uncomfortable passages will be as short as possible. (Mitchell Library, Glasgow)

The Companies' Acts 1862 to 1890.

COMPANY LIMITED BY SHARES.

MEMORANDUM OF ASSOCIATION

OF

The Lanarkshire Gold Mines of Australia, Limited.

I.—The name of the Company is THE LANARKSHIRE GOLD MINES OF AUSTRALIA, LIMITED.

II.—The Registered Office of the Company will be situated in Scotland.

III.—The objects for which the Company is established are :—

(a) Primarily, and without prejudice to the other objects of the Company, to adopt and carry into effect, with or without modification, a Contract, expressed to be made between John Thomson, Mine Manager, Coolgardie, Western Australia, presently residing at Law, by Carluke, in the County of Lanark, Scotland, of the first part ; and Thomas Rae, Solicitor, Wishaw, as Trustee for and on behalf of this Company, of date 3rd May 1898, of the second part ; and to adopt, enter into, and carry into effect any other agreement entered into by these parties or others for and on behalf of the Company.

(b) To prospect and explore for the purpose of obtaining information, and also to acquire under purchase, lease, option, or otherwise, and to develop, work, and turn to account, sell, dispose of, or otherwise deal with lands, mines, mining rights, minerals, forests, claims and property of every kind and description in any part of the world, and particularly, but without prejudice to said generality, lands, mines, and mining, and other properties situated in Australia and the British Colonies, and to enter into treaties and contracts and engagements of any description, and either absolute or conditional with respect thereto.

(c) To search for, prospect, examine, and explore mines and ground supposed to contain minerals or precious stones, and to search for and obtain information in regard to lands, quarries, mines, mining claims, mining districts and localities ; to purchase, take on lease, option, or concession, or otherwise acquire any interest therein, and to hold, sell, dispose of, and deal with lands, forests, mines, and mining rights, and property sup-

75 The thrifty Scottish nation played a disproportionate part in financing the development of imperial resources. Numerous companies for the exploitation of overseas mines, plantations and ranches were launched on the stock exchanges of Glasgow and Edinburgh. This is a typical memorandum of association for one which was founded in 1898 and wound up in 1904. (National Archives of Scotland)

76 Gone more or less completely native, except for perhaps a Victorian reticence about exhibiting too much flesh, Robert Louis Stevenson (1850–1894), barefoot and garlanded, together with his wife Fanny Osbourne and local friends, lolls in the tropical forest of the Marquesas Islands. His splendid house of Vailima, where he died, stands to this day on Samoa. (Trustees of the National Library of Scotland)

77 At the apogee of Empire, in 1901, Glasgow staged an international exhibition which celebrated the city's own place in the grand imperial edifice rather more than any exotic wonders. Beside the Kelvin arose a grand central dome somehow combining the Arabic, the Indian and the Chinese. (Glasgow University Archives)

78 The 2nd Battalion The Black Watch forms the guard of honour at the foot of the throne for the Coronation Durbar in Delhi in 1911, when King George V went to receive the homage of his subjects as Emperor of India. This display of imperial magnificence did not succeed in quelling the disaffection ever more obvious in the sub-continent. (British Library)

79 Gilbert Elliot, 4th Earl of Minto (1847–1914), came of a distinguished proconsular family but preferred polo to politics. All the same he had a real effect on imperial policy. As Governor-general of Canada, he allowed her to go her own way in foreign affairs. As Viceroy of India he brought in the first, cautious forms of constitutional rule. Here he poses with his family outside Government House, Calcutta. (British Library)

80 Scenes of military life: top. 2nd Battalion, The King's Own Scottish Borderers on the North-West Frontier, 1890s (Regimental Headquarters, The King's Own Scottish Borderers); bottom. The Black Watch – looking none too happy – in Boer War uniform, at Wilgo Bridge (The Black Watch Regimental Museum).

81 Scenes of military life (continued): top. Sergeants of the 2nd Battalion, The Black Watch picnic in the Khyber Pass, 1906; bottom. 2nd Battalion, The Black Watch, after Church Parade in the Garrison Chapel, Cherat, India, 1906 or 1907 (both pictures The Black Watch Regimental Museum). **Overleaf**: top. Highland Brigade Gathering, Agra, India, 1914 (competing in the Championship Cup: The Argyll and Sutherland Highlanders, The Black Watch, The Cameron Highlanders, The Highland Light Infantry, The Seaforth Highlanders – The Seaforths won) (The Black Watch Regimental Museum); bottom. Old and New Colour Parties of the 1st Battalion, The Argyll and Sutherland Highlanders after the presentation of New Colours in Cairo, 1926. The CO (centre) is Lt. Col. G.W.Muir, whose son was to win the VC serving with the Argylls in Korea (Regimental Headquarters, The Argyll and Sutherland Highlanders).

jurisdiction over debt for the panchayats, instead of the land courts. All were thrown back at him. In 1887 Wedderburn therefore resigned in his turn.[16]

After that, liberal officials preferred to keep their heads down. A man like the Glaswegian William Hunter, in post till 1895, only revealed his sympathies in orientalist pastimes. His literary output was prodigious. He wrote a novel, *The Old Missionary* (1890), which showed profound disillusion with the efforts to evangelise India. He celebrated traditional ways in his *Annals of Rural Bengal*, and recorded them officially in his *Statistical Account of Bengal*. A further scientific achievement was his comparative dictionary of India's non-Aryan languages. While he corresponded with Mahatma Gandhi, he permitted himself nothing else that could be construed as subversive.

Hume, however, had meanwhile set about founding the Indian National Congress. First, he circularised the graduates of the university of Calcutta. From the response he drew up a preliminary report careful to say that, while reform was necessary, the continued connection of India and Britain remained 'absolutely essential'. On that agenda, he summoned the inaugural meeting to Bombay in December 1885. It had just 70 delegates, mainly lawyers, journalists and schoolmasters, who qualified by paying a small fee. The most important organised element was the Indian Association, grown out of the Brahmo Samaj under the leadership of Banerji, who had turned from government to nationalism. They were all nervous and diffident, protesting their loyalty and more intent, it seemed, on giving thanks for British rule than on demanding changes in it. They would, if he had been willing, have elected as their president Lord Reay, Governor of Bombay. They concluded the proceedings on a restrained note, calling for a Royal Commission on Indian administration, for a cut in military expenditure, for the Viceroy's council to be abolished and some powers to be passed to provincial councils with popular representation. They wanted also greater native recruitment to the Indian Civil Service, and for the judicial bench to be manned from the ranks of barristers, which meant Indians, rather than of officials.

Hume was elected general secretary, a post he retained till 1908. He gave the Congress the air of the idealistic radicalism which he inherited from his father and which now dominated Scottish politics, less radical in deed than in word. The Congress, just as if it had been in Scotland, felt most concerned to put its moral case across to higher authority. It kept on good terms with official India. Once Wedderburn went home in 1889, having just served as president of the fourth Congress, he formed and chaired a British committee, then a parliamentary committee after he was returned as MP for Banffshire in 1892. He found support from, among others, Lord Dalhousie, kinsman of the late Governor-General, W.E. Baxter, one of Dundee's textile tycoons and MP for the city, and Robert Reid, MP for Dumfriesshire and a future Lord Chancellor. Reid urged the importance of introducing an Indian presence at Westminster, achieved in 1895 with the election of a wealthy Parsee, Dadabhai Naoroji. Keir Hardie, entering the House of Commons as Labour's harbinger at the same time, proved to be another ally. To the political convictions of all these Scots, India's backwardness was irrelevant: they saw at least the educated natives not as racially inferior, but as people much like themselves, entitled to the same rights. Other sections of Scottish opinion may have taken no such kindly view, but they certainly left less of an impression. Over the jewel in the Empire's crown, the contest among Scots gave the palm to the liberal side.[17]

The Congress continued as a vehicle for the reasonable, constitutional claims of the new Indian middle class till Lord Curzon's term as Viceroy in 1899–1905. A fresh phase of autocratic, modernising rule with sweeping reforms, partition of Bengal the most hated, at once aroused the opposition of the Congress. By that fact it turned into a movement of the masses. It lurched towards violence with the formation of an anti-European and militantly Hindu wing, the Arya Samaj. This alarmed the moderates, but it did not repel, at least not to the same extent, Hume and Wedderburn, who felt appalled at Curzon's excesses. They published a *Call to Arms* so forthright that the Congress requested its suppression. It enjoined on India the Irish example: 'Be in earnest; disregard all threats – spurn all coercion – prove to the British nation that you really are determined to be fairly dealt with . . . resolved never to give them a day's peace till you *are* so dealt with; that you will spend your time, your money, your lives, if need be'. In its wake, Keir Hardie went to India in 1908, to the dismay of the authorities. He came back with this verdict: 'The Government of India in its present form resembles a huge military despotism tempered somewhat by a civil bureaucracy. Every attempt to win even the smallest modicum of rights is regarded by the Olympians who inhabit the heights of Simla as a menace to the stability of the Empire.' He predicted that the gulf between official and popular India could only widen. He was, of course, right.[18]

CHAPTER TWENTY-SIX

'Thank God we are all Scots here': East Africa

On June 3, 1873, John Kirk, Her Britannic Majesty's consul-general in Zanzibar, presented himself to the ruler of the island, Sultan Barghash. He carried ready with him the text of a treaty between the two monarchs, drafted by the Foreign Office in London, under which the sultan found he was to abolish the slave trade in his realm. Kirk also carried a supplementary telegram straight off the wires saying that, unless Barghash signed, the Royal Navy would mount a blockade and halt the whole of Zanzibar's commerce, in slaves or anything else. What could he do? His economy relied on three things. One was cloves, which his wealthy Arab subjects cultivated on their plantations and exported all over the world. The second was ivory, which they brought down from the interior of Africa. The third was slaves, rounded up there in order to carry the ivory on their own backs; on arrival at the coast, they would be sold for labour on the plantations or transported to the Middle East. Abolition of the slave trade thus seemed bound to ruin the island, not to speak of Barghash himself, for from a duty on it he derived much of his revenue. He tried to argue with Kirk. The British Government's ultimatum broke its existing treaties with his sovereign state and violated the normal international conventions by which monarchs, if in amity, should negotiate as equals. Kirk cut him short, and with less than faultless logic compared the prospective treaty rather to the Peace of Versailles which Germany had imposed on France at the end of their recent war: 'I have come not to discuss, but to dictate,' the Scotsman said. All he would grant was a little time to reflect. In haste the sultan consulted his elders. Some babbled fatuously of fighting. Others thought something might be salvaged if only Barghash could get over to the mainland, to make a stand there or perhaps to find his way to London and put his case. Kirk told him, however, that he would not be allowed to leave the island. If his sovereignty meant so little, there was no choice but surrender. Two days later, he signed the treaty. Messengers were at once dispatched to close down for ever the slave market of Zanzibar. It would be demolished, its ruins in due course to be covered by an ornate Anglican cathedral, with an altar over the spot where the whipping post had stood.[1]

Kirk now became the most powerful political figure in East Africa, an unlikely attainment for this son of a minister of the Free Church of Scotland from Barry, near Dundee. Born in 1832, he had graduated in medicine at the university of Edinburgh, then worked in the Royal Infirmary. But Scottish wanderlust seized him. He went during the Crimean War to serve at a hospital on the Dardanelles, spending his spare time in collection of botanical specimens. That then took him to Kew Gardens in London, where he impressed the director. The result was a recommendation to David Livingstone for Kirk to join him on the ill-fated expedition up the Zambesi. Together, in December 1858, they hauled themselves over blistering rocks to the top of the gorge at Cabora Bassa, to find the river falling steeply through a double bend of rapids which made the higher reaches utterly inaccessible from the lower ones. Kirk knew then that the expedition had failed. He was amazed at Livingstone's deluding himself to the contrary, and trying to delude others. But he kept his thoughts to himself, for he understood that this egotism and petulance were products of humiliation. Kirk soothed it with patient common sense, his first display of the diplomatic skills which would stand him in good stead for the rest of his career. That was lucky for him, because when the two of them returned to Britain to recuperate, he found himself unemployed. It was through Livingstone's good offices that eventually, in 1866, he got a job as medical officer in the British consulate at Zanzibar. They continued to correspond while the doctor wandered round on his final journeys, but did not meet again: except in Westminster Abbey, where Kirk was one of his pall-bearers.[2]

Kirk would make a good deal of what was by any standards a minor post. Except for some moribund Portuguese settlements, the East African coastline offered even now a desolate, not to say dangerous, aspect to foreign eyes. From the southern jungles to the northern deserts it was little marked by contacts with the West; its traditional trade lay with the Arabian Peninsula. As usual, Europeans all the same supposed the unknown interior to hold incalculable riches. To these Zanzibar, the sole entrepot of any importance, must be the key. It already housed American, French and British consulates. The last was the most active, as custodian of relations entered into back in 1798 by the East India Company and Barghash's grandfather, the Sultan of Oman, whose dynasty had seized the island from the Portuguese a century before. The sultan, feeling himself in danger from the Shah of Persia to his north, sought aid from the company. For the sake of political stability along the western littoral of the Arabian Sea, it agreed to help him in return for his co-operation in suppressing piracy. Later, in 1832, Barghash's father, Seyyid Said, moved his capital to Zanzibar. He would be safer there, and the island's trade was making it the richer of the two halves of his realm; since 2500 miles of ocean separated them, he thus became still more dependent on British goodwill. He was not really sovereign in the European sense, for he barely attempted to control his nominal subjects so long as they yielded him revenue. But Britain acknowledged him to be sovereign, at least for the purpose of treaties. These treaties reflected her humanitarian concerns. She did not demand total abolition of slavery, accepting realistically that it was what made Said's odd little polity work. Still, through the stable and tractable regime he created, some pressure might be exerted for restricting the slave trade. Up to his death in 1856, both sides were broadly satisfied with the alliance.

The situation began to alter radically from the period of Kirk's arrival. Said's will had ordained division of his realm, Oman falling to one son, Zanzibar to a second. The Omanis disputed the division, though it seemed to be settled by the time that Barghash, a third son, succeeded as sultan of the island in 1870. Britain anyway recognised him, largely at the behest of Kirk, who thought him more decent than the rest of his plotting kin. He took a benevolent interest in the young man, assuring him of support, even easing at first the pressure against slavery, in the hope of training him up into an amenable but effective ruler as his father had been. Then Zanzibar could look forward all the more to an independent future, which promised also to be a rosy one. The Suez Canal was now open, cutting 4000 miles off the route to Europe. William Mackinnon's British India Steam Navigation Company had already started a regular run to the island. But suddenly disaster struck. In 1872 an epidemic of cholera ravaged Zanzibar, then a hurricane destroyed most of the plantations. Replacement of them required an increased supply of labour, which could only be met by slaves. Britain's worldwide campaign against the slave trade was meanwhile about to move into a final, decisive phase. It had been more or less suppressed in West Africa. Humanitarian interests demanded the same in East Africa. They soon had behind them the popular wave of abolitionist fervour arising from the death of Livingstone in 1873. All this spelt crisis on the island.[3]

It was now that Kirk, having several times been acting consul, secured his official appointment. Almost his first duty was to receive and escort before Barghash a delegation from the British Government proposing that Zanzibar should end the slave trade voluntarily. News of its approach had caused panic among the island's Arabs who, in order to appease Allah, flocked to offer prayers in the mosques and sacrificed cattle and chickens for behoof of the poor. In the event, the delegation won nothing but an unacceptable offer of gradual abolition, and shortly left amid general acrimony. Persuasion having failed, compulsion followed. Kirk got his instructions to present the ultimatum of June 3. After forcing closure of the market on Zanzibar, he had the sultan send out edicts banning slavers from the African mainland and forbidding their seaborne traffic. These were still only partial measures. They did not check domestic servitude on the island, which lasted into the twentieth century. Nor did they prove universally effective, despite Kirk's personal efforts to execute them with flying visits to the coastal towns. At least, however, the Governments of Britain and of Zanzibar were now to follow a common policy on the slave trade.

Yet Kirk had mixed feelings. As an evangelical Scot, he hated slavery. But he feared that his victory against it might prove pyrrhic. He had disliked humiliating Barghash before his own people, without whose loyalty this fragile realm could scarcely endure. The sultan indeed ran a serious risk of being overthrown. Even short of that, he might become embittered enough to cast off British influence and seek another protector. Still, nothing of the sort happened. Kirk used all his kindness and tact to reconcile Barghash to his subordination, which no more than reflected the reality of power. 'I often think how much more easily I could rule the country myself,' he noted in his journal, but Scottish self-discipline forbade him any such ruthless

332 THE SCOTTISH EMPIRE

course. Barghash remained the sovereign, with Kirk henceforth in the role of grand vizier to ensure the upright conduct of government. The regime recalled those of orientalist Scots who had served as residents in the Indian principalities. After the same fashion, it maintained the outward native form of the state and deferred to its subjects' conservatism. The sole innovation came in propelling them towards legitimate commerce, in other words, away from the slave trade.

Kirk soon showed them that this could bring political rewards. Remote as Barghash's realm was, it had enemies. If no real threat came any longer from the elder branch of his line in Oman, another appeared in 1876 from further off, from the modernising Egypt of Khedive Ismail. His territories at the time, before the Mahdi's rebellion a few years later, included the Sudan. The long route up the Nile was impracticable for the province's commerce, so the Khedive wanted to lay down instead an overland route towards the Somali coast. He sent out an expedition under none other than Charles Gordon, the future martyr of Khartoum, then in his service. On the Indian Ocean, it occupied the ports of Brava and Kismayu which by custom and use belonged to Barghash. Two rulers thus came into conflict who, if not without independent discretion, both stood under British tutelage, and it fell to London to arbitrate between them. A strategic question posed itself: the Suez Canal allowed East Africa to be opened up, but should it be done through Egypt or Zanzibar? In dispatches home, Gordon pressed the claims of the first, Kirk those of the second. What tilted the balance in favour of Kirk was his support from humanitarian interests, as Livingstone's disciple and as servant of a state where visible progress against slavery had been made. Britain compelled Ismail to withdraw. Barghash at last became convinced of Kirk's goodwill towards him: he 'had never before understood the force of the disinterested friendship of Her Majesty's Government for his country' and was 'highly delighted'.[4]

Relations could then evolve as Kirk wished: in return for compliance with his bidding on slavery, he would extend Zanzibar's sway and make her the pivot of a new East African economy. While enriching themselves, the sultan and his subjects could act in some sort as agents of civilisation across a backward region. It was in a sense a Livingstonian project, of transforming Africa by commerce, if not yet by Christianity: conversion of Moslems at any rate never proved an easy task. Even so, to men like Kirk legitimate commerce itself represented a Christian value, and the nature of the indigenous authority, as long as it was effective, remained secondary. That view did put him at odds with the Scottish missions just now arriving at the furthest edge of his sphere of influence, on Lake Nyasa. They saw the Arabs as the root of the evil they had come to destroy, and would in the end virtually go to war against it. Whenever Arabs and Africans clashed, the missionaries and the consul took opposite sides. Kirk has been described as a strategist of Empire, but the Empire he had in mind was surely an old Scottish one: an Empire not of territorial occupation and settlement, but of emporium and entrepot preserving the native social forms.[5]

For now, Kirk appeared to have the better measure of the situation. While the missions in the interior struggled, not least in promoting commerce, Zanzibar flourished. Barghash grew eager to import western capital and technology for development of the mainland. To explore there Kirk engaged a young geologist, Joseph Thomson, who went 'as a Christian and a Scotsman, carrying everywhere goodwill and friendship'. In several years of strenuous and often dangerous travels, he filled in many blanks on the map of the region and assessed its economic potential with some exactitude. It was he who discovered the copper in Katanga and the almost temperate setting of the Kenyan Highlands, ideal for European agriculture. Both regions, unfortunately, lay rather far away from Zanzibar. Reports about deposits of coal closer at hand proved false, and Thomson's careful surveys of the soil and mineral outcrops wherever he went served only to show there was nothing of much value in any ground over which the sultan held sway.

Kirk also turned on Barghash's behalf to Mackinnon, already in league with King Leopold II of the Belgians on the ostensibly international scheme for a commercial highway into Africa. The sultan sought more than a road, however, and offered a concession for general development. In 1877, with Kirk as honest broker, negotiations began. Mackinnon thought to drive a hard bargain: he wanted not only the tolls from the road, but also title to the land for four or five miles on either side of it, as well as a lease of the harbour at Dar es Salaam and the right to its customs. Barghash balked. The package, it seemed to him, would in effect rob him of his sovereignty on the mainland for the paltry return of a yearly rental and percentage of the profits. The talks were anyway being sabotaged behind the scenes by the British Foreign Secretary, Lord Salisbury, resolved to ensure that neither Belgians nor anyone else gained a foothold in East Africa which might require some corresponding British commitment. By 1880 the rest had given up. William Gladstone and the Liberals meanwhile returned to office in London in a mood of righteous anti-imperial indignation. Kirk was instructed to forget even a modest plan for a line of posts across the interior to exercise surveillance of illegal slavers' caravans. All that materialised was an agreement for Mackinnon's shipping to serve East African ports, where consular agents responsible to Kirk would reside. It was a worse reverse than he knew for his policy of extending the sultan's rule. Zanzibar would not now become a continental state, but remain a petty insular principality.[6]

For that reason Kirk's endeavours came eventually to nought, because a petty Zanzibar was left exposed to other European powers. This grew clear from 1884, a year of British reverses in Africa, most at German hands. In July, the Kaiser annexed the Cameroons, forestalling Her Majesty's consul by a few days. In September, Britain was obliged to recognise his sovereignty over South-West Africa. In pursuit of his imperial ambitions, he went the length of conspiracy with the French. A demarche by these arch-enemies, all the more perilous for its opportunism, forced Britain to abandon the treaty with Portugal which would have given the latter surrogate control along the lower reaches of the River Congo. France and Germany then blocked a scheme hatched in the City of London to take over the public finances of Egypt. They even plotted against the long-established British presence on the River Niger. The colonial situation had grown so complex, and potentially explosive, that the European governments decided to meet under German chairmanship at the end of the year and settle their differences. Britain, in order to confirm her possession of certain regions, was obliged to give ground in others. Worse, she found herself outmanoeuvred in formulation of the general principles by which the powers agreed, in the Treaty of Berlin, to be henceforth bound in Africa. Under what came to be known as the doctrine of effective occupation, they undertook in their existing or future protectorates to establish sufficient authority to guarantee freedom of trade and transit. This turned out, at least as Germany interpreted it, to have much wider implications. She used it to argue that any lands not yet effectively occupied lay open to annexation. The scramble for Africa was on.

Outside the tropics, too, it had been a bad year for the British, in the Sudan, Egypt and India. Trying both to limit their imperial burdens and to reconcile Germany, they were not disposed to stop her when she tried her luck again in the backwater of East Africa. Agents of her colonial companies prowled round making dubious treaties with coastal chieftains nominally subject to Barghash. His indignation was useless, and Kirk's appeals to London fell on deaf ears. In December, the Kaiser's navy appeared off Zanzibar in order to force the sultan to cede the disputed areas, including the harbour of Dar es Salaam. The Foreign Office explicitly instructed Kirk to co-operate in reaching a peaceful settlement, in case trouble should 'convert a mere commercial speculation into a political question'. Shaken and demoralised, he could do nothing but arrange surrender by a Zanzibari state which was to all intents and purposes his own handiwork.[7]

Surrender did not stop there. Next, the British Government consented to set up with France and Germany – not Zanzibar – a joint commission to determine the extent of Barghash's dominions, presumably with a view to seeing which other parts the respective powers might take over. As a quasi-judicial inquiry it was farcically inconclusive, for he had never exercised sovereignty in the European sense. Kirk became convinced that the Germans were really aiming to control the whole coast: if they did, they could even threaten India. To avert that, he had to deliver the *coup de grâce* to his own creation, and displace the remaining Zanzibari sovereignty on the mainland by a British one. It was done in 1886 by formal partition of East Africa between Britain and Germany, into what later became Kenya and Tanganyika. Kirk then resigned. This was not quite the end of his involvement in the region, but essentially his work lay in ruins. Barghash died in 1888, and two years later Zanzibar's residual independence was extinguished by a British protectorate. An outpost of the Scottish Empire went with it.[8]

The outcome created as many problems as it solved. For the sole purpose of forestalling another power, Britain had acquired vast new territories she did not want. She had no policy there, except the airy and general one of developing commerce and spreading civilisation. If the Zanzibaris were *hors de combat*, who could do it? The explorer Thomson, now home again, went on lecturing tours to warn that the prospects of trade in the region were greatly exaggerated, as were the possibilities of native progress through mere contact with the West. The Government did not listen. Instead it imagined that the territories, and such strategic and economic interests as they represented, could be defended without taking on the duties of administration, or indeed spending a penny on anything. For the purpose it resorted to the old expedient of the chartered company. It was not alone in this: Germany sought to develop her African colonies by the same means, as did other countries. But the modern companies were different from the historic ones. In the past they had at least started out as co-operative means of offsetting risks which single merchants could not face. Now they were rather the instruments of emerging global capitalism, under the control of individual tycoons or large consortiums. In Africa especially, they sought lucrative monopolies excluding the smaller, independent enterprises still important in other regions of the world. They governed as well as traded, since trade could hardly be developed before some form of government was imposed. They became political undertakings, but they were politically irresponsible. They took little enough notice of the governments granting them their privileges. They often brutally mistreated the hapless peoples under their sway. Still, as things turned out they offered no permanent solution to the problems of imperialism, and seldom lasted.

The East African example was, however, the least unpleasant. That may be put down to the good intentions of Mackinnon, who took the lead in it. As a Scot, he had little stomach for the ruthless exploitation which might have brought him even passing success. Nor had he the imagination or, any longer, the energy to direct the enterprise on other terms. His self-confidence and tenacity did get it off the ground. They also drove him beyond the point where his commercial acumen would once have told him to stop. He was after all, as we have seen elsewhere, a limited man. At any rate, in 1887 he organised the British East Africa Association, which elected him chairman. The next year Zanzibar conceded to it her entire possessions on the mainland within the British sphere as defined by the partition. Then a royal charter was granted to what now became the Imperial British East Africa Company. It boasted among its directors not only Mackinnon and Kirk but also Alexander Bruce, brewer in Edinburgh and, more to the point, son-in-law of Livingstone; the Marquis of Lorne, sometime Governor-General of Canada; Sir Donald Stewart, former Commander-in-Chief of India; and Sir George Mackenzie, Britain's greatest expert on Persian affairs. 'Thank God,' the last said, 'we are all Scots here.'[9]

They set themselves aims too various even for such a versatile nation. Their charter laid on them the humanitarian duty of suppressing the slave trade. They shouldered evangelical burdens besides. In 1891 Mackinnon called in James Stewart of Lovedale to found the East African Scottish Industrial Mission at Kibwezi, 150 miles from Mombasa, on the model of the stations by Lake Nyasa. This one would languish, though, stranded in empty territory, till the first large wave of European settlers arrived in Kenya after 1900. Such diversions detracted from the economic viability of the main venture, never clear from the outset. Compared to other regions of the world, East Africa was not an attractive locus for investment. The company's launch appeared successful, but only by sleight of hand: most of the £500,000 of paid-up capital was subscribed by Mackinnon's own subsidiaries. He did have the usual assurance from the Foreign Office of a subsidy for his shipping, to carry the mails between London and Zanzibar. This he needed to compete with the still more heavily subsidised German shipping, though in the event the Treasury refused to hand over as much as he had counted on. Another constraint arose from Britain's obligation under the Treaty of Berlin to maintain free trade, even within a concession such as his.

An old man now, Mackinnon lacked the vigour to surmount these constraints. On the contrary, he ran the business with extreme caution, and Mackenzie, his managing director in Zanzibar, was little better. Co-operating rather than competing with local merchants, he looked for trade not so much to the coast as to the interior, where costs were at their highest and profits at their most meagre. In that case the company, unless it could almost immediately have transformed the region's economy, seemed bound to fail. Such transformation was unavailable, because the company never generated the earnings to finance it, and even more because it depended on the necessarily slow introduction and cultivation of crops for export. The similar failure of the German company confirmed these basic facts. Mackinnon and his directors found that, after laying out their entire capital, they had annual expenditure of £80,000 but income of only £35,000, nearly all in duties on primary products from the interior. In other words, they were getting no real return at all, and heading straight for bankruptcy. They might have been rescued by a scheme for linking up with Cecil Rhodes's British South African Company, after he tried to acquire the African Lakes Company in Nyasaland. But Mackinnon's own friends among the Scots missionaries put a stop to that.[10]

The political miscalculations proved still greater, for Mackinnon was above all no politician. This was a more imperialist venture than the one he had dreamed up with King Leopold, in that it pursued basically national ends through control of territory and of peoples given no say in the matter. But he, or rather his lieutenant Mackenzie, displayed a curious indifference to British interests, at any rate as they would before long come to be seen, in arranging in 1889 for Italy to sublet from the Sultan of Zanzibar the ports along the Somali coast. True, the Government in London preferred the Italians' presence to that of more serious rivals. But the effect would be to alienate part of its sphere of influence, and create a colony for another power. Scots, as elsewhere, were willing to work for foreign empires too. Here, however, they showed less than their usual competence, especially in relations with the indigenous peoples. A dangerous incident occurred at Kismayu in 1891 during a dispute over title to land between the company's administrator, Ross Todd, and the Somalis. The callow Scotsman so outraged them during a palaver that they rushed on and wounded him. He was only saved when Count Lovatelli, an Italian explorer chancing by on a visit, fired off his revolver and scattered the assailants. But in this region the natives were soon in general revolt against the company, and the eventual imposition of regular colonial rule came as a blessing.[11]

From the start, then, the company's objects were mixed up with high policy. Its charter gave it authority to act politically, subject to the Foreign Office's right to intervene in any negotiations and to veto any agreements reached. This official surveillance was imposed because the presence especially of the Germans seemed bound to cause problems. Their company indeed set out at once on a race with Mackinnon's to open up the country. Yet high policy also aimed to accommodate the Germans. Mackinnon, falling between two stools, was left at a loss. He blamed his problems on passivity at home. 'In all directions we are overborne by German officials and startled by new German plans,' he wrote to Salisbury, now Prime Minister, in April 1890, 'and I feel so disheartened by the apparent lukewarmness of the support which we receive from HMG.' This was in its way an accurate assessment, for the Government shrank from offending Germany even while it fretted at Mackinnon's circumspection. In any event he was unlikely to get decisive backing from Salisbury, who heartily disliked the charmless Highlander. 'He has no energy for anything except quarrelling with Germans,' the premier growled. Out of bewilderment in one party and inconsistency in the other, disaster ripened.[12]

One result was to drag the British Government into what it had sought to avoid, direct involvement in East Africa. Probably Salisbury just resigned himself to that. At any rate, he now went over Mackinnon's head to conclude a new treaty with the Germans, defining borders in the region and securing their recognition of the British protectorate in Zanzibar, in return for ceding them Heligoland. The involvement was then bound to go further, for each of the two powers coveted Uganda. More advanced than the coastal region economically and politically, it contained powerful native monarchies. They spent their substance in wars with one another, but could afford to because they had enriched themselves from the consequent supply of slaves to the Arabs of Zanzibar. During the late 1870s a European presence was established in Buganda, biggest of these kingdoms, by German and British missions, among others. Alexander Mackay from Rhynie led the British one. The religious situation in Buganda grew tangled. Protestants vied with Catholics, Moslems with both. Since the Europeans were obviously more powerful than the Arabs, the Kabaka Mutesa converted to Christianity. But his son Mwanga, ascending the throne in 1884, persecuted the missions and their native flock. He thus unleashed civil war, complicated by rivalry among the Christian sects, which was itself a reflection of the scramble for Africa.

Britain possessed a further, strategic interest in Uganda. Much against its will, Gladstone's Ministry had in 1883 occupied Egypt to guard the Suez Canal. It then had to look to the security of the whole valley of the Nile. A catastrophic turn came with the loss of the Sudan to the Mahdi after Gordon's death at Khartoum. But to some that appeared less serious than a possible advance by Germany to the river's headwaters, which issued from Lake Victoria in Bugandan territory. The bizarre idea had taken hold that the flow of the Nile could be halted, and Egypt ruined, by the fiendish technology of the Kaiser's minions. To stop that, again at no cost to itself, Salisbury's Government hoped to rely on Mackinnon, as his concession included the ports from which the headwaters were most accessible. The Foreign Office therefore prodded him up-country. Willingly he went, for he believed Uganda's relative riches could bring him the profit which otherwise eluded him. To get at them, he had to establish legitimate commerce and effective administration across the intervening territory. This would best be done in his view by building a railway. But it required an enormous outlay of capital which his company no longer had. Indeed, by the beginning of 1891, the directors knew they could scarcely get through the year. Their sole remaining hope was an official subsidy for the railway, a slim hope indeed, given Salisbury's impatience with them. They resorted in effect to blackmail, announcing that unless they got help they would withdraw their agents from Buganda and leave the missionaries to be massacred. A public outcry predictably arose. The Foreign Office hastened to respond, accepting that Mackinnon deserved recompense for the money and responsibility he had saved his country. The Treasury grudgingly agreed, again on less generous terms than he expected. The Cabinet, however, could not find time in Parliament for a Bill. At this point the company gave up: it resolved to retire from Uganda by the end of 1892 and liquidate itself.[13]

A General Election now supervened. The Liberals scraped back, dependent for a majority on the Irish Nationalists, in Gladstone's last and professedly most radical Ministry. Its radicalism seemed bound to bring the sorry episode in East Africa to an end. But Lord Rosebery, the new Foreign Secretary and darling of the Scots besides, acted on an agenda of his own. An increasingly committed imperialist, uniting round him most of his party's rising stars, he had rather approved of the outgoing Government's foreign policy. He believed that a great power ought in any event to maintain continuity through the shifts of domestic politics. It followed that he wanted to preserve the British position in Egypt and on the upper Nile, and in the latter case to strengthen it by occupying Uganda permanently.

Rosebery moved at once to postpone the company's withdrawal from the territory. On the pretext of protecting the missions, he gave it the money to stay on for three months, till March 1893, a deadline later extended to the end of the year. In secret he drew up a provisional treaty with the Kabaka, under which British rule was to be imposed. Then he orchestrated a public campaign in favour of what he had already decided to do. When the time came for him to seek the Cabinet's consent, he heavily hinted that he would resign unless he got his way. He thus presented his colleagues, almost to a man anti-imperialist and outraged at his double dealing, with an impossible dilemma. They did not need to be reminded that they had lost the Liberal Unionists over Ireland in 1886. So they could not afford to lose the Liberal imperialists over Uganda now: it would have been the end of the Government, indeed of the party. Rosebery made it crystal-clear that they all depended on him. To rub salt in the wound, he made it equally clear that they must give him a free hand to follow a foreign policy obnoxious to them. And by the way, they would have to accept him as Gladstone's successor.[14]

Britain thus declared a protectorate over Uganda in 1894, and over Kenya in 1895. Mackinnon was by then two years in his grave, but before his death had already disengaged from the affairs of his ruined company. To Rosebery it was worthless except as a stopgap while he made his own arrangements. Then he let it sink. It had seen a trivial return for its vast investment and paid not a single dividend to its shareholders. For £200,000 of official compensation, representing a large loss to all involved, it transferred its powers to the protectorates. The Government still had a bargain, since three-quarters of the sum came from the Sultan of Zanzibar for restoration of his customs. But in some larger sense the company might be said to have fulfilled a task. At a time when politicians refused to meet the cost of colonial expansion, it did secure territories that turned out in the long run not to lack economic and strategic value for Britain. In that, East Africa also illustrated graphically the evolution of Scottish imperial concepts. Under Kirk, the commercial Empire was still at work, modified by Christian ideals. Mackinnon went beyond him, but his own half-baked mixture of commercial and Christian purposes impeded transition to successful imperialism. At last Rosebery overthrew all the old assumptions and ruthlessly asserted power, his own and his country's. The Empire had been contested here, and a new idea of it won.[15]

CHAPTER TWENTY-SEVEN

'A kind of celestial Scotland': South Africa

On the night of December 10, 1899, the Highland Brigade – the Seaforths, the Gordons, the Black Watch, the Argyll and Sutherland Highlanders – floundered in a drenching thunderstorm across the trackless veld near a place called Magersfontein. They were marching under General Andrew Wauchope to the relief of Kimberley, a British outpost besieged since the start of the Boer War in October. The two little Afrikaner republics, the Transvaal and the Orange Free State, had adopted a forward strategy and mounted immediate attacks, in the hope of winning some decisive advantage to forestall the inevitable concentration of imperial power against them. Until that night, they appeared to have failed. The Scottish troops, full of fighting spirit, had moved rapidly north from the Cape Province, crossing the Orange then the Modder Rivers. If they could breach the enemy's position at Magersfontein, Kimberley would be relieved and the high veld would lie open to them.

That was the object of their nocturnal manoeuvre. During the day, their guns had relentlessly bombarded the Boers' entrenchments. Wauchope meant to get within striking distance of them under cover of darkness, then rush them at dawn. It was in any event a risky plan, but the storm ruined it. Rain hampered everything. Lightning affected the officers' compasses. Most companies got lost. As the hour of attack approached, few were near their starting positions, and their order of battle had become hopelessly muddled. But the Afrikaners knew where they were, or at any rate knew better. Familiar with the country, they could afford to wait till daybreak. Then they opened steady fire on the scene of confusion before them. Since nobody on the Scottish side had envisaged such a state of affairs, there were no orders to meet it. Some officers tried to lead their men in an assault, to be mown down at once. Others sought to retire, with the same result. Most could do nothing except take what cover was to be found on the exposed ground, and wait while the African sun mounted the sky. They carried no water, because again it had never been foreseen that they would be trapped like this. By noon their condition was intolerable. Wauchope, crouching in the bush along with the rest, at last decided to order a general retreat. He stood up to direct it – and in the same instant dropped dead, riddled by bullets. Only with nightfall could most of the Scots get away.

News of the disaster was scarcely credited at home. The nation went into mourning: women wept in the streets, social gatherings were cancelled. People said it was the worst reverse to Scottish arms since Culloden. It had not a single redeeming feature. On grief at the loss of so many fine young troops was piled shame that famous regiments with a glorious history had not fought to the last man, but fled the field. Scots found that hard to take: the blame must surely lie elsewhere. There had to be scapegoats, most obviously in an incompetent general staff – full of Englishmen, it was noted. Would they have sent a brigade of their own countrymen so carelessly to its doom?[1]

Scotland has seldom felt so devastated. That brought immediately to a head a complex of emotions about the war, the intensity of which is at first sight surprising. While Scots had been active in South Africa, she housed no great emigrant population of them. Their commercial penetration was deeper elsewhere. Other lands, India or Canada, had always attracted and inspired them more. Yet South Africa now came to represent all they hoped and feared about the Empire, crystallising a contest over it among themselves because this was also a contest over the nature of their own nation: whether Scots should continue to respect the traditions and rights of other races, or could justify subduing them for their own good, to bring them the blessings of progress more quickly. The moral dilemma was therefore caught up with a practical question of national consequence, whether Scotland should act the custodian of timeless values or the pioneer of modernisation. It cannot be said that she gave any coherent answer to this complex of problems. Sure it is, however, that the external conflict waxed so bitter because it expressed an inner conflict.

Scots' activity in South Africa had been marked by two encounters. One was with indigenous society, to which at first they made a fairly clear response. Abhorring savagery, they sought out from its depths universal elements of humanity to form the basis of improvement. In that spirit, the missions of John Philip, Robert Moffat and David Livingstone had done much to foster, especially in Cape Colony, liberalism towards natives. By now the elder generations were gone from the scene, but James Stewart of Lovedale took up the torch. Working in the eastern Cape, a backward region still blessed by its mild government, he resisted segregation and educated Africans as if they had been Scots. A prime aim was religious, to equip them to run a system of presbytery for themselves. It did not in fact amount to a fulfilment of that when the Rev Pambani Mzimba, educated at Lovedale, formed in 1893 the Presbyterian Church of Africa with money he had collected in Edinburgh while there as a delegate to mark the jubilee of the Free Church. His purpose was rather to set up a black denomination to continue in what he saw as necessary reliance on Scotland, because white Presbyterians in South Africa were about to constitute themselves a completely independent body. All the further off lay the missions' social and political aim, to bring blacks up to a level where they might enjoy full citizenship. In this respect even Cape Colony remained far from practising what missionaries preached.

Outside it their aims were of necessity different. Bounds had been set to the advance of liberalism by recognition in 1854 of the Boers' independence on the other side of the Vaal River. They oppressed the indigenous peoples and remained hostile to the British, to missionaries above all. Since these did not regard the Vaal as a border for themselves, conflict became inevitable when they crossed it and tried to uphold racial equality. Philip had proposed how: the Crown, while not annexing tribal lands, should exercise enough supervision to protect them and the missions working in them. The authorities at the Cape took little notice of him, and showed no interest in extending the area of direct rule. But the fluid state of political authority in the region made fixed frontiers meaningless anyway. In reality the British vied with the Afrikaners for effective control up to and even beyond the River Zambesi, while both vied with the blacks, whose tribes in turn warred among themselves.

In a situation of growing complexity towards the end of the century, Philip's ideas were refined by John Mackenzie. Along with Stewart of Lovedale, he had first gone out as a young man in the party accompanying Mrs Mary Livingstone when she rejoined her husband. They arrived at Kuruman, in Bechuana territory, in 1859. Mackenzie struck away by himself, north to the Makololo and the Matabele, before settling at Shoshong among the Bamangwato in 1864–76. Then he returned to Kuruman, to head the institution founded in memory of Moffat for the education of indigenous pastors. As one of the few whites in a remote area, he acquired political influence. Devotion to evangelism made him refuse an official post, but he freely gave advice. He argued that stability could be imposed over the whole tract south of the Zambesi by appointing a Governor-General for it, who would exercise a suzerainty variable according to the condition of its different parts. There were organised native polities in what later became Bechuanaland, Basutoland and Swaziland, where a resident commissioner might suffice to uphold civilised standards among tribal authorities otherwise retaining their powers. The Boers, too, could be left to look after their own internal affairs, so long as they stopped attacking their neighbours.

There was in this little inconsistent with the main departure in actual British policy at the time, annexation of the Transvaal in 1877. The Government in London claimed it was for the republic's own good, and stood ready to grant responsible government back to the Afrikaners, but the annexation did not last long enough for that. It came to a disastrous end within four years, when they rebelled and, after a brief struggle, triumphed at the Battle of Majuba Hill. By now Gladstone was once more in office. In 1882, amid his efforts to cut imperial commitments, he recognised the republic as independent again. This offered no solution either. Immense natural resources were being discovered in South Africa. Britain acquired, beside a missionary or civilising interest, a direct economic one with clear political implications. Cecil Rhodes, already a member of the Cabinet at the Cape, saw them. He wanted, under a sovereignty conciliating the Boers and subjugating the blacks, to develop the region on the grandest scale. If expansion of the sovereignty was thwarted for the time being, he meant at least to keep open a road to the North, and to the riches reputed to lie in the interior of the continent. The road would now have to run along the undefined western border of the Transvaal. It would therefore pass through Kuruman.

Mackenzie, deeply alarmed, set out to block Rhodes. He returned home, to lobby in London and campaign in Scotland on behalf of the indigenous peoples. He aroused enough of a public outcry to extract a decision that Bechuanaland should pass not to the Cape but under the British Government as a Crown colony, with himself as commissioner there. In that capacity he went back in 1884, fending off Rhodes's last effort to dislodge him and annex the region. He thus managed to protect the Bechuanas, and indirectly the Basutos and Swazis too. Their lands became, in accordance with his scheme, the High Commission Territories. The only whites in them were the commissioners, with a few magistrates and policemen. Otherwise paramount chiefs loosely ruled, presiding over assemblies of the lesser chiefs, who in their own districts managed everyday matters of justice, land and so on. Without Mackenzie, nations independent today would almost certainly have been absorbed by South Africa. Instead he preserved a concept of the Scottish Empire.

Rhodes, however, was not so easily foiled. His road to the North stayed open because he soon won at its terminus, in what was to be Rhodesia, the main concession for his British South Africa Company. He did it through the good offices of John Moffat, son of Robert, who inveigled Lobengula, chief of the Matabele, into signing away his lands; which may remind us that missionaries were not always found on the side of the angels. Nor were others of the Scots involved. In 1891 Rhodes appointed as administrator of the territory a son of Edinburgh, Leander Starr Jameson. He acted the wild colonial boy, impulsive, gallant, rascally, a chain-smoker and hard drinker, ever ready to kick over the traces. His job was to organise a colonising drive, give the settlers their head and make this a white man's country. In doing so, he swept aside all the blacks' rights and interests, often by the most brutal means. Nearly 16 million acres, one-sixth of the whole area, were alienated to immigrants, who treated the indigenous peoples as just a pool of cheap labour. By the turn of the century, then, Scottish liberalism towards the natives no longer looked so wholehearted, and was being compromised by instances of plain imperialist oppression. New values corrupted the original character of the encounter.[2]

The Scots' second encounter in South Africa was with the Boers. It gave rise to a still more complex reaction. At one extreme we again find Jameson, who apparently thought little more of Afrikaners than of blacks if their independence clashed with British interests as he saw them. It was he who led the infamous raid into the Transvaal which presaged the Boer War. In the event little more than a drunken frolic – his men drank 36 cases of champagne before they set off at the end of December 1895 – it yet had the all too serious purpose of overthrowing the republic. The *uitlanders*, British for the most part, working its mineral riches, were warily refused rights of citizenship by President Kruger. Jameson meant to provoke among them the rebellion for which he deemed them ripe. At first Rhodes urged him on, but at the last moment drew back and ordered him not to move from the point on the border where he had assembled his gang. He decided to go ahead anyway, and goad the faint-hearted into action by his example. He found he had misjudged both friend and foe. In a few days the Afrikaners surrounded and captured him, then turned him over to the British Government, which sent him to jail. It was a huge embarrassment to imperialists, whose ill-will towards the Boers stood revealed.[3]

War erupted within four years. To the English it may have looked like just another tropical bushfire, through which the Queen's soldiers would march to triumph over a lesser breed. Some Scots agreed, even some missionaries. Stewart of Lovedale, Moderator of the General Assembly of the Free Church in 1899, backed the war: he had given his inaugural address on "Christian Imperialism". A soldier like Douglas Haig could never summon up any sympathy for the Afrikaners, however valiantly they fought him. Yet to a second soldier, Ian Hamilton, things appeared less simple. He already knew the country. An officer in the Gordons, he had been captured at Majuba Hill. As a Scot he at once understood and admired the point when his guards, seeing him downcast, told him that those choosing to fight on the sabbath could expect no other fate. When he arrived back in Cape Town in 1899, now as the Gordons' commander, he was entertained by Alfred Milner, the High Commissioner, who felt certain of swift victory. Hamilton retorted that the Boers on their own ground were the most formidable foe in the world, and noted how he upset his host.

Hamilton's mixed feelings were shared by many of his countrymen. They could not abide a good deal in Afrikaner character, conduct and custom, above all the cruelty towards the blacks. Yet they also felt conscious of affinities. The most obvious one lay in Calvinist religion. We have already seen how early Scots evangelists came to love the Boers as their own people. The tradition continued. The Free Church still freely sent personnel and encouragement to Stellenbosch, the seminary near Cape Town of the Dutch Reformed Church, which mistrusted the more liberal theology of Holland. William Macmillan, who arrived in 1891 with his missionary father, found here 'a community of Scots'. By the time he went home to university in 1903, it was waning under the pressure of Afrikaner nationalism. Meanwhile, though, Jan Smuts, J.B.M. Herzog and D.F. Malan had all received a Presbyterian education. Scots could understand their nationalism because it bore some resemblance to Scottish nationalism: the Boers, too, had against the odds sturdily clung on to their identity. John Buchan came out during the war and later wrote:

> For the veld farmer I acquired a sincere liking and respect. He had many of the traits of my Lowland Scots, keen at a bargain and prepared to imperil his immortal soul for a threepenny bit, but ready to squander pounds in hospitality. When I spent the night at a farm and at family worship, listened to Dutch psalms sung to familiar Scottish psalm-tunes, I might have fancied myself in

Tweedsmuir . . . History has seen many fine stocks brought within the pale of our Empire, but none stronger and finer than this one which turned defeat into victory and led captivity captor.

Buchan thus recognised the war as a tragedy, even by his own imperialist lights. He confessed there were moments when he almost wished to change sides, because 'it must be such a glorious thing to fight a losing battle for what is after all a noble object'. He has won little recognition as a moralist, but to South Africa he brought an atheoretical idealism typical of Scottish moralists. It was the start of his lifelong quest for a human philosophy which, without assurance of any objective correlative, would be grounded in activity, existential in the sense of defining the self and fortifying its integrity. Here it led him to a conclusion that even deluded self-sacrifice in a last stand against impossible odds might be justified. This exemplary Scot, torn as he was between the romantic and the practical, found in the Afrikaners something of what he sought.[4]

They fought hard, and suffered for it. The British expected to beat them easily, indeed within a year of Magersfontein turned the tide and advanced as far as Pretoria. The Boers still would not surrender, but took to the bush as guerrillas. Not till 1903 could they be quelled, and then only by, in the words of the Scots leader of the Liberal opposition at Westminster, Henry Campbell-Bannerman, 'methods of barbarism'. Most notorious were the concentration camps built in haste for the families left behind by Afrikaner menfolk. Buchan had as his first official job to come in and set up a proper administration for them. For public consumption, he denied they were all that bad. In private he admitted that they had made his hair turn grey, and that 'the original policy of forming the camps . . . was certainly not wise'. His ability to clean them up with relative ease tends to show that inefficiency rather than malevolence caused the shambles. Yet 20,000 women and children perished in detention, almost as many as the British troops who died in battle or of disease, and very many more than the 4000 Afrikaner fighters killed.

These and other severities cost the imperialists' cause dear, yet did not shake their faith in its ultimate justice: it was for the good of South Africa to be reconstructed as a dominion of the Crown, by whatever means should prove necessary. To that end, Milner had early on formed his "kindergarten", a group of brilliant and dedicated young men, containing for some reason a high quotient of Scots. One was Buchan, a son of the manse from Glasgow, and an Oxonian with a precocious literary reputation, recruited as Milner's private secretary in place of Patrick Duncan, born in Banffshire. The recruiting sergeant seems to have been a Scottish don, R.S. Rait, at New College, Oxford, who also brought in Philip Kerr. There were others: George Craik from Fife, Dougal Malcolm of Poltalloch and Lord Lovat. The kindergarten proved in almost every case the springboard for a public career of distinction. At the time of Buchan's death in 1940 he was Governor-General of Canada, while Duncan held the same office in South Africa, and Kerr, by then Lord Lothian, was ambassador in Washington.

Buchan and Kerr left extensive records of their labours and motives. They had to expend much effort on problems of fiendishly minute administration. But they set to with the wonderful confidence of youth, heightened by their imperialist idealism. Being imperialists, they were also *dirigistes*. They believed that with thorough analysis and resolute action they could heal the anguish of South Africa, tame her wilderness, strengthen her elements of civilisation and erect on them a durable balance and harmony, thus resolving for a complex society the tensions which had tormented it since its beginning. It was a genuinely altruistic project which discharges them from any accusation of crude racialism, easy though it may be to damn the outlook of their leader Milner in that way. He made no bones about his aim of keeping the British on top, dominating the Boers, let alone the blacks.

But his young men were often more perceptive. They aimed broadly to blur racial divisions damaging in that sense which had produced a plain contradiction in older Scottish attitudes, between liberalism towards the natives and sympathy for the Boers, when the two races were irreconcilable. The key to any progress obviously lay in economic development. Its possibility in South Africa was bound up with questions of labour, questions of which race did what. Kerr, for instance, argued that the line between the work of a white man and the work of a black man ought not to be regarded as the line between skilled and unskilled. Otherwise there could be no answer to the main social problem, as he saw it, the thousands of poor whites trying to live from unimproved agriculture in a country now wasted. Their condition would only grow worse while they thought manual toil beneath them. One answer was to give them an example with progressive farmers brought in from Britain, who might, however, have to displace indigenous peoples from their land. All the relevant questions thus bore on one another.[5]

The members of the kindergarten did share a curious notion that land congenial to Europeans was white man's country, freely open to settlement. Buchan stressed, though, that they should also act as trustees for a civilising mission. The natives would either prove themselves capable of responding or not, and in the latter case were probably doomed to gradual extinction. But until this was demonstrated one way or the other, no rigid social or economic barrier should be placed between them and the whites. Buchan maintained, in words recalling those of Philip long before, that a subject population denied legal rights would degrade the value of human life and depreciate the moral currency. The answer was to 'patiently and skilfully bring to bear upon the black man the solvent and formative influence of civilisation'.

Buchan's outlook is confirmed in his later literary works, where racial conflicts seldom oppose negroes and Europeans as such. Rather they oppose civilisation and savagery, the latter viewed with a mixture of fascination and horror. Such is the case in the prime example, *Prester John* (1910). The hero, David Crawford, hails from Kirkcaple, a typical small town on the east coast of Scotland. It is in his boyhood there that he first meets John Laputa, a black clergyman and guest preacher of the type that missions were in reality sometimes sending home. Quite out of place in a

Scots burgh, Laputa has both a noble and a diabolical side to his character. Later, back in South Africa, he foments a native uprising, in which he proves himself as fine as any white leader could be. He resembles indeed the Montrose of Buchan's later biography in military genius, charisma and religious vision. Yet he perverts these qualities to lead his people back towards barbarism. He fails and dies after a final confrontation with Crawford, who has meanwhile pursued a humdrum trader's career on the veld but unexpectedly excelled himself to foil the revolt. Now he is also persuaded by the higher nature of Laputa that negroes have it in them to break their bounds and aspire towards civilisation. The book closes with scenes of their starting to do so.[6]

Still, when Buchan in his official capacity referred to the racial barrier, he meant the one between Briton and Boer. So did his colleagues. Kerr, at first suspicious of the vanquished enemy, changed his mind and formed, notably with Smuts, fast Afrikaner friendships. Yet he remained didactic in his outlook towards them, a man who knew better. His goodwill arose from a belief that they could learn the Scottish lessons, on the use of education, agricultural improvement and so on, that he meant to teach them. Buchan, too, despite his compassion and sympathy for the Boers, thought they had to be firmly guided by principles bound to strike them at the outset as alien. For instance, he promoted what seemed unmistakably a policy of high imperialism, the encouragement of further British colonisation. He drafted the Settlers' Ordinance of 1902 in the Transvaal, and the Crown Lands Disposal Act, which made land available and regulated its allocation. But there was more than high imperialism to them. Buchan identified a weakness in the society of the Transvaal especially, in the deep rift long obvious between Afrikaner peasants and the commercial or industrial community of *uitlanders*. Immigrants to the land would bring efficient methods with them, allow a larger population to be supported, build up agriculture as a balance to mining and create out of it a group with common interests at once Boer and British. In the event the policy did not succeed very well, drawing only 12,000 people. That does not detract from Buchan's good intentions, to conciliate by creating a social equilibrium previously absent.

South Africa appeared to the kindergarten the place for an even bolder experiment, in imperial federation. She could lead the way through union of the conquered republics and of the British colonies, the Cape and Natal. With the wounds of war still raw, that would mark a yet higher achievement than Canada's of 1867. Kerr dedicated himself to it, in his official duties and well beyond. Though overburdened, he found time to develop his skills as a publicist in setting up a bilingual newspaper to advocate union, *The State* or *Die Staat*, which played a great part in speeding agreement on the South African constitution. His job done, he returned home and set to work just as hard for a wider imperial federation, within which a scheme of Home Rule all round for the United Kingdom might be fitted. Buchan agreed that the Empire could be consciously constructed to benefit every one of its peoples. The British would still be uniquely capable of directing it because of their values. Scots, for the same reason, were most capable of all. Of course they would profit. The real profit would be moral, however, in fostering 'the virtues of the pioneer', as Buchan put it to a Glasgow audience in 1904. Scots might thus fulfil the civilising work begun by their brother Calvinists, the Boers. As the latter's sterling qualities matured, the two would become still firmer friends and partners than before the war. All peoples of European extraction, having civilisation behind them, ought in principle to be trusted in this fashion. The Afrikaners, though forced into the Empire, were just as fit for responsibility as the French Canadians, or indeed the Scots of 1707: they too had been perverse and recalcitrant, yet finally found an equal role in ruling their new country, not to speak of others, without losing their nationality.

Unlike many imperialists, Buchan would thus never oppose colonial nationalism. On the contrary, he welcomed and encouraged it, as rendering the Empire more benevolent, and so more powerful. His own nationalism bore little resemblance to the modern Scottish version, but it was for him the touchstone of his experience in South Africa, and the link with his earliest, most intimate memories. It let him see in her a grander version of his home, with higher mountains and greener glens. And since her crust of civilisation was as yet thin, she offered to his generation what otherwise only long-dead Scots had known, the pride and joy of making a hard land bloom. This was indeed 'a kind of celestial Scotland'.[7]

By the same token, the Empire was essential to it. Buchan would come to equate defence of the Empire with the maintenance of civilisation, and devote himself to that. The link first surfaces in his book, *The Lodge in the Wilderness*. He poured much of himself into it, yet it is a thoughtful rather than a passionate work, consciously so because he wrote it straight after the Liberal victory at the General Election of 1906 to counter the anti-imperialist reaction he now saw in Britain. In spacious conversations the characters take up varied points of view, but feel their way towards an idea that imperialism may be an agent of civilisation, perhaps the start of a new one, with deeper morality, richer creativity, healthier culture. They therefore reject crude jingoism. One figure calls that the stark opposite of imperialism, 'the school of thought which thinks of the Empire as England'. Another hopes that one day imperial patriotism will stand to national as national patriotism now stands to local affection: 'A man is not less of a patriot because the "lone shieling and the misty island" are nearer his heart than the whole of Britain'. But the book reaches higher. The true theme is 'the ethical basis of Empire, and its relation to intellectual and aesthetic progress'. In the end the speakers address no less a problem than the world out of joint, the decadence of the West and the spiritual penury of its peoples, to which imperial activity may offer an existential cure.[8]

Perhaps, if ever fulfilled in this sense, the kindergarten really could have set South Africa on a happier course, and consummated the Scottish encounter with both blacks and Boers. Once peace came, Buchan and his fellows had a free hand so long as Unionist government lasted in London. But after that their chance was gone for, in the first years of the incoming Liberal Ministry, Scots radicals gained the upper hand. No imperialism, however benign, cut any ice with them. They had certainly wanted none of it if the business of Empire was to bully people like the Afrikaners, and their sentiment had hardened as the war dragged on. By exploiting this revulsion, Campbell-Bannerman managed to restore some moral unity to Scottish Liberalism.

So when his party triumphed at the polls in 1906, it broke with what had gone before. It consciously turned from foreign adventures to reform at home, not in order to succour a superior race, as domestic imperialists would have had it, but to improve conditions for the Scots people and meet national aspirations on the Celtic fringe. Policy in the Empire changed accordingly, to take equality and democracy as its watchwords. Campbell-Bannerman spelled it out in 1907 to the Colonial Conference, the now regular meeting of leaders from the Dominions. They had themselves, when gathering under the last Government, usually received with distaste any schemes tending towards imperial federation. The new Prime Minister declared all that over and done with: he stood for their freedom and independence, freedom in their internal affairs, freedom in their relations with each other, and with the mother country. In effect he ruled out imperial federation even as an ultimate goal. He thus reasserted old Scottish values. But events were soon to expose them once again as a less than infallible guide to the modern world.[9]

It followed that the Ministry must accept and respect the right to self-government of colonial communities, which at the time were all white communities. Liberals sensed this might pose a moral dilemma, where a white community also ruled an indigenous one. In practice they did not try to resolve the dilemma, but applied without qualification their general principle. It at once produced an uncomfortable sequel. The first South African crisis the Government faced had nothing to do with the Boers. It arose rather from relations between the English-speakers of Natal and the natives, especially the fierce Zulus. In 1906, imposition of a poll tax caused trouble in the tribal villages. From small beginnings it got quite out of hand because officials on the spot overreacted. The governor immediately declared a state of emergency, and appealed to London for troops. The Colonial Secretary, Lord Elgin, previously a somewhat ineffective Viceroy of India, sent a force. But he intended it as an instrument of reassurance and restraint, warning that he wanted to be consulted about its deployment rather than obliged to look on while a bloodbath ensued. The warning went for nothing. In a critical development, two dozen black leaders were arrested, court-martialled and sentenced to death. When Elgin asked for a stay, the governor resigned in protest at his interference in Natal's internal affairs, and all the Ministers threatened to follow suit. The Colonial Secretary might have had in the last resort the power to impose his views, yet he backed down and the men were shot. Bloodbath duly ensued: 3000 Africans died and Dinizulu, King of the Zulus, was imprisoned. Elgin did not step in again. In effect he fully conceded the principle of non-interference with responsible colonial government, even when it acted against his wishes, and even when to do so it had to rely on imperial soldiers.[10]

That set a pattern for the future of South Africa, which it now fell to the Liberals to decide. The central aim of policy was to treat Boer and Briton as equals. Campbell-Bannerman spoke scathingly of Milner, 'whose idea of making peace in South Africa is to turn the Dutch into English'. Even so, though on different grounds, the Government did desire to bring the two peoples together under a federal authority. The Colonial Secretary expounded his version of the concept in a paper to the Cabinet in June 1906. He laid stress not on grand imperial designs but on the practical problem of a panicky European population 'surrounded by coloured and more or less savage races'. Federation would make it feel safer and stronger, yet benefit the blacks too, because the liberalism of the Cape might then permeate the other territories.

But first it was necessary to grant responsible government to the conquered republics. The Treaty of Vereeniging at the end of the war had vaguely promised it, while giving the Boers no guarantees. Elgin hoped to delay any definite move till a British majority was built up in the country by immigration. The Prime Minister sharply disagreed, citing the results of plantation in Ireland. He insisted that the Cabinet must face, not duck, the question of how much power to hand back to the Afrikaners. On the table lay a draft from the previous Government for a constitution in the Transvaal with a strong executive little amenable to control by an assembly, which would in any case be rigged against the Boers. The Colonial Secretary, supported by imperialist colleagues, sought only to modify it. Campbell-Bannerman again intervened. He personally carried the Cabinet in favour of tearing up the draft and writing a new constitution on the principle of one man, one vote. In the event, it distributed the seats so as to give additional weight to the Rand and the *uitlanders*, though not to deprive the Afrikaners of a majority. It was left to Elgin to match this as best he could with some care for the blacks. Now the Boers insisted that indigenous rights, especially in respect of a franchise, were to be dealt with only after the achievement of self-government by the provinces. In other words, each was to maintain its existing franchise, so in the event there would be no vote for negroes in Natal, the Orange Free State or the Transvaal. In the last case, it was possible to slip in permissive provision for a native trust to look after their interests: it would have been toothless at best, but anyway remained a dead letter because a white initiative was needed to make anything of it. Campbell-Bannerman, in his radical's sympathy for the Afrikaners, had sold out the Africans.[11]

At the time, though, the settlement was hailed as a triumph for magnanimity and justice. The Transvaal's first elections in 1907 gave the British settlers adequate representation, and the Boers their majority, with which they formed a Ministry under General Botha. He ruled in the interests of his own people, but the Ministry in London looked on benignly, thwarting only his wish to annex Swaziland. It then granted a constitution to the Orange Free State, in an even more striking example of the policy of trust. Here there was no chance of a majority other than an Afrikaner one, quite likely intolerant and disaffected. Yet all the Liberals required was some protection for minorities. They had to their own satisfaction solved the problems: the Union of South Africa was formed in 1910.

The Liberal Government of 1906 indeed broke with everything that imperialists stood for: they opted for disintegration and autonomy in the Empire rather than for integration and centralism. We may note, too, since the policy was run by Scotsmen, that it realised old Scottish values. But it also contained a tragic contradiction. The old values had informed both the Scots' encounters in South Africa. It was as natural for them to see themselves in the Boers as to bring enlightenment to the blacks. Yet by the very fact that they now consummated their encounter with the Boers, they failed to consummate their encounter with the blacks. Only transcendent new values might have consummated both: perhaps the rejected values of the imperialists, though even then not certainly. At any rate, without an imperial constraint, white South Africa was free to follow her own path to perdition.[12]

CHAPTER TWENTY-EIGHT

'A movement among the Celtic elements': Imperial Politics

O n the evening of March 7, 1900, a mob of students gathered at a hall in Queen Street, Edinburgh, where a meeting to support the Boers was being held by the Stop-the-War Committee and the Independent Labour Party. They prevented entry by the guest of honour, Samuel Cronwright, a progressive South African politician and husband of the novelist Olive Schreiner. Inside, they shouted down Keir Hardie. Then, armed with clubs, they stormed the platform and attacked the party seated on it, singling out and beating up the kilted Theodore Napier, a 55–year-old Jacobite and Scottish Nationalist born in Ballarat, Australia. The meeting was abandoned, though disorder continued in the street outside. The same thing had happened the previous night in Glasgow. There the ILP's stewarding kept the rioters, again mostly students, out of the hall, but they paraded in front of it before going to wreck the office of the party's newspaper, the *Labour Leader*. And the same thing would happen the next night at a church in Dundee, where more students broke up the meeting, then threw stones at the manse. At that point, Cronwright gave up his Scottish tour. He afterwards published an account of it, under the sardonic title *The Land of Free Speech*, drawing attention to a remarkable degree of organisation among his assailants. His hosts, noting that the police were throughout nowhere to be seen, in turn hinted darkly at official collusion in violence designed to silence critics of British aggression.[1]

What seems more interesting about these incidents today is the role in them of educated youngsters, candidates for the Scottish bourgeoisie (a bourgeois riot does not, after all, often happen in Scotland). We may impute to them a material calculation, that their prospects depended on Empire. But clearly their commitment to it went further: it gripped not only their minds but also their hearts. By now this was true of many Scots, looking to an imperial destiny to consummate their nation's rise since 1707. Yet no older generation had been chauvinist in that sense, even while taking pride in Scotland's commercial, missionary or military prowess, which they could view in detachment from imperialism because of its deep roots in her own history. It had rather confirmed than denied what she thought of as her peculiar values. Thus far, we have mainly surveyed such distinct currents of Scottish sentiment or thinking, and the continuities in them. Here we turn to the discontinuities, and the changes wrought in Scottish politics at the heyday of Empire. Even so, the changes were incomplete, for Scots could no more agree about imperialism than anything else. On the contrary, the changes were contested.

Until now, Scotland had rested secure in her values. If diluted by the pressures of the modern world, they were also more diffused than of old, the property no longer of an elite but of the people. Cults of Robert Burns or Walter Scott flourished under an aura of symbols historic and rustic, above all Highland, which were harmless enough if representing nothing of the nation's urban, industrial reality. Still, they helped to keep alive a certain type of Scottish character, sober, diligent, thrifty, cross-grained, a certain aspect of the Scottish intellect, democratic in tenor, and a certain image of Scottish society, relatively egalitarian. The whole found political expression in the Liberalism of Scotland, grounded in ethical imperatives, rather insensitive to social or economic change and fairly indifferent to the problems of power. It did not wear well as in the last decades of the century it was drawn down divergent roads by fresh ideas often hard to reconcile with what it held dear, ideas which indeed it was finally obliged to leave to rival political forces. Meanwhile they cost it its moral unity, just as they cost it its physical unity, its command over the mass of Scots of every station in life and in every corner of the land.

Imperialism was one of those fresh ideas, its growing appeal to Scots singular because it had first struck them as suspect. Till the day of his death in 1855 the Nestor of the nation's radicals, Joseph Hume, had urged Britain to give up her colonies. Only 16 years later the scholar-politician James Bryce, of a generation that would live into the twentieth century, defined Empire with a shudder as 'the sacrifice of the individual to the mass, the concentration of all legislative and judicial powers in the person of the sovereign, the centralisation of the administrative system, the maintenance of order by a large military force'. Eight years on from that in his Midlothian campaign of 1879, William Gladstone roused Scots' moral outrage against Benjamin Disraeli and the newly imperialist Tories. They had, he charged, almost destroyed the Empire by attempts at central control of it, in contrast to Liberal policy of bolstering colonial loyalty with responsible government and free trade. In his sort of Empire, enhancing the individual's welfare, saving him from the moral evils of the mother country, Scots could still stay true to themselves. But now they needed only to glance across the border to see a different sort of Empire in the making – worse, one that was, in the words of Sir John Seeley, the "expansion of England". The Empire had indeed become again more truly an English one, a big country's Empire of conquest, occupation and settlement which, even if acquired in a fit of absence of mind, transferred English institutions to the colonies or imposed them on lands peopled by alien races. Disraeli struck a chord among the people of England by exploiting all that to save the Tory party from the extinction it might have faced in the dawning democratic age. In order to play a full part in his sort of Empire, even Scots such as David Livingstone and John Buchan were often to exalt English ideals too.[2]

Still, among most of their countrymen Disraeli failed. A year before his death, in

1880, he lost office for the last time to Gladstone, who came back into power as a Scots MP to boot. Whatever they might think in Dalkeith, the new premier found he could not annul imperialism. Adventures or misadventures overseas, culminating in the martyrdom of General Gordon at Khartoum, staggered a Government unready for such traumas. Gladstone's sudden espousal of Irish Home Rule in 1886 finished the classical Liberal party off. In England it also put paid to radicalism for the rest of the century and ushered in the high noon of Empire. In Scotland the outcome again differed. The Liberals' hegemony was shattered for ever, to be sure. Yet, with the deadweight of more cautious colleagues cast off into a Unionist party, the radicals had a last fling. They no longer had to compromise idealism for unity and could give vent to their reforming, democratic, internationalist, pacifist instincts. So the high noon of Empire found them turning more decisively against it: abroad as the oppressor of innocent foreign peoples, at home as the cause of taxes, militarism and an overmighty state sapping national resources and moral fibre. In other words it was a burden and Britain would be better rid of it, though few could say when or how. In practice such questions hardly figured anyway for 20 years, till the keeper of the Gladstonian flame, Henry Campbell-Bannerman, MP for the Stirling Burghs, became Prime Minister and won the Liberals their last great electoral victory in 1906. He saw his prime duty as holding the party together, though, and in the event did little to meet the Scottish radicals' higher hopes.

All the same, they meanwhile enjoyed some domestic success. It altered the Union, and that threw up implications for the Empire. The progress of the Union had been vexing Scots. They expected better of their new rulers after throwing off the Tory yoke in 1832 and with it the last trammels of semi-independence. The victorious Whigs promised to bring them for the first time within the pale of the British constitution. This "Scotch millennium" was to lead onwards and upwards, into a future which, whatever else, could only be unionist. But the new system, founded on the absolute sovereignty of the Parliament at Westminster, turned out in all essentials English, assigning to Scotland a provincial, subaltern role. Its subversion of national institutions generated huge problems. In the worst example, the Disruption of 1843, they set one, the Kirk, at odds with a second, the law, in a dispute which spilled over into a third, the universities. The harmony and balance underpinning the culture were being lost.

Within a decade followed the first modern protests against the progress of the Union. At first they bizarrely brought together the antiquarian patriotism of high Tories and the abstract idealism of wild radicals. The result was a milk-and-water affair compared to contemporary nationalist movements in Europe. Yet if dissolution of the Union barely figured on its agenda, its transcendence of normal differences in the cause of the nation proved significant. The Whigs' work of assimilation was halted, even reversed. That happened notably in the structure of government, the aspect of the Union least pleasing to Scots. They constantly complained about the neglect of their affairs at Westminster and the obstacles even to indispensable

Scottish legislation. The remedy canvassed was restoration of the office of Secretary of State for Scotland, abolished out of misguided spite in 1746. The pressure mounted till it became irresistible, unless Parliament was just to ask for trouble. The Bill to set up the Scottish Office, grudgingly introduced by Gladstone and almost lost at one point, went through unopposed in 1885 under his Conservative successor, Lord Salisbury. This inaugurated Scotland's modern political system. But already, for some Scots, the matter could not stop there: if public opinion had won back an executive, it might win back a legislature too. Gladstone was scarcely in a position to demur after espousing Irish Home Rule. He had stated in Midlothian: 'I will consent to give to Ireland no principle, nothing that is not upon equal terms offered to Scotland and to the different portions of the United Kingdom'.

The episode was a notable victory for the nation. From it indeed Nationalism emerged as a continuous, formally constituted organisation, in the first instance as the Scottish Home Rule Association. Backed by another rag-taggle of enthusiasts, it took on a colour of radical particularism, of anti-statist resistance to the centre. But popular support remained unsure, as Gladstone liked to point out. If he accepted parity of principle between Ireland and Scotland, so that Home Rule for one might lead to Home Rule for the other, he also stressed that Ireland was demanding it whereas Scotland, to date, was not. Putting his Irish Bill to the House of Commons, he seemed to place the neighbour island on a par with the settlements in distant continents rather than with the nations of Great Britain: 'The colonies said: "We do not want your good laws; we want our own." We admitted the reasonableness of that principle, and it is now coming home to us across the seas. We have to consider whether it is applicable to the case of Ireland'.

Gladstone was in fact irked by demands for equal treatment from Scotland, and dismissive of them. They could only be met by toning down his plans, in particular his subordinate proposal to exclude Irish MPs from Westminster. Wanting a bold, simple solution, and in essence wanting it for Ireland alone, he ignored advice to blur its edges and generalise it in a wider scheme. While without the Irish there would have been no devolution for anybody, implications for others could not be ignored. If, for example, Gladstone's plan was to set a precedent for Scots, it would shut them out of imperial affairs, an unacceptable prospect. Yet if it was to avoid the appearance of surrender to Fenian terrorism, Ireland ought not to be offered more than Scotland would in principle ever get. Here lay a recipe for stalemate. Even while being foiled, Irish Home Rule remained the cynosure, though it is worth remembering also that, in the period up to the First World War, Scottish Home Rule went to a vote in the Commons 13 times and on the last eight was carried. From the outset in 1889 a majority of Scots MPs voted for it. That became a majority of the whole House in 1894. But there was little to show except reforms of administration and parliamentary procedure. If nothing could be done for the benighted Irish, the Scots' special pleading inevitably fell on deaf ears.[3]

After all, the United Kingdom had since 1801 been no longer a simple Anglo-

Scottish affair but covered the entire British Isles. What happened in Scotland could be seen as part of a growing riposte from the periphery to centralisation in an imperial state. Nationalism stirred right round the Celtic fringe, with further help from another of Gladstone's parting shots, the Reform Act of 1884. Its biggest innovation lay in introducing a uniform franchise instead of the franchises varied and unequal, according to where the vote was cast, that had survived earlier reforms. Uniformity brought consequences larger in some parts than in others. It raised the electorate by 67 per cent in England and Wales, and by 80 per cent in Scotland, while in Ireland it more than tripled the electorate. Added up, the 700,000 Irishmen, 600,000 Scotsmen and 300,000 Welshmen now enjoying the suffrage formed 30 per cent of the whole electorate. That proportion of non-English voters stayed much the same till the First World War. In no other period have the Celts carried such numerical weight in the British system. For centuries, the trend had been for English dominance to increase; now they hoped to redress the balance, though the dawn proved false. The Liberals, a people's party in Scotland and Wales, could hardly avoid responding to Nationalism, in other words espousing Home Rule, yet they could not afford to annoy the English either. A comprehensive, coherent scheme of devolution adequate to this state of affairs remained elusive.[4]

The smaller nations did not help, for they scarcely made common cause. Scots eloquent in defence of oppressed Poles or Italians often thought the Irish quite a different matter. John Hill Burton, the utilitarian Whig, led till his death in 1881 a school of virulent anti-Celts extolling his compatriots' English connections and their role as partners in British imperialism. Other literati following the fad for scientific racism speculated gloomily on the quality of the nation's blood, whether its solid Lowland qualities were not tainted by too much Celtic unruliness, or whether a weakness for democratic anarchy did not handicap it in the modern world. If confidence in national virtues remained high, disappointments also pointed to vices. Since the Irish were everything the Scots did not want to be, these harped on differences rather than similarities: 'There is no love lost between the two countries', Campbell-Bannerman remarked.

The pair anyway experienced the United Kingdom in starkly different terms. The Union of 1707 was a success, the Union of 1801 a failure. Consensus, concord and confidence marked the Scots, division, discord and diffidence the Irish. Scots governed themselves at local level, and had won back a national administration; the Irish were ruled by alien gentry in the countryside and by Englishmen, sometimes Scots, in Dublin Castle. Scotland was politically serene, every section of society finding a place in the broad Liberal church; popular alienation and protest racked quasi-colonial Ireland. Scotland had her grumbles, yet none so grievous as the complaints of Ireland, all the old ones and then an array of new ones endlessly arising, not least from the coercion needed to keep the place in some sort of order. Scotland stood at the forefront of industry and commerce, while Ireland stayed backward and, next door to an economic superpower, eked out a bare subsistence. If with misgivings, Scots conformed to the interests of the Empire and, conscious of good fortune on that broader scene, kept their disputes domestic. Irish Catholics, even when they left their wretched homes behind, remained absentees at the imperial love-feast. Though in Parliament their Nationalist leaders held to constitutionalism, not demanding independence but accepting dependence as a compromise, they felt driven in frustration to fruitless wrecking of imperial business. Scots could never have acted like this, even the most radical, who with the rest vaunted their people as a loyal, progressive, responsible, successful one.[5]

Differences from Ireland appeared all the less unmistakable for coming home to Scotland in a flood of mainly Catholic immigrants who were poor, ignorant, superstitious and, so far as the natives could see, vicious. If sometimes of use as industrial coolies, these ragged hordes seemed, much more than the casual chauvinism of England, to threaten the Scottish character. In former centuries Scots had deeply influenced the course of Irish history. Now the tables were turned. That sharpened the religious strife which both Celtic nations knew anyway, bringing out the sectarian bitterness so peculiar to their stock and so baffling to the English. In Scotland, this strife had not thus far been strife between races or classes as well, let alone between imperial power and downtrodden masses, but the Irish diaspora brought some semblance of that. Many Scots felt shocked at any idea of granting Home Rule to such a deficient nation. Gladstonians found themselves hard put to explain how what was good for the Irish goose was not yet good for the Scottish gander.[6]

To others who cast off radical blinkers, however, a better idea occurred. Should a remedy for the Irish be necessary, but Gladstone's unacceptable, the whole problem might be looked at under a fresh imperial light. If Ireland could be found a place anchored in the framework of Empire, then the bonds of a Union increasingly rejected by her people would be eased without losing them altogether in an unpredictable and perhaps dangerous way. Ireland had after all posed a danger while she still lay outside the Union of 1801, itself prompted by rebellion and invasion at a time of mortal peril to Britain. Such spectres haunted statesmen yet, and would haunt them till the Second World War. The United Kingdom, once the sole imperial power of any consequence and still mistress of the seas, was meanwhile being challenged by Germany, the United States and other upstarts. It seemed insane for her voluntarily, through Home Rule, to recreate a threat at her own back door.

Scotland had a son eager to find his country a place on this broader scene. More to the point, Archibald Primrose, 5th Earl of Rosebery, was Gladstone's protégé and soon his heir apparent. After an education at Eton and Oxford ended by his preference for his stud over his studies, Rosebery assumed the informal direction of the Scottish Liberal party and in particular the management of the Midlothian campaign. He then set off, not without reluctance, for a career at the centre of imperial power in London. Reform of government being in the air, he manoeuvred to have a post of Minister for Scotland created in his favour. He did not succeed but he did make himself a spokesman for his country, welcomed and often cheered wherever he went.

Rosebery schooled himself consciously to be a Scot, as a man of his background perhaps had to, but he managed it well beyond the sentimental level common then and now. He did not believe his people could live in the past, though they might draw strength from it. He understood how for two or three centuries geostrategic reality had dictated that the future lay with empires rather than mere nations. He reckoned it to the Scots' credit that, despite the pain it caused, they recognised as much, responded and came to terms with the limited size and strength of their nation. They then saw gains, but also losses. Scotland lost in cohesion, in her former freedom of thought and action. A small state, if secure, could know and speak its mind, take broad views from the very narrowness of its territory and the integrity of its values. Enlargement of interest might imply contraction of freedom. Yet an imperial vocation demanded more of the same. As Scotland had been transcended by Britain, so England might be transcended by Empire. Rosebery entertained no doubt that for both the means to maintain or restore freedom and follow their destiny was to work towards realisation of the higher entity, within which he could continue to rest content with his 'lesser patriotism'. If the task must again prove hard for the Scots, it might prove harder yet for the English, they being less aware of the problem. The destiny of his people, Rosebery liked to say, was to 'mould the Empire', while their neighbours often shrank from 'the vigorous embrace of the new world'. On the broader scene, the destiny of Scotland might once again prove as exemplary as it had been to the men of the Enlightenment. Rosebery's patriotism therefore yielded only to his imperialism, 'the dominant passion of my public life'.

Rosebery became a catalyst for new Scottish values rising to compete with the old ones: collectivist, elitist, perhaps racialist, certainly imperialist values, hard to dismiss because they seemed to offer a way through baffling problems where otherwise an impasse had been reached. He readily gathered disciples round him. These Liberal imperialists were often Anglo-Scots, such as Richard Haldane, or English carpet-baggers sitting for Scottish seats, such as Herbert Asquith. While their elitism irritated the rank and file, after 1886 the shattered party could not do without them. Under Rosebery's patronage they embarked on a programme with no less an aim than saving Britain from her domestic and foreign perils.[7]

The special cast of Liberal imperialists' thinking posited that problems at home or abroad could be analysed and solved in much the same way. They made no clean break with the past, and in some respects barely questioned the older orthodoxy. They stuck to its commercial principles: foreign investment, freedom of capital movement, primacy of finance, profits from the carrying trade – in short the whole apparatus of informal Empire – remained for them the bedrock of British prosperity. Their key to the future was not economic but political: new politics would remove the need for new economics. Rosebery himself stressed, a little too much, the role of the leader benign but bold in thought and action. His true switch of emphasis was from morality to expertise, from individualism to organisation, from democratic anarchy to national interest, the whole summed up in his unfortunate watchword of Efficiency. As he and his disciples developed the basic outlook, they proposed that the state should act to remove obstacles by better education and training, industrial reorganisation, more positive social policies. These are the standard recipes of modernisers even today; the difference then lay in their imperial context. Empire was to become the vehicle of modernisation on a global scale.

That, of course, meant reforms at home too. Gladstone had himself lent his weight in Midlothian to the claim that British institutions were creaking: 'The Parliament is overweighted. The Parliament is overwhelmed'; it was necessary to 'take off its shoulders that superfluous weight by the constitution of secondary and subordinate authorities'. Here lay the germ of something to transcend impoverished radical nostrums, the concept of Home Rule all round. It was soon to win support across a wide spectrum of opinion, if with little more help from Gladstone himself. But Liberal imperialists could well see why his scheme of 1886 was not very acceptable to British voters: because its exclusion of Irish MPs from Westminster raised the spectre of separation. Rosebery, while backing him in public, maintained in private that it would be better to keep some. Forced by failure to think again, Gladstone at length agreed there might be ways to let them vote on imperial but not on purely British matters, in which case they could stay. Rosebery encouraged this evolution of his leader's views because he wanted to turn a measure to defuse Nationalism into one to promote imperialism. The virtue for him of the latest refinement was that it preserved Westminster as an imperial Parliament for the common interests of the British Isles. Disciples moved on to propose that each constituent nation should then have its own Parliament for dealing with domestic affairs. Measures to drain Irish bogs, create Scottish crofts or disestablish Welsh Anglicanism were of concern solely in their respective countries, where they should in justice and self-respect be decided. That would at the same time free imperial statesmen of legislative triviality to pursue a higher mission.[8]

Home Rule all round won keen converts among Scots. To Irishmen disaffected from any kind of Union, the precise proposals for devolution perhaps made little difference. With the Welsh the revival of Nationalism was only getting under way, and awaiting the young David Lloyd George to take off. The English, as ever, couldn't have cared less. Of the four nations the Scots, after devoting such huge human, material and emotional resources to both Union and Empire, showed the deepest interest in synthesis of them. Waxing more Scottish the further from home they got, they wanted nothing to narrow their horizons, unlike the Irish. They would surely have rejected self-determination that made of their border anything more than a line on the map. With Home Rule all round, they might control their own agenda in Edinburgh while continuing to play a full role at Westminster.

The most visionary did not see why such a redistribution of power need stop at the United Kingdom. A grander design still might lead on to imperial federation, with the relationship of Westminster to the other Parliaments in the British Isles offering a model for its relationship to the self-governing colonies. As a focus for the whole Empire, a supreme legislature would find enough work to do. Rosebery's mind early moved on these lines, though later he had some second thoughts. But in 1885 he wrote: 'I detest separation and feel that nothing would make me agree to it. Home Rule, however, is a necessity for both us and the Irish. They will have it within two years at the latest. Scotland will follow, then England. When that is accomplished, Imperial Federation will cease to be a dream'.[9]

An imperial solution to the Irish problem seemed propitious in a second way, because the Empire had reached a crucial formative stage. Some developments were negative. British strategy had long consisted in establishing the informal Empire so congenial to Scots. It held distant territories in primarily economic dependence, eschewing formal political sovereignty but keeping rivals out. Now in this system – in Africa especially, though elsewhere too – a major transformation was under way, to Britain's disadvantage. A complex series of events culminated in severe diplomatic defeat for her at the conference held in Berlin in 1884 to settle colonial differences among the European powers. It ended in sanctioning the scramble for Africa, and here her global strategy collapsed, as it did later in the Far East, Oceania and the Middle East. There was the added discomfiture that she had just failed in the First Boer War of 1879–81 to impose her sovereignty on the Afrikaner republics. The time had anyway come to reassess priorities and try to decide what new territories were to be acquired, under what form of authority and, indeed, for what ultimate purpose.

Other developments were more positive. Britain had sent her surplus population to live in distant parts: Canada, Australia, New Zealand, the Cape of Good Hope and so on. These colonies of settlement stayed loyal. If reorganisation should take place, it could start here. Britain was the sole power possessing such colonies. Though dispersed, they might be brought closer together in common structures which could help her to hold her position as an imperial power. But since this was the first time anyone ever thought of them in this way, the tendency of policy had long been opposite. Insofar as Scots could make a difference to it, they accepted not only the right but also the need for colonial societies to choose their own destiny once they reached a certain level of development. Since the 1840s, when the 8th Earl of Elgin led the way in Canada, nearly all had been granted responsible government. Westminster no longer claimed in practice any right to control their internal affairs. It did dispatch governors, but these were as constitutional as the monarch at home, forming ministries out of majorities in elected legislatures answerable in reality to their own populations.

The Canadians had taken a second step in the Confederation of 1867, of which the architect was another Scot, John Macdonald. It came in part as a response to the threat, on the agenda of the United States since 1776, to unite the continent one day. Support existed for such a project inside Canada herself, not just from radical admirers of American democracy but from the Scottish merchant community of

Montreal, who saw their markets of the future as North American rather than European. Macdonald could bring British Columbia and the Maritime Provinces into the Confederation only by heavy-handed manoeuvres, and Manitoba only by suppressing rebellion. Still, when 20 years later people began to ponder how to meet Gladstone's Irish problem without Gladstone's Irish solution, Canada seemed to offer a model. She consisted of disparate, recalcitrant regions not even all contiguous, for British Columbia lay 2000 miles away from the rest and the Canadian Pacific Railway had yet to be built. Yet they had by hook or by crook been persuaded to embark on an experiment which could not possibly end in uniformity: so anomalies were allowed and special provisions made for this and that. It did after a decade or two appear to be working. A new country had been formed which, with due allowance for the French, was recognisably British, owing allegiance to the Crown.

Could it be an example which, on a grander scale, the Empire might follow? With that in mind, the Imperial Federation League was formed in London in 1884. It appealed across the parties, as across the oceans. It certainly appealed to the Canadians, two of whose leaders attended the inauguration. One was Macdonald, now Prime Minister, the other his friend and colleague, former Minister of Finance and now Canada's first High Commissioner to the United Kingdom, fellow-Scotsman besides, Alexander Galt. He favoured boldness. He thought there could be an imperial assembly, with representatives from legislatures in the colonies of British settlement, then from England, Scotland and Ireland. Macdonald showed more caution. He ruled out parliamentary federation as impracticable and a uniform tariff in the Empire as contrary to the colonies' interests. But he saw scope for other forms of agreement on trade and for co-operation on defence, having no doubt that the daughters would always come to the aid of the mother country. This difference of interpretation between the two Canadians can be traced down the history of the issue for the next three decades.[10]

In Rosebery, Scotland had at the time an advocate of imperialist ideas no less eminent, and closer to Galt than to Macdonald. Freed in 1886 from the trammels of office, he became president of the Imperial Federation League. Under him, its aims captured the imagination of many Scots, and of many others. To Scotland indeed, if it had come to anything, the scheme might have offered a happier fate in later times, by averting the disorientation, demoralisation and provincialisation that followed economic collapse after the First World War. The narrower focus of the radical model, dealing discretely with mere local grievances of Scots and Irish, would have been inadequate anyway. This debate about Scotland's identity and role was never carried through to a conclusion, however. After just winning the General Election of 1892, Gladstone brought forward a second Home Rule Bill retaining Irish MPs at Westminster. It met the same fate as the first. At length it sent the Liberals, radicals and imperialists alike, into the wilderness for ten years to fritter away their energies and talents in squabbles with one another.

This time the fuel for dissension came not from nearby Ireland but from faraway

South Africa, as the next great imperial controversy arose with outbreak of the Boer War in 1899. Scots radicals felt outrage at the oppression of sturdy, God-fearing Afrikaners, so like themselves. It offended not only their politics but also their patriotism. To the Young Scots' Society, where a new radical generation was rallying, the journalist Hugh Macpherson declared that if excuses for British aggression were right, 'we who are proud of the long fight for Scottish independence need not denounce England as if she did anything dishonourable in her efforts to annex Scotland. Nor need the Boers feel aggrieved at the annexation of their country'. On the other hand Liberal imperialists could not in all conscience disapprove of the war. And they judged public opinion better: this was the first colonial struggle to arouse popular fervour in Scotland. Rejecting Irish Home Rule had been negative, but fighting for national honour in South Africa appeared positive. Scots did not imagine they were thus casting off their Scottishness; the new values they espoused seemed to them just as fine an expression of it.

At any rate Campbell-Bannerman, now Liberal leader, all but finished himself by a critical but neutral stance on the war, generally expressed through reasoned abstention in the Commons. On one occasion or another the majority of Scots MPs repudiated his line, either by combining with the Unionist Government or by voting against its South African policy. When in 1900 it called the Khaki Election after a run of military success, the Liberals lost their Scottish majority for the first time since 1832. This was unbelievable. Since pro-Boers had suffered most, Rosebery and the imperialists saw the chance of a coup. They set out to infiltrate Scottish Liberalism and take it over. But Campbell-Bannerman, underrated by his foes, came back from the political grave and could call on enough radical reinforcements to fend them off. He was also to be saved by events, by the British Army's dismal performance in South Africa and the infamy of its retribution on civilians. Sensing the turn of the tide, he reunited Liberals by condemning not the war itself but the 'methods of barbarism' used to end it. He isolated Rosebery, then demanded a firm statement of him whether he still counted himself a member of the party. The reply spoke of 'definite separation', if in terms so evasive as to exasperate even imperialists. All Liberals had grown tired of the internal turmoil which appeared to be the sole practical result of Rosebery's olympian concern with the great issues of the time. Campbell-Bannerman allowed that their tradition was open to change but stressed it could not come at the whim of one man.[11]

In fact, however the matter stood among the elite, the run of Scots Liberals never accepted the modernising credentials of imperialism. Progressive in outlook, they might in theory have been amenable to Rosebery's social and economic visions. But the electoral trauma of 1900 if anything drove them back on their old values. It was from a moralising radical platform, directed not least at the iniquities of Empire, that Campbell-Bannerman established his authority, not before time. True, he flattered imperialists with more favour than their numbers or influence now merited, so as to present his party still as a broad church. The tactics were vindicated by his landslide at the polls after the exhausted Unionists handed over power to him at the end of 1905. It was the last great victory for the Liberals, and a victory for the radicals especially. At least they put paid to Rosebery and his long-term aim of bringing together again the forces split in 1886, which is to say, of reuniting the Liberal imperialists with the Liberal Unionists who then deserted Gladstone over Ireland. That would have overborne the radicals, no doubt at the cost of a second schism in the parent party, but established the Empire as the dominant theme of British politics. So much the worse for Rosebery that he could not carry this off before Campbell-Bannerman checkmated him.[12]

As in many internal struggles, the outcome proved in the event to be no great matter. Victory did not really revive the Scots radicals. Their agenda after 1906 owed little to the new century, but fell back on unfinished business of the old; most of it anyway came to nothing. Nor did the imperialists do better, even after Asquith succeeded Campbell-Bannerman on his death in 1908. Over-represented yet in the Cabinet, they hardly fulfilled their earlier promise, the sole exception being Haldane, who as Secretary for War set up an Imperial General Staff, then as Lord Chancellor tried to promote the juridical unity of the Empire with a Supreme Court of Appeal, citing the analogy of Scottish civil appeals to the House of Lords. Otherwise, the imperialists endowed the Government with an overweening air which opened the way to the rise of Labour and eclipse of Liberalism. With or without Rosebery, their force was spent. Home Rule remained on the agenda, but not now linked to any wider scheme, certainly not to imperial federation: Asquith's mature policy in fact turned out closer to Gladstone's than to Rosebery's. He presented a rolling programme of Home Rule all round, first for Ireland, then for Scotland and Wales, though everything had to await passage of the Parliament Act in 1911. That ought to have given time to ruminate on an ideal reform of the British state. The Cabinet entrusted the task to Winston Churchill, after 1908 MP for Dundee and then Home Secretary.

A Minister primarily concerned with England should have been in a position to achieve a better balance than earlier efforts, with benefits for all four nations. But he also had to contend with the first backlash from Englishmen who did not want England, or by extension the Union, to change in any way. And from 1910 England again had a Tory majority. John Gretton, diehard MP for Rutland, warned of 'a widespread movement on foot among the Celtic elements in the UK to assert predominance over the Anglo-Saxon. An understanding exists between the principal Irish, Welsh and Scottish parties to co-operate at the right moment'. In his view the Scottish city of Glasgow and the English city of Liverpool had almost ceased to belong to the Union, forming part instead of some wide Atlantic world. Ireland lay athwart their routes to it, as large Irish minorities in their own populations reminded them: hence their impulse to appease Ireland, which the English should not fall for.

Churchill at length concluded that, while England bulked larger than the other three nations together, it would be undesirable to have sitting in London a

Parliament both for her and for the United Kingdom as a whole. His compromise was to divide England into regions each with its own Parliament. Assessing that the English would never stand for this, Asquith dismissed it out of hand: 'We cannot go back to the heptarchy'. The Cabinet decided to press ahead in Ireland anyway and leave the rest till later. When Asquith introduced the third Irish Home Rule Bill in 1912, he promised it would be 'only the first step in a larger and more comprehensive policy'. No policy as such ever appeared – a pity, because that by definition might have gathered more general support and deterred particularist opposition. Meanwhile under the Parliament Act, the Bill had to pass unamended in three successive sessions to override the inevitable Lords' veto. While the procedure dragged on, Ulstermen girded their loins with such implacable resolve as to daunt all hope of imposing anything on them. If the third Bill got no further than the first two, prospects seemed dire indeed: civil war in Ireland, constitutional crisis at Westminster.[13]

Still, none of this seemed to worry Scots Home Rulers, pursuing what they identified as their best opportunity since devolution had come on the political agenda a quarter-century before. Despite cold blasts of indifference from on high, Liberal backbenchers continued to put down resolutions and draft Bills of their own. At length they won their point to the extent of getting official support for one of these measures. It would have created a Parliament in Edinburgh with authority over such powers as were already transferred to the Scottish Office. It made its desultory way through the session of 1913–14, though it was expected to pass by the end. But as soon as war broke out it lapsed, along with Irish Home Rule.

While the nation's gaze then became riveted on grimmer matters, the lack of regret or resentment seems odd. The reason surely lay again in the limited vision of Home Rule's radical sponsors, their lack of interest in wider repercussions, their preference for moralising rectitude over practical consequence. With the rest of their agenda in a mess, they did need a cause: in fact their warnings that without Home Rule their party had no future proved true in the end. But the public grew alarmed at the direction of devolution, in Ireland towards bloodshed and treason. It appeared a high price to pay for a project which in Scotland promised little more than improved administration. This failure came in part by chance, but also by the bankruptcy of radicalism. On August 4, 1914, there vanished forever, as it turned out, all chance of rational modernisation in Union and Empire. Since they had passed their apogee, this was perhaps as well. Contrary to Scottish expectations, nations were about to start dismantling empires.[14]

There was at any rate no more need for the Left to come to terms with imperialism. It relinquished the cause to the Right where it was appropriated in a form not threatening to the British state. In Scotland the origins of this process can also be traced back to 1886, to the revolt against Gladstone over Irish Home Rule by a large minority of the classical Liberal party. That issued in Unionism, a movement which in contrast to hidebound radicalism seemed assured and open-minded, free of past trammels and eager to embrace the future. By the same token it was attuned to a need for all the peoples of the British Isles, each with their own histories and aspirations, to be sure of proper places in one Union and Empire.

Scots offered a prime example. Unionism's boisterous Britishness was at the same time robustly Scottish in a flag-waving way alien to crabbed Calvinist radicals or to Rosebery's scholarly cultivation of national sensibility. It also displaced the slow-witted, blue-blooded Tory party which was what had remained in Scotland from repeal of the Corn Laws in 1846. In this, Scottish Unionism was to be distinguished from English Unionism, which after its first eruption could seldom be told apart from English Conservatism. The Scots kept an independent mind as well as an independent organisation. Their roots, lying in the old Liberalism, were on that account partly radical. This explained why they pursued certain interests always unsettling to their English allies – in free trade, education, welfare and the land. At any rate they escaped being absorbed by or even subordinated to the Conservatives. Confident of outdoing the English, they also diverged from a third family of Unionists, those in Ireland herself, whose defensiveness made them wary of perfidious Albion. In its essentials this Scottish Unionism would last a long time.

It was above all a populist movement, and the great centre of population lay in Glasgow. In 1886 the city forsook Gladstone to a remarkable extent. It was imperialist because its business relied on Empire: now the Empire's future appeared to hinge on Ireland. The West of Scotland also had old cultural links with Ulster, along with modern material links. The elites of Glasgow and Belfast, making and trading much the same things, found at this crux that they differed little in political outlook either. Nor had there ever been a bar to workers moving back and forth between Lagan and Clyde, so that the Scottish industrial system lay open to the influence of immigrant Ulstermen. They imported the Orange Order, which fostered an evolution of restrictive practices grown in part out of the ancient traditions of indigenous crafts, not yet broken down by a century of *laissez-faire*. While bosses turned a blind eye, trade unionists regulated membership to maintain wages by agreement with foremen who used the Order as a clearing-house for apprenticeships. They confined jobs to an acceptable group, usually sons or relations of men already employed, in any event Protestants, keeping out Catholics ready to work for less. Everyone was happy except the excluded, who did not matter. This role of the Orange Order, as of freemasonry in some sectors, may have been fortuitous, but it forged a link in men's minds between Scottish industry and the higher entities on which they reckoned it depended.

A common interest thus stretched up and down the social scale from manu-facturers and merchants to skilled tradesmen. That alliance of economic elite and protestant proletariat formed the core of Unionism. Even before 1886 Glasgow had cherished a vision of an ideal industrial society where regulation by a paternalist corporation would bring the energy of capitalism and morals of the citizens into a harmony enriched with the best the world offered: the architecture of Europe, arts of the Orient, enterprise of America, products of the Empire. Despite the stark contrasts of rich and poor within its bounds, the city spurned the socialist politics emerging in England and instead sought tranquillity in a system designed to defuse clashes of capital and labour. Unionism in effect took it over, or rather added a political superstructure to it. The result was a broad-based movement of urban and commercial interests understood in the context of Union and Empire.[15]

While in the workshop of the world people knew their prosperity depended on British greatness, they held no less high an idea of Scotland's place among the nations or less firm a resolve to maintain it. The immediate stimulus to Unionism came from Irish Home Rule, but it grew from seeds deep in Scottish soil which had only to be germinated by the sudden change of political climate in 1886. The Irish question was in other words a catalyst for forces anyway transforming Scottish politics, as they had transformed Scottish society and culture.

Scots, after overcoming their initial awe at the scale of the imperial enterprise they entered in 1707, had made themselves a commercial Empire out of it. They rationalised the process into the theory of political economy, vindicated by the loss of the American colonies in 1783. For a period their ideal was then realised in an Empire of free trade sustained by a maritime strategy. Scots set off into it with supreme self-confidence, as authors of its central truths. And those truths at length became almost the official doctrine of the British state, with the repeal of the Corn Law and the Navigation Acts in the mid-nineteenth century. Still the world's leading industrial power, the United Kingdom in effect asserted a right to get cheap food for a burgeoning population from wherever it wanted, without favour to colonial producers – almost claiming its autonomy from the Empire. Fanatical adherence to this doctrine was more a hallmark of the English utilitarianism, however, than of the Scottish political economy which had given it birth and which it now displaced. Scots found it tended to sacrifice their catholic empiricism for rather too much logical rigour.

For example, the Empire of free trade heralded in 1783 had rested on an assumption, at least by Scots, that resources would remain in the hands of alien peoples. It became ever harder to reconcile this with the plain facts of renewed British conquest, occupation and settlement in distant lands. Scots accepted that free trade also went with responsible government, as rendering superfluous any mercantile control of colonial economies. But trade was soon restricted again by colonies' claims for fiscal freedom, that is, for duties on imports from the mother country. London at first disallowed some of those imposed in Australia and New Zealand, but gave way when the more politically formidable Canada followed suit. Having claimed her own independence from the Empire, Britain could hardly refuse it to her eldest surviving daughter, not after the sharp lesson of the American Revolution. An English sort of Empire soon seemed less compatible with free trade than utilitarians assumed in their habitual glib manner. By the turn of the twentieth century, further implications were clear. For Britain the appearance of serious economic rivals posed a question whether she could promote a system of free trade of general benefit to all, rather than of particular profit to herself, when others would not play so fair. But splendid isolation held its own dangers: hence the effort to persuade the Empire to draw closer again, not least economically. Scottish thinking also began to shift away from free trade, at least in the rigid, dogmatic guise that English utilitarianisn had imposed on it.

In the intellectual van stood William Cunningham. Once intended for the ministry of the Free Church, he had then taken Anglican orders and afterwards pursued an academic career at the universities of Cambridge, London and Harvard. He became the British pioneer of economic history, borrowing concepts from Friedrich List and other European national economists to apply to his own country. As it had lost its industrial lead, yet depended on foreign food and raw materials, he doubted if it was still best served by free trade. This caused problems both at home, because workers did not benefit from foreign investments, and overseas, as in Ireland and India. It might still work in the neutral markets of third countries where all had a chance, but in the imperialist scramble for the remaining parts of the globe such markets were vanishing. Cunningham called for a turning back, despite some undoubted costs, towards protectionism. Then James Shield Nicholson, professor of political economy at the university of Edinburgh for 45 years, set out to link such new ideas with native tradition, and explicitly with the passages on colonialism in *The Wealth of Nations*. Since 1776, he affirmed, free trade had 'assumed a dogmatic simplicity and universality not recognised by Adam Smith'. Smith could have possessed no concept of the modern Empire with colonies adopting protectionist policies for their own development. The way to reconcile them with the mother country's interests was by imperial preference, that is to say, by tariffs against imports from foreign countries. With internal free trade and a common external barrier, no part of the Empire could complain of exploitation by another. Nicholson also recalled that Smith had proposed a form of imperial federation, as a logical consequence of his placing defence before opulence. Altogether, he thought, paternalist co-operation for the general welfare would prove more capable than liberal individualism of ensuring social equity.[16]

Still, Scottish Unionism, being above all a populist movement, was not a very intellectual or otherwise a very consistent one. So much became clear when in 1903 it faced a challenge to follow its own economic logic from the irrepressible Joseph Chamberlain, who as chief defector from Gladstone was leader of English Unionism. Now serving as Colonial Secretary under Arthur Balfour, he rent a second Ministry from top to bottom by taking up imperial preference and launching a great campaign for it. He wanted to restore British pre-eminence by forging the Empire into a single trading bloc, the world's mightiest. Interestingly, he set out to do so from Scotland, not from Westminster, nor yet from his own territorial base in his native Birmingham. Instead he chose to launch his campaign from Glasgow, a stronghold of classical political economy where Smith himself had taught. Chamberlain perhaps calculated that, if he could convert Scotland, the rest of Britain would fall into his hands. Scotland, however, remained wary of English dogma.

Chamberlain's chief, Balfour, proved in that respect worthy of his ancestry in the landed gentry of East Lothian, or rather in *nouveaux riches* who had bought their way in on Indian money, enough of it at length to ally themselves by marriage with the neighbour nation's high aristocracy. A Scottish philosopher to trade, Balfour's scepticism was reinforced by the run-down political inheritance from his uncle, Salisbury, to which he had succeeded a year before. He accepted the argument that rigid adherence to free trade was counter-productive in a country at risk from lustier rivals. Still, he distrusted Chamberlain's sweeping remedy, as he distrusted all sweeping remedies. He saw the difficulty of imposing imperial preference on established interests. He doubted if any new system would turn out on balance better than the old, since no magic wand could ever be waved to solve the world's problems. Turning to the wider imperial scene, he understood how little natural harmony existed in it, so that Dominions were unlikely to compromise their interests for the sake of a higher entity, let alone of the mother country. Empire had a certain useful potential, but it could not be realised by forcing the pace. Even so, the boffin in Balfour found the debate beguiling. Odd as it may seem for a beleaguered Prime Minister, he wrote a short theoretical tract of his own, *Economic Notes on Insular Free Trade* (1903). There he balanced the respective arguments in a compromise: the British trading system should remain open in principle while retaliating against less liberal countries if they put tariffs on its products. Probably he had with this more of a political than an economic aim, confronted as he was with a schism not dissimilar to that which had beset Campbell-Bannerman, requiring him to hold the middle against two extremes.

On one side Balfour faced Chamberlain, his most powerful Minister, whose brainchild he thus had to take seriously. His hope lay in persuading him to settle for a policy of retaliation as a practical first instalment on the greater project and hold off from that while opinion matured. So he did not rebuff Chamberlain but told him that if imperial preference was the cause he had at heart, one which formed as yet no part of the Government's programme, he had better resign to conduct his campaign: should he convert a majority of the voters, the rest would follow. On the other side Balfour faced Unionist free traders hostile to all tariffs. He had resistance inside his own Cabinet from a couple of Scots, Charles Ritchie, the Dundonian Chancellor of the Exchequer, and Lord Balfour of Burleigh, the Scottish Secretary. These were lesser men whom he could sacrifice if need be, and in the end they saved him the trouble by resigning. But they did represent Scotland.[17]

When pressed on the matter, Scotland took her stand for free trade. Even Glasgow did: imperial preference could not loosen the hold of political economy on its calculating mind. If the city's elite refused to shift, neither could its Unionist party. The workers, too, still equated free trade with emancipation from effete aristocrats now intent on regaining lost privilege through tariffs to restrict imports and raise living costs in the mother country. But why should imperialist Glaswegians have thought like this? And why should the ideological shift represented by Scottish

Unionism have reached its limits at free trade? A French observer, Victor Bérard, thought he understood why. According to him, free trade offered a rational course for an exporting country with specialised markets, which was to say, a rational course for Scotland. Since English demand for her goods had fallen and no longer absorbed her production, she sent them to America, to other industrialising countries and to new colonies. For example, she sold merchant ships to a range of European customers, while Chile, China, Japan, Portugal and Russia bought as many warships as the British Government. Since Scotland traded more outside the Empire, protectionism would be of less benefit to her than to England. Bérard wrote that Scots did support the Empire, but 'they see all too clearly what they would lose in the event of a militarily and exclusively national Empire being established'. If Bérard was right, he underlines how, even amid decay of a native tradition in political economy, Scots remained independent enough of mind to resist an English sort of Empire.

Chamberlain's campaign failed anyway, leaving nothing to show but more of the disarray in the Government which would call down such retribution from the electorate in 1906, not least in Scotland. By then the people decided the Liberal party alone could be trusted to guarantee cheap food. Glasgow, where Unionists had made a clean sweep in 1900, returned instead a slate of free traders, mostly Liberals. The alliance of 1886 between elite and proletariat cracked. Scottish Unionism was never quite to recover the impetus of its first 20 years.[18]

At least it kept its independence of mind, not just over protectionism but also over Home Rule. In 1886 many Unionists of the first water had taken their stand against the specific terms of Gladstone's proposals for Ireland without prejudice to wider aims of their own. They, too, often thought Scotland's affairs neglected at Westminster, and some favoured Home Rule all round or formal federalism. Less was heard from them after 1895 when Unionists went for the first time to sit on the Tory benches at Westminster. But federal ideas meanwhile made progress in the Empire. Australia federated in 1901. So, after the Boer War, did the four provinces of South Africa, by way of a daunting exercise to reconcile differences between two British colonies and two conquered Afrikaner republics. This was the work of Lord Milner's kindergarten, especially of his young, high-minded Scots and of the idealistic but pragmatic solutions they conceived.

Once home again, it was they rather than distracted Liberal Ministers who sustained intellectual debate on the constitution. Then as now there was a problem in awakening at Westminster any understanding, let alone acceptance, of federalism in the United Kingdom. A time-honoured Scottish response to such obtuseness was to found a journal. In 1911 Philip Kerr set up *The Round Table* for the promotion of 'an organic union to be brought about by the establishment of an Imperial government constitutionally responsible to all the electors of the Empire, with the power to act directly on the individual citizens'. But he feared reality could not measure up to his fine words and high ideals. His friend John Buchan, too, had a respect for nationhood which made him sceptical about unity among peoples lacking it in a form strong and confident enough for self-conscious use. Frederick Oliver was a more ardent Nationalist, something he may have owed to his heredity as a grandson of Duncan McLaren, MP for Edinburgh and pioneer of Home Rule in mid-Victorian times. He insisted that Scotland retained 'every characteristic of a proud and self-reliant nation. Her nationality is no abstraction, but a tingling reality. Her traditions have suffered no wound or injury in loyal co-operation'. He saw the emotional force behind Scottish Nationalism, and the faltering ability of Liberals to harness it. Perhaps, therefore, the Unionists might.[19]

Unionists remained Scots patriots, never to be swayed from that by alliance with English Tories (a lesson which could have been better learned in later times). The party reminded its prospective candidates early in 1914, in time for a General Election which did not look far away, that 'Scottish National sentiment is a strong force in all ranks of Scottish life'. After again rejecting devolution as a threat to business and jobs, this paper took care to distinguish two types of national sentiment: a 'parochial, parish-pump type, based more largely on jealousy of others than on pride in national achievements and capacities', and a better type linked to a 'wider imperial patriotism'. The second type could be enlisted by Unionists. Conspicuous by its absence (compared to corresponding documents in, say, 1997) was any notion of Scottish dependency in the British state: Scots ought to support the existing order not because they were unable to rule themselves or pay their way, but because they possessed an identity so strong as to render it immaterial what government they lived under. They could in any event rejoice at their place in the wider scheme of Union and Empire, loved as they were at home, admired abroad.[20]

So Scots Unionists did not ape English views of relations among the nations of the United Kingdom. That was confirmed during the renewed struggle over Irish Home Rule, the visible cloud on Britain's sunny horizon before 1914. In Scotland, the results of the crisis in 1886 had been internalised. At this third crisis, Scots stepped forth in both Ireland and Great Britain as champions of Ulster. They defended rights for the province which even the rapid development of its own self-consciousness over 30 years did not yet put it in a position to defend for itself.

Scotland's distaste for catholic Ireland was all along stoked by a parallel connection with this second Ireland, largely Scots in ethnic origin, Evangelical in religion, and dating from the plantations and the Covenants. Ulster had yet, as Scottish colonies were wont to do, gone its own way. No more here than in distant continents was a little Scotland replicated. A democratic intellect evolving more radically than its archetype had reached its apogee just before the Union of 1801. Sturdy religious dissent was matched by a secular idealism aiming at both reform and conciliation with Catholics, though Protestant posterity would recall with blushes the brief alliance of 1798 in the cause of the whole Irish nation. Cultural impoverishment followed. The community came to define itself not by nationhood but by religion. By contrast with Scotland, the two were severed. The tragedy and triumph of the Disruption, while destroying the Auld Kirk, galvanised Scots with patriotic and imperial energy. It even jolted Ulstermen: the Irish General Assembly of 1843 called for united Presbyterian pressure to be brought to bear at the point where the Empire's fate was cast, at Westminster. The charge dissipated, however. If Ulster had an equivalent crisis, it came with disestablishment of the Church of Ireland in 1871, and that cost Irish Presbyterians the *regium donum*, their tangible link with the state. They took a long step into the laager of a menaced and intransigent minority. A community voluntary in its religion and provincial in its politics ought still to have felt much in common with Scots radicals, who had shown the same attributes and often been allies. But when the moment of truth came in 1886, most refused to join Ulstermen in rejecting Home Rule. That was explicable given their movement towards a particularist Nationalism of their own, though failure to adapt old loyalties to fresh challenges hinted at a flagging of their vigour. At any rate, Scottish support for the Irish Union had to be drummed up elsewhere. It was found among those expansive Unionists who conceived of a fellow-feeling even with reclusive Ulstermen that others could no longer summon up.[21]

Memories lingered of what they had shared though the reality of it was fading. The emotion of the hour brought it to mind. A popular book, *The Scot in Ulster*, came out in 1888. Its author, John Harrison, was a Scotsman struck on a visit to the province by survivals of immigrant culture from the seventeenth century. He stressed how, as in the mother country, this character had been tempered in the struggles of a heroic Protestantism. While not unsound in his scholarship, he was essentially inspired by the romantic Covenanting historiography of contemporary Scotland. On this side of the water it plucked at the heartstrings and gave devolving statesmen more than they reckoned with when they tried to browbeat Ulstermen. On the further side it restored to the province a heritage lost, or anyway lacking, and one as valid as any to be discerned in the Celtic twilight by Irish Nationalists. The whole at length bore fruit in a potent symbolism uniting the Protestants of Ulster for the struggles they were to face in the twentieth century. As soon as Asquith introduced his third Bill, they set about organising against it under Edward Carson. They summoned a convention to Belfast to voice their protests. It drew up a pledge to fight Home Rule which on "Ulster Day", September 28, 1912, was signed by more than 200,000 people, some in their own blood. They called it their Covenant. Thousands of Scots Unionists signed copies sent across the North Channel.

It was a moment, remembered up to the present, when Scots and Ulstermen stood shoulder to shoulder. But the solidarity hid different motives. Ulstermen valued Union and Empire above all on sectarian criteria as safeguards for their own embattled position. Their stance did not lack support among Scots. It inspired the leader that Unionism brought forth to match the hour. Andrew Bonar Law could always be relied on as a stern and stubborn defender of causes close to his heart, which in the Unionist way often proved to be popular causes. He was himself a Scottish triumphalist. Unlike any other politician since Henry Dundas, he owed nothing to England in background or education. In his blood ran the unyielding

Presbyterianism which united the West of Scotland and Ulster – capable also of export, for he had arrived as a child from New Brunswick, where his father, born at Portrush in Antrim, served as an emigrant minister. He qualified himself for public life by making a fortune in the mercantile elite of Glasgow. Law's Unionism was wedded to imperial commerce, unabashed about riches, egalitarian without being compassionate and tending to rigidity on certain matters of vital concern to itself, not always grasped elsewhere. That meant Ireland *par excellence*, for this Unionism had sprung to life to defend the Irish Union. Law rejoiced to champion his embattled kin in their struggle against Home Rule: there was 'no length of resistance to which Ulster can go in which I would not be prepared to support them'.[22]

The historian Lord Blake called Law the "unknown Prime Minister". Then and since, Englishmen have sought in vain to understand his austere view that, Ulster being right, Ulster had to fight. It was his almost treasonable conduct of opposition in the crisis that made him "unknown", because incomprehensible, to them. Of a man refined by Westminster's parliamentarianism they entertained expectations, not least that he should behave in an English manner. In one or two ways he did. He was a better unifier of his party than the silky Balfour: while he had supported imperial preference and lost his first seat in Glasgow for his pains, he agreed that now was no time to argue about something so secondary as tariffs.

Yet Celtic obduracy and sectarianism formed a stronger part of his make-up, more chilling because unwarmed by the Celtic fire the English could take account of, as in Lloyd George. Instead there was in Law an unsentimental calculation which put the interests of the Second City before those of the First: London lay at the edge of his world, Glasgow at the centre. He did not care a fig what people in London thought about Ireland, or their basic desire that the problem should just go away. He saw Ireland from Glasgow, especially its Presbyterian population in the North, forming one cultural and economic zone with the West of Scotland, washed by the wide Atlantic which represented at the same time opportunities for trade and a threat to security if ever Belfast or Londonderry should fall into the wrong hands. That gives a clue to the ampler motives of Scots, contrasted with Ulstermen, even in the solidarity of this crisis. To Scots it was the crisis not of a province but of an Empire. Law regarded it as such and the fact almost made him, in the strange way a diehard can be, the man to clinch a compromise.

Certainly that seems true in comparison with the weary, disenchanted Balfour. He, too, had personal experience of both countries: after his native land had launched his ministerial career in 1886 when he became Scottish Secretary, he went on to serve as Chief Secretary for Ireland and earn the nickname of Bloody Balfour for his readiness to coerce. In him the contrast between the two deepened a much more philosophical sense of the Scots as an exemplary people who, with a separate and troubled history, now reinforced Union and Empire through their multiple loyalties. 'It is only by following the example that we have set that the future of the Empire can be made absolutely secure,' he told them, looking forward 'to a time when Irish patriotism will as easily combine with British patriotism as Scottish patriotism does now.' Set against that ideal he found the Ulster Unionists almost as wanting as the Irish Nationalists, and would take no chances for Ireland. In 1910, while still leader at Westminster, he received an intriguing message from Lloyd George. The Welshman feared that, with the Lords about to lose their veto, the two big parties had doomed themselves to a fight to the death over Home Rule. To that he preferred coalition. He proposed a basis for it in a hybrid programme which borrowed devolution, welfare and national insurance from his own side, military national service and imperial reorganisation, political or economic, from the other. Lloyd George and Balfour held secret talks, letting very few others into their confidence – though one was Law, whom they wanted to consult for his ties to federal Canada as well as to Ulster and Scotland. Yet it all came to nothing. Balfour, recalling the fate in 1846 of Peel and a Tory party that abandoned a great principle, in the end told Lloyd George to forget it.[23]

But Law did not forget it. He had succeeded Balfour as leader of the opposition by the time the Irish Home Rule Bill went in 1913 from the Commons to the Lords, who took just nine days to throw it out. A long hiatus had to follow while the Parliament Act was invoked, in which any kind of trouble might blow up. The grim prospect gave everyone pause, not least Law. He wrote in September to King George V urging a way out through 'a scheme of devolution which would apply not only to Ireland but to the whole of the United Kingdom'. In other words he wanted His Majesty's Ministers to make a reality of their promises on Home Rule all round which they had forgotten in a quest for easier options. Law declared, by contrast, that a comprehensive scheme was still something he could consider with an open mind. Here was a Scots Unionist receptive to ideas for a new status in a new order for his nation: but it had to be an enhanced status in a rational order with benefits for everyone, rather than a device to avoid English Liberal embarrassment. For this as for all such ideas, however, time was running out. Law would yet bring the same broad view to the changed circumstances after 1918. No man then did more to create the political entity of Northern Ireland, under a regime of Home Rule he had earlier rejected for the island as a whole, the difference now being that it would be set up separately in both parts. This monument to him survives into the new millennium, but it was not a model that would serve beyond Ulster.[24]

Hence it was the sole form of Home Rule possible in the United Kingdom till the end of the twentieth century. That does not mean the devolutionary ideas produced in the ferment of three decades between 1886 and 1914 were bad, for the inertia of people and institutions means many good ideas are stillborn. The men involved lived after all in a Britain not too remote from ours, with some of the same problems, of an advanced industrial society trying to cope with fierce international competititon. They had to consider what political apparatus was best for doing so and they wondered whether a broader framework than the United Kingdom was the right one. In the days of the Empire that led straight on, as it does now in Europe, to the issue of parliamentary sovereignty. The basic question these men faced was whether they should embark on systematic reform of the British state, interrupt its organic growth (or habit of mend-and-make-do) and set the whole thing on a rational basis calculated to meet the problems arising by very virtue of its global eminence, of the Empire in particular. To that question, Gladstone, Campbell-Bannerman and the radicals said there should be internal reform but not external reform; Chamberlain and the English jingos said there should be external reform but not internal reform; Rosebery and his imperialists said there should be both; Balfour and the Conservatives said there should be neither.

As for Scotland, her devolutionary aspirations widened only to narrow again. They narrowed indeed almost to nothingness, not to revive for 60 years. The ideological contests of the earlier period, if pregnant, proved barren. That spelled also the end of a greater project, of reconstructing the Empire according to Scottish ideas as some sort of federation: at the imperial noontide, Scots would have settled a score dating back to 1707. Though this arose from a movement among the Celtic elements, it was not in motivation necessarily anti-English. Scots by now accepted a community of interest with England seldom shaken even by vexation with the English. Some of the vexation was provoked by the sloppiness of an Empire functioning as a quasi-federation where nobody knew how far loose central authority tempered large local autonomy. Worse, by the end of the nineteenth century that authority was tightening inside the United Kingdom while it slackened beyond. How were the positions of Scotland, Ireland and Wales to be reconciled with those of Canada or Australia? Yet Scots could not see, probably did not want to see, that there was no need to do anything while the status quo remained acceptable to the colonies. Once the status quo became unacceptable, the Empire just dissolved. In reality it could never have been unified even in a limited fashion. Before long the evolution of the old Dominions into independent states, with secession of southern Ireland from the United Kingdom, demolished imperial federation as a halfway house to Scottish sovereignty.

If not anti-English, and indeed meant to be congruent with British patriotism, the greater project would yet have been bound to reduce English domination of the whole, or at least to deflate the pretensions to absolute sovereignty at Westminster. Above all it would have aimed at a rational result dispelling imperial absence of mind. That result would not have been an English sort of Empire but a Scottish sort of Empire. The notion was a spectacular example of contemporary Scottish self-confidence. As so often, though, Scottish self-confidence outreached reality. We might say with hindsight that an ultimately sterile argument thus ran its course. Home Rule would only have been possible at the end of one of two processes: either of breaking the British state down, as radicals wanted, or of building it up, as imperialists wanted. Neither happened. The British state never did reform itself and the old order straggled through by its own lights to a new era.[25]

Part Four

A Crumbling Empire

CHAPTER TWENTY-NINE

'A mother state': Imperial Politics

A t half past five on the morning of April 9, 1917, Easter Monday, the flower of Scotland's youth sprang from the trenches defending Arras in northern France, and advanced towards the Germans investing the town. The Scots saw round them only a dark mist flecked with snowflakes, falling since an hour before the bitterly cold dawn. They heard only the thunder of guns, in the greatest barrage of the war to date, and the shriek of shells that it sent overhead. When they got to the enemy's front line, they found it no longer existed. There was just a hummocky waste of craters and broken wire, all of which they had occupied just 40 minutes after the assault began. With the barrage creeping ahead of them, they moved on against a second line, to be met with the same scene. It was theirs by half past nine. They pressed forward again and, as evening fell, captured much of a third line. They had gone four miles, by the standards of this war a stupendous gain. It was one of the deceptive moments when breakthrough on the western front looked possible.

The Germans' resistance seemed indeed to be crumbling. They were caught out with nothing now to halt the onslaught short of a fourth, incomplete entrenchment six miles back. They had been at work since the New Year building this system, the Hindenburg Line, at a distance sometimes 30 miles behind their previous positions. They willingly yielded the ground: from the four zones of defence, linking Arras with the heights of the Aisne round Laon about 60 miles to the south-east, they aimed to launch an offensive mighty enough to split the British from the French army and defeat each separately. Their retirement to it had taken place in February, in an operation of such precision that the Allies did not at first understand what was happening. They found, all of a sudden, nothing in front of them. They probed cautiously forward, then decided to try a bigger push.[1]

General Douglas Haig, the Scot commanding the British army, accepted the plan of his French counterpart, General Robert Nivelle, for a combined attack on the enemy's flanks: with both ends of the Hindenburg Line captured, it would collapse and open up a vast breach. Haig would strike out from Arras on a front of 12 miles, though this was to be in the nature of a feint, to draw the Germans northwards and weaken them for the smashing blow which the French would deliver by storming the heights of the Aisne. Even so, he gathered the largest concentration of forces since the Battle of the Somme nine months before, 14 divisions comprising 120 battalions of infantry. Of these, 44 were Scottish, 38 from the homeland, the rest from the diaspora. They numbered more than the whole British army engaged at Waterloo, and were seven times the size of Robert Bruce's army at Bannockburn. Arras was the biggest battle Scotland ever fought.

Scotland won the first day. On the second, the attack petered out. Many units saw clear ground in front of them, but had no orders to go on, nor behind them any large reserves to press home the assault. Problems abounded, of course. In the awful weather, the earth was sodden. During the deadlock on the western front, infantry had become the handmaiden of artillery, and it took a while to bring up the ordnance thought necessary to let the soldiers advance further. Enemy machine-gunners held out in pockets, making the use of cavalry impossible; in any case there was again none to go through, and no light tank available as a substitute. Altogether, failure to follow up the initial victory must be put down to feeble staffwork. The unimaginative High Command had never expected its own troops to do so well. Knowing this to be only a diversion, it felt satisfied when the gains sufficed to make the shaken Germans draw on their reserve. It thus lost its chance. Now there could be no more than minor operations to round off the territory won, and the usual conditions of the war descended again.[2]

One operation which may serve for an example was directed at the village of Roeux, on the River Scarpe just beyond the new front line. It had not been a pretty place, but a grim industrial settlement typical of the region, living off a chemical works. It became the scene of bitter fighting, above all by Scottish divisions, the 9th, 15th and 51st. In this stubborn struggle Haig, pinning his faith on his countrymen, kept them continuously engaged. Unfortunately, the enemy concentrated against them a huge array of machine-guns: it was the first battle in which these proved decisive. Three days after the original advance, the 11th and 12th Royal Scots attacked the works. They had to cross a wide open space in full view of the Germans with no artillery to support them. Yet at one point it looked as if the lads of the Lothians might perform a miracle. After their previous triumph, they felt invincible. They went on and on till both battalions had been reduced to 100 men. Following them came companies of the Canadian Seaforths which suffered casualties of 93 per cent, including all their officers. The most heroic, Lieutenant Donald Mackintosh, was last seen, thrice wounded and covered in blood, pulling himself to the top of a German trench to urge his men forward; he won a posthumous Victoria Cross. The survivors returned from the carnage undaunted, but those looking on could only deplore such useless sacrifice. The works remained in enemy hands.

Minor operations gradually extended into more ambitious ones, with a cost in lives to match. On April 23, battalions of the 51st Division renewed the onslaught, faced now by some of the toughest Prussian troops. The 6th Gordons, advancing through a hail of automatic fire, all but disintegrated as a unit. Small parties still pressed on, reached the works and drove out the enemy. They held on till dark against furious counter-attacks. The closeness and ferocity of fighting round the village may be gauged from a gruesome scene discovered afterwards. On the steps of the cemetery an enemy soldier and a sergeant of the Argylls were found locked in death, the German with his teeth in the Scot's wrist, the Scot with his in the German's throat. Both had been killed by a shell. On April 28, the 15th and 16th Royal Scots assaulted Roeux itself. Each was down to 400 men, half the original strength. The 16th would lose another 200 in this action, and the 15th another 300, including their commander, Captain Gavin Pagan, formerly minister of St George's, Edinburgh. They actually occupied the village, after penetrating a wood in 'crazy fighting' and breaking through into the ruined streets. There they suddenly found no more resistance. It seemed odd that the British barrage was now falling in their rear. They waited in vain for a regiment of the Lincolns who were supposed to come up and join them. Then the truth dawned. They had gone through the front lines and were cut off. The enemy saw this too. While the remnants of the Royal Scots reformed along a road between the village and the river, they were attacked from three sides. One chance remained: to slide into the water and swim back under cover of the bank towards Arras. About 30 soldiers tried, but most were wounded, and the effort proved beyond them. Germans appeared, hauled out the exhausted survivors and made them prisoner. On May 3, a fresh assault captured Roeux, again at enormous sacrifice, only to see it retaken the same day. In fact this was a defeat, and marked the end of the whole offensive.

Meanwhile, on April 16, the French strike to the south had failed, despite deployment of every available division. The results of Nivelle's master-plan turned out to be an advance of 600 yards and such horrifying slaughter that the French army mutinied. The British had got further, but with little else to show. In less than a month of fighting they suffered losses of 150,000. If we assume that to this, at a minimum, the Scots' casualties stood in the same proportion as their membership of the whole army, then 60,000 men were killed, wounded or went missing. With the appalling haemorrhage on such blood-soaked fields the Empire, British and Scottish, began to die too.[3]

It may seem odd for any Scot, in telling this story, to have omitted the total of casualties, and stressed instead the booty won from the enemy. But that is what we discover in John Buchan's official history of the war, from which the account above largely comes. In this work his range is comprehensive, his narrative gripping, but he remains reticent on the numbers killed. Perhaps he felt remorse for having failed in some sense a supreme test which others met, including his own younger brother, Alastair, a lieutenant in the Royal Scots Fusiliers who fell at Arras that very Easter Monday. Buchan had tried to enlist, and got into the Intelligence Corps. His poor health made conditions on the front intolerable for him, however. He was posted back to London to become director of the new Department of Information, in charge of propaganda, a job extended by the commission for the official history. Though his duties proved demanding, he may still have blamed himself.

At any rate it is not only in the history that, after the war, we hear an altered tone in his literary voice. In previous novels the central figures, often placed in an imperial setting, had been essentially aristocratic, if sprung in several cases from the Anglo-

Scottish *haute bourgeoisie*. They were the sort of men the author had mixed with, and become one of, in South Africa. Though looking like amateurs, they knew their business backwards and conducted it with superb skill, whether building a great commercial combine or ruling a conquered territory. In them Buchan did much to create an important image of imperial Britain, of a trading nation's solid virtues raised to a higher plane by a noble ideal. For Scots who partook of it, the ideal was more austere yet: personal ethos, educated intellect and technical proficiency stood to be proven in the crucible of the fallen world, issuing in a stoical devotion, a kind of secular Covenanting. To Buchan, if not to every one of his countrymen, this Empire fulfilled above all the destiny of Scotland.

But the war marks a caesura between the earlier and the later works. Nobility had then gone for little, or at least victory exacted such a price of it as to cast doubt on its moral value. Buchan's favourites, Richard Hannay, Sandy Arbuthnot and Edward Leithen, still figure, only now afflicted by malaise. The vitality is displayed by a new set of characters, representing Scottishness in more authentic, not to say humane, form: Dickson McCunn, a Glasgow grocer, and the Gorbals Diehards inseparable from him. They never appeared, and would have been scarcely conceivable, in the previous novels. In place of nobility, then, we see bourgeois morality and solid proletarian worth. These are still Scottish values, though, and capable of sublimation.[4]

Surely Buchan's moral odyssey represented something wider in the experience of his nation. In high patriotic spirit, with no disaffection from the British state, it had fought a tragic and wasteful war to the end. For Scotland the peace turned out tragic and wasteful too, if in a different way, with economic disaster on a scale rendering her comparable to those societies which in consequence suffered collapse and revolution. To that extremity she was never reduced, despite brief stirrings in the Glasgow of January 1919. But grand old ideals, combining romantic nationalism with imperial aspiration, dissolved.

Scots thus felt forced to take stock of their identity, and seek ways to renew it. One possible way was to redefine the nation so as to make it more distinctive from the British and imperial context in which for two centuries it had flourished. Not surprisingly, this proved no easy task. Modern Scottish Nationalism, with formal origins in the political upheaval of 1886, had to that extent itself grown out of imperial aspiration. Right up to 1914, when only the outbreak of hostilities halted passage of a Home Rule Bill, Scots still thought this a means to get the Empire working better. Nor did the war quite kill the idea. Some saw in the common struggle still greater reason for a more equitable arrangement among the nations of the United Kingdom, and among the Dominions. It 'has made us feel, as nothing else has ever done, that we are in truth all members one of another,' wrote Murray Macdonald, Liberal MP for the Falkirk Burghs, in proposing yet another scheme of imperial federation and Home Rule all round in 1917.[5]

But several developments combined to halt progress in this direction. One was that for the Dominions a more equitable arrangement of a wholly different kind would soon be found. They were nations in embryo, as Scottish philosophy had predicted they would become and as Scots felt ready to acknowledge. Before the war imperialists of every political hue had assumed that some central authority could guide the destiny of an Empire where the white races would continue to rule. After the war, those assumptions vanished into thin air. Buchan's later memoirs seemed almost to deny that they had ever been real: 'Our creed was not based on antagonism to any other people, it was humanitarian and international; we believed that we were laying the foundation of a better world'. Now, at any rate, he and his fellows expressly advocated not dominance by Britain but her partnership with the Dominions, all working together for peace through the League of Nations. Buchan, appalled during the war by the racialism of the Germans and impressed by the gallantry of Indian and African troops, abandoned his other earlier certainties of which peoples were superior and which inferior. He no longer excluded the possibility that they might in time be every one capable of governing themselves.

The Dominions, however, were not satisfied with airy generalities. They had freely rallied round Britain in 1914. They still felt galled that they were not actually asked to: King George V simply declared war against Germany on their behalf. Their feats of arms and sacrifices strengthened their sense of nationhood. This altered mood might have been mollified by their individual membership of the League of Nations. But Britain would still not countenance separate diplomatic representation for them in foreign capitals, and in the 1920s she tried to draw them into a scheme of imperial preference with an insistence which reminded them that she had never formally renounced her sovereignty over them. Given these niggling grievances, nobody could be sure how the Empire was going to develop.

It might even have fallen apart, for several Dominions elected governments of a nationalist kidney, under William Cosgrave in the Irish Free State, General J.B.M. Herzog in South Africa and William Mackenzie King in Canada. Each sought explicit change in the constitution of the Empire. Cosgrave resented being held inside a supposedly voluntary association. Herzog wanted a positive right to secede from it. King strained at an imperial leash he found binding him during a quarrel with his Governor-General, who refused him a dissolution when he lost his parliamentary majority but granted one to the opposition after it failed to form a new Ministry. King won the ensuing election, and vowed never again to suffer such an insult to Canadian democracy from some British fuddy-duddy. Whitehall could not be unaware of these rumblings. Largely out of anxiety about them no new Imperial Conference, a regular event before the war, was called till 1926. Before they left home for the mother country, the Prime Ministers let it be known that they would insist on clearing up the question of their sovereignty.

The time had come for the English to do something of which they were always wary, and define a constitutional doctrine. When finally forced to in this case they turned to a Scotsman, Arthur Balfour. He had, while Prime Minister after the turn of the century, taken a wholly pragmatic, not to say cynical, line on imperial relations, falling neither for the dogmatism of free trade nor for quixotic schemes of federation. In his view the Dominions were sure to go their own way in the end, and nothing much could be done to stop them. Yet bonds of goodwill might be maintained, a 'sense of unity and the necessity on great occasions of making a common effort'. His task now was to cast that sense in 'some complete and perfect form', though Balfour's ideas of completion and perfection turned out as usual more blurred than others'. He was asked anyway to draft for the conference a statement meeting the Prime Ministers' wishes. Even the hostile Cosgrave and Herzog would accept it as their formal resolution at the end of the proceedings.[6]

The statement defined the Dominions as autonomous and equal in status, not subordinate to one another in their internal or external affairs, but united by allegiance to the Crown and freely associated in the British Commonwealth. It sounded platitudinous, and was meant to be, as Balfour conceded in expository speeches. Common loyalty, freedom and ideals were the bond of Empire, he told the House of Lords: 'If that is not enough, nothing else is enough'. Its members stood on a footing of equality and felt responsibility for one another, but 'as to what that equality involves, as to exactly what degree of responsibility each has for the other, on that I personally think very little is to be gained by refining, discussing or defining'. Before an audience in Edinburgh, he asked aloud whether his arrangement was the best: 'The question is, in my opinion, an idle question, because the constitution now formally declared is absolutely the only constitution which is possible if the British Empire is to exist'. It would be enshrined in the Statute of Westminster (1931), the legal basis of the Commonwealth.[7]

Vague as it was, it did make a difference. That became clear just five years later at the abdication of Edward VIII. This was not taken to be a matter solely for the Parliament at Westminster. Separate legislation had to be passed in each Dominion. Visibly now, the monarchy was no longer a unity, as it had been when George V declared war. And eventually the capacious official doctrine would make room in the Commonwealth for nations quite alien in character from the old Dominions which prompted its framing. That things might turn out so probably never occurred to Balfour, yet this lasting achievement must be ascribed primarily to him. A Scottish philosopher apart from everything else, he saw through the received wisdom and transient circumstances to define as precisely as was possible the stage which the Empire had now reached.

By so doing he quashed one Scottish hope, of a United Kingdom recast by Home Rule all round within an Empire recast by federation. In a sort of stadial theory, the hope posited ultimate reconciliation of nationalism and imperialism. As the peoples of the different territories passed up the scale of development, their growing communal self-consciousness could, instead of dividing them, be transcended. In fact the opposite happened. Nationalism displaced imperialism, and the Dominions claimed their sovereign independence. The prospect of federation was gone for good.

With it went the counterpart of Home Rule all round. In practice, though, it had already vanished off the agenda because of events inside the British Isles.

There the project of general devolution died in Ireland, the very country for which it was designed. The war and its aftermath saw the ruin of Irish constitutional nationalism, seizure of the initiative by revolutionaries, and secession from the United Kingdom of the 26 counties. Scots still found it hard to shake off a notion that the two Celtic nations might somehow set an example for each other. Even on the Unionist side, Balfour had till 1914 argued that they shared a common destiny: the Irish were bound to follow the Scots, if somewhat behindhand, in achieving full integration in the British state. In a sense this was what his adversaries on the Left argued, except they thought it would be helped, not hindered, by Home Rule all round. They too showed some impatience with Irishmen envisaging a different outcome. They were thus unready for, and felt horrified by, the Easter Rising of 1916. One Liberal theorist of the imperial constitution yet capable of thinking things through was Arthur Keith, professor of Sanskrit in the university of Edinburgh and former civil servant in the Colonial Office. He recognised that, from a Scottish as well as a British point of view, Irish nationalism had now turned pernicious. At this stage he still believed an independent Ireland unlikely because of the strategic threat she would pose: she would not want to be an ally of Great Britain and could become a grave menace. Yet there was no question of restoring the *status quo ante*. 'We must concede to Ireland a measure of self-government which will go far beyond what I desire to see secured for Scotland, and when Ireland has that we shall be driven into demanding more than I personally desire to see given'. He did not draw the alternative conclusion that Scots might prefer to forget the whole business.[8]

In 1918, however, both countries stood according to official doctrine in the same position as in 1914: they were alike candidates for Home Rule all round. For Ireland, Sinn Fein's victory at the election straight after the armistice prompted a rapid legislative response on those lines. Its inadequacy in the face of nationalist claims was not at once widely understood. One who did understand it was the young Walter Elliot, in this his first Parliament. During the debates, he constantly moved amendments tending to grant powers worthy of sovereign bodies in a new state. 'Are you afraid of an Irish Republic? Why, I should threaten them with an Irish Republic if they didn't behave,' he said. Perhaps the future Secretary of State for Scotland – and in that post a pragmatic devolutionist – sought to set precedents for his own nation in case, after all, the Union was not so much dissolving as undergoing radical reform.

Scotland did begin to move slowly forward in tandem. Action for her of some sort had been endorsed not only by Elliot but by most Unionists elected in 1918, as part of their pact with the National Liberals inside Lloyd George's coalition. A Speaker's Conference on Scottish Home Rule was called in 1920, and at length drew up a plausible scheme. It need not have bothered. The Government of Ireland Act, passed the same year, never worked. It was not repealed but simply overtaken by events, in particular by Sinn Fein's assumption of authority *de facto* in the 26 counties. The Ministry's most trusted adviser, John Anderson, the formidable Scottish mandarin in charge at Dublin Castle, still urged Home Rule for a united Ireland as the least of the available evils, the solution likely to minimise violence. But his compatriot in the Cabinet, Andrew Bonar Law, stood firm on the rights of Ulster, in other words on partition. The Prime Minister, despite his own perennially open mind, saw no choice but to go along with his Unionist colleagues, who not only had exceptionally strong feelings on the matter but also formed the greater part of his parliamentary majority. The Act was thus superseded by the Treaty of 1921, which set up a Free State in the South and granted Home Rule to the North, pending a final all-Irish settlement perforce postponed by civil war and in the event never to come.

From all this we may safely conclude that Scotland showed no unity of view about Ireland, and that any sense of a common destiny had evaporated. Scots did not wish to follow the example of the Free State. They were if anything glad to see the back of the Irish, once these came out in their true anti-imperialist colours. The partition drew on the map a line long felt, far above any sense of Celtic fraternity, to be there, between the feckless, superstitious papists of the 26 counties and the Scots themselves with their cousins in Ulster, all God-fearing, hard-working Protestants: hence the new virulence in Scotland against Catholic immigrants or their offspring during the 1920s. This was odd at a time when the immigration had in fact dried up, though only after creating a community which amounted to about one-sixth of the population. Some now hoped to get rid of it, especially certain luminaries of the Church of Scotland. The leading clerical figure of the era, the Rev John White, displayed an anti-Irish rancour matched only by his zeal for reunion with the Free Church. This he engineered in 1929, finally healing the wounds of the Disruption and recreating one Kirk for the nation. In his mind, hostility to Ireland formed part and parcel of renewed Scottish identity.

Events did nothing to dispel the link. From the start the Free State showed an independent spirit and soon, under the Statute of Westminster, had an independent status. That was still not enough for Eamonn de Valera's extreme nationalists, who lost the civil war but before long won power democratically and set out to secure sovereignty without qualification. To do the business in such messy circumstances it has always been useful to call on a dispassionate Scot. Malcolm MacDonald, Secretary of State for the Dominions from 1935, spent three years negotiating the terms on which an Irish Republic might eventually be constituted: by staying in the Commonwealth, recognising the king as its head, and accepting that a united Ireland would only come about with Ulster's consent. He could not have known that his concessions on sovereignty were to be used by de Valera to stay neutral during the Second World War. This strained even MacDonald's composure. In June 1940, he went on a secret mission to Dublin, trying to bring Ireland into the war. In return, Winston Churchill offered military aid for defence of the whole island, which was to be conducted by a joint council from both its Governments. He further authorised

MacDonald to say that an accord on these lines could be the first step to reunification. Britain was ready to accept it in principle without prejudice to the details. But the mission failed. The commitments were still not hard enough for de Valera, who refused to abandon his neutrality. As a consummation of Ireland's nationalism and independence, that left little room for regret on either side when, now indeed a republic, she left the Commonwealth in 1949.[9]

No more than the Dàil in Dublin did Stormont in Belfast offer a useful precedent for Scots. The point may be surprising. Ulster, tied to Scotland by blood, culture and religion, showed Home Rule of a sort to be feasible. Yet in fact, of the United Kingdom's constituent countries it was the least fit for a devolved parliament just because it also contained a large, disaffected minority belonging to Catholic Ireland. The purposes to which the system then had to be put discouraged confidence, remote though they were from anything Scots Home Rulers had in mind. Of course, divergence in the evolution of the mother country and of this, as of all Scottish colonies, had continued. Ulster's frustrations since 1801, brought to the pitch of paranoia in 1886 and 1914, made for an especially sharp contrast with the progress and optimism of Scotland over the same period. Scotsmen opened their minds on a global scale, but Ulstermen closed their minds. They came to judge every great matter, the very fate of the Empire, solely on its utility to them in warding off the papist threat to home and hearth. Protesting loyalty to a greater whole, they in fact steadily set themselves apart. In 1921, Westminster sealed this anomalous status. If Northern Ireland's relations with the Free State remained murky, its relations with the mainland were clear. It would not be integrated into the British state, and British politics would not operate there. The dominant party of Ulster Unionists was complicit in this, for it granted their wish: to run what James Craig, their leader in the formative years, lauded as 'a Protestant Parliament for a Protestant people'. For half a century they succeeded, with results sufficiently well-known.

While during that period the English gladly forgot Northern Ireland, the Scots never quite did. The province could not be considered fully anomalous by them, because they had some of the same ethnic and religious divisions on their own soil. But their responses underlined the divergence between the mother country and the colony. There were, admittedly, a few similar responses. Presbyterian anti-papist diatribes of the 1920s found an echo well beyond douce, churchgoing circles. In the mean streets of the West of Scotland especially, the Orange Order, the Freemasons and the Boys' Brigade raucously amplified them. These were authentic proletarian movements of long standing, given a new impetus by defiant solidarity among Scots workers as economic disaster beset them. They were also common to the Protestant communities on either side of the North Channel, and they turned the solidarity into ferocious discrimination against Irish Catholics in the workplace and elsewhere. This paid off for Unionist politicians. In Northern Ireland it did so by committing the populace to political institutions which they had never actually asked for. In Scotland it did so because it impeded the conversion of the proletariat to socialism, especially as employers connived in the restrictive practices. Surely nothing could be more Celtic, less English, than this bigotry. Yet by dint of condemning all things Irish it celebrated all things British, underwrote the Union and incidentally rejected Scottish Nationalism.[10]

Still, differences between the two Unionisms remained stronger. Scottish Unionism had long outgrown its origins in the Irish crisis of 1886 and developed an outlook relevant to its own circumstances. It aimed to identify the interests of Scottish capital and of the British state. Victorian values were vanishing, with the whole nation undergoing a shift from individualism to collectivism. Unionists had been collectivists from the start, if seldom in the paternal manner of English Tories. The businessmen who bankrolled the party also carried about with them enough Scottish democracy to make it now both an asylum for homeless Liberals and a bandwagon for bigoted workers. Of course it would never let the grassroots actually influence the exercise of power. In 1921, having negotiated the Irish treaty, it ignored howls of protest from the Orangemen and, when they broke off relations, coolly left them to it. Unionism's stock as a defence against Irish disloyalty and subversion was not to be so easily exhausted. Yet its Ministers at the Scottish Office adopted notably progressive policies in education, housing and welfare, all on public monies won from London, which were of special benefit to the depressed Catholic community and indeed began its eventually successful integration. To the stricken private sector of industry, meanwhile, Unionists proposed the remedy of more formal organisation in cartels and the like, forging links to the state which in turn designed instruments to overcome the economic crisis. The programme, generous and popular, was a fine political balancing act. It gave Unionism its electoral dominance between the wars.

If eminently pragmatic, the programme also touched deeper chords. The answer it offered to questions of Scotland's identity was to affirm her place as a constituent of the British state and resolve remaining doubts by developing the benefits of centralisation. Crucially, enemies of Unionism took their stand primarily on grounds neither of religion nor yet of nation, but of class. Even when attacked, therefore, it fulfilled its purpose by contributing to the realignments which now brought Scottish politics more in line with English politics than ever before. The programme would in the long run have its limits. It reduced national interests to regional ones. It at last even rendered contemptible the figures of the Scottish establishment who devised it, after the British state decided they were incapable of delivering full employment and took over the job itself. But exactly the same thing happened in Northern Ireland – and Stormont made no difference. In reality an absolutely sovereign Westminster could not be stopped, even by the existence of a parliament, from giving the law at will to a peculiar province. Yet perversely, as the episode of 1940 showed, the parliament might serve to cut Ulster out of Westminster's long-term calculations. There was simply nothing for Scots in that sort of devolution, the only sort of devolution around.[11]

By comparison with neither half of Ireland, then, can Scotland be said to have lost much by settling for what she had after the First World War. We find few contemporary statements of the choice as, *faute de mieux*, the most acceptable; searchers of Scotland's soul were more likely to dwell on decline and exhaustion. But it may be significant that Buchan wrote during these years a novel, *Midwinter* (1923), which he set at a crux of Scottish history, in 1745, the time of the last Jacobite rebellion and the last threat to the Union. Two heroes figure in it, a gallant Highland officer and Dr Samuel Johnson, both profoundly attached to the House of Stewart. At the end each decides to take a different path, but each has despite himself become aware that their old loyalties are giving way to new ones in a new nation, comprehending both Scotland and England. And this seems to offer a better guarantee of peace, prosperity and civilisation than anything they can propose instead.

Buchan became a politician too, as Unionist MP for the Scottish Universities in 1927–35. He showed little taste for the hurly-burly of Westminster, and found no preferment from the Governments he supported, perhaps because he formed friendships on all sides and made non-partisan speeches. He made one of the best on November 24, 1932, about Scottish Home Rule. The Union he called 'a blessing beyond doubt', but he said he still hated some of the arguments advanced against reforms of it. 'I believe that every Scotsman should be a Scottish Nationalist,' he went on. Since Scotland's problems were neglected by a Government concerned mainly with England, she paid a high price for her present status. Moreover, 'the Scottish people, with a long tradition of democracy in their bones, are at least as capable of running a Parliament successfully as any other race.' If it could be proved that a Parliament in Edinburgh was desirable, Scotsmen should support it; even if it could not be so proved, but was still desired by a majority of Scots, then they should be allowed to make the experiment. Curiously Buchan added that, since these two conditions had not been met, he did not himself support such a Parliament. He thought it wrong to break up a successful social and political unit into which Scotland was integrated. But what clinched the argument for him was her share in the management of the Empire: 'Why should we want to be a daughter state when we are a mother state?'[12]

Too big a man to make a good politician, Buchan may yet be taken as a representative figure. So long as the Empire lasted - and there were few visible signs at this stage of its dissolution – it seemed to most Scots only sensible to work within that framework, despite the doubt cast on imperial idealism by the war. It was much the same as settling for the United Kingdom. Even those rejecting the minor premise might accept the major one. The National Party of Scotland, founded in 1928, crystallised what had been a broad current of opinion into a separate political force for the first time. Its members easily agreed on breaking away from England, but not from the Empire. While it contained a few anti-imperialists, most seconded the opinion of its leading intellectual, Andrew Dewar Gibb, professor of law at the University of Glasgow. He called Scotland and England two imperial 'mother nations', the 'defenders and begetters' of the Empire; self-government would strengthen that status. His view was inscribed in the fundamental doctrines of the Scottish National Party as defined on the reorganisation and union of earlier groups in 1934, the formal origin of the movement we know today. Its declared aim was 'self-government for Scotland on a basis which will enable Scotland as a partner in the British Empire with the same status as England to develop its National Life to the fullest advantage'.[13]

Labour, also seeking a fresh start for Scotland, had through Keir Hardie a strong tradition of anti-imperialism. It waned as the party grew into a contender for power. Since it identified the state as saviour, it naturally had to be ready to assume all the state's responsibilities, including the Empire. Thomas Johnston, later Secretary of State for Scotland, made this a special interest. He took Labour's economic orthodoxy, the under-consumptionist theory of J.A. Hobson, and gave it an imperial application. He proposed a new trading policy under which Britain and the Dominions would set up an official agency to purchase food or raw materials and exchange surpluses among themselves. The Empire would function as a single economic unit, cutting out capitalist middlemen and speculators. In effect, this was a socialist form of imperial preference. Johnston's ideas also had a political aspect, conceived to counter Unionist appropriation of Empire and to offer something positive from the Left on a subject about which Liberals or Communists had little to say. He thought, for example, that Labour might work with the fraternal parties powerful in certain Dominions against exploitation. Perhaps one day they could all come together in a federal imperial Parliament, which 'might be made the greatest lever for human emancipation the world has ever known'. In Britain it would be supplemented by Home Rule all round. But Scots had been here before.[14]

In these realities of politics, the resurrection of the nation and the exaltation of the worker, we have a parallel to what Buchan set out in literary form. They were efforts, on the one side bourgeois and on the other proletarian, to sublimate Scottish values in a new system to replace spent imperialist heroism. Neither prevailed, though they offered many something to live by in times at best humdrum and at worst desperate. But it was not an epoch favouring renewal. Most Scots held on to what they could from the past. Of that past, obscured by the dust and smoke of Arras and a thousand other battlefields, the Union and the Empire seemed to have been sure foundations. The visions they now offered were narrower, just as expectations of them were lower. But the time for conceiving of a Scotland outside the scope of imperial politics had not yet come.

CHAPTER THIRTY

'A national home for the Jewish people': Palestine

N ebi Samwil, at 3000 feet the highest of the Judaean hills, is a brilliant white, conical peak overlooking Jerusalem four miles away. Called after the prophet Samuel, who found there his last resting place, it became the Mizpeh or watch-tower of the tribe of Benjamin and the Mountjoye of the Crusaders. They gave it that name because, like many other conquerors, they had from the summit inspired themselves with the sight of the Holy City before moving on to take it. On November 21, 1917, Scots of the 52nd Lowland Division occupied the mountain.

Their action was crucial to General Sir Edward Allenby's campaign for Palestine. In this sideshow to the First World War he had the slenderest resources to work with, but the 52nd made up for many deficiencies. It had long faced the Turks, starting at Gallipoli. Transferred to Egypt, it crossed Sinai and fought three battles round Gaza before advancing into the hills. It suffered 700 casualties, men who at such a distance from base could not be replaced. Still, the division was never decimated, as it would have been in France, and so did not see its Scots character diluted by helter-skelter drafting of recruits from anywhere. It continued to uphold the high patriotic spirit and the stern Presbyterian discipline of the homeland.[1]

Those qualities were vindicated on Nebi Samwil. The 52nd's salient stretched no wider than a single ridge, where stood a mosque and a small village amid its gardens. Yet from here the troops commanded the country all about Jerusalem. The Turks, believing it both possible and necessary to retake the position, set out to do so the very day after the Scots arrived. As the sun went down, 500 of them launched an attack. They were stopped by a single company of the 7th Cameronians, reduced by losses to 30 but luckily in possession of a Lewis gun. With it five men held the foe at bay on a narrow track, as others protected them from walls and roofs. Further fighting was bound to disclose the defenders' weakness, hidden for the present by the falling darkness, so the assailants had not just to be checked but routed. A second company of the Cameronians, no more than 70 strong, did the job. They scaled a low cliff on the flank, fixing their bayonets as they scrambled up. Then they hurled themselves into a fierce hand-to-hand struggle with 200 of the enemy still milling round the mosque. The Turks fled.

After five days, indeed, they gave up and withdrew from Nebi Samwil. Two weeks later Allenby marched into the Holy City. There are moments in every campaign when a crucial part may be played by a few, and here 100 Cameronians were the key to victory. They held on and saved a position which could have turned in the enemy's favour. That was why Jerusalem fell when it did. The Scots felt all the more disappointed that they had meanwhile been ordered to pull back, and missed the honour of taking part in the ceremonial entry. Like Moses, the divisional history records, they were only allowed to see the promised land from far off.[2]

We may well believe that Scots soldiers still turned to scripture in moments of strong emotion, for the Holy City and the Holy Land had always aroused the Christian devotion of their nation. On the first crusade there went one Robert, son of Godwine, a knight with lands in the Lothians; taken by Saracens, he was martyred for his faith. Scots then joined in every crusade up to the seventh, when a troop of chivalrous paladins included Robert Bruce, Earl of Carrick, the Competitor of 1290 and grandfather of King Robert I. The king himself always wished to reach the Holy Sepulchre, and asked for his heart to be cut out and carried there after his death. One other Scotsman went in peace. In the winter of 1228–9 the Emperor Frederick II visited Jerusalem, not to fight but on a mission of diplomacy. He admired the Arabs, as they knew, and persuaded them to hand over the city for a brief while to the Christians. In his entourage he took along his physician, Michael Scot. This man's learning and skill so overawed his age that he was to be depicted as a wizard in Dante's *Inferno*, the sole son of his nation to appear there, damned to shuffle round with face and feet turned in opposite directions. His reputation reached back to his native heath, where fellow Borderers imputed to him the splitting of the Eildon Hills in three. He was no doubt accounted devilish because, like his master, he had acquired languages and science from a superior Islamic civilisation.[3]

The great physician thus presaged the new mentality of the Renaissance, which sanctioned intellectual inquiry through encounters with other worlds, not only the ancient world but also the contemporary non-European world. One Scot who penetrated it was William Lithgow who, aged 28, set out from his native Lanark in 1610 and covered 36,000 miles, mainly on foot. In his later account, *Rare Adventures* (1623), he told how he entered Jerusalem singing the 103rd psalm on Palm Sunday, 1612. He lodged with friars, not revealing he was a Protestant, and 'they mightily rejoiced that a Christian had come from such a far country as Scotia to visit Jerusalem'. But his real interest lay in secular things, or rather in satisfaction of his curiosity. His work forms part of the literature of travel and wonders which helped to fire Europe's imagination and stimulate further encounters. As such, it may not have met with entire approval from those of his compatriots representing a second mentality, shaped in the Reformation, rigid Calvinists who wanted to change the world rather than just understand it. The Holy Land lay close to their hearts, for to them the National Covenant of 1638 put Scots on a par with the ancient Israelites as the only two sworn nations of the Lord. Scotland, so often alone in the world, might even find a worthy ally if redeemed Jews could be restored to Palestine. This last point, which rested on a reading of scripture (Romans xi, 25–6) that the Second Coming would not occur till God's chosen people were converted to Christianity, turned into a minor obsession of Scots.[4]

82 The Rev. John Faulds, from Ardrossan, minister of the Scots Kirk in Kandy, Ceylon, 1909–1920, prepares to leave the manse with his wife for tea with friends. Tea (inset) had been introduced to the island by Scots from the West Indies, where the old plantations had been ruined by the abolition of slavery. Sir Thomas Lipton of Glasgow became the greatest plantation owner on Ceylon by the end of the nineteenth century. (St Andrews University Library)

83 William Macmillan (1885–1974), born to Scots missionaries near Cape Town, played a key role in two different spheres, in giving South Africa a modern historiography, and then, with the politician Malcolm MacDonald, in turning British imperial policy from administration to development. He had a profound intellectual influence on the winding down of Empire. (Private collection)

84 In the late nineteenth and early twentieth centuries, four Scots Prime Ministers played a major part in imperial development. Archibald Primrose, Earl of Rosebery (1847–1929) (above), headed a Liberal Government which lasted little over a year in 1894–5. The rest of his career he devoted largely to expanding the Empire and encouraging the white dominions to form some sort of imperial federation. (SNPG)

85 Arthur Balfour (1848–1908) (right) led a Unionist Ministry in 1902–5 deeply divided on the question of imperial preference, a concept which sought to bring the far-flung territories of the Empire into a single economic bloc. As Prime Minister and an agnostic on the question, Balfour sought to balance the parties to the dispute, but only paved the way for his Government's defeat. (SNPG)

86 Sir Henry Campbell-Bannerman (1836–1908) was a down-to-earth Glaswegian representing the radical wing of Liberalism which was sceptical of Empire. His brief Ministry in 1906–8 abandoned all idea of imperial unity in either a political or an economic sense. It moved rather towards greater colonial autonomy, with proposals for a Union of South Africa and for limited constitutional government in India. (SNPG)

87 Andrew Bonar Law (1858–1923) was a Glaswegian of the hardbitten sort, who made a fortune on the city's Iron Ring before going into politics. He reached No. 10 Downing Street just a few months before his death. An intransigent Unionist who favoured imperial preference and opposed Home Rule for Ireland, let alone Scotland, he was yet largely responsible for creating the political entity of Northern Ireland under its own Parliament. (SNPG)

88 Thomas Sutherland (1832–1922) built up one great commercial enterprise of the Scottish Empire, the Peninsular & Oriental shipping line, originally founded by the Shetlander, Arthur Anderson, and helped to create another, the Hongkong and Shanghai Banking Corporation, which was to be run on 'Scottish principles': that is, as a note-issuing institution without a central bank in control of it. (HSBC Holdings plc)

89 By the First World War, the chain-smoking James Mackay, Lord Inchcape (1852–1932), was the greatest Scottish tycoon and one of the wealthiest men in the world. Born illegitimate at Arbroath, he worked his way up and made a fortune from shipping, oil, banking and a host of other interests. After the war, though he declined the Crown of Albania, he gave more time to government than to business. (National Portrait Gallery, London)

90 The *Benlomond* I (above) at Hong Kong harbour, 1890. The Ben Line, founded in 1839 by Alexander and William Thomson of Leith, specialised in the tramping trade.(By kind permission of William Thomson) The Scottish Empire is alive and well on the Bund in Shanghai in 1927 (below), despite the chaos and mayhem in the rest of the warlords' China. In prime position overlooking the waterfront of the River Yangtze are the offices of the Hongkong and Shanghai Bank, under the dome in the centre, and of Jardine Matheson, in the building with columns second from the right. (Private collection)

91 In 1902, James Stewart Lockhart (1858–1937) had just arrived in the newly leased territory of Weihaiwei. Here he holds his first meeting with the headmen of its various villages and he preserves so far as possible the outward forms of official life in imperial China, himself playing the role of the Confucian 'mother and father' magistrate. (The Education Board of the Merchant Company of Edinburgh and the School Governing Council of George Watson's College)

92 In a final flourish of Scottish orientalism, Reginald Johnston (1874–1938) sports a mandarin's uniform somewhere in the Forbidden City of Peking. After serving in Hong Kong, and as the commissioner in charge of the territory of Weihaiwei, he became tutor to the last Emperor, Pu-yi. On his return home, he renewed British sinology. (The Education Board of the Merchant Company of Edinburgh and the School Governing Council of George Watson's College)

93 James Frazer (1854–1941) was a pupil of William Robertson Smith (plate 65) who, in his voluminous *Golden Bough*, popularised his master's work. He revealed to a wide public how much of their social behaviour was symbolic, which on analysis exposed the dark depths of the individual sub-conscious. This mild-mannered scholar, drawing on data borne home from Empire, showed how the savage still lived inside the civilised man. (SNPG)

94 Workshop of Empire. Locomotives from the North British Locomotive Company works at Springburn, Glasgow are loaded aboard the *City of Barcelona* for export to India (above), and discharged at Bombay (below). (Glasgow University Archives)

95 (Top:) Scottish emigrants at Quebec, 1911. After Confederation, Scottish emigration to Canada continued, but mainly to Ontario and the West instead of Atlantic Canada. Scottish influence on Canada continued between 1871 and 1914, with 320,000 Scots arriving. (National Archives of Canada) (below:) Emigrants dance a Highland fling aboard a Canadian Pacific liner, during the 1920s. The prewar industrial might of Scotland collapsed during this decade, producing high unemployment and heavy emigration, often under schemes of assisted passages (facing, top). The Scottish population dropped for the first time since records began. (Below and facing, left: Trustees of the National Library of Scotland; facing, right: Glasgow University Archives)

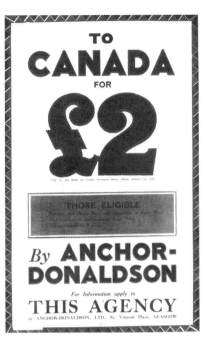

96 The Roman severity, the spare idealism of John Buchan (1875–1940) (Governor-general of Canada, 1935–1940) are captured in Thomas Clapperton's head. He was also a romantic drawn by the grandeur of Empire, and a sensitive artist who at length realised, chiefly through experience of the First World War, that grand ideals can demand too much of us. In his books he ceased to extol heroism in order to explore instead a more generous, if more fatalistic, humanity. (SNPG)

97 The horrific losses of the First World War called forth the construction of one of the most striking pieces of modern Scottish architecture, the Scottish National War Memorial in Edinburgh Castle by Robert Lorimer, built in 1923–7. This solemn and beautiful shrine mirrors the mood of its time, forsaking the individual heroics of an earlier era to stress the collective sacrifice of the Scots people. (Royal Commission on the Ancient and Historical Monuments of Scotland)

98 Scottish soldiers stand warily to one side on the outskirts of Jerusalem in 1937 as Jewish settlers demonstrate about one of their many grievances under the British mandate in Palestine. Scots' sympathy for Zionism, as in A.J.Balfour's Declaration of 1917 in favour of a national home for the Jewish people, allowed them no moderating role in the intractable problems of the Middle East. (The Black Watch Regimental Museum)

99 The first of the great imperial retreats: The Black Watch, who had been stationed at Peshawar on the North-West Frontier, march past the new President of Pakistan, Mohammed Ali Jinnah, before embarking for home at Karachi in 1947. The regiment had first served in India during the Mutiny of 1857. It was the last unit of the British army to leave this half of the partitioned sub-continent. (The Black Watch Regimental Museum)

100 The Scottish jute industry in Calcutta near the end of its era, during the 1930s. Scots, nearly all Dundonians, and none looking too happy with Indian style, still form a majority of management. But there are already bright-eyed Bengalis sitting alongside them, and plenty of smart young chaps coming up behind. Within a decade, the Scots commercial community in this emporium will have all but vanished. (Dundee University Archives)

101 Lieutenant-Colonel Colin Mitchell ('Mad Mitch') organised the last of the classic imperial police actions when he led his regiment of Argylls to re-occupy the town of Crater in the Crown colony of Aden so as to make sure of an orderly end to British rule in 1967. It was a task congenial to Scots, who have always liked a quick brawl which leaves the beaten foe to carry on in his own way. (Regimental Headquarters, The Argyll and Sutherland Highlanders)

102 Six fathers of modern Africa have had the benefit of a Scottish education: Jomo Kenyatta (1893–1978) of Kenya (above, left), Hastings Banda (1902–1997) of Malawi (above, right), Kwame Nkrumah (1909–1972) of Ghana (overleaf, top left), Nelson Mandela (b.1918) of South Africa (overleaf, top right) and Kenneth Kaunda (b.1924) of Zambia (overleaf, bottom left) all attended missionary schools or colleges, while Julius Nyerere (1921–1999) of Tanzania (overleaf, bottom right) went to university in Edinburgh. (Nelson Mandela: Press Association; others: Hulton Getty)

103 The very heavens wept at the final fanfare for Empire, when Britain handed over Hong Kong to China on June 30, 1997. The colony had been a largely Scottish creation in 1842, and Scots had played a huge role in its economy and government. It was therefore fitting that the Empire should be played out by a Scottish regiment, The Black Watch. (The Black Watch Regimental Museum)

104 Eduardo Paolozzi (1924–), born in Leith, has created this vigorous composition, 'The Wealth of Nations' (1993), to express the economic values given to the world by his native land. It seems to celebrate primarily the work of hand and machine, so the erection of the sculpture in a new financial district on the western side of the Scottish capital may be something of an irony. (M.K.Jackson)

It was still working on them 200 years later. Lord Lindsay used his Indian service for wide oriental travels and published a book on the Near East in 1838. Not content with description, he surmised that, given the decay of the Ottoman Empire and rise of western influence, Palestine might 'again become a civilised country' and the Jews, 'so wonderfully preserved, may yet have another stage of national influence opened to them; that they may once more obtain possession of their native land, and invest it with an interest greater than it could have under any other circumstance'. In his footsteps followed the artist, David Wilkie, son of the manse and devout Presbyterian. Wishing to portray authentic biblical scenes, he went to Palestine during 1840–1. He had been accustomed to paint in a sober manner, reminiscent of the Dutch masters whose Calvinist culture he shared. This contact with the Orient seemed to free him from them and inspire him to a blaze of colour. Whether the change would have been permanent we cannot tell, for he died off Gibraltar sailing home, an event commemorated in J.M.W. Turner's canvas, *Peace: Burial at Sea*. Palestine had the same effect on a second Scottish artist, David Roberts, and made his reputation. His unpromising start in Edinburgh, as a dauber of backdrops for circuses, at least aroused enough taste for the exotic to send him away. He travelled to the Middle East in style, attired in Arab dress at the head of a caravan. He produced vivid records of the Holy Land much prized by Palestinians today as showing that it was not then a desert, but boasted architectural and scenic wonders long before imperialists or Zionists left a mark. From the work of Roberts images of an ancient, unified culture emerge uncluttered by painterly clichés of his time, the depictions of the harem or of Arab cruelty that so affront Islamic sensibility. The Scottish cultural response had shifted from the evangelical to one that was, in the best sense, orientalist.[5]

The main Scottish response remained evangelical all the same. Some high-flying Presbyterians conceived out of their exegesis an intense curiosity about the remnant of Palestinian Jewry. The Emperor Titus had not exiled the Hebrews to the last man, and over the ages others had found a way back. Their descendants, by the nineteenth century numbering some thousands, lived on in the Holy Land waiting for the Messiah. Getting in touch with them required organisation, and the sole possible vehicle for it was the Church of Scotland. Among the evangelical leaders figured the sprightly but single-minded Rev Robert Candlish. In 1838 he persuaded the General Assembly to appoint him convener of a Committee for the Conversion of the Jews. This was not the only national Church of the epoch to set up such a body, though others tended to limit their efforts to their own territories. But few Jews lived in Scotland. If any purpose was to be served, the committee had to look abroad. By a stroke of luck, it got a bequest from the will of a pious lady. Candlish approached a rising clerical star from Dundee, the Rev Robert M'Cheyne, and in effect offered him leadership of an expedition to ascertain the condition of the Palestinian Jews. It would be composed of another young man, the Rev Andrew Bonar of Collace, and then of more senior ministers, the Rev Alexander Black, professor of divinity at Marischal College, Aberdeen, and the Rev Alexander Keith of St Cyrus, author also of *The Evidences of Prophecy.* M'Cheyne, just 25 years old and suffering from consumption which needed to be soothed in a warmer clime, still felt confident and energetic enough to accept the onerous charge.[6]

In April 1839 the party set out through England and France, then sailed from Marseille to Alexandria, hoping to continue coastwise to Jaffa or Beirut. But there was plague in Egypt, and quarantine on travellers by ship. To avoid wasting time, the Scots hired rowing boats to get across the delta of the River Nile, and camels to journey through Sinai. It heartened them that they were then retracing the footsteps of Moses. They still found the going hard. During several gruelling days in the desert, Professor Black fell off his mount and never felt right again. Insisting on strict observance of the sabbath, the ministers quarrelled with their impatient Arab porters. But they all cheered up at Gaza, gateway to the Holy Land. Now the clergymen could relieve the tedium in an edifying manner by observations of how biblical prophecy had been fulfilled, with the expert Dr Keith pointing out the desolation of this sinful place or that. They arrived in Jerusalem on June 7, 1839. They stayed 12 days, visiting the Holy Places, searching out synagogues and engaging worshippers in discussion. Like many missionaries in far different circumstances, they felt dismay at the indifference to their good news. But they were not downhearted. They rode on through Samaria to Haifa, then sailed to Beirut. Black and Keith had had enough by now. They left for Constantinople and went up the River Danube to Budapest where, to their surprise, they discovered a large number of Jews. It was on their proposal that the General Assembly would afterwards send a mission to the city, which lasted till the Second World War. Meanwhile, the other two bore inland to Galilee and spent a month there. M'Cheyne's sickness told on him, however. The pair returned to Beirut and followed their colleagues as far as the coast of the Black Sea, before striking out on a more northerly route. They visited Jewish communities in the eastern marches of the Austrian Empire and in Prussian Poland, and tried in vain to get a visa for Russia. Back in Scotland, M'Cheyne and Bonar sat down to write a report on all they had seen. They reckoned that Palestine housed 10,000 to 12,000 Jews. Apart from Jerusalem, most lived in Galilee. Because of its equable climate this, the ministers suggested, would be the best place for a mission. They delivered their report to the General Assembly of 1842, which authorised it to be published. It aroused a good deal of interest, going through three editions in a year. But this year was also the last before the Disruption, and the Kirk had other things on its mind.[7]

Since most evangelical ministers went into the Free Church in 1843, the Jewish Committee could be reconstituted there. It did dispatch a few missionaries, to continental cities and to Mediterranean ports. But the General Assembly had to devote most of its energy and nearly all of its money to making good its claim to represent the true Kirk, so that it found little left over for more speculative projects. The Palestinian one could begin to prosper only with the fresh missionary impetus given by the martyrdom of David Livingstone. M'Cheyne died young, but Bonar lived to serve as Moderator of the General Assembly in 1878. He dusted off their original plan, and in 1884 the Jewish Committee sent Dr David Torrance to found a school and hospital at Tiberias on the Sea of Galilee. Returning Jews had gathered in the town because it was where, according to Hebrew legend, the Messiah would first set foot after rising out of the lake. Their communal life was supported from the charitable donations of Jews abroad who thus gained religious merit. It could be reinforced by sanctions, for the rabbis of Tiberias administered all monies. When they found Torrance had come for evangelical as well as humane purposes, they cut off anybody in contact with him. Converts were therefore even fewer here than elsewhere. Still, one would distinguish himself on a wider scene. This was Leon Levison. The Free Church brought him to Glasgow to receive instruction, then sent him back to Palestine as a missionary. He would attain the presidency of the International Christian Hebrew Alliance, though he was also a Zionist. His son Frederick settled in Scotland and became a minister. Torrance, though, had after years of toil little else to show in souls saved or even minds opened, since the rabbis treated his educational efforts with equal suspicion. He made no more progress against their ancient faith than his brethren did against the cults of India, and he stoically spent his time curing the sick. This religious mission perhaps had more effect at home, in helping to resurrect the historic Calvinist identification with Israel.[8]

There was also a secular mission from Scotland to Palestine. It sprang from the fertile brain of Laurence Oliphant, whom we have met as the 8th Earl of Elgin's secretary in Canada and China. He was a true scion of the Scottish Empire. Born in Cape Town in 1829, son of the colony's Attorney-General, he grew up in Ceylon, where his father had become Chief Justice. His employment by Elgin included a spell in Japan and narrow escape from a samurai's sword. Then he came back to Scotland to qualify for the bar and dabble in Liberal politics: he sat as MP for the Stirling Burghs till beaten by the more radical Henry Campbell-Bannerman in 1868. But Oliphant was best known as a man about town, at least until he turned to spiritualism. He joined the Brotherhood of the New Life, a sect founded by a guru from Aberdeenshire, Thomas Davidson, later also founder of the Fabian Society. Oliphant's beliefs apparently forbade him to consummate his subsequent marriage.

He therefore had plenty of energy left for his pet project of settling more Jews in Palestine. But his basic concern was his own country's strategic interests. Russia, plotting to seize the Holy Places, needed to dismember the Ottoman Empire. Britain could not allow her presence to lower over the routes to the Orient, so she had to buttress the Sublime Porte. Russia was able, however, to exploit unrest among Armenian, Kurdish and Syrian minorities under Turkish sway. Oliphant believed Britain could counter this by strengthening the Jewish minority, with refugees from Russian pogroms who would be glad of a new home and would at the same time form a bulwark against Czarism. During Benjamin Disraeli's Ministry of 1874–80,

Oliphant managed to arouse some serious political interest in the scheme. In 1878 he submitted a memorandum proposing to found a Palestine Development Company. It would operate under Ottoman sovereignty but be a front for British penetration. He hoped to obtain from the Turks a concession for 25 years, and afterwards raise funds through contributions and subscriptions. With a touch of his old flippancy, he wrote: 'Any amount of money can be raised upon it, owing to the belief which people have that they would be fulfilling prophecy and bringing on the end of the world. I don't know why they are so anxious for this latter event'.

The response was positive enough to send Oliphant off on his travels again. He visited Romania and the Ukraine to recruit emigrants. He proceeded to Palestine and found what he was seeking, suitable terrain for systematic colonisation. It lay, 1.5 million acres of it, east of the River Jordan in the ancient land of Gilead. It was relatively fertile. It was near the Dead Sea, where minerals might be mined. It was not too remote or rugged to be linked to the outside world by rail. Oliphant went to Constantinople to write a book about his project and lobby for it. His hopes were dashed by the return to power of William Gladstone in 1880, heading a Ministry anti-imperialist and anti-Ottoman besides. The Sublime Porte clanged shut against all British counsel. Oliphant was left to go it alone. In 1882 he made his home in Haifa. He meant to aid the small but growing stream of Jewish immigrants, yet got along best with the obscure sect of Druses, by whom his memory is still revered. There he died six years later. If he achieved little, he had a more acute perception of one aspect of imperial policy than his Government. Much against its will, it had meanwhile had to occupy Egypt in order to safeguard the Suez Canal. But the canal could not be safe without making sure of Sinai and the territory beyond.[9]

We have seen at work two main modern Scottish attitudes to Palestine, an evangelical, even millenarian, attitude and a secular, imperialist one. What they had in common (as opposed to a weaker third attitude of cultural orientalism) was the wish to change Palestinian reality. Improbable as it might have seemed that they could devise something like a joint programme for changing that reality, in fact they did. It might have seemed even more improbable that what they had in common would be drawn out by Arthur Balfour, yet this happened too.

Balfour had an inquisitive and speculative brain which ranged over matters remote from politics. His deepest concern was with the possibility of religious belief in a scientific age. His *Defence of Philosophic Doubt* (1879) held the bases of science to be no stronger than those of religion. He was probably a believer. At any rate, as a boy in East Lothian, he had been brought up a Presbyterian. His Scottish training would have woven the Old Testament into the texture of his mind. His niece and biographer, Blanche Dugdale, testifies that it did, so as to give him a lifelong interest in the Jews. Imperialism formed another element of Balfour's thinking, though not for lack of critical scrutiny did he accept it into his canon. In his era it was a fact of life, and he espoused it on those grounds. Yet given the chance to push its bounds out beyond what was practicable, as in 1903 and 1926, he always demurred.

And he fell far short of claiming by *force majeure* a right to oppress alien peoples. The patriotism and pride of race that he would have thought justified in a Briton, above all in a Scot, rested rather on spiritual and intellectual qualities. They might be linked with material advance and political power, but not necessarily so. Small nations, for example, could forge an identity out of their spiritual and intellectual exertions, yet still have to battle against the odds to preserve it. One such case, of old, had been the Scots. Another, in his own time, was the Jews. Empire had performed a service by changing reality in favour of the Scots. Perhaps it could do the same for the Jews, who had a greater claim on imperialist indulgence because of their yet unhappier history.[10]

Balfour's cast of mind on such points turned out to be of historical importance because it enticed him towards a movement, Zionism, seeking to fulfil hopes he was disposed to respect. None of this bore fruit till his maturity, indeed till, aged 57, he was near the end of his prime ministerial career. He sat at the time for a constituency in Manchester housing many Jews. In 1905 one of them introduced him to Chaim Weizmann, the apostle of Zionism just arrived from Russia. A General Election loomed. One issue threatening to blow up and sway the Jewish vote in Balfour's marginal seat was the Aliens Act which his Government had passed. It imposed restrictions on immigration aimed, though not in so many words, at the thousands of Jews fleeing Czarist oppression. The meeting may therefore have been set up as an electoral ploy: if Balfour could put it across to Weizmann that discrimination not made explicit was not discrimination at all, the word might spread.

However that may have been, at this and a second interview the pair of them got on famously, launching into long discussions of Jewish destiny. Weizmann apparently convinced Balfour this could be fulfilled nowhere but in Palestine. He made such an impression that, though they did not meet again till 1914, Balfour at once recalled who he was and what he wanted. Weizmann then told him how he had bumped into Cosima Wagner, of all people, at Bayreuth two years before. She had said that no contribution by Jews to German greatness could ever persuade her they were Germans. Balfour found it hard to restrain his tears, and Weizmann easily steered the conversation once more on to the subject of Zionism. As they parted, Balfour said: 'Mind you come again to see me. I am deeply moved and interested, it is not a dream, it is a great cause and I understand it'. He was by now only leader of the opposition in the House of Lords, but his career took off again at the end of 1916. Lloyd George then formed a coalition with Balfour as Foreign Secretary. In that capacity he would give his name to the declaration which altered the course of Palestinian history.[11]

In the meantime the end had come for the British policy of a century, of keeping the moribund Ottoman Empire alive. When it threw in its lot with the Germans in 1914, the policy could change, indeed had to. How, though? Thanks to French mediation, King George V was now the ally of Czar Nicholas II, but that meant no objection could be raised if Russia at the end of a victorious war seized Constantinople. France herself had long been infiltrating Syria. The Arabs were in revolt against the Sublime Porte. It was by no means clear if all these claims could be reconciled with British interests in the Middle East, centred on the security of the Suez Canal.

In the Foreign Office in London, one idea bandied about was Oliphant's, of stabilising the country through Jewish settlement. This proved no easier now than 30 years before. Balfour's interest remained as yet a personal matter. The Zionists had not aligned themselves with the Allies. Why should they? The Government they hated most was the Czar's, and they did not care if the Kaiser beat him. They rejoiced at the first Russian Revolution of March 1917, which toppled Nicholas II, scattered his armies, liberated the Pale and licensed the Bolsheviks, many of whom were Jews. Even American Jews seemed lukewarm about the United States' entry into the war in April. International Jewry, if such a thing existed, might almost have been supposed unfriendly to the Allied cause. The Germans hoped so. Pointing to the prosperous, even privileged status of their own Jews, they tried to win over the Zionists. Wilhelm II's press dropped heavy hints about a future Jewish Palestine under his protection, an outcome he would either impose in case of victory or demand in case of a negotiated peace.

So long as the issue of the struggle could not be taken for granted, all this alarmed Balfour. But he thought he might save the day if he could actually do something about creating a Jewish national home. The fall of Czarism, disastrous in other respects, at least freed his hands there: he no longer had to defer to Russian views on the future of Palestine or anything else. He invited the Zionist Organisation to submit a draft of what undertakings it would like to see from His Majesty's Government. In July 1917 Lord Rothschild carried the answer to Whitehall in person. Long months of deliberation followed. Balfour remained somewhat wary of a document he had not himself drafted. Moreover, against his generality that explicit Jewish support would be useful in the war, a strong particular objection was raised by non-Zionist Jews inside and outside the Government. They feared that creation of a national home would compromise members of their race who wished to go on living in the lands of their birth, to which they gave their first allegiance. The objection wrought the main change in the draft. It had foreseen quick establishment of an autonomous Jewish state, with the protecting power as no more than a policeman. The final version turned out much more ambiguous. It perhaps reflected less any real discord among those poring over the text than a desire to avoid offending the non-Zionist Jews: if they could be mollified, then indeed all Jewry would in some sense have rallied round. That formed the whole point of making a public declaration, as opposed to the secret accords by which the Allies were otherwise carving up the Middle East.[12]

At last, in November, everybody concerned did reach agreement. Published in the form of a letter from Balfour to Rothschild, the declaration read:

His Majesty's Government view with favour the establishment in Palestine of a national home for the Jewish people, and will use their best endeavours to facilitate the achievement of this object, it being clearly understood that nothing shall be done which may prejudice the civil and religious rights of the existing non-Jewish communities in Palestine, or the rights and political status enjoyed by Jews in any other country.

It was a document admitting of a good deal of interpretation. When pressed, John Buchan, Director of Information, hesitated yet surmised that the Government had no objection to a Jewish Palestine as such, at any rate to the establishment in Palestine of a very large Jewish colony, but that public announcement whether it should be a sovereign Jewish state or a British protectorate was undesirable. As official adviser, George Adam Smith said it was idle to compare the claims of the Jews on Palestine with the rights of, say, the Belgians to Belgium; while Jewish immigration would doubtless rise, it could not justify more than a certain degree of autonomy for the community it created. At the other extreme high imperialists such as Philip Kerr, now working in Lloyd George's secretariat, envisaged a protectorate which, peopled by Jews, would grow into a dominion. The blunt fact was that nobody knew what they had let themselves in for.[13]

At least one certainty emerged from the whole business, however, that the Zionists supported the Allies. With the peace, they claimed their prize. Allenby had conquered Palestine, and on strategic grounds Britain decided to keep the territory. Existing international law allowed, by right of conquest, a protectorate or even annexation. But the war to end wars had just been fought for the principle of self-determination. The path of virtue was to link that acquisition with this principle. Zionism, and the introduction of presumably pro-British Jewish settlers, would help. The mandate approved by the League of Nations in 1922 at any rate directed His Majesty's Government to implement the Balfour Declaration west of the Jordan.

Though merely mandated, Palestine became in effect part of the Empire. At first all went well. Jewish immigration surged, but things remained peaceful enough for military occupation to end and initial ideas on self-government to be worked out. One High Commissioner, a cool and capable soldier from an old family in Lanarkshire, John Chancellor of Shieldhill, was keen to press ahead. He had done this sort of thing before, and done it well, as the first Governor of Southern Rhodesia, where in 1923 he established a constitution. In the summer of 1929 he returned from Jerusalem to London with plans in his pocket for setting up a legislative council. On the way he stopped in Geneva to assure officials of the League of Nations that communal relations were improving. While there, he heard news of a horrific outburst of violence between Jews and Arabs after an incident at the Wailing Wall. He hurried back and restored order, but could not stop the vicious circle of revenge which followed. He concluded that the Balfour Declaration had been a 'colossal blunder', unjust to the Arabs and impossible of fulfilment in its own terms.[14]

Even so, that hardly damped the spirits of his successor in 1932, Arthur Wauchope. He was a Scottish soldier as well, but of a wholly different type, wizened, untidy, literate, musical, bibulous and talkative. He fell in love with Palestine. The kibbutzim delighted him, as a farmer himself or rather a laird in Midlothian. He also had a progressive outlook, a sympathy for the Labour party, an interest in Russia, a penchant for artists and heretics. So he liked Jews anyway. That coloured his genuine wish to better the lot of all Palestine's peoples. He had commanded the British forces of occupation in Germany after the war and had a good idea what Adolf Hitler's anti-semitism would mean. When Nazi persecution of the Jews started, he knew that Palestine must become an asylum. He therefore regarded the mandate for a national home as the most important part of his task. That contradicted the latest official British policy, however, of not allowing the Jews to become a majority or even a large enough minority to open up the possibility of a Jewish state. In truth neither he nor his superiors grasped the scale of the calamity they faced from potential millions of desperate refugees with nowhere else to go. But Arabs could easily see the possibility of being outnumbered and dispossessed.

For a time, though, Wauchope carried his tasks off, well enough to get a second tour of duty in 1936. He wanted to use this to revive the plan for self-government. He thought he could bring it about through an array of checks and balances, yet a legislature had in the end to give somebody control. Wauchope tried to allay the Arabs' fears by in effect guaranteeing a majority for Moslems and Christians. That only outraged the Jews. They mobilised Zionists overseas, including a lobby at Westminster. The Government stalled by appointing a royal commission, which would at length recommend partition of the country. It was a blow to Wauchope who, amid yet more violence, gave up and resigned. While he had tried to be impartial, he lost the trust of both sides. He mistook for mere growing pains in a new society what were in fact yawning and soon unbridgeable divisions between two enemy races. Nothing remained of his efforts. A brother Scot, Malcolm MacDonald, now became Colonial Secretary. Another friend of Weizmann, he had once counted himself a Zionist too, yet after a visit to Palestine he imposed formal limits on immigration, to the fresh fury of the Jews. A conference of all sides called early in 1939 collapsed. During the Second World War, MacDonald was accused of betraying the Jews left to their fate in Europe. But the cupboard had finally been stripped bare of Palestinian solutions. In 1948 the Government pretended to push the scheme of partition through, while in reality just walking away from the problem – not so much laying down the mandate as flinging it aside. Britain thus freed herself of the unhappy promise to the Jews, yet without regaining the friendship of the Arabs, and suffered a signal defeat.[15]

Several strands of the Scottish imperial experience were woven together in Palestine. Surprisingly, what stood out was the evangelical one, the impulse to change reality in a manner agreeable to the divine plan, an impulse which in most other parts of the globe had lost vigour well before the First World War. Often it only kept going so long through an afflatus of high imperialism. In significant cases, the performance of a religious duty had then brought a secular result, with Presbyterianism yielding to colonial officialdom. But this was the last such case. Britain's assumption of the Palestinian mandate reflected a feeling that, despite the horrors of war, she was still marching towards her imperial pinnacle, her golden age, and that Zionism would be part of it. The feeling even overcame Balfour, or at least let his Calvinist inner promptings get the better of his diplomacy. And he shared that feeling with many Scots. In changing reality here, they followed their God and chose the Jews. But this was not the way to peace in Palestine. Anyway the Empire, now at its greatest territorial extent, appearing stronger and more durable than ever before, had in fact entered its decline. Among the first omens was the shattering of Scottish hopes for the Holy Land.

CHAPTER THIRTY-ONE

'On the look out for some stigma': African Colonisation

J ust before nine o'clock on the evening of Saturday, January 23, 1915, William Livingstone lay on his bed dandling his new baby son, while his wee daughter played round them and his wife got ready to take a bath next door. The only odd thing about this scene of Scottish domestic bliss was its location: the Livingstones' home stood close to their nation's oldest site in Central Africa, at Magomero where Charles Mackenzie had tried in vain to set up a mission in 1861. It was now a plantation belonging to Alexander Bruce, grandson of David Livingstone, part of his estate of 169,000 acres, the biggest in Nyasaland. William Livingstone, another kinsman, acted as manager. Like Scots in all times and places, they preferred to keep things in the family. For one thing, it rendered the business of exploitation so much easier. This pair meant to show how with modern methods they could make the wilderness bloom. Half a century after being opened up and latterly under regular imperial government, the territory might then enjoy the prospect of growing into a colony of settlement. For that, though, more planters would have to dispossess more blacks and reduce them to landless labourers. Bruce and Livingstone had shown the way by dint of barely legal expropriation and of harsh discipline.

Livingstone's domestic bliss was about to be shattered. His wife noticed the cat was still inside and asked him to put it out for the night. As he opened the front door to shoo it through, half a dozen natives pushed their way in and one thrust a spear into his right side. Probably he recognised them as his own workers. He was able to seize his rifle, but had no time to load it and used it as a club while he fought them through three rooms. Then he collapsed. Just at that moment Duncan MacCormick, the friend of his childhood on Lismore and his neighbour here, lurched in wounded through the heart. He had immediately heard of the trouble from his house-boys and come over to see what was afoot. He brought no gun because, he said, he could settle any difficulty with his fists. On the way he ran into more negroes skulking in the compound, who speared him. Now he too lay dying. One of the intruders finished Livingstone off by burying an axe in his skull, then severed his head, drenching his daughter in the blood. The heroically level-headed Mrs Livingstone went back into the bedroom to see about the baby, and found him still lying safely there. She picked him up and began to argue with the Africans, as she would argue all night, asking why they had murdered her husband. They just replied that he would not be the only one. While she still talked, they hurried her and the children away into the bush.

They set off on a march which continued till the morning, but treated their captives as kindly as they could. They bought them milk and eggs, and as the sun rose held broad leaves over their heads to shade them. All would be rescued unharmed.

What the natives said about more whites being killed was true. A few miles away, at the plantation of Mwanje, a second attack had taken place. Armed natives appeared and severely wounded the Scots manager, Robert Ferguson, who managed to stagger to the nearby home of his countryman, John Robertson. He was in turn speared while standing at his door, but banged it shut and saved himself. When the negroes milling round in front set light to the house, he and his wife slipped out the back and hid in a field of cotton. Ferguson, laid on a settee in the living room, was cremated in the blaze. The alarm spread among the settlers for 50 miles around. Through the darkness they fled for their lives to the tiny townships of the territory, most to Blantyre, headquarters of the Church of Scotland's mission. There also, the African Lakes Company had its stores and armoury. They might have been a special target if this was the great black uprising that Europeans in Africa eternally dreaded; only five years before, John Buchan's *Prester John* had played on the fears of terrible forces welling up out of the depths of the dark continent. Here, however, the violence died away as suddenly as it had erupted.[1]

Instead the next day, the sabbath, saw a peaceful if gruesome scene at the church of the Rev John Chilembwe, founder of a native congregation at Mbombwe, just outside the boundary of Bruce's estate. He was the product of a Scottish education – or rather, some would now say, of how it was going wrong. Schooled by the Free Church, he had been sent to complete his studies at a Negro Baptist seminary in the United States. There he fell under the influence of Ethiopian Christianity. On his return, he found that no mission would give him the position that his undoubted abilities merited. So he set up his own sect and built his own place of worship from funds raised locally, quite an achievement in a poor country. But his experiences twisted the character of this once pleasant and straightforward man. He bitterly resented his treatment at white hands. He resolved to save his people from their oppressions. He it was who organised the revolt in Nyasaland, the first against established British rule anywhere in Africa. Many of his flock worked at Magomero, and hated Livingstone. Chilembwe could easily incite them to murder, and persuade them that this would spark off a general rebellion. He himself drew up a list of Europeans in the colony, marking down those who would be killed out of hand, then those, including the women and children, who would be spared to go in peace, and finally those who would be given leave to stay on as pedagogical helots, continuing to teach the blacks but not otherwise exercising any power.

Now, on the morning after, Chilembwe was calmly prepared to preach his regular sermon, amid surroundings unusual only in that he had Livingstone's bloody, cloven, severed head stuck up on a pole by the pulpit. He was triumphant but, pointing to the grisly sight beside him, prophesied also that the deeds of the night would be avenged. In this case, the believers' part was to bear witness to the just necessity of those deeds by meeting their fate with courage and resignation. In fact Chilembwe must already have known they were all doomed. There would be no general rebellion. Chiefs in the surrounding districts who had promised help sat tight. The insurgent tribesmen missed their chance to capture Blantyre before the Europeans could concentrate there such strength as they possessed. Soon they would recover from their shock and strike back. When they did, they found Chilembwe's people almost defenceless and easily hunted them down. He himself was killed a few days later while trying to get across the border to Mozambique. The colonial authorities set out to obliterate his memory. They blew up his church. They executed 20 of his followers, and sentenced others to long terms in prison.[2]

That could not, however, mark the end of the affair. For five months Britain had been fighting the Great War in defence not just of herself but also of her far-flung imperial possessions. Even in this backwater she was vulnerable. The enemy, striking from German East Africa, had already essayed an attack on the Scottish missionary station of Karonga, sited strategically at the northern tip of Lake Nyasa. The war really had come to Central Africa, and young blacks were the only ones available to defend it. Recruitment of them caused a shortage of manpower, with wider disruption of the rudimentary economy. The African Lakes Company all but ceased trading. The Free Churchmen at Livingstonia especially felt the pinch. Their mission had so far been one of the best organised in the whole continent. Now they faced problems of every kind.

Chilembwe's rising turned the problems into a political crisis. Not since the institution of colonial government about the turn of the century had the missionaries been fully free to pursue their own aims for indigenous society. They had instead to co-ordinate those aims with imperial policy, and if need be subordinate them to it. One sporadic imperial policy was to settle people of British stock in suitable spots round the globe. It entailed the selection, at will and without reference to the natives, of large tracts of white man's country. Buchan had organised it in South Africa. In Rhodesia it was promoted by another Scots graduate of Lord Milner's kindergarten, Dougal Malcolm. The highlands of Kenya looked especially fit for colonisation. And though conditions proved less favourable here, to some extent Nyasaland followed the trend. Men such as Bruce had already acquired 60 per cent of the land. The destruction of an existing way of life and its replacement with something altogether different ran counter to Scottish imperial tradition. But by the early twentieth century Scottish traditions of every kind were enfeebled and fragmented. The most forward-looking Scots had few qualms about adopting the purposes of an English sort of Empire.

Bruce thought of himself as forward-looking, and even with his Presbyterian credentials he did not now spare the missionaries. These were widely regarded, often regarded themselves and indeed had an official status as leaders of the blacks. Up to 1913 the Rev Alexander Hetherwick, head of the station at Blantyre, and after that the Rev Robert Laws, his counterpart at Livingstonia, were nominated as native members, that is to say, representatives of the negroes in the legislative council of Nyasaland. Bruce was also a member, and when it came to discuss the uprising he laid the blame squarely on clerical influence. He claimed that nearly every rebel of note had been educated at a mission and proposed in response that all African schools should be closed forthwith. If Bruce was rich and powerful, Laws commanded his own kind of respect, as a man of vision and common sense who had doggedly pursued progress in stability. He reacted with such horror that Bruce never put his motion. Still, the missionaries could be left in no doubt about the strength of feeling among whites, officials and settlers alike. A district commissioner summed it up: 'It is a peculiar thing that almost every highly educated native of the Livingstonia mission is politically minded and race conscious and always on the look out for some stigma. At the back of their minds is an intolerance of the Europeans and their creed is "Africa for the Africans" '.

Laws and Hetherwick countered by calling for an official inquiry. The authorities agreed, though pointedly omitting to place any Scots missionaries on the committee then set up. It had a wide remit to investigate the effect of education on blacks. But when it reported in 1917, it chose the easy target of the small, independent sects, proposing a power to ban them if their credentials did not bear examination. Strictures on the Scots could all the same be read between the lines. One aim at Livingstonia and Blantyre was to train indigenous teachers. The report dropped heavy hints about the dangers of their spreading 'undesirable political propaganda'. It noted that this was not a feature of Anglican or Roman Catholic missions. 'That Protestant methods open a door to disloyalty, which is closed by Romanism and Anglicanism, is a doctrine new to us,' the missionary journal of Nyasaland thundered back. Among Scots the whole business was soon being portrayed as an erastian plot, the sort of thing the nation had been fighting for 300 years. The Churches felt obliged to recall that the Treaty of Berlin (1885) guaranteed freedom of religion in Central Africa. All the same, the Scottish mission scarcely ran any serious risk. In the midst of war the Empire faced many worse problems, and nobody dared offend public opinion in Scotland again.[3]

In any event, she could still call on many imperialist idealists and ideologues well placed at the centre of affairs to defend her interests. Just when the report on Nyasaland was published, the Government in London had a Scotsman, Arthur Steel Maitland, as Under-Secretary for the Colonies. A hawkish disciple of Joseph Chamberlain, he yet made sure the committee's findings were quietly shelved. Scots like him, if attached to the Right, often still showed a relatively liberal outlook by the standards of the day. Philip Kerr, for example, warned about the danger of perverting the legacy of the kindergarten, where he and his fellows had aspired to 'justice and opportunity and freedom, not for one race, or the other, but for both'. This liberalism was also being passed on to a younger generation with little or no experience overseas. Walter Elliot would concede that the Empire must come to an end one day. It should respect indigenous forms of government because 'in 20 or 30 years the European will have gone home and he will never return' – though here Elliot indeed referred to territories without white settlement.

In the circumstances, it was perhaps natural for Scottish missions to respond in a spirit of compromise to the evolution of British imperialism, to tone down their original ambitions for the natives to a level no longer likely to cause embarrassment. That seemed to be the message from the Very Rev James Ogilvie, convener of the Foreign Missions Committee of the Church of Scotland, when he gave the Duff Missionary Lectures in 1923. He chose the theme of "The Empire's Debt to Missions", meaning to show that the two had much in common. In reference to the delicate matter of Nyasaland, he pointed out that evangelists were at work on a long-term project of moulding the negroes which had far to go and which meanwhile called for caution in applying European standards. He denied that missionary education disrupted and damaged tribal communities. On the contrary, its purpose was to strengthen them, and if that did not work, the causes were usually to be found outside the missions. In Nyasaland, nobody could demonstrate that evangelism had generated political problems. Unrest was just a feature of the age, or perhaps evidence of growing racial tension, against which missions offered the main hope of peace. Critics should anyway look at the other side of the coin. The missions held moral ideals before the eyes of both colonial officials and white settlers. They campaigned against wrongs of every kind, formerly slavery, now 'liquor, land and labour'. They formed a link, as nobody else could, between the imperial authorities and the indigenous races, so keeping alive the Empire's ideal of trusteeship. In return, they were entitled to ask for protection, co-operation and appreciation.[4]

The appeal was all the more heartfelt because the missions' crisis had not ended with the war, and global depression would soon make it worse. Their commitments were huge. At its height, Scotland raised £300,000 a year to support 750 missionaries teaching a worldwide total of 170,000 pupils. The will and means to sustain this effort were now to be severely tested. In Nyasaland, which alone had 850 Scottish schools with an enrolment of 55,000, it was all anyone could do with shrunken resources to stop the standards dropping, let alone raise them. An optimistic gesture came in 1924 with the constitution of the ostensibly self-governing, self-supporting Central African Church, under a synod with the two presbyteries of Livingstonia and Blantyre. The Free Church of Scotland, which had spiritual independence so much at heart, insisted on pushing this through. But it seemed hasty and premature even to some missionaries, who thought the black ministry still left a little to be desired. Besides putting on its new, native face, Presbyterianism also showed a less gladdening, more imperialist side. There was now no reason for places of worship in Zomba and Blantyre, the main centres of white settlement, to continue admitting negroes. So they were segregated. That went down badly in the villages beyond and fostered the further growth of Ethiopian Christianity, where blacks dissatisfied with or rejected by the missions could seek salvation. When Hetherwick retired in 1928 and Laws in 1929, they departed to acclaim but left behind a sense that the pioneers' glad, confident morning was over. Their final goal, the transformation of African society through an African Kirk, clearly lay some way off yet.[5]

Nyasaland was not the sole territory in which the aim of an indigenous Presbyterianism became confused with less benign imperial trends. The eastern Cape housed at Lovedale the continent's oldest Scottish station, headed since the death of the veteran James Stewart in 1905 by the Rev James Henderson. In 1923 he helped to set up the Bantu Presbyterian Church of South Africa. It took out of the dominion's Kirk, separately constituted since 1897, all the black congregations that had, with a commendable desire for independence from the missions, originally opted to enter it. So this latest move also amounted to a segregation, rather than a secession. Yet Henderson's purposes were hardly reactionary. With his other hand he had been working to give the indigenous peoples access to higher education in an institution specially for them. The South African Native College, at Fort Hare nearby, opened its doors in 1916 under Dr Alexander Kerr as principal, and now attained the full status of a university. A beacon of African learning, it offered a haven to scholars who could scarcely have made an academic living otherwise, such as Prof Zachariah Matthews, a social anthropologist, its first black graduate and later its principal himself, or Prof Davidson Jabaru, who taught Xhosa and Latin. The educational complex round Lovedale was without parallel in the continent, yet apparently made little difference to the cultural level of the region. A visiting Scot, Victor Murray, compared this to the Highlands in its backwardness. Here too, land remained the basis of existence and determinant of the social structure. It evoked in the indigenous people the same outlook as in any scion of the clansmen who 'insists on being given land in his own district, and would rather have a hopeless patch on his own native heath than a fair holding in a strange glen'. Against this uncivilised background, it seemed natural to Henderson and Kerr that Africans should practise their Presbyterianism separately from Europeans.[6]

More encouraging examples were not lacking, however. Missions after all spanned the globe and could pool the best practice – especially now that the international council planned at the conference in Edinburgh in 1910 had finally, since 1921, set to work. In the Gold Coast, for example, several influences came together to give a happy turn to a new Kirk. Calvinism had been represented here for the best part of a century by Swiss evangelists, whom George Maclean's Merchant Government had first invited in. In 1914 they were all, rather unjustly, expelled for alleged German sympathies. Workers from Calabar under the Rev Arthur Wilkie replaced them in the meantime. But, because of the upheaval, blacks had to be brought into the government of the Church from the moment a synod was formed in 1918. For once, the thousands of natives more or less took over from the handful of colonialists: God was praised in Twi, Ga and Ewe rather than in English. The smooth transition impressed the Rev Alexander Fraser, appointed head of Achimota College, near Accra, in 1924. He arrived from a background which was, besides Scottish, Asian. The son of a Governor of Bengal, he had started work in Ceylon, and to Africa he brought missionary attitudes current in the East: deeper awareness of obstacles to conversion, appreciation of its social as well as spiritual dimension, understanding that alien cultures might have something to offer westerners. Now in charge of the territory's training of secondary teachers, he insisted that whites could not just dictate an education to blacks: both must co-operate. This remained as yet barely thinkable in Nyasaland but Fraser, through his influence on a close friend at Livingstonia, the Rev Cullen Young, helped to shift Presbyterianism towards greater faith in native self-sufficiency. On retiral in 1932, Fraser went home to apply the same philosophy to the workers of Scotland, as first principal of Newbattle Abbey.[7]

But there were also contrary examples. In East Africa the missionaries' compromise with the imperialists went too far. Presbyterianism had had a chequered history in Kenya since its introduction by the ubiquitous Stewart of Lovedale. He appeared in 1891 with £10,000 in his pocket from William Mackinnon and Alexander Bruce to set up a station at Kibwezi, in a rather bleak district on the road from Mombasa to the highlands. The collapse of the Imperial East Africa Company left it stranded. So the evangelists pressed on up-country, to establish a chain of stations among the Kikuyu, the country's main tribe. They still did not prosper. In 1901, with just one of the six pioneers left alive, the Church of Scotland had to come to the rescue.[8]

The Kirk first used the mission as a bolthole for the Rev David Clement Scott, after he was more or less drummed out of Blantyre. He brought with him his hope of preserving but purifying indigenous life through the agency of "new men". It proved equally quixotic here, as the country underwent a western onslaught: in rapid succession came imperial sovereignty, the entry of missions and a start to systematic white settlement. Presbyterians indeed formed part of the onslaught. The mission itself owned 70,000 acres, which its original benefactors had assumed were theirs to give away. At the expense of natives believing themselves to have been robbed, it was thus among the biggest and richest landlords in the colony. Its later heads, the Rev Henry Scott from 1907 and the Rev John Arthur from 1911, no doubt disapproved of excesses in expropriation by others. Unlike their brethren in Nyasaland, however, they avoided all controversy over this or any public question. If they too aimed to create an African Church, it would be in the form of a quiescent and loyal Christianity for blacks taking their place as obedient coolies in a white man's country. From this prospect, even more than in other colonies, the indigenous peoples soon drew away to seek a more dignified and independent place on their own soil.[9]

Condemnation of the kind of society being created in Kenya came not so much from evangelists as from renegade officials. Norman Leys, born in Lanarkshire, was a member of the medical service till transferred because of his protests at dispossession of the Masai. He accused greedy settlers of seizing so much good land that the natives could only be reduced to poor tenants and labourers: this was not trusteeship but exploitation. McGregor Ross, from a Highland background, served 17 years as Kenya's director of public works and was actually a member of the executive council till his politics ended his career. He then wrote, mainly for leftist journals in Britain, scathing indictments of the situation he had left behind, of corruption and injustice on one hand, helplessness and outrage on the other. To the two Scots this was an English sort of Empire, with race replacing class as the criterion of inequality. They staked their careers on fighting it, lost their local confrontations but took revenge once they got home. Their exact local knowledge meant they could not be dismissed as pontificating do-gooders: in liberal circles, at least, they succeeded in giving Kenya a worse reputation than almost any other colony, as the one with the widest gap between imperial rhetoric and reality. Even the British Government restrained the settlers. In a statement of policy penned in 1927 by the Under-Secretary for the Dominions, Lord Lovat, another Scottish graduate of Milner's kindergarten, he set out the principle that 'Kenya is primarily an African territory, and the interests of the African natives must be paramount. If and when these interests and the interests of the immigrant races should conflict, the former must prevail'.[10]

Only the Scots missionaries kept quiet. They soon had to pay. While they had won enough converts to form a presbytery by 1920, they remained displeased by the moral condition of the people. It was over this, rather than the land, that crisis blew up. Among the Kikuyu, rites of initiation included circumcision for both boys and girls. In the latter case it was a dangerous operation with durably painful effects. The missionaries set out to suppress this offensive heathen custom, hallowed by tribal tradition though it was. They won political support from Britain, notably from the first Scottish woman MP, the Duchess of Atholl. They forced a showdown in the autumn of 1929. Arthur, as head of the mission, ordered that at services on Sunday, November 1, all members of presbyterian congregations should be required, before being admitted to communion, to take a vow on their faith as Christians to cease female circumcision. At once the main station lost 90 per cent of the 2500 communicants on its roll, and others saw an exodus as staggering. Kenyan Presbyterianism collapsed. The ministers could hardly grasp the fact. One, Horace Philp, solemnly put it down to the 'subversive Bolshevik propaganda going on among the natives of Kenya, inspired from outside the country'. The losses would never be made good. When a presbytery of Kenya was re-erected in 1935, it catered only for whites. The Kikuyu demonstrated meanwhile that they were quite capable of running their own Churches and schools, and forgot any debt of gratitude they owed to those who had first shown them how. Not till the 1950s, with the Rev David Steel's efforts at conciliation, did the Kirk again attract enough negroes to form united congregations.[11]

Overall in the British African territories between the wars, it cannot have seemed that missionary leadership and guidance were going to lead soon, or perhaps ever, to equality even for those blacks who learned their lessons. They had been taught that all Christians were equal, and that Africans possessed the same capacities as Scots. Not consigned like the rest of their peoples to casual labour, the pupils of missions grew up to be teachers, engineers, overseers, tradesmen, shopkeepers, interpreters, clerks, drivers and so on. Yet they were still kept down and, if they murmured against their subordination, missionaries usually told them to look first to the cure of their souls or the irenic example of their native pastors. Meanwhile, European laymen often picked out educated negroes for the most blatant discrimination, cruelly mocking their habits and language. What was the use, then, of their technical skills, linguistic ability and knowledge of European ways? The answer lay in the fact that, if they could not rule their country or in practice even their Church, they did dominate the congregations in the villages. There they formed a new social group with its own ideas of how to practise what the missions preached.

It was the wellspring of black nationalism. The sentiment first began to well up in the so-called native associations, most of them spontaneously formed by Presbyterian tribesmen for pastimes from sport to debating. The earliest seems to have been the North Nyasa Native Association, dating from 1912. But this was probably one of several founded in the years just before the First World War round Livingstonia and Karonga. They quickly spread over Nyasaland, then across the artificial colonial boundary to the part of Northern Rhodesia east of the Copperbelt, in due course to other territories. They were not always treated with suspicion by missionaries or even by officials. Laws welcomed them as 'safety valves': since negroes paid taxes, for example, they were entitled to discuss whether the money could be best spent on a road or a hospital.[12]

The war again widened Africans' horizons. Actively recruited for it, they matured during their service, saw something of the world and measured themselves against people in faraway places, black and white. None of that severed them from tribal society. But it did spur them after returning to keep in touch with those from different backgrounds who had shared their experiences. They then sought a forum outside traditional circles for opinions which might be taken inside them as indecorous, opinions they had formed through comradeship in exertions beyond their elders' ken. The associations offered that forum. Here young negroes could forget ancestral enmities for common interests. As they defined those interests, they also gained the confidence to represent them to officialdom. During the 1920s, while economic conditions worsened, the associations called for better education from the missions, higher wages from the planters, economic aid from the authorities. Black leaders of later times were thus trained to organise and negotiate.[13]

They proved especially forward in Kenya. The Kikuyu Central Association was a prop to the tribe's morale in hard times, as the prospect loomed of losing its land and pride. Faced with a menial future in a white man's country, the association was the reverse of defeatist, however. It challenged Europeans to make a reality of their vaunted trusteeship. If they really wanted to modernise old ways of life, they should assure rights to property for the indigenous peoples. If they really wanted to foster new ways of life, they should give natives access to higher education. In 1930, in a move unprecedented in Africa, the association stumped up the cost of sending delegates all the way to lobby in Britain for the redress of grievances. They got a cool reception from the Colonial Office, but in Scotland a warmer one from the Labour Party and from the Foreign Missions Committee of the Kirk – to the discomfort of Arthur back in Kenya, who had denounced the initiative. On their return he tried to woo the delegates, hoping through them to reach out again to the lost converts from his ruined mission. They spurned him. To their surprise, their efforts brought no result otherwise. It had not occurred to them that the British Government would ignore evidence of injustice.[14]

More forward still were the first steps in South Africa. The continent's most advanced country lured blacks who had been able to equip themselves for a role in the free markets of an international economy. Many arrived from Nyasaland, where the African Lakes Company forged commercial links and the Overtoun Institute taught industrial skills. The missionaries had hardly foreseen that their greatest gift to trained natives would be mobility. Yet it followed from the course the country had taken since the imposition of imperial government, when development became the prerogative of white settlers rather than of negro peasants. Ambitious Africans actually did best to leave. The missions, embarrassed at the lack of local opportunity, often stimulated the movement and even acted as recruiting agencies for the booming industries of the Rand.

One young migrant was Clements Kadalie, a favourite of Laws who after finishing school had served as his private secretary. Later Kadalie moved to teaching and clerical jobs, ending up in Cape Town. There in 1919 he led a successful strike for higher wages by black and coloured dockworkers, which gained a certain degree of support even from white labour. The ringleaders then set about planning a general union, with the aim of improving conditions among both skilled and unskilled in all branches of the economy. Under Kadalie as national secretary, they launched the Industrial and Commercial Workers' Union in 1920. This was the first time outside their tribes that South African blacks had combined for any purpose, but they suffered from inexperience of how to operate in a society run by Europeans. Against the hostility of government and business, the union's efforts to forge alliances were shifting, uncertain and ill-judged. In the General Election of 1924, for example, it supported the Afrikaner Nationalist, J.B.M. Herzog, rather than the somewhat more liberal Jan Smuts.

By 1927 the union was caught in a vicious circle: with recruitment low, it had little money, so no way of sustaining strikes and nothing to attract more members. In fact it was teetering on the verge of collapse. At this point sympathisers arranged for Kadalie to go on a fraternal trip and seek help in Scotland. Warmly welcomed, he found it intriguing that his hosts showed more interest in him as a product of the missions than as a leader of the workers. Still, they collected enough to pay for an adviser on finance and organisation to return with him. The man chosen was William Ballinger, aged 35, who had started life as a plasterers' apprentice in Motherwell and was now making his way up inside the Independent Labour Party, as councillor and leader of the trades council in his hometown. It shocked him on his arrival in South Africa to find not what he expected – a growing, solvent if unseasoned union – but sheer chaos. He tried valiantly to import the best practice from Scotland, on the model of the ILP with its tending of the grassroots in municipal, educational and cultural endeavours. Ballinger had a clear goal: a moderate, respectable trade unionism which would allay enmity and win sympathy from whites. But he could hardly get started without some minimum of internal discipline. Kadalie was fitted neither to provide it himself nor to call it forth from others. He and Ballinger were besides touchy and tactless men, unable to work together. The latter soon saw the task was hopeless. He advised withdrawal of the sponsorship, and the union folded.[15]

All the same, Ballinger decided to stay on in South Africa. He fell in love with a Scots girl, Peggy Hodgson. Born in Glasgow, she had emigrated with her family in the 1890s; her father actually fought with the Boers and was surprised to be called a traitor when he later went home on holiday. His daughter grew up brilliant and eloquent, though handicapped in old-fashioned South Africa by her sex. A graduate of Oxford, she could have got a job in Britain, but preferred to return to her adopted country. One light in her life was the personal patronage of William Macmillan, whom we have already met as a scion of the Scottish evangelical and academic community at the University of Stellenbosch. He was now a professor at Witwatersrand. The three Scots formed an enlightened circle which made a worthy successor to the one a century before round John Philip – of whom Macmillan wrote the biography.

The new circle had, like the old, both an intellectual and a political side. Macmillan's talents stretched in the old Scots way across the social sciences. He owed a flying start in his career to the publication in 1919 of *The South African Agrarian Problem and its Historical Development*. It sparked off a national debate about the most pressing predicament perceived at the time, that of the Afrikaner poor whites. Macmillan described the forces reducing these *bywoners*, or tenant farmers, to proletarian status. Comparing the process to the industrial revolution in Britain, he forecast the growth of 'social caste, the landlord and the landless', with political tensions to match. All this meant that 'the point on which to concentrate is not the colour of a man's skin but his standard of life and his wage'. In other words, race lost relevance when members of every race might have to face similar problems. With this and later works, Macmillan overturned the conventional wisdom of South Africa, that the country was built on the victory of colonialism over savagery. He constructed a new historiography based essentially on the missionary tradition which went back to Philip and which accorded equal importance to blacks and whites. He argued indeed that every one of the country's several races merited mutual respect. They could learn it from studying their contributions to their life together in South Africa for, if she had peculiar difficulties, none was closed to analysis on principles universally acceptable as scientific. It says a good deal about her ever uglier politics, however, that by 1933

Macmillan no longer wanted to stay. He returned to Britain, and a further career which we shall have occasion to survey below.

He left Peggy Ballinger as acting head of his department at Witwatersrand. She was refused the chair on grounds of her sex. So she turned to politics, drawn anyway by indignation at moves to quash the relative liberalism of Cape Province. There, thanks originally to Philip and Fairbairn, blacks had long been able to enjoy civil rights, including the franchise. But from 1936 they were placed on a separate electoral roll entitling them to choose a handful of white representatives in the provincial and federal Parliaments. The Ballingers, having led and lost the struggle against the change, stood for these seats and won, Peggy for the house of assembly, William for the senate. She especially found her métier as a campaigning politician, with a remarkable skill at turning debates on control of the indigenous population into discussions of its welfare. Against the odds she got through some small improvements from time to time. She impressed Patrick Duncan, yet another Scots graduate of Milner's kindergarten, now Governor-General. He used his supposedly neutral position to warn against economic oppression of negroes, if not in the end to much effect. Even after 1948, when the Nationalists came to power and imposed apartheid, the Ballingers battled on. In 1953 they formed the South African Liberal Party, and continued to serve in Parliament till the abolition of their seats in 1960. The Government only brought their careers to a close when it outlawed the party in 1968.[16]

They were not missionaries, yet through Macmillan they owed much to the Scots missionary tradition. They also showed its limits, by their inability to lift white oppression: in the end this would yield only to black resistance. The resistance, though soon developing independently, owed much to the missions' influence too. Five African presidents had a Scottish education. Nelson Mandela of South Africa attended Fort Hare, but left after a dispute with Principal Kerr. Jomo Kenyatta of Kenya gave up his apprenticeship without fulfilling the requirements, perhaps because of his liking for drink and women, whereupon Arthur refused him a reference for employers. Hastings Kamuzu Banda of Nyasaland was thrown out of an examination for cheating by the invigilator, Cullen Young. At least the other pair were good boys: Kwame Nkrumah of Ghana, personally selected for training by Principal Fraser of Achimota, and Kenneth Kaunda of Zambia, son of a presbyterian minister. They had all learned they were the equals of the European. In later careers they proved to him that Africa was not for him to dispose of as he wished. Until their generation came along, no terminus to imperial government had been foreseen, and talk remained rife of turning large tracts of the continent into white man's country. Once their generation came along, imperial government was doomed and the continent destined to return one day to the rule of its own people.

CHAPTER THIRTY-TWO

'Someone must speak for them':
African Decolonisation

J ust after midnight on March 3, 1959, the English Governor of Nyasaland, Sir Robert Armitage, declared an emergency, being by his own account faced with a revolt of the blacks and massacre of the whites. Before sunrise, a convoy of troops and police screeched to a halt outside the modest home in the township of Limbe belonging to Dr Hastings Kamuzu Banda, leader of the Nyasaland African Congress. A picked group of commandoes stalked up to the house with every precaution against violent resistance. When they burst in they found Banda fast asleep in bed. He had time to cover his pyjamas in an elegant dressing gown before they drove him away to the tiny airport at Blantyre: the very spot where eight months before, in his more usual dark suit, Homburg hat and fly-whisk, he had arrived back from four decades of exile to his people's acclaim as hero and saviour. Now he was bundled on a plane which flew him to jail in Southern Rhodesia.

That marked merely the start of Operation Sunrise, as Armitage dubbed it. He also banned the Congress, suspended civil rights, enforced censorship of the press, rushed in military reinforcements and ordered the arrest of 1500 people. The round-up cost 50 lives. All those killed were Africans; no European died or even suffered serious injury. Of the detainees, one in three was freed in a few days but the rest, reckoned the hard core of troublemakers, remained in custody in an improvised camp at Kanjedza. To a remarkable extent, Presbyterians formed this hard core. The Rev Andrew Ross, sent to minister to them, found about 700 inmates to be members of the Church of Central Africa: 'There was a sufficient number of Church elders in the camp to enable it to be treated in practice as a congregation of the Blantyre synod'.[1]

Armitage, so far from suppressing black nationalism, set Nyasaland off along the final stretch of road leading to independence five years later. Its attainment was in many ways a triumph for Presbyterian democracy, of which Banda had made himself a symbol. One reason for his personal influence was that Scots missionaries had built him up as a paragon of his race. That may be hard to credit, given the depths to which his reputation has since sunk, but in several respects he had appeared an answer to their prayers. Among other distinctions in a long career he gave them a plausible account of the spiritual condition of the black mind. Over that they had continued to agonise as much as David Livingstone, John Philip or John Campbell ever did. Could indigenous peoples believe in God in the same way as Europeans? In other words, would their conversion be a true one, to a concept of deity that saved their souls? In that case, what sort of moral state had stood revealed in the political consciousness of a John Chilembwe?

Banda made the connections, explained it all and so, after many false dawns, brought missionary perplexity to an end. This had lasted well into the 1930s, when the Rev Alexander Hetherwick of Blantyre expressed a qualified optimism that negroes would come to the gospel through their 'belief in the existence of spirit as the mystic essence in the world'. He conceded that they lacked ethics, or even a conscience in a Christian sense: though tribal law prescribed atonement for wrongs, crime remained a civil matter and sin had no moral value. Yet, he finished weakly, an evangelist might appeal to 'the native instinct for character as evidenced in the character of the convert and our Lord's own life'. The next generation felt little more sanguine. The Rev Cullen Young, head of the Overtoun Institute, loved negroes. But he could not help asking himself if the mission had instilled in them a sufficient sense of sin. He pursued the point through intensive studies of their history and customs, which turned him in effect into an anthropologist. He affirmed that the great thing to Africans was their community. They lived in the bush by values far from primitive, though lacking a divine sanction and therefore different from Christian values. Still, Young did not argue that the first ought just to be displaced by the second. The aim should be a new ethical system encompassing both. Some practices had to be condemned and rooted out as impossible to christianise: rites of initiation, bawdy and bloody at once, with all else in 'the scrub and undergrowth of charm, spell and tabu'. But other traditions might be accepted. In any event religion's progress among blacks could never, Young thought, 'take any path but through the thought area occupied by the ancestors'. Given their central place in communal values, the missionary must try to show that an infusion of Christianity would not deform but develop indigenous reverence for them: 'Ancestral guardianship must be not so much obliterated as expanded into a vision of God as the great ancestor . . . carrying the old clan comradeship and loyalty out into the larger family, not destroyed but enlarged'. Yet Young was perhaps still not quite persuaded in his own mind by the time he returned home.

A few years later, in 1938, Banda arrived in Scotland to finish his training as a medical missionary. His Presbyterian allegiance had wavered in the two decades since he left Nyasaland for South Africa and America. Now he was back in the fold, soon as an elder of Guthrie Memorial Church, Easter Road, Edinburgh. He met missionary veterans and reminded Young, who did not remember the incident, that they had parted in anger long before. Banda, over 40 but in his own words 'still absurdly youthful-looking', was wilful as ever. The eccentricities beneath his placid exterior amazed his friends. As divines they were hardly debauched, yet his puritanism far exceeded theirs. He had been horrified on landing from a steamship in Glasgow to find a Presbyterian city with so many pubs. In Edinburgh, too, 'the very home and Mecca of the Church of Scotland', it shocked him to see unmarried men and women holding each other for the purpose of dancing in ballrooms; he recalled how missionaries had denounced Chewa revelries as savage and sinful. Even in the straitlaced Scottish capital this obsessive prudery seemed absurd, though for him it had its uses: he was able to make a specialism of something unmentionable, the treatment of sailors with venereal disease. His moral energy carried him otherwise beyond the call of duty. Towards the end of his three years in Edinburgh he began visiting the sick in poor districts, for experience but also from a genuine desire to ease suffering.

Young and Banda put the past behind them to become friends, then collaborators in editing a volume of essays by articulate blacks from Nyasaland, *Our African Way of Life* (1944). It was a milestone, the first time natives of enough intellectual training had been able to work out with a European of enough sympathetic understanding an account of tribal mentality which might be of value to scientific inquiry. Banda and Young translated the essays from the original Chichewa and wrote a preface. The expression here may have been Young's but he often let Banda put words in his mouth. At the same time, Banda's contact with Young's thinking was to leave a lasting impression on him.

The book covered many large questions, including religion. Young rejoiced that Banda unlocked to him the secret of what Africans believed. It was a faith in *Mulungu*, a supreme being, as well as in *mizimu*, or spirits: 'We never thought that spirits were gods . . . The spirits of one's ancestors had to be prayed to, not because they were themselves the deities, but rather because they were the means of approaching the Deity, who was above everything else, including the spirits themselves'. If terse, the statement outlined what is taken as an axiom in progressive Christianity today: that blacks had worshipped the true God before they ever received a revelation, which they were then entitled to combine with older religious practice just as converted Europeans had done a millennium before. Ross, for example, later felt proud of bringing into the open 'the village life of the Christian Church which had been hidden. There was already an African theology being lived in the villages, but nobody had articulated it in words'. As for Mulungu, 'that's the word we have chosen to translate the Bible now that we have accepted that Africans were worshipping God, but needed the thing to be developed. They grasped after a God whom they knew but did not know. African traditional religion is mixed in with Christianity now, inextricably'.[2]

Banda's statement in the book also served a greater purpose of Young's: to set out a general vindication of black culture. The pair conceded on behalf of indigenous peoples 'that much in their community thought and communal life has been judged unfitting and detrimental to progress'. Yet, despite official and missionary efforts, natives felt 'there is so much in the new culture that seems, not merely no better but actually less good than what they know of the old'. One answer might be to reverse the process of instruction, 'to get through to the European mind some inkling of their African truth, their African scale of values, their African social ethic'. This assertion of cultural nationalism would form a permanent part of Banda's politics. It was not, however, quite identical with Young's more ambiguous outlook. He preferred his black men authentic, sons of the soil rather than westernised sophisticates. In that, while no racist, he almost echoed white settlers. He could commend nothing more than a moderate nationalist line, given the basic benevolence of British colonialism. The big defect was its complacency: 'What does one do when the less fortunate, those over whom one rules, refuse to be treated as primarily "backward"? That is the point at which we stand today'. A first step should be to co-opt into government the most able natives, such as Banda.[3]

Banda's politics went further because he had to put up with things far beyond Young's ken. A doctor in Edinburgh lived a normal bourgeois life, yet that helped not one whit when, after gaining his degree, Banda had to turn and face African reality. Hearing of his prospective return, nurses at Livingstonia wrote into headquarters in Edinburgh saying they would not serve under a black. He took the blow with dignity. He tried for a job with the Government of Nyasaland, to be offered one on condition that he would not seek to mix with white doctors. This he refused. In other words, he relinquished his ambition of becoming a medical missionary, to which he had given years of hard work, fêted the while as a nonpareil of his people. It was a cruel outcome, for which Scotland offered no redress. In 1941 Banda moved to a practice in Liverpool. And he began to involve himself, so far as distance allowed, in his country's politics, by helping to found the Nyasaland African Congress. Towards the end of the Second World War, nationalist movements were being formed for several British colonies, often by expatriates: a Pan-African Congress took place in Manchester in 1945. There Hastings Banda met Jomo Kenyatta and Kwame Nkrumah. He had much in common with them, though not the socialism they absorbed at the London School of Economics, meat far too strong for a conservative, Presbyterian Chewa.[4]

In Britain a new political era dawned with Labour's landslide in the General Election at the close of the war. The party stayed true enough to its anti-imperialist tradition to grant independence to India, but appeared in no great hurry elsewhere. In reality it had complex attitudes towards Empire. It suffered delusions about the strength of an unconquered Britain. Up to the 1930s she had remained the sole global power of any importance, attempting in that decade to forge through imperial preference an economic bloc of her own in response to depression. Times had changed, but they proved not at all easy to read. Atlanticism was still untried outside the special case of military alliance. A Europe in ruins held out no sort of alternative. The Government had at least half a mind to revitalise Empire once again, to embark on a new era which would bring, at the outset anyway, a yet more intense relationship between the mother country and its dependencies, till at length it set them on their own feet.

Several strands of imperial thinking intertwined here, though not in the event into a very robust fabric. The strongest strand of Scottish thinking anyway implied that the whole lot would sooner or later unravel. In Scotland war, sacrifice and hard-won victory boosted British patriotism. They did not avert defeat for the Unionist party, a surer sign that Scotland could now only with difficulty think of herself as an imperial nation in the way she still had done in 1918. The change of heart may have arisen not so much from Empire's objective decline, at the time not conspicuous, as from the thoroughness with which Scotland had been reduced economically, and had reduced herself politically, to provincial dependence, intent above all on winning largesse from London. Such was the course set by her new political masters in the Labour Party, of which she became, as she remained, a fief. This new domestic orthodoxy, anyway somewhat inarticulate, showed few points of connection or agreement with the part of the official mind in Whitehall which thought of revitalising Empire. It is here, in a withering of imperialist populism, and a lack of interest or aspiration left behind it, that we may mark how different Scotland had become from her old self, at home and in relation to the world.[5]

But Scots had already fed into the latest evolution of imperial policy a crucial ingredient, nourished out of the missionary impulse, or rather a secular derivative of it. Its creators were a professor, William Macmillan, and a politician, Malcolm MacDonald. Macmillan had returned to Britain in 1933 after abandoning South Africa in disgust at growing racism there. He then took a long, hard look at Empire, trying to develop a coherent critique of it and devise a fresh approach on liberal lines which might yet appeal to broad currents of opinion. Through his work he got to know, and became an adviser of, MacDonald. The son of Labour's first Prime Minister, he too went into the National Labour Party in 1931 and on that ticket afterwards won election for Ross and Cromarty. He served as a Minister in the Dominions and in the Colonial Offices. A political lightweight, elevated to the Cabinet in 1935 to keep alive a fiction of some share by the Left in the National Government, he all the same combined unconventional thinking with a discreet, conciliatory manner. And in the Commonwealth he found his life's work.

In 1936 a sudden explosion of violence in Jamaica shook the whole West Indies. The appalled Colonial Office set up an inquiry, but the findings reflected its cautious, even grudging view of the world, concerned to keep its territories quiet and their administration cheap. It placed all blame on a global depression quite beyond its own control: the one conceivable remedy lay in piecemeal improvement financed out of local revenues. But, with Macmillan at his elbow, MacDonald was coming to suspect that colonial tranquillity and imperial parsimony might in the long run be contrary principles. What if depression was not the cause of the trouble? These economies had flagged ever since abolition of slavery. If they were going to revive under the natural operation of markets, they ought to have done so long ago. For Britain to discharge her responsibility of setting colonial peoples on their own feet, she might have to seek some other method than forcing them into self-sufficiency by refusing to spend any money on them.

MacDonald therefore appointed a royal commission on the West Indies. As often with such bodies, it told the Secretary of State what he wanted to hear, and in a tone rather different from the Colonial Office's. Its report concluded that development should no longer be self-financing. Instead, the British Government ought to pay for whatever social or economic schemes were deemed necessary under a comprehensive plan, through a regional fund at the disposal of a comptroller answerable to the Secretary of State. By these means, the islands could at last be prepared for independence. The scheme was in force by 1940, though nothing much happened till after the war.[6]

It might have been a mere footnote in the history of Empire. In fact it marked a crux matching the advent of Keynesian economics at home. MacDonald and Macmillan became advocates for much more active development of colonies, hand-in-hand with greater political autonomy. Imperial preference was failing to solve the problems. In agriculture, for example, regulation of output and marketing often foundered on inefficiencies among the peasantry, due in turn to rigid land-holding traditions. In the absence of mechanisms to set aside such obstacles, the grand strategy could be sure neither of meeting the needs of industrial workers and consumers nor of raising the standard of living for backward tillers of the soil. Left to itself no scheme, liberal or protectionist, could foster growth and welfare. These, dependent on each other, had to be promoted at lower levels by more and cheaper aid, without worrying about balancing colonial budgets or securing a return to British taxpayers. To set the ball rolling, MacDonald proposed to create a Colonial Research Fund which could identify projects beneficial in the long term even if not at once self-sufficient on existing criteria. It sounded virtuous enough, but his real aim, owed to Macmillan, was to prise open the Treasury and crack the problem of capital, lack of which had always constrained development. Instead the Colonial Office would itself become arbiter of a pattern of higher spending in all its territories. MacDonald was ready to bring his scheme before Cabinet in September 1939.

War did not stifle his ambitions. While India seethed and the whole oriental Empire awaited its doom, Britain's enemies cast her imperial record in her face. It seemed high time to refurbish her image, to give subject races an incentive for joining in the struggle, to nip their discontents in the bud and to prepare for fending off decolonising pressures after the peace. Introducing his legislation in the fateful month of May 1940, MacDonald spoke of 'the duty of taxpayers in this country to contribute directly and for its own sake towards the development in the widest sense of the word of the colonial peoples for whose good government the taxpayers of this country are ultimately responsible'. Parliament voted MacDonald's fund an annual £10 million over ten years. Though he was then shoved sideways by Winston Churchill, who had rather different imperial ideas, and some months later put out of the Cabinet altogether, his work with Macmillan thus survived. The Colonial Office was equipped to press on with it as soon as normality returned.[7]

That was Scotland's main contribution to the jetsam of imperial ideas left by the ebb of war. She always harboured an undercurrent of radical, anti-colonial sentiment which, now the tide of imperialist populism had turned, rose to the surface again. After 1945 it was enriched by a flow of young African intellectuals who started coming over on scholarships to finish their education. Afire with nationalism, they won a ready response from their hosts. In Edinburgh they were welcomed by David Carmichael of the British Council and by Kenneth Little, later professor of social anthropology and first chairman of the Centre for African Studies, who held a seminar for them on the roots of colonialism. He was author of the earliest study of *Negroes in Britain* (1948), which treated racial prejudice as a variant of the conflict among classes which had developed, especially in England, during the industrial revolution. But sympathy extended well beyond academic circles. It found a focus in the Scottish Council for African Questions, chaired by Gordon Lethem, a former colonial governor and Liberal parliamentary candidate. Less conventional in its liberalism was the Capricorn Group set up by Colonel David Stirling of Keir, founder of the Special Armed Services. He had retired after the war to Africa and been disturbed at the outlook for the lands of European settlement. He hoped harmony might yet prevail if anti-racist whites aired their views, and meant his group as a platform for that. He found common ground with Scottish political parties, newspapers and other organs of opinion, above all with active Presbyterians. They knew Africa well after a century of mission, and many supported black nationalism.[8]

Nowhere was their attention so fixed as on Nyasaland. If in most colonies the future offered a straight contest between imperial power and native aspiration, the condition of this one was more complex. Here the people had to contend not just with their own governors but also with the aggrandisement of Southern Rhodesia, which wanted to dominate and if possible absorb the two territories nearby. The means would be federation, which had gained some currency as an antidote to variegated ethnic tensions at this end of the continent. The model was, of course, the Union of South Africa, cobbled together from disparate provinces after the Boer War. Despite Afrikaner rumblings it held together, and there seemed no special reason why it should not in time expand to take in Basutoland, Bechuanaland and Swaziland, then places further north. That idea had gone on Jan Smuts's agenda as early as 1923, when Southern Rhodesia attained responsible government. He put it to Howard Moffat, scion of the Scots missionary clan and Prime Minister of the colony in 1927–33. 'If I could have Moffat I could have Rhodesia,' said Smuts, though he got neither.[9]

One reason why Moffat grasped at the notion of a federal Central Africa was to fend off these unwelcome attentions. Vulnerable alone, Southern Rhodesia joined with two neighbours might become the keystone of a new dominion robust enough to stand on its own – and more loyal to Empire because the European population would be British. In economic terms this made some sense, by linking the broad farmlands of Southern Rhodesia and mines of Northern Rhodesia with a pool of labour in Nyasaland. But in political terms it meant bringing together an ensemble which could never be white man's country. Moffat himself felt easy enough with that. No racist, he aspired by the undemanding standards his day to be a protector of blacks and promoter of their development. If relatively liberal, he was still not liberal enough, because opponents of his plan managed to kill it for the present.

In Northern Rhodesia, which lacked any direct indigenous representation, opposition came from two sound and sensible Scots governors. James Maxwell had begun his career as a medical officer in Sierra Leone and his profession influenced his politics. Interested in racial theory, he worried that Europeans might over generations in the tropics lose their vigour. But his notorious parsimony gave him greater reason to turn away white settlers, by refusing to let them appropriate land in anything less than economic units: in his view colonisation must remain an experiment rather than a policy till they proved they could outdo native peasants. His successor John Maybin temporised too. He impeded European immigration, while in his dispatches dwelling on the incompatibility of three territories with such disparate racial composition. As for his own, many of its able-bodied men had worked on the other side of the River Zambesi and knew just what to expect in a federation run from Salisbury: 'Though their views may not have been formed with the clarity of a jurist or the profundity of a political philosopher, they were held none the less stoutly and they were unanimously opposed to amalgamation with Southern Rhodesia'.[10]

In Nyasaland, resistance to federation could rely on the Scots Presbyterians, who made up one-third of the white population. While they were transients, their mission had a permanent presence with a precise vision: of a non-racial society under its own African leaders, educated, skilled, Christian, an example to the whole Empire. On this view, it was morally indefensible and politically disastrous even to contemplate any link with lands of white supremacy. Missionaries stood ready to repel fresh advances from that quarter as they had repelled, and defeated, all others since the days of Harry Johnston in the 1890s. If the British Government should be inclined to manipulate the situation in the three territories by consulting just their Europeans, in Nyasaland a white majority against federation was quite possible.

After 1945, new policies of indigenous development and political advance soon carried some colonies, those without white settlers, to independence: the first, Ghana, won it under Nkrumah in 1957. Meanwhile in Central Africa, however, high imperialism enjoyed a last fling. Local economies had thriven in war and continued doing so. Here and elsewhere the Colonial Office could now start spending MacDonald's fund on roads, bridges, dams, hospitals, schools, agricultural research, technical training and so on. Towns were modernised, rural areas opened to the market and native skills enhanced. But the economic boom carried a political cost, in a great expansion of the expatriate personnel for colonial government, then in a further and more general distribution of the British stock overseas. Southern Rhodesia received a heavy inflow of white immigration, Northern Rhodesia a lesser but still large one, while the biggest numbers of all went to South Africa. They were mainly skilled workers whose arrival at once delayed the need to train blacks and strengthened the whites' stake in political control. It would be fair to say all the same that Whitehall felt dismayed by the electoral victory in 1948 of the Nationalist Party in South Africa and the institution of apartheid in an anti-British atmosphere. At any rate, this complex of trends set off another search for the right structure in Central Africa. The project of federation was dusted down.

It won no instant welcome. Whites in Southern Rhodesia were more worried about their privileges than new-fangled blueprints for the Empire. The same held true in Northern Rhodesia. Here the same wariness was displayed from the opposite point of view by the native member of the legislative council, John Moffat, one more scion of the missionary clan, who formed a Liberal Party to advocate racial partnership and black enfranchisement. And in Nyasaland, too, missions remained hostile. If mediocrity and compromise had marked them since Laws and Hetherwick retired a quarter-century before, their old radicalism came to life again in a new generation: the Revs Andrew Doig, Neil Barnard, Thomas Colvin, Michael Scott and Andrew Ross, most of them supporters of Labour at home. Doig was their doyen. He had arrived just before the war, served as a military chaplain, then been appointed native member of the legislative council in 1947. He harped on two points embarrassing to the British Government. First, the territory's formal status of protectorate (rather than colony) must mean something, for instance that it could not be federated against its will. Secondly, blacks who had helped to defend the Empire deserved better than to see their homeland turned into white man's country. Indulgence towards him and the others by the head of Livingstonia, the Rev Fergus Macpherson, gave them a free hand. It also assured support from the General Assembly which warned in 1952, as plans for federation matured, that 'no scheme should be adopted without the consent and co-operation of the Africans'.[11]

In 1953, the Central African Federation came all the same. The recent electoral victory in Britain of the Conservative party had been decisive, with a right wing eager to uphold imperial rule. Before Rhodesian whites this Government dangled the bait of a federal constitution which, amid its complexities, excluded all political expression by blacks save through a toothless African Affairs Board. Local politicians, their appetite whetted, went on to call for Southern Rhodesia to be declared a dominion or Northern Rhodesia to be granted responsible government so that, with control from London curtailed, white supremacy could be entrenched in both. The Secretary of State for Commonwealth Relations from 1957, the Earl of Home, did not demur. Identified at the time with the Right, he dissented from his homeland's general outlook; he later put on record his view that the Kirk preached the Christian doctrine of equality 'with little political sense'. In 1958 he sanctioned two new policies of the federal Government, a cut in African representation and a deployment of Southern Rhodesian bureaucrats and policemen in the other territories, which might prepare for their taking over in due course from the British colonial authorities.

Doig at once resigned from both the federal Parliament and the African Affairs Board. He took instead the post of general secretary to the synod of the Church of

Central Africa. It promptly passed resolutions implying that these were racist measures which had been taken to soften up Nyasaland for a future as native reserve on the South African pattern: 'The synod therefore feels it urgently necessary to say that it is unanimously opposed to federation'. The sudden peril provoked unmistakable hostility from blacks, and so repaired one flaw in the missions' case hitherto. Ross explained it like this: 'Nyasaland Africans, even the nationalists, had right up until the 1940s really felt that Britain was their friend . . . Nyasaland was made to join the Central African Federation against its will and Africans really felt betrayed'. He and his colleagues now threw themselves into organisation and propaganda for the Nyasaland African Congress. Settlers complained that ministers 'did not hesitate to preach African nationalism from the pulpit and have allowed and encouraged Congressmen to initiate political discussion after their services on Sunday'.[12]

Then, in July 1958, Banda returned. He arrived not just with sympathy from the Church of Scotland but with its active blessing and support: the Moderator of the General Assembly and founder of the Iona Community, the Rev George Macleod, saw him off. When he touched down at Blantyre, some of his jubilant people hailed him as a reincarnation of Chilembwe, risen again to bring freedom to Nyasaland. Banda took a more sober line: 'Everyone expects that I have come with self-government in my handbag, but we will have to struggle for it'. Still, his Calvinist faith left him in no doubt of having God on his side, while his experience as an elder equipped him to run the numerous committees of a nationalist movement largely Presbyterian in personnel. His strategy was to conduct a peaceful campaign for universal suffrage while dropping hints that, if frustrated, it might degenerate into violence; his own behaviour remained moderate beyond reproach, yet he did little to discourage hotheads. Universal suffrage, besides being an end in itself, also offered Nyasaland a way out of federation, for the people would secede as soon as they could and seek independence alone. In these circumstances Banda judged that matters were best brought to a head in case the chance should be lost. He got the Congress to agree. Subsequent disturbances led straight to Armitage's declaration of an emergency eight months later.[13]

No hard evidence ever surfaced of the imminent rising or massacre by which the governor justified his move. The country stayed on the whole peaceable and law-abiding. But its march towards freedom did not stop. This was because a second centre of nationalist agitation existed in Scotland: Scots argued with equal force the case that native detainees would at liberty have argued for themselves. Nyasaland stood at the top of the agenda for the General Assembly of 1959, soon after Banda's arrest. As Moderator, Macleod struck just the right note. His speech started off conciliatory in tone, recognising what Europeans had done in Africa. 'But,' he went on, 'it seems to us that Europeans have plenty to speak for them. We believe that for the time being someone must speak for the African – and that someone will be the General Assembly of the Church of Scotland.' Then he spoke for them himself: 'If I were an African in Nyasaland, I would rather risk sedition than allow myself to be further merged with the white minority in Southern Rhodesia'. To stormy applause, a huge majority approved a deliverance calling for black power. The Prime Minister, Harold Macmillan, later acknowledged that this had tipped the balance against the previous British policy of upholding federation.[14]

That Macmillan was anyway revising the policy showed itself after he won a General Election later that year. In 1960 he set off on a tour of Africa, to speak in Cape Town of the winds of change blowing through the continent. He put into the Colonial Office, to balance Home at Commonwealth Relations, a man intent on liquidating the Empire or at least on being, as he said, 'the last Colonial Secretary'. Iain Macleod, if born in England, was son of a Lewisman and proud of it. Political history has revealed during these 13 years of Tory rule the presence in the Cabinet of "hidden Scots" assuring generous treatment for the ingrate land of their fathers. Their liberality extended to Africa. Both Macmillan and Macleod, according to the latter's biographer, 'had a sense of the outsider about them. They had at least some understanding from their family's collective memory of what it meant to be under the yoke of English rule'. Macleod brought in two more Scots, the Earl of Perth and Hugh Fraser, to work with him. They aimed to proceed towards independence while averting racial war. They therefore differed from Home, who believed white rule the guarantee of peace and stability. The respective departments often backed different protégés on the ground, but Macleod seized the initiative.

The big problem lay in the intransigent white settlers, who so far had managed to blackmail the Tory Government in London. They even hindered progress in the territories of East Africa housing no permanent European population but held in a loose union with others which did, on the grounds that any concession would open the floodgates. Now in Uganda, Macleod swept that obstacle aside. In Tanganyika, he favoured another Scot, Richard Turnbull, who since arriving as governor in 1958 had never ceased to spell out in dispatches how only political advance could avert violence. This meant encouraging young Julius Nyerere, a former student in Edinburgh, who might otherwise have to give way to extremists or be tempted into extremism himself. With Macleod's ear, Turnbull could go further than encouragement and make Nyerere his Prime Minister. Working together, they passed through the intermediate stages of drafting a constitution, holding elections and receiving internal self-government, till Tanganyika won independence in 1961. In Kenya conditions were trickier, because of the state of emergency imposed a decade before against the Mau Mau. Macleod at once ended it. By 1963, when Malcolm MacDonald performed his imperial swansong and went out to be Governor of Kenya, the country was ready for rapid transition too. He put his trust in Jomo Kenyatta, a man still suspect in Britain, and urged other leaders to sink their differences, especially tribal ones, under the veteran's direction, even if this implied an eventual one-party state. Whatever the ultimate wisdom of the policy, it allowed MacDonald and Kenyatta to co-operate in achieving independence within 12 months.[15]

But Central Africa was the key. There the political brew had been rich or, rather, indigestible. Mixed together came schemes of development to benefit blacks, if not so much as they benefited whites, and projects of self-rule overtaken by novel imperial structures preserving the settlers' power. The ingredients never jelled, and now they separated, with Nyasaland the solvent. While Home had charge of relations with self-governing Southern Rhodesia, Macleod was responsible for the other two territories. This proved crucial when he freed Banda. From then on federation unravelled, with help from a royal commission's hostile report again telling the Secretary of State what he wanted to hear. In a few months Banda was sitting as leader of the nationalist delegation at a constitutional conference. By 1961 he won universal suffrage, by 1962 a right of secession and by 1964 independence, with himself as first President of Malawi. Progress was slower in Northern Rhodesia, which Southern Rhodesia wanted to keep for the copper. But the territory also had a vigorous African National Congress under Kenneth Kaunda, who could not be long denied. He left the federation in 1963 and led Zambia to independence in 1964. Home tried but failed to get from the prime minister of Southern Rhodesia, Sir Roy Welensky, nominal concessions which could justify her independence while keeping blacks in their place. But even gestures proved beyond the country's whites, who took their own path to perdition.

The Church of Scotland supported black nationalism all through the final stages of these struggles. It cast off its earlier compromises with imperialists. Meanwhile it had backed an official policy of racial partnership or multiracialism, with equal weight for various groups even where indigenous peoples formed an overwhelming majority. But now the Kirk came to regard this too as a fraudulent idea. In the end it advocated African independence pure and simple, not just declining to hinder it but actively promoting it. Since white supremacy brought advantages for missions, their stance cannot have been owing to a calculation but to a belief. The belief concerned religion rather than race: pagan Africans remained inferior on account of their ignorance, but converted Africans were equal, as all Christians were equal.

What were the ultimate consequences of the belief? Answers offered by the era since independence give little comfort, or at least show how deep the divide between Scottish and alien cultures remained after a century of exchange. Banda used his country's independence to institute personal dictatorship, exploiting inherited colonial laws with the refinement that, as he boasted, he fed his foes to crocodiles. One definition of his Malawi might be of a land ruled by a stern Presbyterian elder, moulding a still benighted people into puritanical, disciplined conservatives. Conspicuous anyway by its absence was criticism from the Church of Scotland of his excesses, which far surpassed the colonial regime's; though to some ministers this is now a matter of public reproach. By 1992 his people had had enough. That year saw riots, strikes, demonstrations, formation of new political groups and the Government's assent to a referendum on the one-party system, a prelude to democratic elections and the end of Banda's rule in 1994. But the first impetus was given by the

Roman Catholic bishops in a pastoral letter condemning abuses, though indeed Presbyterians and other denominations afterwards helped to sustain progress.

Another definition of Banda's Malawi might be of a typical African tyranny. It had its peculiar features: the ban on all forms of western sexual liberation, the Kamuzu Academy where favoured children learned Latin and Greek, the South African aid in return for diplomatic support. But the eccentricities were never such as to counter the usual effect of tyranny, the demoralisation arising from economic failure under corrupt, dictatorial rule by a single party, which left this among the poorest countries on the continent when Banda fell. Yet benevolent despots such as Kaunda and Nyerere fared no better. They wanted to preserve an African spirit of community, exalted by Christian socialism. But the co-operation had to be enforced, while competition, elitism or accumulation of personal wealth were banned. One positive result followed: removal of tribalism from politics. But negative results, similar to Malawi's, prevailed. Scots who trained the pioneers of freedom had not provided them with all the moral and practical equipment they needed to avoid the pitfalls.

If their contribution has proved disappointing, Nelson Mandela still found reason to praise the Scots: 'The missionaries built and ran schools when the government was unwilling or unable to do so. The learning environment in the missionary schools, while often morally rigid, was far more open than the racist principles underlying government schools'. In other words, Scots brought about modest African progress when few others wished or bothered to bring it about. As ever, Scottish aspirations outran Scottish resources, but the hopes are always high, and the goals worthy of respect.[16]

CHAPTER THIRTY-THREE

'The oracle is dumb': India

On May 9, 1934, Sir John Anderson, Governor of Bengal, accompanied by his daughter Mary and Miss Nellie Mackenzie, drove in semi-state to Calcutta's racecourse at Lebong for one of his regular public appearances, at the spring meeting. On arrival, he and the rest of the official party took their places in his personal box by the winning post. Next to them the stand overlooking the final furlong was already full. On the other side of the track lay a cheap public enclosure, still more crowded. Everyone had come to watch the main event, the popular Governor's Cup. When it was over, with cheers ringing out, Anderson stood up in his seat to see the winner led in. Excited Indians from the enclosure surged across towards him. With them came two assassins. The first pushed his way through the press till he was only three feet from Sir John. He took out a gun and, resting his arm on the rail of the stand, fired. Tandy Green, the starter, saw the boy's movement and jumped on him just too late, but they fell over together and he wrested the weapon away. The bullet missed. It passed between Anderson and Miss Mackenzie, to wound in the foot an Anglo-Indian girl standing behind. An instant later, the second assassin fired from even closer. He missed too, and his gun jammed as he tried again. The Rajah of Barwari, 'with the plucky assistance of the Rani of Nazarganj', overpowered him. Anderson had had a lucky escape.

Perhaps this was a warning to keep away from the races, for Anderson did not make a raffish kind of governor. He was what some might call a true son of Edinburgh, bred by its schools and university to be composed, diligent and reliable, qualities which in time had evolved towards the overbearing, pedantic and self-satisfied. We last left him at Dublin Castle, just before the British evacuated it for ever, trying vainly to prevent civil war in Ireland. For him his efforts paid off all the same, because he was then promoted, aged only 40, straight to Permanent Secretary at the Home Office. There he served for ten years till Bengal beckoned; he was the first member of the Home Civil Service ever transferred to India. On returning in 1938 he entered Parliament as MP for the Scottish Universities. The climax of his career would come in Winston Churchill's War Cabinet, as the Home Secretary who invented the Anderson shelter and the Chancellor of the Exchequer who in every extremity kept the finances of the state in order. He would end up a peer of the realm, taking his title of Viscount Waverley from the Scottish capital's main railway station. The Bengalis ought to have counted themselves lucky to be touched by the wings of so high a flyer. Yet to them he looked like just another imperialist oppressor.[1]

After the Viceroy, the Governor of Bengal had the biggest job in the sub-continent. His province was vast and its people volatile, led on by an elite educated in European ways for over a century. John Buchan had noted the effect of learning the Whig doctrines of Thomas Macaulay and John Stuart Mill, fine old doctrines, though hardly suitable to an autocracy: 'The Bengali is not a strong man, but he has an ingenious and receptive brain, and has absorbed this kind of western learning far faster than the average Englishman' – a pointed remark if ever there was one. As soon as the Bengali mastered the discourse of human rights and constitutional principles, 'he began to ask himself why he had no equal share with the British in the government of his own country – why, indeed, the British were there at all'. Anderson did not mean to offer answers to such questions. He had been briefed to perform certain tasks and he set about doing so in his wonted impartial and efficient manner. He had the prime duty of keeping the province quiet until new and, it was hoped, definitive legislation for the future of India could be prepared in London. That required him above all to suppress political violence. He called in more troops, ordered a stricter regime for suspects detained without trial and imposed collective fines on areas which sheltered terrorists. The attempt on his life at Lebong would have been a reminder that he had a long way to go.[2]

This sort of thing seems a sorry finale to the Scottish encounter with India. If it at last amounted to mechanical execution of futile orders from 9000 miles away, we may well ask what good had come of it. Was nothing special left from two centuries of rich exchange between a great, ancient civilisation and a small, distant nation? At Anderson's level, perhaps not: there is no sign that Indians saw in him or ought to have seen in him anyone other than a typical member of the British ruling caste. Nor, lower down, is the evidence reassuring. When the novelist Eric Linklater came on a tour in the 1930s he recorded that, 'having seen something of the way in which we behaved in India – of the insensate pretence to superiority that white people, of no intrinsic distinction, exhibited in their dealing with Indians – I left Bombay with a feeling of uneasiness, related to guilt, of which I had been innocent when I arrived'. Eugenie Fraser's charming memoir of the Scots who made up much of the commercial community in Calcutta regrets how little of the country she or the rest of them saw. As for the Indians, 'I do not think we ever really got to know them'.[3]

The story may still be instructive if we recall that the progress of the Scottish encounter with India almost mirrored the philosophical history of Scotland herself. Though Scots in the end stood perplexed at the ultimately unknowable nature of an alien civilisation, or dismayed by the unforeseen consequences of western irruption into it, they were surely also vindicated in the moderation and toleration with which they had once applied to it their theories of social development and political economy. At any rate, hindsight casts in a much worse light the newer and narrower doctrines of utilitarianism or evangelical religion used afterwards to justify a secular mission, then a military despotism. Scottish philosophy meanwhile crumbled, but left habits of thought which raised doubts among at least some of its students about the conventional wisdom of high imperialism in an increasingly English sort of Empire. As this, in turn, succumbed to the stresses of the twentieth century, Scots still offered a running if now scarcely coherent critique of it. Yet we cannot deny that, as the quality of their own culture declined, so did the richness of their encounter with India.

Scottish orientalism had had built into it from the outset a fatalistic resignation towards the impermanence of Empire. True to form, the Scots who founded the Indian National Congress in 1885 well knew there could be nothing durable about their leadership and that they would be replaced by natives, as indeed happened while Lord Curzon was Viceroy in 1899–1905. Resistance to his high-handedness, especially in partitioning Bengal, turned the Congress into a movement of the masses and spawned a revolutionary wing, in part militantly Hindu, in part terrorist. With this fresh configuration, it set out on its own course.

The Scottish Congressmen, Allan Octavian Hume, William Wedderburn and George Yule, may have seemed like wild-eyed radicals at home but in the new Indian context they were moderates, alarmed that the situation might run away from indigenous leaders who thought like them. 'Surely these men deserve some recognition and support,' wrote Wedderburn, 'but so far as they are concerned, the oracle is dumb, and they write to me almost in despair.' Yet the Congress's future had to lie in direct action inside India rather than in appeals to Britain's better nature, which was where the Scots thought to help. If instead there ensued a straight contest between imperial power and native aspiration, they would find much less to do. Yule, both an economic and a political liberal, was the one with the deepest stake in the country, running in effect an Indian company except in its senior personnel. Like every head of an agency house he looked after his own first, but he freely entered into local partnerships. After he died in 1902, however, the third head of the dynasty, his nephew David, could never find so much common ground with native capitalists. As for Hume and Wedderburn, their authority rested on their official distinction, yet that had not let them hold down jobs in the Indian Civil Service. Transients in the sub-continent, they espoused at home a truly Scottish but by now rather old-fashioned internationalist radicalism which would not survive into the new century much beyond their own respective deaths in 1912 and 1918. By then, the esteem and gratitude they enjoyed among Indians probably stood in inverse proportion to their domestic influence.

No doubt they rejoiced in 1906 when, after a decade of Unionist rule, the Liberal party swept back to power under Henry Campbell-Bannerman, a brother Scot rather of their own kidney. They ought also to have found an ally in his Secretary of State for India, John Morley, an Englishman but about as near to a Scotsman as he could get without actually being one. Like many of his now elderly generation, he hero-worshipped William Gladstone. He saw himself as keeper of the Gladstonian flame, and had already written the first biography of the great man. In Parliament he sat for the Montrose Burghs, one of several carpetbaggers to have sought refuge north of the border in Liberalism's dark days. They found a welcome because their views were usually consonant with their constituents', and they took care to underline the fact. Morley told the good people of Arbroath in October 1907 that 'we English, Scotch and Irish are in India because we are not Orientals. We are representatives not of oriental civilisation but of western civilisation, of its methods, its principles, its practices'. But this was just why he would now achieve less than he hoped. He abhorred oppression of foreign peoples, disliked imperialism generally and would be one of two Ministers to resign rather than fight the First World War. Yet he still stood, as if nothing had happened in almost a century, for the secular mission, the drive to transform India by application of radical axioms from afar.

Morley at once met a stumbling block, the more fixed for being outwardly so yielding, in the Viceroy, the 4th Earl of Minto, whom we have already met as Governor-General of Canada. His relations with London were bound to be delicate. Sent to Calcutta in the very last days of the outgoing Ministry, Minto could have been recalled by the Liberals but they let his appointment stand. He has usually been described as a Conservative, yet this is not strictly true. He was a Scots Liberal Unionist, something rather different, a member of a progressive, collectivist party stressing civic duty and social responsibility from the local to the imperial level, yet suspicious of starry-eyed idealism. In Canada, Minto had cast off his own imperialist delusions and come to a realistic assessment of what that colonial community felt and thought about the Empire. India demanded no less. The Viceroy disliked radicalism, whether of a British Liberal or an Indian nationalist hue, and feared its implications for an alien, ancient and ever more restive land.

In dealing with his masters in London, Minto followed an old Scots maxim of Indian administration, that those on the spot knew best. If it irked Morley, the Raj was well-versed in oriental tactics of obstructing him. Plenty of people inside the India Office in London sided with the Viceroy, while he personally enjoyed enough official and social standing to communicate directly with the King. The Secretary of State for his part complained of the 'cool indifference of your officers and ministers to what is said or done in Parliament'. When he took it into his head to visit India in person, Minto fobbed him off. In the end Morley was bound to have his way, of course, but that could not stop the Viceroy and his entourage forming their own views and exerting some influence on policy. In dealing with his subjects in India, Minto showed himself just as hard-headed. He did not deign to prettify the realities of power: 'We are here a small British garrison, surrounded by millions composed of factors of an inflammability unknown to the western world, unsuited to western forms of government, and we must be physically strong or go to the wall'. So he was more severe on nationalism than his Secretary of State would have liked. He refused to contemplate reversing the partition of Bengal, and deported local politicians who demanded it. When trouble flared in the Punjab too, he arrested several leading Congressmen. Yet he granted British India her first constitution.

The impulse may have come from Morley, but Minto worked to realise the concept with a will which a reluctant reformer could hardly have shown. Once that grew clear, his Secretary of State left him to it, aware that no Bill without his blessing could be piloted through the House of Lords anyway. The result has been dubbed a constitutional autocracy. 'We have distinctly maintained,' said Minto in his address inaugurating the system in 1910, 'that representative government in the western sense is totally inapplicable to the Indian Empire and would be uncongenial to the traditions of eastern populations.' He may himself have hankered romantically after the Moghul Empire, where the durbar of ruler and notables was always the main transaction of state. He allowed a special position to Moslems, the ruling class of old, on the axiom that 'We must safeguard communities'; though he may have attached more weight to the fact that the Moslem League, unlike the Congress, supported the Raj. Yet he also found scope for innovation. He brought an Indian into the Government of India, creating the post of native member on his executive council for Satyendra Sinha, Congressman and barrister from Calcutta. He gave Indians some direct representation, if only through a minority of members in a legislative council with a nominated official majority; the provincial councils, though, were to have unofficial majorities. With cautious acceptance of the elective principle in a stronger legislature, he crossed the line from consultation to deliberation. It would be idle to call this a new political orientalism, a revival of the work of Thomas Munro, John Malcolm and Mountstuart Elphinstone. But if Minto lacked their knowledge or love of India and her culture, he showed something of the same concern to respond to her peculiarities. He was not, like Morley, ready to treat Indians as candidates for western liberal democracy. But he did temper the military despotism.[4]

Those orientalist Scots of old had often done their best work at the provincial level, and so did their latter-day successors. To Madras in 1912 came Lord Pentland, straight from the Scottish Office he had headed for seven years. The former John Sinclair, a soldier chosen by Campbell-Bannerman as private secretary, he too was an old-fashioned radical and had run his administration in that spirit. He thus fell foul of his patron's successor at No 10 Downing Street, Herbert Asquith, who at length shoved him sideways to India. Pentland brought this peculiar radical spirit with him. He declared sympathy for Indian aspirations, cultivated Congressmen and offered himself as a figure of authority for once ready to listen to nationalists. In other ways, too, he remained intensely Scottish. At home he had been obsessed with the land and reform of the law concerning it. He was delighted to find how Scots had always indulged the same obsession in India. For his province he drew up a programme of aid for mechanisation, co-operative societies and other agricultural improvements. Education was a second major interest. He made lavish use of his cultural patronage, for example, to revive the venerable but moribund Madras Literary Society. Above all, in 1914 he summoned the wayward genius of Patrick Geddes to come out from Edinburgh and 'enlighten the municipal administration of India'.

Geddes made the remarkable contribution of drawing attention for the first time to the effects of colonialism on the manmade fabric of the sub-continent. Three of the four great Indian cities – Calcutta, Bombay and Madras – were in effect British foundations and creations. Each imposed an alien pattern on indigenous life, setting an example which cast a long shadow over public planning, such as it was. Two official aims seemed to Geddes bizarre: in the villages to fill in the tanks, a rendezvous for daily work and play, because they bred mosquitoes; and in the towns to drive needlessly wide roads through poor quarters, displacing the people along with their evolved social patterns. Clearly, such crassness arose from western assumptions. On the plains round Madras, by contrast, Geddes found a uniquely Indian urban form in the great temple-cities of Dravidian culture, physical expressions of a way of life imbued with religion and history. Here was an exotic analogue of the socio-biological approach he had worked out in his civic studies in Scotland, and a chance to show how, in the union of the robust Scots intellect and the earthy Tamil spirituality, renewal could come by interaction of the world's marginalised cultures.

He set off on a search for methods of reviving Indian urban forms. He personally drew up reports on 50 cities, in varying degrees of detail, showing how they might be improved without violence to their inherited structures, and in another series worked out ideas to sustain the villages. He eagerly sought the opinion and advice of Indian intellectuals. His open-minded enthusiasm impressed Chandra Bose, Rabindranath Tagore and above all Mahatma Gandhi, who told him: 'You could not be more pained than I am over our base imitation of the West'. Geddes felt especially anxious that Delhi, the fourth great city of the sub-continent and from 1911 again its capital, should not ape the others. As it happened, a brother Scot, John Begg, consulting architect to the Government of India, agreed. He too had been working to preserve old crafts and modernise living traditions rather than impose European formalism, which amounted to a 'western occupation' of the country. Both Scots were dismayed at Sir Edwin Lutyens's grandiose plans for New Delhi, in which they saw the unseemly symbol of a Raj nearer its end than a new beginning. 'Why should the style of our Capital be such as to express most strongly those alien characteristics in the administration which every year tend more and more to disappear?' Begg asked. Lutyens lost his temper at his impudence, but the domes and vistas of his New Delhi would anyway arise in due course, and posterity has approved his taste.

Geddes was all the same a breath of fresh air in stuffy official India, and his patron Pentland showed that the Raj even at this stage need not be hidebound. But when the First World War broke out, the old soldier in him felt progressive policies had to be played down: the Indians' first duty was to defend the Empire, though that might take them to fight far away, even to Europe. This was a view of their duty that the British generally sought to impress on the Indians. On neither side, apparently, had much influence been exerted by the military orientalism of the late Charles MacGregor, who envisaged the defence of India as the defence of a nation. At any rate nobody had carried this far-sighted Scot's work forward after his untimely death, and Whitehall continued to regard the Indian Army as an auxiliary of the

British one. Douglas Haig, who had served in India as chief of the general staff, felt no qualms about transferring native divisions straight to the western front in France during the early months of the war. This was one reason why Pentland, who with others gave effect to that policy, left not much of a liberal reputation behind him when he returned home in 1919.[5]

In another old field of endeavour, commerce, the intimacy of Scots and Indians also loosened. Yule's offered a good example. David Yule, aged only 44 on coming into his inheritance in 1902, still acted the Victorian patriarch, treating his companies as personal fiefs and running them himself. In a familiar extension of the role he was also a philanthropist, paying much heed to the less obviously profitable sectors of agriculture and forestry, donating generously to roads, schools or hospitals. His name entitled him to a high place in the society of Bengal, and seats on many boards. By any standards extremely wealthy, he was admired and deferred to. Yet it seems clear with hindsight that under him his agency house went into relative decline. He never had to face that. In 1920 he retired home laden with honours and bought a couple of newspapers to amuse his leisure. He could afford to because he had just sold out to Americans, to the firm of J.P. Morgan, known in Britain as Morgan Grenfell. It maintained Scottish appearances by putting in its own rising star, Thomas Catto from Peterhead, who had made his name and fortune convoying supplies from the United States to Europe during the war. He shook Yule's up, turned it into a modern business and eventually, in 1933, floated it as a public company. For him the chairmanship of Morgan Grenfell had followed. It raised him into the City of London's elite and won him a peerage in 1936. In 1940 he became Financial Adviser to the Chancellor of the Exchequer, working alongside John Maynard Keynes, and in 1944 Governor of the Bank of England, which he guided through nationalisation. His last public service came in chairing a royal commission on the finances of the Union, which concluded in 1952 that Scotland got much more out of it than she put in. One would not want to begrudge him this dazzling career. But, as for Yule's, he left behind a business which no longer belonged either to Scotland, where the proprietary link was broken, or to India, where it at length disposed of its assets.

This history summed up the agencies' fate. In 1931, India's five biggest commercial groups were, in order of size, Tata, Andrew Yule, Inchcape, James Finlay and Burn & Co, the first Indian, the rest Scottish in origin. A majority even of the country's top 20 groups had a similar Scottish origin. They owned 400 subsidiaries dominating jute, tea, sugar, metals, coal, electricity, transport and general investment. Yet within two decades they had all but vanished.[6]

One reason lay, probably, outside their control. The global economy was undergoing a deep shift away from the system of the nineteenth century, where the houses had fitted in so well. The era of free trade in staple commodities from exotic parts, dominated by British merchants, would soon be over. After 1945 it yielded to the age of the consumer, with production for the masses organised by multinational corporations in varied structures, against an economic and financial background of equal complexity. It was not perhaps beyond the agencies to understand and meet this, though in general they did not. Some set up new manufacturing subsidiaries in joint ventures with firms from home. But most stuck to the staples or, what amounted to much the same thing, to heavy industries of the sort in which their cousins in Scotland also grimly persevered, against problems just as intractable. The houses' conservatism is of a piece with the end of the Scottish way of doing business and with the nation's general lack of enterprise in the period.

More especially, the agencies fell behind Indian rivals. At home and abroad, Scots were now tending to counter commercial threats with cartel or combination. Such devices could protect them for a while but, through relieving them of the discipline of the market, seldom saved them in the long run. It may well be asked if India had ever known free trade in the classic sense, but by the 1930s the suppression of competition could no longer rescue expatriate hegemony. In industry after industry the houses either failed to move into new processes and products or, if they did, failed to match the natives. It was as if the economic system of the Raj inevitably tipped the balance of commercial power at last towards Indians. These banded together all the more closely. In 1927 they set up the Federation of Indian Chambers of Commerce, in opposition to the British-dominated Associated Chambers of Commerce, of which the weightiest member was the Bengali chamber, where Scots reigned supreme. The Government of India, always ready to intervene in the economy, now had to respond to an indigenous, indeed a nationalist voice, since the same rich Indians bankrolled the Congress. What was now the point of holding on? Perhaps Scots had already gone subconsciously into retreat, anticipating an independent India where they would be less welcome. Indians at any rate remembered their lessons. They set up after 1947 a system of protection and subsidy of which their Scottish mentors would have been proud. It meant India's industry afterwards fared no better than Scotland's.[7]

Of those four great Scots agencies in the India of 1931, only Finlay's survives today in anything like the same form. Though a limited company since 1909, it contrived also to remain a closed corporation even by Scottish standards, under the control of a few men usually unconnected to other groups. Perhaps this updated version of private partnership was the key to self-preservation. At any rate the house held its own till the independence of India. Then her new masters imposed consciously nationalist controls on the old exploiters, so burdensome as to force them out before long, unless they turned themselves over to local ownership. Many just went into liquidation. But Finlay's sought pastures new, notably in Africa, while steadily ridding itself of wasting assets. Even at home, it allowed no exception to that rule: by 1971 it closed down its mills at Catrine and Neilston, where it had processed cotton for 150 years, retaining then in Scotland only its headquarters and its stake in the North Sea.

Existing commercial relationships on the sub-continent had thus been eroded in two ways, on the Indian side by a nationalist desire to settle old scores and on the

Scottish side by the inability of a faltering system to modernise itself. The economic interests of Scotland and India, once happily married, drifted apart. Nor in fast-changing conditions was there much chance that political efforts could save the marriage.[8]

The efforts arose from the best of motives. If Scotland's radical fire still burned, it did so not among the exhausted Liberals but in the Labour Party. Even there, though, quick success in taking over as the main force on the Left after 1918 exacted a cost of earlier innocent ideals. Believing in the state, Labour felt an obligation to assume all the state's responsibilities, including imperial ones. Keir Hardie had gone out to India and been appalled, but his successor as leader, Ramsay MacDonald, by no means rejected the Raj. He wrote that 'for many a long year British sovereignty will be necessary for India . . . Britain is the nurse of India'. For him and his comrades, the condition of workers in the sub-continent had direct relevance to their aims at home. India was similar to other colonies in being a supplier of raw materials to the industries of the metropolis. Yet she differed in being also, at least in certain sectors, an industrial power in her own right, with a non-white workforce giving her a structure of costs cheaper than that of western competitors. The point cut little ice with socialists. On the axiom that capitalism was irrational, they saw no justification for inequalities in pay. Rather they meant to correct such blemishes by political action, here by bringing about common imperial standards in conditions of employment. They tackled the task as soon as they could. The National Government of wartime had included a few members of the Labour Party, notably George Barnes, general secretary of the Associated Society of Engineers, MP for Gorbals and Minister of Pensions. In 1918 he also joined the British delegation negotiating the peace at Versailles. The conference offered ample scope for do-gooding. Barnes sought out representatives of the Government of India, which had a separate seat, and urged them to work with him on joint regulation of labour. But his initiative did little more than reveal vast complexities.

To see them, Barnes had only to look as far as Dundee and its competition in jute with Calcutta. The industry remained as important to the one as to the other, something replicated nowhere else in the Empire. Calcutta was now, because of lower costs, much the bigger centre of production and set the global prices for finished goods. A boom in the 1920s saw profits, productivity, capacity and employment all rise. Yule's mills, for example, often declared dividends of 100 per cent, sometimes more. Dundee did well enough too, when high demand could not be satisfied in India and switched for a while to Scotland. But the general outlook remained much as ever: under pressure, the Dundonian industry stagnated. In all except one year, output and trade fell below the level of 1914. So there could be no opportunity to improve the city's terrible working conditions.

This posed the kind of problem that Labour thought it existed to solve. In Thomas Johnston, MP for Dundee and imperial expert besides, it had a man who saw socialism as nothing if not economically ingenious. He felt sure he could find a way out of the rut in which wicked Dundonian capitalists exported investment to Calcutta in order to exploit the underpaid coolies' still worse conditions, then used them to hold down the wages of Scots. The result was to depress living standards in both cities and stop the imperial economy flourishing as it might. In 1925 Johnston went out to India to find facts and propose solutions. Duly shocked at what he saw, he proposed as a remedy that Indian workers should form unions. They would then be better paid and consume more. The costs of production, as between Calcutta and Dundee, would be evened out too, easing the squeeze on Scots. The snag was that employers did not allow Indian workers to form unions. Until that changed, then, their British brothers should boycott goods from Calcutta. This did not seem very sensible, for in good times there would be other markets and in bad times the coolies would suffer. Those not knowing Johnston might have thought him more mischievous than ingenious. His trip was anyway viewed with intense suspicion by officials of the Raj, as by Dundonian Communists who inquired of Indian comrades if he had indulged in 'corrupt banquets and hospitality'. He also got a cool welcome from capitalist Congressmen. For his part he found them disagreeably indifferent to the poverty around them. On this score, even British management seemed preferable. Johnston began after all to see some virtue in a Raj he deplored in principle. He could not doubt that self-government would provide the ultimate cure for injustice, but meanwhile a professional, impartial British administration was guilty of less oppression than appeared likely should Indians be ruled by Indians. So Johnston returned orthodox rather than radical on India, and without answers for the problems he wanted to tackle.[9]

The depression of the 1930s made those problems worse. In Calcutta, Scots at last understood that Indian competitors had their measure. A half-century of operation was not enough to save the restrictive practices run by the Jute Mills Association, the combination of expatriate firms. When they proposed alternative means of limiting production, Indians refused to co-operate. Some of these, adding insult to injury, still earned profits even in the worst years. Not only in manufacturing but also in exports of raw jute they destroyed Scottish dominance, setting up their own cartel with better contacts up-country and abroad. All the Scots' chickens came home to roost: their small pool of talent, their duplication of effort, their neglect of new products and markets, their disregard of marketing or research. Their only virtue seemed to lie in tenacity: in 1939, 110 mills were still working with no upward trend in production. This could not last beyond 1947. Scots would have been squeezed out of jute as out of everything else, but the partition of India anyway divided the mills along the River Hooghly from their main source of supply, four-fifths of the crop being grown in what became East Pakistan. Dundonians stayed on in management of companies usually owned by Indians till the 1960s. Then most of the industry surviving in Calcutta was finally shut down by Pakistani competition.

Meanwhile in the depression, Dundee must have been the only place actually to suffer from the general effort by British and colonial economic interests to seek salvation in the Empire. This culminated at the Imperial Conference of 1931 in Ottawa, which agreed on a system of preferences. But that ruled out any protection for Dundee from the cheaper exports of Calcutta. Dundonian capitalists could hardly pay their workers less, or cut the cost of their material inputs: by contrast with critical points in the past, no fibre inferior to jute was now to be found for production of a cheaper, coarser article. So their axe fell on employment, which dropped by one-third. At least they did then start reorganising an industry which under its founding families remained much as it had been for 100 years. They co-operated, specialised and invested more, aided by official direction in the Second World War. When Indian independence came, it made little difference to a Dundee now producing only one-twelfth of the world's processed jute. The mills shifted from foreign to domestic markets, accepting that these had to be free rather than protected. In short they readied themselves for a final run of modest prosperity which lasted into the 1960s. But the strange tale of a single industry shared by two cities 9000 miles apart reached its end.[10]

The severance of Scotland and India was, of course, finally a political one. In the antepenultimate stage of the Raj the sub-continent came under Scottish influence greater than any since the days of the Dundases. In 1935–40 the Secretary of State in London, the Marquis of Zetland, was actually a member of the Anglo-Scottish branch of that family. He possessed impeccable Indian credentials. As Earl of Ronaldshay, before succeeding to the marquisate, he had served as Governor of Bengal in 1916–22. A scholar of Sanskrit himself, he was astonished to find that the local universities taught their undergraduates an exclusively western curriculum with no reference to Hindu thought. His efforts to promote study of the Indian classics prompted a conference of pandits to award him the title of Darshanambudhi, Ocean of Philosophy. In calling for the whole system of higher education to be made more Indian, he in effect rejected westernisation: 'To suppose that it is possible perma-nently to turn 320 millions of people, having behind them many centuries of history and the tradition of a distinctive culture and civilisation, into imitation Europeans, is to indulge in an idle dream'. This principle, he afterwards declared, should inform the Government of India too.[11]

It proved easier to set out principles than derive policies from them, but the prospects still seemed tolerable when the Marquis of Linlithgow arrived as Viceroy in 1936. His family, the Hopes of Hopetoun, boasted an outstanding record of imperial service. His father, before becoming Secretary of State for Scotland in 1905, had launched the federation of Australia, and the son hoped to perform the same service here. He had already served as chairman of the select committee which drafted the India Act (1935), a measure which with hindsight looks paltry and fussy in equal measure but at the time was confidently expected to chart the course of the Raj for years ahead. Unfortunately, Linlithgow turned out to be not really the man for the job in New Delhi. Though diligent and honest, he was too cold and shy for the mercurial sub-continent, too cautious and scrupulous to deal with the nationalists now seeing the end of British rule in sight, the unfathomable Mahatma Gandhi and the suavely ruthless Jawaharlal Nehru.

The Act's centrepiece was a federation of the provinces of British India with the princely states, creating political unity as the basis for constitutional progress. In practice, three groups had to be squared: the princes, the Congress and the Moslems. Zetland and Linlithgow knew that determined opposition from any one of the trio would make the whole scheme unworkable, and their time was taken up with rather fruitless juggling of them. Even so, from 1937 the federalising provisions began to take effect in stages. Each of the provinces, with combined voters' rolls swollen to 30 million, was to elect an assembly ready for responsible government. The Congress had opposed the Act as a matter of course but still took to the hustings. It won in five provinces, and emerged as the largest party in two more. After a tussle with the Viceroy over technicalities, enough Congressmen accepted office to inaugurate the provincial part of the constitution. He could then move on to the princes, meant to furnish conservative ballast in the federation. He dangled before them a fresh financial settlement, but their greed yielded to their fear when the Congress barged in on this wheeler-dealing. Suddenly it demanded that the future federal authority should have the power to intervene in the undemocratic princely states, something not envisaged in the Act. As a result, many princes refused to commit themselves. They were in reality consigning themselves to oblivion by passing up their guaranteed place in a new India. It was enough for the Congress, however, that they should frustrate Linlithgow – and even before he could get to work on the Moslems, who by 1938 were calling for a Pakistan.[12]

On September 3, 1939, the Viceroy had anyway to shelve everything. His declaration of war on Germany, by his own fiat and without consulting any Indians, was constitutional but unfortunate. It turned out to be the proximate cause of breakdown in relations between the Raj and the Congress. Linlithgow talked of fresh advance once peace came, even announced the goal of making India a dominion. But all he could offer for the time being was an advisory council on conduct of the war to be drawn from various sections of opinion. The Congress countered with a demand for responsible government at once and rapid progress towards independence. Since, predictably, it had no response by the end of the year, its provincial Ministers resigned. Gandhi ordered civil disobedience, and Nehru was arrested. Strains appeared between the Viceroy and the Secretary of State. Zetland wanted 'immediate action' to call the Indian political leaders together and work out a constitution for a dominion to be created 'not later than the end of the war'. Linlithgow refused to move 'at any pace faster than that we regard as best calculated, on a long view, to hold India to the Empire'.

In May 1940 Zetland, just after escaping an Indian assassin in London, got the sack. He presumed this was because the new Prime Minister, Winston Churchill, regarded him as too liberal. Churchill had indeed always been a reactionary on the Raj, but he could not ease things for Linlithgow. On the contrary, the Viceroy came under greater pressure because of Labour's presence in a reshuffled National Government. The pressure did not make him more flexible, however. He met the Congress's Quit India campaign with a huge wave of arrests. He had Gandhi himself put in detention. Violence and sabotage followed. Famine visited Bengal, a deep disgrace after Britain had ruled the province for a quarter of a millennium, and Linlithgow mishandled the relief. He was still able to treat with the Moslems, but gave hostages to fortune for fear of communal mayhem. In fact he set off an irreversible trend towards bloody partition. He himself wrote: 'India is hopelessly . . . split by racial and religious divisions which we cannot bridge, and which become more and more acute as any real transfer of power by us draws near'. He maintained that it was therefore better to face the troubles than to make concessions. But his policy collapsed within four years of his departure in 1943. He was the longest-serving and last Scottish viceroy. His rule finished in exhaustion. At the very end of Scotland's encounter with India, a spectral orientalism and a haggard despotism entered the lists against one another for the last time. The contest was bound to be drawn, for their force had been spent. India's destiny lay in other hands.[13]

CHAPTER THIRTY-FOUR

'As loyal as the Highlanders': China

The Chinese Revolution entered its final phase on December 6, 1911. In Peking the Manchu regime, long tottering, began to collapse. The Regent for the infant Emperor Pu-yi, Prince Ch'un, abdicated and the formidable Empress Dowager, Lung-yu, banned him from politics. Instead she called on General Yuan Shih-k'ai, till then fully engaged in fending off any northward advance by insurgents who had seized control in the provinces of central China. Now he was promoted Prime Minister and plenipotentiary negotiator. On December 18, he met rebel leaders inside the British concession in Shanghai. The two sides were expected to settle on a constitutional monarchy. Instead they proclaimed a republic. What game was Yuan playing?

Sun Yat-sen, hope of Chinese liberals, hurried home from exile in the United States to become President of the Republic on January 1, 1912. His new era lasted less than three months. The overbearing Yuan relentlessly badgered him. Sun sought to allay the clash of personalities by stepping down on condition of free elections. But all he did in the event was hand over power to Yuan. To corner Sun like this had been the aim of the devious 53–year-old soldier from the start. He was perhaps so hard to fathom because he stood poised between the ancient and the modern China. An ambitious and decisive man in certain respects, he had distinguished himself as a military moderniser. For his pains he lost his command in 1908, but he waited in the wings while the Manchu regime crumbled, accepting now that in the end it would have to be overthrown. Yet he was himself a scion of the ruling class, and it seems clear with hindsight that he meant to found a new dynasty. His reverence for the history of the Middle Kingdom showed itself after Lung-yu had summoned him back to Peking amid that final crisis at the end of 1911, when he neither mounted a coup nor even issued a manifesto. Instead he made a classical allusion, pledging that he would not betray the child on the throne or his mother, and become another Wang Mang, remembered by the Chinese as the most notorious usurper ever, for having robbed just such a widow and infant of the imperial dignity in 6 AD. In abetting revolution, Yuan yet grasped at the straws of tradition and precedent.[1]

It happened that Yuan had made himself well known to the Scots of China. He was not their man but, for his part, he appeared to prefer them to more rapacious foreigners. The Scottish connection dated back to a previous stage of his career, when at the turn of the century he was for three years Governor of Shantung, a province stretching along the southern shores of the Yellow Sea, commanding the maritime approaches to Peking. He went there just as, in 1898, the British took a lease of a portion of the province at Weihaiwei. This tract of 300 square miles housed 128,000 people and a fine harbour which, renamed Port Edward, proved its worth as a naval base and commercial entrepot. Enjoying a pleasant climate in summer – rare for China – it became a resort for those on leave from steamier postings; in winter, its scattered crofts nestling from icy winds in the folds of rocky moors reminded Scots of Sutherland.

Weihaiwei was one of the acquisitions that marked Britain's response to sharpening rivalry among the imperialist powers. Her earlier policy of holding aloof imposed special penalties in the Far East, where she was used to enjoying a monopoly of political and economic influence over the Manchu regime. Since its humiliation in the Sino-Japanese War of 1894–5, western vultures had flocked round its twitching body. The Russians extorted a lease of Port Arthur, on the northern coast of the Yellow Sea, and transformed it into a huge fortress. The Germans extorted a lease of Tsingtao, in southern Shantung, and built a railway running inland. The British had to counter these moves, and did so with the base at Weihaiwei. Occupied at the same time and under much the same conditions as the New Territories of Hong Kong, it yet met a different fate from theirs. They were in effect annexed by Britain, but at Weihaiwei she strictly observed the terms of the lease: though she exercised jurisdiction, this was not a colony but foreign territory and its people did not become the Queen's subjects. The Scot who was Foreign Secretary at the time, Arthur Balfour, felt anxious, beyond the special case of Hong Kong, to preserve China's territorial integrity and avoid setting a precedent for other powers to follow.[2]

The man the British had to deal with on the spot was Yuan. Knowing China's plight, he kept face by conducting relations under a veneer of exemplary politeness. He caused no trouble and never whipped up hostility to the foreign devils: nor, however, did he damp down the outrage felt by ordinary Chinese against them. He liked to stress tacitly that the Emperor remained sovereign in Weihaiwei, so that his governor could not be taken for granted. After the two sides reached an accord on the boundaries, he temporised about appointing commissioners to go out with their British counterparts and set up the markers. Again, the question arose whether locals owed taxes to their old or to their new masters. Yuan just refused to give a ruling, or offer any guidance to his officials. It was the sort of diplomatic irritation that westerners had come to expect of mandarins. If Yuan was adept at legal pettifogging and bureaucratic cavil, he still did not overdo things. His point made, he issued an edict exhorting the people to the obedience and tranquillity which were their duty as loyal subjects, for the territory would return to the Emperor's rule once the lease expired. With that, he left the British to it. He was right to assess them as less hostile than other Europeans, which in the distracted state of the Middle Kingdom represented as much amity as it could hope for. At Kiaochow, by contrast, he showed himself bolder, even defiant, towards the Germans, who were more aggressive and contemptuous of Chinese interests. In a hopeless situation, Yuan saw the chance of at least earning a reputation as leader of resistance to imperialism. Such subtlety gladdened the men to whom he perforce yielded his authority in Weihaiwei.[3]

For almost the whole time until the lease was surrendered, Scots would rule the territory. From 1902 to 1921 the civil commissioner, to give him his proper title, was James Stewart Lockhart, who arrived with a quarter-century in the Hong Kong Civil Service behind him, since 1895 as Colonial Secretary, second to the Governor. Following in his footsteps from Hong Kong, and before that from the University of Edinburgh, came Reginald Johnston, who for years would serve as his right-hand man. Both pursued not only the same professional but also the same intellectual odyssey. As cadets in Hong Kong, under the rules owed to James Legge, they had to make a thorough study of local language, history and culture before being allowed to do anything else. That introduced them to an ancient civilisation which enthralled them. Lockhart's way of life became, in its mingling of government and scholarship, veritably Confucian; outside the line of duty he composed works on Chinese linguistics, folklore, numismatics and painting. The volatile Johnston had still more eclectic interests: besides loving the Chinese drama, he felt himself in spirit, if not in observance, a Buddhist, who detested missions, rejected Christianity's 'bloodthirsty deity' and rejoiced to see brother Scots 'throw off the shackles of the horrible creed inherited by them from their forefathers'. He would break his career in 1918 for a bizarre interlude in the Forbidden City as tutor to the now nominal Emperor Pu-yi. He succeeded as civil commissioner at Weihaiwei in 1927 and stayed till the end of the lease in 1930.

Lockhart was selected to inaugurate British rule because, just before, he had worked out the agreement with Peking on the New Territories and set up an administration for them in the face of fierce local hostility. He succeeded partly by his brilliant linguistic gifts, perhaps owed to his upbringing in Argyll with Gaelic as mother tongue, and partly because he had learned to respect not only the historical achievements of the Chinese but also their present aspirations. In contrast to the run of officials in Hong Kong, he looked beyond the circles of transient European businessmen to the indigenous commercial elite now emerging. In it he perceived the key to future prosperity, to which the style of government would have to adapt. If not, if it failed to safeguard the people's interests, it would render itself unjust and unacceptable.

Weihaiwei's society had much deeper roots than Hong Kong's. The territory, unlike other European outposts in China, remained rustic, untouched by western influence. Lockhart and Johnston sought to keep it so. If a single feature more than any other delighted them, it was that Shantung had been the native province of Confucius. They saw all the more reason for upholding the social order sanctioned by the sage's teaching, with each man's place hallowed in an age-old hierarchy. 'The people are governed in accordance with their own immemorial customs,' declared Johnston. True, for the Emperor as guardian of the peace a more remote British power had to stand in. But if the two Scots were its agents, they obscured the fact. They took the part not of alien colonialists but of the magistrates who had always represented benevolent despotism in every corner of the Middle Kingdom. For the routines of law and order, they relied on the traditional headmen in the villages, whom they would reward for special zeal with a medal and a public citation, just as under the Manchus. In evoking an encounter with these worthies, where all would exchange compliments and ceremonially drink tea before broaching a leisurely discussion and recording the results in elegant calligraphy, Lockhart's biographer wrote: 'The Scot is transformed into the true Chinese official'.

Lockhart and Johnston played the role with aplomb and to the general satisfaction of the people, who in their turn expected magistrates to be "father and mother officials". By tradition, these guided their charges with a mixture of kindness and reproof to encourage virtue and promote harmony. In practice the two Scots had little serious crime to deal with, so they spent most of their time on civil cases, indeed on trivial quarrels. For example, they were often called on to tame shrews, since by local custom wives could be much older than their husbands and cause trouble accordingly. So long as he was 'rigidly just', Johnston recalled, the Chinese treated him as they would a mandarin, perhaps with a little less fear. And he 'frequently in delivering judgments, in both civil and criminal cases, used appropriate texts either from the Confucian classics themselves or from the Sacred Edict for the purposes of giving hearers little moral discourses on points suggested by the cases'. The qualifications for the job were 'not so much a knowledge of the law and legal procedure as a ready acquaintance with the language, customs, religious ideas and ordinary mode of life of the people and an ability to sympathise with or at least understand their prejudices and points of view', especially their 'peculiarities of thought and speech'.[4]

This government represented in all a last blossoming of Scottish orientalism. And that had always had the purpose not only of preserving but also of renewing, of giving fresh expression to ancient virtues. In Weihaiwei it also meant finding a way forward which skirted the growing chaos in the rest of China. One path lay through development of commerce, making the best of the territory's slender resources. Exports of peanuts boomed. New factories made silk into industrial thread, and into lace or stockings for tourists. When revolutionary zeal moved the mass of Chinese to cut off their pigtails, the nimble-fingered ladies of Port Edward turned them into hairnets for American housewives. Lockhart and Johnston were, as usual, required to ensure that their territory cost His Majesty's Treasury nothing. They followed the Manchu practice of levying tax on a whole village, rather than on individual peasants, and when they needed money, for public investment in roads or shipping facilities, they made sure to consult the headmen about which imposts would be most acceptable. The principal guaranteed fiscal stream came from the official monopoly of opium, venerable enough for Lockhart to maintain. More important was that the Chinese Government treated Weihaiwei as a foreign port, with imports free of duty.

Along with its trade, its banking and other services expanded to produce a healthy balance of payments. A chamber of commerce was formed in 1916, and the end of the First World War found the territory thriving.

Again, renewal could come through education, something for which China had no less respect than Scotland. It was customary even in poor villages for peasants to club together and set up a school where their own children could acquire the rudiments of learning. The last thing Lockhart and Johnston wanted was to interfere with such frugal habits, but these schools always threw up a few bright pupils capable of higher things. One well-beaten path for the Chinese lad o'pairts, through public competitive examination to the mandarinate, had petered out. Lockhart found a substitute in scholarships for sons of needy families, by which they could also learn English. His scheme came nowhere near meeting the demand for western education, so at length he set up a free school at Port Edward, offering instruction in both English and Chinese. More boldly, he encouraged a girls' school. For everybody there was education in public health, backed up by free hospitals, campaigns of vaccination and training in western medicine. Weihaiwei counted in the end more literate citizens than jobs for them. Some got out by joining the police in Hong Kong, but the rest had just to go back to their villages; where, however, their skills surely proved beneficial.

Lockhart and Johnston thought it a drawback of progress that Weihaiwei also acquired something of a political life. At first it consisted in little more than the annual exchange of visits, with elaborate displays of courtesy, between the civil commissioner and the Governor of Shantung. When the revolution came, the Scots deplored the fall of the Emperor and voiced their dislike of Sun, in which they felt themselves at one with the people. Johnston sensed a silent incredulity: 'Enthusiasm for the revolution was wholly lacking in that little section of Confucius's native province, and probably not 50 of its inhabitants had the slightest conception of what a republic was'. As the original democratic impetus then ran out, the Scots joined in on the conservative side. They arrested liberals who fled to Weihaiwei, if on the pretext of keeping out every faction rather than of favouring one over another. As anarchy spread, a stream of refugees made for this safe haven. In 1918 British troops had to be stationed there for the first time. On Lockhart's retiral in 1921, however, he bade farewell in terms suggesting that little had changed, that he still saw himself as the overlord of a rude, hardy peasantry linked to his retinue through a web of personal relationships, like a Scots chieftain of old: 'I regard myself as fortunate in having always had to deal with the affairs of such an eminently reasonable and lovable race as the Chinese whom I have always found as loyal as the Highlanders of my own country and ever ready to lend their assistance in sunshine and storm'.[5]

Johnston had to face the reality: an irreversible revolution which, if displaying any single character beneath the prevalent mayhem, was moulding a modern nationalism. He wrote that 'the educated people of Weihaiwei, while conspicuously law-abiding and submissive to our rule, remain true Chinese at heart, and make no pretence of being sentimentally attached to the British flag'. But the results were little to his taste. The main political movement, the Kuomintang, condemned the ways of the Middle Kingdom as outmoded. Instead, following the western model, it aimed to encourage the people's participation in politics so that they would identify the public interest with their own. Sun believed self-government could be stimulated from on high by passing down commands through the bureaucracy to the masses. By the same token, he saw in the peasant's spirit of independence a defect and obstacle to a strong, cohesive nation-state. Johnston admired just the qualities that Sun deplored.

But since the tide of history had turned, it seemed to the civil commissioner sensible to surrender the lease. He pointed out in his dispatches home that Britain possessed far more important strategic interests in the region: with any threat from Russia and Germany evaporated, continued occupation of a territory which remained legally Chinese was provocative. The Kuomintang said the same. Anti-imperialist slogans could be found daubed even in the streets of Port Edward. Rather than await a crisis, Johnston forestalled it. He opened negotiations, reached agreement with the republican authorities and handed Weihaiwei over to them on October 1, 1930. As the last garrison, of Argyll and Sutherland Highlanders, played *Auld Lang Syne*, only the locals felt unhappy. They regretted British rule from the moment incompetent native officials took over. Prosperity vanished too with the status of free port. And all this formed just a prelude to the real chapter of miseries under the Japanese occupation of 1938–45.

Lockhart and Johnston never meant to westernise or modernise but just to rule economically and well until the time came when, with renewal, China could again govern herself. They saw themselves as custodians, with a task rising above administrative routine, of a corner of the Middle Kingdom which elswhere was in full dissolution. Their masters in Whitehall often suspected that they, like the Chinese themselves, thought this culture superior to the West's. So Lockhart, marked down as a weird egghead, never got promotion, while Johnston left the Colonial Office believing he had no future there: true enough, for its reports called him a 'deranged old man'. The benefits of their rule proved hard to assess anyway, not least because they took no further interest in imperial policy after returning home. They spent their time instead reviving Chinese studies, which in Britain had flagged since the death of Legge in 1897. They headed new academic departments and sought to arouse wider public attention for their work. In the long, difficult history of relations between China and the West, this may not have counted for much. Yet the Scots of Weihaiwei had also shown something rare in the heyday of the Empire: an ability to care for its peoples without impugning their identity.[6]

But revolution was hardly solving China's problems either. The great national reproach against the Manchus, of demeaning the Middle Kingdom before the foreign devils, found no remedy. On the contrary, the republic stood if anything in still greater need of international support. Here was a sphere where different Scottish precepts could come into play. A friend of Lockhart's and Johnston's, Charles Addis, the leading figure in the Hongkong and Shanghai Bank, showed how.[7]

His bank was, even more than other colonial banks, a Scottish institution. Its origins lay back, half-a-century earlier, in the expansion of Peninsular & Orient under Thomas Sutherland, who launched in Hong Kong the career that took him to chairmanship of the shipping line. As business in the Orient grew more complex, it needed a sound banking system. Sutherland met the need by masterminding the foundation of the Hongkong and Shanghai Bank in 1864, in co-operation with several brother Scots, notably William Adamson, local manager of the Borneo Company, who had introduced Anna to the King of Siam. Jardine Matheson at first kept its distance, for among the commercial feuds it habitually conducted was one with Sutherland; it had, a few years before, embarrassed him by arranging for illegal opium to be placed aboard one of his steamers, then informing on him to the Chinese authorities. The princely hong changed its tune with the bank's success. When the first public loan to China was issued in London in 1875, no question arose of its being managed by any other than Matheson & Co, the house acting for the taipan in the East. But after a decade of such loans the Hongkong and Shanghai Bank was making the running, thanks to its formidable agent in the City, Harry Panmure Gordon, a son of Perthshire and sometime commander of the Shanghai Mounted Volunteers. By 1898, Jardine Matheson felt eager to co-operate with the bank in the British and Chinese Corporation, set up to win commercial concessions from the imperial regime. The principal directors were Ewan Cameron, the bank's senior manager in London, and William Keswick of the princely hong; the bank put up the money, while the hong acted as contractor. They at once landed the concessions for all railways in the valley of the Yangtse Kiang and the southern provinces, plus a connection to Peking. From now on, in almost every aspect of Chinese finance, the bank led and the rest followed.[8]

In this first period of spectacular expansion, the bank's success was in great part due to the fact that Sutherland established it on "Scottish principles", following the system in Scotland before the Banking Act (1845). He intended, in other words, a joint-stock company acting as bank of issue through a wide network of branches. If Hong Kong lay under English rather than Scots law, Scottish practice proved in the conditions superior, indeed necessary. A tiny colonial outpost had no political authority competent to regulate a bank of issue, or in modern terms, no state to support a monetary system. Its position was thus similar to that of banks in the old Scotland, obliged to keep assets and liabilities so balanced as at once to make a profit and maintain the value of the currency.

Sutherland judged shrewdly, for the bank in the long run throve better even than its Scottish models. Its notes displaced the silver dollar to become the preferred currency in Hong Kong, in neighbouring provinces and in cities further north. It thus won a semi-official position, in the Middle Kingdom as much as in the colony. It became banker to the Imperial Chinese Maritime Customs, which happened to be run by James Campbell, one of the Scots who failed the examination for the Indian Civil Service; he went instead to the Treasury, and was seconded to Peking. The customs represented the biggest, most reliable security available to the Manchus now that they had to prop themselves up with borrowing. The bank often led the syndicates offering these so-called imperial loans, so it had a stake on both sides of the balance sheet. Before long, it was in effect underwriting the entire informal Empire in the East. That laid the foundation for its modern development into an international financial institution of the first rank.[9]

Because of its origins and the nature of its business, the bank remained largely Scots in personnel. It appointed agents in Scotland, and opened a branch in Edinburgh in 1874. The country had no end of bright youngsters fitted by a commercial education for life abroad, and at once familiar with the banking practice they found in China. The anecdote went round about a captain on the Yangtse Kiang surprised to find one of his passengers was a banker and English: he 'had thought all bank men were Scotch'. More unlikely was the tale of the porridge trap, how agents dug pits on desolate moors in Scotland, where they placed bowls of porridge to trap unwary native youths searching for food: the captives were sent to London for training as oriental bankers.

Addis needed no such bait. A son of the manse, he had rebelled and sown his wild oats. There was then nothing for it but a career in business to make him respectable. He took the hint, for on sailing away to join the Hongkong and Shanghai Bank in 1880 he carried in his trunk a complete set of the Waverley Novels; later, seeking a wife, he went back to Saltcoats and wooed the provost's daughter. His couthiness stretched to a kindly moral rectitude with high hopes of capitalism's hidden hand and a deep dislike of exploitation. Unusually in the banking world, he turned out after all to be an intellectual and later caught up on what he had missed. While on furlough in 1899–1900 he matriculated at the university of Edinburgh to read political economy under Shield Nicholson, the imperialist disciple of Adam Smith. Even before this, Addis had been leapfrogging up the management of his bank. After his return to the Orient, he took charge there.

The Manchus were now, after defeat in the Sino-Japanese War of 1894–5, on their last legs. That only prompted westerners to turn up the pressure, mainly in the quest for concessions, the monopolistic right to execute and exploit major public works such as railways and mining. Swarms of entrepreneurs, or rather speculators, came swooping in from many nations. With the backing of their governments at home and their legations in Peking, they cajoled harassed mandarins into authorising huge borrowings. It was, at one remove, a scramble for China, an imperialist race for influence and territory. Britain felt she had no choice but to join in, yet she did not want to forsake the dynasty, symbol of national integrity, bulwark against chaos and guarantee of her own traditional favoured status. Her attitude paid off in that, thanks largely to her Scotsmen on the make, she yet carried away the lion's share of opportunities in the face of so many rivals. But it still looked as if the Middle

Kingdom would be partitioned unless it modernised itself soon enough. Of course, that His Majesty's Treasury should spend anything to promote this purpose was nevertheless unthinkable. Only private hands could help the Chinese to help themselves.[10]

In the event, those hands were Addis's. By himself he set out to change western policy so that the Chinese might begin to get something back from it too. He was first of all the man behind Britain's revision of her several treaties with the Celestial Empire, the oldest dating back 60 years, into what was meant to be a comprehensive settlement for the new century. In 1902 the Foreign Office entrusted the actual negotiations to James Mackay, the shipping magnate, but asked Addis to draft his instructions. They offered China many technical improvements in trade in return for internal reforms which would lay the foundations of a modern economy as then conceived: a uniform currency, a national bank and, in due course, adherence to the gold standard. The next step came after Addis moved to London in 1905. One task here was the formation of the bankers' consortium. This group of financial houses in different countries came together to regulate the Manchu regime's relations with its creditors and keep it solvent. In managing it, Addis again worked hand-in-glove with Whitehall. As a sort of financial ambassador, he would stop by on his frequent trips abroad at the Quai d'Orsay or the Wilhelmstrasse in order to keep the European powers in line on their Chinese commercial policies. There could have been nothing more congenial to an old Scots banker than to foster economic growth, to embark for that purpose on monetarising the resources of a developing country, to free it from exploitation by richer and stronger powers, to offer it order and stability through a place in the global trading system. During his travels to the Orient, however, it struck Addis that he was running out of time. He had always counselled support for the Manchus, but now he realised they would not survive. He started offering his Government different advice, that it should remain neutral among the various factions of a growing opposition (this while the legation in Peking and the Foreign Office were still trying to pretend they did not exist). Before the end, Addis had invited Sun to his home in London to talk about the financial needs of a new order. Yet the revolution of 1911 still took him by surprise.

If Addis afterwards saw his plans blighted, it was not for want of co-operation from the bold Yuan. Once he seized power he did not tarry in reviving his Scottish contacts, with promises to meet the Middle Kingdom's obligations and keep an open door to foreign investors. Addis responded at once on behalf of his own bank, then worked to bring the consortium into line. He brought Russia and Japan into it, not because they had money to lend but in order to allay their potential belligerence towards the Chinese Republic. By May 1912, six powers stood ready with a Reorganisation Loan of £25 million for Yuan. It was almost too good to be true: he actually made a show of breaking off talks lest fellow revolutionaries wonder if their struggle against foreign devils had been in vain. Addis bore with him as the main hope for unity, stability and peace. Indeed he urged that the market had to be preserved for the strongman, as for the house representing his interests, the Hongkong and Shanghai Bank. The Foreign Office, impressed with Addis's percipience, put pressure on the City of London to hold up other Chinese loans until this one was underwritten, as its failure could not be contemplated. The financiers complied with gritted teeth, but raised such an outcry afterwards that the authorities never tried the trick again. Here, Addis quite overturned the norms of Victorian Britain, with their strict distinction of public and private. But on this point Scots never were utilitarian dogmatists.[11]

Yuan, however, had his own ideas of what to do with the money. He called elections of a sort, which the Kuomintang won, only to make itself the object of his wrath. He ordered the assassination of its parliamentary leader, and purged its deputies in the new National Assembly. He sent his armies to attack its main base of Nanking. He forced Sun into exile again. This was a second revolution, only possible because of the loan, which suppressed such democratic tendencies as the first had shown. Yuan was now a military dictator. More than that, he aspired to restore the monarchy in his own person. In 1915 he proclaimed himself Emperor. But his struggles had exhausted him, and he died within a year. Addis backed him throughout, even for the imperial dignity, and kept the Foreign Office behind him too. They just failed to consolidate his rule. Now, however, the game was up: central government in China became a fiction, and power rested with warlords.

The tireless Addis succeeded in many things. In his profession he was the most distinguished figure of his time. Already the senior manager in London, at his apogee he became in 1918 the first man from a joint-stock institution to be elected a director of the Bank of England. At the Royal Economic Society he got to know John Maynard Keynes. A crony of Montagu Norman in stern support of the gold standard and free trade, he was called on as adviser to the Government right through the 1920s. Only in 1932, when past 70, did he retire, after delicate hints that perhaps his day was done. But what made him stand out from the pinstriped ranks was his extraordinary influence on British policy in China, greater than any other private individual's before or since. Like Lockhart and Johnston, he loved the country, its language and people. Still, more than they, he remained during a long life the idealistic Scot of the era of his youth, a Calvinist of strict morality and high sense of duty, tempering incessant calculation with a sense of mission. He championed political economy as valid for all places and times. He did see, though, that its triumph in China would require a single market under a central government, in other words a modern state, strong, efficient and independent. He understood, too, that for this purpose he had to turn predatory foreigners from competition to co-operation. So he bent every effort to induce them to lend in a controlled and apolitical rather than chaotic and self-interested fashion. In the true spirit of the Scottish Empire, he wanted not territory but progress.

Yet, while Addis succeeded in many particular things, he failed in his grand design. China continued to evolve in ways that neither he nor any foreigner could control. In reality the scope of the task he set himself proved too disruptive to be tolerated by the borrowers, and too demanding to be accomplished by the lenders, backed though they were by the panoply of western finance and technology, by political and in the last resort by military power. China was not as Addis or other well-wishers perceived her to be, and they could not remake her in their own image. The revolution would frustrate what they worked for because it marked the real turning point in the historical interlude of foreign domination. This then went into slow decline, at first hidden by China's internal agony between the two World Wars, compounded when Japan again attacked her, in a conflict absorbed at length into a global one. But after 1945 western influence, so far from being restored, collapsed.[12]

Till the end the British remained the foremost foreign investors, with three Scottish houses pre-eminent. The largest was the Hongkong and Shanghai Bank, which sustained some semblance of a financial system. The newest was the Inchcape Group; it had a personal link to the bank's founder, Sutherland, through its head, the former John Mackay, now Lord Inchcape, who had taken over P & O from him, then revived the combine's interests in the East through acquisition of the Chartered Bank. The oldest, Jardine Matheson, was no longer supreme, but its scions must have carried oriental acumen in their genes. Keswick, taipan of the Victorian epoch, had handed over to his son Henry, who died young in 1928. Married solidly into the gentry of Dumfriesshire, he left three sons of his own. John, the youngest and most capable, was chosen to inherit three-quarters of the princely hong's equity on coming of age. During the Second World War, he served with Lord Mountbatten, commander-in-chief in the East, then in the embassy at Chungking, temporary headquarters of the Chinese Government. He returned in 1945 to Shanghai, to be elected chairman of the international chamber of commerce; with a brother in charge of the China Association at home, Jardine Matheson again dominated the Chinese lobby in Britain. The old days seemed almost to be back. In a speech to the Rotary Club of Shanghai, Keswick recalled the taipan's habitual advice to new recruits: 'Remember young man, when you get to China, to keep the sabbath and anything you can lay your hands on'. He reflected more ruefully on fresh stormclouds, now of civil war, gathering round: 'If you are an old China hand and have stood sufficiently long at the Club bar, you could convince yourself that the Communists will never come to Shanghai'.

Yet by May 1949 they were there. Like others, Keswick found it hard to grasp that the old days would never return. So far from fleeing, most stayed put in the expectation of somehow carrying on. An awed brother Scot, David Urquhart, consul-general in Shanghai, found the taipan a tower of strength for the European community, yet could not help noting his 'disappointing traits', his ruthless defence of the princely hong's interests. It did no good. Keswick met a blank in efforts to get in touch with the Communists. They grimly took their revenge, not by outright confiscation but by making it impossible for westerners to trade while in effect holding them and their assets hostage. Each company, though earning nothing, still had to pay wages, rents, bills and taxes, or else face harassment and huge fines. With the banks stopped too, they soon exhausted their local reserves and saleable stocks, to become reliant on remittances from home. By the end of the year Jardine Matheson alone was remitting £50,000 a month. This could not continue, but the final twist was to block the foreign devils' exit when they at last gave up. In 1952 the Scottish houses announced they were going. They took another three years to win the necessary permission, and then on most unfavourable terms. Jardine Matheson left behind property estimated at £30 million. Keswick personally lost £1 million in Shanghai.[13]

With China closed again, each house had to seek pastures new. P & O carried on as the grandest British shipping line, no more tied to Hong Kong than to a score of other exotic ports. The Hongkong and Shanghai Bank was of most potential use to the Communists once they got over their first fury. It won leave to send a delegation to the mainland in 1954, and re-established a limited presence. Yet its future lay elsewhere, if not far away. Financiers in the City of London had been accustomed to look down on it as a stolid outfit manned by upright and hard-working Scots, a bit out of its depth on the international scene. That judgment reckoned without the rise of the tiger economies, in the final quarter of the twentieth century the fastest growing in the world. Among them the bank held a prime position, and expanded apace. It continued to derive two-fifths of its profits from Hong Kong, however, and the slow imperial sunset there imposed further adjustment. In 1991, it got itself listed as a British company, coming home, or at least to London, after more than a century, still standing to gain because the City kept stronger links with the Orient than any other European financial centre.

Jardine Matheson had more to worry about, the Chinese never having forgiven it for the Opium Wars. After banishment from the mainland, it underwent the structural change forced on every Scottish agency house before it. In 1961 it ceased to be a pure partnership, and sold off shares representing one-quarter of the issued capital. Today, the founding families control only 5 per cent of it. While their position is partly protected by a complex corporate structure, they could not alone repel a serious attack. So they are always scared of takeover, especially by Chinese businessmen who since the 1980s have seemed intent on ousting the British. The wealthiest of all, Sir Yue Kong Pao, shocked Jardine Matheson by snapping up one of its offshoots, a company owning wharves and godowns – and, ominously, doing so with money from the Hongkong and Shanghai Bank. Diversification has been the princely hong's second defence. The bulk of its assets long remained in Hong Kong, where its own and its subsidiaries' shares accounted for one-eighth of the total value of securities on the stock exchange. But fresh expansion took place elsewhere in South-East Asia and the Pacific region. Then, in 1984, Jardine Matheson shifted its registered office to Bermuda. Its main listing moved to London in 1992. So the princely hong, too, prepared for the end of Empire.[14]

In the last British colony of any importance, Scots figured till the curtain fell. Two played a prime role in the peaceful disengagement. Murray Maclehose, in 1978 the first Governor of Hong Kong to visit Peking, took the chance to launch serious talks about the future, to the surprise of his hosts. Having not yet thought much about it, they were won over to his formula of "one country, two systems": in other words, this should remain a capitalist enclave once returned to China. The result was the Joint Declaration of 1984, under which the handover proceeded, not without difficulty. In fact the Chinese scarcely regarded it as a joint undertaking, rather as a painless way to get the British out. So much became clear during the governorship of David Wilson in 1978–81. He deferred to Peking in postponing a transition to democracy, but his efforts to win in return guarantees of rights for the people of Hong Kong made little headway, in the face of China's view that this was no business of his.

The Scots' economic achievement remained. It does not mean, however, that political economy has engulfed the society to which they applied its laws. To China it proved impossible, even at the point of the bayonet, just to dictate terms. And no official action, but spontaneous commercial change, turned Hong Kong from a British dependency into a Chinese society. Indigenous hongs arose in imitation of European ones and displaced them by tremendous expansion inside and outside the colony. Long before the end of imperial rule they came to dominate its commerce. Today they traffic across the globe with the canniness and flair of the Scots who showed them how, but following the principles of political economy in Confucian form. They even stand ready to bring China herself into the global system, now that Maoism has given way to the drive for modernisation which foreigners helped to start. Surely little lies beyond the reach of a people whose innate commercial genius matches or surpasses any in the West. The whole prospect would have delighted the Scottish philosophers. It is in lessons well-taught that something of Scotland may survive on the other side of the world, long after another tartan-clad regiment, the Black Watch, played the Empire out with *Auld Lang Syne* on June 30, 1997.[15]

CHAPTER THIRTY-FIVE

'Lying in the centre of trade': Malaysia

O n December 11, 1948, in the late afternoon, 7 platoon, G company of the 2nd battalion, the Scots Guards, drove up to a group of huts, so-called labour lines, on a remote plantation, Sungei Remok, in the Malayan state of Selangor. The patrol consisted of a sergeant and 13 soldiers, raw National Servicemen, accompanied by detectives of the Special Branch. They were helping to fight Britain's war against Communist guerrillas. This special assignment proved harrowing. On their way into the jungle the troops had already been ambushed, and seen a lieutenant killed. In immediate retaliation they picked on two youths they happened to meet along the road and accused them of carrying supplies to the rebels. These, despite frantic protestations of innocence, they shot dead. Next they arrested another man, who saved his life by offering to help them. He led them to Sungei Remok, a settlement for poor Chinese labourers who might well sympathise with the insurgency. He pointed out one woman as a definite suspect. Terrified, she informed on others, who were shut in a hut for questioning. The villagers grew so agitated that the young Scots, nervous and untrained for such a testing situation, could think of nothing better than firing in the air to scare them. The tension grew in the tropical twilight, when a captive tried to escape; he too was shot and killed. At nightfall, the guardsmen decided it would be better to lock up the women and children too. Next morning they let out everyone under guard. While the helpless menfolk looked on, their distracted families were loaded on a lorry. As it rumbled away, the soldiers set light to the labour lines. In one hut explosives were hidden, not with any sinister purpose but for the villagers' use in their fishing. Sudden detonations amid the smoke and flames made the troops panic. They thought this another ambush, and opened fire on their prisoners. These took to their heels, but at close quarters they were easily hit, most in the back. All died.

The next day brought an official statement saying a band of 24 guerrillas had been wiped out. This ought by any standards to have counted as a remarkable success. Normally the army boasted of its kills and, as this time there were no survivors, even wounded ones, the terse report seemed odd. The police looked into the circumstances, to find at once how unusual they were. The Attorney-General of Malaya was called in. After ten days he declared himself satisfied that the deaths resulted from an attempted escape, despite having no photographs, no names and no evidence of the victims' alleged Communist connections. The official account stands to this day. But different ones have surfaced over the years. In 1969, Scottish newspapers ran stories contradicting the Attorney-General's verdict: four guardsmen admitted they had killed villagers in cold blood. Labour's Foreign Secretary, George Brown, set up a committee of inquiry. Its members interviewed people in Britain, and in June 1970 were about to fly to Malaysia to follow up their leads. But the new Conservative Government, elected that month, called a halt on the grounds that the evidence gathered to date yielded no reliable evidence of a massacre. There the matter rests.[1]

Such a picture of the Scottish Empire in action, eight years before Malaya's independence, is not flattering. Nor, however, is it representative of the role Scots had played in this part of the world for a quarter of a millennium. Here again, their first contacts predated the Union. On his voyages round the East Indies, the traveller Alexander Hamilton kept running into compatriots. In 1701 he chanced on that ship of the Company of Scotland which got stranded at Malacca, where its men idled away their time awaiting rescue: two were smitten by a common strumpet who fed them potions alternately to rouse their lust and to kill them in hope of the treasure she supposed them to be hiding. Then in 1703, in a strange presage of what was to come, Hamilton had Singapore offered him by the Sultan of Johore. He thought it 'a proper place for a company to settle a colony in, lying in the centre of trade'. But the time could not have been less ripe for an oriental Darien. Rather, after 1707, it was the Scots' infiltration of the English East India Company that gave them a fresh start. England had been till then largely shut out of the Malay-speaking world by the Dutch. Scots opened it up again.[2]

The boldest was Alexander Dalrymple, brother of the judge and antiquarian, Lord Hailes. Like many younger sons of lairds looking for a place in life, he signed on with the company and, as a cadet of 15, went out to Madras. He reacted like a Scot against 'the odious superiority which too often prevails with Europeans over natives in all parts of India'. For his part, he was fascinated by the local history of his post and burrowed through its records. He found Madras had once carried on a brisker trade to South-East Asia than it did now. He fancied he could revive this traffic, and pressed his employers to let him try. In 1759 they lent him a small ship, on which he set off through the Straits of Malacca, called at Cochin China, then landed on Hainan before wintering at Macao. The next spring he sailed out to Manila, which the British had just seized from the Spaniards, their enemies in the Seven Years' War. He turned south till he reached Sulu, a group of islands stretching between the Philippines and Borneo. They formed a sultanate which, on the edge of both the Spanish and Dutch spheres of influence, had managed to maintain its independence. Dalrymple, with the Scot's eye for an emporium, at once saw the possibilities. The islands grew pepper, cinnamon and sugar. The natives were friendly, hoping for British protection from more rapacious Europeans. Their home lay within reach of Batavia, Manila and Canton, while being free of the restrictions imposed by the authorities at each of those ports. Perhaps an oriental Darien might be possible after all. Dalrymple drew up a treaty of friendship with the Sultan of Sulu. He sped back to Madras and persuaded the council of the presidency to ratify it. Then he returned to receive in 1763 formal cession of Balembangan, an islet off North Borneo, with rights over 20,000 square miles of the adjacent coast. This was the company's first possession in the South China Sea and, Dalrymple promised, the natural focus for a maritime, commercial empire in the Far East.[3]

But events thwarted him. Till a European peace was concluded, it remained unclear whether or not the Philippines would be handed back to Spain; if not, there was no need for a station at Balembangan. Dalrymple went to Manila to assess matters, but the sole definite outcome of the visit was his discovery of the real Sultan of Sulu; the one he had been dealing with was a usurping nephew. Dalrymple took the old man home and reconciled the pair, further cementing the people's affections for himself. To gratify them, and to clinch matters, he decided he had to bring Balembangan to the attention of the company's directors in London rather than rely on his superiors in India. Back in Britain in 1765, he was still frustrated. The company accepted the acquisition, but made nothing of it. A couple of agents sent there fell out with the natives, and a few years later had the place burned down about their ears; Sulu retreated again into isolation, where it would remain till subdued by the Americans under General Pershing in 1910.

Dalrymple turned elsewhere. His historical reputation rests on his achievements as the father of hydrography, but in his time he was most famous as the world's greatest expert on the Pacific Ocean. He argued that a great, undiscovered southern continent must exist, otherwise the Earth would be unbalanced by the weight of land in the northern hemisphere; one purpose of Captain James Cook's voyages was to test this theory. If disproved, it did lead Europeans to a reasonable conception of Pacific geography. It is pleasant to record, however, that Dalrymple's concept of a chain of emporiums would be later realised in the Straits Settlements. And his toehold in Borneo prefigured British control of its northern portion. These two factors helped to form the modern Malaysia, straddling 400 miles of sea.[4]

As ever, commercial Scottish interest in a distant land soon turned intellectual. The Malay tongues with their unique syntax fascinated philologists. John Leyden, who shared the enthusiasm of Walter Scott for the collection of ballads, and who placed his polymathy at the disposal of Francis Jeffrey in the *Edinburgh Review*, later went out to Calcutta. Though a physician, he spent most of his time on linguistic study. This brought him the chair of Hindustani and Persian at the College of Fort William and made him an ornament of Lord Minto's orientalist court. He accompanied the Governor-General on the expedition to Java in 1811, with the prospect of becoming secretary to the new administration of the island. For it he had a political vision, as centre of a Malay Empire to be erected under British protection. He had also an immediate scholarly project, to explore the archives of Batavia. The first man ashore, he went straight to the manuscript library, but 'with fatal inadvertence he entered it, without using the precaution of having it aired, although it had been shut up for some time, and the confined air was strongly impregnated with the poisonous quality which has made Batavia the grave of so many Europeans'. Leyden died.[5]

With him on that expedition was John Crawford, another physician turned courtier in Calcutta. He has already appeared in these pages during his later career as a westerniser of India and as an ethnologist in London. Java found him midway on his odyssey from orientalism to scientific racism. He travelled to other islands to gather material which he wrote up in a *History of the Indian Archipelago* (1820). This, while dismissive of native culture, did not exonerate the colonial powers for sapping the will of indigenous peoples to improve themselves. The next Governor-General, Lord Moira, sent Crawford to Siam and Cochin China. His recommendation that Britain should annex the two countries fell on deaf ears. He had one further posting in the East, as resident in Singapore in 1823–6, though he was 'not a popular man' in the infant settlement.

Britain's acquisition of the island followed on, in tortuous fashion, from a policy of renouncing wider sovereignty in South-East Asia. At the end of the French wars there had been nothing to stop her keeping Java. Yet by the Treaty of Vienna she handed it back to Holland. She did not thereby signify any indifference to the area's commerce. That, on the contrary, she intended to dominate, but by means of trading stations rather than of territorial occupation. Once she decided how, she just dictated the appropriate terms to her economic client, the new Kingdom of the Netherlands. Crawford drafted these terms in a treaty of 1824 which declared the Malay Peninsula to be a British sphere of influence and the archipelago beyond (except Borneo) a Dutch one. He negotiated a second treaty with the Sultan of Johore for definitive cession of Singapore. The Straits Settlements then came into being in 1826. They united three separate outposts into a single colony, of which the administration was inaugurated by yet another Scot, Robert Fullerton. No disposition could have been more congenial to his countrymen.

From the start Scots played a large role in the outposts. Least of them was the island of Penang which, occupied in 1786, came under regular government in 1801 in the person of George Leith. He purchased Province Wellesley on the mainland opposite from the Sultan of Kedah. His successor was William Farquhar, who tried in 1803 to enlarge his realm by refounding the factory at Balembangan, to be slapped down by the East India Company. In 1805 it erected Penang into a presidency, with the aim of developing it into the major naval base of the eastern seas. Renamed Prince of Wales Island, it received as its first governor Philip Dundas, nephew of Scotland's great imperial statesman.

At the time, the main city on the straits was Malacca, to which a colourful history had given a Chinese population with a Malay minority and smaller communities of Indians, Portuguese and Dutch. Britain seized it, along with other Dutch colonies, in 1795. She returned it, more slowly than Java, in 1818. But then, by the treaty of 1824, she took it back again. The most obvious Scottish presence in Malacca was a missionary one. William Milne had arrived in 1814, expelled from Macao. He brought a printing press, and finished translating the Old Testament into Chinese before his death in 1822. Meanwhile, in 1818, the London Missionary Society set up a college. The evangelists made little progress with conversions in the city itself, since the Malays were Moslems and most of the Chinese impervious to their good news. But anyway the main aim was, through such contact with the latter as could be made, to prepare missionaries against the day when the Middle Kingdom would no longer be closed. To this college in 1839 came Henry Legge, father of British sinology. On the acquisition of Hong Kong in 1841, he transferred his staff there.[6]

The youngest, but burgeoning and soon most important of the Straits Settlements, was Singapore. Its foundation on February 6, 1819, is always credited to Sir Stamford Raffles. He stayed, though, just one night, leaving his colleague Farquhar in charge, to be succeeded by Crawford. Wearily predictable as the pattern must have seemed to critics of the Scots' clannishness, a procession of them arrived to seize at once the prime commercial presence too. The first merchants to land bore the names Hay, Johnston, Napier and Scott. Out of 17 partnerships formed in the colony by 1834, Scots accounted for 12. Already the biggest was Guthrie & Co, founded in 1821 by Alexander Guthrie, a youth from Brechin, cousin to Dr Guthrie of the ragged schools; control of the firm would, in the habitual way, remain in the family for a century. Most of the pioneers came thinking they were going to deal above all with China which, if officially closed, in fact lay wide open to a range of merchandise from British cotton to Indian opium. Some sought sidelines, however. In 1824, Robert Hunter left to set up as the sole foreign merchant in Bangkok, where he introduced opium and discovered the earliest recorded Siamese twins, Chang and Eng, whom he took to exhibit in America. In the Philippines also a Scottish house, Smith, Bell & Co, and in the Dutch East Indies three more, Maclaine & Co, McNeill & Co, and Fraser Eaton & Co, established themselves. Within a couple of decades the flimsy barriers to the Celestial Empire fell. With that, the need for an entrepot on the straits might have vanished. Instead the Scots continued to open whole new lines of trade all over southern Asia and the islands: coffee, sugar, spices, vegetable oils, guttapercha, metals, minerals.[7]

The best illustration of the difference this made came on Borneo, in which Scots have taken an extraordinary interest: it was uncharted, exotic, rugged, peopled by the proud, warlike tribes of Dyaks. A no man's land under the treaty of 1824, it might without constitution of the Straits Settlements have remained so much longer, since the Dutch had hardly ventured there. But, with Singapore's capital and enterprise on its doorstep, exploitation of its natural resources began. This would lead at length to partition of Borneo between Britain and Holland, another step towards formation of today's Malaysia.

If Scots had had their way, they might have overrun the whole of Borneo. The Dutch at any rate found it hard to keep them out. In 1816, their officials got to Pontianak on the western coast just before Farquhar landed there. A fresh intrusion came 20 years later from James Erskine Murray, who won the local sultan's permission to settle at Samarinda on the eastern coast. An irate Governor-General in Batavia asserted his doubtful suzerainty and demanded the expulsion of Murray.

Mercenaries shortly killed the unwelcome Scotsman. So it was from the north, already known to Dalrymple, that the mysterious interior had to be penetrated. In efforts to suppress piracy by Sea Dyaks, a flotilla of the Royal Navy under Admiral Thomas Cochrane attacked and occupied Brunei in 1846. The sultan was forced to sign a treaty of friendship with Britain which also ceded the offshore island of Labuan. The next year merchant princes of Glasgow, with their partners in Singapore, sent a trading mission there. In charge of it they put one Robert Burns, an illegitimate grandson of the bard.

In Burns, too, strange places awakened an intellectual as well as commercial interest. He was a keen, not to say ruthless, trader. He confirmed the rumoured existence in Borneo of rich deposits of antimony, sought after as lead for pencils. But he was also fascinated by its unknown peoples. He found their character, so far from savage, superior to the 'mean servility' of coastal Malays. He published perceptive papers on their tribal structure, customs and languages, material now prized by historians as a record of unspoiled indigenous society on the eve of the European impact. Having carried out his commission, he was authorised by his employers to obtain a lease of the mineral-bearing lands. Here, however, he ran foul of James Brooke, the Englishman who had set himself up as white rajah of Sarawak in 1841. Brooke sought to keep out commercial competitors, not just from his own fief but from the rest of Borneo. He created such a fuss, locally and in London, that the Glaswegians had to abandon their scheme. But Burns defied him. He wrote a sharp protest to the Foreign Secretary, Lord Palmerston. He carried on looking for new tribes and trading on his own account. His travels came to an abrupt end in 1851, however, when he was murdered by pirates. Meanwhile, even Brooke had to turn to Scots for development of his domain. He granted a concession to an agency house, W.R. Paterson & Co of Glasgow and Singapore, which after typical mutations of membership transformed itself into the Borneo Company in 1851. It built the port of Kuching, and a big exporting business. It remained under Scottish direction till the 1930s.[8]

We have seen in India and China the agencies' versatility. Here they excelled themselves again. One reason was that they entered a political vacuum, an archipelago divided among weak states with vague boundaries and murky relations to reluctant imperial powers. The houses stepped into the gap. In the 1870s, for example, Sulu came under pressure again from the Spaniards in the Philippines. It held out with help from the Labuan Trading Company of Singapore, especially from the Scot who was its manager for Borneo, William Cowie. The sultan granted him a depot in the isolated Sandakan Bay on the eastern coast, where he could carry on regular commerce in full view of prying eyes, but augment it out of sight with gun-running through the Spanish blockade round the islands to the north. So lucrative was this double-dealing that Cowie, on the winding up of his own house, commandeered one of its steamers and went into partnership with the sultan. In a few years he made a fortune and retired home.

But he was one of the Scots who could not stay away from Borneo. In 1881 its political geography underwent another change. The Sultan of Brunei was pressed into ceding the territory of North Borneo (now Sabah) to a British chartered company, a favoured vehicle of informal empire at the time; behind it stood Dent's, the Chinese hong. Since Sandakan was held to fall within the boundaries, Cowie offered himself as an adviser, and in 1895 got elected to the court of directors. A cuckoo in the nest, he pushed out Dent's and took control himself. He was able to do so because other shareholders had become dissatisfied by meagre dividends from a slow process of development. He embarked instead on a lavish spending programme to link Sandakan across country with Brunei and Labuan by a grand trunk road, a telegraph and even a railway. Investors seemed unaware that this meant traversing unexplored mountain and jungle. They took Cowie's word for it that the interior housed a large population eager for industry and commerce. In fact it was thinly peopled with tribes wanting only to live the lives of their ancestors, and therefore uninterested in either. Cowie claimed, for instance, that the telegraph could be laid in a few months for £5000. It actually took three years and set the company back £20,000. As it was hardly used, the running costs proved prohibitive too. To meet them, a tax had to be put on rice, the staple food of the inhabitants, both of the natives and of the Chinese brought in to supply their lack of skills. The Chinese stopped coming, while the natives rose in revolt.

A moment of truth arrived for the company: it had no men or arms to fight rebels, and no cash to buy any. Cowie was obliged to go out and treat in person with the leader of the uprising, whom he fobbed off with an award of land the company did not own. When this became known, the shareholders at last saw the light and started to get out. Somehow, Cowie pressed on regardless. He invested yet more in his imaginary railway. He sought to imitate the Dutch culture system by directing the natives to grow tobacco. Noting the start of Malaya's boom in rubber, he offered planters absurd inducements to come to North Borneo. His efforts were only cut short by his death in 1910. In 15 years he had doubled the territory's trade, though at untold cost, for in real terms his schemes can hardly have been profitable. Here was a Scotsman on the make who never made it. New directors at least ended his misrule, so that they were able to maintain the company's government till 1946. Then, bankrupted by war, it ceded North Borneo to the Crown.[9]

Still, before his end Cowie had in his reckless way almost hit upon the role this area finally came to play in imperial commerce. It would be transformed into an economy of plantations, the Scots contributing by one of the extraordinary pieces of colonial cross-fertilisation for which they were sometimes responsible. With such an economy, in particular of sugar, they had first made acquaintance in the West Indies two centuries before. But, resting there on slavery, it failed after the emancipation of 1833. Among the Scots who faced ruin was Robert Tytler from Peterhead. He just carried on in a new way and a new colony. In 1837 he went to Ceylon and set about a scientific search for crops suited to the climate and labour available. That took time, perhaps 40 years for real economic success in a setting of social stability, with Tytler and other Scotsmen by then among the biggest landowners. Their compatriots had first arrived on the island at the turn of the century, and its development since mirrored the evolution of Scottish imperial attitudes, in small compass and speeded up. During the first decade, "King Tom" Maitland had as governor run an orientalist regime leaving the life of the people on the whole alone. In the second decade, under Alexander Johnston, benevolent despotism gave way to a more regular bureaucracy concerned with securing native rights, though also letting Europeans acquire land. By the fourth decade utilitarian doctrines were spreading across the strait from India, notably in the person of Charles Hay Cameron, who followed his colleague Alexander Ross in Bengal in seeking to make legal reform an instrument of social change. One set of legislation dealt with the land, among other things allowing for the empty interior to be parcelled up and sold off in order to promote cultivation of tradable crops. When Tytler arrived, the time was thus ripe for economic innovation, to replace primitive subsistence by plantations geared to demand in the West.

Tytler himself introduced cacao and coffee, the latter becoming by mid-century Ceylon's foremost crop. But a human import proved as valuable. Tytler kept in touch with the old country, with the shrewd farmers and fabricators of the North-East of Scotland. In their clannish way, some of the most enterprising followed him to the island. James Taylor started growing cinchona and tea. James and Graeme Elphinstone planted coconuts. John Brown built a modern system of irrigation. By 1875, perhaps half the managers of Celanese plantations hailed from Aberdeenshire and Kincardineshire. This influence later faded. The home region lacked the economic depth to sustain further development at long distance. Exchange of commodities passed not through Aberdeen but through London, whence most new capital came. But Glaswegians moved in as well: Thomas Lipton spent £75,000 in 1890 on making himself the largest single proprietor on Ceylon, and brought a decisive switch to tea. James Finlay & Co, itself an old West Indian house, has stayed on to this day, long after the rest of the Scottish holdings have been swallowed by others or nationalised. It manages 22 estates producing a million tons of tea a year, about 5 per cent of the country's total. The tea-gardens of Sri Lanka still bear names, Balmoral, Blinkbonny and many more, evoking these links.[10]

The cross-fertilisation did not stop there, for the Scots planters transferred their techniques onwards to Malaya. From the outposts on the straits, imperial power had permeated the whole peninsula, mainly to secure its tin, and brought most of the sultans into a loose federation, in practice controlled by British residents. Much land remained virgin, and here the planters could by the same process of trial and error continue their search for the best crops. First they tried coffee, then pepper, then oil-palms. From the 1880s they triumphed with rubber. Till then it had almost all come from Brazil, where it grew wild. Export of the trees was forbidden, but somebody smuggled one out to see if it would flourish in a similar tropical clime. It did: and Malaya, now with a renewable resource, never looked back.

Among the investors was the family of Lockhart. Their matriach bought a plantation for £25,000 and sent out a son to run it. Almost ruined by a slump in coffee, he switched to become one of the first growers of rubber. The young man, among many others, earned a fortune. He rewarded his granny by making her the so-called Rubber Queen of Edinburgh, worth more than £500,000. A grandson, Bruce Lockhart, later more famous as a spy in Russia, followed in his uncle's footsteps in 1908. He befriended the natives and had his first romance 'by carrying off Amai, the beautiful ward of Dato Klana, the local Malay prince'. His offer to convert to Islam could not appease her family. Their life together ended when he fell ill: 'The doctors pronounced malaria, but there were many people who said that I had been poisoned'. Packed off home, Lockhart gave in his later memoirs of these 'misspent years' a vivid picture of the Scots, more than 2000 of them, who formed perhaps one-third of the planter class. He noted their resemblance to the Dutch across the straits: 'They had the same virtues: thrift, grit, clear-headedness and an immense capacity for work. But they also had the same Calvinistic worship of wealth and the same ruthless determination in their pursuit of it'. Somerset Maugham, passing through, recorded a different impression: 'The greater number of them are rough common men of something below the middle class, and they speak English with a vile accent, or broad Scotch'.

From 1905 the boom in Malayan rubber waxed so tremendous that it could not remain a matter of individual enterprise, however swashbuckling. Individuals just lacked the resources to power such expansion. So, for its own reasons, this pioneering work was to follow the general evolution of Scottish business in the period. A different structure of limited companies had to finance the spread of plantations over the jungles of southern and western Malaya, since a new estate could not be tapped for five or six years. The companies came in two guises. They could be either so-called sterling companies registered in Britain, the first of which, Selangor Rubber, was set up in Glasgow, precursor of many more. Or else they could be rupee companies registered in an Asian dependency, with Singapore pre-eminent. New horizons opened for the agency houses.[11]

Guthrie's stood at their forefront still. Like the Indian and Chinese agencies, it was now involved in banking, insurance, railways, steamships, docks, telegraphs and so on. From 1896 it went into rubber, which would make it as great as any of them. In buying up huge holdings of plantations, it followed the organisational precedent of the houses in Calcutta or Shanghai. For each one it formed a separate company, with its own capital or by flotation on stock exchanges overseas. In either case, its position as agent for the companies put it in effective control of them. It did not own them, but it governed their policy, purchases and sales. In Malaya, it could offer all the usual services, with the addition of actual management of the estates. That proved perfect for the conditions, conferring benefits of scale on an industry composed of small, distinct units. The drawback was that such corporate proliferation, with the attendant directorships, commissions and fees, created vested interests which hindered rationalisation later. But amid the boom it mattered little. Not long after the First World War the houses, Guthrie's in the lead, were dominating the industry.

Then, as in Scotland, repeated slumps pushed forward the process of concentration in another form. Producers of rubber first tried to restrict output by voluntary agreement. When that failed, they appealed for official intervention. In 1921 the British Government appointed a committee under James Stevenson, former managing director of Johnnie Walker at Kilmarnock, one of many Scottish businessmen who had taken on public duties during the war. He proposed an elaborate regime of control based on the previous production of each plantation. It could not be worked without co-operation from the Dutch in the East Indies, which they refused. Though put into force regardless for the British Empire alone in 1922, it broke down in six years. When the great depression came in the 1930s, the practical results of regulation in Malaya were seen to be meagre. What did follow was nemesis for such dashing pioneers as had hung on. Whole families were ruined, including the Lockharts. Having enriched themselves on rubber, they could not believe it would let them down, and they refused to sell out till the disastrous collapse of their markets left them no choice. Bruce Lockhart's friend, Freddie Cunningham, was then the sole proprietary planter left.

In fact, regulation proved wrong for rubber. This industry suffered from depression with the rest, yet was among the first to recover. Advanced technology needed its products. Demand from the western masses for cars, and so for tyres, heralded better times. Before long rubber was again a commodity actively traded on growing international markets, many of them more buoyant than Britain's. Americans, Europeans and Japanese sent exports in exchange, widening the agencies' range of goods. That was the reason for the quirk that in 1932, alone in the Empire, Singapore rejected the preferential duties approved as a panacea at the Imperial Conference in Ottawa, where Britain tried to tie her dominions and dependencies into one economic bloc. Even the Federated Malay States, just as reliant on rubber, deferred. But, egged on by her merchants, Singapore flouted the mother country's will, and for good measure refused to be pushed into a customs union with Malaya. Guthrie's supported the position with a public declaration that it needed both imperial and non-imperial trade which, if free from interference, would reinforce each other. The view seemed vindicated when a new accord on quotas for rubber, this time covering Britain, France, Holland and Siam, collapsed in its turn. The discomfited Government in London could only urge the houses of Singapore to find more openings for British manufactures.

The Second World War caused still another economic upheaval. In the level of global activity, reconstruction brought quick recovery, hastening a further evolution of global structure, with emergence of the multinational company as the most powerful corporate form. Many national companies, in Britain and the Empire, succumbed to the process. But the best went with it, adapted and survived. Guthrie's was one, though as in other cases this entailed cutting its last links with Scotland, weakened anyway in a diversifying business soon run from either London or Kuala Lumpur. While the parent partnership had moved towards limited liability as early as 1903, that hardly affected the rule of the intermarried founding clans. Their last scion stepped down in 1923, however, in favour of an Aberdonian managing director, John George Hay; with no kin, he at least favoured the kith and always recruited from Scottish universities. Still, he could not last for ever, and 30 years later he turned his mind to what would happen on his retiral, when legally the dormant progeny of the founders had to resume control. This would not do. Hay proposed that the sundry companies making up Guthrie's should establish an organisation, owned in proportion by each, for the services provided to them by an even yet unincorporated central agency. It would nowadays be called a buy-out by the management. So the Guthrie Group formed in 1961, with Hay as caretaker while a successor was groomed. After his death it became in 1967 the Guthrie Corporation. He had been the last Scot in charge. What was now the biggest owner of plantations in the world continued under non-Scottish management.[12]

The war left a turbulent political legacy too. When Japan conquered Malaya and most of the East Indies in 1942, she unleashed their pent-up nationalism. Despite her own defeat, she rendered impossible the full restoration of imperial power. That power could still defeat the Malayan Communists in their turn. But this was a separate matter, which did not stop the British starting to prepare for disengagement. The reality could be read in the posting of Malcolm MacDonald as Commissioner-General to deal with the special problems of South-east Asia in 1948, complete with his own court at Johore beside the causeway to Singapore. Here he practised what he preached: that the mother country should not be the exploiter but the trustee of its colonies. While he at once declared an emergency, he tempered it with the promise of eventual independence. He thought the timetable had to be shortened to 15 years from the 25 so far assumed; a new generation of native leaders, loyal during the war, would not stand for anything longer. Independence was to follow in half the time he set.

But progress proved far from straightforward. Lying in the centre of trade, and after centuries of imperialism, MacDonald's realm had turned into a racial jumble. Not least, there were white settlers, whose hauteur he deplored: 'In the light of the admirably gifted characters of the local Asian peoples, it seemed almost incredible'. He replaced the planters' domination with a more progressive and tolerant regime of respect for the natives. The crucial political concession was his acceptance that their interests mattered. Yet they proved hard to reconcile. Indigenous Malays disliked every immigrant group, especially the Chinese who formed a majority in Singapore. They also looked down on the more backward branches of their own stock in Sarawak and North Borneo, now ceded to the Crown. Because of the threat from an aggressive and tyrannical Indonesia next door, MacDonald felt alarmed about these lands and their people, 'the happiest I had ever known'. He wanted to form all the British territories in the area into a federation founded on equality and strong enough to stand on its own feet. The Government in London accepted his reasoning. By the time he left in 1955, he had become the architect of Malaysia.

Disparate in character, however, the country had to be constructed step by step. The Federated Malay States, with the inclusion of Malacca and Penang, achieved independence in 1957. Singapore, Sarawak and Sabah followed in 1963, all joining the federation. But Singapore seceded just two years later, in effect pushed out by the federal authorities who did not want so many Chinese. Its leaders were mortified, but have since built their own successful city-state. The Malays show few regrets, for they wish to be masters in their own house. They have laid a heavy hand on Sarawak, where half the population is Dyak and much of the rest Chinese. From the time federation was mooted, many hated the idea, longing rather for the return of their white rajahs. The colonial administration installed after the war took no notice. One result was that in 1949 a reckless young man made the point in the most horrible way, by assassinating the new governor, Duncan Stewart, a son of Argyll. The killer and three fellow conspirators were hanged, 15 others imprisoned. The habit of ruling the territory with a rod of iron outlasted independence. At that point it had a Chinese premier, whom the federal authorities removed in 1968. They seized the chance also to get rid of some Europeans who had stayed on, seen as troublemakers for defending the Dyaks.[13]

The plight of this people, once magnificent, now demoralised by drink, disease and ignorance, moved a Scot, John Wilson. He came out to run a teachers' training college but in 1954 resigned to go to a village on the Budu River in the interior. It worried him that schooling seemed to damage traditional society, for the best youngsters left their homes never to return. He thought there must be some way to develop primitive peoples without destroying their morale. He set up a sort of secular mission, not to convert them to a new way of life but to instill pride in their old one. To be sure, Presbyterian prejudices were at work too: the puritan Wilson felt nobody should get something for nothing, so he asked everyone to bring at least a cup of rice or a handful of vegetables to pay for a lesson or hire some tools. But simple improvements in hygiene or agriculture made a world of difference, and the experiment sustained itself except for a few helpers from Scotland. Even these Wilson meant in time to replace with Dyaks trained up in principles of which he approved. To that end, he sent some pupils all the way to Nairn Academy, and one to the University of Aberdeen. By 1957, he had his scheme operating in three villages for 400 families. His unorthodox methods were already causing friction with the colonial administration, but it would be Sarawak's independence and federation that ruined him. Though an opponent of Malaysia, he rallied round when in 1963 Indonesia went to war to enforce her claim to the whole of Borneo, and took command of a group of scouts on the border. One defensive tactic devised in Kuala Lumpur was to corral the people into fortified settlements. This seemed to Wilson to negate his work, and he would have nothing to do with it. For that he was expelled in 1968. In a personal tragedy for him, his efforts came to nothing.[14]

Once again the Scot's instinct to save what was authentic, to find means for lagging societies to renew themselves on their own terms, was defeated by larger, impersonal historical forces: perhaps a paradigm of Scotland's own fate. The violence of the old imperialism, in which her sons had played their part, could often be matched by the violence of the new nationalism. Yet at the end of the turbulent twentieth century, the former British colonies in this quarter of the globe had emerged as islands of stability, prosperity and good government amid a sea of troubles. Basic to their achievement was industrial and commercial success, as they plied both old and new sea-lanes, the old opened up in time immemorial by Asians among themselves and the new in the global economy. Imperialism created the conjoint network. But it had not brought the Asiatic nations under an alien yoke for good. After it was over, they resumed the traffic of the ages, ruled their own waves and even swept the wondering West with the products of their refreshed ingenuity. Here was a maritime empire like that of which Dalrymple had dreamed, not an empire of conquest and domination, but of peaceful exchange and mutual advantage, a Scottish Empire after all, though Scots are long gone from it.

CHAPTER THIRTY-SIX

'A kingdom of the mind': Canada

It was summer and I was deeply in love. One day the object of my love, a compact, golden-haired girl who lived on Willey's Sideroad, a half mile away, came over to visit my sisters. They were away and we walked together through the orchard and climbed on to a rail fence which overlooked a small field between our place and Bert McCallum's. Our cows were pasturing on the second-growth clover in front of us. The hot summer afternoon lay quiet all around.

With the cows was a white bull named O.A.C. Pride for the Ontario Agricultural College where my father had bid him in at auction. As we perched there the bull served his purpose by serving a heifer which was in season.

Noticing that my companion was watching with evident interest, and with some sense of my own courage, I said: 'I think it would be fun to do that.'

She replied: 'Well, it's your cow.'

This comes from the account by Professor John Kenneth Galbraith of his own people, the Scotch. They were descendants of Highlanders settled in the 1820s on the northern shore of Lake Erie, where he grew up nearly a century later. He writes of them not without affection, if not without a degree of irony suitable to one who has got well away from all that, to the sophistication of Harvard. His anecdote brings out two of their traits, their matter-of-fact acceptance of brute nature and their sexual reticence towards one another: stark contrasts to the life lived nowadays by the banks of the Charles River. The Scotch yet seem to have been confident in their narrow but robust values. We may infer that these were much the same as they had brought from the mother country three or four generations before, unattractive perhaps to outsiders, but preserved in an agrarian community having, and wanting, little to do with such.[1]

Another reason may be that the Canada of the period offered few values of her own to overlay inherited ones. In 1903, five years before Galbraith's birth, a certain Alexander Fraser, addressing the Caledonian Society of Montreal, had adverted to the theme: 'Canadian nationality! What is it? There is no answer forthcoming. It is a question without an answer, for Canadian nationality has as yet no existence'. According to him, the country was a mere random assemblage of peoples. Only the slow working of time could at some future stage weld them into a national type 'racy of the soil and congenial to the civilisation of the day'. To this end, Fraser saw a need for revival of Scottish sentiment: 'It is rapidly dying out. Every year shows a deplorable difference, and only pensive thoughts arise in the contemplation of a vanishing influence'. If Canada wished to find an identity of her own, above all to remain different from the great republic to the south, she ought to cultivate the seeds of Scottishness already implanted in her. Fraser's sentiments were typical of the Scots who had long pondered nationality, and how progress formed or transformed it. In Canada especially, that had intrigued them from the beginning of their colonisation.

Some Scots came to preserve a life under threat, or already lost, in the Old World. This was an aim more attainable here than in the revolutionary society of the United States. Where they settled together, even in the midst of other ethnic groups, they could often keep up their religion, customs and language. In the Maritime Provinces, or in pockets of Quebec, Ontario and Manitoba, communities of them were living at the turn of the twentieth century much as they had lived since their arrival, much indeed as they would have wanted to live had they been able to stay in Scotland. As late as the 1950s, Charles Dunn picked out among Nova Scotians many customs that their Highland forebears must have brought along with them. They maintained close ties of kinship, especially through complex traditional patterns of marriage. They could often trace lines of descent back to their ancestral glens. Without documents, Canadians of the third or fourth generation stationed as soldiers in Scotland during the World Wars had been able to find remote relations. The people still showed a zest for music, poetry, strong drink and wry humour, not least at funerals. Many spoke Gaelic, and since 1921 they had even been able to study it at school. Books, mainly of a devotional nature, were actually published in the language, more so than in Scotland. Dunn's sanguine survey felt all the same forced to note that the inheritance from the homeland was being eroded by onward migration into the interior of the continent.

A different story had anyway emerged from the literature of Canadian Scots, quite a rich genre. If the mother country was old and the daughter Dominion young, their culture still showed something in common. In order to set it off against a stronger neighbouring one, writers in both searched for characteristic themes and forms, which they often chose to express through a native persona. While Scots of Scotland tended to dwell on the persona's pawky character and language, with the typical virtues they articulated, Scots of Canada stressed rather the landscape where the persona moved, even exaggerating its wild, eerie desolation; though this motif might strike foreigners more by its emptiness and poverty, its lack of historical or legendary reference. The whole trend, reliant on models rather than observation, anyway threatened to disjoin life and image of life, to muffle individual voices and to weaken contact with more universally acceptable literary standards. So self-conscious patriotism may have helped to produce deficient literature.

Certainly in Victorian times the kailyard sprouted in Canada as wantonly as at home, tended by numerous couthy poets. Novels in the same vein were still being written after the turn of the twentieth century by Robert Knowles, presbyterian minister of Galt, Ontario. Though his characters have settled in Canada for good, they constantly reaffirm their original nationality, vindicated by the hard times they knew before leaving and during the early days in a new country. It binds them together in a sort of self-created ghetto, as much like Scotland as they can manage. Knowles writes of his congregation in *St Cuthbert's of the West* (1905): 'They were stern men . . . They nipped contumacy in the bud. The greater number of them had been born in bonnie Scotland, and all of them, even those who had never seen their ancestral home, spoke and lived and thought as though they had just come from the heathery hills'. The key to their happiness and success is to accept this inviolable character and preserve it on an understanding that good will come of it. Mere acceptance leads, however, to a second-hand, commonplace, derivative quality in their lives, as it does in this literature concerning them.

Still, the note is struck again in the novels, of a later date, by Frederick Niven. Born in Chile, he was educated in Glasgow, then lived both there and in Canada. In *The Flying Years* (1935), the main character says on eviction from his croft: 'Scotland. Just a few sad songs and old ballads! That's all. I see it getting worse every year. God knows what the end will be. And yet – and yet – we'll take Scotland with us: a kingdom of the mind'. *The Transplanted* (1944) lays even stronger stress on the compatibility of a Scottish existence in Scotland or in Canada. Its emigrant hero is happy in both. He can conceive, on return to his birthplace, equal feeling for both: 'Perhaps too much was made, in all lands, of nationalism. Granting the existence of national characteristics, racial traits, surely racial traits – of any race – if worthy of retention could survive corporeal transportation'. At his second departure, 'he had the feeling of leaving home for home'. Hugh MacDiarmid read these books and did not spare them: 'Niven now lives in Canada – but it must be said that Canada has not quickened his art in any way. Rather the reverse'. The bard acidly observed that Scots emigrants served the colonies in all but culture. With no realistic interest in their surroundings, they contributed little to creation of independent literatures, nor indeed gave creditable expression to their doubtless enhanced affection for Scotland. As MacDiarmid knew and lamented from experience in the mother country, however, the kailyard proved long-lived.[2]

At least the daughter Dominion in the end offers a more worthy literary memorial to what has been lost, in the elegiac stories of Alastair MacLeod, collected in *The Lost Salt Gift of Blood* (1988). They are set on Cape Breton Island, where Gaelic is still spoken, songs are still sung, legends live on and a sense pervades the mainly Scots people of a way of life grown out of deep roots in the Old World. In one tale, a grandfather describes to his grandsons a Canadian island named Canna, after its Hebridean counterpart. But all the people there, he says, are gone:

'You mean dead?' they asked.

'Well, some of them, yes,' he said, 'but I mean gone from there, scattered all over the world. That is why this place is called Canna and we carry certain things within us. Sometimes there are things within us which we do not know or fully understand and sometimes it is hard to stamp out what you cannot see.'

This story, *Vision*, plays on the second sight, but in the very place-name a historical destiny recurs, with the linking of two dispossessions, a physical and a linguistic. The same motif appears in different forms throughout the sequence. In *The Closing Down of Summer*, for example, migrant workers are forced to seek a livelihood far away. After coal had been found in Nova Scotia at the turn of the century, many Gaels took to mining: as it fostered close-knit communities too, it did not damage their culture's integrity. But now that the seams are exhausted, these men know their way of life will pass away with them: 'It is unlikely we will be replaced in the shaft's bottom by members of our own flesh and bone. For such replacement, like our Gaelic, seems to be of the past and largely over'. When they go to work in South Africa they carry sprigs of spruce, as their 'Highland ancestors, for centuries, fashioned crude badges of heather or of whortleberries to accompany them on the battlefields of the world. Perhaps so that in the closeness of their work with death they might find nearness to their homes and an intensified realisation of themselves'. The emotions are in a sense wasted, because unable to break a cycle which inexorably repeats itself, without obvious meaning, in changing times and circumstances: the ancestors' leaving of Scotland is annually re-enacted in the descendants' leaving of Nova Scotia.

The cycle closes in another story, *The Tuning of Perfection*, which demonstrates the internal decay even of the community left behind. A family is induced to take part in a Celtic Revival: 'It was as if we were parodies of ourselves . . . It was as if it were everything that song should not be, contrived and artificial and non-spontaneous and lacking in communication'. MacLeod offers moving images from a dying culture, yet a more detached and sceptical view may not be illegitimate. Rory Maclean, author of the novel-cum-travelogue, *The Oatmeal Ark* (1998), also springs from roots in the Gaelic diaspora but is intent less on elegy than on definition of its cultural failure. He has a similar scene of a ceilidh, one where the characters are by turns more bland and blemished, more cynical and selfish, more prosaic and penetrating than MacLeod's. The author assigns a bleak reason for their laments: 'All the songs were about Scotland and the pain of diaspora, providing solace in a place which had been economically deprived for generations'.[3]

The later twentieth century has indeed seen these communities break down, something which can no longer be hidden, as for Dunn, by a few survivals. A more recent and rigorous study, of Pictou Island since 1945, demonstrates how every structural shift in the Canadian economy, every technical innovation and every advance of the welfare state, though useful to individuals, has appeared to loosen their links with one another. Social disintegration, slow and never traumatic, met no resistance. On the contrary, people gladly accepted most improvements because at first they seemed beneficial. But when less welcome changes arrived, such as the consolidation of schools which robbed the island of its children, their reaction was fatalistic: the same kind of reaction as from the Highlanders of Scotland amid the same kind of change. Once set off, the disintegration could not be halted. Kinship had performed among the islanders a vital function, not only through personal bonds, but also for practical purposes, to ensure the efficient communal effort needed for survival amid a harsh pioneering environment. As families left off intermarrying on the old patterns, they grew apart and lost what they had in common, especially the Gaelic language. There was then much less incentive for them to stay together, so that emigration swelled. Some farms are still worked jointly, and reluctantly sold, but agriculture on any scale has almost ceased, while waged employment is now normal. The land acquired by the first colonists and held through several generations passes to strangers, to white settlers as they would be called in Scotland. The future seems to lie in tourism: that would complete the transition of a formerly self-sufficient community into one wholly dependent on the outside world. The emigrants, cut off from their roots, had not in the end been able to avoid absorption into North American culture. They then succumbed to that rootlessness which specially distinguishes it from the culture of the Old World, where most people, if under no compulsion, live and die in or near the places where they were born. Tradition, vulnerable even in narrow Europe, melts away in the wide, open spaces of the New World.[4]

The fact is capable of shocking Scots who arrive there with native preconceptions. The critic David Craig set off *On the Crofters' Trail* (1990) with the myths of Scottish emigration in his baggage. He felt puzzled when the settlers' posterity would not confirm them: 'The people we met were proud to have been part of the migration rather than troubled that it had ever been necessary'. He found it odd of them to insist that their forefathers had not been cleared, but had come of their own free will and made the most of things: 'I now began to work out a theory of why clearance material was more elusive than that of more voluntary emigration . . . From that point on we suspected that the hardest thing to find in Canada would be memoirs of veritable eviction'. And thus it proved. Amid allusions likening the Highlanders to the Jews in the Holocaust, he was reduced to fulmination to authenticate his thesis that willing migrants had been cleared: 'Apologists for clearance sometimes emphasise that hundreds on Barra and South Uist "petitioned" to leave. So why the brutal compulsions at the last minute? Conditions as well as estate heavies (and the occasional minister) were *driving* them out'. No wonder that the ambition and mobility of the colonist escaped him: 'I had not expected . . . that the Scottish settlers would move on, most of them, so soon, having used Cape Breton as a stepping stone to the American Middle West, the Canadian prairies, British Columbia'.[5]

Still, other Scots had from the outset foreseen that their way of life could not survive amid the alien corn. Dilution and fragmentation often started at once. We have an early witness of the process in the novelist, John Galt, a restless soul ever ready to shake the dust of Scotland off his feet, and encourage others to do so. He himself became a Canadian pioneer in the 1820s. He led parties to clear the primeval forest and to found a largely Scots community at Guelph, Ontario. He knew, if they did not, that social change here was bound to be real, for he remained also an acutely conservative observer of Scotland. In *Annals of the Parish* he showed the deep changes going on in her traditional society: the original balance is destroyed without anyone especially wishing it. In Canada he noted 'an obvious tendency in the state of things . . . to favour a relapse into barbarity', and drew a parallel with the United States, where 'nothing is less disputable than that the backwoodsmen . . . have declined from the civilisation of their progenitors'. But as an enlightened Scot, seeing in man a social animal, Galt was not downcast.

His Canadian novel, *Bogle Corbet*, the one dealing with a youngster who abandons the hopeless corruption of Jamaica, shows what can still be done by a fresh start in the freedom of the wilderness. The Scots colonists whom Corbet joins are at first daunted by it, but they soon adjust, learn to subsist, found families, build communities. Galt stresses not so much individual success as co-operative development under paternalist leadership, yet he is no facile optimist. The settlers have to struggle. Corbet himself heads a long line of Canadian literary anti-heroes, given to melancholy, irony and self-mockery. The work offers a sharply realistic alternative to the heroic adventures on the frontier which Americans imagined as a realisation of their ideology. But it is not quite anti-American either, for it criticises illiberal British treatment of Canada. These are interesting tensions, which reflect Scottish preoccupations. They offer two views of human nature, which it falls to the Canadian lot to attempt to reconcile. This is the earliest work of any substance to define Canadianism by reference to them. It shows us that, if Gaelic tenacity could be transplanted, so could the *perfervidum ingenium Scotorum*. North American culture favoured the latter, which prevailed and allowed the immigrants to adapt to their environment.[6]

The realities have borne out Galt's judgment. One example is to be found in the formerly sizeable Scots population of the Eastern Townships of Quebec, now known as Les Cantons de l'Est. Here, south of the St Lawrence River near the frontier with the United States, Hebrideans felled the primeval forest in the middle of the nineteenth century. By its end 12,000 of them occupied the land. But, as often in this quarter of the continent, it was not very fertile. With little reason to stay, from the 1930s they began to depart eastwards to New England and westwards to the prairies. Meanwhile, since about 1900, the provincial government of Quebec had pursued a policy of settling the fecund French in peripheral districts. The policy came under furious attack from one Robert Sellar in a tract notorious right up to the present day, *The Tragedy of Quebec* (1907). The author identified himself as a 'Scotch radical': half a century before, George Brown had given him his first job in Canada on the *Globe* of Toronto. Sellar espoused all the causes of his patron and hero, from free trade to the separation of Church and state. In Quebec he discerned a conspiracy to expel Protestant farmers from the land they had won. To some his outpouring was a timely restatement of the papist menace, to others the essence of bigoted francophobia among English-speaking Canadians.

Yet it protested too much. The first of the French, arriving amid a Highland community, actually learned Gaelic, though as their numbers grew they had no further need to. The language fell into disuse anyway beyond the second generation after colonisation, through marriages between Gael and non-Gael. Once the balance tipped, decay was rapid: the last Gaelic-speaking minister left in 1942. By 1980, 80 per cent of the people were French, and these incomers, in occupation for decades, had no cause to remember who once opened up a country they now called their own. Only about 100 descendants of the pioneers survived: 40 could speak Gaelic but, thinking it backward and primitive, used English as a first language. Proud of their community still, they knew all the same that it was about to die. Sellar, however, in predicting this fate and ascribing it to inadequate Presbyterian vigilance, had missed the point.

The real point finds confirmation in a more local study of Winslow, part of the Eastern Townships away from the main area of Gaelic settlement. Here, one group was not simply swamped by the other. Scots and French arrived together in the mid-nineteenth century and co-existed without mixing, each tied together by its own system of kinship, community and tradition, which long let them also resist the allurements of the prairies and the cities. Even so, the Scots left in the early twentieth century, to scatter widely over North America, including the United States. Scarcely any remain today. This suggests that while the French came to stay, they never pushed the Scots out. The case in the rest of the Eastern Townships was surely at bottom much the same. If their Scottishness died not quite a natural death, because caused in part by public policy, there was no foul play either. We might rather conclude that the Scots vanished because they acted on their own assumptions and impulses, markedly divergent from those of the Roman Catholic culture amid which they at length found themselves. It was not just a religious matter. Quebec owes every major social movement, in welfare, education and labour, to clerical initiative and priestly direction of obedient flocks. Presbyterianism, by contrast, accords equal weight to the laity in the Church and holds that merit lies in people who look after themselves. The ultimate contrast is between dependence and independence: the French remained where they were put, while the Scots followed the opportunities of the New World.[7]

The culture of the New World was then bound to impose itself. Self-conscious allegiance to little Scotlands beyond the seas seems seldom to have lasted beyond a generation or two, and many Scots must have become Canadians sooner. What else can explain the fate of their Presbyterianism, once so cherished, yet all but voluntarily disbanded in 1925? About two-thirds of its adherents then joined Congregationalists and Methodists in the United Church of Canada. It had the aim, in a fast-growing country with a need to define itself, of fostering Christian nationalism, neither papist and universal on the one hand nor Anglican and colonial on the other. This purpose was not easy to formulate: the three Churches had started negotiating at the turn of the century. Even after they laboriously reached agreement, the definition of a true, united Protestantism was not good enough for some Presbyterians. Believing everything Scottish superior, they remained convinced that Canada was what loyal Scots had made her. A rump of them stayed aloof and, with heavy historical symbolism, signed a covenant to preserve their own Church. But it has not grown with the country. Its membership remains in absolute numbers about the same as in 1925, so that its share of the population has halved to 4 per cent. Today it is more Scottish than ever, an ethnic Church, often of recent immigrants.[8]

As for the corresponding secular evolution, none illustrates it better than the most eminent of Canadian Scots, William Mackenzie King, the Prime Minister who dominated three decades of his country's politics till 1950. He espoused a nationalism rather hostile to the imperial power, as an obstacle to Canada's independence. He may have owed that to a beloved mother who imbued him with the memory of injustices done to his grandfather, William Lyon Mackenzie. In any event he recorded that 'my father would speak of the Mother Country because his parents had been born in Scotland . . . My mother would have thought in a similar way, but . . . the next and third generation did not think of Britain or Scotland as the mother country'. That he could not bring himself to mention England, contrary to normal North American usage, perhaps itself identifies the main object of his mistrust. If the form of a small nation's mentality remained, however, its content entirely changed.[9]

That becomes explicit in a writer sprung from those Nova Scotians who, in their relative isolation and self-sufficiency, had been atypically sedentary. Hugh MacLennan remarks that his people owed the same passionate loyalty as their ancestors to the hills of home. 'The knowledge that I am three-quarters Scotch, and Highland at that, seems like a kind of doom from which I am too Scotch even to think of praying for deliverance,' but 'I belong to the last Canadian generation raised with a Highland nostalgia.' His conclusion that the links have now been broken is set out in *Scotchman's Return* (1958), composed after a visit to the land of his fathers: 'Am I wrong, or is it true that it is only now, after so many years of not knowing who we are or wanted to be, that we Canadians of Scotch descent are truly at home in the northern half of North America?'

But if Canada's random assemblage of peoples was to develop, she had to look beyond the inevitable early communalism towards the construction of a new nationality. Scots, with their interest in nationality and in how progress formed or transformed it, often understood this. So we find, for example, that even the strand in them of Presbyterian intransigence, with its bitter hostility to papists, had never fully displaced the admiration for the brave pioneers of New France among Scotsmen arriving straight after the conquest. The esteem expressed by James Murray, first Governor of Quebec, was echoed by John Buchan, Governor-General of Canada in 1935–40. A character in his last, great, Canadian novel, *Sick Heart River* (1941), praises this 'fine European stock planted out in a new country and toughened by two centuries of hardship and war. They keep their close family life and their religion intact and don't give a cent for what we call progress. Yet all the time they have a pretty serious fight with nature, so there is nothing soft in them'. The French journalist, André Siegfried, on a visit from the metropole in 1946, explained the affinity by the fact that Scots were 'démocrates de tempérament, par contraste avec cet esprit d'hiérarchie dont les anglais, même d'extrême gauche, ne se défont jamais qu'avec peine'.

Buchan's own national consciousness relieved him of any assumption that English ways were the norm. During journeys round the country, he was often struck by how Scots it could be. On Prince Edward Island, repeatedly addressed in the Gaelic he did not know, he wrote: 'I felt during my visit as if I had suddenly been transported to a Scottish parish'. He saw how in this alien environment a new nationality was unlikely just to duplicate that of the imperial power. But he found profound new allegiances as yet unformed: the people were 'very loyal to Britain and very loyal to their own province but not so loyal to Canada as a whole . . . Each province tends to regard itself as a separate unit and to look at a policy on the narrowest grounds, without any consideration of Canada as a whole'. The likeness to Scotland might suggest a remedy: in his own country, Highland and Lowland races had fused so that Scots had multiple loyalties. 'A man can never have too many loyalties,' he told the people of Prince Edward Island. It should therefore be a matter of pride that Canada housed such diverse cultures. If she could gain more confidence, more sense of herself and of her history, it was something to unite the provinces rather than drive them apart.

Buchan thus descried here yet another Scotland on a grander scale, like South Africa. Each of these countries showed strong parallels with the others: they had, beside a good deal of shared history, (at least) two languages and two cultures. Without suppression or distortion, belonging to an Empire of diversity in unity could help them. During a speech in Montreal in 1937, Buchan said Canada was by now 'a sovereign nation and cannot take her attitude to the world docilely from Britain, or from the United States, or from anybody else. A Canadian's first loyalty is not to the British Commonwealth of Nations, but to Canada and to Canada's King'. The statement might now be taken for granted, and Buchan himself explained he was only trying to bring out for his listeners the practical implications of the Statute of Westminster. But at the time it sounded a note of nationalism radical almost to the point of subversion: and from the Governor-General too![10]

As Buchan's feelings for the country grew deeper and more complex, they affected his general outlook. In *Sick Heart River* he gave them literary expression. Finished shortly before his death, the novel is largely confessional, fixing its gaze on ultimate things, God and world, man and society, blind and inscrutable forces of life and death amid a savage landscape. It also carries the idealist in Buchan beyond imperialism, a term which may perhaps never have quite captured his inner self anyway. At the close of his oeuvre, he resolves the dilemma forced on him by the First World War, between the hero's calling and its devastating impact on the little lives of common men whom it is supposed to uplift and redeem. The hero can now be allowed a calling again. But, whether to Empire or anything else, it is less important than his character, his conduct and above all the effect they create, of reminding people round him, and us, of their higher nature, wakening the best in himself and curbing the worst. A sign of the change comes in the absence from this work of casual racism. Buchan's favourite, Edward Leithen, appears for the last time amid a cast of others caught like him between two cultures. He says to one, Lew Frizell, a half-caste Indian-Scot: 'I come from England. I'm Scots same as you'. But in the final moving pages, a sort of celebration in the face of personal doom dissolves these differences and frees them all to confront what truly counts in their existence under the aspect of eternity. And they set about saving individuals rather than the Empire. Canada had cured Buchan of his grand theories.[11]

Yet with our hindsight Buchan's ambition for Canada, let alone South Africa, must look as sanguine as his view of contemporary Scotland. To his mind his homeland had risen above its troubled past to attain a settled nationhood, exemplary for the younger countries. Half a century after his death, however, Scotland had if anything reverted to Canada's condition of uncertainty, with a chronic crisis of confidence, a blurred identity and no guarantee for the integrity of the state to which she belonged: this may be changed by the new Parliament in Edinburgh or perhaps not. In both Scotland and Canada, meanwhile, an ambiguous nationhood seems neither capable of perfection nor yet disposed to self-effacement. One Nova Scotian draws a parallel between the pair of them more by way of warning than example. MacLennan recalls of his own folk: 'We had in our collective consciousness memory of Scotland's loss to England. It accounts for our profound distrust of any expression of self-confident rational nationalism'. All four peoples who had come together in 1867, the French, the Loyalists, the Scots and the Irish, 'were the children of four separate defeats and abandonments'. So Canadians felt 'a fear close to taboo of offering to Canada an undivided loyalty'. Since his forebears had offered such loyalty to lost causes, 'what more natural for a Scotch Canadian to feel that a total commitment of loyalty to Canada, as weak relative to the US as Scotland had been weak relative to England, would end in a personal disaster?' Still, he set great store by the end of Empire, which he thought would make Canadians see the reality of their situation: they now had no choice but to feel at home in North America, and if they faced it they might find it at last matching some inner conviction.[12]

That was written in 1954. But by 1972, when Margaret Atwood published *Survival*, her thematic guide to Canadian literature, the national condition seemed barely to have improved. She described it in terms that might well ring true to Scots. She found Canada had deep feelings of inadequacy nourished by two still deeper forces, which also nourished each other: Calvinism told people they were doomed, while colonialism told them they were powerless. Before country and culture could mature, those forces had to be overcome. As yet they were barely articulated, however, except in immature exhibitionism. With no more useful expressions of national sentiment apparent, Atwood had to go along with the idea of Canadians as losers, less confident and powerful than the peoples with whom they most readily compared themselves. Under such conditions, what mattered most was indeed survival, 'hanging on, staying alive'. It made for a jejune conclusion, though even then not so bleak as the analogous pessimism in much newer Scottish writing – which, incidentally, usually employs Canada or other lands of exile as metaphors for pure, unredeemed loss.[13]

In any event, Canadian nationhood has found no ratification in the end of Empire. The country is after all there not through geographical or ethnic necessity but because of a connection with Britain now over. To be sure, it has made something of that. In good measure Canadians fulfil the ideals written for them into the preamble of the British North America Act of 1867, promising 'peace, order and good government' in conscious contrast to 'life, liberty and the pursuit of happiness' in the American Declaration of Independence. Compared to the United States, theirs is a country free of racialism or violence, generous in provision of public services and welfare. But the intended final consummation was for Canada in some way to realise herself, in Buchan's ideal to transcend her domestic differences and achieve a fusion. This has never happened, or anyway has not gone far enough to guarantee national integrity. If fusion there be, it is rather on the North American scale, fusion into a culture where local, let alone regional or national, variation is hard to find. Canada's major links reach across the border rather than from sea to sea. Canadians can, if they wish, go to live in the United States and blend in with greater ease than Scots in England, since there is no great distinction even in accent. Visiting Americans, on the other hand, encounter territory not foreign, or only in the most reassuring way, for it hardly diverges from their own. So the British connection amounts to little in the end. Canadians alone, it appears, are really capable of telling their country from the great republic to the south, and then in no more than cultural terms. This, however, remains a culture that has constantly to ask how it can define itself over against a larger and more dynamic neighbour speaking the same language. The end of Empire has brought it face to face with that unpalatable and intractable reality.

Something of the same holds for Scotland. Here again is the problem of the southern neighbour, though objectively it ought to be no problem, since on almost every measure Scottish society grows more and more like British society, and has done so for over a century. Besides, English or Anglo-British culture is itself under pressure from the post-modern culture shared by both Europe and North America, to some extent by almost the whole globe. Against its force Scotland has (and has to offer Canadian Scots) only a few fragments of her ancient self. The prospect appears rather for the universal victory of a bourgeois order varying only in degrees of disposable income. A flight of five hours will verify that circumstances on each side of the Atlantic Ocean are much the same, or else will make the transition quick and easy in the case of real partiality for one or the other. There is nothing like the deliberate and unconditional choices of olden times which, once made, may paradoxically have rendered the adaptation more bearable.

Yet the Old World remains in a special sense profoundly different from the New World. As Scots long posited, there is in fact little continuity between mother country and colony. For one thing, in Scotland the end of Empire has ratified nationhood, or ratified it again, since it never really died away. Scots of earlier generations may have cherished a vision of the future that lay with empires rather than with mere nations, though perhaps it was wishful thinking, or a need to compensate for modernity's undermining of their ancient nationhood. In this vision, Scots and English would transcend themselves on a higher plane. Yet transcendence never took place, not in the Empire, nor even fully in the Union. Rather to her surprise, Scotland at length found that the cultural autonomy secured in 1707 remained the most vital fact of her existence. Whatever else might fail, that kept up a certain continuity, a certain balance between old and new, a certain sense of responsibility in Scots for their own country. If often diminished or distorted, this sense yet offered hope and vision in a way that eludes Canada.

The comparison is apt because the period of that Scottish rediscovery, the last third of the twentieth century, has also been an epoch in Canadian history. It started when Pierre Elliot Trudeau became Prime Minister in 1968. Of French and Scots parentage, he was bilingual and to that extent equipped to deal with the rising tide of nationalism in Quebec. He had also been educated on both sides of the Atlantic and, as a liberal alike in the North American and the European sense, seemed to offer a new way forward. For him, while the individual took precedence over the collective, legally enforceable human rights were to be widely defined, in particular so as to include linguistic rights. With these rights the French could acquire a fresh identity in a multicultural society resting on equal status at least for the two founding nations, and ultimately for all other groups that had meanwhile immigrated and were still immigrating. Bizarrely, this entailed official extinction of the Scots, who were wiped out by mere administrative fiat. In 1961, at the last census recording the category, nearly two million Canadians declared themselves to be of Scottish descent, the third largest ethnic group after the English and French. By the time of the census of 1971 they, along with the other peoples of the British Isles, including even the Irish, had been reclassified as British. Most of the existing population was thus reduced to the two founding nations required for the policy of bilingualism. Thus did Canada casually dispense with the traces on her soil of little Scotlands beyond the seas.

But Trudeau, too, had a higher vision. He wanted at last to define Canada over against her southern neighbour, where the melting pot remained as yet the prevalent doctrine of nation-building. He also set the final seal on independence from Britain by repatriating the Canadian constitution. Freed of these trammels, his people could leave narrower nationalisms behind and achieve a novel, multicultural fusion. The concept has meanwhile become a global cult, yet in Canada it proved barren. Meant .to counter Quebec's claims for special status, it did not bring out what the French shared with fellow citizens but rather reinforced their differences and even created new ones. Meant to validate an ideal of unity in diversity, it only underlined the amorphous, rootless qualities of an explicitly immigrant society liable to be changed by every newcomer.

There is no transcendence, no fusion and, worse, nothing to fall back on when these fail. Canada, if in geography as in character the closest of the New World to the Old, yet belongs unequivocally to the New. Maclean writes: 'No one on this continent could drink from a river that was part of himself or grasp a handful of soil and say, "I am of this earth" '. Here lies the deep difference from Scotland, however transformed or even deformed by her history she has been. Amid those wide open spaces, she must ever remain a mere kingdom of the mind.[14]

CHAPTER THIRTY-SEVEN

'Traitors to Scotland': Imperial Economics

At breakfast on March 17, 1981, Alexander Fletcher, Minister for Industry at the Scottish Office, opened the papers to read bad news – the Royal Bank of Scotland had agreed to merge with the Standard Chartered Bank. The first was his country's biggest bank. The second was one which did not really belong anywhere: though registered in the United Kingdom, it conducted little business there, and most of its interests lay in Asia or Africa. That did not worry Fletcher so much as the stingy deal it was offering, 148p per share or £300 million, rather below the net value of the Royal Bank's assets. Even with eight Scottish directors on the board of Standard Chartered to be thrown in, it seemed meagre recompense for effective removal of control over a Scottish bank to London – if that was, as seemed likely, where the merged headquarters would go.[1]

Fletcher, a chummy chap, knew everybody that mattered on the Scottish economic and political scene. He found his own dismay reflected among friends in the financial circles of Edinburgh. His colleagues at Westminster appeared less concerned. The 21 Scots Tory MPs were, but for a couple of obvious high-flyers, a mediocre bunch. They had little liking for the ideology of the free market prevalent in their own Government. Yet they felt wary of making common cause with Labour and the Scottish National Party, both immediately up in arms. Instead Fletcher enlisted the support of his own boss, the Secretary of State for Scotland, George Younger, and of the new Secretary of State for Trade, John Biffen. Biffen had earlier, during Labour's first attempt at devolution, pondered that political question from a frame of mind which was unionist without being hostile to Scots. As a sympathetic Englishman, he thought more could be done to meet their grievances within the existing constitution, and here was an example. Fletcher did well to win him over, for Biffen bore the responsibility of deciding whether to let the merger go ahead or refer it to the Monopolies Commission.

Fletcher chose the position of his ambush with care, yet it contained a flaw, that grounds for referral to the commission were not salient. The proposed merger had after all been agreed by the parties to it. And no monopoly, or risk of monopoly, existed in British banking. Cartels existed, but that was a different matter. A cartel existed among the four English clearing banks, while the fifth, Williams & Glyn's, was linked to the Royal Bank, and so to the cartel of three Scottish clearing banks. One tacit rule of the cartels was that neither should encroach far on the territory of the other. A little competitive pressure was still thought desirable, in the cautious manner of those days. It had long been expected that a "fifth force" in British banking would emerge, though nobody could say quite how. A certain potential for it lay among the Scottish banks, yet none was strong enough to pull itself up by its own bootstraps, and merger with some third party seemed to be the way forward.

At least, that was how it seemed to the chairman of the Royal Bank, Michael Herries. For some years he had been seeking a partner, and put out several feelers. One was to the English bank, Lloyd's, which already owned 16 per cent of ordinary shares in the Royal Bank, though this looked likely to be ruled out on monopolistic grounds. Other possibilities were more outlandish: the Standard Chartered Bank and the Hongkong and Shanghai Bank, old imperial banks which, after the Empire had been lost or nearly so, still needed to find a role. In particular they needed to get into markets from which their history had shut them out, into America and into Europe, for preference into Britain. Into this last the obvious way was the Royal Bank. But it bristled with obstacles. The Bank of England had since the First World War insisted on separation of banking at home and abroad, letting no company from overseas acquire a British clearer. While Herries hoped to change that, he had to choose his ground, to find the right partner and to work out the right partnership. His own background helped: ancestry in the landed gentry of Dumfriesshire had been his ticket into Jardine Matheson, where he at length rose to be taipan. So he knew at first hand the operations of the Hongkong and Shanghai Bank and for some reason did not like what he saw, especially the face of its chairman, Michael Sandberg. Herries thus came readily to the conclusion that Standard Chartered was a better fit for the Royal Bank, each being able to give the other what it lacked, a network abroad in return for an established position at home. And though Standard Chartered was bigger than the Royal Bank, their respective global rankings being 52nd and 125th, the link could be dressed up as a merger rather than a takeover. For all this, by dint of deferring at every turn, Herries at length won round the Governor of the Bank of England, Gordon Richardson.

Yet Herries appeared unaware of one problem arising not down in Threadneedle Street but in a place visible from his own desk, New St Andrew's House, seat of the Scottish Office. It arose from the question whether a merged corporation would be run from Edinburgh or London. As to the first, Herries was unwilling to give any commitments, lest it render the status of fifth force elusive; as to the second, it became clear that Scots would not accept Britain's gain being Scotland's loss. That is to say, it was a political problem, as such identified by Fletcher. His cronies, Peter de Vink and Ian Noble, set out to mobilise resistance. But the lines of battle were hardly formed when they had to wheel about and face an onslaught from Hong Kong. Sandberg could not afford to stand by, since for him too the obvious way into Britain was the Royal Bank. He outbid Standard Chartered with an offer of 221p a share, worth £500 million. He and his executives flew over to woo Edinburgh with a package much more winsome than the limp surrender to English financial imperialism implicit in Standard Chartered's. Theirs held promises to preserve Scottish banking autonomy and make the Royal Bank the European flagship of their group, more of a partner than a subsidiary. As far as it went, the ploy succeeded: if the choice lay between those two, then on the whole Scottish opinion probably did favour the Hongkong and Shanghai Bank. But Sandberg could not sweeten Herries. That meant he could not sweeten Richardson either, not when he was challenging the original offer with fresh terms that made it look stupid. The Governor asked Sandberg to desist. When ignored, he did all in his power to block the rival bid. The first step was for Standard Chartered to raise its own price to 215p.

As a hue and cry rose in Scotland, Herries and Richardson found the situation spinning out of their control. There could no longer be a clandestine coupling, but only a battle in the open marketplace, no cosy merger, but a hard-fought takeover. Willy-nilly it then became a matter for Scotland, not just for shareholders. Various institutions took their stand, from the Scottish Office down, this with a discreet lead from Younger and with scarcely repressed rabble-rousing from Fletcher, who went round Edinburgh calling the directors of the Royal Bank 'traitors to Scotland'. The usual Scottish claque of press, political parties and pressure groups joined in. Not least among these was the Bank of Scotland, junior only to the Royal Bank, and owned to the extent of 35 per cent by Barclays Bank: it feared that, if the integrity of the domestic system could not hold, predators would soon arrive at its own door. Even the Tory MPs grew restive. The Government realised it might face a Scottish crisis. Evasive action was necessary, and the portals of the Monopolies Commission stood open. Biffen overruled reservations from its officials to declare that there was a public interest at stake beyond the private interests of the parties involved. In reaching his conclusion, he took account of Edinburgh's importance as a financial centre and of a strong banking system for the Scottish economy: an unmistakable echo of Fletcher's views. On May 1, Biffen referred both bids to the Commission.

Its deliberations proved lengthy and complex. Given an anomalous referral, not clearly covered by the statute, the terms of the argument defied easy definition. Both suitors felt frustrated at being asked to respond to unspecified imputations which were to be adjudged on unknown criteria. At least Richardson had a clear line: at all costs to stop the Hongkong and Shanghai Bank. His spokesmen argued that, being based overseas, it was not properly subject to supervision by the Bank of England, though in fact it had co-operated freely almost since its foundation. Heavy hints fell, too, that the regulatory regime under which it did come, albeit in a Crown colony, left something to be desired; yet it had actually made a rather better job of running the local monetary system than the Bank of England had of the British one. The fundamental objection, however, was that Richardson's authority in the City of London would be weakened should his will be flouted. The Commission might have adjusted the terms of one or other offer, rather than rejected either or both out of hand. But Richardson's enmity towards the Hongkong and Shanghai Bank tended not so much to favour Standard Chartered as to bring out the Scottish claims for the Royal Bank. In the end the Commission's task resolved itself into deciding whether the advantages of a British fifth force, based in London, outweighed a different case for diversity, to keep and develop Edinburgh as a financial centre. In January 1982 the Commission turned down both bids. Despite the arguments it had heard to the contrary, it agreed that a change of ownership would remove control of the Royal Bank from Scotland, do damage by closing off careers previously open to her talents, damp down enterprise and hinder the general development of the economy. It also accepted the case against allowing control of a clearing bank to pass outside the United Kingdom. It ruled, in other words, for the independence of the Royal Bank.[2]

Nobody emerged unbloodied from this battle. The two bidder banks had spent much time and money to no purpose. The Bank of England had, just for the sake of Standard Chartered, abandoned its long-standing segregation of internal and external banking, only to see its designs foiled. The Royal Bank was forced to find some new blueprint for the future; it meanwhile turned itself into the first Anglo-Scottish bank, but whether that could be a permanent solution remained unclear. The Scottish establishment was left with egg all over its face. The national system of interlocking interests, where directors from different companies sat on each other's boards, comprehended all the men behind Herries. He himself became chairman of Scottish Widows right in the middle of the rumpus. His deputy at the Royal Bank, Peter Balfour, was chairman of Scottish & Newcastle Breweries too; he also headed the Scottish Council, a body representative of both private and public sectors, which had been complaining about a stampede of decision-makers to London. Another director of the Royal Bank, Robin Duthie, doubled as chairman of the Scottish Development Agency and in that capacity had just denounced the ignorance of people in London about anywhere north of Watford. Yet where were these, and others, when the time came to stand up and be counted over the Royal Bank? They endorsed the deal with Standard Chartered. This establishment, wholly unionist in politics, seemed indifferent to the wider interest of Scotland as revealed by general indignation over their schemes. They had to give way to it in the end, but with an ill grace that still left a bad impression. The one man of similar standing to break ranks was Lord Clydesmuir, Governor of the Bank of Scotland. Otherwise, the semi-victorious campaign against Herries relied on outsiders such as de Vink and Noble, or indeed on Fletcher himself, a Tory Minister born within sight of the shipyards of Greenock, where his father worked. Nationalism was not their prime motive, yet not absent from what they did, or of no help to them.

Their semi-victory raised wider questions still. Scotland took away from the affair a bad impression not only of her great and good but also of the free market. Yet if her banks had now in effect been declared immune from takeover, an essential discipline of capitalism was lost, because the natural selection by which fit companies devoured unfit no longer worked. This may be less important in a financial system as deregulated as that of the United Kingdom has since become. But the lesson was not lost elsewhere. Appeals to the national interest arose as a matter of routine whenever takeovers in any Scottish sector threatened during the 1980s, though assuredly the economy cannot survive on special pleading. After all, if the identity of the Royal Bank was deemed decisive, it could also appear a bit spurious. Most shareholders lived outside Scotland, the two biggest national groups being English and Arab.

A case could be and was made for calling the Hongkong and Shanghai Bank a Scottish outfit too, in its origins, ethos and personnel. As the emblem of British financial power in the Orient, it actually offered a better example than the domestic banks of how well "Scottish principles" in banking had worked in freely evolving conditions: to have been regarded as foreign was bad enough, but to have been defeated by Scottish Nationalism added insult to injury. Sandberg, while not a Scot, was an odd man out in the succession of chairmen. He would be followed by William Purves, a son of Kelso who rose in classic fashion from teaboy to taipan. He crowned his career by leading vigorous expansion on global markets in the course of which he did after all push through a British acquisition, of the Midland Bank. His own corporation's links with the homeland were such that it could not be forever shut out, and Richardson's intrigues against it finally went for nothing. In less degree, Standard Chartered had claims to Scottishness too, again most obviously in its senior personnel. It was a merger, dating from 1969, of the Standard Bank and the Chartered Bank, the latter a foundation of the hatter from Hawick, James Wilson, which grew into the biggest in India and was lured into Lord Inchcape's maw in the 1920s. Today, 25,000 of its 30,000 employees, together with three-fifths of its assets, remain outside the United Kingdom, so it has not yet managed to repatriate itself in the same way as its rival suitor of 1981. The fact remains that two prodigal sons of Scotland had then come home and been not so much as recognised. The battle for the Royal Bank perhaps also brought a semi-victory for a younger generation of parochial Scots over an older generation of imperial Scots.[3]

It spoke volumes, too, that the decisive interventions came from the British state or its agents. During the twentieth century they had always treated Scotland as a mere regional problem. She, willingly placing herself in ever greater dependency on them, came to see matters in the same light. The question whether the benefits also entailed penalties seldom occurred, since other methods of managing the economy seemed to be ruled out. Penalties appeared early all the same. In the First World War, the state's organisation of production had a varying impact but a net effect of boosting heavy industry. Given the loss of foreign customers, this was a formula for slump once peace came. In other sectors secular decline continued, and in the case of textiles, for example, quickened. Altogether the economic structure was so distorted that if by 1918 most still subscribed in theory to *laissez-faire*, in practice a return to it proved impossible. As a matter of fact Scots capitalists had found co-operation with government congenial and were content to continue it, for the purpose not now of fighting a war but of streamlining and sustaining economic activity.[4]

The change of heart was presaged by the findings of an official committee under Lord Balfour of Burleigh, former Scottish Secretary, set up to consider the impact of peace on industry. He noted that even before 1914 the economy had been losing breadth, and if anything relying more on traditional staples. To foreign, especially German, competition it abandoned certain sectors and markets in third countries. The sectors were often of advanced technology, and lack of self-sufficiency in their products had become a real embarrassment in the war. An answer might now lie in consciously countering the deficiencies, perhaps on an imperial scale. One means could be tariffs, with a list of commodities deemed vital to national security as the basis for some type of imperial preference. Another means could be industrial combinations: 'If this country is to maintain its commercial position and effectively compete for its share of the trade of the world many industries must be organised on more modern lines, and often on a larger scale than has been the case in past years'. The policy might be carried out through support of companies in the favoured sectors, through direct action by the Government and through individual or general agreement with the Dominions.[5]

Scots capitalists could not yet swallow this prescription whole. Quite what they did want was harder to pin down, if not plainly contradictory. Like others in Britain, they also cherished a hope of return to the good old days, for example in resuming the Victorian practice of strict economy by the state, abandoned in the war. Peace did at least restore a clearer division between the private and public sectors. In 1919 the Prime Minister, David Lloyd George, gave new jobs, as Minister of Munitions and of Reconstruction respectively, to Andrew Weir and Auckland Geddes, two of several Scots he had lured from industry into government. One of their prime tasks was to disengage the state from its many commercial contracts. Yet their colleague William Weir pulled in the opposite direction, creating new corporations, or their surrogates in cartels, to run electricity, railways, shipping and so on.

Again, Robert Horne, MP for Hillhead, who become Chancellor of the Exchequer in 1921, made a major effort at retrenchment. He entrusted the detail to Eric Geddes, brother of Auckland, who with a committee manned by several more Scots wielded a notorious axe on public spending in 1923. They did not long hold up its expansion. People also wanted to restore sterling to former glory. Horne, himself head of a paper-making concern, remained sensitive to the needs of industry and wary of going back on gold. The enmity he thus aroused in the City of London blocked his reinstatement at the Treasury when the Unionists, after the gap of Labour's first Ministry under Ramsay MacDonald, came in once more at the end of 1924. In Horne's place, Winston Churchill did go back on gold, at a rate overvaluing the pound. This, meant above all to rescue London's financial standing, boosted imports and hit exports, to the detriment of industry in other parts of the country. Even as depression loomed, the Labour Government of 1929 clung to gold and free trade, amid the mounting disgust of its rank-and-file. At the Imperial Conference of 1930, MacDonald ignored the Dominions' call for preference. But Max Aitken, Lord Beaverbrook, a son of the manse from New Brunswick, had launched a campaign for Empire Free Trade, preference in all but name. It may now have commended itself just because it had not been tried and no other expedient was working. The National Government of 1931 revived protectionism in an imperial form. Bringing some domestic respite, this time it managed to strike a chord in Scotland too: when Glasgow pulled itself together enough to mount a great exhibition in 1938, Empire was the explicit theme. But an imperial bloc was of no great help to the recovery of global trade. The economy's other international links weakened and broke. Amid general industrial calamity that counted for much because a small country like Scotland could only ever thrive on external markets. This prelude to total economic mobilisation in the Second World War also sowed the seed of socialist planning and controls afterwards.[6]

It cannot be said that Scots otherwise contributed much to the economic debates of the era. All hands were rather set to the practical task of restoring the international pre-eminence which Scottish industry had once regarded as its own. The effort failed. Capital and labour seemed scarcely able any longer to combine on mutually acceptable terms. The obvious sign of it was unemployment stubbornly stuck at what once would have been unimaginable levels of 25 per cent or more. Heavy emigration followed and, during the 1920s, the first actual drop in population of modern times.

Still, Scotland's human resources cannot have suddenly become so impoverished. One vital ingredient, the native breed of imperial or indeed global tycoons, continued to reproduce itself. The brothers Geddes offered an example. In 1925 Auckland became chairman of Rio Tinto, a sort of collateral descendant of Jardine Matheson. He revived the flagging company and moved it into the front rank of the mining and metallurgical industries by a novel strategy of marketing, diversification and joint ventures, with heavy investment in chemicals and systematic exploitation primarily of copper in Rhodesia. Eric meanwhile headed Dunlop, which he made into one of the biggest British multinationals. From 1924 he was also chairman of Imperial Airways, at first part-time because it involved mainly the public advocacy of routes spanning the Empire, and the negotiation of laborious agreements with third countries: it took years to set up a run to India, later extended eastwards. He thus pioneered the modern freedom of the skies under an international authority. Long bargaining proved necessary even for the Empire Air Mail Scheme, to carry first-class mail without surcharge on a subvention from the Post Office: an exact counterpart for a new age of old subsidies to shipping lines. There were still Scots able enough, if with the prop of official encouragement, to exploit such imperial character as the economy retained.

Scotland's capital resources could not have been so inadequate either. A huge repatriation of investments had followed the outbreak of hostilities in 1914, never to be fully corrected by peace. The prodigious waste of war reduced supply of capital, while more violent cycles of boom and bust in commodities afterwards destabilised demand for it. On both counts, the flow of funds to primary producing colonies fell. The Scots' other favourite locus for investment, the United States, turned perma-

484   THE SCOTTISH EMPIRE

nently into a creditor country. Altogether their portfolio probably ceased to be so profitable, which may have worsened the dislocation at home. Yet international capital mechanisms remained in working order and constant use. There was even an effort to enlarge them. In 1918 the British Linen Bank and the Union Bank shook off the long lethargy induced in their industry by the Act of 1845 to promote a scheme for a Scottish Foreign Exchange Bank, to be owned jointly by all the banks. Others could not rouse themselves, and the idea flopped. The reward was that in subsequent crises the banks which did do international business, all in London, were now 'better informed on conditions in Latin America than in Scotland'. On the other hand investment trusts resumed expansion on rising markets in the 1920s. By the end of the decade, 47 new ones had been formed, making 73 altogether. They may have attracted mainly Scots investors even now: for example, of the ordinary stock of the Alliance Trust, only about one-quarter was held outside Scotland. But the small individual holdings of earlier times gave way to big institutional ones.

Outflows in the nineteenth century took place alongside stupendous demand for capital at home: there was evidently more than enough to invest. Now that the tables had turned, Scotland found herself the one starved of funds. Investors espoused an attitude which was perhaps always implicit, but which in better times they had never had to articulate. Trusts, for instance, defined their responsibility as being strictly to their own shareholders rather than to some wider group of companies or industries; they recognised, that is to say, no public interest of a Scottish or any other kind. It was seldom spelled out at the time, but by 1955 we find a manager stating that

> faced with two investment opportunities, one of which is in Scotland and the other not even in North America but in England, [he] will disregard all considerations of patriotism or nationalism and will select whichever is in his opinion a better proposition from the point of view of a stockholder with a completely mercenary outlook.

While he did concede the need for higher investment in Scotland, he held that, if it had to be financed on a non-commercial basis, it must come from the Government.[7]

There we see how in the twentieth century Scottish capital abandoned Scotland, in the sense of leaving a country where it was not in surplus. There can hardly have been any technical impediment to deploying it at home: institutions integrated into financial systems at least British, often imperial and latterly global, could invest efficiently anywhere. If sentiment had counted, it probably would have worked in favour of Scotland. Yet the manager's arguments show that it did not. What counted for him were the inadequate domestic returns on capital. The theoretical answer would have been a drop in the price of labour, and so in living standards, even more drastic than the one that occurred. It was no surprise that Scots preferred intervention by the state.

Such intervention thus became respectable as it had not been for a century. Once Scotland's ability and will to get on without it flagged, she could not regain her former place at the forefront of capitalism and she dropped out of its development. At any rate she missed the benefits of a major secular change in its morphology, away from the Victorian era's individual buccaneering towards greater formality and scale of organisation. This had started in the United States, then spread to England and some European countries, and has culminated today in the dominance of the global economy by multinational companies. They take many forms, but the most advanced and dynamic have often become altogether impersonal, in the sense of not being tied down in any respect to particular owners, workers, operations, products or countries. Instead they appear free to evolve in every mode capable of sustaining their existence in an almost spontaneous fashion. Scotland has scarcely any based on her own soil. It may be misleading to conclude that this is a function of her size. Small countries elsewhere have not only generated multinationals but also kept them as sources of domestic employment and income: Holland houses Philips, Shell and Unilever, Sweden houses Electrolux, Saab and Volvo, Switzerland houses Nestlé and Roche.

Scots had often been able to bear home the benefits of their economic skills, especially of high mobility. If they no longer could, one reason was this failure to adapt to new demands of scale. True, cosy old partnerships did, with official approval for concentration, yield more readily to modern combines. The prime example was Distillers Company, which through such means grew 30 times in 30 years, but by definition Distillers had to remain a domestic producer. For the rest it was too much. In the notorious instance of British Dynamite or Nobel, already cited, imperial operation apparently required headquarters to be moved from Glasgow to London. In shipping, to which Scots had made a vast contribution, the lines suffered worse than ever from the trade cycle and foreign competition. The outcome of a welter of rationalisation, liquidation and amalgamation was that Scotland, and so Glasgow in particular, ceased to be a major centre of shipping. A general effect was for dominant shareholding interests to become interlocked still more densely. We cannot be sure that on this account momentum faltered. But certainly native enterprise was eclipsed in an economy less flexible and responsive than of old. Without its former robust independence, industry cartelised and fossilised itself, offering little competition to new manufacturing in the South of England. Local ownership and control were then bound to go sooner or later. The ensemble, beyond the usual cyclical or generational changes, spelled doom for the Scottish way of doing business.[8]

Even where problems of scale could be met, the results might otherwise give little comfort. The textile business of Coats had been founded and run over several generations by a family whose successive heads were the very wealthiest Victorian Scots, largely responsible to boot for the existence of modern Paisley. Their sector always remained difficult, yet they never let themselves be held back by a small domestic market. They began expansion overseas in the 1860s, and half a century later theirs was one of the world's largest companies, certainly the largest in the

United Kingdom. Between the wars it grew little, however, and kept afloat by avoiding dependence on British or American markets while moving to fresh fields, mainly in Asia. Relatively it lost ground and slid down the multinational scale, until in 1960 its capital structure was overhauled by merger with a rival to form Coats Patons. Since then it has again joined the ranks of the advanced multinationals, making one-fifth of all the thread sold in the world, among other things. In practice still run by Scots, and keeping its headquarters in Glasgow, the local employment it offers is yet tiny compared to that in the 30 developing countries where it has set up and where it earns 80 per cent of its profits. The chairman said in 1981: 'We follow growth. Our investment will inevitably be foreign, and our rationalisation will inevitably be in the EEC'.[9]

On the more general corporate pattern, Scots roots withered away entirely. In 1918 one of the world's great tycoons, certainly the greatest in Scotland, was Inchcape, born James Mackay of Arbroath. His power rested on the grandest of shipping lines, Peninsular & Orient. If often run by Scotsmen, it had always been based in London, forming there part of the imperial establishment, complaisant to the state in return for favours received. This hardly fostered a competitive spirit, and Inchcape had had to rescue it through a takeover by his own British India Steam Navigation Company in 1914. The combine, still bearing the name of P & O, bolstered its position during the war, not least through Inchcape's own public service in the vital organisation of shipping to and from the British Isles. Like other lines, it suffered heavy losses, but also made enormous profits. Amid the industry's upheavals after the peace, Inchcape was able to expand again through acquisition. By the same token, however, he suffered a loss of financial security. He succeeded in limiting his debts, to his own satisfaction at least. It helped that he was a director of the Bank of England, of the Royal Bank of Scotland and, ever since 1893, of the Chartered Bank. These links proved vital as the problems of other subsidiaries grew. In the course of repeated restructuring Inchcape set up a P & O Banking Corporation. This was acquired by the Chartered Bank in 1927. Since it controlled the finances of the whole group, the move could just as well have been called a fresh takeover of P & O. At any rate, it let Inchcape maintain dividends, ignore deep problems and keep things going in the old way till his death in 1932. His son, the 2nd Lord Inchcape, and son-in-law, Alexander Shaw, Lord Craigmyle, then had to exert themselves to the utmost to keep afloat, and one price was that P & O otherwise ceased to be a Scottish company. Once they were gone, the English took charge.[10]

Inchcape produced the same effect elsewhere. He liked to spend his last years controlling his conglomerate from his estate of Glenapp in Ayrshire. Yet he had come to belong not really to Scotland, nor perhaps even to the City of London, but rather to Westminster and Whitehall, where business and government now interpenetrated. If he was scathing about politicians who meddled with him, he never balked at meddling with them. In time it seemed less bothersome to him to immerse himself in public affairs than to give his attention to the businesses of his own that might have benefited from it. He sat on many official bodies, advised the British Government on international economic relations and became a trusted, pivotal figure. He might have aspired yet higher. In 1921 he had the crown of Albania in his grasp, though that political temptation he did resist: it would fall to his heir to make the family's blood blue by marrying a daughter of the Rajah of Sarawak. The Albanian diversion was suggested to him so that Britain might win concessions for oilfields supposed to lie under the Tyrrhenian Sea. Here lay its link with the biggest national problem that he did solve.[11]

The Empire needed oil, for modern shipping, above all for the Royal Navy, and for new industries. But it controlled few supplies of its own. Before the war, global production had amounted to 50 million tons, of which 65 per cent came from the United States and just 2 per cent from British territory, most from Burma, followed by Scotland (from the shale of West Lothian), Canada and Sarawak. The great hope was the Middle East, where the Glasgow enterprise, Burmah Oil, had made a strike on the shores of the Persian Gulf. The Shah insisted on having a separate corporation formed to exploit his country's resources. In 1911 the Anglo-Persian Oil Company was set up. It might better have been dubbed Scoto-Persian, at least till the British Government acquired a big stake in it during the First World War. Half its early directors came supplied by Burmah, while its inaugural chairman was Lord Strathcona, formerly Donald Smith of the Hudson's Bay Company. Inchcape succeeded him in 1914. He was already battening on the Ottoman Government for concessions in these parts. He could dispense with such niceties once the British occupied Mesopotamia in 1917. Amid moves which made him economic overlord of the territory, he enlisted the state's help to transform Anglo-Persian into British Petroleum. Despite the change of name, the state nearly always used its resulting patronage to prefer Englishmen as directors.

While BP thus set a course towards multinational status, its Scottish parent drifted. Burmah had an energetic managing director, Robert Watson, who set out to extend its commercial networks. He thought official pressure might bring BP into some further connection with the partly Dutch company of Shell, to produce a corporation big enough to compete with the Americans. His promptings fell on deaf ears in Whitehall. With his taste for combination and merger whetted, however, he indulged it so far that Burmah lost almost all operational independence and became mainly a vehicle for investment. It was nominally run by Glaswegians such as Campbell Finlay, bearer of a famous mercantile name, and John Cargill, son of the founder, already elderly in the 1920s but with two decades of chairmanship still before him. A pillar of his city, he sought no influence beyond it, resting content with the presence of family and friends round him on the board, where they could enjoy themselves at full-dress occasions such as the annual general meeting. The business they conducted seldom rose above the routine. From his base in London, Watson informed them of some, if by no means all, of his decisions. Though he often spoke of his beloved Scotland, he left an Englishman in charge of the company when he died in 1947. At this juncture its official history notes the 'weakness that not all functions were even yet housed in London'.[12]

Burmah did later reassert some independence by diversifying. It hoped in 1963 to enter a new era, marked by final withdrawal from the now independent republic of Burma, and turning instead to the North Sea. There it helped to form a group for exploration which discovered the first crude oil in 1966. It was stopped in its tracks, however, by crisis in the Middle East, by war between Israel and the Arabs and by a quadrupling of the price of oil in 1973. The new era ended. Burmah had to be rescued by the Bank of England at the cost of selling its stake in BP, with other assets, £900 million in all. It survived, eventually as quite a strong and compact group for the international manufacture, marketing and transport of specialised products. But at that moment of truth, it had severed its last links with its Glaswegian origins, and seen nipped in the bud any chance of becoming an integrated company for exploitation of the North Sea. Scots have remained unrepresented in oil, the biggest natural resource discovered in their country during the twentieth century, except on a small scale in consortia. Had things gone otherwise after the First World War they might, through Burmah, have been there among the Seven Sisters now dominating the industry they originally founded.[13]

Nearly all the companies which made Scotland an economic power a century ago have declined in one way or another, and many have indeed died. Of the old commercial Empire only a few outposts remain, such as James Finlay and Jardine Matheson. The meagre remainder, if often showing high proportions of Scottish shareholders, keep little more than registration in their country of origin. Where there is growth, it tends to take place somewhere else. Nor has there been much fresh formation outside the thinned ranks of the Victorian corporate legacy. Instead, vigour is injected through foreign investment lured by subsidy. Scotland, once the thrusting junior partner in the general business of Anglo-Scottish imperialism, is today rather a colony of new economic empires.

At home meanwhile, it has been received wisdom that the state must run the economy ever since Labour took office in 1945. This Government saw the key in nationalisation. But in Scotland, as Walter Elliot remarked, 'nationalisation means denationalisation'. There duly followed an attrition of remaining large Scottish enterprise, as control of companies passing into public ownership was vested not in the people but in Whitehall. A late burst of relative prosperity for the heavy industries failed to bring about decisive recovery from decades of the doldrums. Subsidy did not help either, to improve efficiency, to give workers a high standard of living or even to save their jobs in the end. Scotland failed to catch up again with England, while seeing former markets in the Empire vanish and losing too often in competition with international rivals who reappeared. Not till the 1980s were the frontiers of the state rolled back somewhat. The economy did then regain a certain impetus, steadily marking up higher growth than England's, not least through the contribution of two industries, oil and finance, depending not at all on largesse from the state. But Thatcherite reforms were also held up at the Border. For example Scotland kept a public agency charged with economic development, especially by enticing foreign multinationals, right through to the advent of New Labour in 1997.[14]

Even so, not all has been lost. As multinational business emerged, Scots helped to set its standards on the principles of political economy and in the structures of commerce and finance. Some citadels of global capitalism – Montreal, Hong Kong, Calcutta, Singapore – owe their existence largely to Scots, who have seldom been absent from any of the others either. Vigorous Scottish networking forged links among them all, a practice imitated by later diasporas like the Asian ones. Combining a cosmopolitan acceptance of change with durable values and sense of community, these diasporas may be able to moderate the potential extremes of creative destruction in capitalism and produce for all peoples a happier outcome than is often forecast. If most Scots preferred to turn at mid-century into the dead end of dependency, the outward movement of others from the narrow homeland never ceased. It preceded globalisation and is probably quickening again now. It could recreate opportunities missed meanwhile. Some diasporas, of the Jews, Chinese, Indians, Irish or Armenians, spring from violence and issue in trauma. Yet others, like the Scottish one, have by and large been voluntary. This diaspora belongs to the history of a people who have always been inventive, energetic, adaptable and mobile. Revived, those qualities would bode well for Scotland in the new millennium.

CHAPTER THIRTY-EIGHT

'Not solely Scottish': The End of Empire

In the darkness before dawn on July 3, 1967, the Argyll and Sutherland Highlanders under the command of Lieutenant-Colonel Colin Mitchell advanced behind their pipers into the town of Crater in the Crown colony of Aden. Expecting stiff resistance, in the event they exchanged just a few shots with Arab snipers and killed but a single one of them. Their mere appearance sufficed to restore law and order where anarchy had been reigning. As the sun rose, the Scots wakened the locals with a ceremonial reveille. One celebrant of this deed called it 'an act of redemption'. Britain's dominion in the Middle East was about to end and long past counting for much anyway. The previous month she had exerted no influence on events during the Six-Day War between Israel and neighbouring countries. Even here, on sovereign territory, she was scarcely able to contain the whirlwind of nationalist revolution or determine what would come afterwards. It could have been a shameful finale without that show of strength by the Argylls.

They had arrived a fortnight before, walking straight into a mutiny of the native army and police who were supposed to be taking over security from British forces. Three Scots soldiers at once died in an ambush. This enraged the 43–year-old Mitchell, anyway contemptuous of the authorities for their patent failures in the last sector of a territory they were meant to be ruling. The insurgents' impudence portended humiliation unless he took matters in hand. It was as much as anything to save his men's morale that on his own initiative he marched them into Crater, only afterwards letting the world know through a dramatic announcement by himself. From then on he became Mad Mitch, and his Argylls in their turn lived up to his reputation: 'The Adenis realised that we were different from any British troops they had seen in our methods and behaviour; my rumour soon spread that we were wild Beduin tribesmen from the Scottish Highlands who could get very rough indeed if provoked'. An outcry arose over certain incidents: the shooting of three suspects just as they sought sanctuary in a mosque, the killings carried out in apparent revenge for a grenade thrown at Mitchell. They brought down reproaches from other British officers or officials: 'One rather moth-eaten person from the High Commission had the impertinence to refer to my Jocks as "Glasgow thugs",' Mitchell recalled. 'I told him that "poor white trash" such as he should be careful where he used such words in Crater'.

If the town remained tense, Mitchell proved to his own satisfaction that the Arabs would respect firmness. What he had done was direct the last of the classic imperial police actions, an exercise in restoring order rather than imposing occupation, always congenial to Scots. He still made no difference in the end. The Government in London wanted to get out as fast as possible. It had had enough of Aden, one of those awkward imperial outposts where traditional chieftains lay under a loose protectorate in territory which here stretched up 600 miles from the colony on the coast. In its teeming streets nationalism seethed, and the faint hope was to restrain it by forming a federation of the town and the tribes, weighted by the departing British in favour of the latter. Two organisations set out to thwart them: the Front for the Liberation of South Yemen enjoying the support of President Nasser of Egypt, and the National Liberation Front which found favour with the royal house of Saud. By 1967 both were mounting attacks in the hinterland and in Aden itself, where they also shot it out between themselves. The issue was actually to be settled by their sponsors, who reconciled themselves in the wake of the Six-Day War. The Saudis exacted the sacrifice of FLOSY, which the Egyptians abandoned.

With the internal dispute thus resolved after a fashion, the Foreign Secretary, George Brown, blandly announced in July that the territory needed no more protection, only a bit of aid at most, and could move to independence within five months. He finalised the details at a conference hastily convened in Geneva with Aden's new masters-in-waiting. The British withdrew into the port, leaving native authorities to cope as best they could – which was not at all. Complete breakdown threatened when the federal army, created to guard the hapless amirs, understandably threw in its lot with the NLF. This was the point at which the Argylls arrived. Their coup in Crater did no more than maintain the timetable for evacuation and removal of the base which Britain had established here 128 years ago. The perimeter was gradually drawn in till it ringed only the barracks and airfield. The High Commissioner left with the rearguard on November 29, flown out by helicopter to a naval taskforce assembled in the harbour. The triumphant nationalists moved in. Colonial rule ended. The British presence east of Suez all but vanished.[1]

Yet Scots felt proud. A tangible result was salvation of the Argylls as an independent regiment. Back home, Mitchell lost no chance to recall that they faced the loss of their identity in a reorganisation of the army. Protests waxed so fierce that the Government gave way. For the colonel this was the prelude to a brief career as Conservative MP for West Aberdeenshire, which returned him at the General Election of 1970. But he never felt at home in the House of Commons and did not fight the seat again. The real political ramifications lay elsewhere. During that last month of British rule in Aden, on November 2, 1967, Mrs Winifred Ewing, the Nationalist candidate, had won the by-election at Hamilton, beating Labour in its safest Scottish constituency. Though the conjunction has been little remarked, it gave evidence of a turning point in the history of Scotland.

The history of Scotland, however, is today a field contested among schools of thought diverse even by the standards of the Caledonian antisyzygy – the principle that, whatever may be asserted of the Scots, the opposite may be asserted with equal force and truth. It is not the sole reason that the recent revival in Scottish historiography has so far failed to offer a convincing account of why this small country on the edge of Europe, once apparently content with steady assimilation to the wider entities of Union and Empire, should instead have begun to re-emerge as a nation in its own right and to advance into a future which, to say the least, remains open. Most western countries can be reasonably sure that, even while times move on, they will in 10 or 20 years look much as they do now. Scots have no idea how their country will look by then, the potential extremes ranging from dingy province to harebrained republic (though several more pleasant possibilities lie in between). So nobody knows what the end of the history of Scotland is going to be and, depending on the outcome, future historians will have to pick out from our past and present quite different features as possessed of the greatest significance.

Yet many recent works of Scottish history continue to assume explicitly or implicitly that assimilation, into the Union if no longer into the Empire, is a norm, representing a true history of Scotland. The bias arises from the largely social and economic nature of the historiography. It produces a literature inevitably showing the history of Scotland to be a mere variant on the greater history of Britain, because that is what the social and economic history of Scotland has in fact been. The literature then goes to show not how Scotland is different, but how Scotland is the same as somewhere else – an unhelpful result when she finds herself in the throes of a unique development. It may reasonably be concluded that what makes Scotland Scotland is not to be found in her social and economic history.

The unique development of the present day is pre-eminently political, with the rise of Nationalism and the restoration of the Scottish Parliament. Still, admission of that fact does not necessarily take us much further, since its causes remain obscure to political science as practised in Britain since 1945. This has assumed the electoral context of its birth to be a constant and so has worked on a theory of British uniformity. In such light the development of Scotland cannot be unique, but is at most a special case of the general evolution in a reforming modern state or perhaps of a wider move towards regionalism in Europe. The theory of political uniformity then still obtains, with Scotland again a mere variant on a greater defining framework. In other words, even from such political science there is little to be learned about what makes Scotland Scotland.

Yet Scottish nationhood is older and bigger than any party or constitutional arrangement. It is, at its simplest and grandest, what links the Scots' past and present. After 1707 it was without political form and the Scots soon ceased to miss that. But it maintained itself in the cultural autonomy they desired. How and how far they have preserved this cultural autonomy are the most interesting questions about the modern nation. It is true that the culture, if institutionally guaranteed by the Treaty of Union, and if capable of sustaining a high degree of integrity for over a century afterwards, has since grown more fragmented and enfeebled. Still, it is hard to think of another label than cultural autonomy that can reasonably be put on the differences from the English which Scots today see in themselves and use to justify their political autonomy. Scholars have hardly begun to explore such links between Scotland's culture and politics, though analogous ones were the basis of classical historiography in Britain, as in other European countries.

One aim here has been to explore those links in a particular aspect, broad though not, of course, complete in itself. Indeed I have drawn my bounds more narrowly than previous histories of the Scots beyond Scotland, which are in general organised on the theme of diaspora. For my purposes this was too diffuse, giving scope for not much more than *res gestae* of notable Scots almost in the uncritical tradition of Victorian biography. The theme of Scottish Empire, however, can be at once cultural and political: it comprises both the Scots' encounter with the diversity of cultures among mankind and the continual reflection this prompted on their own place in the world. In that case the imperial experience must surely have counted towards their cultural and political uniqueness, towards making Scotland Scotland. It sets the nation apart from mere regions, while bringing to light parallels with the history of other small nations. It sets the Scots apart also from the English, though much imperial experience was apparently common to both. And it has represented a particular kind of fulfilment of Scotland, even if that fulfilment proved, in the light of history, impermanent. As the rule is for Scotland to feel unfulfilled, this exception to it should not be forgotten. What do they know of Scotland who only Scotland know?

England celebrated the high noon of Empire round the turn of the twentieth century with a dithyrambic triumphalism which would echo yet amid the lengthening shadows after 1918. English elites then still set blithely about preserving to posterity an official view of their own genius and power, for example, with the narratives developed in volume after volume of imperial historical series churned out at the ancient English universities – often giving Scotland less notice than, say, Newfoundland. Unluckily for the authors, the series took so long to write that the sun set on the Empire before they could be finished. One reason for its eclipse was that it had anyway never been, in any sense those works implied, a monolith. It existed in many forms which looked different according to the origin, status and activity of the individual or collective spectators. The surprise would be if the Scots had not found there some self-expression to match their formidable self-consciousness.

To be sure Scotland was, like any small nation, never fully master of her destiny. At times she did risk becoming an object of imperialism. In 1707 she had entered an expanding imperial system in the hope of prompting large changes at home, even while she sought in the Treaty to set limits to them. This English Empire had already emerged as an Empire of conquest, occupation and settlement, thus not one specially suiting Scots. With no great surplus of people they were slow to emigrate, and could neither conquer nor occupy nor settle. Besides, the lands where that happened, notably America and Ireland, set uncongenial examples. For some time ahead they occasionally put the English in a mind to reduce Scotland to the same condition, whatever was said in the Treaty. America at length brusquely solved the problem by casting off colonial status, while Ireland moved in the opposite direction towards complete dependency.

Neither fate awaited Scotland. If no longer independent, she did not lose all ability to shape her own fate. Unity never meant uniformity and there was seldom any risk of her just succumbing to metropolitan power. Despite England's greater wealth and the obvious dominance of London, Scotland avoided debasement to a colonial or arguably even a provincial level, since colonies or provinces seldom have cultures complete with laws, religion, learning and ethos outshining at times anything in the metropolis. This culture not only survived the Union but also found in itself a capacity for spectacular renewal. By origin Calvinist, it had always shown more interest in general principle than in particularist identity, in social science than in ethnic uniqueness, in humanity than in nationality, though such interests had usually remained secondary or latent in a small, narrow Scotland. In a new Scotland of broad horizons they attained a cosmopolitan universalism, drawn from many sources yet legislating for all.[2]

Of its power there could be no better proof than the Scots' ability to start changing somewhat the Empire they had entered, faster after the incubus of the American colonies was removed from it. That brought to an end the first Empire, still basically English. The second Empire proved much more congenial to Scots. It was an Empire no longer of the land, of conquest, occupation and settlement, of exclusion and privilege, rather of the sea, of temperance and tolerance, of transience and trading posts, of freedom of movement. It beckoned Scots to exotic climes where they did their business and left, content that they had achieved what they could, for they knew commerce to be the vehicle of progress. In a sense it turned out that the great advantage of the Union was to make more Dariens possible, now successful because of English co-operation.

Cosmopolitan universalism informed in particular the narrative of humanity constructed by Scottish philosophers, using among others the materials furnished by a truly British Empire. In the narrative, imperialism figured conspicuously. It had, after all, recurred throughout history and was legible in the record of nearly every nation having a history. Over millennia empires rose and fell, most leaving just ruins behind. But now had come something new: the extension of empire to distant continents as Europeans embarked on a great adventure which would alter every facet of human society. For David Hume it was 'really the commencement of modern history', and for William Robertson the point 'when Providence decreed that men were to pass the limits within which they had been so long confined, and open themselves to a more ample field wherein to display their talents, their enterprise and their courage'. Europeans conquered not necessarily because they were more advanced but rather because they introduced novel values subversive of older cultures and of their peoples' allegiance to them. Among those values, self-conscious liberty proved to be the most important.[3]

From this the Scots learned large lessons. For example, they found that traditional societies remained nevertheless resilient, whether in their dotage, as in the Orient, or yet to advance to higher stages of civilisation, as in Africa. The non-western world was not in the end just to be westernised, but to work towards a more eclectic amalgam. So the philosophers began to seek out from myriads of contingent facts the most significant in the slow working of time, whether arisen out of nature and unamenable to human design, or out of human action with its traces in monuments, muniments and survivals from earlier stages. The apparent proof on every hand of the principles of conjectural history vindicated also the cautionary aspect of the philosophy, its sense of how complex and precarious progress could be, given the law of unintended consequence. That affirmed Scots' wariness of altering exotic societies on a rigid model. They rather grew skilled at comparative application of their native principles: studying and understanding those societies, Scots could help them to study and understand themselves, to find their place in a universal scheme. Colonies, too, must go their own way rather than replicate the mother country. Scots were too few to determine the course of the second Empire, which yielded at length to another phase of conquest, occupation and settlement, with less benign faces of institutional uniformity, extractive exploitation and enmity to nationalism. But Scots could exert an influence, or at the least prove to their own satisfaction the philosophical point that there remained something irreducible in the diversity of cultures among mankind.[4]

This, after all, Scots not only wrote but lived. Their narrative of humanity included the history of themselves. It even seemed to them exemplary because its stages had accelerated, propelling them in little more than a generation from burning witches to building the New Town of Edinburgh. The material could in its turn be used comparatively to endow the two members of the Union with a common history, though one which often showed Scotland to disadvantage. In practice Scots, too, suffered encroachments by a British imperial state setting its bounds wider still and wider. Sometimes in manifest breach of the articles of Union, it subverted central elements of Scottishness and locked others tartan-clad into the kailyard. Before long the industrial revolution was transforming Scotland as well, obliterating old ways of life and creating new ones hard to distinguish from those of England. There followed George Davie's 'failure of nerve', feelings of inferiority and fears that Scottish society had to be recast on English, at any rate British, models. To some Scots it appeared as if their nation was being overwhelmed by modernity, that their history had ended and that they could at best recollect it elegiacally.[5]

But to others such integration meant more than English hegemony. It was what beckoned them to meet their destiny by going forwards, not looking backwards, into a future that lay with empires rather than mere nations. They made the most of the choice. The classic age of heroic regiments, skirling pipes and bold tartans reconstituted the identity of a country loving nothing so much as its own divisions. Right at the end of Empire it remained strong enough to move Mad Mitch: 'Our patriotism was not solely Scottish. We felt immense pride in the British Empire and believed with a self-confidence that was almost Roman that it was entirely right that the British should rule a large part of the world'.[6]

Symbols for yet another new Scotland were required, and this time Scots chose the sword rather than the pen. To spur them towards the imperial future, they summoned up a martial tradition which stretched back into time immemorial. In the old days they had happily filled with fighting one another the rare interludes free of a need for desperate defence of the homeland. After 1707 the former was undesirable, the latter unnecessary, yet in tandem they turned out to have been a school of virtue, taming the undoubted darker side of the national character and training it to the higher challenges of combat without the baser temptations of conquest. The philosophers could then demonstrate why the poor, backward partner in the Union was a better defender of Empire and generally of British freedom than an England corrupted by luxury. An honourable profession of arms built itself into the identity: by the nineteenth century, missionaries were carrying rifles too. It offered just the most vivid example of Scotland's past merging with Britain's present. The urge in a small country to act like a big country was not always a pretty sight, but at this imperial moment it seemed to itself to be realising its hopes and dreams in everything from high theory to gaudy popular culture. The ensemble flourished at all levels across the country, in the Highlands yet more than in the Lowlands, an inspiration as much for the elite, to civic duty and social responsibility, as for the man in the street, to work, sport and war.[7]

So it is odd of historians to conclude that Scotland suffered a lack of Nationalism during her prolonged Victorian orgy of self-esteem. To give a different example of present relevance, it was then that the question of Scottish self-government first came on the British political agenda, with constitutional ideas to meet the needs of an imperial state bearing a remarkable resemblance to ideas today to meet the needs of a post-imperial state: the constant lies in the espousal of a higher good where Scots will play a bigger part. To be sure, Scottish Nationalism in that era hardly measured up as a movement to its contemporary counterparts in Europe. But there, too, patriotic sentiment often found a cultural rather than political outlet. Only the most heroic subject peoples revolted against hegemony before their chance came with the collapse of the old order in 1918. That was unpredictable, so Scots cannot have been exceptional or perverse to rest content with an assertion of nationhood on the cultural plane, where they anyway remained most autonomous. If translated from culture into politics, it often emerged as imperialism. And Scots believed they possessed better ideas about Empire than the English, who notoriously had acquired it in a fit of absence of mind. An idea about Empire, a modern evolution of the kind sought by all progressive Scotsmen, was how pioneers of Home Rule conceived of their project. So Scottish Nationalism grew up compatible with Empire.[8]

Even when, after the imperial apogee had passed, Scottish Nationalism assumed more diverse forms, still the leaders saw little future for Scotland outside the Empire.

But there did come a reaction, reaching an extreme in Hugh MacDiarmid's 'bitter realisation that the subjugation of Scotland was the completest triumph of British imperialism'. As Empire failed to take the shape Scots had envisaged, they began to suspect that their sacrifice of the nation to it was really just a sacrifice to England, after all. By the time of Mad Mitch and Winnie Ewing the reaction chimed in with a general recoil among western peoples against their history of discovery and expansion, expressed in post-colonial theory and a burgeoning literature on the Third World. There was a reception in Scotland not wholly derisive for Americans who came over to apply a notion of internal colonialism in a country they supposed to be as subject to England as theirs had been before 1776. Australians pondering Scotland from afar felt by contrast able, though they placed themselves among the oppressed, to place Scots as firmly among the oppressors: 'While it is possible to argue that [Scots, Welsh and Irish] societies were the first victims of English expansion, their subsequent complicity in the British imperial enterprise makes it difficult for colonised peoples outside Britain to accept their identity as post-colonial'.[9]

That thought no doubt went down especially well with the Irish, but it also discomfited Scots starting to stress the egalitarianism and democracy which set them apart from a patently imperial people like the English. If few native intellectuals could honestly bring themselves to think of Scotland as colonial, they preferred not to think of her as complicit either. What clarified matters was the stubborn refusal of the British imperial state to pass away with Empire. If anything it continued to overreach itself with too many commitments, not least those to Scots. At any rate, right up to the end of unionist Scotland in 1997 Margaret Thatcher and John Major continued to exert their authority over a Scottish electorate which time and again refused them a mandate.[10]

The British imperial state thus ceased to be compatible with Scottish Nationalism. Today we have, at least for the time being, a compromise which casts off the obsolete pretensions of the first without admitting the further claims of the second. It remains to be seen how stable devolved Scotland will prove. But it is England that has in the first instance encountered the greater problems in adjusting to this, as to a more ample continuum of novel and unwelcome realities. Enoch Powell, a modern English seer, said of Empire: 'The nationhood of the mother country remained unaltered through it all, almost unconscious of the strange fantastic structure built around her. The continuity of her existence was unbroken when the lesser connections which had linked her with distant continents and strange races fell away'. Perhaps so, but England now shows an unmistakable sense of injury to national self-esteem and a certain sullying of national ethos. Once noted for tolerance, the English today resent former subject peoples. When these immigrate, they may be confined in an underclass suffering discrimination and even violence which make of race a perennial presence in politics. The symptoms surely betray a frustrated nationalism, vented in tempered form on Europeans too.[11]

Little of this exists in Scotland, and it is tempting to posit a link between her relative serenity and the happier evolution she is undergoing. A cynical idea persists that Scots exchanged national independence for imperial profit 300 years ago and now, seeing no more profit in prospect, promptly reverse their loyalties. It would be kinder to say that their status as junior partners has let them salvage some self-respect from an enterprise which served them well but leaves them with no illusions about the fact and consequences of its end. In any event, Scotland can never be all that content with the ambiguities of her existence, which generate another kind of insecurity below any superficial composure.[12]

For example, nobody could sensibly claim that Scotland had been other than transformed beyond recognition by Empire. We see it everywhere from the empty glens of Sutherland to the silent shipyards of the River Clyde, or in the very expanse of the great cosmopolis of the West as in the commercial palaces of the capital. There never was in Powell's sense an unbroken continuity of existence here. Perhaps the essence of Scotland's nationhood lies in a history of somehow surviving against the odds, despite horrendous losses. Quite what survives may not be, indeed seldom is, tangible – not this thing or that thing, not this glen or that shipyard. Rather it is metaphysical and protean, a Caledonian antisyzygy, an interplay of opposites, perhaps captured only in hopes and dreams. So with the Empire: Scotland, neither fully nation nor fully province but both, was also neither fully coloniser nor fully colonised but both, yet at the end vindicated herself by rising anew from amid the desecration of just about every altar in her hallowed precincts. In that light Empire is to be seen not as deviant or accessory but as integral to her history. We must regard it, with Reformation, Union and Enlightenment, as one of the great formative experiences of a nation now facing a fresh future.[13]

There is in it one redeeming feature which may even have rendered Empire the most formative of all those experiences. It has in a way made again of Scottish history, for the first time since the eighteenth century, something exemplary. The expansion of Europe generated today's universal culture in which people, goods, money, fashions, ideas and creeds submerge frontiers and erode the distinct marks of nations, even of civilisations – even of the original European civilisation, now recolonised from America. The mechanisms of all this remain somewhat mysterious, as military might or political power cannot fully account for it. When the formal empires ended in the late twentieth century, the floodgates of the larger movement had hardly opened, while the torrent has swollen only since the imperial flags were finally lowered. But if anything has earned the accolade of revolution, once so glibly claimed for more militant doctrines, it is this. In it, however, no iron law defines imperial or subject races. It generally depends on the abilities of a few whether at any given time the many belong to the one or the other. In the end imperialism has turned out a matter of the individual and contingent rather than of the impersonal and inevitable, of the human condition rather than of laws of history. Historical stages succeed one another but nations, or even persons such as politicians and philosophers, have been able to affect encounters at different levels and turn them towards exchange rather than hegemony, in a pluralist (or in political terms a federal) kind of relationship. For themselves and others, Scots at least strove to make it so.[14]

The central dilemma of our age, of how to sustain community amid globalism, Scots have faced since 1707 – and, we may say today, not without success. Historical, political and economic conditions always made strangely intangible Scotland's sense of herself, compelling her people to search elsewhere for promises of fulfilment: her patriotism was never solely Scottish. But now, enriched, the Scots can bring it all back to redirect their hopes and dreams in a way which may once again be of some consequence also to humanity. From the great adventure – more than they were before and surely never again content to be less – the Scots come home.

Notes

INTRODUCTION (pp.1–3)

1. Agricola, Ch.x.
2. Gathorne-Hardy (1921), 25, 40, 57, 271.
3. Quoted, Dickinson, Donaldson & Milne (1952), 1, 153.

1. 'THE SPECIAL FRIENDSHIP': IRELAND (pp.7–18)

1. Mac Iomhair (1967), 194–204.
2. Lydon (1987), 293–4; (1992), 2.
3. Otway-Ruthven (1968), 224–30; Barrow (1988), 316.
4. Barrow, 314; Otway-Ruthven, 224; Freeman (1944), 249; Edwards (1972), 44.
5. Otway-Ruthven, *loc.cit*; Hill (1873), 35–7, 52; (1877), 73; Dunlop (1925), 51, 212; Curtis (1936), 175; Hayes-McCoy (1937), 5; Perceval-Maxwell (1973), 12; Stevenson, (1981), 1.
6. Perceval-Maxwell, 71, 184, 310; Woodburn (1914), 57; Crawford (1983), 57; Levack (1987), 2.
7. Woodburn, 93; Stevenson, 11; Stewart (1907), 26, 39; Beckett (1972), 30–1; Byrne, Martin & Moody (1976), 267–8; Gillespie (1985), 33, 143.
8. Stewart, 40; Woodburn, 102; Beckett, 40; Stevenson, 100–265.
9. Byrne, Martin & Moody, xliii.
10. Stewart, 59; Edwards, 118.
11. Stewart, 66–75; Beckett, 35–9; Byrne, Martin & Moody, 437; Stevenson, 245.
12. Stewart, 75, 91, 103; Woodburn, 172; Beckett, 40; Moody & Vaughan (1986), 23; Canny (1991), 65–6.
13. Stewart, 106–15; Woodburn, 206; Beckett (1948), 99; Elliot (1982), 20; Crawford (1983), 67; Moody & Vaughan, lii, 99, 441.
14. Beckett, 14, 144.
15. Woodburn, 212–24; Ford (1915), 165.
16. Stewart, 123; Woodburn, 236, 247; Perceval-Maxwell, 316; Elliot, 20; Browning (1886), 308; Fry (1992b), 63–4.
17. Stewart, 129; Woodburn, 250–72; Fry, 235–9; Brown (1999), 10.

2. 'THE KEY OF THE UNIVERSE': DARIEN (pp.19–30)

1. Keith (1909), 32, 34; Johnson (1911), 327; Insh (1922), 89–90, 100; Jackson (1995a), 49; Bielinski (1996), 6; Thór (1996), 127; Law (n.d.), 3.
2. Keith, *op.cit.*, 36–7; (1913), 690; (1930), 71–2; Anon. (1703), 11; *Acts of the Parliament, of Scotland* (1820), viii, 63; Bingham (1906), 210; Japikse (1906), 161 *et seqq*; Heckscher (1955), 103–4; Smout (1960), 208; (1968), 56; Butt & Lythe (1975), 64; Calder (1981), 129; Karras (1992), 32–3.
3. Insh (1922), 47, 59; (1928), 59; Roger (1877), 62, 107–8; Willson (1956), 331–2; Lythe (1960), 65, 70.
4. Alexander (1624), 32–5; Insh (1922), 62, 72, 74, 78, 80, 85; Laing (1867), 80; Reid (1977), 42–7; Perceval-Maxwell (1981), 14–22; Reid (1981), xiv; Griffiths & Reid (1992), 492–500.

5. Jackson (1995a), 72–5.
6. Scot (1685), 2; Insh, *op.cit.*, 237 *et seqq*; (1928a), 60; (1928b), 98 *et seqq*; (1932), 15; Donaldson (1966), 35; Riley (1978), 209; Brock (1982), 5–6; Landsman (1985), 106–10, 125.
7. Scott (1904), 175–82; (1905), xliv; Insh (1932), 25; Marshall (1992), 130–3, 271.
8. Insh, *op.cit.*, 125–8; Riley, 210; Calder, 378; Prebble (1968), 13; Furber (1976), 99 *et seqq*; Evans (1986), 84 *et seqq*; Armitage (1992), 127–8.
9. Anon. (1700a), 79; Bingham, 217; Prebble, 38; Insh, *op.cit.*, 41–60.
10. Jackson, 77.
11. Anon. (1700c), 41; Insh (1924), 9, 27, 221; (1932), 73, 86–7; Furber, 217; Armitage, 136.
12. Anon. (1699b), Chs v, vi; Ferguson (1699), *passim*; Prebble, 114 et seqq; Armitage, 140.
13. Ibid., 193 *et seqq*.
14. Ibid., 9; Furber, *loc.cit*; Anon. (1700b), 29; Byres (1702), 51; Macleod (1893), 240–5; Barbour (1907), 142; Insh (1924), ix-xvi; (1932), 33, 245–9; Graham (1992), 104.

3. 'NOBODY WISHES US WELL': THE EUROPEAN CONTEXT (pp.31–43)

1. Cullinan (1993), *passim*.
2. Diffie & Winius (1972), 46, 57, 160, 195–206, 220–8, 245, 256, 296, 332–5, 432; Bender (1978), xix; Newitt (1980), 21; Rothermund (1988), 11–12.
3. Thévet (1575), 665; Léry (1578), preface; Buchanan (1725), I, praefatio; II, 293; Southey (1810), I, 270–9; Insh (1928a), 58; Priestley (1939), 47; Biéler (1961), 174–8; McFarlane (1981), 95; Williamson (1996), 46–63, 70–83.
4. Boxer (1958), 2, 16, 32, 35; (1960), 15, 46, 65, 78–85, 95, 107–23; (1964), 49; (1979), 11; Fieldhouse (1966), 29–31; Souza (1986), 213–7; Law (n.d.), 5–17.
5. Pagden (1982), 38–40; Williamson, (1996), 22–3.
6. Hewitson (1993), 1–2; Udall (n.d.), 73–5.
7. Braudel (1972), I, 139; Hewitson (1993), 12–13; Leiper (1997), 8.
8. Vilar (1962), i, 535; iii, 445 *et seqq*; Lythe (1960), 186–8; Thomson (1989), *passim*; Dickson (1992), 135.
9. Laude, I, 23–31, 110, 217; Hertz (1907), 258–65, 269–76; Emmer (1980), 465; Lenman (1990), 59; Robertson (1997), 83–117.
10. Alexander (1624), 45; Paterson (1701), 104; Buist (1974), 4–5, 82; Lenman (1990), 100–1; (1995), 25; Enthoven (1996), 211.
11. Fieldhouse, 52, 134–9, 144; Vlekke (1946), 65–70; Geyl (1961), 163, 176–9, 186, 198; Boxer (1965), 22, 29; Gaastra & van den Boogart (1980), 175, 198–200, 211.
12. Lenman, 60; Cormack (1967–8), 38–46; *Den Svenska Historien* (1967), iv, 182, 187; vi, 158, 160–1; vii, 88–90; Lundkvist (1973), 57; Scott (1977), 192–4; Roberts (1979), 1–2, 21, 39–43, 51–5, 64–71, 101.
13. Hauch-Fausbøll (1930), 22–6; Lauring (1960), 204; Mentze (1981), 7–8, 72; Jensen *et al* (1983), 21, 147–9; Agnarsdottir (1992), 83–8.
14. Law, 17; Zenner (1720), 153–62; Henderson (1938), 1 *et seqq*; (1962), 1 *et seqq*; Laude (1944), 27; Craig (1984), 21.
15. Vlekke, 87; Geyl, 158–60, 181–2, 209–10; Boxer, 84, 92–9, 102–5, 107–13, 214, 223, 289; Emmer, 482; Rothermund, 12; Carter (1953), 339–40; Schama (1987), 230; Israel (1989), 275.
16. Boxer (1979), 3–17; Steensgaard (1981), 245–59; Young (1992), I, 54.

4. 'THE TRUE INTEREST OF A COUNTRY': THE SCOTTISH DEBATE (pp.44–56)

1. Anon. (1701), passim.
2. Becker (1950), III; Davis (1991), 3.
3. Scott (1904), 174–84.
4. Law (1705), 18, 24; (1751), 58; Burton (1864), 259, 267; Hyde (1948), 64, 53, 59, 79, 114; Scott (1992), 51–3; Pagden (1995), 118–9.

5. Donaldson (1700), 66–79; Spreul (1705), 3; Smout (1960), 211; (1963), 261; (1972), 225; Bannister (1968), I, 1, 27, 50, 61: III, 75; Ferguson (1977), 241–3; Riley (1978), 201, 210; Evans (1986), 84 *et seqq*; Levack (1987), 153; Jackson (1995a), 7 *et seqq*.

6. Perrels (1903), 82; Carstairs (1955), 65; Smout (1963), 261; Cowan (1981), 5.

7. Scott, 191; Keith (1930), 305; Smout (1963), 261; Armitage (1996), 18; Saville (1999), 6–21.

8. Sen (1957), 64; Burrell (1960), 130–7; Steuart (1966), I, 284, 296; Semmel (1970), 18; Barker (1975), 74–81, 118–23; Hutchison (1988), 348; Skinner (1993), 123; Raynor & Skinner (1994), 755.

9. Hutcheson (1755), III, 308–9; Scott (1900), 242; Robbins (1954), 214 *et seqq*; Rotwein (1955), 61, 78–9; Semmel (1970), 14; Lehmann (1971), 76; Ross (1972), 342; Paglin (1973), 90; Venning (1976), 79 *et seqq*; Coleman (1987), 8–12.

10. Fay (1934), 73.

11. Smith (1976) II, 564, 569, 571–2, 575–6, 582.

12. *Ibid.*, 584–8, 590–616, 946–7; Semmel, 24–8; Winslow (1948), 22; Koebner (1961), 219; Kittrell (1965), 48; Winch (1965), 6, 16; Weiss (1968), 33; Stevens (1975), 206; Stone (1992), 80.

13. Dalrymple (1770), xxviii-xxix; Trevelyan (1878), 207; Harlow (1952), I, 37–8; Colley (1992), 116, 131.

14. Sinclair (1790), II, 101; Corbett (1913), *passim*; Benians, Holland Rose & Newton (1940), II, 24; Cowan (1961), 14; Bumsted (1982), 79; Fry (1992a), 199, 210.

15. Semmel, 44; Brougham (1803), 7, 107–8, 148; Fetter (1957), 124; Fontana (1985), 59, 68.

16. Davie, (1961), xv; Mackenzie (1992), 17.

5. 'A NATION NO LONGER': AMERICA (pp.57–69)

1. Ferguson (1888), 55–62, 96–113; Moss (1979) 72–3, 240, 538–9.

2. Wood, 195; Bailyn & Clive (1954), 200–13; Hook (1966–7, 519 *et seqq*; (1990), *passim*; Schlenter (1976), 137 *et seqq*; Bailyn & Morgan (1991), 12–24.

3. Schlenter, 144; Wood, 240; Woods (1907), 160 et seqq; Trinterud (1949), 263; Pryde (1957), 2–29; Wright (1969), 30; Scott (1970), 205; Rouse (1971), 5, 200; Sloan (1971), 38; Daiches (1991), 164.

4. Landsman (1990), 29–40.

5. Woods, 186, 193, 210, 214; Adair (1956–7), 348; Shepperson (1977), 9; Wills (1978), 173, 182, 198, 217, 225, 237; Draper (1982), 34 *et seqq*; Turnbull (1986), 137, 143; Howe (1989), 586–7; Diamond (1990), 115; Sher (1990), 52–3; Stimson (1990), 193; Fechner (1992), *passim*; Pagden (1997), 188.

6. Fagerstrom (1954), 256–7, 265; Knorr (1964), 68; Greig (1969), II, 301–3; Werner (1972), 445–6; Berry (1974), 255; Livingston (1990), 17; Smitten (1990), 167; Colley (1992), 140.

7. Barker (1931), 124; Brock (1982), 13; Akenson (1984), 103; Purvis (1984), 95–6; Bailyn (1986), 9–45.

8. Johnson 86,90; MacLean (1900), 114; Graham (1956), 22; Meyer (1957), 119; Richards (1985), II, 180; Macinnes (1988), 86.

9. Bailyn, 46–54, 67–70, 92, 108–9; Johnson (1924), 86, 119; Fry (1992b), 65–7.

10. Bailyn, 129, 196–9. 373. 398–9, 604, 635; Alden (1944), 139, 277; Wood (1980), 173; Lenman (1992), 67–75; Cashin (1992), *passim*.

11. Carstairs (1955), 68; Soltow (1955–6), 90–6; Hamilton (1963), 255; Campbell (1965), 43; Price (1967), 299–395; (1980), 24, 29; (1984), 27; Devine (1975), 11, 56; (1976b), 3; Slaven (1975), 20–1; Lenman (1976), 91; (1981), 23–4, 42–7; Dell (1982), 1; Wood (1992), 143.

12. Knox (1784), xliii; Devine (1971), 205, 234; (1973), 50 *et seqq*; (1974), 113–26; (1975), 18, 130, 157–8, 161, 171–3; (1976a), 11; (1977), 177 *et seqq*; Butler (1978), *passim*; Karras (1992), 191, 202.

13. Robson (1951), xxiii; Meyer (1957), 157 *et seqq*; Nelson (1961), 90, 110; Brown (1969), 46–50; Hamowy (1979), 503 et seqq; Hast (1979), 9; Landsman (1985), 165, 256–8; Rankin (1986), *passim*.

6. 'THE GREATER BARBARIANS': THE WEST INDIES (pp.70–82)

1. Price (1992), 50–6.
2. Brougham (1803), 75, 81; Checkland (1954–5), *passim*; (1957), 127–32; Hamilton (1963), 262; Campbell (1965), 77; Slaven (1975), 24; Butt (1977), *passim*; Lenman (1977), 91; Duffy (1987), 18–9; Karras (1992), 7, 32–3;
3. Anon. (1961), 34–43; Smout (1961), 240–50; Sheridan (1975), 31; Devine (1978), 40–3, 52; Maxwell, J. (1982), 12–3: Hunter (1993), 83.
4. Long, II, 286; Brougham (1803), 46; Chambers (1867), 42; Sheridan (1960–1), 342 *et seqq*; (1965), 306; (1975), 197–200, 369; Kup (1974–5), 328–47; Hargreaves (11), 3; Drinkall (1991), 58; Karras (1987), 53 *et seqq*; (1992), 49, 119, 177.
5. Long (1773), II, 286; Campbell (1828), 18; Devine (1978), 51–2; Karras, 20–1, 46–7, 54.
6. Bridges (1828), II, 136; Grierson (1925), *passim*; Burns (1949), 123; Allan (1952), 53–8; Dobson (1973), 51; Setzekorn (1975), 128; Graham-Yooll (1981), 162–7; Rheinheimer (1988), 56–66, 123.
7. Williamson (1801), 9–11; Schaw (1921), 81; Rinn (1980), 16–9; Slade (1984), 481 *et seqq*; Morgan (1991), 197; Marx (1992), 135–6.
8. Hancock (1995), Ch.vi.
9. Checkland (1954–5), 218; Curtin (1965), 246; Akinjogbun (1966), 67 *et seqq*; Gladstone & Cropper (1972), 1–22; Rice (1975), 171; Hume (1985), 208, 384 *et seqq*: Wokler (1988), 155–6.
10. Booth (1934), 4–11.
11. Ramsay (1784a) 1–7; (1784b), 14; (1785), 21; Wedderburn (1824), *passim*
12. Hutcheson, I, 302–3; Beattie (1807), II, 24, 55, 65; Davis (18), 433–6; Rice (1975), 168–71.
13. Booth, 20–3, 42–55, 69–72, 113; Williamson, 100, 138; Karras, 6; Marjoribanks (1792), 4; Brougham (1803), 68; (1807), *passim;* Anon. (1962), 37; Hargreaves (1981), 5; Fontana (1985), 63; Morgan (1991), 193.
14. Schutz (1950), 145–7; Bradley (1972), 866 *et seqq*; Rice (1972), 69; (1983), 121–36; Shyllon (1977), *passim*; McCalman (1991), 47.
15. Slade, 483; Galt (n.d.), I, 305; Walrond (1872), 27; Morison (1928), 45–6; Checkland (1954–5), 222; (1971), 316–24; Rice (1972), 70.
16. Noel (1866), 14; Gorrie (1867), 29–32, 52; Olivier (1933), 19–25, 92–6; Lorimer (1978), 178–87; Heuman (1994), 150.

7. 'COMPASSION FOR FALLEN GREATNESS': INDIA (pp.83–95)

1. Wilkin (1912), 33, 67–76; Campbell (1919), 3–5; Mackenzie (1992).
2. Hamilton (1744), I, 256; II, 83 *et seqq*; Dodwell (1929), 97; Furber (1976), 366; Cain (1986), 11.
3. Cain, 12, 16; Marshall (1976), 12, 214, 231; Bryant (1985), 40; Parker (1985), 192–3; Riddy (1989), 42; Maan (1992), 39.
4. Fry (1992b),111–29, 216–23.
5. Ramsay (1772), iii; Steuart (1772), 56–7; Smith, A. (1776), II, 637–41; Gleig (1830), II, 260; Narain (1950), *passim*; Dwyer (1987), 44; Lenman (1990), 183.
6. Smith, V, 550 *et seqq*; Bute (1858), 73, 128–9, 156; Minto (1880), 63–8, 246, 349, 371–2; Mackenzie (1952), 10, 177; Rocher (1968), 6, 34; Edney (1997), 155; Trautmann (1997), 30–5.
7. Narain, op.cit; Robertson (1791), 262, 335–6; Woodruff (1953), 238; Bearce (1961), 24; Rendall (1980), 43–59; Hambly (1990), 36; Smitten (1992), 11–18.
8. Cain, 29; Trautmann, 84–7; Hunter (1896), 57; Lord (1897), 118; Dixon (1939), 7–13, 34, 49–63, 76–83, 102; Kopf (1969), 146–53; Keay (1981), 82–228, 275; Thomson (1981), 13–14; Vicziany (1986), 649.
9. Mackintosh (1835), 226, 239; Smith 1958), 568 *et seqq*; Mehta (1986), passim; Datta (1987), 41–4; O'Leary (1989), 78.
10. Gleig, III, 57; Woodruff, 190; Bearce, 122; Arbuthnot (1881), I, clxxxii; Stokes (1959), xvi, 9–20; Philip (1961), 221; Beaglehole (1966), 80 *et seqq*; Stein (1989), 12.

11. Woodruff, 206; Stokes, 17, 141; Kaye (1856), I, 49, 89, 137, 155, 415; II, 307, 324, 365, 374, 559.

12. Rendall, 64; Philip, 222; Bearce, 131; Stokes, 148; Woodruff, 240; Colebrooke (1884), I, 102; II, 142; Cotton (1892), 17, 75, 121–36, 187; Radcliffe (1962), 8–12, 23–4; Choksey (1971), 139, 193, 213, 423.

13. Colebrooke, II, 142, 154–9; Choksey, 230–9, 374; Bearce, 146–7; Cotton, 186; Rendall, 69; McCully (1940), 28; Anon. (1969), 28; Rothermund (1988), 47; Bayly (1989), 157, 210.

8. 'IN TRUE HIGHLAND STYLE': CANADA (pp.96–107)

1. Macleod & Morton (1963), IX, 1–6, 24, 48.

2. Macleod & Morton, IX, 52; Halkett (1817), 4–13, 88; Ross (1856), 33; Gray (1963), 33.

3. Waller (1960), 1, 94–104, 253, 269–77.

4. Mahon (1921), 330–8, 349–50; Roy (1947), 61; Crowe, McNaught & Reid (1959), 52; Macmillan (1972), 63; Calder (1979), 424–5; Macmillan (1985), 46–53; Fryer (1987), 15, 148.

5. Macmillan, *loc.cit*; Doughty & Shortt (1914), XI, 41; Benians, Holland Rose & Newton (1930), 188; Roy (1947), 61; Rea (1974), 1; Duncan (1976), 52–4; Robertson (1977), 227 et seqq; Bumsted (1978a), 511 *et seqq*; (1978b), 76–8; Bailyn (1986), 373, 398; McLean (1991), 1245–7, 202.

6. Doughty & Shortt, XIII, 232; Galt (1831), 307; Hogg (1874), 426; Fraser (1899), 1, 102, 197, 213; Cowan (1961), 14, 22; Bumsted (1981), 66, 77–85; (1982), 79, 145; Murison (1987), 268.

7. Doughty & Shortt, XVII, 77–88; Lamond (1821), 1–7, 25; Aberdeen (1826), 152; Galt (1826), 306, 471; (1831), III, 13, 75; Lizars (1906), I, 379: Cameron (197), *passim*; Vance (1992), 37–54.

8. Wallace (1928), 31; (1934), 1–10; Campbell (1957), 19, 52–6, 67, 105; (1962), 11, 27–9, 45, 95; Lamb (1960), 11; (1970), 6 *et seqq*; Woodcock (1964), 335–7; Macmillan (1972), 62; Mitchell (1976), 36; Calder (1986), 97.

9. Wallace (1934), 19; Campbell (1962), 96, 123–35, 153, 182–3, 196–7; Macmillan (1972), 45–6; Mitchell (1976), 36–8.

10. Doughty & Shortt, XIX, 18; Davidson (1918), 144; Macdonald (1939), 165–6; Campbell (1957), 196–7; (1962), 135; Rich (1960), I, 82, 377, 389, 498–9; II, 128, 274; Mitchell (1976), 41.

11. Fetter (1957), 122; Gray (1963), 7–17, 46; Selkirk (1984), I, 35–7, 48–9, 100; II, 74; Murison (1987), 270–2; Lenman (1990), 189–90.

12. Gray, 53–67, 79, 92–6, 109; Macleod & Morton, 16; Doughty & Shortt, XIX, 16; XX, 370; Martin (1916), 55–60, 77–80; Campbell (1957), 200; (1962), 213.

13. Gray, 111, 122, 155–65, 213, 342; Martin, 96, 108, 119–29, 158, 171; Campbell (1962), 229–33, 244–52, 264.

14. Wallace, 25–8; Bryce (1905), 212.

9. 'THRIVING IN THE PRODUCE OF FLOCKS': AUSTRALIA (pp.108–118)

1. Cox (1973), 16, 150; Gardner (1980), 47–50; Watson (1984), 165–6.

2. Johnston (1839), 38; Bride (1899), 79; Duffield (1988), 17.

3. Benians, Holland Rose & Newton (1933), 77; Clark (1952), I< 92–3; Shaw 1966), 21, 36, 165; Bewley (1981), *passim*; Donnachie (1984), 21–5.

4. Barry (1958), *passim*; Bateson (1966), 106–8, 168.

5. Roberts (1924), 19; Ellis (1947), *passim*; Ritchie (1986), *passim*; Bayly (1909). 207.

6. Kiston (1985), 91–9.

7. Steven (1965), passim; Macmillan (1967), 319.

8. Brown (1941), I, xi, 3; II, xvii, 53, 128; Bailey (1966), 24; Macmillan (1960), 16–29; (1967a), 323–36; (1967b), 132 *et seqq*.

9. Cox, 109; Jay (1957), 42; Macmillan (1960), 5–7, 24, 42; (1967b), 323.

10. Macmillan, 79; Newman (1961), 218; Richards (1978), 2 et seqq; (1978), 35.

11. Murray (1853), 147; Kiddle (1961), 14 *et seqq*; Roberts (1964), 127–42.

12. Brown, VI, 3, 401; VII, xxiii; Cox, 131; Waterson, 1–2; Cockburn (1900), 147; Foster (1978), xii, 31, 77–80, 95.
13. Hattersley (1945), i, xvi-xvii.
14. Baster (1929), 148–9; Cottrell (1975), 23, 37; Michie (1983), 128–37; Richards (1985), 146–7.
15. Brown (1935), 149, 361; Brown (1940), II, 190–1; III, xxv, 159; IV, xvii; Dyster (1967), 63; Waterson (1968), 25, 135; de Serville (1980), 171 *et seqq.*
16. Cox, 131; Waterson, 1; de Serville (1991), 149, 164.

10. 'OCCASIONAL SCENES OF THE BROADEST FARCE': THE MEDITERRANEAN (pp.119–131)

1. Kirkwall (1864), 227–8.
2. Lord (1896), 141–4; Mahon (1921), 379–386, 429; Dickson (1992), 135, 150–3.
3. Minto (1874), II, 211–7, 237, 254–62; Attard (1988), 6–18.
4. Galt (1812), 120, 137; Grierson (1937), xii, 39; Parker (1946), 198–202; Seward (1972), 269, 298; Bezzina (1985), 56, 144.
5. Dixon (1939), 131: Pratt (1978), 104: Bayly (1989), 112, 130, 197.
6. Bezzina, 38.
7. Bayly, 201; Lord (1897), 148; Jackson (1995b), 220.
8. Dixon, 103, 137; Bezzina, 144, 168: Attard, 37–41; Bayly, 198–9.
9. Kirkwall, 75–86; Pratt, 96–100; Bayly, 198.
10. Pratt, 105–6; Bayly, 199.
11. Kirkwall, 89–102; Lord, 195 *et seqq;* Pratt, 109–12.
12. Napier (1835), 50–3; Napier (1857), I, 285, 304–7.
13. Napier (1835), 29–38; Napier (1857), 309–10, 352–60; Pratt, 112, 171; Bayly, 157.
14. Pratt, 124; Moore (1875), 983; Ferriman (1918), 50–8.
15. Napier (1857), 372–5; Moore, 977; Lord, 256; Dixon, 212; Pratt, 125; Grimble (1978), 291–7; Thomas (1980), 295–302.
16. Napier, 313; Kirkwall, 111–24; Grierson, xii, 43; Pratt, 112–8, 172; von Reumont (1855), 22.
17. Kirkwall, 136–53, 216–29; Pratt, 109, 125–30; Chapman (1964), 12–13.

11. 'SCATTERING THE SEEDS OF CIVILISATION': SOUTH AFRICA (pp.135–147)

1. Martin (1931), 121–3.
2. White, 111–2; Kirkwood (1706), 2; Ramsay (1949), 184; Phillipson (1996), 64–71.
3. Chalmers (1815), 14; Bulloch & Drummond (1975), 155.
4. Lovett (1899), I, 75; Warneck (1901), 96; White (1976), 120.
5. Chalmers (1878), *passim;* Cousins (1897), 14, 53–9, 81; Shepherd (1941), 64, 80–6; Hewat (1960), 175.
6. Walker (1963), 259, 880–7; de Klerk (1976), 30, 138; Ross (1993), 150–7.
7. Campbell (1822), II, 2; Philip (1841) 331, 420.
8. Bulloch & Drummond, 157; Calder (1945), 29; Macmillan (1963), 9–11; (1967), 95; Ross (1986), 53–97.
9. Philip, II, 363–4; Elbourne & Ross (1997), 36–8.
10. Philip (1828), I, ix, xxx, 142, 159, 175, 277, 367–81; II, 327.
11. Brock (1974), *passim.*
12. Walker (1963), 238; Pringle (1966), xxi, 1–6, 175–94, 321; Meiring (1968), 54; Calder (1988), 198–205.
13. Macmillan, 122–4, 137; Ross, 106, 192–3; Gailey (1962), 419 *et seqq;* Davenport (1997), 53.
14. Anon. (1837), 307–19; Du Plessis (1920), 15–25, 424, 460; Chamberlain (1983), 275.
15. Gailey, 422–32; Ross, 141, 158; Macmillan (1963), 18, 96–9, 222–3, 248–61, 278–85, 307, 327.
16. Ross, 158–63; Mackinnon (1887), 96; Fraser (1922), passim; Buchan (1928), 16.

12. 'COMMERCE AND CHRISTIANITY': DAVID LIVINGSTONE (pp.148–160)

1. Mackenzie (1990), 24–7.
2. Holmes, 67.
3. Moffat (1842), 199; Wallis (1945), I, 21, 318.
4. Moffat, 236–46, 261–2; Campbell (1827), II,2; Maclean (1992), 86.
5. Schapera (1951), xxvii; Northcott (1961), 11, 75; Bulloch & Drummond (1970), 160; Holmes (1993). 35.
6. Holmes, 35, 58.
7. Livingstone (1857), 157, 187; Chamberlin (1940), 95–105; Schapera (1959), I, 100; (1961), 6, 18, 103; Teal (1973), 54.
8. Holmes, 67.
9. Livingston, 116; Chamberlin , 255; Teal, 104–9; Oliver (1951), 10; Schapera (1959), I, 122; (1961), 177–85; (1963), 226; Foskett (1965), II, 599.
10. Livingstone, 28.
11. Livingstone, 37, 92; Schapera, 243, 303; Coupland (1928), 135–6; Shepperson (1960), 120; Ransford (1978), 159–62.
12. Holmes, 146; Wallis (1956), 51, 136–7; Butt (1963), 378–82.
13. Holmes, 200.
14. Holmes, 135, 192–6.
15. Mackenzie 18–19.

13. 'THE VOICE OF SCOTLAND': CENTRAL AFRICA (pp.161–171)

1. Chirnside (1880), 13.
2. Hanna (1956), 13–30; McCracken (1967), 65–7; Ross (1973), 196–200.
3. Hanna, 30–2, 41; Ross (1966), 334; (1972), 57–9; (1973), 204–5.
4. Hanna, 9–10; Wells (1908), 50 *et seqq*, 72–81, 101, 113; Oliver (1951), 14; McCracken (1977), 22 *et seqq*; Brock (1986), 75–80.
5. Wells, 128–39; McCracken (1967), 1; (1973a), 222; (1977), 23–31; Brock (1974), *passim*; Hargreaves (1981), 22.
6. Oliver, 65; Crawford (1912), 204; Laws (1934), 15; Rothberg (1965), 11–12; McCracken (1973a), 218–25; (1973b), 190; (1977), 69–76, 196.
7. Moir (1923), *passim*; Macmillan (1970), 13–14; McCracken (1973a), 226; (1977), 44–50.
8. Moir, 135–40; Macmillan, 14; McCracken, 77–101; Hetherwick (1932), 47–59; Rotberg (1966), 12.
9. Hetherwick, 6–7; Rotberg, 12; Livingstone (1931), 49–54; Ross (1966), 333 *et seq*.
10. Hetherwick, 83; Livingstone, 134; Hanna, 41, 205; Macmillan, 14; Rankine (1896), 237; Ross (1968), 250 *et seqq*; Harvie (1977), 108.
11. Moir, 175–6; Macmillan, 14; Ross (1966), 336–40, 346–7; (1968), 200 *et seqq*.
12. Livingstone, 106; Hetherwick, 124, 169; Oliver, 217; McCracken (1977), 113–73; Williams (1978), 52.
13. Macmillan, 15; McCracken (1977a), 179–80; (1977b), 204–8.
14. Hetherwick, 182; McCracken (1967), iii; (1977a), 189–201; Ross (1973), 212; Thompson (1980), 22–3.

14. 'AN INCIPENT CIVILISATION': WEST AFRICA (pp.172–184)

1. Livingstone (1916), 129–30.
2. Booth (1954), 23, 42–55.
3. Shepherd (1941), 23–8; Mair (1973), 28; (1984), vi; Stewart (1993), 158–60; Fyfe, *passim*.
4. Metcalfe (1962), 1, 34–41, 71–80, 106–19, 148–53.
5. Metcalfe, 169–73, 294, 334–7; Laird & Oldfield (1837); Sarbah (1910), 349–51.

6. Ullendorf (1953), 128–43; Bovill (1964), 132–49, 179, 313; Langley (1971), 426–9; Lupton (1979), 36, 58.
7. Cruickshank (1966), 8–10; Thompson (1970), 6; Onyeidu (1985–7), 30–3.
8. Laird & Oldfield, 277.
9. King (1850), 93 et seqq; Kilpatrick (1943), 42–5; Hewat (1960), 14 et seqq; Okon (1972), ii; Buchan (1980), 37.
10. Waddell (1863), 1, 50 et seqq; Curtin (1955), 35, 115.
11. Kilpatrick, 46; Hewat, 20; McFarlan (1946), 2–10, 24–52; Bulloch & Drummond (1975), 153–4.
12. Okon, 201, 262, 305; Waddell (1863), 552–4; Marwick (1897), 303, 375; Taylor (1985), 40–4.
13. Okon, ii; Bulloch & Drummond, loc.cit; Taylor, loc.cit.
14. Okon, 174, 191–5, 208–15, 234, 377; Ajayi (1965), 102.
15. McFarlan, 65; Taylor (1981), 24–5; (1985), 42–4.
16. Livingstone, 33, 61, 86–90; Taylor, 44; Ajayi, 264–5.
17. Livingstone, 128–9, 155; Okon, 448; Hargreaves (1981), 37.
18. Tamuno (1962), 168–79, 196; Perham (1960), II, 406; Joyce (1971), 219–45, 272, 299, 375.

15. 'INTO THE STYGIAN POOL': INDIA, THE RELIGIOUS MISSION (pp.185–196)

1. Youngson (1897), 70.
2. Mitchell (1805), 224; Pearson (1817), 2, 177, 213, 306; Smith (1879), 37–9; Morris (1904), 236–73; Ingham (1956), 33 et seqq; Embree (1962), 145, 175, 262; Thornton (1965), 165–6; Carnall (1997), 219; Trautmann (1997), 102–8.
3. Smith, G., I, 1, 32, 52, 72, 83; (1888), 104; Day (1879), 53–6; Paton (1923), 39; Mayhew (1926), 12; Sharpe (1965), 36; Laird (1970), 14–15: (1972), 223; Kopf (1979), 44.
4. Kopf (1969a), 151–5; (1969b), 100 et seqq; Laird (1972), 198; Rao (1993), 266; Maxwell (1995), 121–8; Robertson (1995), 5–18.
5. Duff (1840).
6. Sharpe, 68; Duff, 518–9; Smith (1878), 93; Laird (1970), 12; (1972), 207–23; Walls (1995), 101–3.
7. Sharpe (1965), 63; Laird (1970), 11–12, 16 et seqq; (1972), 203–6, 225; Kopf (1969b), 44–5, 159–60.
8. Smith, 189, 210, 222, 271; Day, 148; Mayhew, loc.cit; Laird (1970), loc.cit.
9. Laird, 223; Murdoch (1870), 2; Kopf (1969a), 55; (1979), 44–5.
10. Smith (1880), 8; Warneck (1901), 99; Hewat (1960), 67; Roxborough (1978), 387; Kopf (1979b), 159; Forrester (1980), 28–30.
11. Smith II, 13–20, 42, 307, 316–7, 328, 396, 459; Hunter 91873), 27; Mackichan (1927), 116; Bulloch & Drummond (1975), 176.
12. Gehani, ii, lvi, 48–51, 68; McCully (1940), 396; O'Malley (1941), 489, 517–27; Orr (1967), Pt.I, passim; Laird (1970), loc.cit; Porter (1988), 39–49.
13. Sharpe, 82–5; Gehani, 405, 532–3, 546; Orr (1967), Pt.2; Jeyasekeram (1988–9), 42–7.

16. 'I HAVE SINNED': INDIA, THE SECULAR MISSION (pp.197–208)

1. Kaye (1867), II, 353–7, 379–82.
2. Munro (1883), 120.
3. Duff (1858), 245; Campbell (1893), 281, 295; Chalmers (1904), 9.
4. Forbes (1895), 127; Alexander (1898), 104; Thomson (1981), 61–9; Sykes (1992), 47.
5. Morris (1904), 315 et seqq; Bearce (1961), 71–7; Philip (1961), 217–20; Winch (1965), 160; Burrow (1970), 18, 28, 44–8; Carnall (1997), 221–2.
6. Campbell, 138; Stokes, 234.
7. Stokes (1959), 53; Trevelyan (1878), I, 410; Pinney (1976), III, 138.
8. Bearce, 63–70; Trautmann, 161, 182; Crawford (1828), 27, 47–8; Stokes, 53.

9. Goldsmid (1880), I, 7–10, 39, 72–9, 98, 154, 213, 228–32, 286–96; Lambrick (1952), 33, 59–79, 120–35, 150.
10. Goldsmid, I, 311–2; II, 26, 53, 93, 108–12; Lambrick, 183–99, 314.
11. Hunter (1890), 20–37.
12. Hunter, 76–92; Arnold (1862), 168; Trotter (1889), 64; Lee-Warner (1904), I, 303–9, 411; Hall (1932), 99.
13. Hunter, 124, 180; Lee-Warner, II, 106–17, 131–4, 157, 182–6, 232, 342, 361–3, 381; Ramsay (1882), I, 226.
14. Macaulay *et al*, (1855), 12–13; Trotter (1889), 125; Davie (1961), 42–4; Kopf (1969), 244.
15. Smith (1878), 6, 72–81, 97, 141, 179, 213, 237, 317–20, 377, 480, 530, 605, 624; (1880), 1–2, 73, 259; Torrance (1902), 30; Gehani (1966), 219; Trautmann (1997), 145–64.

17. 'WE ARE TOO SCOTCH': CANADA (pp.209–218)

1. Carlyle (1897), 144; Wrong (1905), 455–6.
2. Walrond (1872), 81–9.
3. Morison (1928), 87–97.
4. Morison, 103–10.
5. Morison, 122; Henderson (1969), 1–15; Moir (1979), 64–6; Abbott (1981), 27–39.
6. Henderson, 30, 48; Moir (1956), 47; (1979), 68; James (1965), 221; Darroch (1971), 110–8, 159, 171; Rea (1974), ix, 128.
7. Moir, 68; Manning (1965), 91; Whitelaw (1978), I, 21; III, 5, 22.
8. M'Kerrow (1867), 5; Gregg (1895), 55, 353–4, 560; Macdonald (1939), 423; Moir (1978), 36; (1979), 70.
9. M'Kerrow, 353, 560; Moir (1978), 37; (1979), 75; Vaudry (189), 15–7; Murison (1993), 6.
10. Murison, *passim*; Moir (1975), 39.
11. Vaudry, 41–50, 65–7, 111–29; Lewis (1926), 1–10, 55; Underhill (1929), 106–9; Moir (1956), 61; (1959), 7; (1975), 49; (1978), 37; (1979), 75; Careless (1959), I, 12–21, 33, 125.
12. Vaudry, 127–30; Moir (1975), 49; (1978), 37.
13. Moir (1975), *loc.cit*; Gill (1985), 181.
14. Lewis, 33, 61, 101, 132, 255; Careless, I, 88–96, 153, 232, 269, 307; II, 9, 109–10, 366; Morison (1919), 187 *et seqq*; (1928), 122; Keith (1928), 17.

18. 'BOTHWELL BRIG FACES': AUSTRALASIA (pp.219–228)

1. Morrison (1933), 79–82; McPherson (1962), 71, 108.
2. McPherson, 140–53; Prentis (1983) 81; Stewart (1909), 4; Macmillan (1972), 1, 23.
3. Lang (1972), 144, 196.
4. Baker (1985), 107, 172, 223, 258–68, 442.
5. Lang, 107–14; Baker, 75–6, 86, 98, 223; Nadel (1957), 36–9, 224; Macmillan (1962), 6–12.
6. Lang, 29–38, 61–5, 78, 95–8.
7. Lang, 89.
8. Stewart, 4, 23; Lang, 144; Baker, 143, 162–7, 181–8, 202, 220, 375, 453, 489; Prentis, 81; Macmillan (1967), 308; Lemon (1982), 21; Murison (1993), 19–28; Cumming (1993). 22–5.
9. Merrington (1929), 60; Pearce (1976), 51–2; Richards (1982), 27.
10. Merrington, 12–21, 37, 53–83, 105, 126, 169; Pearce, 53–4.
11. Merrington, 109, 218; Pearce, 56–60; McLintock (1949), 269, 346; Brooking (1985), 159.
12. Pearce, 61–3, 77; Begg (1874), 11.
13. McPherson, 35, 71–3, 85, 100–10; Pearce, 65–72.
14. Morrison, 81; Pearce, 72; Molloy (1986), 221, 239–40.

19. 'THE TRUE ART OF THE MISSIONARY': OCEANIA (pp.229–239)

1. Lovett (1903), 353, 472–93.
2. Paton, J. (1889), 3, 208; Paton, M. (1894), 131–3; Gunn (1914), 14, 159; Fleming (1927), 148; Garrett (1982), 4–17, 74, 126, 156, 173, 293.
3. Balfour (1901), II, 193; Colvin (1911), II, 223; Hennessy (1974), 205–6.
4. Pearce (1976), 104.
5. Colvin, XIX, 62; XXX, 158; Hennessy, 240; Theroux (1992), 440; Stevenson (1896), 14; Linklater (1953), 194; Bell (1992), 259.
6. Murray, 404; Monckton (n.d.), 1.
7. Garrett, 177–8; McIntyre (1967), 242, 379.
8. Porteous (1978), 145–6.
9. Day (1984), 1, 23, 114, 132, 270; Theroux, 699–700; Tabrah (1987), 91.
10. Chapman (1964), 102, 155–60, 183–93, 210–3, 234–41, 263–79, 296; Knaplund (1961), 62–9, 81–90.
11. Monckton, 9, 73, 94; Lovett, 238–46; Macmillan (1957), 4–10, 60, 71, 138; Joyce (1971), 22–9, 40–2, 95–109.
12. Joyce, 126–41, 167, 213; Macgregor (1897), 32; Young (1944), 1.
13. Monckton, 1; Joyce, 137; Bell, 265; Stevenson (1892), 117; Calder (1980), 308–10.
14. Stevenson (1892), 39–41, 97, 274.

20. 'FITTED TO POLLUTE PUBLIC SENTIMENT': THE SCOTTISH DEBATE (pp.240–251)

1. Bryce (1903), 311; Black & Chrystal (1912a), 381–2; (1912b), 476–83; Riesen (1981), 269.
2. Hume (1757), 27 et seqq, 41 et seqq; Burrow (1966), 14; Manuel (1967), 168–83; Hitchen (1984), 615; Ackerman (1991), 10–11.
3. McLennan (1876), 14, 27, 68–9, 85, 101, 123, 145–6, 154, 231, 282, 465; Lowie (1937), 44; Ackerman (1987), 80–1.
4. Ackerman (1987), 150–1; (1991), 33; Davie (1991), 119.
5. Knox (1850), passim; Rae (1964); Collinson (1990).
6. Ackerman, 41; Beidelman (1974), 18, 30–9.
7. Beidelman, 32–9, 53, 65–6; Ackerman (1987), 150; (1991), 41–2; Said (1991), 235.
8. Crawford (1990), 35; Cioffi (2000), passim; Clack (2000), passim.
9. Lowie, 197–212; Beidelman, 25, 42, 58–60; Davie, 123; Jones (1984), 35–55.
10. Beidelman, 27; Black & Chrystal (1912b), 484 et seqq; Ackerman (1991), 41–3.
11. Davie, 139: Ajayi (1965), 264; Sharpe (1965), 283–7, 347; Orr (1967), 41; Cox (1977), 18–19; Dow (1977), 69, 115; Garrett (1992), 303–5; Walls (1995), 101–3.
12. Sharpe, 87, 109, 124, 164–72, 199, 278–96, 310–4, 329–47; Farquhar (1908), 24; Gairdner (1910), 37, 274; Miège (1973), 162, 256.

21. 'USING THE SAFE AND SMALL': IMPERIAL ECONOMICS (pp.255–277)

1. Trotter (1938), I, 20–3, 52–4; Reader (1970), 24–5; Stopford (1974), 319.
2. Burton (1849), 336–7.
3. Donaldson (1966), 76, 91; Thomas (1973), 64; Flinn (1977), 14, 441–3; Wood (1980), 74; Devine (1988), 198, 245; (1992), 1–12.
4. Wood, 175; Stevenson (1885), 43.
5. Gallagher & Robinson (1953), 1–4.
6. Nicolson (1932), 27, 39; Bolitho (1936), 26–39; Cable (1937), 6–13, 65, 133–8, 162; Blake (1956), 15, 33; Orbell (1978), 34; Payne (1980), 66; Jones (1989), 67–71; Strachan (1992), 5; Jackson (1995b), 229–33.
7. Hyde (1975), 8–24.

8. Munro (1983), 1–4.
9. Blake, 6–15, 38–47, 111; Strachan, 6; Cornford (1925), 24–6, 38; McLellan (1956), 13, 36; Laird (1961), 11, 41, 49; Milne (1967), 345–9; McAlister (1976), 3–4; Kent (1976), 190; Orbell (1978), 1–5.
10. Orbell, 14–35; Benians, Butler & Carrington (1959), III, 465; Corley (1983), 1–14, 25–32.
11. Butt & Lythe (1975), 237; Michie (1981), 247–8; Campbell (1985), 113–6.
12. Morison (1912?), 17; McCalla (1979), 114–7, 158; Macmillan (1972), 154.
13. Anon. (1884), 468–79; Cairncross (1953), 25–6; Fieldhouse (1964), 84; Campbell (1965), 79–83; Butt & Lythe (1975), 235; Cottrell (1975), 25; Slaven (1975), 27.
14. Gladstone, 75; Cairncross, 89; Mackenzie (1954), 2–20; Checkland (1975), 513, 561–2; Dickson (1980), 193; Treble (1980), 170–85; Jones (1986), I, 28, 57, 143, 272; Cain & Hopkins (1993a), 118, 146, 172; Jones (1993), 15–16, 50, 62.
15. Thomas (1973), 300; Payne (1980), 73; Michie (1983), 125–7; (1985), 65–7.
16. Rankin, 270; Longhurst (1956), 70; Payne (1967), 519–29; Macmillan (1970), 102–15.
17. Thomas, 300–11: Lenman (1977), 192; Davis & Huttenback (1986), 214; Schmitz (1988), 22–6.
18. Cairncross, 89; Campbell, 79; Dickson, 79; Marwick (1935–6), 111; Gilbert (1939), 5–13, 52, 102; Bailey (1959–60), 268–77; Payne (1980), 60; Cassis (1990), 141–2; Schmitz (1993), i-ii, 3, 13.
19. Jones (1989), 2; Munro (n.d.), *passim.*
20. Davies & Muir (1978), 89. 216; Porter (1986), 13, 46, 52, 77, 144, 182; Munro (1983), 73–85.
21. Bolitho, 110; Harcourt (1981), 16; Munro (1983), 8; Jones (1987), 86; (1989), 4–39, 50–62, 77.
22. Cable, 206; Blake, 174; Milne (1967), 349–53; Jones (1986), 29–35; (1989), 67–71.
23. Hyde, 39, 94–100, 119, 139–51; Cornford, 68–9; Cooper, 174–5; Strachan, 159; Orbell, 40–61; Armstrong (1991), 56–9.
24. Robertson (1974), 36–47; (1976), 36 *et seqq*; Cooper (1989), 166 *et seqq*; Kim & Slaven (1994), 153.
25. Macrosty (1907), 42–66, 92, 125–31, 241; Payne (1967), 539; Mackenzie (1992), 16.

22. 'LES PEUPLES DE SECOND RANG': THE EUROPEAN CONTEXT (pp.278–289)

1. Hansard, I, 1909, cols. 948–9.
2. Curtis & Nadel (1964), 21; Fieldhouse (1966), 362; Cooksey (1968), 91–132; Kiernan (1969), 235.
3. Galbraith (1972) 377–98; Roeykens (1954), 29, 123, 273; Kiewiet (1955), 15–16, 24, 46, 57; Anstey (1962), 67–79, 127–37, 168, 208; Ascherson (1963), 16–23, 57, 92–102, 132, 186; Stengers (1972), 248 *et seqq*; Kossman (1978), 381, 392.
4. Hutchison & Martelli (1971), 9–15, 110–26, 146–77; Katzenellenbogen (1973), 21–45, 130–5; Clarence-Smith (1978), 174; Hargreaves (1981), 41 *et seqq*.
5. Hargreaves, 50–6; Newitt (1981), 35; Kuitenbrouwer (1991), 355.
6. Ascherson, 50; Stengers, 263 *et seqq*; Clarence-Smith, 174; Kuitenbrouwer, 349–52.
7. Majumdar (1962), 3, 451–2, 471–3, 506, 518; Fasseur (1980), XI, 348; Baud (1983), I, 50; III, 54; Macinnes (1994), 25.
8. Knight (1894), 287, 392–3; Bryce (1921), 1–3.
9. Fieldhouse, 327; Fasseur, 350–62; Edwardes (1967), 27.
10. Edwardes, 28–32, 174; Kossman, 398–406; Fasseur, 367; Benda (1958), 340–5.
11. Thornton (1965), 44; Dekker (1967), 7–15.
12. Brown (1901), Ch.xi; Dekker (1987), 20.

23. 'THE MOST PROPER PERSONS FOR THIS COUNTRY': CANADA (pp.290–302)

1. Bowsfield (1971), 23–46.
2. Ross (1856), 208; Bryce (1905), 212; (1911), 193, 225; Macnaughton (1926), 105; Galbraith (1976), 11.

3. Macleod & Morton (1963), 107, 122–3; Woodstock (1964), 339; Mitchell (1976), 41; Goldring (1979), 83, 96; (1980), 23.
4. Woodcock, 339–40; Galbraith, 30, 48–71; Mitchell, 43; Wallace (1934), 28; Rich (1940), xiii; Richards (1975), 176–91; Calder (1986), 98–102.
5. Galbraith, 72, 87, 98, 132–40; Thrum (1911), 35; Wilson (1919), 21; Lewis & Murakami (1923), 23, 152; Voght (1973), 137; Williams (1973), xliii-lii; Seymour (1979), *passim.*
6. Thrum, 39–49; Galbraith, 154, 180–1, 199; Coats & Goswell (19080, III, 188, 207.
7. Woodcock, 341; Bowsfield, 39–61; Begg (1871), 1, 70, 93, 218, 262–3, 330–6; Doughty & Shortt (1914), VI, 33–7: XX, 283; Innis (1956), 358; Turner (1976), 76–85; Jarvenpa & Zenner (1980), 198.
8. Doughty & Shortt, VII, 548; Wood (1984), 79 *et seqq;* Norton (1991), 16 *et seqq.*
9. Chamberlain (1983), 281; Kilbourn (1958), 13, 99–108, 178, 200, 213–20, 236–44; Donnelly (1987), 62–70.
10. Walrond (1872), 126; Morison (1912), 6, 17; (1928), 156; Curtis & Nadel (1964), 20; Macmillan (1972), 154; McCalla (1979), 103, 114–7, 158; Hobsbawm (1990), 24–9.
11. McCalla, 61; Skelton (1920), 33, 48, 145, 220–1, 328; Huttenback (1966), 36.
12. Willson (1915), 374, 455, 480, 553; Donald (1952), 1, 130, 158–62, 287, 380, 489; Gilbert (1973), 177–93; (1976), 1, 16, 63, 75–105.
13. Skelton, 523; Pope (1894), I, 312; II, 214–5; Long (1931), 23–5; Stewart (1954), 119.
14. Pope, 214–21; Skelton, 523–39; Saywell & Stevens (1981), xiii-xxiii; Smith (1891), 267–8; Buckingham & Ross (1892), 407; Buchan (1924), 159; Underhill (1959), 127; Saywell (1960), xxxix, 6, 233; Grant (1965), 3–4; Kennedy (1976), 124; Miller (1980), 81, 96, 119–31, 158, 173, 192.

24. 'OUR PRINCIPAL RELIANCE IS ON OPIUM': CHINA (pp.303-315)

1. Oliphant (1860), 29, 114; Walrond (1872), 215, 240; Wrong (1905), 254–5; Lumby (1960), 479–84; Taylor (1982), 1.
2. Wrong, 256; Morison (1928), 218–25; Knollys (1894), 187–9; Loch (1900), 106–7; Walrond (1972), 251, 361–6; Welsh (1993), 207; Checkland (1988), 140, 154–60, 174.
3. Fairbank, I, 60; Chambers (1757 & 1772), *passim;* Campbell (1903), 498; Greenberg (1951), 25; Dermigny (1964), II, 642, 659; III, 941, 968, 1242, 1246; Harris (1970), 4–5; Brown & Cherry (1978), 41–3; Cheong (1979), 9–12; White (1990), 71.
4. Nightingale (1970), 50; Fry (1992b), 126–7; Welsh, 2, 59–60; Fairbank (1953), 70.
5. Greenberg, 74, 104–5,; Fairbank I, 63–6; Cheong, 6–8; Sayer (1937), 12; Coates (1966), 137–41; Crisswell (1981), 20–7.
6. Greenberg, 150, 167–85; Cheong, 121–37, 181–7, 207, 263–70; Crisswell, 27–33; Allen & Donnithorne (1954), 35; Maxwell (1982), 14.
7. Greenberg, 191–3; Crisswell, 45; Fairbank, 69–79; Blake (1960), 1, 13; Collis (1965), 6, 121–84; Coates (1966), 143, 170.
8. Greenberg, 198–202; Crisswell, 40; Fairbank, 80.
9. Collis, 206–98; Cheong, 142–4, 155–67, 181–7; Maxwell, *loc.cit;* Greenberg, 202–8.
10. Greenberg, 209–13; Crisswell, 4, 59; Fairbank, 80–2; Blake, 52–7; Eitel (1895), 163–72; Welsh (1993), 1.
11. Greenberg, 170, 214; Crisswell, 66; Fairbank, II, 56; Harvey (1981), 5–6; Keswick (1982), 27; Chapman (1985), 234.
12. Bonar (1861), *passim;* Burns (1870), 257, 338, 386, 467, 528; Legge (1905), 1, 27, 206, 327; Stewart (1909), 92; Latourette (1929), 246, 396, 665; Fulton (1967), xv, 25; Mackenzie (1971), II; Lau (1994), 225 *et seqq;* Bickley (1997); Girardot (1997); Sweeting (1997).
13. Greenberg, 95–101, 137, 174; Checkland (1971), 323.
14. Fairbank (1953), 463–4; Allen & Donnithorne (1954), 65; Liu (1962), 138; Hou (1965), 85, 118; Crisswell (1981), 120; Keswick (1982), 171; Chapman (1985), 233; Lefevour (1970) 2–4, 24–30, 48–60, 129–33.

25. 'A HUGE MILITARY DESPOTISM': INDIA (pp.316–328)

1. Swinson (1967), 232, 246–8.
2. Swinson, 251.
3. Hopkirk (1990), 22–5, 31–5, 67–8, 139–51, 237–8, 433, 485.
4. Preston (1969), 58–73.
5. Preston, 58,77; Hopkirk, 422, 519; Thornton (1895), 297–301; Charteris (1920), 48–57; Macdiarmid (1923), 87; Woodruff (1953), II, 142.
6. Dilke (1868), II, 353; Chaudhuri (1971), 18–19; Parker (1985), 206–8.
7. Anon. (1951), 3–15, 45–51; Jeffery (1982), 24.
8. Anon. (1908), 116; (1959), 15, 34–49; (1980), 1–6: Gladstone (1910), 1–11, 42, 53, 79, 93; Lokanathan (1935), 45; Longhurst (1956), 17, 34, 70; Pointon (1964), 1–5, 32, 50.
9. Lokanathan (1953), 163; Parker (1985), 191; Rothermund (1988), 59–63.
10. Checkland (1976), 220; Jones (1987), 95; (1989), 28.
11. Rothermund, 57; Brand & Woodhouse (1934), 18; Marwick (1935), 109; Chapman (1938–9), 35–50; Anstey (1952), 279–80; Gadgil (1971), 57–8; Bagchi (1972), 262–71.
12. Wallace (1928), 53–7, 87; Clapham (1938), III, 127; Saul (1960), 193; Spear (1961), 287; Anon. (1980), 23; Munro (1983), 9; Stewart (1998), 4.
13. Wilson (1885), 6–9, 20; Skrine (1901), 136, 440; Howe (1949), 55; Woodruff (1953), II, 15; Wilson (1984), vii, 48, 140, 232.
14. Campbell (1893), II, 25–35, 86, 166–79, 107, 228.
15. Woodruff, 164; Wedderburn (1913), 1, 32–47; Ambirejan (1978), 265.
16. Ratcliffe (1923), 13–14, 26–51.
17. Wedderburn, 47–60, 87; Ratcliffe, 70, 102; Wasti (1964), 10.
18. Wasti, 3; Hardie (1917), 80, 115; Moulton (1974), 26, 38.

26. 'THANK GOD WE ARE ALL SCOTS HERE': EAST AFRICA (pp.329–339)

1. Coupland (1936), 206–8; Gaving (1962), 146; Gray (1963), 239; Bennett (1978), 96; Holmes (1993), 334–5.
2. Coupland (1928), 48, 135–6; (1939), 38–41.
3. Gray, 234–40; Bennet, 92–6.
4. Gray, 240; Bennett, 100–9; Flint (1963), 359.
5. Bennett, 99, 121; Holmes, 334; Oliver (1951), 84; Galbraith (1972), 156–7.
6. Coupland, 378; Flint, 361; Gray, 250; Bennett, 106, 121; Galbraith (1971), 374; Munro (1983), 4; Liebowitz (1999), 214–9.
7. Flint, 366; Bennett, 127; Kiewiet (1955), 57.
8. Coupland, 480; Flint, 373; Bennett, 128.
9. Flint, 373; Kiewiet, 92–3; Thomson (1886), 65–78; Thomson (1896), 73; Gibb (1937), 142; Thompson (1970), 142; Galbraith (1972), 89.
10. Flint, 380; Galbraith, 29–33, 132–41; Munro, 4; McIntosh (1969), 33.
11. Drysdale (1964), 36; Lewis (1980), 51; Laitin & Samatar (1987), 51.
12. Kiewiet, 230; Galbraith, 141–91; Gallagher & Robinson (1961), 307.
13. Kiewiet, 268; McIntosh, i-xx, i, 14, 159–63; Galbraith, 193–225; Munro, 5; Oliver, 170; Rotberg (1971), 68.
14. Gallagher & Robinson, 309–23.
15. Kiewiet, 304; Galbraith, 226–39.

27. 'A KIND OF CELESTIAL SCOTLAND': SOUTH AFRICA (pp.340–351)

1. Baird (1901), 178–92; Royle (1982), 32, 107.
2. Ballantyne (1879), 43–4; Mackenzie (1887), II, 461; (1902), 352; (1921), 1, 26–8; Wells (1908), 242, 302; Shepherd (1941), 217; Bolt (1971), 121; Northcott (1972), 280, 319, 330, 656 *et seqq.*

3. Pakenham (1960), 75–94; Butler (1968), 10–11; Palmer (1972), 300–9.
4. Bryce (1897), 489; Campbell (1900), 131; Macmillan (1975), 7, 41–3, 80; Hamilton (1966), 41, 125; Sixsmith (1970), 34.
5. Butler (1960), 15–32; Smith (1965), 110–25; Nimocks (1968), 25, 42; Kruse (1989), 21–9, 41–53.
6. Smith, 124, 144; Buchan (1903), 207; (1940), 109–12; Hyam (1968), 66–90.
7. Smith, 122–30; Kruse, 9, 54–77; Buchan (1903), 395; (1906), 213; (1910), 189; (1940), 114–20; Sandison (1967), 149–52.
8. Buchan (1906), 37, 98, 124, 165, 332–41, 361; Daniell (1975), 94–111; (1984), 102.
9. Brown (1992), 183.
10. Hyam, 238–58, 278, *et seqq*; Checkland, 249; Pyrah (1955), 179; Shinn (1990), 91.
11. Hyam, 102, 119–42, 158–82; Checkland (1988), 248–51; Wilson (1973), 476–89.
12. Hyam, 289, 330; Shinn, 121–2.

28. 'A MOVEMENT AMONG THE CELTIC ELEMENTS': IMPERIAL POLITICS (pp.352–374)

1. Brown (1992), 168–9.
2. Bryce (1871), 375; Knaplund (1927), 145; Magnus (1954), 287; Taylor (1957), 86–7; Gallagher & Robinson (1961), 123, 138–40; Hanham (1969), 91–9; Hechter (1975), 235–6; McLeod (1976), 221–6; Harvie (1977), 90; Donaldson (1989), 1, 27, 86.
3. Magnus, 250 *et seqq*; Naylor (1985), 21; Fry (1987), 92, 104.
4. Craig (1981), 66–8; Kearney (1989), 149–74.
5. Naylor, 435; Ferguson (1998), 287.
6. Naylor, 106–7; Handley (1946), *passim*; Walker (1972), *passim*.
7. Fry, 88–119; Scottish Home Rule Association (1891), 2; Raymond (1923), 51–2, 93; Crewe (1931), I, 149 *et seqq*; James (1963), 157; Thornton (1965), 89; Jacobson (1973), 83.
8. Jenkins (1964), 40 *et seqq*; Searle (1971), 98 *et seqq*; Matthew (1973), 98–9.
9. Mitchell (1892), 156; Hamer (1972), 156; Winch (1965), 167; Jalland (1979), 757–60.
10. Pope (1894), I, 312; II, 214–20; Skelton (1920), 523; Gallagher & Robinson (1953), 1–15.
11. Thornton, 87; Hanham, 93; Searle, 109, 122; Matthew, 260; McLeod, 217–31; Naylor, 307–8, 423; Macpherson (1902), 3; Spender (1923), 297; Price (1972), 101–10; Wilson (1973), 342–65; Barker (1975), 66–8; Koss (1985), 22.
12. James, 453; Searle, 109; Wilson, 387.
13. Haldane (1902), 141; Maurice (1937), I, 103–11, 135, 274–81, 325; II, 86; Dunlop (1938), 244–50; Sommer (1960), 161, 193, 236; Mackintosh (1962), 496–500; Hamilton (1966), 255–6.
14. Hansard, xxvi, col.1399; Naylor, 421.
15. Smart (1894–5), 36; Woodburn (1914), 264; Checkland (1976), 29; Dickson (1980), 251–2; McFarland (1990), 43; Walker (1991), 50–9.
16. Nicholson (1909), 42–3, 60, 204–6, 270; (1910), 161 *et seqq*; Cunningham (1911), 10–13, 87; Semmel (1960), 188–200; (197), 226; Wood (1983), 146–65, 198–204.
17. Mackintosh, 494; Balfour (1905), 22; Amery & Garvin (1935–69), V, 255; VI, 474; Hanham (1973), 163; Zebel (1973), 128.
18. Wilson 371–81, 407; Bérard (1915), 185, 235–6; Haldane (1923), 157; Tyler (1938–9), 257; Young (1963), 210; Gollin (1965), 28; Judd (1968), 37–55, 74, 113–5; Rempel (1972), 225; Sykes (1979), 207; Levy (1983), 378, 402.
19. Balfour (1927), 15 *et seqq*, 51 *et seqq*; Pyrah (1955), 7; Butler (1960), 35–47, 223–4; Kruse (1989), 85–8; Adams (1999), 160.
20. Naylor (1985), 6; Walker (1994), 97–115; Officer & Walker (1998), 19–20.
21. Stewart (1907), 158–71; Woodburn (1914), 318, 342–52; Brooke (1987), 136, 171, 190–3.
22. Officer & Walker, 14–15; Adams, 109.
23. Naylor, 437–440; McFarland (1995), 37, 233–43; Loughlin (1999), 118–9.

24. Balfour (1913), 23; Blake (1955), 44, 105, 116–7; Robbins (1984), 287–91; Adams (1999), 40–1, 116–25.
25. Jalland, 765–84; Hyam & Martin (1975), 121–2; Lunney (1994), 69.

29. 'A MOTHER STATE': IMPERIAL POLITICS (pp.377–388)

1. Buchan (1923), III, 452; Oatts (1969), 77.
2. Buchan, 453; Ewing (1921), 200–1; Lindsay (1925), 139; Falls (1958), 129; Sym (1962), 192–4.
3. Ewing (1921), 212; (1925), 409–10, 426–7; Lindsay, 144; Sym, 194; Farrell (1920), 23; Sinclair-Stevenson (1968), 101–6; Grant (1972), 23.
4. Sandison (1967), 167–8; Kruse (1989), 188–91.
5. Macdonald (1917), 7.
6. Balfour (1927), 174 *et seqq*; Young (1963), 449; Huttenback (1966), 168; MacDonald (1970), 1–2; Zebel (1973), 287; Egremont (1980), 333–4.
7. Balfour (1927), 65 *et seqq*; Butler (1960), 57, 134–41.
8. Keith (1928), 39; (1936), 52.
9. Garner (1978), 115–9, 240.
10. Wheeler-Bennet (1962), 70; Bruce (1990), 234; (1992), 155–65; McFarland (1990), 203–15; Shinn (1990), 183–6; Walker (1990), 89.
11. Brooke (1987), 210; Bruce (1990), 240–52; (1992), 157–65; McFarland (1990), 215; Kay (1994), 88–94; Dew, Gibbon & Paterson (1995), 159.
12. Hansard, vol.272 (1932–3), cols. 259–67; Kruse, 12–41, 170–1.
13. Lynch (1991), xx, 433; Finlay.
14. Johnston (1952), 51–2, 67; Walker (1988), 59–90.

30. 'A NATIONAL HOME FOR THE JEWISH PEOPLE': PALESTINE (pp.389–399)

1. Thompson (1923), 424–6, 440–1, 469; Kernohan (1995), 100.
2. Thompson, 441–5, 457–8.
3. Macquarrie (1985), 11–36, 47–57, 76, 125.
4. Lithgow (1623), 194; Williamson (1993), 21; Sim (1969), 308, 365.
5. Lindsay (1838), 7; Caw (1908), 108; McDougall (1941), 23–5; Irwin (1975), 183–5, 207–8, 331; Macmillan (1990), 182; Lawson (1994), 17–26.
6. Kernohan, 18–19.
7. Bonar (1842), 1, 175, 197; (1894), 96–9; Kernohan (1995), 18–28.
8. Kernohan, 75–6; Lindsay (1854), 15–16; Jewish Committee of the Free Church (1895), 16–25, 153; Torrance (1902), 88; Hyamson (1950), 4; Livingstone (1923), 32–42, 59, 82, 134–44, 223; Levison (1989), 1, 15–24, 50, 63, 310, 323.
9. Oliphant, L. (1880), 284, 302,341: Oliphant, M. (1891), I, 71, II, 169; Knight (1907), 6; Hendrson (1956), 1–4, 105, 134, 188, 203–5, 230; Vereté (1970), 50; Taylor (1982), 1, 190, 290; Sanders (1983), 16–17; Friedman (1992), xxxix-xlv.
10. Dugdale (1930), I, 43.
11. Kernohan, 95; Sanders, 87–95, 116–9, 164, 191; Stein (1961), 147–60; Fromkin (1989), 97.
12. Kernohan, 195–7.
13. Kernohan, 108–12; Stein, 161; Marlowe (1959), 25–7; Kimche (1968), 76; Sanders (1983), xvii, 435, 491, 559, 581–91, 611, 658; Friedman (1992), 39, 129, 264–5, 278–87.
14. Friedman, 250–1, 287, 305; Livingstone, 261; Hyamson (1950), 118; Bentwich (1965), 129–31, 146–7; Fromkin (1989), 293–5, 526, 554–61; Sherman (1997), 85.
15. Bentwich, 149–56; Kernohan, 127; Sanger, 86–93, 159–75; Sherman, 12, 90; Fergusson (1970), 31–2;

516 THE SCOTTISH EMPIRE

31. 'ON THE LOOK OUT FOR SOME STIGMA': AFRICAN COLONISATION (pp.400–411)

1. Leys (1924), 328; Price & Shepperson (1958), 269–74; White (1987), 136–7.
2. Price & Shepperson, 1–4, 276–85, 316.
3. Price & Shepperson. 363–72; Grau (1960), 135; Rotberg (1965), 36, 116; McCracken (1967), iii; Mufuka (1977), 68, 105–13; Forster (1989), 6.
4. Ogilvie (1924), 179–255.
5. Mackichan (1927), 131; Livingstone (1931), 197; Hetherwick (1932b), 246; Laws (1934), 194; Malcolm (1939), 11; Rotberg (1966), 116–8; Ross (1968), 344; McCracken (1977), 221–91.
6. McCracken, 195–208; Ogilvie (1925), 234–6; Murray (1929), 40; Shepherd (1941), 275, 342; Mandela (1994), 41–3.
7. Davidson (1973), 23; Agyemang (1978), i, 1–4, 30; Gyang-Duah (1996), 160.
8. Murray-Brown (1972), 40.
9. McIntosh (1969), 1, 197–9; Pickard (1996), 5–12.
10. Wylie (1976–7), 294–305; Flint (1989), 213–4; Royle (1996), 24.
11. McIntosh, 218, 414; Pickard, 58–70; Leys (1931), 9–13; Scott (1932), 299–300; Philp (1936), 165; Murray-Brown, 40, 90, 115.
12. Macpherson (1974), 38–9; Hatch (1976), 17, 37.
13. Cook (1975), 98–108, 125.
14. Pickard, 33–44.
15. Johns (1970), 739–45; Kadalie (1970), 11, 31, 117, 178; Gupta (1975), 242.
16. Hargreaves (1981), 78–9; Rich (1989), 193.

32. 'SOMEONE MUST SPEAK FOR THEM': AFRICAN DECOLONISATION (pp.412–424)

1. Short (1974), 105–15; Royle (1996), 224.
2. Ross (1993), 37–41.
3. Banda & Young (1946), 6.
4. Rotberg (1960), 188; Short (1974), 28–39.
5. Newman (1989), 155–60; Cain & Hopkins (1993b), 5–6, 234.
6. Porter & Stockwell (1983), I, 16–29, 97; Constantine (1984), 52, 233–57, 303; Cain & Hopkins (1993b), 232.
7. Porter & Stockwell (1987), 9–16, 117; Sanger (1995), 146–55; Flint (1989), 213.
8. Little (1948), ix–x; Hatch (1976), 14, 29; Hoe (1992), 274, 286.
9. Northcott (1961), 333–5; Lwanda (1993), 42.
10. Gann & Gelfand (1964), 74–91; Gunn (1964), 214–5, 228, 245–9, 277, 303, 331; Mufuka (1977), 115, 147.
11. Mufuka, 150–64; Northcott. 333; Rotberg, 111, 238–9; Doig (1993), 25.
12. Moffatt (1960), 13; Mufuka (1975), 54–9; Douglas-Home (1976), 125; Ross (1993), 28; Thorpe (1997), 196.
13. Hanna (1969), 252–3; Royle (1996), 221.
14. Mufuka, 179–98; Royle, 231; Welensky (1964), 172; Ross (1968), vi; Hatch (1976), 29; Ferguson (1990), 299.
15. Doig, 45; Taylor (1963), 165–80. 196, 221; MacDonald (1972), 239–49; Bates (1976), 191, 279–80; Pratt (1976), I, 42–50; Garner (1978), 377; Shepherd (1994), 151–67; Sanger (1995), 357; Royle (1996), 203.
16. Lwanda, 118, 214; Royle, 232; Young (1970), 114–20; Bates (1972), 191; Hatch (1976), xiv; Pratt (1976), I, 42–50; Holland (1991), 334; Mandela (1994), 42; Newell (1995), 243; Ross (1997), 284 *et seqq*.

33. 'THE ORACLE IS DUMB': INDIA (pp.425–437)

1. Wheeler-Bennett (1962), 70, 118, 131–5.
2. Buchan (1924), 105; Singh (1971), 4.
3. Linklater (1970), 91; Fraser (1989), 23, 109–10, 123, 140, 202–3, 264.
4. Buchan, 85, 104–5, 223, 235; Morley (1909), 39; Minto (1934), 28, 48; Spear (1961), 325; Wasti (1964), 11, 145, 193, 217; Das (1965), 53–5, 202; Wolpert (1967), 43–7, 61–139, 150–77, 189–99; Singh (1976), 2, 13, 102, 116, 129; Bence-Jones (1982), 197–207.
5. Preston, 58, 77; Hopkirk, 422, 519; Thornton (1895), 297–301; Charteris (1920), 48–57; Macdiarmid (1923), 87; Pentland (1928), 142–4, 180, 213–26, 243–52, 272; Carmichael (1930), 238; Woodruff (1953), II, 142; Kitchen (1975), 249–59, 288; Metcalf (1989), 94, 214; Meller (1990), 217–21.
6. Anstey (1952), 279–81; Mackenzie (1954), 179–90; Gadgil (1971), 270–3; Bagchi (1972), 275–8; Rothermund (1988), 88–92, 108.
7. Lokanathan (1935), 115; Pointon (1964), 101; Anon. (1951), vi, 110, 121; Anon. (1959), 117, 132, 164; Anon. (1980), 12–23; Blake (1956), 250; Laird (1961), 215; McCrae & Prentice (1978), 58; Jeffery (1982), 25–37; Stewart (1998), 232.
8. Anstey (1952), 281; Carstairs & Cole (1960), 117–32; Tomlinson (1981), 455–69; Markovits (1985), appendix.
9. Gupta (1975), 10–12, 63, 80–1, 116; Dowds (1984), 6–14.
10. Lenman, 211; Chapman & Menzies (1946), 239–47; Anstey (1952), 281; Carstairs & Cole (1960), 117–32; Gauldie (1969), xxvii; Gadgil (1971), 270–3; Bagchi (1972), 278–87; Flinn (1977), 289; Walker (1979), 194–5, 529; Campbell (1988), 188; Rothermund (1988), 88–92, 107–8; Tomlinson (1981), 455–69.
11. Zetland (1926), 25–8; (1956), 82, 98, 130, 149.
12. Spear, 390–5; Zetland (1938), 19; (1956), 197–204, 232, 245–51; Butler (1960), 175; Rizvi (1978), 1–17, 36–43, 55–9, 70, 172; Bence-Jones (1982), 273 *et seqq.*
13. Spear, 392; Zetland, 255–7, 277–96; Rizvi, 88–9, 107, 123–52, 177–8, 195, 223; Huttenbach (1966), 190.

34. 'AS LOYAL AS THE HIGHLANDERS': CHINA (pp.438–450)

1. Ch'en (1961), 115–8.
2. Bolitho (1936), 201; Atwell (1985), xvi, 5–12, 39; Behr (1987), 9, 144, 155; Miners (1987), 294; Airlie (1989), 4, 26–43, 57, 76, 93, 113; Hou (1995), 17.
3. Atwell, 37, 60; Airlie, 163.
4. Atwell, 39–50, 103, 115–6.
5. Atwell, 67–8, 102–22; Airlie, 183.
6. Atwell, 81, 94, 146–78, 208–10; Airlie, 163–71, 269, 289; Johnston (1918), xxv, 80.
7. Dayer (1988), 65.
8. Fairbank (1963), 362; Harcourt (1981), 15; Cain & Hopkins (1993a), I, 433–9.
9. Cain & Hopkins, I, 433–9.
10. Bolitho, 201; Dayer, 36; McLean (1973), i–vi; (1976), 301–4; King (1988a), 222; (1988b), 170.
11. Dayer, 1–19, 33–6, 66–70, 86; Cain & Hopkins, I, 426–40; McLean (1983), i–ix, 12–18l (1976), 301–4; King (1987), 602; (1988a), 222; (1988b), 149–50, 169–70, 185.
12. King (1988b), 517–9.
13. Remer (1933), 339; McLean (1973), 2; Crisswell (1981), 227–9; Hooper (1986), 7–25, 51, 95–108; Shao (1981), 60, 76, 138.
14. Shao, 27; Shai (1989), 90–108; Blyth & Wotherspoon (1997), 192.
15. Welsh, 461–503; Lethbridge (1980), 204; Barber (1981), 175–90; Keswick (1982), 234, 255.

35. 'LYING IN THE CENTRE OF TRADE': MALAYSIA (pp.451–463)

1. Blaxland (1971), 166; Miller (1972), 49–50; Short (1975), 167–8; Royle (1987), 202–3; Jackson (1991), 45.
2. Hamilton (1744), II, 83; Harlow (1955), 445–50.
3. Fry (1970), xiii-xxi, 15–25; Braddell, Brooke & Makepeace (1991), I, 6.
4. Fry, 53, 75, 100–10, 121, 135.
5. Calder (1970), 709.
6. Braddell, Brooke & Makepeace, I, 8, 41, 73–9, 147; Morton (1825), 1, 22–36, 52, 70, 82; Crawfurd (1915), 45–6; Marcus (1954), 1–6; Greer (1956), 29; Harrison (1961), 23; Tarling (1972), 18; Roxborough (1988–9), 71.
7. Braddell, Brooke & Makepeace, I, 8–10, 74–82; Majumdar (1962), 3, 451–2, 471–3, 506, 518; Anderson (1965), 7; Cunyngham-Brown (1971), 1, 58–63, 77, 94–6, 117–25, 147–59, 173; Bristowe (1974), 88–93; Anon. (1978), 1–7; Fasseur (1980), XI, 348; Baud (1983), I, 50; III, 54; Macinnes (1994), 25.
8. Longhurst (1956), 17, 34, 70; Kratoska (1983), 223; King (1995), xii, xv, 159–86, 211.
9. Tregonning (1956), 236–43; (1958), 10–20, 35–42, 54–63, 86, 137.
10. Ferguson (1894), *passim*; Lord (1897), 81, 118; Dixon (1939), 23–34; Ward (1965), 35; Michie (1985), 68–70, 81–2; Hargreaves (1994), 67–9.
11. Couperus (1924), 17; Lockhart (1936), 4, 39, 74, 141–2, 176–89, 248; Butcher (1978), 25–39.
12. Cunyngham-Brown, 194, 249, 289–93, 306–9; Butcher, 46; Stillson (1971), 592; Drabble (1973), 81–5; Drabble & Drake (1981), 306–13, 328; Jones & Van Helten (1989), 171–3.
13. Garner (1978), 377; Porter & Stockwell (1987), I, 63; Sanger (1995), 271, 283, 297, 308, 335–8.
14. Wong (1960), 13–15; MacDonald (1986), 1; Wilson (1960), vii-viii, 2–3, 43, 198; Dickson (1971), I, 38, 52–75, 110, 150, 173, 210–4, 227–39.

36. 'A KINGDOM OF THE MIND': CANADA (pp.464–476)

1. Galbraith (1964), 32–3 and *passim*. I am grateful to Professor Galbraith for his kind permission to use this short passage as epigraph to the present chapter.
2. Fraser (1903), 6–19; Knowles (1905), 37; Grieve (1926), 85; Niven (1935), 15–19; (1944), 20–2; Campbell (1981), 163–73; Knowles (1981), 2–15, 392–7; Wagner (1984), 4.
3. MacLeod (1991), 106, 163, 217; Maclean (1998), 98–104.
4. Dunn (1953), 74, 123, 138–46; Ommer (1986), 121–38; Ross (1987), 6, 21–32; Davidson (1988), 32 *et seqq*.
5. Craig (1990), 88, 102, 190–1, 272.
6. Campbell, 174; Galt (1831), Ch.29; Reid (1979), 119; Scott (1985), 102; Cowan (1992), 75.
7. Sellar (1974), vii-ix; Cameron (1978), 146–6, 262–4; Doucette (1980), 20–39, 146–56; Little (1991), 1, 13, 27, 77, 102.
8. Reid (1976), 125; Moir (1978), 34–40.
9. Pickersgill (1960), I, 666; Grant (1965), 50.
10. Buchan (1941), 39; Siegfried (1947), 74; Smith (1965), 375, 396, 406, 420; Best (1976), 15; Lownie (1995), 264–5.
11. Buchan, 81; Lownie, 286; Sandison (1967), 171–9; Daniell (1975), 197; Harvie (1991), 52–4.
12. MacLennan (1951), iii.
13. Atwood (1972), 36, 62, 93.
14. Maclean, 9, 309–16; Bumsted (1982), 13; Kennedy (1976), 112; McLean (1991), 213; McRoberts (1998), 300 *et seqq*.

37. 'TRAITORS TO SCOTLAND': IMPERIAL ECONOMICS (pp.447–489)

1. King (1991), 891–3.
2. King, 895–6; Longbridge (1980), 204; Barber (1981), 175–80; Keswick (1982), 234, 255; Welsh (1993), 501–3, 532.
3. Jones (1993), 344–5.
4. Flinn (1977), 211; Lenman (1977), 288.
5. Committee on Commercial and Industrial Polucy (1918), 21–48.
6. Beaverbrook (1934), 11–13; Fry (1987), 139; Kinchin & Kinchin (1988), 35–6, 129–36; Cain & Hopkins (1993), 13, 30, 47, 73; Kim & Slaven (1994), *passim.*
7. Marwick (1935–6), 115–6; Gilbert (1939), 9–10, 120; Donald (1956), 203–6; Treble (1980), 185; Thomas (1973), 316–7.
8. Cable (1937), 218; Trotter (1938), 226–35; Blake (1956), 180; McLellan (1956), 58, 94–104; Hannah (1976), 187–91; Muir & Davies (1978), 217; Orbell (1978), 70–7; Strachan (1992), 11.
9. Harvey (1981), 208–15; Grieves (1989), 108, 125–45.
10. Jones (1986), 238; (1987), 119; (1989), 134–48.
11. Swire (1929), xxi; Bolitho (1936), 160–1, 177; Mackenzie (1954), 179; Pollo & Puto (1981), 181; Jones (1989), 155–6.
12. Anon. (1938), 10, 30, 56–62; Hunt (1951), 11, 28, 120, 179, 211; Mejcher (1972), 380; Kent (1976), 190.
13. Corley (1983), 6–10, 67, 144–7, 162–4, 217, 239, 265–70, 308, 362, 377, 388.
14. Campbell (1965), 245; Flinn (1966), 233; Hume & Moss (1977), 10; Maxwell (1982), 22.

38. 'NOT SOLELY SCOTTISH': THE END OF EMPIRE (pp.490–499)

1. Mitchell (1969), 192–7, 225, 241; Paget (1969), 218–37, 250; Blaxland (1971), 456 *et seqq*; Gavin (1975), 349; Harper (1978), 111–5; Balfour-Paul (1991), 88–90; Holland (1991), 336.
2. Wormald (1992), 93; Williamson (1993), *passim*; (1996), *passim.*
3. Robertson (1777), I, 55; Greig (1969), I, 245; Lüthy (1964), 28–30; Pagden (1995), 2–10.
4. Armitage (1997), *passim.*
5. Davie (1961), Ch.1; Pittock (1991), 54.
6. Mitchell, 21.
7. Kendrick & McCrone (1989), 595; McCrone (1992), 46–69, 158, 209; Kidd (1993), 213–5.
8. Robbins (1983), 92–3.
9. MacDiarmid (1972), 233–4; Hechter (1985), 20; Ashcroft, Griffith & Tiffin (1989), 15; Marr (1992), 73.
10. Robertson (1994), 225; Finlay (1997), 13.
11. Powell (1969), 255.
12. Dunlop & Mills (1986), 25–7; (1987), 119–32.
13. Keating (1988), 27, 96–7.
14. Lüthy, *loc.cit.*

Bibliography

Abbott, L.W., 'James McGill (1744–1813)', *Scottish Tradition*, xi, 1981

Aberdein, J.W., *John Galt* (Oxford, 1926)

Ackerman, R., *J.G. Frazer, his life and work* (Cambridge, 1987)

Adair, D., '"That Politics may be Reduced to a Science" – David Hume, James Madison and the Tenth *Federalist*', *Huntington Library Quarterly*, xx, 1956–7

Adam, M.I., 'The Highland Emigration of 1770', *Scottish Historical Review*, xvi, 1919

——, 'The Causes of the Highland Emigrations of 1783–1803', *Scottish Historical Review*, xvii, 1920

Adams, I. & Somerville, M., *Cargoes of Hope and Despair, Scottish emigration to North America*, 1603–1803 (Edinburgh, 1993)

Adams, J.T., 'On the Term "British Empire"', *American Historical Review*, xxvii, 1919

Adams, R.G., 'Two Documents on the Battle of King's Mountain', *North Carolina Historical Review*, viii, 1931

Adams, R.J.Q., *Bonar Law* (London, 1999)

Agnarsdottir, A., 'Scottish Plans for the Annexation of Iceland, 1785–1813', *Northern Studies*, xxix, 1992

Agyemang, F., *We Presbyterians* (Accra, 1978)

Airlie, S., *Thistle and Bamboo, the life and time of Sir James Stewart Lockhart* (Hong Kong, 1989)

Ajayi, J.F.A., *Christian Missions in Nigeria, 1841–1891 (Evanston, 1965)*

Akenson, D.H., 'Why the Accepted Estimates of the Ethnicity of the American People, 1790, are Unacceptable', *William and Mary Quarterly*, xli, 1984

Akinjogbin, I.A., 'Archibald Dalzel, slave trader and historian of Dahomey', *Journal of African History*, vii, 1966

Alden, J.R., *John Stuart and the Southern Colonial Frontier* (Ann Arbor, 1944)

Alexander, Sir W., *An Encouragement to Colonies* (London, 1624)

Alexander, W.G., *Recollections of a Highland Subaltern* (London, 1898)

Allan, V., 'The Prince of Poyais', *History Today*, ii, 1952

Allen, G.C. & Donnithorne, A.G., *Western Enterprise in Far Eastern Economic Development* (London, 1954)

Ambirajan, S., *Classical Political Economy and British Policy in India* (Cambridge, 1978)

Amery, J. & Garvin, J., *Life of Joseph Chamberlain* (London, 1935–69)

Amoh, Y. & Fagg, J.B., 'Adam Ferguson's Rules of War', *Eighteenth-Century Scotland*, v, 1991

Anderson, J., *Political and Commercial Considerations relative to the Malayan Peninsula* (Singapore, 1965; first published, 1824)

Anderson, M. & Morse, D.J., 'The People', in Fraser & Morris (1990)

Anon., *A List of the Subscribers to the Company of Scotland Trading to Africa and the Indies* (Edinburgh, 1696)

——, *Some Seasonable and Modest Thoughts partly occasioned by and partly concerning the Scots East India Company* (Edinburgh, 1699a)

——, *The History of Caledonia* (London, 1699b)

——, *A Full and Exact Collection of all the Public Papers relating to the Company of Scotland Trading to Africa and the Indies* (n.p., 1700a)

——, *An Enquiry into the Caledonian Project* (London, 1700b)

——, *The Original Papers and Letters relating to the Scots Company Trading to Africa and the Indies* (n.p., 1700c)

——, *The Arraignment, Trial and Condemnation of Captain William Kidd for Murder and Piracy* (London, 1701)

——, *The Case of Scotsmen residing in England and in the English Plantations* (Edinburgh, 1703)

——, *The State of Controversy betwixt United and Separate Parliaments* (Edinburgh, 1706)

——, *Opinions of the Hon Mountstuart Elphinstone examined and compared with those of the late Sir Thomas Munro and Sir John Malcolm* (London, 1831)

——, *The Wrongs of the Caffre Nation* (London, 1837)

——, 'Scottish Capital Abroad', *Blackwood's Edinburgh Magazine*, cxxxvi, 1884

——, 'The Scot Abroad', *Scottish Geographical Magazine*, ii, 1885

——, 'Founder of Burn & Co', *Burn's Monthly Magazine*, ii, 1908

——, *Federation and Home Rule* (London, 1910)

——, *The History of Smith, Mackenzie & Co* (London, 1938)

——, *James Finlay & Co Ltd, 1750–1950* (Glasgow, 1951)

——, *The Duncan Group* (London, 1959)

——, 'The Rise of Glasgow's West Indian Trade', *Three Banks Review*, li, 1961

——, 'An Early Glasgow-West Indian Miscellany', *Three Banks Review*, liv, 1962

——, *The House of Binny* (Madras, 1969)

——, *Under Four Flags, the story of Smith, Bell & Company in the Philippines* (Bristol, 1978)

——, *Andrew Yule & Co Ltd* (Edinburgh, 1980)

Anstey, R., *Britain and the Congo in the Nineteenth Century* (Oxford, 1962)

——, *King Leopold's Legacy* (Oxford, 1966)

Anstey, V., *The Economic Development of India* (London, 1952)

Apter, D., *The Political Kingdom in Buganda* (Princeton & London, 1964)

Arasthi, A. & Sinha, R.M., *Elphinstone Correspondence, 1804–1808* (Nagpur, 1961)

Arbuthnot, Sir A.J., *Major-General Sir Thomas Munro* (London, 1881)

Argyll, Duke of, *India under Dalhousie and Canning* (London, 1865)

Armitage, D., The British Empire and the Civic Tradition 1656–1742, unpublished D.Phil. thesis, University of Cambridge, 1992

——, 'The Scottish Vision of Empire, intellectual origins of the Darien venture', in Robertson (1995)

——, Colonial Theory in a Provincial Society, Scotland before 1707, unpublished paper, 1996

——, 'Making the Empire British, Scotland in the Atlantic world, 1542–1707', *Past and Present*, clv, 1997

Armstrong, J., 'Conferences in British Nineteenth-century Coastal Shipping', *Mariner's Mirror*, lxxvii, 1991

Arnold, E., *The Marquis of Dalhousie's Administration of British India* (London, 1862)

Ascherson, N., *The King Incorporated* (London, 1963)

Ashcroft, B., Griffith, G., & Tiffin, A., *The Empire Writes Back, theory and practice in post-colonial literatures* (London & New York, 1989)

Asquith, C. & Spender, J.A., *Life of Lord Oxford & Asquith* (London, 1932)

Asquith, M., *Autobiography* (London, 1962)

Attard, J., *Britain and Malta* (Marsa, 1988)

Atwell, P., *British Mandarins and Chinese Reformers* (Hong Kong, 1985)

Atwood, M., *Survival, a thematic guide to Canadian literature* (Toronto, 1972)

Auld, J.W., 'The Liberal Pro-Boers', *Journal of British Studies*, xiv, 1975

Austin, J.H.E., 'Recruiting in Scotland', *Journal of the Royal Army Medical Corps*, xxiii, 1914

Bagchi, A.K., *Private Investment in India, 1900–1939* (Cambridge, 1972)

Bailey, J.D., 'Australian Borrowing in Scotland in the Nineteenth Century', *Economic History Review*, xii, 1959–60

——, *A Hundred Years of Pastoral Banking* (Oxford, 1966)

Bailyn, B., *Voyagers to the West* (New York, 1986)

& Clive, J., 'England's Cultural Provinces, Scotland and America', *William and Mary Quarterly*, xi, 1954

& Morgan, P.D. (eds.), *Strangers within the Realm, cultural margins of the first British Empire* (Williamsburg, 1991)

Bain, A., *James Mill, a biography* (London, 1882)

Baird, J.G.A. (ed.), *Private Letters of the Marquess of Dalhousie* (Edinburgh & London, 1910)

Baird, W., *General Wauchope* (Edinburgh & London, 1901)

Baker, D.W.A., *Days of Wrath, a life of John Dunmore Lang* (Melbourne, 1981)

Baker, P., *Attitudes to Coloured People in Glasgow* (Glasgow, 1970)

Balfour, A.J., *A Defence of Philosophic Doubt* (London, 1879)

——, *Economic Notes on Insular Free Trade* (London, 1903)

——, *Negotiation and Imperial Trade* (London, 1904)

——, *Imperial Defence* (London, 1905)
——, *Imperial Preference* (London, 1911)
——, *Nationality and Home Rule* (London, 1913)
——, *Opinions and Arguments from Speeches and Addresses* (London, 1927)
Balfour, G., *The Life of Robert Louis Stevenson* (London, 1901)
Balfour, R.G., *Presbyterianism in the Colonies* (Edinburgh, 1899)
Balfour-Paul, G., *The End of Empire in the Middle East* (Cambridge, 1991)
Ballantyne, M.M.S. & Shepherd, R.H.W., *Forerunners of Modern Malawi, the early missionary adventures of Dr James Henderson* (Lovedale, 1968)
Ballantyne, R.M., *Six Months at the Cape* (London, 1879)
Banda, H.K. & Young, T.C., *Our African Way of Life* (London & Redhill, 1946)
Banerjea, P., *Indian Finance in the Days of the Company* (London, 1928)
Bannister, S. (ed.), *The Writings of William Paterson* (New York, 1968; first published, 1859)
Barber, L., 'The Scottish Economy at Mid-Term, more than an invisible hand at work', in Drucker, H.M. & N.L. (1981)
Barber, W.J., *British Economic Thought and India* (Oxford, 1975)
Barbour, J.S., *A History of William Paterson and the Darien Company* (Edinburgh & London, 1907)
Barker, H.F., *National Stocks in the Population of the United States as Indicated by Surnames in the Census of 1790*, Annual Report of the American Historical Association, 1931
Barker, M., *Gladstone and Radicalism* (Hassocks, 1975)
Barnard, M., *History of Australia* (Sydney, 1962)
Barrow, G.W.S., *Robert Bruce and the Community of the Realm of Scotland* (Edinburgh, 1965)
Barry, J.V., *Alexander Maconochie of Norfolk Island* (Melbourne, 1958)
Bartlett, C.J., *Great Britain and Sea Power, 1815–1853* (Oxford, 1963)
Bartley, J.O., *Teague, Shenkin and Sawney* (Cork, 1954)
Baster, A.J., *The Imperial Banks* (London, 1929)
Bates, D., *A Gust of Plumes* (London, 1972)
Bates, M., 'Social Engineering, Multiracialism and the Rise of TANU, the trust territory of Tanganyika, 1945–1961', in Low & Smith (1976)
Bateson, C., *Patrick Logan* (Sydney, 1966)
Baud, W.A., *De Semi-officiele en Particuliere Briefwisseling tussen J.C. Baud en J.J. Rochussen* (Assen, 1983)
Bayly, C., *Imperial Meridian, the British Empire and the world, 1780–1830* (London & New York, 1989)
Baynes, J., *The History of the Cameronians (Scottish Rifles), iv, 1948–1968* (London, 1971)
——, *Soldiers of Scotland* (London, 1988)
Beaglehole, T.H., *Thomas Munro and the Development of Administrative Policy in Madras, 1792–1818* (Cambridge, 1966)
Bearce, G.D., *British Attitudes to India, 1784–1858* (Oxford, 1961)
Beattie, J., *Elements of Moral Science* (Edinburgh, 1807)
Beaverbrook, Lord, *The Resources of the British Empire* (London, 1934)
Becker, H., *Through Values to Social Interpretation* (Durham, NC, 1950)
Beckett, J.C., *Protestant Dissent in Ireland, 1687–1780* (London, 1948)
——, *Confrontations, studies in Irish history* (London, 1972)
Begg, A., *The Creation of Manitoba* (Toronto, 1871)
Begg, J., *A Visit to New Zealand* (Edinburgh, 1874)
Behr, E., *The Last Emperor* (London, 1987)
Beidelman, T.O., *W. Robertson Smith and the Sociological Study of Religion* (Chicago, 1974)
Bell, I., *Robert Louis Stevenson, dreams of exile* (Edinburgh, 1992)
Bence-Jones, M., *The Viceroys of India* (London, 1982)
Benda, H.J., 'Christiaan Snouck Hurgronje and the Foundations of Dutch Islamic Policy in Indonesia', *Journal of Modern History*, xxx, 1958
Bender, G.J., *Angola under the Portuguese* (London, 1978)
Benians, E.A., Butler, Sir J. & Carrington, C.E. (eds.), *The Cambridge History of the British Empire*, iii, *The Empire – Commonwealth* (Cambridge, 1959)
Benians, E.A., Holland Rose, J. & Newton, A.P. (eds.), *The Cambridge History of the British Empire*, I, *The Old Empire* (Cambridge, 1929)
——, *II, The New Empire* (Cambridge, 1940)
——, *VI, Canada and Newfoundland* (Cambridge, 1930)

——, *VII, Pt. 1, Australia* (Cambridge, 1933)

——, *VII, Pt. 2, New Zealand* (Cambridge, 1933)

Bennett, N.R., *A History of the Arab State of Zanzibar* (London, 1978)

Bentwich, H. & N., *Mandate Memories, 1918–1948* (London, 1965)

Bérard, V., *L'Angleterre et l'impérialisme* (London, 1906)

Berry, C.J., 'James Dunbar and the American War of Independence', *Aberdeen University Review*, xlv, 1974

Best, H.B.M., 'The Auld Alliance in New France', in Reid (1976)

Bew, P. Gibbon, P. & Patterson, H., *Northern Ireland, 1921–1994* (London, 1995)

Bewley, C., *Muir of Huntershill* (Oxford, 1981)

Bezzina, J., *Religion and Politics in a Crown Colony* (Valletta, 1985)

Bickley, G., The Hong Kong Government Central School and the New Hong Kong Government Education System, the relative contributions of James Legge, George Smith and Frederick Stewart, unpublished paper, 1997

——, *The Golden Needle, the biography of Frederick Stewart, 1835–1889* (Hong Kong, 1997)

Biéler, A., *La Pensée Economique et Sociale de Calvin* (Geneva, 1961)

Bielinski, S., Scottish-Dutch Intermarriage in Colonial New York, unpublished paper, 1996

Bingham, H., 'The Early History of the Scots Darien Company', *Scottish Historical Review*, iii, 1906

Birch, D. & Macmillan, D.S., *Wealth and Progress, studies in Australian business history* (Sydney, 1967)

Black, G.F., *Scotland's Mark on America* (New York, 1921)

Black, J., 'The Tory View of Eighteenth-Century British Foreign Policy', *Historical Journal*, xxxi, 1988

Black, J.S. & Chrystal, G., *The Life of William Robertson Smith* (London, 1912a)

(eds.), *Lectures and Essays of William Robertson Smith* (London, 1912b)

Blake, C., *Charles Elliot, RN, 1801–1875* (London, 1960)

Blake, G., *B.I. Centenary, 1856–1956* (London, 1956)

——, *The Ben Line* (London, 1956)

Blake, R., *The Unknown Prime Minister* (London, 1955)

Blaxland, G., *The Regiments Depart* (London, 1971)

Blewett, N., 'Free Fooders, Balfourites, Whole Hoggers, factionalism within the Unionist party, 1906–1910', *Historical Journal*, xi, 1968

Blundell, Sir M., *So Rough a Wind* (London, 1964)

Blussé, L. & Gaastra, F., *Companies and Trade* (Leiden, 1981)

Blyth, S. & Wotherspoon, I., *Hong Kong Remembers* (Hong Kong, 1996)

Bodelsen, C.A., *Studies in Mid-Victorian Imperialism* (London, 1960)

Bolitho, H.H., *James Lyle Mackay, First Earl of Inchcape* (London, 1936)

Bolt, C., *Victorian Attitudes to Race* (London & Toronto, 1971)

Bolton, G.C., 'The Rise of Burns, Philp 1873–1893', in Birch & Macmillan (1967)

Bonar, A.A., *Narrative of a Mission of Inquiry to the Jews* (Edinburgh, 1842)

——, *Memoir of the Rev David Sandeman* (London, 1861)

Booth, C., *Zachary Macaulay* (London, 1934)

Boswell, J., *Account of Corsica* (London, 1768)

——, *Journal of a Tour to the Hebrides* (Oxford, 1924; first published, 1786)

Bourne, K., *Britain and the Balance of Power in North America, 1815–1908* (London, 1967)

Bovill, E.W., *Missions to the Niger* (Cambridge, 1964)

Bowsfield, H., *Louis Riel, the rebel and the hero* (Toronto, 1971)

Boxer, C.R., *Portuguese and Dutch Colonial Rivalry* (Lisbon, 1958)

——, *The Portuguese Seaborne Empire* (London, 1960)

——, *Race Relations in the Portuguese Colonial Empire, 1415–1825* (Oxford, 1963)

——, 'The Portuguese in Brazil', in Curtis & Nadel (1964)

——, *The Dutch Seaborne Empire* (London, 1965)

——, 'War and Trade in the Indian Ocean and the South China Sea', *Journal of the Australian Association for Maritime History*, i, 1979

Boyce, D.G. & Stubbs, J.O., 'F.S. Oliver, Lord Selborne and Federation', *Journal of Imperial and Commonwealth Affairs*, v, 1976–7

Bradley, I., 'James Ramsay and the Slave Trade', *History Today*, xxii, 1972

Brady, C. & Gillespie, R., *Natives and Newcomers, essays on the making of Irish colonial society* (Bungay, 1986)

Brand, A. & Woodhouse, T., *A Century's Progress in Jute Manufacture* (Dundee, 1934)
Branson, R., 'James Madison and the Scottish Enlightenment', *Journal of the History of Ideas*, xi, 1979
Bride, T.F. (ed.), *Letters from Victorian Pioneers* (Melbourne, 1899)
Bridges, G.W., *The Annals of Jamaica* (London, 1828)
Brock, R.A. (ed.), *The Official Records of Robert Dinwiddie* (Richmond, Va., 1883)
Brock, S.M., James Stewart and Lovedale, unpublished Ph.D. thesis, University of Edinburgh, 1974
Brock, W.R., *Scotus Americanus* (Edinburgh, 1982)
Bromley, J.S. & Kossman, E.H. (eds.), *Britain and the Netherlands in Europe and Asia* (London, 1968)
Brooke, P., *Ulster Presbyterianism* (Dublin, 1987)
Brooking, T., 'Tam McCanny and Kitty Clydeside', the Scots in New Zealand', in Cage (1985)
Brougham, H., *An Inquiry into the Colonial Policy of the European Powers* (Edinburgh, 1803)
——, *A Concise Statement of the Question regarding the Abolition of the Slave Trade* (London, 1807)
Brown, D., *Life of Dr John Duncan* (Edinburgh, 1872)
Brown, G. Douglas, *The House with the Green Shutters* (London, 1901)
Brown, I.G. & Cherry, T.A., *Scottish Architects at Home and Abroad* (Edinburgh, 1978)
Brown, P.L. (ed.), *The Narrative of George Russell of Golf Hill* (Oxford, 1935)
——, *Clyde Company Papers* (Oxford, 1941)
Brown, R. & Stokes, E. (eds.), *The Zambesian Past* (Manchester, 1966)
Brown, S.J., ' "Echoes of Midlothian", Scottish Liberalism and the South African war', *Scottish Historical Review*, lxxi, 1992
' "Outside the Covenant", the Scottish presbyterian Churches and Irish immigration 1922–1938', *Innes Review*, xlii, 1991
(ed.), *William Robertson and the Expansion of Europe* (Cambridge, 1996)
——, The Idea of an Established Church in Eighteenth-century Irish Presbyterianism, unpublished paper, 1999
& Fry, M.R.G. (eds.), *Scotland in the Age of the Disruption* (Edinburgh, 1993)
Brown, W., *The Good Americans, the loyalists in the American Revolution* (New York, 1969)
Browning, O., 'Adam Smith and Free Trade for Ireland', *English Historical Review*, i, 1886
Bruce, A.L., *The Cape to Cairo* (Edinburgh, 1892)
Bruce, J., *Historical View of Plans for the Government of British India* (London, 1798)
——, *Report on the Negotiations between the Honourable East India Company and the Public, respecting the renewal of the Company's exclusive privileges of trade, for 20 years from March 1794* (London, 1811)
Bruce, S., 'The Ulster Connection', in Gallagher & Walker (1990)
Bryant, G.J., 'Scots in India in the Eighteenth Century', *Scottish Historical Review*, lxiv, 1985
Bryce, G., *Mackenzie, Selkirk, Simpson* (London, 1905)
——, *The Scotsman in Canada, ii, Western Canada* (London, 1911)
Bryce, J., *A History of the Holy Roman Empire* (London, 1871)
——, *Impressions of South Africa* (London, 1897)
——, *The Relations of the Advanced and Backward Races of Mankind* (Oxford, 1902)
——, *Studies in Contemporary Biography* (London, 1903)
——, *Lord Reay, 1839–1921* (London, 1921)
Buchan, J., *The African Colony* (Edinburgh & London, 1903)
——, *A Lodge in the Wilderness* (Edinburgh & London, 1906)
——, *Prester John* (London, 1910)
——, *Salute to Adventurers* (London, 1917)
——, *The History of the South African Forces in France* (Cape Town, 1921)
——, *Midwinter* (London, 1923)
——, *A History of the Great War* (London, 1923)
——, *Lord Minto, a memoir* (London, 1924)
——, *The Runagates Club* (London, 1928)
——, *Comment and Characters* (London, 1940)
——, *Memory Hold-the-Door* (London, 1940)
——, *Sick Heart River* (London, 1941)
Buchan, J., *The Expendable Mary Slessor* (Edinburgh, 1980)
Buchanan, G., *Opera Omnia* (Leiden, 1725)
Buchanan, J., *The Shire Highlands as Colony and Mission* (Edinburgh & London, 1885)
Buckingham, W. & Ross, G.W., *The Hon Alexander Mackenzie, his life and times* (Toronto, 1892)

Budge, I. & Urwin, D.W., *Scottish Political Behaviour* (London, 1966)

Buist, M., *At Spes non Fracta, Hope & Co, 1770–1815* (The Hague, 1974)

Bulloch, J. & Drummond, A.L., *The Church in Victorian Scotland* (Edinburgh, 1975)

Bumsted, J.M., 'Highland Emigration to the Island of St John and the Scottish Catholic Church, 1769–1774', *Dalhousie Review*, lviii, 1978

——, 'Sir James Montgomery and Prince Edward Island, 1767–1803', *Acadiensis*, vii, 1978

——, 'Scottish Emigration to the Maritimes, 1770–1815, a new look at an old theme', *Acadiensis*, x, 1981

——, *The People's Clearance, Highland emigration to British North America, 1770–1815* (Edinburgh & Winnipeg, 1982)

——, *The Scots in Canada* (Ottawa, 1982)

Burne, Sir O.T., *Clyde and Strathnairn* (Oxford, 1891)

Burns, Sir A., *Colonial Civil Servant* (London, 1949)

Burns, I., *Memoir of the Rev William C. Burns* (London, 1870)

Burns, R.F., *The Life and Times of the Rev Robert Burns* (Toronto, 1872)

Burrell, S.A., 'Calvinism, Capitalism and the Middle Classes', *Journal of Modern History*, xxxii, 1960

Burrow, J.W., *Evolution and Society* (Cambridge, 1970)

Burton, J.H., *Political and Social Economy* (Edinburgh, 1849)

——, *The Darien Papers* (Edinburgh, 1849)

——, *The Scot Abroad* (Edinburgh & London, 1864)

Bute, Marchioness of, *The Private Journal of the Marquess of Hastings* (London, 1858)

Butcher, J.G., *The British in Malaya* (Kuala Lumpur, 1982)

Butler, J., *The Liberal Party and the Jameson Raid* (Oxford, 1968)

Butler, J.R.M., *Lord Lothian* (London, 1960)

Butler, S.M., The Glasgow Tobacco Merchants and the American Revolution, unpublished Ph.D. thesis, University of St Andrews 1978

Butt, J., 'David Livingstone and the Idea of African Evolution', *History Today*, xiii, 1963

——, 'The Scottish Cotton Industry during the Industrial Revolution, 1780–1840', in Cullen & Smout (1977)

& Lythe, S.G.E., *An Economic History of Scotland, 1100–1939* (Glasgow & London, 1975)

Byres, J., *A Letter to a Friend at Edinburgh* (n.p., 1702)

Byrne, F.J., Martin, F.X. & Moody, T.W. (eds.), *A New History of Ireland, III, Early Modern Ireland, 1534–1691* (Oxford, 1976)

Cable, B., *A Hundred Year History of the P & O* (London, 1937)

Cage, R.A., *The Scots Abroad, labour, capital and enterprise, 1750–1914* (London, 1985)

Cain, A.M., *The Cornchest for Scotland, Scots in India* (Edinburgh, 1986)

Cain, P.J. & Hopkins, A.G., *British Imperialism, innovation and expansion, 1688–1914* (London & New York, 1993a)

——, *British Imperialism, crisis and deconstruction* (London & New York, 1993b)

Cairncross, A.K., *Home and Foreign Investment, 1870–1913* (Cambridge, 1953)

Calder, A., *Revolutionary Empire, the rise of the English-speaking empires from the fifteenth century to the 1780s* (London, 1981)

——, 'Thomas Pringle (1789–1834), a Scottish poet in South Africa', in Riemenschneider (1988)

——, 'The Great Days, and Now?' *The Raven*, xviii, 1992

——, 'The Disruption in Fiction', in Brown & Fry (1993)

——, *Revolving Culture, notes from the Scottish republic* (London & New York, 1994)

Calder, J., *Scotland's March Past, the share of Scottish missionaries in the London Missionary Society* (London, 1945)

Calder, J., *RLS, a life study* (London, 1980)

(ed.), *The Enterprising Scot* (Edinburgh, 1986)

——, 'Andrew Bell, an experiment in India', in the above

——, 'Perilous Enterprises, Scottish explorers in the Arctic', in the above

Cameron, E. (ed.), *The Other Side of Hugh MacLennan, selected essays old and new* (Toronto, 1978)

Cameron, J.M., A Study of the Factors that Assisted and Directed Scottish Emigration to Upper Canada, 1815–1855, unpublished Ph.D. thesis, University of Glasgow, 1970

Cameron, N., *Barbarians and Mandarins* (Hong Kong, 1989)

Campbell, A., *A Voyage round the World* (Edinburgh, 1810)

Campbell, C., *Memoirs* (Glasgow, 1828)

Campbell, D., *General Hector A. Macdonald* (London, 1900)

Campbell, D. & MacLean, R.A., *Beyond the Atlantic Roar, a study of the Nova Scotia Scots* (Toronto, 1975)

Campbell, Sir G., *Memoirs of my Indian Career* (London, 1893)

Campbell, I., 'Knowles of Galt (1868–1944)', *Scottish Tradition*, xi, 1981

Campbell, J., *The Spanish Empire in America* (London, 1747)

——, *An Account of the Spanish Settlements in America* (Edinburgh, 1762)

Campbell, J., *Travels in South Africa* (London, 1822)

Campbell, M.W., *The North West Company* (Toronto, 1957)

——, *McGillivray, Lord of the Northwest* (Toronto, 1962)

Campbell, R.H., *Tippoo Sultan, the Fall of Seringapatam and the Restoration of the Hindu Raj* (Bangalore, 1919)

Campbell, R.H., *Scotland since 1707, the rise of an industrial society* (Oxford, 1965)

& Skinner, A.S. (eds.), *The Origins and Nature of the Scottish Enlightenment* (Edinburgh, 1982)

Campbell, R.R., *James Duncan Campbell* (Cambridge, Mass., 1970)

Campbell, W., *Formosa under the Dutch* (London, 1903)

Canny, N., 'The Marginal Kingdom, Ireland as a problem in the first British Empire', in Bailyn & Morgan (1991)

Careless, J.H.S., *Brown of the Globe* (Toronto, 1959)

Carlyle, T., *Occasional Discourse on the Nigger Question* (London, 1853)

——, *Latter-Day Pamphlets* (London, 1897)

Carmichael, Lady M., *Lord Carmichael of Skirling* (London, 1930)

Carnall, G., 'Robertson and Contemporary Images of India', in Brown (1997)

& Nicholson, C. (eds), *The Impeachment of Warren Hastings* (Edinburgh, 1989)

Carr, J.D., *The Life of Sir Arthur Conan Doyle* (London, 1949)

Carstairs, A.M., 'Some Economic Aspects of the Union of Parliaments', *Scottish Journal of Political Economy*, ii, 1955

& Cole, A.V., 'Recent Developments in the Jute Industry', *Scottish Journal of Political Economy*, vii, 1960

Carter, A., 'Dutch Foreign Investment, 1738–1800', *Economica*, xx, 1953

Carter, J.J. & Pittock, J.H. (eds.), *Aberdeen and the Enlightenment* (Aberdeen, 1987)

Cashin, E., *Lachlan McGillivray, Indian trader* (Athens, Ga., 1992)

Cassis, Y., 'The Emergence of a New Financial Institution, investment trusts in Britain, 1870–1939', in the following

& Van Helten, J.J. (eds.), *Capitalism in a Mature Economy* (Aldershot, 1990)

Caw, J.L., *Scottish Painters, past and present* (Edinburgh, 1908)

Chadwick, O., *Mackenzie's Grave* (London, 1959)

Chalmers, J., *Letters written from India during the Mutiny and Waziri Campaigns* (Edinburgh, 1904)

Chalmers, J.A., *Tiyo Soga* (Edinburgh., 1878)

Chalmers, T., *The Utility of Missions Ascertained by Experience* (Edinburgh, 1815)

Chaloner, W.H. & Ratcliffe, B.M., *Trade and Transport* (Manchester, 1977)

Chamberlain, M.E., *Lord Aberdeen, a political biography* (London & New York, 1983)

Chamberlin, D. (ed.), *Some Letters from Livingstone, 1840–1872* (Oxford, 1940)

Chambers, D., Mission and Party in the Church of Scotland 1810–1843, unpublished thesis, University of Cambridge, 1973

Chambers, R., *Smollett* (Edinburgh & London, 1867)

Chambers, W., *Designs of Chinese Buildings* (London, 1757)

——, *Dissertation on Oriental Gardening* (London, 1772)

Chancellor, V., *The Political Life of Joseph Hume, 1777–1855* (London, 1986)

Chapman, D., 'The Establishment of the Jute Industry', *Review of Economic Studies*, vi, 1938–9

& Menzies, I.E.P., 'The Jute Industry', in Silverman (1946)

Chapman, J.K., *The Career of Arthur Hamilton Gordon, First Lord Stanmore* (Toronto, 1964)

Chapman, S.D., 'British-based Investment before 1914', *Economic History Review*, xxxviii, 1985

Charteris, J., *Field-Marshal Earl Haig* (London, 1920)

Chaudhuri, R.N., *The Economic Development of India under the East India Company, 1814–1858* (Cambridge, 1971)

Checkland, O. & S.G., *Industry and Ethos, Scotland 1832–1914* (London, 1984)

Checkland, S.G., 'John Gladstone as Trader and Planter', *Economic History Review*, vii, 1954–5

——, 'Two Scottish West Indian Liquidations after 1793', *Scottish Journal of Political Economy*, iv, 1957

——, *The Gladstones* (Cambridge, 1971)

——, *The Upas Tree, Glasgow 1875–1975* (Glasgow, 1976)

——, *The Elgins, 1766–1917* (Aberdeen, 1988)

Ch'en, J., *Yuan Shih-K'ai* (London, 1961)

Cheong, W.E., *Mandarins and Merchants – Jardine, Matheson & Co, a China agency of the early nineteenth century* (London & Malmo, 1979)

Chirnside, A., *The Blantyre Missionaries* (London, 1880)

Chisholm, A.H., *Scots Wha Hae, history of the Royal Caledonian Society of Melbourne* (Sydney, 1950)

Choksey, R.D., *Mountstuart Elphinstone* (Bombay, 1971)

Cioffi, F., *Wittgenstein on Freud and Frazer* (Cambridge, 2000)

Clack, B.R., *Wittgenstein, Frazer and Religion* (Cambridge, 2000)

Clapham, J.H., *An Economic History of Modern Britain* (Cambridge, 1938)

Clarence-Smith, W.G., 'The Myth of Uneconomic Imperialism, the Portuguese in Angola, 1836–1926', *Journal of Southern Economic Studies*, v, 1978

——, *The Third Portuguese Empire, 1825–1975* (Manchester, 1985)

Clark, C.M.H., *A History of Australia* (Melbourne, 1962)

Cloet, M. et al (eds.), *Algemene Geschiedenis der Nederlanden* (Haarlem, 1980)

Coates, A., *Prelude to Hongkong* (London, 1966)

Coats, R.H. & Gosnell, R.E., *Sir James Douglas* (Toronto, 1908)

Cochut, P.A., *Law, son système et son époque* (Paris, 1853)

Cockburn, F.J. *Recollections of an Indian Civilian* (London, 1900)

Cockburn, J., *The Evolution of Empire* (London, 1905)

Colebrooke, Sir T.E., *Life of Mountstuart Elphinstone* (London, 1884)

Coleman, D.C., *History and the Economic Past* (Oxford, 1987)

Colley, L., 'Radical Patriotism in Eighteenth-century England', in Samuel (1989)

——, *Britons, forging the nation 1707–1837* (New Haven & London, 1992)

Collinson, S., 'Robert Knox, anatomy of race', *History Today*, xl, 1990

Collis, M., *Foreign Mud* (London, 1964)

——, *Wayfoong, the Hongkong and Shanghai Banking Corporation* (London, 1965)

Colvin, S. (ed.), *Letters of Robert Louis Stevenson* (London, 1911)

Committee on Commercial and Industrial Policy, *Commercial and Industrial Policy after the War*, Cmnd 9035, 1918

Connolly, S.J. (ed.), *Kingdoms United? Great Britain and Ireland since 1500* (Dublin, 1999)

Constantine, S., *The Making of British Colonial Development Policy, 1914–1940* (London, 1984)

Cook, D.J., 'The Influence of Livingstonia Mission upon the Formation of Welfare Associations in Zambia, 1912–1931', in Ranger & Weller (1975)

Cooksey, S.J.S., *Britain and the Congo Question* (New York, 1968)

Cooper, M., 'McGregor Gow and the Glen Line', *Journal of Transport History*, x, 1989

Coote, C., *A Companion of Honour, the story of Walter Elliot* (London, 1965)

Corbett, J.S. (ed.), *Private Papers of George, 2nd Earl Spencer, 1794–1801* (Navy Records Office, 1913)

Corley, T.A.B., *A History of the Burmah Oil Company, 1886–1924* (London, 1983)

Cormack, A.A., 'Scots in the Swedish East India Company', *Aberdeen University Review*, xlii, 1967–8

Cornford, L.C., *The Aberdeen Line* (Aberdeen, 1925)

Cosgrove, A. (ed.), *A New History of Ireland, II, Medieval Ireland* (Oxford, 1987)

Cotton, J.S., *Mountstuart Elphinstone* (Oxford, 1892)

Cottrell, P.L., *British Overseas Investment in the Nineteenth Century* (London, 1975)

Couperus, L., *Oostwarts* (The Hague, 1924)

Coupland, Sir R., *Kirk on the Zambesi* (Oxford, 1928)

——, *The Exploitation of East Africa, 1856–1890* (London, 1939)

——, *Livingstone's Last Journey* (London, 1945)

Cousins, H.T., *Tiyo Soga, the model Kafir missionary* (London, 1897)

Cowan, E.J., 'From the Southern Uplands to Southern Ontario, nineteenth-century emigration from the Scottish Borders', in Devine (1992)

Cowan, H.I., *British Emigration to North America* (Toronto, 1961)

Cowan, I.B., 'The Inevitability of Union – a historical fallacy?' *Scotia*, v, 1981

Cox, J.L., The Development of A.G. Hogg's Theology in relation to Non-Christian Faith, its significance for the Tambaram meeting of the International Missionary Council 1938, unpublished Ph.D. thesis, University of Aberdeen, 1977

Cox, K., *Angus McMillan* (Olinda, Victoria, 1973)

Craig, D., *On the Crofters' Trail* (London, 1990)

Craig, F.W.S., *British Electoral Facts, 1832–1960* (Chichester, 1981)

Crawford, D., *Thinking Black* (London, 1912)

Crawford, J., *History of the Indian Archipelago* (London, 1820)

——, *A View of the Present State and Future Prospects of the Free Trade and Colonisation of India* (London, 1828)

——, *The Plurality of the Races of Man* (London, 1867)

——, *Journal of an Embassy from the Governor-general of India to the Courts of Siam and Cochin China* (Bangkok, 1915)

Crawford, Q., *Sketches relating chiefly to the . . . Hindus* (London, 1790)

Crawford, R., 'Frazer and Scottish Romanticism, Scott, Stevenson and *The Golden Bough*', in Fraser, R. (1990)

Crawford, W.H., 'Ulster as a Mirror of the Two Societies', in Devine & Dickson (1983)

Creighton, D.G., 'The Victorians and the Empire', *Canadian Historical Review*, xix, 1938

Crewe, Marquis of, *Lord Rosebery* (London, 1931)

Crisswell, C.N., *The Taipans* (Hong Kong, 1981)

Cromb, D., *Hector Macdonald* (Stirling, 1903)

Cronwright, S., *The Land of Free Speech* (London, 1900)

Cropper, J. & Gladstone, J., *Correspondence on the Present State of Slavery in the British West Indies and in the United States of America* (Shannon, 1972; first published, 1824)

Crouse, N.M., *The Search for the North-west Passage* (New York, 1934)

Crowder, M., *The Story of Nigeria* (London, 1962)

Crowe, H.S., McNaught, K. & Reid, J.H.S. (eds.), *A Source-book of Canadian History* (Toronto, 1959)

Cruickshank, B., *Eighteen Years on the Gold Coast of Africa* (London, 1966; first published, 1853)

Cullen, L.M. & Smout, T.C. (eds.), *Comparative Aspects of Scottish and Irish Economic and Social History, 1600–1900* (Edinburgh, 1977)

Cullinan, P., *Robert Jacob Gordon, 1743–1795, the man and his travels at the Cape* (Cape Town, 1993)

Cumming, G., 'Scottish National Identity in an Australian Colony', *Scottish Historical Review*, lxxii, 1993

Cundall, F., *The Darien Venture* (New York, 1926)

Cunningham, A., *William Cunningham* (London, 1950)

Cunningham, J., *The Church History of Scotland* (Edinburgh, 1882)

Cunningham, W., *The Wisdom of the Wise, three lectures on free trade imperialism* (Cambridge, 1906)

——, *The Case against Free Trade* (London, 1911)

Cunyngham-Brown, S., *The Traders* (London, 1971)

Curtin, P.D., *Two Jamaicas, the role of ideas in a tropical colony* (Cambridge, Mass., 1955)

——, *The Image of Africa, British ideas and action, 1780–1850* (London, 1965)

Curtis, E., *A History of Ireland* (London, 1936)

Curtis, P. & Nadel, G.H., *Imperialism and Colonialism* (New York, 1964)

Daiches, D. (ed.), *A Companion to Scottish Culture* (London, 1981)

——, 'John Witherspoon, James Wilson and the Influence of Scottish Rhetoric on America', *Eighteenth-Century Life*, xv, 1991

with Jones, J. & Jones, P. (eds.), *A Hotbed of Genius, the Scottish Enlightenment* (Edinburgh, 1986)

Dalrymple, A., *An Historical Collection of the Several Voyages and Discoveries in the South Pacific Ocean* (London, 1770)

Dalton, Sir C.N., *The Real Captain Kidd* (London, 1911)

Dalzel, A., *History of Dahomey* (London, 1793)

Daniell, D., *The Interpreter's House, a critical assessment of John Buchan* (London, 1975)

(ed.), *The Best Short Stories of John Buchan* (London, 1984)

Darroch, L., *Robert Gourlay* (Thornhill, Ontario, 1971)

Das, M.N., *India under Morley and Minto* (London, 1965)

Datta, K., 'James Mackintosh, Learned Societies and Enlightenment Ideas', in Carter & Pittock (1987)

Davenport, R., 'Settlement, Conquest and Theological Controversy, the Churches of nineteenth-century European immigrants', in Davenport & Elphick (1997)

& Elphick, R. (eds.), *Christianity in South Africa* (Cape Town & Oxford, 1997)

Davidson, A.E., 'As Birds Bring Forth the Sun, the elusive art of Alistair MacLeod', *Canadian Literature*, cxix, 1988

Davidson, B., *Black Star, a view of the life and times of Kwame Nkrumah* (London, 1973)

Davidson, G.C., *The North West Company* (New York, 1918)

Davidson, J. & Gray, A., *The Scottish Staple at Veere* (London, 1909)

Davie, G.E., *The Democratic Intellect* (Edinburgh, 1961)

——, *The Scottish Enlightenment and Other Essays* (Edinburgh, 1991)

Davies, M. & Muir, A., *A Victorian Shipowner* (London, 1978)

Davis, D.B., *The Problem of Slavery in Western Culture*, (Ithaca, NY, 1968)

——, 'New Sidelights on Early Antislavery Radicalism', *William & Mary Quarterly*, xxviii, 1971

Davis, L.E. & Huttenback, R.A., *Mammon and the Pursuit of Empire* (Cambridge, 1986)

Day, A.G., *Hawaii and its People* (New York, 1955)

Day, L.B., *Recollections of Alexander Duff* (London, 1879)

Dayer, R.A., 'The Young Charles S. Addis, poet or banker', in King (1983)

——, *Finance and Empire, Sir Charles Addis, 1861–1945* (London, 1988)

De, B., 'A Note on the Melville Manuscripts in the National Library of Scotland', *The Indian Archives*, x, 1956

——, Henry Dundas and the Government of India 1773–1801, a study in constitutional ideas, unpublished D. Phil. thesis, University of Oxford, 1961

De Groot, G.J., '"We are Safe Whatever Happens", Douglas Haig, the Rev George Duncan and the conduct of war 1916–1918"', in Macdougall (1991)

De Jong, G.F., *The Dutch in America, 1609–1674* (Boston, 1975)

De Kiewiet, M.J., History of the Imperial British East Africa Company, unpublished Ph.D. thesis, University of London, 1955

Dekker, E.D., *Max Havelaar, of de Koffyveilingen der Nederlandsche Handelmaatschappij* (London, 1987; first published, 1860)

De Klerk, W.W., *The Puritans in Africa* (London, 1976)

Dell, R.F., 'The Operational Record of the Clyde Tobacco Fleet, 1747–1775', *Scottish Economic and Social History*, ii, 1982

Den Otter, A.A., *Civilising the West, the Galts and the development of western Canada* (Edmonton, Alberta, 1982)

Dermigny, L., *La Chine et l'Occident* (Paris, 1964)

De Serville, P., *Port Phillip Gentlemen* (Melbourne, 1980)

——, *Pounds and Pedigrees, the upper class in Victoria, 1850–1880* (Oxford, 1991)

Devine, T.M., 'Glasgow Colonial Merchants and Land 1770–1815', in Ward & Wilson (1971)

——, 'Glasgow Merchants and the Collapse of the Tobacco Trade, 1775–1783', *Scottish Historical Review*, lii, 1973

——, Sources of Capital for the Glasgow Tobacco Trade, 1740–1780, *Business History*, xvi, 1974

——, *The Tobacco Lords* (Edinburgh, 1975)

——, 'A Glasgow Tobacco Merchant during the American War of Independence, Alexander Speirs of Elderslie 1775–1781', *William and Mary Quarterly*, xxxiii, 1976

——, 'The Colonial Trades and Industrial Investment in Scotland', *Economic History Review*, xxix, 1976

——, 'Colonial Commerce and the Scottish Economy, 1730–1815', in Cullen & Smout (1977)

——, 'An Eighteenth-century Business Elite, Glasgow-West India merchants, 1750–1815', *Scottish Historical Review*, lvii, 1978

——, 'Migration', in Daiches (1981)

——, 'The Scottish Merchant Community, 1680–1740', in Campbell & Skinner (1982)

——, *The Great Highland Famine, hunger, emigration and the Scottish Highlands in the nineteenth century* (Edinburgh, 1988)

(ed.), *Irish Immigrants and Scottish Society in the Nineteenth and Twentieth Centuries* (Edinburgh, 1991)

(ed.), *Scottish Emigration and Scottish Society* (Edinburgh, 1992)

(ed.), *Scottish Elites* (Edinburgh, 1994)

& Dickson, D. (eds.), *Ireland and Scotland, 1600–1850* (Edinburgh, 1983)

& Jackson, G, (eds.), *Glasgow, I, the beginnings to 1830* (Manchester, 1995)

& Mitchison, R. (eds.), *People and Society in Scotland, I, 1760–1830* (Edinburgh, 1988)

& Young, J.R. (eds.), *Eighteenth-century Scotland, new perspectives* (East Linton, 1999)

Diamond, P.J., 'Witherspoon, William Smith and the Scottish Philosophy in Revolutionary America', in Sher & Smitten' (1990)

Dickinson, W.C. Donaldson, G. & Milne, I.A. (eds.), *A Source Book of Scottish History* (London & Edinburgh, 1952)

Dickson, A. & Treble, J.H. (eds.), *People and Society in Scotland, III, 1914–1990* (Edinburgh, 1992)

Dickson, M., *Longhouse in Sarawak* (London, 1971)

Dickson, P., *Red John of the Battles, John, 2nd Duke of Argyll, 1680–1743* (London, 1982)

Dickson, R.J., *Ulster Emigration to Colonial America, 1718–1775* (London, 1966)

Dickson, T., *Scottish Capitalism* (London, 1980)

Diffie, B.W. & Winius, G.D., *Foundations of the Portuguese Empire, 1415–1520* (St Paul, 1977)

Dilke, C., *Greater Britain* (London, 1868)

Dixon, C.W., *The Colonial Administration of Sir Thomas Maitland* (London, 1939)

Dobson, N., *A History of Belize* (London, 1973)

Dodwell, H.A. (ed.), *The Cambridge History of the British Empire, IV, British India, 1497–1858* (Cambridge, 1929)

Doig, A., Malawi *1939–1961*, in National Library of Scotland (1993)

Donald, D.M.C., 'Scottish Investment Trusts', *Scottish Bankers' Magazine*, xlvii, 1956

Donald, H.M., Life of Lord Mount Stephen (1829–1921), unpublished Ph.D. thesis, University of London, 1952

Donaldson, G., *The Scots Overseas* (London, 1966)

Donaldson, J., *The Undoubted Art of Thriving* (Edinburgh, 1700)

Donnachie, I., 'Scottish Criminals and Transportation to Australia, 1786–1852', *Scottish Economic and Social History*, iv, 1984

——, *Scotland and Australia, 1901–1988*, (HMSO, 1988)

Donnelly, F.K, 'The British Background of William Lyon Mackenzie', *British Journal of Canadian Studies*, ii, 1987

Doucette, L., *Cultural Retention and Demographic Change, studies of the Hebridean Scots in the Eastern Townships of Quebec* (Ottawa, 1980)

Douds, G., 'Tom Johnston in India', *Scottish Labour History Society Journal*, xix, 1984

Doughty, Sir A.G. (ed,), *The Elgin-Grey Papers, 1846–1852* (Ottawa, 1937)

& Shortt, A. (eds.), *Canada and its Provinces* (Toronto, 1914)

Douglas, C.H., *Fifty Years of Social Credit* (Mexborough, Yorks., 1973; first published, 1959)

Douglas, J., *Bombay and Western India* (London, 1893)

Douglas-Home, Sir A., *The Modern Commonwealth* (London, 1971)

——, *The Way the Wind Blows* (London, 1976)

Dow, D.A., Domestic Response and Reaction to the Foreign Missionary Enterprises of the Principal Scottish Presbyterian Churches, 1873–1929, unpublished Ph.D. thesis, University of Glasgow, 1977

——, *The influence of Scottish Medicine* (Carnforth, 1988)

Downie, R.A., *Frazer and the Golden Bough* (London, 1970)

Drabble, J.H., *Rubber in Malaya, 1876–1922* (Oxford, 1973)

& Drake, P.J., 'The British Agency Houses in Malaysia, survival in a changing world', *Journal of South East Asian Studies*, xii, 1981

Draper, T., 'Hume and Madison, the secrets of Federalist Paper no. 10', *Encounter*, lviii, 1982

Drinkall, S., 'The Jamaican Plantation House, Scottish influence', *Architectural Heritage*, ii, 1991

Drooglever, P.J., 'Dekolonisatie van Oost- en West-Indië', in Cloet et al (1980), xiv

Drucker, H.M. & N.L. (eds.), *The Scottish Government Yearbook 1982* (Edinburgh, 1981)

Duff, A., *India and India Missions* (Edinburgh, 1840)

——, *The Indian Rebellion* (London, 1858)

Duffield, I., 'Some Reflections on Scottish Convicts Transported to Australia', *Scottish Records Association, conference report*, x, 1988

Duffy, M., *Soldiers, Sugar and Seapower, the British expeditions to the West Indies and the war against revolutionary France* (Oxford, 1987)

Duncan, K.J., 'Patterns of Settlement in the East', in Reid (1976)

Dundas, H., *Letters from the Rt Hon Henry Dundas to the Chairman of the Court of Directors of the East India Company upon an Open Trade to India* (London, 1813)

Dunlop, A. & Mills, R., 'The Racialisation of Politics in Britain, why Scotland is different', *Patterns of Prejudice*, xx, 1986

'Racism in Britain, the Scottish dimension', in Jackson (1987)

Dunlop, J.K., *The Development of the British Army, 1899–1914* (London, 1938)

Dunlop, R., 'Sixteenth Century Schemes for the Plantation of Ulster', *Scottish Historical Review*, xxii, 1925

Dunn, C.W., *Highland Settler* (Toronto, 1953)

Du Plessis, J., *The Life of Andrew Murray of South Africa* (London, 1920)

Dwyer, J., *Virtuous Discourse, sensibility and community in late eighteenth-century Scotland* (Edinburgh, 1987)

Dyster, B., 'Prosperity, Prostration, Prudence – business and investment in Sydney, 1838–1851', in Birch & Macmillan (1967)

Edgar, W.B. (ed.), *The Letterbook of Robert Pringle* (Columbia, SC, 1972)

Edney, M.H., *Mapping an Empire, the geographical construction of British India, 1765–1843* (Chicago, 1997)

Edwardes, M., *The West in Asia, 1850–1914* (New York, 1967)

Edwards, P., *The Early African Presence in the British Isles* (Edinburgh, 1990)

Edwards, R.D., *A New History of Ireland* (Dublin, 1972)

Egremont, M., *Balfour* (London, 1980)

Eitel, E.J., *Europe in China, the history of Hongkong* (London & Hong Kong, 1895)

Elbourne, E. & Ross, R., 'Combatting Spiritual and Social Bondage, early missions in the Cape Colony', in Davenport & Elphick (1997)

Elliott, M., *Partners in Revolution* (New Haven & London, 1982)

Ellis, M.H., *Lachlan Macquarie* (Sydney, 1947)

Elphinstone, M., *Report on the Territories conquered from the Paishwa* (Calcutta, 1821)

Embree, A.T., *Charles Grant and British Rule in India* (London, 1962)

Emmer, P.C., 'Suiker, Goud en Slaven, de Republiek in West-Africa en West-Indië', in Cloet *et al*, X (1980)

Enthoven, V., 'The Last Straw, trade contacts along the North Sea coast: the Scottish staple at Veere', in Heerma van Voss & Roding (1966)

Erskine, H., *The Emigrant* (n.p., n.d.)

Evans, A.M.M., 'The Scot as Politician', in Reid (1976)

Evans, J.W., 'William Paterson of Skipmyre', *Transactions of the Dumfriesshire and Galloway Natural History and Antiquarian Society*, lxi, 1986

Ewing, J., *The History of the 9th (Scottish) Division* (London, 1921)

——, *The Royal Scots, 1914–1919* (Edinburgh, 1925)

Faber, R., *The Vision and the Need, late Victorian imperialist aims* (London, 1966)

Fage, J.D. & Oliver, R. (eds.), *The Cambridge History of Africa* (London, 1986)

Fagerstrom, D.I., The American Revolutionary Movement in Scottish Opinion, 1763–1783, unpublished Ph.D. thesis, University of Edinburgh, 1951

——, 'Scottish Opinion and the American Revolution', *William and Mary Quarterly*, xi, 1954

Fairbank, J.K., *Trade and Diplomacy on the China Coast* (Cambridge, Mass., 1953)

Falls, C., *The Gordon Highlanders in the First World War* (Aberdeen, 1958)

Farquhar, J.N., *Christianity in India* (London, 1908)

——, *The Crown of Hinduism* (London, 1913)

Farrell, F.A., *The 51st (Highland) Division, war sketches* (Edinburgh, 1920)

Fasseur, C., 'De Nederlandse Kolonien, 1795–1914', in Cloet et al., XI (1980)

Fay, C.R., *Imperial Economy and its Place in the Formation of Economic Doctrine* (Oxford, 1934)

Fechner, R., From Paisley to Princeton to Philadelphia – John Witherspoon as Preacher, Professor and Politician, unpublished paper, 1992

Ferguson, J., *Two Scottish Soldiers* (Aberdeen, 1888)

Ferguson, J., *Pioneers of the Planting Enterprise in Ceylon* (Colombo, 1894)

Ferguson, R., *A Just and Modest Vindication of the Scots Design for Having Established a Colony at Darien* (n.p., 1699)

Ferguson, R., *George MacLeod* (London, 1990)

Ferguson, W., *Scotland's Relations with England* (Edinburgh, 1977)

——, *The Identity of the Scottish Nation* (Edinburgh, 1998)

Fergusson, B., *The Trumpet in the Hall* (London, 1970)

Ferriman, Z.D., *Thomas Gordon* (London, 1918)

Fetter, F.W. (ed.), *The Economic Writings of Francis Horner* (London, 1957)

Fieldhouse, D.K., 'The New Imperialism, the Lenin-Hobson thesis revisited', in Curtis & Nadel (1964)

——, '*The Colonial Empires, a comparative survey from the eighteenth century* (London, 1966)

Finlay, R.J., 'Nationalism, Race, Religion and the Irish Question in Interwar Scotland', *Innes Review*, xlii, 1991

——, 'For or against?' Scottish nationalists and the British Empire', *Scottish Historical Review*, lxxi, 1992

——, 'Controlling the Past, Scottish historiography and Scottish identity in the nineteenth and twentieth centuries', *Scottish Affairs*, ix, 1994

——, *Independent and Free, Scottish politics and the origin of the Scottish National Party* (Edinburgh, 1994)

——, 'The Rise and Fall of Popular Imperialism in Scotland, 1850–1950', *Scottish Geographical Magazine*, cxiii, 1997

Firth, C.H., 'The British Empire', *Scottish Historical Review*, xv, 1918

Fisher, H.A.L., *James Bryce* (London, 1927)

Fisher, S. (ed.), *Studies in British Privateering, Trading Enterprise and Seamen's Welfare, 1755–1900* (Exeter, 1987)

Fleming, J.R., *A History of the Church in Scotland, 1843–1874* (Edinburgh, 1927)

Fletcher, A., *Political Works* (Cambridge, 1997)

Flinn, M.W., 'The Overseas Trade of Scottish Ports', *Scottish Journal of Political Economy*, xiii, 1966

——, 'Exports and the Scottish Economy in the Depression of the 1930s', in Chaloner & Ratcliffe (1977) (ed.), *Scottish Population History* (Cambridge, 1977)

Flint, J., 'The Wider Background to Partition and Colonial Occupation', in Mathew & Oliver (1963)

——, 'Macmillan as a Critic of Empire, the impact of an historian on colonial policy', in Macmillan & Marks (1989)

Fontana, B., *Rethinking the Politics of Commercial Society, the Edinburgh Review, 1802–1832* (Cambridge, 1985)

Foot, H., *A Start in Freedom* (London, 1964)

Foot, M.R.D., *War and Society* (London, 1973)

Ford, H.J., *The Scotch-Irish in America* (Princeton, 1915)

Forbes, A., *Colin Campbell, Lord Clyde* (London, 1895)

Forrest, Sir G., *Selections from the State Papers of the Governors-general of India – Lord Cornwallis* (Oxford, 1926)

Forrester, D., *Caste and Christianity* (London & Dublin, 1980)

Forster, R.G., *T. Cullen Young, missionary and anthropologist* (Hull, 1989)

Forsyth, D., 'Empire and Union, imperial and national identity in nineteenth-century Scotland', *Scottish Geographical Magazine*, cxiii, 1997

Foskett, R., 'Some Scottish Episcopalians in the North American Colonies, 1675–1750', *Records of the Scottish Church History Society*, xiv, 1960–3

(ed.), *The Zambesi Doctors, David Livingstone's Letters to John Kirk, 1858–1872* (Edinburgh, 1964)

(ed.), *The Zambesi Journal and Letters of Dr John Kirk, 1858–1863* (Edinburgh & London, 1965)

Foster, S.G., *Colonial Improver, Edward Deas Thomson, 1800–1879* (Melbourne, 1978)

Foster, W., 'James Mill in Leadenhall Street, 1819–1836', *Scottish Historical Review*, x, 1912

Fotheringham, L.M., *Adventures in Nyassaland* (London, 1891)

Fraser, A., *The Last Laird of MacNab* (Toronto, 1899)

Fraser, A.L., *The Mission of the Scot in Canada* (Toronto, 1903)

Fraser, E., *A House by the Hooghly* (Edinburgh, 1989)

Fraser, J.G., *Episodes in My Life* (Cape Town, 1922)

Fraser, R. (ed.), *Sir James Frazer and the Literary Imagination* (London, 1990)

Fraser, W.H. & Morris, R.J. (eds.), *People and Society in Scotland, II, 1830–1914* (Edinburgh, 1990)

Frazer, J.F., *The Golden Bough* (London, 1906)

Freeman, A.M., *The Annals of Connacht* (Dublin, 1944)

Friedman, I., *The Question of Palestine, British-Jewish-Arab relations, 1914–1918* (New Brunswick, NJ and London, 1992)

Fromkin, D., *A Peace to End All Peace* (New York, 1989)

Fry, H.T., *Alexander Dalrymple (1737–1808) and the Expansion of British Trade* (London, 1970)

Fry, M.R.G., *Patronage and Principle, a political history of modern Scotland* (Aberdeen, 1987)

(ed.), *Adam Smith's Legacy* (London, 1992a)

——, *The Dundas Despotism* (Edinburgh, 1992b)

Fryer, M.B., *Allan Maclean, Jacobite General* (Toronto, 1987)

Fulton, A., *Through Earthquake, Wind and Fire, Church and Mission in Manchuria, 1867–1950* (Edinburgh, 1967)

Furber, H. (ed.), *An Indian Governor-generalship, 1793–1798* (Cambridge, Mass., 1933)

———, 'The East India Directors in 1784', *Journal of Modern History*, v, 1933

———, *John Company at Work* (Cambridge, 1948)

———, *Rival Empires of Trade in the Orient, 1600–1800* (Minneapolis, 1976)

Fyfe, C., *Africanus Horton, 1835–1883* (Oxford, 1972)

———, *Race, Empire and Post-Empire* (Edinburgh, 1982)

Gaastra, F.S., 'De VOC in Azië, 1680–1795', in Cloet *et al*, IX (1980)

& van den Boogart, E., 'Overseeze Geschiedenis', in Cloet *et al*, VII (1980)

Gadgil, D.R., *The Industrial Evolution of India in Recent Times, 1860–1939* (Bombay, 1971)

Gailey, H.E., 'John Philip's Role in Hottentot Emancipation', *Journal of African History*, iii, 1962

Gairdner, W.H.T., *Edinburgh 1910, an account and interpretation of the world missionary conference* (Edinburgh & London, *1910*)

Galbraith, J.K., *Made to Last* (London, 1964)

Galbraith, J.S., 'Gordon, Mackinnon and Leopold, the scramble for Africa 1876–1884', *Victorian Studies*, xiv, 1971

———, *Mackinnon and East Africa* (Cambridge, 1972)

———, *The Little Emperor, Governor Simpson of the Hudson's Bay Company* (Toronto, 1976)

Gallagher, J. & Robinson, R., 'The Imperialism of Free Trade', *Economic History Review*, vi, 1953

———, *Africa and the Victorians* (London, 1961)

Gallagher, T. & Walker, G., *Sermons and Battle Hymns, Protestant popular culture in modern Scotland* (Edinburgh, 1990)

Galt, J., *Voyages and Travels in the Years 1809, 1810 and 1811* (London, 1812)

———, *The Last of the Lairds* (Edinburgh, 1936; first published, 1826)

———, 'Bandana on Colonial Undertakings', *Blackwood's Edinburgh Magazine*, cxv, 1826

———, Bandana on Emigration, Blackwood's Edinburgh Magazine, cxv, 1826

———, *Bogle Corbet* (London, 1831)

Gann, L.H., *A History of Northern Rhodesia* (London, 1964)

Gardner, P., 'The Warrigal Creek Massacre', *Journal of the Royal Australian Historical Society*, lxvi, 1980

Garner, J., *The Commonwealth Office, 1925–1968* (London, 1978)

Garrett, J., *To Live among the Stars, Christian origins in Oceania* (Geneva & Suva, 1982)

———, *Footsteps in the Sea, Christianity in Oceania to World War II* (Geneva & Suva, 1992)

Gathorne-Hardy, G.M., *The Norse Discoverers of America* (Oxford, 1921)

Gauldie, E. (ed.), *The Dundee Textile Industry, 1790–1885, from the papers of Peter Carmichael of Arthurstone* (Edinburgh, 1969)

Gavin, R.J., 'The Bartle Frere Mission to Zanzibar in 1873', *Historical Journal*, v, 1962

———, *Aden under British Rule, 1839–1967* (London, 1975)

Gegenheimer, A.F., *William Smith, educator and churchman* (Philadelphia, 1943)

Geggus, D.P., *Slavery, War and Revolution* (Oxford, 1982)

Gehani, T.G., A Critical Review of the Work of Scottish Presbyterian Missions in India, 1878–1914, unpublished Ph.D. thesis, Strathclyde University, 1966

Gelfand, M., *Livingstone the Doctor* (Oxford, 1957)

Geyl, P., *The Netherlands in the Seventeenth Century, 1609–1648* (London, 1961)

Ghosh, R.P., 'The Colonisation Controversy', *Economica*, xxxi, 1964

Gibb, A. Dewar, *Scotland in Eclipse* (London, 1931)

———, *Scottish Empire* (London, 1937)

———, *Scotland Resurgent* (Stirling, 1950)

Gilbert, J.C., *A History of Investment Trusts in Dundee* (London, 1939)

Gilbert, M., *Servant of India* (London, 1966)

———, 'Mount Stephen, a study in environments', *Northern Scotland*, i, 1973

———, *Awakening Continent, the life of Lord Mount Stephen* (Aberdeen, 1976)

Gill, S.D., ' "We are too Scotch", the Rev William Proudfoot and the United Secession Mission to Canada', *Records of the Scottish Church History Society*, xxii, 1985

Gillespie, R., *Colonial Ulster* (Cork, 1985)

Girardot, N., James Legge and the Strange Saga of Sinological Orientalism and the Comparative Science of Religions in the Nineteenth Century, unpublished paper, 1997

Gladstone, J.S., *History of Gillanders, Arbuthnot & Co and Ogilvy, Gillanders & Co* (London, 1910)

Gladstone, W.E., *Midlothian Campaign* (Edinburgh, 1880)

Gleig, G.R., *The Life of Major-general Sir Thomas Munro* (London, 1830)

Glen, D. (ed.), *Selected Essays of Hugh Macdiarmid* (London, 1969)

Goldring, P., 'Scottish Recruiting for the Hudson's Bay Company, 1821–1880', *Scottish Tradition*, ix, 1979

——, 'Lewis and the Hudson's Bay Company in the Nineteenth Century', *Scottish Studies*, xxiv, 1980

Goldsmid, Sir F.J., *James Outram, a biography* (London, 1880)

Gollin, A.M., *Proconsul in Politics* (London, 1964)

——, *Balfour's Burden, Arthur Balfour and imperial preference* (London, 1965)

Gordon, Sir R., *Encouragements for such as shall have Intention to be Undertakers in the New Plantation of Cape Breton* (Edinburgh, 1625)

Gorrie, J., *Illustrations of Martial Law in Jamaica* (London, 1867)

Gould, C., 'Scottish Printers and Booksellers in Charleston, South Carolina', *Studies in Scottish Literature*, xv, 1980

Gouldesborough, P., 'An Attempted Scottish Voyage to New York in 1669', *Scottish Historical Review*, xl, 1961

Graham, E.J., 'In Defence of the Scottish Maritime Interest, 1681–1713', *Scottish Historical Review*, lxxi, 1992

Graham, I.G.C., *Colonists from Scotland* (Ithaca, NY, 1956)

Graham-Yooll, A., *The Forgotten Colony* (London, 1981)

Grant, Sir A., *How the Ancient Romans Governed their Provinces* (Bombay, 1862)

Grant, C., *Observations on the State of Society among the Asiatic Subjects of Great Britain, particularly with respect to morals; and on the means of improving it* (London, 1797)

Grant, C., *Royal Scots Greys* (Reading, 1972)

Grant, G., *Lament for a Nation* (Princeton, 1965)

Grant, J., *The Old Scots Navy* (Navy Records Society, 1914)

Grant, R., *The Expediency Maintained of Continuing the System by which the Trade and Government of India are now Regulated* (London, 1813)

Grant-Duff, M., *Notes of an Indian Journey* (London, 1876)

Gray, J.M., *Lord Selkirk of Red River* (London, 1963)

——, 'Zanzibar and the Coastal Belt', in Mathew & Oliver (1963)

Gray, M., *Scots on the Move – Scots migrants 1750–1914* (Edinburgh, 1974)

Gray, R., *The Two Nations, aspects of the development of race relations in the Rhodesias and Nyasaland* (Oxford, 1960)

Green, E.R.R., *Essays in Scotch-Irish History* (London, 1969)

Greenberg, M.M., *British Trade and the Opening of China, 1800–1842* (Cambridge, 1951)

Greer, R.M., *A History of the Presbyterian Church in Singapore* (Singapore, 1956)

Gregg, W., *History of the Presbyterian Church in the Dominion of Canada* (Toronto, 1895)

Greig, J.Y.T. (ed.), *The Letters of David Hume* (Oxford, 1969)

Grierson, C., *Colonia de Monte Grande, primera y unica colonia formada par escoceses en la Argentina* (Buenos Aires, 1925)

Grierson, Sir H. (ed.), *The Letters of Sir Walter Scott* (London, 1937)

Grieve, C.M. (Hugh Macdiarmid), *Contemporary Scottish Studies* (London, 1926)

——, *Lucky Poet* (Berkeley & Los Angeles, 1972; first published, 1943)

——, 'The Quality of Scots Internationalism', in Glen (1969)

Grieves, K., *Sir Eric Geddes* (Manchester, 1989),

Griffiths, N.E.S. & Reid, J., 'New Evidence on New Scotland', *William & Mary Quarterly*, xxxix, 1992

Grimble, I., 'Emigration in the Time of Rob Donn, 1714–1778', *Scottish Studies*, vii, 1963

——, *The Sea Wolf, the life of Admiral Cochrane* (Colchester, 1978)

Gull, E.M., *British Economic Interests in the Far East* (Oxford, 1943)

Gunn, W., *The Gospel in Futuna* (London, 1914)

Gupta, P.S., *Imperialism and the British Labour Movement* (London, 1975)

Guthrie, E., *Home Rule, Federation and the Crown* (London, 1889)

Guttridge, G.H., 'Adam Smith on the American Revolution, an unpublished memorial', *American Historical Review*, xxviii, 1933

Gutzke, D.W., 'Rosebery and Ireland, 1898–1903, a reappraisal', *Bulletin of the Institute of Historical Research*, liii, 1980

Gwynn, S. (ed.), *The Anvil of War, letters between F.S. Oliver and his brother, 1914–1918* (London, 1936)

Gyang-Duah, C., The Scottish Mission Factor in the Development of the Presbyterian Church of Ghana, unpublished Ph.D. thesis, University of Edinburgh, 1996

Hair, P.E.H., 'A Scottish Missionary in the Caucasus, Henry Brunton', *Bulletin of the Scottish Institute of Missionary Studies*, xiii, 1973

——, *New Introduction to the Second Edition* [of Brunton's Grammar of the Susu Language] (n.p., 1984)

Haldane, R.B., *Education and Empire* (London, 1902)

——, *An Autobiography* (London, 1929)

Halkett, J., *Statement respecting the Earl of Selkirk's Settlement upon the Red River* (London, 1817)

Hall, D.G.E. (ed.), *The Dalhousie-Phayre Correspondence, 1852–1856* (Oxford, 1932)

——, *Historians of South-east Asia* (Oxford, 1961)

——, *A History of South-east Asia* (London, 1968)

Hamer, D.A., *John Morley* (Oxford, 1968)

——, *Liberal Politics in the Age of Gladstone and Rosebery* (Oxford, 1972)

Hamilton, A., *A New Account of the East Indies* (London, 1744)

Hamilton, H., *An Economic History of Scotland in the Eighteenth Century* (Oxford, 1963)

Hamilton, I.B.M., *The Happy Warrior, a life of General Sir Ian Hamilton* (London, 1960)

Hamowy, R., 'Jefferson and the Scottish Enlightenment', *William and Mary Quarterly*, xxxvi, 1979

Hancock, D., *Citizens of the World, London merchants and the integration of the British Atlantic community, 1745–1785* (Cambridge, 1995)

Handley, J., *The Irish in Modern Scotland* (Cork, 1946)

Hanham, H., *Scottish Nationalism* (London, 1969)

——, 'Religion and Nationality in the Mid-Victorian Army', in Foot (1973)

Hanley, E., 'Immigrants and the Scots Nats', *Race Today*, i, 1969

Hanna, A.J., *The Beginnings of Nyasaland and North-eastern Rhodesia, 1859–1895* (Oxford, 1956)

——, *The Story of the Rhodesias and Nyasaland* (London, 1960)

Hanna, C.A., *The Scotch-Irish* (New York & London, 1902)

Hannah, L., *The Rise of the Corporate Economy* (London, 1976)

Harcourt, F., 'The P & O Company, flagships of imperialism', in Palmer & Williams (1981)

Harcus, A.D., *History of the Presbyterian Church in Malaya* (London, 1954)

Hardie, J.K., *India, impressions and suggestions* (London, 1909)

Hargreaves, J.D., *Aberdeenshire to Africa, North-east Scots and British overseas expansion* (Aberdeen, 1981)

——, *Academe and Empire, some overseas connections of Aberdeen University* (Aberdeen, 1994)

Harlow, V.T., *The Founding of the Second British Empire, 1763–1793* (London, 1952)

——, 'Early British Pioneers in Borneo', *Sarawak Museum Journal*, vi, 1955

& Madden, F., *British Colonial Developments, 1774–1834* (Oxford, 1953)

Harper, M., 'Emigration from North-east Scotland in the Nineteenth Century', *Northern Scotland*, vi, 1985

——, *Emigration from North-east Scotland* (Aberdeen, 1988)

Harper, S., *Last Sunset* (London, 1978)

Harris, J., *Navigantium atque Itinerantium Bibliotheca* (London, 1705)

Harris, J.F. & Hazlehurst, C., 'Campbell-Bannerman as Prime Minister', *History*, iv, 1970

Harris, R.C., 'The Simplification of Europe Overseas', *Annals of the Association of American Geographers*, lxvii, 1977

Harrison, B., 'English Historians of "the Indian Archipelago", Crawford & St John', in Hall (1961)

Harrison, J., *The Scot in Ulster* (Edinburgh, 1888)

Harrison, J.W., *A.M. Mackay, pioneer missionary of the Church Missionary Society to Uganda* (London, 1890)

Harris-Smith, M. & Thomson, J., *Ulu, an African romance* (London, 1888)

Harsgor, M., 'After-effects of an "Exemplary Decolonisation"', *Journal of Contemporary History*, xv, 1980

Hart, F.R., *The Disaster of Darien* (n.p., 1930)

Harvey, C.E., *The Rio Tinto Company* (Penzance, 1981)

Harvie, C., *Scotland and Nationalism* (London, 1977)

——, *No Gods and Precious Few Heroes, Scotland 1914–1980* (London, 1981)

——, 'Second Thoughts of a Scotsman on the Make, politics, nationalism and myth in John Buchan', *Scottish Historical Review*, lxx, 1991

Hast, A., *Loyalism in Revolutionary Virginia* (Ann Arbor, 1979)

Hatch, J., *Two African Statesman, Kaunda of Zambia and Nyerere of Tanzania* (London, 1976)

Hattersley, A.F., *The British Settlement of Natal* (Cambridge, 1950)

(ed.), *John Shedden Dobie, South African journal 1862–1866* (Cape Town, 1945)

Hauch-FausbØll, *Records of the Browns of Colstoun House* (Copenhagen, 1930)

Haws, C., *Scots in the Old Dominion, 1685–1800* (Edinburgh, 1980)

Hayes-McCoy, G.A., *Scots Mercenary Forces in Ireland, 1565–1603* (Dublin & London, 1937)

Hayton, D. & Szechi, D., 'John Bull's Other Kingdoms, the English government of Scotland and Ireland', in Jones (1987)

Hechter, M., *Internal Colonialism, the Celtic fringe in British national development* (London, 1975)

——, 'Internal Colonialism Revisited', in Rogowski & Tiryakian (1985)

Heckscher, E.F., *Mercantilism* (London, 1955)

Heerma van Voss, L. & Roding, J., *The North Sea and Culture* (Hilversum, 1996)

Henderson, D.M., *Highland Soldier* (Edinburgh, 1989)

Henderson, J.L.H., *John Strachan, 1778–1867* (Toronto, 1969)

Henderson, P., *The Life of Laurence Oliphant* (London, 1956)

Hennessey, J.P., *Robert Louis Stevenson* (London, 1974)

HMSO, *That Land of Exiles, Scots in Australia* (Edinburgh, 1988)

Hertz, G.B., 'England and the Ostend Company', *English Historical Review*, xxii, 1907

Hetherington, S.J., *Against the Tide, Katharine Atholl, 1874–1960* (Edinburgh, 1988)

Hetherwick, A., *The Gospel and the African* (Edinburgh, 1932a)

——, *The Romance of Blantyre* (London, 1932b)

Heuman, G., *The Killing Time, the Morant Bay rebellion in Jamaica* (London, 1994)

Hewat, E.G.K., *Vision and Achievement, 1796–1856, a history of the foreign missions of the Churches united in the Church of Scotland* (London, 1960)

Hewitson, J., *Tam Blake & Co, the story of Scots in America* (Edinburgh, 1993)

Hibbert, C., *The Great Mutiny, India 1857* (London, 1978)

Hill, G., *An Historical Account of the Macdonnells of Antrim* (Belfast, 1873)

——, *An Historical Account of the Plantation in Ulster* (Belfast, 1877)

Hitchen, J.M., Formation of the Nineteenth Century Missionary Worldview, the case of James Chalmers, unpublished Ph.D. thesis, University of Aberdeen, 1984

Hobson, J.A., *Imperialism, a study* (London, 1902)

Hobsbawm, E., *Nations and Nationalism since 1780* (Cambridge, 1980)

Hoe, A., *David Stirling* (London, 1992)

Hogg, J., *The Works of the Ettrick Shepherd* (London, 1874)

Holland, R., *The Pursuit of Greatness, Britain and the world role, 1900–1970* (London, 1991)

& Porter, A. (eds.), *Theory and Practice in the History of European Expansion* (London, 1988)

Holmes, T., *Journey to Livingstone* (Edinburgh, 1993)

Hook, A.D., 'Scottish Contributions to the American Enlightenment', *Texas Studies in Literature and Language*, viii, 1966–7

——, *Scotland and America, a study of cultural relations* (Glasgow & London, 1975)

——, 'Philadelphia, Edinburgh and the Scottish Enlightenment', in Sher & Smitten (Edinburgh, 1990)

——, The Scottish Invention of the USA, unpublished paper, 1992

Hooper, B., *China Stands Up, the end of the Western presence* (Sydney, 1986)

Hopkirk, P., *The Great Game* (Oxford, 1990)

Hoskins, H.L., *British Routes to India* (New York & London, 1928)

Hou, C., *Foreign Investment and Economic Development in China* (Cambridge, Mass., 1965)

Howarth, D. & S., *The Story of P & O* (London, 1986)

Howe, D.W., 'Why the Scottish Enlightenment was Useful to the Framers of the American Constitution', *Comparative Studies in Society and History*, xxxi, 1989

Howe, S., *Novels of Empire* (New York, 1949)

Hughes, C.A. & Nicolson, I.F., 'A Provenance of Proconsuls, British colonial governors 1900–1960', *Journal of Imperial & Commonwealth History*, iv, 1975

Hume, D., *Political Discourses* (Edinburgh, 1752)

——, *The Natural History of Religion* (London, 1956; first published, 1757)

——, *Essays, moral, political and literary* (Indianapolis, 1985)

Hume, J.R. & Moss, M.S., *Workshop of the British Empire, engineering and shipbuilding in the West of Scotland* (London & Edinburgh, 1977)

Humphreys, R.A., *William Robertson and his 'History of America'* (London, 1954)

Hunt, W., *Heirs of Great Adventure, the history of Balfour, Williamson & Co Ltd* (London, 1951)

Hunter, J., *A Dance Called America: The Scottish Highlands, the United States and Canada* (Edinburgh & London, 1994)

Hunter, R., *History of the Missions of the Free Church of Scotland in India and Africa* (London, 1873)

Hunter, R.J., 'Scotland and the Atlantic, the voyage of the *Jonet* of Leith', December 1611, *Mariners' Mirror*, lxxix, 1993

Hunter, Sir W.W., *The Marquess of Dalhousie* (Oxford, 1890)

——, *The Old Missionary* (London, 1890)

——, *Life of Brian Houghton Hodgson* (London, 1896)

Hutcheson, F., *A System of Moral Philosophy* (London, 1755)

Hutchison, I.G.C., *A Political History of Scotland, 1832–1924* (Edinburgh, 1986)

Hutchison, R. & Martelli, G., *Robert's People, the life of Sir Robert Williams* (London, 1971)

Hutchison, T., *Before Adam Smith, the emergence of political economy, 1662–1776* (Oxford, 1988)

Huttenback, R.A., *The British Imperial Experience* (London & New York, 1966)

Huxley, E., *Four Guineas*, a journey through West Africa (London, 1954)

Hyam, R., *Elgin and Churchill at the Colonial Office* (London, 1968)

& Martin, G, *Reappraisals in British Imperial History* (London, 1975)

Hyde, F.E., *Cunard and the North Atlantic, 1840–1973* (London, 1975)

Hyde, H.M., *John Law* (Amsterdam, 1948)

Ingham, K., *Reformers in India, 1793–1833* (Cambridge, 1956)

——, *The Making of Modern Uganda* (London, 1958)

——, *A History of East Africa* (London, 1962)

Ingram, E. (ed.), *Two Views of British India* (Bath, 1970)

——, *Commitment to Empire* (Oxford, 1981)

Innis, H.A., *The Fur Trade in Canada* (Toronto, 1956)

Insh, G.P., *Scottish Colonial Schemes, 1620–1686* (Glasgow, 1922)

——, *Papers relating to the Ships and Voyages of the Company of Scotland trading to Africa and the Indies, 1696–1707* (Edinburgh, 1924)

——, 'Some Notes on the Literature of Scots Colonisation', *Records of the Glasgow Bibliographical Society*, vii, 1928

——, 'The *Carolina Merchant, advice of arrival*', *Scottish Historical Review*, xxv, 1928

——, *The Company of Scotland trading to Africa and the Indies* (London & New York, 1932)

——, *The Scot in the Modern World* (Edinburgh, 1932)

Irvine, A., *An Inquiry into the Causes and Effects of Emigration from the Highlands* (Edinburgh, 1802)

Irwin, D. & F., *Scottish Painters at Home and Abroad, 1700–1900* (London, 1975)

Isaac, J., *British Post-War Migration* (Cambridge, 1954)

Israel, J.I., *Dutch Primacy in World Trade, 1585–1740* (Oxford, 1989)

Jackson, G., 'Glasgow in Transition, 1660–1740', in Devine & Jackson (1995a)

——, 'New Horizons in Trade', in Devine & Jackson (1995b)

Jackson, K. & Marré, J., *New Zealand* (London, 1969)

Jackson, P., *Race and Racism* (London, 1987)

Jackson, R., *The Malayan Emergency* (London & New York, 1991)

Jackson, W.T., *The Enterprising Scot* (Edinburgh, 1968)

Jacobson, P.D., 'Rosebery and Liberal Imperialism, 1899–1903', *Journal of British Studies*, xiii, 1973

Jalland, P., 'United Kingdom Devolution 1910–1914, political panacea or tactical diversion?', *English Historical Review* xciv, 1979

James, R.R., *Rosebery* (London, 1963)

James, R.W., *John Rae, political economist* (Toronto, 1965)

Japikse, N., 'De Prins van Oranje en de Schotsche Stapel te Vere in 1668', *Archief van het Zeeuwsch Genootschap*, 1906

Jarvenpa, R. & Zenner, W.P., 'Scots of the Northern Fur Trade, a middleman minority perspective', *Ethnic Groups*, ii, 1980

Jay, L.J., 'Pioneer Settlement on the Darling Downs, a Scottish contribution to Australian colonisation', *Scottish Geographical Magazine*, lxxii, 1957

Jeal, T., *Livingstone* (London, 1973)

Jeffery, R., 'Merchant Capital and the End of Empire – James Finlay, merchant adventurers', in Maxwell (1982)

Jeffreys-Jones, R., 'The Inestimable Advantage of not being English, Lord Lothian's ambassadorship 1939–1940', *Scottish Historical Review*, lxiii, 1984

Jenkins, R., *Asquith* (London, 1964)

Jensen, P.H. et al (eds.), *Dansk Kolonihistorie, indføring og studier* (Aarhus, 1983)

Jewish Committee of the Free Church of Scotland, *The Sea of Galilee Mission* (Edinburgh & London, 1895)

Jeyasekeran, T.A., 'William Miller and the Meaning of Christian Education in India', *Bulletin of the Scottish Institute of Missionary Studies*, n.s., iv–v, 1988–9

Johns, S.W., 'Trade Union, Political Pressure Group or Mass Movement? The Industrial & Commercial Workers' Union of Africa', in Mazrui & Rotberg (1970)

Johnson, A., *The Swedish Settlements on the Delaware* (New York, 1911)

Johnson, H.G., *Economic Nationalism in Old and New States* (London, 1968)

Johnson, P., *The Birth of the Modern World Society, 1815–1830* (London, 1991)

Johnson, S., *A Journey to the Western Islands of Scotland* (Oxford, 1924; first published, 1775)

Johnston, J.G., *The Truth, consisting of letters just received from emigrants to the Australian colonies* (Edinburgh, 1839)

Johnston, R.F., *Lion and Dragon in Northern China* (London, 1910)

——, *Letters to a Missionary* (London, 1918)

Johnston, S.H.F., *The History of the Cameronians (Scottish Rifles), i, 1689–1910* (Aldershot, 1957)

Johnston, T., *Memories* (London, 1952)

Johnstone, W. (ed.), *William Robertson Smith, essays in reassessment* (Sheffield, 1995)

Jones, C. (ed.), *Britain in the First Age of Party* (London & Roncevert, 1987)

Jones, G., *Banking and Empire in Iran* (Cambridge, 1986)

——, *British Multinational Banking, 1830–1990* (Oxford, 1993)

& Davenport-Hines, R.P.T. (eds.), *British Business in Asia since 1860* (Cambridge, 1989)

& van Helten, J.J., 'British Business in Malaysia and Singapore since the 1870s', in the above

Jones, M.A., 'The Scotch-Irish in British America', in Bailyn & Morgan (1991)

Jones, P. (ed.), *Philosophy and Science in the Scottish Enlightenment* (Edinburgh, 1988)

Jones, R.A., 'Robertson Smith and James Frazer on Religion', in Stocking (1984)

Jones, S., *Two Centuries of Trading, the origins and growth of the Inchcape Group* (London, 1986)

——, 'British Mercantile Enterprise Overseas in the Nineteenth Century, the example of James Lyle Mackay, 1st Earl of Inchcape', in Fisher (1987)

——, *Trade and Shipping, Lord Inchcape 1852–1932* (Manchester, 1989)

Joyce, R.B., *Sir William MacGregor* (Melbourne, 1971)

Judd, D., *Balfour and the British Empire* (London, 1968)

Kadalie, C., *My Life and the ICU* (London, 1970)

Karras, A.L., 'The World of Alexander Johnston, the creolization of ambition 1762–1787', *Historical Journal*, xxx, 1987

——, *Sojourners in the Sun, Scottish migrants in Jamaica and the Chesapeake, 1740–1800* (Ithaca & London, 1992)

Katzenellenbogen, S.E., *Railways and the Copper Mines of Katanga* (Oxford, 1973)

Kay, B., 'The Scots ower the Sleuch', in Wood (1994)

Kaye, J.W., *Life and Correspondence of Sir John Malcolm* (n.p., 1856)

——, *Lives of Indian Officers* (London, 1867)

Kearney, H., *The British Isles, a history of four nations* (Cambridge, 1989)

Keating, M., *State and Regional Nationalism* (Hemel Hempstead, 1988)

Keay, J., *India Discovered* (Leicester, 1981)

Keith, A.B., *Imperial Unity and the Dominions* (Oxford, 1916)

——, *Responsible Government in the Dominions* (Oxford, 1928)

——, *Constitutional History of the First British Empire* (Oxford, 1930)

——, *Letters and Essays on Current Imperial and International Problems* (Oxford, 1936)

Keith, T., 'Scottish Trade with the Plantations before 1707', *Scottish Historical Review*, vi, 1909

——, 'The Trading Privileges of the Royal Burghs of Scotland', *English Historical Review*, xxviii, 1913

Kellas, J.G., *The Politics of Nationalism and Ethnicity* (Basingstoke, 1991)

Kendle, J.E., 'The Round Table Movement and "Home Rule All Round" ', *Historical Journal*, xi, 1968

——, *The Round Table Movement and Imperial Union* (Toronto, 1975)

Kendrick, S. & McCrone, D., 'Politics in a Cold Climate, the Conservative decline in Scotland', *Political Studies*, xxxvii, 1989

Kennedy, P., The Canadian Identity as a Focus for the Study of the Scots in Canada, unpublished M. Litt. thesis, University of Edinburgh, 1976

Kennedy, P.M., *The Rise and Fall of British Naval Mastery* (London, 1976)

Kent, M., *Oil and Empire* (London, 1976)

Ker, J., *Memoirs* (London, 1727)

Ker, J., *Scottish Nationality and Other Papers* (n.p., 1887)

Kernohan, R., *The Road to Zion* (Carberry, 1995)

Keswick, M., *The Thistle and the Jade, a celebration of 150 years of Jardine, Matheson & Co* (London, 1982)

Kidd, C., *Subverting Scotland's Past* (Cambridge, 1993)

——, 'Teutonist Ethnology and Scottish Nationalist Inhibition 1780–1880', *Scottish Historical Review*, lxxiv, 1994

Kiddle, M., *Men of Yesterday, a social history of the western district of Victoria, 1834–1890* (Melbourne, 1961)

Kiernan, V.G., *The Lords of Human Kind* (London, 1969)

Kilbourn, W., *The Firebrand, William Lyon Mackenzie and the rebellion in Upper Canada* (London, 1958)

Kilpatrick, J.W., Protestant Missions in Jamaica, unpublished Ph.D. thesis, University of Edinburgh, 1943

Kim, D.-W. & Slaven, A., 'The Origins and Economic and Social Roles of Scottish Business Leaders, 1860–1960', in Devine (1994)

Kimche, J., *The Unromantics, the great powers and the Balfour declaration* (London, 1968)

Kinchin, J. & P., *Glasgow's Great Exhibitions* (Bicester, 1988)

King, D., *The State and Prospects of Jamaica* (London, 1850)

King, F.H.H. (ed.), *Eastern Banking* (London, 1983)

——, *The Hongkong Bank in Late Imperial China, 1864–1902* (Cambridge, 1987)

——, *The Hongkong Bank in the Period of Imperialism and War, 1895–1918* (Cambridge, 1988)

——, *The Hongkong Bank between the Wars and the Bank Interned, 1919–1945* (Cambridge, 1988)

——, *The Hongkong Bank in the Period of Development and Nationalism, 1941–1984* (Cambridge, 1991)

King, V.T., *Explorers of South-east Asia* (Kuala Lumpur, 1995)

Kirkwall, Viscount, *Four Years in the Ionian Islands* (London, 1864)

Kirkwood, J., *Proposals concerning the Propagation of Christian Knowledge in the Highlands and Islands and Foreign Parts of the World* (Edinburgh, 1706)

Kitchen, P., *A Most Unsettling Person, an introduction to the ideas and life of Patrick Geddes* (London, 1975)

Kittrell, F.R., 'The Development of the Theory of Colonisation in English Classical Political Economy', *Southern Economic Journal*, xxxi, 1965

Knaplund, P., *Gladstone and Britain's Imperial Policy* (London, 1927)

(ed.), 'Gladstone-Gordon Correspondence', *Transactions of the American Philosophical Society*, n.s., li, 1961

Knight, W. (ed.), *Rectorial Addresses Delivered at the University of St Andrews, 1863–1893* (London, 1894)

——, *Memorials of Thomas Davidson* (Boston & London, 1907)

Knollys, H. (ed.), *Life of General Sir Hope Grant* (Edinburgh & London, 1894)

Knorr, K.E., *British Colonial Theories, 1570–1850* (Toronto, 1944)

——, 'The Fall of the First British Empire', in Curtis & Nadel (1964)

Knowles, L.C., In Search of a National Voice, some similarities between Scottish and Canadian poetry, unpublished Ph.D. thesis, University of St Andrews, 1981

Knowles, R., *St Cuthbert's of the West* (Edinburgh & London, 1905)

Knox. J., *View of the British Empire* (Edinburgh, 1784)

Knox, R., *The Races of Man* (London, 1850)

Koebner, R., *Empire* (Cambridge, 1961)

& Schmidt, H.D., *Imperialism* (Cambridge, 1964)

Kopf, D. (ed.), *Bengal Regional Identity* (East Lansing, 1969)

——, 'Rammohun Roy's Historical Quest for an Identity in the Modern World', in the above

——, *British Orientalism and the Bengal Renaissance* (Berkeley & Los Angeles, 1969)

——, *The Brahmo Samaj and the Shaping of the Modern Indian Mind* (Princeton, 1979)

Koss, S., *Asquith* (London, 1985)

Kossman, E.H., *The Low Countries, 1780–1940* (Oxford, 1978)

Kotkin, J., *Tribes* (New York, 1992)

Kratoska, P.H. (ed.), *Honourable Intentions* (Singapore, 1983)

Kruse, J., *John Buchan (1875–1940) and the Idea of Empire* (Lampeter, 1989)

Kuitenbouwer, M., *The Netherlands and the Rise of Modern Imperialism* (New York & Oxford, 1991)

Kumar, D. (ed.), *The Cambridge Economic History of India, II, 1757–1970* (Cambridge, 1983)

Kup, A.P., 'Alexander Lindsay, 6th Earl of Balcarres, Lieutenant-governor of Jamaica 1794–1801', *Bulletin of the John Rylands Library*, lvii, 1974–5

Laing, D. (ed.), *Royal Letters, Charters and Tracts relating to the Colonization of New Scotland* (Edinburgh, 1867)

Laird, B., *Paddy Henderson* (Glasgow, 1961)

Laird, M. & Oldfield, R.A.K., *Narrative of an Expedition into the Interior of Africa* (London, 1837)

Laird, M.A., 'Alexander Duff and Scottish Educational Influences in Bengal during Bentinck's Administration', *Scottish Educational Studies*, ii, 1970

——, *Missionaries and Education in Bengal* (Oxford, 1972)

Lamb, W.K. (ed.), *The Letters and Journals of Simon Fraser, 1806–1808* (Toronto, 1960)

——, *The Journals and Letters of Sir Alexander Mackenzie* (Cambridge, 1970)

Lambrick, H.T., *Sir Charles Napier and Sind* (Oxford, 1952)

Lamond, R., *A Narrative of the Rise and Progress of Emigration from the Counties of Lanark and Renfrew to the New Settlements in Upper Canada* (Glasgow, 1821)

Lamont-Brown, R., *Tutor to the Dragon Emperor, the life of Sir Reginald Fleming Johnston at the court of the last Emperor of China* (Stroud, 1993)

La Nauze, J.A. *et al*, *Six Great Australians* (Melbourne, 1962)

Landsman, N.C., *Scotland and its First American Colony, 1683–1765* (Princeton, 1985)

——, 'Religion and Revolution, the two worlds of John Witherspoon', in Sher & Smitten (1990)

Lang, J.D., *Reminiscences of My Life and Times* (Melbourne, 1972)

Langley, M., 'The Last Journey of Mungo Park', *History Today*, xxi, 1971

Latourette, K.S., *A History of Christian Missions in China* (London, 1929)

Lau, T.Y., James Legge (1815–1897) and Chinese Culture, unpublished Ph.D. thesis, University of Edinburgh, 1994

Laude, N., *La Compagnie d'Ostende et son Activité Coloniale au Bengale* (Brussels, 1944)

Laurence, M., *The Diviners* (London, 1974)

Laurie, W.F.B., *Sketches of Some Distinguished Anglo-Indians* (London, 1887)

Lauring, P., *A History of the Kingdom of Denmark* (Copenhagen, 1960)

Law, J., *Proposals and Reasons for Constituting a Council of Trade in Scotland* (Glasgow, 1751; first published, 1700)

——, *Money and Trade Considered* (Edinburgh, 1705)

——, *Oeuvres Complètes* (Paris, 1934)

Law, R., 'The First Scottish Guinea Company, 1634–1639', *Scottish Historical Review*, lxxvi, 1997

Laws, R., *Reminiscences of Livingstonia* (Edinburgh & London, 1934)

Lawson, J., *The Painter's Vision* (Scottish National Portrait Gallery, 1994)

Lawson, P. & Lenman, B.P., 'Robert Clive, the 'Black Jagir' and British Politics', *Historical Journal*, xxvi, 1983

Leckie, G.F., *An Historical Survey of the Foreign Affairs of Great Britain* (London, 1808)

Leder, L.H., *Robert Livingston (1654–1728) and the Politics of Colonial New York* (Chapel Hill, 1961)

Lee-Warner, Sir W., *The Life of the Marquis of Dalhousie* (London, 1904)

LeFevour, E., *Western Enterprise in Late Ch'ing China, a selective survey of Jardine, Matheson & Company's operations, 1842–1895* (Cambridge, Mass., 1970)

Legge, H.E., *James Legge* (London, 1905)

Legge, J., *The Chinese Classics* (Hong Kong, 1960; first published, 1861)

Lehmann, E., *Henry Home, Lord Kames, and the Scottish Enlightenment* (The Hague, 1971)

Leiper, S., *Precious Cargo, Scots and the China trade* (Edinburgh, 1997)

Leith-Ross, F., *Money Talks, 50 years of international finance* (London, 1968)

Lemon, A., *The Young Man from Home, James Balfour 1830–1913* (Melbourne, 1982)

Lenman, B.P., *An Economic History of Modern Scotland* (London, 1977)
——, *Integration, Enlightenment and Industrialisation, Scotland 1746–1832* (London, 1981)
——, 'The East India Companies', in Maccubbin & Phillips (1989)
——, 'The English and Dutch East India Companies and the Birth of Consumerism in the Augustan World', *Eighteenth-Century Life*, xiv, 1990
——, 'Aristocratic "Country" Whiggery in Scotland and the American Revolution', in Sher & Smitten (1990)
——, 'The Transition to European Military Ascendancy in India, 1600–1800', in Lynn (1990)
——, 'Garrison Government'? – Governor Alexander Spotswood and Empire', in Simpson (1992)
——, *The Jacobite Clans of the Great Glen* (Aberdeen, 1995)
Léry, J. de, *Histoire d'un Voyage fait en la Terre du Brésil* (La Rochelle, 1578)
Lethbridge, D.G., *Hong Kong, stability and change* (Hong Kong, 1978)
——, *The Business Environment in Hong Kong* (Hong Kong, 1980)
Levack, B.P., *The Formation of the British State* (Oxford, 1987)
Levison, F., *Christian and Jew, the life of Leon Levison 1881–1936* (Edinburgh, 1989)
Levy, C.B., Conservative and Liberal Unionism in Glasgow 1874–1912, unpublished Ph.D. thesis, University of Dundee, 1983
Lewis, J., *George Brown* (London & Toronto, 1926)
Lewis, W.S. & Murakami, N. (eds.), *Ranald MacDonald* (Spokane, 1923)
Leyburn, J.G., *The Scotch-Irish* (Chapel Hill, 1962)
Leys, N., *Kenya* (London, 1924)
——, *A Last Chance in Kenya* (London, 1931)
Liebowitz, D., *The Physician and the Slave Trade, John Kirk, the Livingstone expeditions and the crusade against slavery in East Africa* (New York, 1999)
Lijphart, A., *The Trauma of Decolonisation* (New Haven & London, 1966)
Lindley, Sir F., *Lord Lovat* (London, 1935)
Lindsay, A., *A Letter to Alexander Duff* (Edinburgh, 1854)
Lindsay, Lord, *Letters on Egypt, Edom and the Holy Land* (London, 1838)
Linklater, E., *A Year of Space* (London, 1953)
——, *Fanfare for a Tin Hat* (London, 1970)
Liston, C., 'Sir Thomas Brisbane in New South Wales', *Journal of the Royal Australian Historical Society*, lxxi, 1985
Listowel, J., *The Other Livingstone* (Lewes, 1974)
Lithgow, W., *Rare Adventures* (London, 1623)
Little, J.I., *Crofters and Habitants, settler society, economy and culture in a Quebec township, 1848–1881* (Montreal & Kingston, 1991)
Little, K., *Negroes in Britain* (London, 1948)
Liu, K.-C., *Anglo-American Steamship Rivalry in China* (Cambridge, Mass., 1962)
Livingston, D.W., 'Hume, English Barbarism and American Independence', in Sher & Smitten (1990)
Livingstone, D., *Missionary Travels and Researches in South Africa* (London, 1857)
Livingstone, W.P., *Mary Slessor of Calabar* (London, 1916)
——, *Laws of Livingstonia* (London, 1921)
——, *A Galilee Doctor* (London, 1923)
——, *A Prince of Missionaries, the Rev Alexander Hetherwick* (London, 1931)
Lizars, R. & K., *In the Days of the Canada Company* (Toronto, 1896)
Lloyd, C., 'Dr Baikie and the Niger', *History Today*, xxi, 1971
Loch, H., *Personal Narrative of Occurrences during Lord Elgin's Second Embassy to China in 1860* (London, 1900)
Lockhart, R.H.B., *Memoirs of a British Agent* (London & New York, 1932)
——, *Return to Malaya* (London, 1936)
Logan, J., *Notes of a Journey through Canada, the United States of America and the West Indies* (Edinburgh, 1838)
Lokanathan, P.S., *Industrial Organisation in India* (London, 1935)
Long, E., *The History of Jamaica* (London, 1774)
Long, M.H., 'Sir John Rose and the Informal Beginnings of the Canadian High Commissionership', *Canadian Historical Review*, xii, 1931
Longhurst, H., *The Borneo Story* (London, 1956)

Lord, W.F., *The Lost Possessions of England* (London, 1896)

——, *Sir Thomas Maitland* (London, 1897)

Lorimer, D.A., *Colour, Class and the Victorians* (Leicester, 1978)

Lorne, Marquis of, *Imperial Federation* (London, 1885)

Loughlin, J., ' "Imagining Ulster", the North of Ireland and British national identity 1880–1921', in Connolly (1999)

Louvisbury, R.G., *The British Fishery at Newfoundland, 1634–1763* (New Haven, 1934)

Lovett, R., *The History of the London Missionary Society, 1795–1845* (London, 1899)

(ed.), *James Chalmers, his autobiography and letters* (London, 1903)

Low, D.A. & Smith, A. (eds.), *History of East Africa* (Oxford, 1976)

Lowie, R.H. *The History of Ethnographical Theory* (New York, 1937)

Lownie, A., *John Buchan, the presbyterian cavalier* (London, 1995)

Lucas, D., *The Welsh, Irish, Scots and English in Australia* (Canberra, 1987)

Lumby, E.W.R., 'Lord Elgin and the Burning of the Summer Palace', *History Today*, x, 1960

Lundkvist, S., 'The Experience of Empire, Sweden as a great power', in Roberts (1973)

Lunney, L., 'Ulster Attitudes to Scottishness, the eighteenth century and after', in Wood (1994)

Lupton, K., *Mungo Park* (Oxford, 1979)

Lüthy, H., 'Colonisation and the Making of Mankind', in Curtis & Nadel (1964)

Lwanda, J.L., *Kamuzu Banda of Malawi* (Glasgow, 1993)

Lydon, J., 'The Impact of the Bruce Invasion, 1315–1327', in Cosgrove (1987)

——, 'The Scottish Soldier in Medieval Ireland, the Bruce invasion and the galloglass', in Simpson (1992)

Lynn, J.A. (ed.), *Tools of War* (Urbana, Ill., 1990)

Lythe, S.G.E., *The Economy of Scotland in its European Setting, 1550–1625* (Edinburgh & London, 1960)

Maan, B., *The New Scots* (Edinburgh, 1992)

McAlister, A.A., *A Short History of H. Hogarth & Sons Ltd* (Kendal, 1976)

Macalister, F., *Memoir of the Rt Hon Sir John McNeill* (London, 1910)

Macaulay, T.B. *et al*, *The Indian Civil Service, report to the Rt Hon Charles Wood* (London, 1855)

MaCaffrey, J.F., 'The Origins of Liberal Unionism in the West of Scotland', *Scottish Historical Review*, I, 1971

McCalla, D., *The Upper Canada Trade, 1834–1872* (Toronto, 1979)

McCalman, I. (ed.), *The Horrors of Slavery and Other Writings by Robert Wedderburn* (Edinburgh, 1991)

McCracken, J., Livingstonia Mission and the evolution of Malawi 1875–1939, unpublished D. Phil. thesis, University of Cambridge, 1967

——, 'Livingstone and the Aftermath, the origins and development of Livingstonia Mission', in Pachai (1973)

——, 'Scottish Medical Missionaries in Central Africa', *Medical History*, xvii, 1973

——, *Politics and Christianity in Malawi, 1875–1940* (Cambridge, 1977)

——, 'Underdevelopment in Malawi, the missionary contribution', *African Affairs*, lxxvi, 1977

McCrae, A., *Scots in Burma* (Edinburgh, 1990)

& Prentice, A., *Irrawaddy Flotilla* (Paisley, 1978)

McCrone, D., *Understanding Scotland, the sociology of a stateless nation* (London & New York, 1992)

——, 'Towards a Principled Society, Scottish elites in the twentieth century', in Dickson & Treble (1992)

Maccubbin, R.P. & Phillips, M.H., *The Age of William III and Mary II* (College of William and Mary and Grolier Club, 1989)

McCulloch, S.C. (ed.), *British Humanitarianism* (Philadelphia, 1950)

McCully, B.T., *English Education and the Origins of Indian Nationalism* (New York, 1940)

Macdiarmid, D.S., *The Life of Lieutenant-general Sir James Moncrieff Grierson* (London, 1923)

Macdonald, C.M.M. (ed.), *Unionist Scotland, 1800–1997* (Edinburgh, 1998)

Macdonald, D., *Africana* (London, 1882)

McDonald, E.S. & F., 'The Ethnic Origins of the American People, 1790', *William and Mary Quarterly*, xxxvii, 1980

McDonald, F. & McWhiney, G., 'The Celtic South', *History Today*, xxx, 1980

Macdonald, J.A.M., *Notes on the Constitutional Reconstruction of the Empire* (London, 1917)

Macdonald, J.R., *Labour and the Empire* (London, 1907)

MacDonald, M., *Borneo People* (London, 1956)

——, *The Evolving Commonwealth* (Ditchley Park, 1970)

——, *Titans and Others* (London, 1972)

Macdonald, N., *Canada 1763–1841, immigration and settlement* (London, 1939)

McDougall, D., *In Search of Israel* (London, 1941)

McDougall, E.A.K. & Moir, J.S. (eds.), *Selected Correspondence of the Glasgow Colonial Society, 1825–1840* (Toronto, 1994)

Macdougall, N. (ed.), *Scotland and War* (Edinburgh, 1991)

McDougall, R.L., 'The Literary Influence of Sir Walter Scott in Canada', *British Journal of Canadian Studies*, ii, 1987

McFarlan, D.M., *Calabar, the Church of Scotland mission* (Edinburgh & London, 1946)

McFarland, E., *Protestants First, Orangeism in Nineteenth-century Scotland* (Edinburgh, 1990)

——, *Ireland and Scotland in the Age of Revolution* (Edinburgh, 1995)

McFarlane, I.D., *Buchanan* (London, 1981)

McGilvary, G.K., East India Patronage and the Political Management of Scotland 1720–1774, unpublished Ph.D. thesis, Open University, 1989

Mcgrail, T.H., *Sir William Alexander, first Earl of Stirling* (Edinburgh & London, 1940)

McGrath, J., 'The Medieval and Early Modern Burgh', in Devine & Jackson (1995)

MacGregor, C., *Mountain Warfare* (London, 1866)

Macgregor, Sir W., *British New Guinea* (London, 1897)

Macinnes, A.I., 'Scottish Gaeldom, the first phase of clearance', in Devine & Mitchison (1988)

——, 'Landownership, Land Use and Elite Enterprise in Scottish Gaeldom, from clanship to clearance in Argyllshire 1688–1858', in Devine (1994)

McIntosh, B.G., The Scottish Mission in Kenya, 1891–1923, unpublished Ph.D. thesis, University of Edinburgh, 1969

McIntyre, W.D., *The Imperial Frontier in the Tropics, 1865–1875* (London, 1967)

Mac Iomhair, D., 'The Battle of Fochart, 1318', *Irish Sword*, viii, 1967

Mackenzie, Sir C., *Realms of Silver* (London, 1954)

Mackenzie, J., *Austral Africa, losing or ruling it* (London, 1887)

Mackenzie, J.M., *The Empire of Nature* (Manchester, 1988)

——, 'David Livingstone, the construction of the myth', in Gallagher & Walker (1990)

——, Scotland and the Empire, inaugural lecture delivered at the university of Lancaster, 1992 (ed.), *David Livingstone and the Victorian Encounter with Africa* (London, 1996)

Mackenzie, J.N., *An Autobiography* (London, 1971)

Mackenzie, W.C., *Andrew Fletcher of Saltoun* (Edinburgh, 1935)

——, *Colonel Colin Mackenzie, First Surveyor-general of India* (Edinburgh & London, 1952)

Mackenzie, W.D., *John Mackenzie* (London, 1902)

M'Kerrow, J., *History of the Foreign Missions of the Secession and United Presbyterian Church* (Edinburgh, 1867)

Mackesy, P., *The War in the Mediterranean, 1803–1810* (London, 1957)

——, *Statesmen at War, the strategy of overthrow 1798–1799* (London, 1974)

——, *War without Victory, the downfall of Pitt 1799–1802* (Oxford, 1984)

Mackichan, D., *The Missionary Ideal in the Scottish Churches* (Edinburgh, 1927)

Mackinnon, J., *South African Traits* (Edinburgh, 1887)

Mackintosh, K.J. (ed.), *Memoirs of the Life of Sir James Mackintosh* (London, 1835)

McLean, D.A., British Banking and Government in China, the Foreign Office and the Hongkong & Shanghai Bank 1895–1914, unpublished D. Phil. thesis, University of Cambridge, 1973

——, 'Finance and "Informal Empire" before the First World War', *Economic History Review*, xxix, 1976

——, 'International Banking and its Political Implications, the Hongkong & Shanghai Banking Corporation and the Imperial Bank of Persia, 1889–1914', in King (1983)

Maclean, J.M., *Recollections of Westminster and India* (Manchester, 1902)

MacLean, J.P., *Scotch Highlanders in America* (Glasgow, 1900)

——, *Flora Macdonald in America* (Lumberton, NC, 1909)

McLean, M., 'In the new land a new Glengarry', migration from the Scottish Highlands to Upper Canada, unpublished Ph.D. thesis, University of Edinburgh, 1982

——, *The People of Glengarry, Highlanders in transition, 1745–1820* (Montreal & Kingston, 1991)

Maclean, R., *The Oatmeal Ark* (London, 1998)

McLellan, R.S., *Anchor Line, 1856–1956* (Glasgow, 1956)

MacLennan, H., *Each Man's Son* (Toronto, 1951)
——, *Scotchman's Return* (Toronto, 1958)
McLennan, J.F., *Studies in Ancient History, comprising a reprint of Primitive Marriage* (London, 1876)
MacLeod, A., *The Lost Salt Gift of Blood* (London, 1991)
McLeod, I., Scotland and the Liberal Party 1880–1900 – Church, Ireland and Empire, a family affair, unpublished M. Litt. thesis, University of Glasgow, 1976
MacLeod, M.A. & Morton, W.L., *Cuthbert Grant of Grantown* (Toronto, 1963)
Macleod, N., *Address on Christian Missions to India* (Edinburgh & London, 1868)
MacLeod, W. (ed.), *Journal of the Hon John Erskine of Carnock, 1683–1687* (Edinburgh, 1893)
McLintock, A.H., *The History of Otago* (Dunedin, 1949)
Macmillan, D., *Scottish Art, 1460–1990* (Edinburgh, 1990)
Macmillan, D.S., *The Squatter Went to Sea, the story of Sir William Macleay's New Guinea expedition (1875) and his life in Sydney* (Sydney, 1957)
——, *The Debtor's War, Scottish capitalists and the economic crisis in Australia, 1841–1846* (Melbourne, 1960)
——, 'The Scottish Australian Company, 1840–1850', *Scottish Historical Review*, xxxix, 1960
——, 'John Dunmore Lang', in La Nauze *et al* (1962)
——, 'Scottish Enterprise in Australia, 1798–1879', in Payne (1967)
——, *Scotland and Australia, 1788–1850* (Oxford, 1967)
——, 'The Transfer of Company Control from Scotland to London in the Nineteenth Century, the case of the Scottish Australian Company 1853', *Business History*, xii, 1970
(ed.), *Canadian Business History, selected studies, 1497–1971* (Toronto, 1972)
——, 'The "New Men" in Action, Scottish mercantile and shipping operations in the North American Colonies 1760–1825', in the above
——, 'Scottish Enterprise and Influences in Canada, 1620–1900', in Cage (1985)
Macmillan, H.W., The Origins and Development of the African Lakes Company, 1878–1908, unpublished Ph.D. thesis, University of Edinburgh, 1970
& Marks, S., *Africa and Empire* (London, 1989)
Macmillan, W.M., *The South African Agrarian Problem and its Historical Development* (Cape Town, 1919)
——, *Bantu, Boer and Briton* (Oxford, 1963)
——, *The Cape Colour Question* (London & New York, 1967)
——, *My South African Years* (Cape Town, 1975)
Macnair, J.I., *The Story of the Scottish National Memorial to David Livingstone* (Blantyre, 1951)
Macnaughton, J., *Lord Strathcona* (London & Toronto, 1926)
McNeill, W.A., (ed.), 'Papers of a Dundee Shipping Dispute, 1600–1604', *Scottish History Society Miscellany X*, (1965)
Macphail, A., *The Master's Wife* (Montreal, 1939)
Macpherson, F., *Kenneth Kaunda of Zambia* (Lusaka, 1974)
McPherson, F., *Watchman against the World, the story of Norman McLeod and his people* (London, 1962)
Macpherson, H., *The Gospel of Force* (Edinburgh, 1902)
Macquarrie, A., *Scotland and the Crusades* (Edinburgh, 1985)
McRoberts, K., *Misconceiving Canada, the struggle for national unity* (Oxford, 1998)
Macrosty, H.W., *The Trust Movement in British Industry* (London, 1907)
Magnus, Sir P., *Gladstone, a biography* (London, 1954)
Mahon, R.H., *Life of General the Hon James Murray* (London, 1921)
Major, E., *Viscount Morley and Indian Reform* (London, 1910)
Majumdar, A., Lord Minto's Administration in India, 1807–1813, unpublished D.Phil. thesis, University of Oxford, 1962
Malcolm, D.O., *The British South Africa Company* (London, 1939)
Malhotra, P., *The Administration of Lord Elgin in India, 1894–1899* (New Delhi, 1979)
Mandela, N., *Long Walk to Freedom* (London, 1994)
Manning, H.T., 'Who Ran the British Empire, 1830–1850?', *Journal of British Studies*, v, 1965
Manuel, F., *The Eighteenth Century Confronts the Gods* (New York, 1967)
Marjoribanks, J., *Slavery* (Edinburgh, 1792)
Markovits, C., *Indian Business and Nationalist Politics, 1931–1939* (Cambridge, 1985)
Marlowe, J.W., *The Seat of Pilate, an account of the Palestine mandate* (London, 1959)
Marr, A., *The Battle for Scotland* (London, 1992)

Marshall, G., 'David Hume and Political Scepticism', *Philosophical Quarterly*, iv, 1954

——, *Presbyteries and Profits, Calvinism and the development of capitalism in Scotland, 1560–1707* (Edinburgh, 1992)

Marshall, P.J., *East India Fortunes, the British in Bengal in the eighteenth century* (Oxford, 1976)

Marshman, J.C., *History of India* (London, 1867)

Martelli, G., *Livingstone's River, a history of the Zambesi expedition, 1858–1864* (London, 1970)

Martin, A.D., *Doctor Vanderkemp* (London, 1931)

Martin, C., *Lord Selkirk's Work in Canada* (Oxford, 1916)

Martin, G., 'Empire Federalism and Imperial Parliamentary Union, 1820–1870', *Historical Journal*, xvi, 1973

Martin, M. (ed.), *The Despatches, Minutes and Correspondence of the Marquis of Wellesley* (London, 1837)

Marwick, W., *William and Louisa Anderson* (Edinburgh, 1897)

Marwick, W.H., 'Scottish Overseas Investment in the Nineteenth Century', *Scottish Bankers' Magazine*, xxvii, 1935–6

Masson, C.R., *Les Bourgeois de la Compagnie du Nord-Ouest* (New York, 1960; first published 1889–90)

Mathew, G. & Oliver, R., *History of East Africa* (Oxford, 1963)

Matthew, H.C.G., *The Liberal Imperialists* (Oxford, 1973)

Maurice, Sir F., *Haldane* (London, 1937)

Maxwell, I.D., Alexander Duff and the Theological and Philosophical Background to the General Assembly's Mission in Calcutta to 1840, unpublished Ph.D. thesis, University of Edinburgh, 1995

Maxwell, J., 'Scotland's Commercial Empire, an historical perspective on Scotland's relations with the Third World', in Maxwell (1982)

Maxwell, S., *Scotland, Multinationals and the Third World* (Edinburgh, 1982)

Mayhew, A., *The Education of India* (London, 1926)

Mazrui, A.A. & Rotberg, R.I. (eds.), *Protest and Power in Black Africa* (New York, 1970)

Mehta, M.S., *Lord Hastings and the Indian States* (Delhi, 1986)

Meiring, J., *Thomas Pringle* (Cape Town & Amsterdam, 1968)

Mejcher, H., 'Oil and British Policy towards Mesopotamia, 1914–1918', *Middle Eastern Studies*, viii, 1972

Meller, H., *Patrick Geddes* (London & New York, 1990)

Mentze, E., *Dansk Vestindien* (n.p., 1981)

Merrington, E.N., *A Great Coloniser, the Rev Dr Thomas Burns* (Dunedin, 1929)

Metcalf, T.R., *An Imperial Vision, Indian architecture and Britain's Raj* (London, 1989)

Metcalfe, G.E., *Maclean of the Gold Coast* (Oxford, 1962)

Meyer, D., *The Highland Scots of North Carolina, 1732–1776* (Chapel Hill, 1957)

Michie, R.C., 'Aberdeen and Ceylon, economic links in the nineteenth century', *Northern Scotland*, iv, 1981

——, *Money, Mania and Markets* (Edinburgh, 1981)

——, 'Crisis and Opportunity, the formation and operation of the British Assets Trust, 1897–1914', *Business History*, xxv, 1983

——, The London Stock Exchange and the British Securities Market, 1850–1914, *Economic History Review*, xxxviii, 1985

Miège, J.L., *Expansion Européenne et Décolonisation, de 1870 à nos jours* (Paris, 1973)

Mill, J., *History of British India* (London, 1840)

Mill, J.S., *Considerations on Representative Government* (London, 1906)

Millar, J., *Observations concerning Distinctions of Ranks in Society* (London, 1771)

Miller, C., *The Canadian Career of the Fourth Earl of Minto* (Waterloo, Ontario, 1980)

Miller, H., *Jungle War in Malaya* (London, 1972)

Miller, H., *The Revolutionary College, American presbyterian higher education, 1707–1837* (New York, 1976)

Miller, J.C., *Alexander Hamilton* (New York, 1959)

Miller, J.D.B., 'The End of Bombast and Pessimism?', *Journal of Contemporary History*, xv, 1980

Milne, T.E., 'British Shipping in the Nineteenth Century, a study of the Ben Line papers', in Payne (1967)

Miners, N., *Hong Kong under Imperial Rule, 1912–1941* (Hong Kong, 1987)

Minto, Countess of, *Lord Minto in India* (London, 1880)

Minto, Mary, Countess of, *India, Minto and Morley, 1905–1910* (London, 1934)

Misra, B.B., *The Central Administration of the East India Company, 1773–1834* (Manchester, 1959)

Mitchell, C., *Having Been a Soldier* (London, 1969)

Mitchell, E.A., 'The Scot in the Fur Trade', in Reid (1976)

Mitchell, J., *An Essay on the Best Means of Civilising the Subjects of the British Empire in India* (Edinburgh, 1805)

Mitchell, J., *Conservatives and the Union* (Edinburgh, 1990)

——, *Constitutional Conventions and the Scottish National Movement, origins, agendas and outcomes* (Glasgow, 1991)

Mitchell, W., *Home Rule for Scotland and Imperial Federation* (Edinburgh, 1982)

Mizuta, H. & Sugiyama, C. (eds.), *Adam Smith, international perspectives* (New York, 1993)

Moffat, Sir J., 'The Stalemate over Dr Banda', *Central African Examiner*, iii, 1960

Moffat, J.S., *The Lives of Robert and Mary Moffat* (London, 1889)

Moffat, R., *Missionary Labours and Scenes in Southern Africa* (London, 1842)

Moir, F.L.M., *After Livingstone* (London, 1923)

Moir, J.S., 'The Settlement of the Clergy Reserves, 1840–1855', *Canadian Historical Review*, xxxvii, 1956

——, *Church and State in Canada West* (Toronto, 1959)

——, '"The Quay of Greenock", jurisdiction and nationality in the Canadian presbyterian disruption of 1844', *Scottish Tradition*, v, 1975

——, 'Scottish Influences on Canadian Presbyterianism', *Scotia*, ii, 1978

——, '"Loyalty and Respectability", the campaign for co-establishment of the Church of Scotland in Canada', *Scottish Tradition*, ix, 1979

Molloy, M., '"No Inclination to Mix with Strangers", marriage patterns among Highland Scots migrants to Cape Breton and New Zealand, 1800–1916', *Journal of Family History*, xi, 1986

Monckton, C.A.W., *Some Experiences of a New Guinea Resident Magistrate* (London & New York, n.d.)

Monopolies and Mergers Commission, *Hongkong & Shanghai Banking Corporation, Standard Chartered Bank Ltd, Royal Bank of Scotland Group Ltd, a report on the proposed mergers*, Cmnd 8472, 1982

Moody, T.W. & Vaughan, W.E. (eds.), *New History of Ireland, IV, Eighteenth-century Ireland* (Oxford, 1986)

Moore, T. (ed.), *The Letters and Journals of Lord Byron* (London, 1875)

Moorhouse, G., *India Britannica* (London, 1983)

Morgan, P.D., 'British Encounters with Africans and African-Americans, circa 1600–1780', in Bailyn & Morgan (1991)

Morison, J.L., 'Lord Elgin in Canada, 1847–1854', *Scottish Historical Review*, x, 1912

——, *British Supremacy and Canadian Self-Government* (Glasgow, 1919)

——, *The Eighth Earl of Elgin* (London, 1928)

Morley, J., *The Life of William Ewart Gladstone* (London, 1903)

——, *Indian Speeches, 1907–1909* (London, 1909)

——, *Recollections* (London, 1918)

Morris, A.J.A. (ed.), *Edwardian Radicalism* (London, 1974)

Morris, H., *The Life of Charles Grant* (London, 1904)

Morris, J., *The Venetian Empire* (London, 1980)

Morrison, J.H., *Streams in the Desert* (London, 1919)

Morrison, M.D., 'The Migration of Scotch Settlers from St Ann's, Nova Scotia, to New Zealand 1851–1869', *Collections of the Nova Scotia Historical Society*, xxii, 1933

Morton, J., *Memoirs of the Life and Writings of the Celebrated Literary Character, the late Dr John Leyden* (Calcutta, 1825)

Morton, W.L., *Alexander Begg's Red River Journal* (Toronto, 1954)

Morwood, W., *Traveller in a Vanished Landscape, the life and times of David Douglas* (New York, 1973)

Moss, B.G., 'The Roles of the Scots and Scotch-Irishmen in the Southern Campaigns in the War of American Independence, 1780–1783, unpublished Ph.D. thesis, University of St Andrews, 1979

Moulton, E.C., 'British Radicals and India in the Early Twentieth Century', in Morris (1974)

Mufuka, K.N., 'Militant Scottish Missionaries in Malawi, 1953–1963', *Scottish Tradition*, v, 1975

——, *Missions and Politics in Malawi* (Kingston, Ontario, 1977)

Mui, H.C. & L.H., 'Smuggling and the British Tea Trade before 1784', *American Historical Review*, lxxiv, 1968

——, (eds.), *William Melrose in China 1845–1855, the letters of a Scottish tea merchant* (Edinburgh, 1973)

Muir, J., *An Essay on Reconciliation* (London, 1858)

——, *Original Sanskrit Texts* (London, 1869–70)

Mungeam, G.H., *British Rule in Kenya, 1895–1912* (Oxford, 1966)

Munro, J.F., *Scottish 'Business Imperialism', Sir William Mackinnon and the development of trade and shipping in the Indian Ocean* (London, 1983)

——, 'Scottish Overseas Empire and the Lure of London, the Mackinnon Shipping Group 1847–1893', *Scottish Economic and Social History*, viii, 1988

——, Clydeside, the Indian Ocean and the City, the Mackinnon investment group 1847–1893, unpublished paper, n.d.

Munro, W., *Reminiscences of Military Service with the 93rd Sutherland Highlanders* (London, 1883)

Munro, W.T., *Madrasiana* (Madras, 1868)

Murdoch, J., *Indian Missionary Manual* (London, 1870)

Muramatsu, S., Jacobitism and Some Types of National Interest in the Union of 1707, unpublished paper, 1995

Murison, B., 'Poverty, Philanthropy and Emigration to British North America, changing attitudes in Scotland in the early nineteenth century', *British Journal of Canadian Studies*, ii, 1987

——, 'The Disruption and the Colonies of Scottish Settlement', in Brown & Fry (1993)

Murray, A.C., *Master and Brother* (London, 1945)

Murray, A.V., *The School in the Bush* (London, 1929)

Murray, A.W., *Forty Years' Mission Work in Polynesia and New Guinea* (London, 1876)

Murray, H., *Enquiries Historical and Moral respecting the Character of Nations and the Progress of Society* (Edinburgh, 1808)

Murray, J., *An Impartial History of the Present War in America* (London, 1778)

Murray, R.D., *A Summer at Port Phillip* (Edinburgh, 1843)

Murray-Brown, J., *Kenyatta* (London, 1972)

Nadel, G., *Australia's Colonial Culture* (Melbourne, 1957)

Nairn, T., *The Break-up of Britain, crisis and neo-nationalism* (London, 1977)

Napier, Sir C., *The Colonies, treating of their value generally, and of the Ionian Islands in particular* (London, 1833)

——, *Colonisation* (1835)

Napier, P., *I Have Sind, Charles Napier in India, 1841–1844* (Salisbury, England, 1990)

——, *Raven Castle, Charles Napier in India, 1844–1851* (Salisbury, England, 1991)

Napier, Sir W., *The Life and Opinions of General Sir Charles James Napier* (London, 1857)

Napier, W., *The Transvaal in 1876* (Grahamstown, 1881)

Narain, V.A., *Jonathan Duncan and Varanasi* (Calcutta, 1959)

Nash, R.C., 'The English and Scottish Tobacco Trades in the Seventeenth and Eighteenth Centuries, legal and illegal trade', *Economic History Review*, xxxv, 1982

National Library of Scotland, *Scottish Decolonisation Project* (Edinburgh, 1993)

Naylor, A.C.I., Scottish Attitudes to Ireland, 1880–1914, unpublished Ph.D. thesis, University of Edinburgh, 1985

Neil, W. (ed.), *The Cleghorn Papers* (London, 1927)

Nelson, W.H., *The American Tory* (Oxford, 1961)

Newell, J., ' "A Moment of Truth"? The Church and political change in Malawi, 1992', *Journal of Modern African Studies*, xxxiii, 1995

Newitt, M., 'Portuguese Conquistadores in Eastern Africa', *History Today*, xxx, 1980

——, *Portugal in Africa* (London, 1981)

Newman, C.E.T., *The Spirit of Wharf House* (Sydney, 1961)

Newman, M., *John Strachey* (Manchester, 1989)

Nicholas, S. (ed.), *Convict Workers, reinterpreting Australia's past* (Cambridge, 1988)

Nicholson, J.S., *A Project of Empire* (London, 1909)

——, 'The Economics of Imperialism', *Economic Journal*, xx, 1910

Nicolson, J., *Arthur Anderson* (Lerwick, 1932)

Nightingale, P., *Trade and Empire in Western India, 1784–1806* (Cambridge, 1970)

Nimocks, W., *Milner's Young Men* (Durham, NC, 1968)

Niven, F., *The Flying Years* (London, 1935)

——, *The Transplanted* (London, 1944)

Noel, B.W., *The Case of George William Gordon, Esq. of Jamaica* (London, 1866)

Northcott, C., *Robert Moffat, pioneer in Africa, 1817–1870* (London, 1966)

——, 'John Mackenzie and Southern Africa', *History Today*, xxii, 1972

Norton, W., 'Malcolm McNeill and the Emigrationist Alternative to Highland Land Reform, 1886–1893', *Scottish Historical Review*, lxx, 1991

Oatts, L.B., *The Highland Light Infantry* (London, 1969)

O'Brien, C.C., 'Warren Hastings in Burke's Great Melody', in Carnall & Nicholson (1989)

Officer, D. & Walker, G., 'Scottish Unionism and the Ulster Question', in Macdonald (1998)

Ogilvie, J.N., *An Indian Pilgrimage* (Edinburgh, 1922)

——, *Our Empire's Debt to Missions* (London, 1924)

——, *The Presbyterian Churches of Christendom* (Edinburgh & London, 1925)

Okon, A.A., The Church of Scotland and the Development of British Influence in Southern Nigeria, 1846–1885, unpublished Ph.D. thesis, University of London, 1972

O'Leary, P., *Sir James Mackintosh, the Whig Cicero* (Aberdeen, 1989)

Oliphant, L., *Narrative of the Earl of Elgin's Mission to China and Japan* (London, 1860)

——, *The Land of Gilead* (Edinburgh & London, 1880)

——, *Episodes in a Life of Adventure* (Edinburgh & London, 1887)

Oliphant, M.O.W., *Memoir of the Life of Laurence Oliphant* (Edinburgh & London, 1891)

Oliver, R., *The Missionary Factor in East Africa* (London, 1951)

Olivier, Lord, *The Myth of Governor Eyre* (London, 1933)

O'Malley, L.S.S., *Modern India and the West* (London, 1941)

Ommer, R.E., 'Primitive Accumulation and the Scottish *clann* in the Old World and the New', *Journal of Historical Geography*, xii, 1986

Onyeidu, S.O., 'William Balfour Baikie as Missionary, 1854–1864', *Bulletin of the Scottish Institute of Missionary Studies*, n.s., iii–iv, 1985–7

Orbell, J., *From Cape to Cape, the history of the Lyle Shipping Company* (Edinburgh, 1978)

Orr, J.M., The Contribution of Scottish Missions to the Rise of Responsible Churches in India, unpublished Ph.D. thesis, University of Edinburgh, 1967

Otway-Ruthven, A.J., *A History of Medieval Ireland* (London, 1968)

Outram, J., *The Conquest of Scinde* (London, 1846)

Owen, R. & Sutcliffe, B. (eds.), *Studies in the Theory of Imperialism* (London, 1972)

Pachai, B. (ed.), *The Early History of Malawi* (London, 1972)

——, (ed.), *Livingstone, Man of Africa* (London, 1973)

Pagden, A., *The Fall of Natural Man* (Cambridge, 1982)

——, *Lords of All the World, ideologies of empire in Spain, Britain and France, 1500–1800* (New Haven & London, 1995)

Paget, J., *Last Post, Aden 1964–1967* (London, 1969)

Paglin, M., *Malthus and Lauderdale* (Clifton, NJ, 1973)

Pakenham, E., *Jameson's Raid* (London, 1960)

Palmer, S., 'Johnston and Jameson, a comparative study in the imposition of colonial rule', in Pachai (1972)

& Williams, G., *Charted and Uncharted Waters* (London, 1981)

Parker, J.G., 'Scottish Enterprise in India, 1750–1914', in Cage (1985)

Parker, W.M. (ed.), *The Journal of Sir Walter Scott* (Edinburgh & London, 1946)

Parliamentary Papers, *Report from the Select Committee on Emigration, Scotland*, vi, 1841

Paterson, L., *The Autonomy of Modern Scotland* (Edinburgh, 1994)

Paterson, W., *Proposals and Reasons for Constituting a Council of Trade* (Edinburgh, 1701)

Paton, J., *John G. Paton* (London, 1889)

Paton, M., *Letters and Sketches from the New Hebrides* (London, 1894)

Paton, W., *Alexander Duff* (London, 1923)

Payne, P.L., *Studies in Scottish Business History* (London, 1967)

——, 'The Emergence of the Large-scale Company in Great Britain, 1870–1914', *Economic History Review*, xx, 1967

——, *The Early Scottish Limited Companies, 1856–1895* (Edinburgh, 1980)

Pearce, G.L., *The Scots of New Zealand* (Auckland & London, 1976)

Pearson, H., *Memoirs of the Life and Writings of the Rev Claudius Buchanan* (Oxford, 1817)

Pelcovits, N.A., *Old China Hands and the Foreign Office* (New York, 1948)

Pentland, M. Sinclair, Lady, *The Rt Hon John Sinclair, Lord Pentland, a memoir* (London, 1928)

——, *A Bonnie Fechter, the life of Ishbel Marjoribanks, Marchioness of Aberdeen and Temair* (London, 1952)

Perceval-Maxwell, M., *The Scottish Migration to Ulster in the Reign of James I* (London, 1973)
——, 'Sir William Alexander of Menstrie', *Scottish Tradition*, xi, 1981
Perham, M., *Lugard* (London, 1960)
Perrels, J.W., 'Bijdragen tot de Geschiedenis van den Schotschen Stapel te Vere', *Archief van het Zeeuwsch Genootschap*, 1903
Philip, J., *Researches in South Africa* (London, 1828)
Philip, R., *The Life, Times and Missionary Enterprises of the Rev John Campbell* (London, 1841)
Philips, C.H., *The East India Company, 1784–1834* (Manchester, 1940)
——, 'The New East India Board and the Court of Directors, 1784', *English Historical Review*, iv, 1940
(ed.), *The Correspondence of David Scott, 1787–1805* (London, 1951)
(ed.), *Historians of India, Pakistan and Ceylon* (Oxford, 1961)
——, 'James Mill, Mountstuart Elphinstone and the History of India', in the above
Phillipson, N.T., 'Providence and Progress, an introduction to the historical thought of William Robertson', in Brown (1996)
Philp, H.R.A., *A New Day in Kenya* (London, 1936)
Pickard, R.J., The Church of Scotland in Kenya from First Beginnings to the Mau Mau Emergency, unpublished M.A. dissertation, University of Aberdeen, 1996
Pickersgill, J.W., *The Mackenzie King Record* (Chicago & Toronto, 1960)
Pinney, T. (ed.), *The Letters of Thomas Babington Macaulay* (London, 1976)
Pi-Sunyer, O., 'Catalan Nationalism', in Rogowski & Tiryakian (1985)
Pittock, M., *The Invention of Scotland* (London, 1991)
Pointon, A.C., *The Bombay Burmah Trading Corporation Ltd, 1863–1963* (Southampton, 1964)
Pollo, S. & Puto, A., *The History of Albania* (London, 1981)
Pope, J., *Memoirs of the Rt Hon Sir John Alexander Macdonald* (London, 1894)
Porteous, J.D., 'Easter Island, the Scottish connection', *Geographical Review*, lxviii, 1978
Porter, A., *Victorian Shipping, Business and Imperial Policy, Donald Currie, the Castle Line and southern Africa* (Woodbridge, Suffolk, 1986)
——, 'Scottish Missions and Education in Nineteenth-Century India, the changing face of "trusteeship" ', in Holland & Porter (1988)
& Stockwell, A.J., *British Imperial Policy and Decolonisation, 1938–1964* (London, 1987)
Porter, B., *Critics of Empire* (London, 1968)
Powell, J.E., *Freedom and Reality* (London, 1969)
Prakash, O., *The Dutch East India Company and the Economy of Bengal, 1630–1720* (Princeton, 1985)
Pratt, C., *The Critical Phase in Tanzania, 1945–1968* (Cambridge, 1976)
Pratt, M., *Britain's Greek Empire* (London, 1978)
Prebble, J., *The Highland Clearances* (London, 1963)
——, *The Darien Disaster* (London, 1968)
Prentis, M.D., 'The Emigrants of the Highland and Island Emigration Society, 1852–1857', *Journal of the Royal Australian Historical Society* lxix, 1983
——, *The Scots in Australia* (Sydney, 1983)
Preston, A., 'Sir Charles MacGregor and the Defence of India, 1857–1887', *Historical Journal*, xii, 1969
Preston, B.W., 'Nova Scotia', in Daiches (1981)
Price, J.M., 'The Rise of Glasgow in the Chesapeake Tobacco Trade, 1707–1775', in Payne (1967)
——, *Capital and Credit in British Overseas Trade, the view from the Chesapeake, 1700–1776* (Cambridge, Mass., 1980)
——, 'Glasgow, the Tobacco Trade and the Scottish Customs, 1707–1730', *Scottish Historical Review*, lxiii, 1984
Price, R., *An Imperial War and the British Working Class* (London, 1972)
Price, R. & S., *Stedman's Surinam, life in an eighteenth-century slave society* (Baltimore & London, 1992)
Price, T. & Shepperson, G., *Independent African* (Edinburgh, 1958)
Pringle, T., *African Sketches* (Cape Town, 1834)
——, *Narrative of a Residence in South Africa* (Cape Town, 1966; first published, 1835)
Pryde, G.S., *The Scottish Universities and the Colleges of Colonial America* (Glasgow, 1957)
Purvis, T.L., 'The European Ancestry of the United States Population, 1790', *William and Mary Quarterly*, xli, 1984
Pyrah, G.B., *Imperial Policy and South Africa* (Oxford, 1955)
Radcliffe of Werneth, Lord: *Mountstuart Elphinstone* (Oxford, 1962)

Rae, I., *Knox the Anatomist* (Edinburgh & London, 1964)

Ramsay, A., *An Enquiry into the Rights of the East India Company* (London, 1772)

——, *A Succinct Review of the American Contest* (London, n.d.)

Ramsay, B.D.W., *Rough Recollections of Military Service and Society* (Edinburgh & London, 1882)

Ramsay, J., *Enquiry on the Treatment and Conversion of African Slaves in the British Sugar Colonies* (London, 1784a)

——, *Objections to the Abolition of the Slave Trade, with Answers* (London, 1784b)

——, *A Reply to the Personal Invectives and Objections contained in two Answers . . . to an Essay on the Treatment and Conversion of African Slaves* (London, 1785)

Ramsay, J.C., The Darien Scheme and the Church of Scotland, unpublished Ph.D. thesis, University of Edinburgh, 1949

Ranger, T.O. & Weller, J. (eds.), *Themes in the Christian History of Central Africa* (London, 1975)

Rankin, H.F., *The Moore's Creek Bridge Campaign* (Conhoshocken, Pa., 1986)

Rankin, J., *A History of our Firm* (Liverpool, 1908)

Rankine, W.H., *A Hero of the Dark Continent, memoir of Rev William Affleck Scott* (Edinburgh & London, 1896)

Ransford, O., *David Livingstone, the dark interior* (London, 1978)

Rao, J.S.N., 'Adam Smith in India', in Mizuta & Sugiyama (1993)

Ratcliffe, S.K., *Sir William Wedderburn and the Indian Reform Movement* (London, 1923)

Raymond, E.T., *The Life of Lord Rosebery* (New York, 1923)

Raynor, D. & Skinner, A., 'Sir James Steuart, nine letters on the American conflict, 1775–1778', *William and Mary Quarterly*, li, 1994

Rea, J.E., *Bishop Alexander Macdonnell and the Politics of Upper Canada* (Toronto, 1974)

Reader, W.J., *Imperial Chemical Industries, a history* (Oxford, 1970)

Reese, G. & Van Horne, J.C. (eds.), *The Letter Book of James Abercromby, colonial agent (1751–1773)* (Richmond, Va., 1991)

Reid, J.G., 'The Scots Crown and the Restitution of Port Royal, 1629–1632', *Acadiensis*, vi, 1977

——, *Acadia, Maine and New Scotland, marginal colonies in the seventeenth century* (Toronto, 1981)

Reid, R., 'The Rev William Bell, one emigrant's adjustment to Upper Canada', *Scottish Tradition*, ix, 1979

Reid, W.S. (ed.), *The Scottish Tradition in Canada* (Toronto, 1976)

——, 'The Scottish Protestant Tradition', in the above

Reith, J., *Life and Writings of Rev Alexander Murray* (Dumfries, 1903)

Remer, C.F., *Foreign Investments in China* (New York, 1933)

Rempel, R.A., *Unionists Divided* (Newton Abbot, 1972)

Rendall, J., 'Scottish Orientalism from Robertson to James Mill', *Historical Journal*, xxv, 1982

Rheinheimer, H.P., *Topo, the story of a Scottish colony near Caracas, 1825–1827* (Edinburgh, 1988)

Rice, C.D., 'Abolitionists and Abolitionism in Aberdeen', *Northern Scotland*, i, 1972

——, *The Rise and Fall of Black Slavery* (London, 1975)

——, 'Archibald Dalzel, the Scottish Intelligentsia and the Problem of Slavery', *Scottish Historical Review*, lxii, 1983

Rich, E.E. (ed.), *Journal of Occurrences in the Athabasca Department by George Simpson, 1820 & 1821* (Toronto, 1938)

——, *Colin Robertson's Correspondence Book, September 1817 to September 1822* (London, 1940)

——, *Hudson's Bay Company, 1670–1870* (New York, 1960)

Rich, P.B., *Race and Empire in British Politics* (Cambridge, 1990)

——, 'W.M. Macmillan, South African Segregation and Commonwealth Race Relations, 1919–1938', in Macmillan & Marks (1989)

Richards, E., The Highland Scots of South Australia, paper presented to the Royal Caledonian Society of South Australia, August 4, 1978

——, 'Highland Emigrants to South Australia in the 1850s', *Northern Scotland*, v, 1982

——, *A History of the Highland Clearances* (London, 1985)

——, 'Australia and the Scottish Connection, 1788–1914', in Cage (1985)

——, *Scottish Australia* (HMSO, 1988)

——, 'Scotland and the Uses of the Atlantic Empire', in Bailyn & Morgan (1991)

Richards, R.L., 'Rae of the Arctic', *Medical History*, xix, 1975

Riddy, J., 'Warren Hastings – Scotland's benefactor?', in Carnall & Nicholson (1989)

Ride, R., 'Biographical Note [on James Legge]', in Legge (1960)

Riemenschneider, D. (ed.), *The History and Historiography of Commonwealth Literature* (Tübingen, 1988)

Riesen, R.A., Faith and Criticism in Post-Disruption Scotland, unpublished Ph.D. thesis, University of Edinburgh, 1981

Riley, P.W.J., *The Union of England and Scotland* (Manchester, 1978)

Rinn, J.A., 'Scots in Bondage', *History Today*, xxx, 1980

Ritchie, J., *Lachlan Macquarie* (Melbourne, 1986)

Rizvi, G., *Linlithgow and India* (London, 1978)

Robbins, C., '"When it is that Colonies may Turn Independent", an analysis of the environment and politics of Francis Hutcheson (1694–1746)', *William and Mary Quarterly*, xi, 1954

Robbins, K., '"The Grubby Wreck of Old Glories", the United Kingdom and the end of the British Empire', *Journal of Contemporary History*, xv, 1980

——, 'Core and Periphery in Modern British History', *Proceedings of the British Academy*, lxx, 1984

——, 'Wales and the Scottish Connexion', *Trafodion Anrhydeddus Gymdeithas y Cymmrodorion*, 1985

Roberts, M. (ed.), *Sweden's Age of Greatness* (London, 1973)

——, *The Swedish Imperial Experience* (Cambridge, 1979)

Roberts, P.E., *India under Wellesley* (London, 1929)

Roberts, S.H., *History of Australian Land Settlement, 1788–1920* (Melbourne, 1924)

——, *The Squatting Age in Australia* (Melbourne, 1964)

Robertson, B.C., *Raja Rammohun Roy, the father of modern India* (Delhi, 1995)

Robertson, I.R., 'Highlanders, Irishmen and the Land Question in Nineteenth-century Prince Edward Island', in Cullen & Smout (1977)

Robertson, J., 'Union, State and Empire', in Stone (1994)

——, (ed.), *A Union for Empire* (Cambridge, 1995)

——, (ed.), *Andrew Fletcher, political works* (Cambridge, 1997)

Robertson, N., *Not as Strangers* (Auckland, 1967)

Robertson, P.L., 'Shipping and Shipbuilding, the case of William Denny & Brothers', *Business History*, xvi, 1974

Robertson, W., *The Situation of the World at the Time of Christ's Appearance* (Edinburgh, 1755)

——, *The History of America* (London & Edinburgh, 1777)

——, *An Historical Disquisition concerning the Knowledge which the Ancients had of India* (London, 1791)

Robson, E. (ed.), *Letters from America, 1773–1780* (Manchester, 1951)

Robson, J., *Hinduism and its Relations to Christianity* (Edinburgh, 1874)

Robson, J., *Ion Keith-Falconer of Arabia* (London, 1924)

Rocher, R., *Alexander Hamilton (1762–1824), a chapter in the early history of Sanskrit philology* (New Haven, 1968)

Roeykens, P.A., *Les débuts de l'oeuvre africaine de Léopold II, 1875–1879* (Brussels, 1954)

Rogers, C., *Memorials of the Earl of Stirling* (Edinburgh, 1877)

Rogowski, R. & Tiryakian, E.A. (eds.), *New Nationalisms of the Developed West* (Boston, 1985)

Ross, A., *The Red River Settlement* (London, 1856)

Ross, A.C., 'The African – a Child or a Man? The quarrel between the Blantyre Mission of the Church of Scotland and the British Central Africa administration, 1890–1905', in Brown & Stokes (1966)

——, The Origins and Development of the Church of Scotland Mission, Blantyre, Nyasaland 1875–1926, unpublished Ph.D. thesis, University of Edinburgh, 1968

——, 'Scottish Missionary Concern 1874–1919, a golden era?', *Scottish Historical Review*, li, 1972

——, 'Livingstone and the Aftermath, the origins and development of the Blantyre Mission', in Pachai (1973)

——, *John Philip, 1775–1851* (Aberdeen, 1986)

——, 'The Scottish Missionary Doctor', in Dow (1988)

——, Nyasaland, 1958–1965, in National Library of Scotland (1993)

——, 'The Dutch Reformed Church of South Africa, a product of the Disruption?', in Brown & Fry (1993)

Ross, C. (ed.), *Correspondence of Charles, First Marquis Cornwallis* (London, 1859)

Ross, E., *Pictou Island, Nova Scotia, the rise and fall of an island community* (Victoria BC, 1987)

Ross, I.S., *Lord Kames and the Scotland of his Day* (Oxford, 1972)

Ross, K.R., 'Malawi's Peaceful Revolution 1992–1994, the role of the Church of Scotland', *Records of the Scottish Church History Society*, xxvii, 1997

Rotberg, R.I., *Christian Missionaries and the Creation of Northern Rhodesia, 1880–1924* (Princeton, 1965)

——, *The Rise of Nationalism in Central Africa* (Cambridge, Mass., 1966)

——, *Joseph Thomson and the Exploration of Africa* (London, 1971)

Rothermund, D., *An Economic History of India* (London & New York, 1988)

Rotwein, E. (ed.), *David Hume, writings on economics* (Edinburgh & London, 1955)

Rouse, P., *James Blair of Virginia* (Chapel Hill, 1971)

Roxborough, W.J., Thomas Chalmers and the Mission of the Church, unpublished Ph.D. thesis, University of Aberdeen, 1978

——, 'Presbyterianism in Malaysia', *Bulletin of the Scottish Institute of Missionary Studies*, n.s., iv-v, 1988–9

Roy, J.A., *The Scot and Canada* (Toronto, 1947)

Royle, T., *War Report, the war correspondents' view of battle from the Crimea to the Falklands* (Edinburgh, 1987)

——, *Winds of Change, the end of Empire in Africa* (London, 1996)

Rush, J.R. & Winks, R.W. (eds.), *Asia in Western Fiction* (Manchester, 1990)

Russell, M., *Palestine* (Edinburgh, 1831)

Said, E.W., *Orientalism* (London, 1978)

——, *Culture and Imperialism* (London, 1993)

St Clair, T., *A Soldier's Recollections of the West Indies and America* (London, 1834)

Samuel, R., *Patriotism, the making and unmaking of British national identity* (London & New York, 1989)

Sanders, R., *The High Walls of Jerusalem, a history of the Balfour Declaration and the birth of the British mandate for Palestine* (New York, 1983)

Sandison, A., *The Wheel of Empire* (London, 1967)

Sanger, C., *Malcolm MacDonald, bringing an end to Empire* (Liverpool, 1995)

Sarbah, J.M., 'Maclean and Gold Coast Judicial Assessors', *Journal of the African Society*, ix, 1910

Saul, S.B., *Studies in British Overseas Trade, 1870–1914* (Liverpool, 1960)

Saunders, C., 'A Liberal Descent? W.M. Macmillan, C.W. de Kiewiet and the history of South Africa', in Macmillan & Marks (1989)

Saville, R., 'Scottish Modernisation prior to the Industrial Revolution', in Devine & Young (1999)

Saywell, J.T. (ed.), *The Canadian Journal of Lady Aberdeen, 1893–1898* (Toronto, 1960)

& Stevens, P. (eds.), *Lord Minto's Canadian Papers* (Toronto, 1981)

Schama, S., *The Embarrassment of Riches* (London, 1987)

Schapera, I. (ed.), *Apprenticeship at Kuruman, being the journals and letters of Robert and Mary Moffat, 1820–1828* (London, 1951)

——, (ed.), *David Livingstone, family letters 1841–1856* (London, 1959)

——, (ed.), *Livingstone's Missionary Correspondence, 1841–1856* (London, 1961)

——, (ed.), *Livingstone's African Journal, 1853–1856* (London, 1963)

——, (ed.), *Livingstone's Private Journals, 1851–1853* (London, 1966)

——, (ed.), *David Livingstone, South African papers* (Cape Town, 1974)

Schaw, J., *Journal of a Lady of Quality* (New Haven, 1921)

Schlenter, B.S., 'Scottish Influences, especially Religious, in Colonial America', *Records of the Scottish Church History Society*, xix, 1976

Schmitz, C., 'Scottish Investors in Australian Mining, 1870–1920', Scottish Records Association conference report, x, 1988

——, Patterns of Scottish Portfolio Investment, 1860–1914, unpublished paper, 1993

Schutz, J.A., 'James Ramsay, essayist, aggressive humanitarian', in McCulloch (1950)

Scot, G., *A Brief Advertisement, concerning East New Jersey, in America* (Edinburgh, 1685)

Scott, F.D., *Sweden, the nation's history* (Minneapolis, 1977)

Scott, H.E., *A Saint in Kenya, the life of Marion Scott Stevenson* (London, 1932)

Scott, P.G., 'An Edinburgh Graduate in Virginia, the educational influence of James Blair', *University of Edinburgh Journal*, xxvii, 1976

Scott, P.H., *John Galt* (Edinburgh, 1985)

——, *Andrew Fletcher and the Treaty of Union* (Edinburgh, 1992)

Scott, W.R., *Francis Hutcheson* (Cambridge, 1900)

——, 'The Fiscal Policy of Scotland before the Union', *Scottish Historical Review*, i, 1904

——, *The Records of a Scottish Cloth Manufactory at New Mills, Haddingtonshire, 1681–1703* (Edinburgh, 1905)

Scottish Home Rule Association, *Appeal to the Scot Abroad* (Edinburgh, 1891)

Scottish National Portrait Gallery, *Visions of the Ottoman Empire* (Edinburgh, 1994)

Scottish Office, *Ethnic Minorities in Scotland* (Edinburgh, 1983)

Searle, G.R., *The Quest for National Efficiency, a study in British politics and political thought, 1899–1914* (Oxford, 1971)

Seed, G., *James Wilson* (Millwood, NY, 1978)

——, 'James Wilson, founding father', *History Today*, xxx, 1980

Sefton, H.R., 'The Scotch Society in the American Colonies in the Eighteenth Century', *Records of the Scottish Church History Society*, xvii, 1971

Selkirk, T. Douglas, Earl of, *Collected Writings* (Winnipeg, 1984)

Sellar, R., *The Tragedy of Quebec, the expulsion of its protestant farmers* (Toronto, 1974; first published, 1907)

Semmel, B., *Imperialism and Social Reform* (London, 1960)

——, *The Rise of Free Trade Imperialism* (Cambridge, 1970)

Sen, S.R., *The Economics of Sir James Steuart* (London, 1957)

Senior, E., 'The Glengarry Highlanders and the Suppression of the Rebellions in Lower Canada, 1837–1838', *Journal of the Society for Army Historical Research*, lvi, 1978

Setzekorn, W.D., *Formerly British Honduras* (Athens, Ohio, 1975)

Seward, D., *The Monks of War* (London, 1972)

Seymour, W., 'Botanist Explorers of Two Continents', *History Today*, xxix, 1979

Shai, A., 'Imperialism Imprisoned, the closure of British firms in the People's Republic of China', *English Historical Review*, civ, 1989

Shao, W., *China, Britain and Businessmen, political and commercial relations 1949–1957* (London, 1991)

Sharpe, E.J., *Not to Destroy but to Fulfil, the contribution of J.N. Farquhar to protestant missionary thought in India before 1914* (Uppsala, 1965)

Shaw, A.G.L., *Convicts and the Colonies* (London, 1966)

——, *Great Britain and the Colonies, 1815–1865* (London, 1970)

Shepherd, R., *Iain Macleod* (London, 1994)

Shepherd, R.H.W., *Lovedale* (Lovedale, 1941)

Shepperson, G., 'David Livingstone the Scot', *Scottish Historical Review*, xxxix, 1960

(ed.), *David Livingstone and the Rovuma* (Edinburgh, 1965)

——, 'The American Revolution and Scotland', *Scotia*, i, 1977

——, 'Scots Abroad', in Daiches (1981)

Shepperson, W.S., *British Emigration to North America* (Oxford, 1957)

Sher, R.B., 'Witherspoon's *Dominion of Providence* and the Scottish Jeremiad Tradition', in Sher & Smitten (1990)

——, 'An "Agreable and Instructive Society" – Benjamin Franklin in Scotland', *Eighteenth-Century Life*, xv, 1991

& Smitten, J.R., (eds.), *Scotland and America in the Age of the Enlightenment* (Edinburgh, 1990)

Sherman, A.J., *Mandate Days, British lives in Palestine, 1918–1948* (London, 1997)

Sheridan, R.B., 'The Rise of a Colonial Gentry, a case study of Antigua, 1730–1775,' *Economic History Review*, xiii, 1960–1

——, 'The Wealth of Jamaica in the Eighteenth Century', *Economic History Review*, xviii, 1965

——, *Sugar and Slavery, an economic history of the British West Indies, 1623–1775* (Barbados, 1975)

Shinn, R.F., *Arthur Berriedale Keith, 1879–1944* (Aberdeen, 1990)

Short, A., *The Communist Insurrection in Malaya, 1948–1960* (London, 1975)

Short, P., *Banda* (London, 1974)

Shyllon, F., *James Ramsay, the unknown abolitionist* (Edinburgh, 1977)

Siegfried, A., *Le Canada* (Paris, 1947)

Silverman, H.A., *Studies in Industrial Organisation* (London, 1946)

Simpson, G.G. (ed.), *The Scottish Soldier Abroad, 1247–1967* (Edinburgh, 1992)

Sinclair, Sir J., *The History of the Public Revenue of the British Empire* (London, 1970)

Sinclair-Stevenson, C., *The Gordon Highlanders* (London, 1968)

Singh, P., *Lord Minto and Indian Nationalism, 1905–1910* (Allahabad, 1976)

Sinker, R., *Memorials of the Hon Ion Keith-Falconer* (Cambridge, 1903)

Sixsmith, E.K.G., *Douglas Haig* (London, 1970)

Skelley, A.R., *The Victorian Army at Home* (London, 1977)

Skelton, O.D., *The Life and Times of Sir Alexander Tilloch Galt* (Toronto, 1920)

Skinner, A.S., 'Adam Smith and the American Economic Community, an essay in applied economics', *Journal of the History of Ideas*, xxxvii, 1976

——, *A System of Social Science, papers relating to Adam Smith* (Oxford, 1979)

——, 'Sir James Steuart, economic theory and policy', in Jones (1988)

——, 'Adam Smith and America, the political economy of conflict', in Sher & Smitten (1990)

——, 'The Shaping of Political Economy in the Enlightenment', in Mizuta & Sugiyama (1993)

& Wilson, T., *Essays on Adam Smith* (Oxford, 1975)

Skrine, F.H., *Sir William Wilson Hunter* (London, 1901)

Slade, H.G., 'Craigston and Meldrum Estates, Carriacou, 1769–1841', *Proceedings of the Society of Antiquaries of Scotland*, cxiv, 1984

Slade, R., *King Leopold's Congo* (Oxford, 1962)

Slaven, A., *The Development of the West of Scotland, 1750–1960* (London, 1975)

Sloan, D., *The Scottish Enlightenment and the American College Ideal* (New York, 1971)

Smart, D., *The Life and Art of Allan Ramsay* (London, 1952)

Smart, W., 'The Municipal Industries of Glasgow', *Proceedings of the Philosophical Society of Glasgow*, xxvi, 1894–5

Smith, A., *An Inquiry into the Nature and Causes of the Wealth of Nations* (Oxford, 1976; first published, 1776)

Smith, E.W., *African Ideas of God* (London, 1950)

Smith, G., *The Life of John Wilson* (London, 1878)

——, *The Life of Alexander Duff* (London, 1879)

——, *Fifty Years of Foreign Missions* (Edinburgh, 1880)

——, *Stephen Hislop* (London, 1888)

——, *A Modern Apostle, Alexander N. Somerville 1813–1889* (London, 1891)

Smith, G., *Canada and the Canadian Question* (Toronto, 1891)

Smith, G. Adam, *Historical Geography of the Holy Land* (Edinburgh, 1892)

Smith, G.H., *With the Scottish Rifle Volunteers at the Front* (Glasgow & Edinburgh, 1901)

Smith, J. Adam, *John Buchan, a biography* (London, 1965)

Smith, J.N., The Presbyterian Church of Ghana, 1835–1960, unpublished Ph.D. thesis, University of Edinburgh, 1963

Smith, P., *Ethnic Minorities in Scotland* (Edinburgh, 1991)

Smith, V.A., *The Oxford History of India* (Oxford, 1958)

Smith, W., Robertson, *The Prophets of Israel* (Edinburgh, 1882)

——, *The Religion of the Semites* (Edinburgh, 1889)

Smitten, J.R., 'Moderatism and History, William Robertson's Unfinished History of British America', in Sher & Smitten (1990)

——, Power and Authority in William Robertson's *Historical Disquisition concerning India* (1791), unpublished paper, 1992

Smout, T.C., 'The Development and Enterprise of Glasgow, 1556–1707', *Scottish Journal of Political Economy*, vii, 1960

——, 'The Early Scottish Sugar Houses, 1660–1720', *Economic History Review*, xi, 1961

——, *Scottish Trade on the Eve of the Union* (Edinburgh, 1963)

——, 'The Glasgow Merchant Community in the Seventeenth Century', *Scottish Historical Review*, xlvii, 1968

——, *History of the Scottish People, 1560–1830* (London, 1972)

——, (ed.), *Scotland and the Sea* (Edinburgh, 1992)

Soltow, J.H., 'Scottish Traders in Virginia', *Economic History Review*, xii, 1959–60

Sommer, D., *Haldane of Cloan* (London, 1960)

Southey, R., *History of Brazil* (London, 1810)

Souza, G.B., *The Survival of Empire, Portuguese trade and society in China and the South China Sea, 1630–1754* (Cambridge, 1986)

Spear, P., *India, a modern history* (Ann Arbor, 1961)

Spender, J.A., *The Life of the Rt Hon Sir Henry Campbell-Bannerman* (London, 1923)

Spooner, F.C., *Risks at Sea, Amsterdam insurance and maritime Europe, 1766–1780* (Cambridge, 1983)

Spilhans, M.W., *South Africa in the Making, 1652–1806* (Cape Town, 1966)

Spreul, J., *An Accompt Current betwixt Scotland and England Balanced* (Edinburgh, 1705)

Stansky, P., *Ambitions and Strategies, the struggle for the leadership of the Liberal party in the* 1890s (Oxford, 1964)

Steensgaard, N., 'The Companies as a Specific Institution in the History of European Expansion', in Blussé & Gaastra (1981)

Stein, B., *Thomas Munro* (Oxford, 1989)

Stein, L., *The Balfour Declaration* (London, 1961)

Stengers, J., 'King Leopold's Imperialism', in Owen & Sutcliffe (1972)

Steuart, Sir J., *The Principle of Money applied to the Present State of the Coin of Bengal* (n.p., 1772)

——, *An Inquiry into the Principles of Political Oeconomy* (Edinburgh & London, 1966)

Steven, M., *Merchant Campbell, 1769–1846* (Melbourne, 1965)

Stevens, D., 'Adam Smith and the Colonial Disturbances', in Skinner & Wilson (1975)

Stevenson, D., *Scottish Covenanters and Irish Confederates* (Belfast, 1981)

Stevenson, R.L., *The Amateur Emigrant* (London, 1885)

——, *A Footnote to History, eight years of trouble in Samoa* (London, 1892)

——, *In the South Seas* (Edinburgh, 1896)

——, *Vailima Papers* (London, 1925)

——, *Letters, 1891–1894* (London, 1926)

Stewart, A.R., 'Sir John A. Macdonald and the Imperial Defence Commission of 1879', *Canadian Historical Review*, xxv, 1954

Stewart, D., *Sketches of the Character, Manners and Present State of the Highlanders of Scotland* (Edinburgh, 1822)

Stewart, D., *History and Principles of the Presbyterian Church in Ireland* (Belfast, 1907)

Stewart, D.M., *The Presbyterian Church of Victoria, 1859–1909* (Melbourne, 1909).

Stewart, G.T., *Jute and Empire* (Manchester, 1998)

Stewart, J., *A View of the Past and Present State of the Island of Jamaica* (Edinburgh, 1823)

Stewart, J., *Dawn in the Dark Continent* (Edinburgh & London, 1903)

Stillson, R.T., 'The Financing of Malayan Rubber, 1905–1928', *Economic History Review* xxiv, 1971

Stimson, S.C., 'A Jury of the Country', common sense philosophy and the jurisprudence of James Wilson', in Sher & Smitten (1990)

Stocking, G., *Functionalism Historicised* (Madison, Wisconsin, 1984)

Stokes, E., *The English Utilitarians and India* (Oxford, 1959)

Stone, L., *An Imperial State at War* (London & New York, 1994)

Stone, Sir R., 'Public Economic Policy', in Fry (1992a)

Stopford, J.M., 'The Origins of British-based Multinational Manufacturing Enterprises', *Business History Review*, xlviii, 1974

Strachan, M., *The Ben Line, 1825–1982* (Norwich, 1992)

Sulté, B., 'Les Ecossais au Canada', *Revue des Deux Frances*, xi, 1898

Sutherland, L.S., *The East India Company in Eighteenth-century Politics* (Oxford, 1952)

Den Svenska Historien, IV, Gustav Adolfs och Kristinas tid, 1611–1654; VI, Frihetstiden, 1719–1772; VII, Gustavianska tiden, 1772–1809; ix, Industri och folkrörelser (Stockholm, 1967–8)

Sweeting, A., 'With the ease and grace of a born bishop', James Legge's contributions to religious and secular education in Hong Kong, unpublished paper, 1997

Swinney, G.N., 'Robert Neill, artist and naturalist', in Calder (1986)

Swinson, A, *North-War Frontier, people and events, 1839–1847* (London, 1967)

Swire, J., *Albania* (London, 1929)

Sykes, A., *Tariff Reform in British Politics* (Oxford, 1979)

Sykes, L., *Calcutta through British Eyes* (Madras, 1992)

Sym, J., *Seaforth Highlanders* (Aldershot, 1962)

Tabrah, R., *Ni'ihau* (Kailua, Hawaii, 1987)

Tamuno, S.M., The Development of British Control of Southern Nigeria, 1900–1912, unpublished Ph.D. thesis, University of London, 1962

Tarling, N., *Britain, the Brookes and Brunei* (Kuala Lumpur, 1982)

Taylor, A., *Laurence Oliphant, 1829–1888* (Oxford, 1982)

Taylor, A.J.P., *The Trouble Makers* (London, 1957)

Taylor, B., 'A Scottish Contribution to Eastern Nigeria's Educational Development', *Scottish Educational Review*, xvii, 1985

Taylor, J.C., *The Political Development of Tanganyika* (Stanford, 1963)

Taylor, W.H., Calabar, an educational experiment in Nigeria, unpublished Ph.D, thesis, University of Exeter, 1981

Terpstra, C., David Bogue, DD, 1750–1825, pioneer and missionary educator, unpublished Ph.D. thesis, University of Edinburgh, 1959

Theroux, P., *The Happy Isles of Oceania* (London, 1992)

Thévet, A., *Cosmographie Universelle* (Paris, 1575)

Thomas, B., *Migration and Economic Growth, a study of Great Britain and the Atlantic economy* (Cambridge, 1973)

Thomas, C., *Margaret Laurence* (Toronto, 1969)

Thomas, D., *Cochrane* (London, 1980)

Thomas, W.A., *The Provincial Stock Exchanges* (London, 1973)

Thompson, R.R., *The Fifty-second (Lowland) Division, 1914–1918* (Glasgow, 1923)

Thompson, T.J., Fraser and the Ngoni, a study in the growth of Christianity among the Ngoni of northern Malawi 1878–1933, with special reference to the work of Donald Fraser, unpublished Ph.D. thesis, University of Edinburgh, 1980

Thompson, W., Glasgow and Africa, connexions and attitudes, unpublished Ph.D. thesis, Strathclyde University, 1970

Thomson, D.C., *Alexander Mackenzie* (Toronto, 1960)

Thomson, J., 'East Central Africa and its Commercial Outlook', *Scottish Geographical Magazine*, ii, 1886

Thomson, J.B., *Joseph Thomson, African explorer* (London, 1896)

Thomson, L.K.J., 'Scotland and Catalonia and the American Market in the Eighteenth Century', *Scottish Economic and Social History*, ix, 1989

Thór, J.T., 'Foreign Fisheries off Iceland, c. 1400–1800', in Heerma van Voss & Roding (1996)

Thornton, A.P., *The Imperial Idea and its Enemies* (London, 1959)

——, *Doctrines of Imperialism* (New York, 1965)

——, 'Scotland, 1789–1832', problems of a political satellite, *Queen's Quarterly*, xci, 1984

Thornton, T.H., *Colonel Sir Robert Sandeman* (London, 1895)

Thorpe, D.R., *Alec Douglas-Home* (London, 1997)

Thrum, T.C., *History of the Hudson Bay Company's Agency in Honolulu*, Annual Report of the Hawaiian Historical Society, xviii, 1911

Tiffany, N.M., *Letters of James Murray, loyalist* (Boston, 1901)

Tomlinson, B.R., 'Colonial Firms and the Decline of Colonialism in India, 1914–1947', *Modern Asian Studies*, xv, 1981

Torrance, J., *The Story of our Maratha Missions* (Edinburgh, 1902)

Trautmann, T.R., *Aryans and British India* (Berkeley & Los Angeles, 1997)

Treble, J.H., 'The Pattern of Investment of the Standard Life Assurance Company, 1875–1914', *Business History* xxii, 1980

Tregonning, K.G., *Under Chartered Company Rule, North Borneo 1881–1946* (Singapore, 1958)

——, 'The Mat Salleh Revolt, 1894–1905', *Journal of the Malayan Branch of the Royal Asiatic Society*, xxix, 1956

Trevelyan, G.O., *Life and Letters of Lord Macaulay* (London, 1878)

Trinterud, L.J., *The Forming of an American Tradition* (Philadelphia, 1949)

Tripathi, A., *Trade and Finance in the Bengal Presidency, 1793–1833* (Bombay, 1950)

Trotter, L.J., *Life of the Marquis of Dalhousie* (London, 1889)

——, *A Life of General Sir James Outram* (Edinburgh & London, 1893)

Trotter, R. (ed.), *Imperial Chemical Industries Ltd and its Founding Companies* (London, 1938)

Turnbull, A., 'Scotland and America', in Daiches, Jones & Jones (1986)

Turner, A.R., 'Scottish Settlement of the West', in Reid (1976)

Tweed, J., *Considerations and Remarks on the Present State of the Trade to Africa* (London, 1771)

Tyler, J.E., 'Campbell–Bannerman and the Liberal Imperialists, 1906–1908', *History*, xxiii, 1938–9

Udall, S.L., *To the Inland Empire, Coronado and our Spanish legacy* (New York, n.d.)

Ullendorf, E., 'James Bruce of Kinnaird', *Scottish Historical Review*, xxii, 1953

Underhill, F.H., 'Canada's Relations with the Empire as seen by the *Toronto Globe*, 1857–1867', *Canadian Historical Review*, x, 1929

——, 'Lord Minto on his Governor-generalship', *Canadian Historical Review*, xl, 1959

Usherwood, S., 'The Abolitionists' Debt to Lord Mansfield', *History Today*, xxxi, 1981

Vance, M.E., 'The Politics of Emigration, Scotland and assisted emigration to Upper Canada 1815–1826', in Devine (1992)

Van der Wal, S.L., 'The Netherlands as an Imperial Power in South-east Asia in the Nineteenth Century and After', in Bromley & Kossman (1968)

——, 'Nederland en Nederlandsch–Indië, 1914–1942', in Cloet *et al* (1980), XIV

Van Kley, E.J., 'The Effect of the Discoveries on Seventeenth-century Dutch Popular Culture', *Terrae Incognitae*, viii, 1976

Vaudry, R.W., *The Free Church in Victorian Canada, 1844–1861* (Waterloo, Ontario, 1989)

Vellut, J.L., 'Dekolonisatie van Kongo, 1914–1942', in Cloet *et al* (1980), XIV

Venning, C., 'Hume on Property, Commerce and Empire in the Good Society, the role of historical necessity', *Journal of the History of Ideas*, xxxvii, 1976

Vereté, M., 'The Balfour Declaration and its Makers', *Middle Eastern Studies*, vi, 1970

Vicziany, M., 'Imperialism, Botany and Statistics in Early Nineteenth-century India, the surveys of Francis Buchanan (1762–1829)', *Modern Asian Studies*, xx, 1986

Vilar, P., *La Catalogne dans l'Espagne Moderne* (Paris, 1962)

Vlekke, B.H.M., *The Story of the Dutch East Indies* (Cambridge, Mass., 1946)

Von Reumont, A., *General the Right Honourable Sir Frederick Adam* (London, 1855)

Von Zugbach, R.G.L., *Power and Prestige in the British Army* (Aldershot, 1982)

Voght, M., 'Scots in Hispanic California', *Scottish Historical Review*, lii, 1973

Waddell, H.M., *Twenty-nine Years in the West Indies and Central Africa* (London, 1863)

Wagner, J.M., 'The Two Worlds of Frederick Niven', *Scottish Tradition*, xiii, 1984

Walker, E.A. (ed.), *The Cambridge History of the British Empire, VIII, South Africa* (Cambridge, 1963)

Walker, G., *Thomas Johnston* (Manchester, 1988)

——, 'Protestantism and Political Culture, 1890–1990', in Gallagher & Walker (1990)

——, 'The Protestant Irish in Scotland', in Devine (1991)

——, 'The Orange Order in Scotland between the Wars', *International Review of Social History*, xxxvii, 1992

——, 'Empire, Religion and Nationality in Scotland and Ulster before the First World War', in Wood (1994)

——, *Intimate Strangers, Scotland and Northern Ireland* (Edinburgh, 1995)

Walker, W.M., 'Irish Immigrants in Scotland, their priests, politics and parochial life', *Historical Journal*, xv, 1972

——, *Juteopolis, Dundee and its textile workers, 1885–1923* (Edinburgh, 1979)

Wallace, D.R., *The Romance of Jute* (London, 1928)

Wallace, J.N., 'The Explorer of Finlay River in 1824', *Canadian Historical Review*, ix, 1928

Wallace, W.S. (ed.), *John McLean's Notes of a 25 Years' Service in the Hudson's Bay Territory* (Toronto, 1932)

——, *Documents relating to the North-West Company* (Toronto, 1934)

Waller, G.M., *Samuel Vetch, colonial enterpriser* (Chapel Hill, 1960)

Waller, H. (ed.), *The Last Journals of David Livingstone* (London, 1874)

Wallis, J.P.R. (ed.), *The Matabele Journals of Robert Moffat, 1829–1860* (London, 1945)

(ed.), *The Zambezi Expedition of David Livingstone, journals* (London, 1956)

Walls, A.F., 'William Robertson Smith and the Missionary Movement', in Johnstone (1995)

Walrond, T. (ed.), *Letters and Journals of James, Eight Earl of Elgin* (London, 1872)

Ward, J. & Wilson, R.G., *Land and Industry* (Newton Abbot, 1971)

Ward, W.E.F., *Fraser of Trinity and Achimota* (Ghana Universities Press, 1965)

Warneck, G., *Outline of a History of Protestant Missions* (Edinburgh & London, 1901)

Wasti, S.R., *Lord Minto and the Indian Nationalist Movement, 1905–1910* (Oxford, 1964)

Waterson, D.B., *Squatter, Selector and Storekeeper* (Sydney, 1968)

Watson, D., *Caledonia Australis* (Sydney, 1984)

Waugh, D.L., *Three Years' Practical Experience of a Settler in New South Wales* (Edinburgh, 1838)

Wedderburn, R., *The Horrors of Slavery* (London, 1824)

Wedderburn, Sir W., *Allan Octavian Hume* (London, 1913)

Weiss, R.W., 'Economic Nationalism in Britain in the Nineteenth Century', in Johnson (1968)

Welensky, Sir R., *Welensky's 4000 Days* (London, 1964)

Wellesley, Richard, Marquis, *The Wellesley Papers* (London, 1914)

Wells, J., *Stewart of Lovedale* (London, 1908)

Welsh, F., *History of Hong Kong* (London, 1993)

Wesseling, H.L., 'Post-imperial Holland', *Journal of Contemporary History*, xv, 1980

——, 'The Giant that was a Dwarf, or the strange history of Dutch imperialism', in Holland & Porter (1988)

Werner, J.H., 'David Hume and America', *Journal of the History of Ideas*, xxxiii, 1972

Whatley, C.A., *'Bought and Sold for English Gold'?* (East Linton, 2001)

Wheeler, J.T., *Short History of India* (London, 1880)

Wheeler-Bennett, Sir J.W., *John Anderson, Viscount Waverley* (London, 1962)

Whelan, F.G., Hume and the Non-western World, unpublished paper, 1996

White, G., ' "Highly Preposterous" – origins of Scottish missions', *Records of the Scottish Church History Society*, xix, 1976

——, 'The Consecration of Bishop Seabury', *Scottish Historical Review*, lxiii, 1984

White, K., *Pilgrim of the Void* (Edinburgh & London, 1990)

White, L., *Magomero, portrait of an African village* (Cambridge, 1987)

White, M., *The Philosophy of the American Revolution* (New York, 1978)

Whitelaw, M. (ed.), *The Dalhousie Journals* (n.p., 1978)

Wilkie, J., *Metagama, a journey from Lewis to the New World* (Edinburgh, 1987)

Wilkins, W.H. (ed.): *South Africa a Century Ago, letters written from the Cape of Good Hope (1797–1801) by Lady Anne Barnard* (London, 1901)

——, *The Life of Sir David Baird* (London, 1912)

Williams, G. (ed.), *London Correspondence Inward from Sir George Simpson, 1841–2* (Toronto, 1938)

Williams, T.D., *Malawi, the politics of despair* (Ithaca & London, 1978)

Williamson, A.H., 'A Patriot Nobility? Calvinism, kin-ties and civic humanism', *Scottish Historical Review*, lxxii, 1993

——, 'Scots, Indians and Empire: the Scottish politics of civilisation', *Past and Present*, cl, 1996

Williamson, P., *The Life and Curious Adventures of Peter Williamson* (Aberdeen, 1801)

Wills, G., *Inventing America, Jefferson's Declaration of Independence* (Garden City, NY, 1978)

Willson, B., *The Life of Lord Strathcona and Mount Royal* (London, 1915)

Willson, P.H., *King James VI & I* (London, 1956)

Wilson, A., *Letters from India* (London, 1984)

Wilson, C., *Anglo-Dutch Commerce and Finance in the Eighteenth Century* (Cambridge, 1941)

——, *Mercantilism*, Historical Association pamphlet, general series, no. 37, 1947

Wilson, J., *The Indian Civil Service as a Career for Scotsmen* (Edinburgh, 1885)

Wilson, J., *CB, the life of Sir Henry Campbell-Bannerman* (London, 1973)

Wilson, J.K., *Budu, or 20 years in Sarawak* (North Berwick, 1969)

Wilson, W.F., *David Douglas, botanist at Hawaii* (Honolulu, 1919)

Winch, D., *Classical Political Economy and the Colonies* (London, 1965)

Winslow, E.M., *The Pattern of Imperialism* (New York, 1948)

Witherspoon, J., *Address to the Inhabitants of Jamaica* (Philadelphia, 1772)

Wokler, R., 'Apes and Races in the Scottish Enlightenment', in Jones (1988)

Wolpert, S.A., *Morley and India, 1906–1910* (Berkeley and Los Angeles, 1967)

Wong, K.F., *Pagan Innocence* (London, 1960)

Wood, G.S., *The Radicalism of the American Revolution* (New York, 1992)

Wood, I.S. (ed.), *Scotland and Ulster* (Edinburgh, 1994)

Wood, J.C., *British Economists and the Empire* (London & Canberra, 1983)

Wood, J.D., 'Scottish Migration Overseas', *Scottish Geographical Magazine*, lxxx, 1980

——, 'Transatlantic Land Reform, America and the crofters' revolt, 1878–1888', *Scottish Historical Review*, lxiii, 1984

Woodburn, J.B., *The Ulster Scot* (London, 1914)

Woodcock, G., 'Alexander Mackenzie and the River of Disappointment', *History Today*, xiv, 1964

Woodruff, P., *The Men who Ruled India* (London, 1953)

Woods, D.W., *John Witherspoon* (New York, 1907)

Wormald, J., 'The Creation of Britain, multiple kingdoms or core and colonies?', *Transactions of the Royal Historical Society*, 6th series, ii, 1992

Wright, E., 'Education in the American Colonies, the impact of Scotland', in Green (1969)

Wrong, G.M., *The Earl of Elgin* (London, 1905)

Wylie, D., 'Norman Leys and McGregor Ross, a case study in the conscience of African empire 1900–1939', *Journal of Imperial and Commonwealth History*, v, 1976–7

Young, K., *Arthur James Balfour* (London, 1963)

——, *Sir Alec Douglas–Home* (London, 1970)

Young, M.D. (ed.), *The Parliaments of Scotland* (Edinburgh, 1992)

Young, T.C., *Herrenvolk and Sahib-log* (London, 1944)

——, 'The Idea of God in Northern Nyasaland', in Smith (1950)

Youngson, J.P.W., *Forty Years of the Panjab Mission of the Church of Scotland, 1855–1895* (Edinburgh, 1897)

Zebel, S.H., *Balfour, a political biography* (Cambridge, 1973)

Zenner, G., *Neu-Europa* (Leipzig, 1720)

Zetland, J.L.L. Dundas, Marquis of (*prius* Earl of Ronaldshay): *The Heart of Aryavarta, a study of the psychology of Indian unrest* (London, 1925)

——, *India* (Cambridge, 1926)

——, *India, retrospect and prospect* (Nottingham, 1935)

——, *Essayez* (London, 1956)

Index

Entries in bold type indicate a chapter on the subject

Shoshong, mission, 342
Sialkot, mission, 185, 194
Sicily, 119, 120
Siegfried, André, journalist, 472
Sierra Leone, 75, 173
Sikh War, 206
Simpson, George, governor, 107, 290–1, 292–3, 294
Sinclair, Elizabeth, colonist, 235
Sinclair, Henry, Earl of Orkney, 20
Sinclair, John, Lord Pentland, politician, 429, 430, 431
Sind, 203–5
Singapore, 452, 454, 455, 456, 460, 461, 462, 489
Sinha, Satyendra, barrister, 429
Slavery and slave trade, 25, 75–80, 155, 166, 173, 176, 177–8, 234, 278, 281, 329, 330, 331, 332, 404, 416, 457
Slessor, Mary, missionary, 172, 179, 181–3
Small, William, professor, 60
Smith, Adam, economist, 15, 16, 37, 50, 51–3, 54, 59, 62, 78, 86–7, 88, 94, 141, 202, 242, 298, 367, 445
Smith, Donald, Lord Strathcona, businessman, 295–6, 299, 487
Smith, Rev George Adam, 247, 248, 397
Smith, Goldwin, journalist, 301
Smith, William Robertson, critic, 240–1, 245–7, 248, 249, 312
Smith, Bell & Co, 455
Smollett, Tobias, novelist, 73
Smuggling, 45, 52, 305
Smuts, Jan, statesman, 344, 347, 409, 418
Society in Scotland for the Propagation of Christian Knowledge, 136, 219
Soga, Rev Tiyo, missionary, 138
Solomos, Dionysios, poet, 130
Somerset, Lord Charles, governor, 142, 144
South Africa, 31–2, **135–47**, 152, 156, 168, 270, 282, 302, **340–51**, 362, 369, 379, 381, 402, 409–11, 413, 416, 418, 419, 420, 421, 467, 473
South African College, Cape Town, 143
South African Native College, Fort Hare, 405, 411
Spain, 29, 32, 34, 35–7, 119, 136, 456
Spens, David, slave, 76
Spotswood, Alexander, governor, 65
Spreul, John, merchant, 47, 49

Squatters, 108, 112, 114–17, 222, 234
Standard Chartered Bank, 267, 477, 479, 1 48
Standard Life Assurance Company, 267
Stanley, Henry Morton, explorer, 148, 149, 159, 281
Statute of Westminster (1931), 382, 384
Stedman, John Gabriel, mercenary, 70–1, 77, 136
Steel, Rev David, 407
Stellenbosch, university of, 146, 344, 410
Stephen, Alexander, shipbuilder, 263
Stephen, George, Lord Mountstephen, businessman, 299
Steuart, Sir James, economist, 50–1
Stevenson, James, manager, 460
Stevenson, John, missionary, 190
Stevenson, Robert Louis, novelist, 229, 231, 232–3, 238–9, 258
Stewart, Donald, general, 318, 335
Stewart, Dugald, philosopher, 54, 90, 242, 243
Stewart, Duncan, governor, 462
Stewart, Frederick, teacher, 312
Stewart, Henry, Cardinal of York, 123
Stewart, James, Duke of Berwick, general, 36
Stewart, James, missionary, 163–4, 165–6, 335, 341, 342, 344, 405, 406
Steyn, Marthinus, President, 146
Stirling, David, colonel, 418
Strachan, John, bishop, 212
Straits Settlements, 453, 454, 455
Stuart, John, superintendent, 65
Sugar, trade and manufacture, 71
Sulu Islands, 452, 453, 456
Summer Palace, Peking, 303–4
Sungei Remok, massacre at (1948), 451–2
Sun Yat-sen, President, 438, 442, 446, 447
Surinam, 70
Sutherland, Hugh, settler, 290
Sutherland, James, journalist, 188
Sutherland, Thomas, shipowner, 261, 267, 273, 444, 448
Sutherland Highlanders, *see* Argyll and Sutherland Highlanders
Swat, Mad Mullah of, 316
Swaziland and Swazis, 342, 343, 350
Sweden, 39–40, 485
Switzerland, 485
Sydney, 110, 111, 113, 220, 221, 222